Best of Game Programming Gems

Edited by
Mark DeLoura

Charles River Media
A part of Course Technology, Cengage Learning

COURSE TECHNOLOGY
CENGAGE Learning™

Australia • Brazil • Japan • Korea • Mexico • Singapore • Spain • United Kingdom • United States

COURSE TECHNOLOGY
CENGAGE Learning™

Publisher and General Manager, Course Technology PTR: Stacy L. Hiquet

Associate Director of Marketing: Sarah Panella

Manager of Editorial Services: Heather Talbot

Marketing Manager: Jordan Casey

Senior Acquisitions Editor: Emi Smith

Project Editor: Kim Benbow

Technical Reviewer: Mark DeLoura

CRM Editorial Services Coordinator: Jen Blaney

Interior Layout Tech: Judith Littlefield

Cover Designer: Mike Tanamachi

CD-ROM Producer: Brandon Penticuff

Indexer: Larry Sweazy

Proofreaders: Michael Beady and Heather Urschel

Library of Congress Control Number: 2008928531
ISBN-13: 978-1-58450-571-6
ISBN-10: 1-58450-571-0

Course Technology
25 Thomson Place
Boston, MA 02210
USA

Cengage Learning is a leading provider of customized learning solutions with office locations around the globe, including Singapore, the United Kingdom, Australia, Mexico, Brazil, and Japan. Locate your local office at: **international.cengage.com/region**

Cengage Learning products are represented in Canada by Nelson Education, Ltd.

For your lifelong learning solutions, visit **courseptr.com**
Visit our corporate website at **cengage.com**

Printed in the United States of America
1 2 3 4 5 6 7 11 10 09 08

To game developers world-wide...especially to those whose games we have yet to play!

Contents

Acknowledgments

The original volume of *Game Programming Gems* was created by a small team, compared to the size of many game development teams today. But it never would have happened without the generous leadership of Jenifer Niles and David Pallai from Charles River Media, who were willing to jump off the cliff with me. The 40 contributors to the original volume who joined us on the journey of creation are life-long friends.

The book editors who directed the series for *Gems 3* through *Gems 6* brought their own talents, background, and flavor to the series and spent just as many sleepless nights working on it as I did. What makes the *Gems* series powerful is that many voices are brought together into one place, and the following four individuals each took on the huge task of distilling the combined wisdom of the game programming community down into a single volume. I owe them each my gratitude:

- *Game Programming Gems 3*, Dante Treglia
- *Game Programming Gems 4*, Andrew Kirmse
- *Game Programming Gems 5*, Kim Pallister
- *Game Programming Gems 6*, Mike Dickheiser

The army of contributors to the series over the years is why *Game Programming Gems* is valuable. I consider all of the authors my extended family. To each of you who have written for the series, you have my profound thanks, and I hope that you're all continuing to write and speak and share your wisdom!

Lastly, my thanks to the new stewards of the *Game Programming Gems* series at Course Technology PTR, Cengage Learning, especially Jennifer Blaney and Kim Benbow, who helped me out so much with this volume. Thank you for keeping the series alive!

About the Authors

James Boer

james@boarslair.com

James Boer began his game development career by delving inside the mind of white-tailed deer in order to develop AI for the surprise hit game *Deer Hunter*. After his eventual capture, return to civilization, and re-education, he worked on a number of games, including *Rocky Mountain Trophy Hunter*, *Deer Hunter II*, *Pro Bass Fishing*, *Microsoft Baseball 2000*, *Tex Atomic's Big Bot Battles*, *Digimon Rumble Arena 2*, and *Lord of the Rings: Tactics*. His writing credits include a number of *Game Programming Gems* articles, co-authoring *DirectX Complete*, a few assorted articles in *Game Developer* magazine, and his own book, *Game Audio Programming*. ArenaNet currently employs him as a network and server programmer for their new game, *Guild Wars*.

Bill Budge

billbudge@hotmail.com

Bill Budge knew at age three that building things would be his life's work. Since then he has moved from blocks to object-oriented design, but amazingly he is still having lots of fun playing with interesting new forms of construction. When not coding, he spends time with his family, perfects his barista skills, runs, and reads every interesting software blog he can find.

Jamie Cheng

jamie.cheng@kleientertainment.com

Jamie got his start as an AI programmer at Relic Entertainment, where he worked on PC, Xbox, and Xbox 360 titles. His credits include *Warhammer 40,000: Dawn of War* and *The Outfit* for the Xbox 360. At the age of 24, Jamie self-funded Klei Entertainment Inc., which has subsequently created award-winning titles for the PC and Xbox 360 Live Arcade. Currently, his studio is partnered with Nexon to create free-to-play online games.

Christopher Christensen

christopher_christensen@naughtydog.com

Christopher first started programming in 1982 on an Apple II+ machine. In 1994, despite having recently gotten a master's degree in computer engineering, he took a job programming PC role-playing games at Interplay Productions. He has been in the game industry ever since and currently is a programmer at Naughty Dog in Santa Monica, California.

Peter Dalton

pdalton@madprog.com

Peter Dalton is Senior Programmer for Smart Bomb Interactive. He has been happily working in the industry for more than seven years with his main focus revolving around engine architecture and the many subsystems that go into making a game engine function. Over the past seven years he has contributed to such titles as *Advent Rising*, *Pac-Man World Rally*, and *Snoopy vs. the Red Baron*, targeting every major console to come out within that time frame. Currently he is working with a very talented group of individuals at Smart Bomb Interactive, focused on building a powerful new gaming engine to allow the studio to create cutting-edge games for the Xbox 360 and PlayStation 3.

Mark DeLoura

mdeloura@satori.org

Mark is the creator and series editor of the *Game Programming Gems* series of books. In his role as Vice President of Technology for GreenScreen Interactive, Mark focuses on pushing the boundaries of technology for games and making great games more efficiently. Over his 15+ years in the games industry, Mark has served in a variety of technology-related roles at Nintendo, Sony, Ubisoft, *Game Developer* magazine, and as an independent consultant. He is an adamant believer in sharing and reusing technology, and he believes that everyone should be able to make games. He maintains a website at www.satori.org.

Eric Dybsand

Eric Dybsand was a contributor to the first *Game Programming Gems* book and has been involved with the computer game industry since 1987. He has worked on a variety of games, developing an NPC AI for the game *Men of Valor* and developing a race car AI for several racing games that shipped in 2001. During 2000, he consulted on the strategic AI for the space strategy game *Master of Orion 3*. Eric also consulted on AI for baseball and wrestling games. He designed and developed the AI opponents for the Windward Studios RTS game *Enemy Nations* and for the Fenris Wolfe FPS games *Rebel Moon Revolution* and *War In Heaven*. Prior to those works, he developed and marketed a line of shareware, turn-based and real-time war and strategy games, and provided testing services on the turn-based war games *Empire Deluxe* and *The Perfect General*. Eric was a favored AI roundtable moderator for five Game Developers Conferences, as well as a CGDC lecturer. Eric was also an excellent and attentive moderator of the Gamasutra "AI Programming" and IGDA "AI in Games" forums on the web. Eric lived in Glendale, Colorado, where, when not working on a game, he enjoyed skiing, biking, hiking, and enjoying the great Colorado outdoors. Eric passed away very suddenly of an aneurysm on April 15, 2004. He is sorely missed by those lucky enough to have been his friends.

Thomas Engel

thomas.engel@factor5.com

Thomas Engel is director of technology and one of the founders of Factor 5, LLC. He has been working in the industry for more than 10 years with his main focus being the technology behind the game play. One of his projects over the last years has been Factor 5's MusyX sound system. Currently, he is busy developing both audio and graphics technologies for next-generation consoles.

Peter Freese

peter@hiddenpath.com

Peter has been active in the game industry since the early 1990s, when he decided he'd rather make games than graphics tools for database programmers. After developing several award-winning educational games, Peter founded Q Studios in 1994 with former Edmark colleague Nick Newhard and led development on the campy 3D shooter *Blood*, which launched publisher Monolith into the spotlight. After developing the graphics engine behind Sierra Studio's final adventure game, *Gabriel Knight 3*, Peter joined the *Ultima Online 2* team at Origin Systems to learn all the joys and trials of MMP game development. In 2001, Peter established a Core Technology group for NCsoft in Austin, Texas, where he directs development on the state-of-the-art graphics engine technology behind many of NCsoft's new online games.

Byon Garrabrant

byon@byonics.com

Byon Garrabrant has been programming games professionally since 1988, starting with PC conversions of coin-op arcade machines. He created *Castles*, *Castles II*, and *Conquest of the New World* for Interplay before joining Westwood Studios in 1997 to co-lead programming on *Command & Conquer Renegade*.

Miguel Gomez

kikomu@seanet.com

Miguel Gomez is a software engineer at the SAAM institute, a developer of modeling and analysis software for medical research. His previous experience includes graphics and physics programming for *PGA Tour '96* (Electronic Arts), *Hyperblade* (Activision), *Baseball 3D* (Microsoft), and *Destruction Derby 64* (Psygnosis). He holds a bachelor's degree in physics and a master's degree in applied mathematics, both from the University of Washington.

Robin Green

rgreen@google.com

Robin Green has worked in the games industry since 1994, starting at Electronic Arts U.K. Studios, then moving on to R&D at Bullfrog Productions, R&D at Sony Computer Entertainment America, and has worked as an engineer at Google, Inc. He has contributed steering behaviors for *Dungeon Keeper 2* and *Sim Theme Park*, presented the GDC lectures "Programming PS2," "Faster Math Functions," and "Spherical Harmonic Lighting: The Gritty Details." He has also sat as a designer and chair for the COLLADA FX Working Group under Khronos. He is a keen digital DJ spinning house classics and techno "on the 1s and 0s" and enjoys designing and building his own MIDI DJ controllers.

Jim Greer

jim@kongregate.com

Jim Greer is the co-founder and CEO of Kongregate, a startup that combines user-submitted Flash games with achievements, high scores, chat, and other community features. Developers share in ad and microtransaction revenue and retain the rights to their games. Before founding Kongregate in June 2006, Jim was Technical Director for Pogo at Electronic Arts. He started in the game industry in 1991 at Origin Systems, where he worked on *Ultima VII* and *Ultima VIII.*

Julien Hamaide

julien.hamaide@gmail.com

Julien started programming a text game on his Commodore 64 at the age of eight. His first assembly programs would follow soon after. He has always been self-taught, reading all the books his parents were able to buy. He graduated as a multimedia electrical engineer at the Faculté Polytechnique de Mons (Belgium) at the age of 21. After two years working on speech and image processing at TCTS/Multitel and three years working on next-generation consoles at Elsewhere Entertainment (www.elsewhere-entertainment.com), Julien started his own studio called Fishing Cactus (www.fishingcactus.com) with two associates. He has published in *Game Programming Gems 5, 6,* and *7,* as well as *AI Programming Wisdom 4,* and has presented at GDC 2008.

Sami Hamlaoui

disk_disaster@hotmail.com

Obsessed by AI, Sami was—and still is—unsure why he wrote an article about audio for *Game Programming Gems 5*. When not going off topic, he continues to spend most of his time trying to make 500 bots look smart while keeping the frame rate in frames-per-second and not seconds-per-frame. He is approximately 5% closer to this goal than he was three years ago and plans to be finished right before the singularity is achieved.

Søren Hannibal

sorenhan@yahoo.com

Søren Hannibal has been programming almost continually since 1985, taking short breaks to sleep, eat, and study when it has been absolutely necessary. Søren wrote a good chunk of the Shiny Entertainment engine and is currently busy cracking the whip as Technical Director for Double Helix Games' engine department.

Greg Hjelstrom

greg@hjelstrom.com

Greg Hjelstrom is the Technical Director at Petroglyph. He has been in the games industry for 13 years and has worked on rendering and physics code used in many games. His first project was to port *Command & Conquer* to the Sega Saturn. He was a co-lead programmer for the first-person shooter *Command & Conquer Renegade*. His most recent projects were real-time strategy games: *Star Wars: Empire at War* and *Universe at War*. He has worked on a variety of console and PC platforms during his career.

Naty Hoffman

gpg@renderwonk.com

Naty Hoffman is currently at SCEA working on *God of War III* for the PS3. He has been developing games for over 10 years. Prior to that he worked at Intel, where he was the lead architect for the first MMX microprocessor and at least partly to blame for the MMX, SSE, and SSE2 instruction set extensions. Naty is particularly interested in physically based real-time rendering methods, on which he has published several articles. He has also taught classes at SIGGRAPH, I3D, GDC, and Meltdown. He is a co-author (with Tomas Moller and Eric Haines) of the third edition of the book *Real-Time Rendering*.

Pete Isensee

pkisensee@msn.com

Pete Isensee manages game technology teams at Microsoft. He's a regular speaker at GDC and a regular contributor to the *Game Programming Gems* series. He enjoys discussing C++ performance issues, particularly over a glass of Bordeaux.

John Isidoro

jisidoro@csa.bu.edu

John Isidoro is part of the 3D Application Research Group at ATI and is simultaneously working toward a Ph.D. in computer science at Boston University. At ATI, he co-developed the Radeon 8500 technology demos and screen savers, as well as many other applications. His research interests are real-time graphics, shader programming, image-based rendering, multi-view reconstruction, non-rigid region tracking, and using graphics hardware in new and innovative ways. He was published at ICCV '98 and CVPR '00, and his contributions to books include *Game Programming Gems 2* and *ShaderX* (Wordware Publishing, Inc.).

Toby Jones

thjones@microsoft.com

Toby Jones is Senior Development Lead in the Windows Experience team at Microsoft. He has been working in the multimedia/games space for nearly 10 years and has written code for Windows Media Player, *Prey*, *Dead Man's Hand* on Xbox, Vegas Video, and Sound Forge. Toby irregularly publishes articles in the *Game Programming Gems* series and elsewhere, and you can usually find him huddled over his laptop muttering things about Lisp, invariants, and other nonsense. He lives in Redmond, Washington, with his wife Jessica and their two cats, who shed enough hair to start a wig factory for balding felines.

Jan Kautz

j.kautz@cs.ucl.ac.uk

Jan is Assistant Professor at the University College London in the Virtual Environments and Computer Graphics Group. Before that he was a Post-Doc with the graphics group at the Massachusetts Institute of Technology. He received his Ph.D. from the Max-Planck-Institut für Informatik, Germany. He is particularly interested in realistic rendering, on which he has published several articles at various conferences, including SIGGRAPH.

Andrew Kirmse

ark@alum.mit.edu

Andrew was the co-inventor and director of *Meridian 59* (1996) and the graphics programmer on *Star Wars: Starfighter* (2001). He has degrees in physics, mathematics, and computer science from the Massachusetts Institute of Technology. Andrew has contributed to each of the *Game Programming Gems* books. He now works at Google and plays with his son Evan.

Eric Lengyel

lengyel@terathon.com

Eric Lengyel is a 12-year veteran of the computer games industry and currently heads up development of the C4 Engine at Terathon Software. He is the author of the best-selling book *Mathematics for 3D Game Programming and Computer Graphics*, and he has written many articles for industry publications, ranging from gamasutra.com to the *Game Programming Gems* series. In the 1990s, Eric was a lead programmer at Yosemite Entertainment, and he later worked in the advanced technology group at Naughty Dog.

Noel Llopis

llopis@convexhull.com

Noel Llopis is following his lifelong dream of being an indie game developer and cofounded Power of Two Games. He is hoping to prove that, even today, it is still possible to create great games with small teams and lots of enthusiasm. He is a member of the Game Developer Conference Advisory Board and a regular columnist for *Game Developer* magazine. He is the author of the book *C++ for Game Programmers*. Some of his past titles include *The Bourne Conspiracy*, *Darkwatch*, and the *MechAssault* series. He earned a master's degree from the University of North Carolina at Chapel Hill and a bachelor's from the University of Massachusetts, Amherst.

Kenny Mitchell

kmitchell@ea.com

Kenny Mitchell's first game was a *Scramble* clone on ZX81, which he coded to run in just under 256 bytes in 1982. As an undergrad in 1991, he developed a constant time voxel ray-tracing engine for implicit surfaces, which, 17 years later, runs in real time. His Ph.D. dissertation introduced a novel recursive perspective projection method for visualization of multidimensional data. As a technical lead at Electronic Arts for 10 years, he's their most prolific contributor to the internal EA Journal. He has presented many times at GDC and authored articles on lighting, displacement mapping, higher order surfaces, streaming, and ray tracing. He is active in developing new IP to showcase development talent profitably, and his most recently shipped game in the *Harry Potter* series fits in just under 24 gigabytes.

Jack Moffitt

jack@chesspark.com

Jack Moffitt founded the Icecast project in late 1998 and has played pivotal roles in several early Internet radio startups, including Green Witch Internet Radio and iCast, a CMGi company, and is widely regarded as one of the leading industry experts in streaming media. His experience in the areas of software development, databases, load management and scaling, streaming media, system administration, architecture, and security is extensive. Jack also founded the Xiph.org foundation, a nonprofit focused on interoperable and patent-free multimedia technologies and standards. He is currently exploring instant messaging technologies and gaming with his new startup Chesspark.

Chris Oat

chris@chrisoat.com

Chris Oat is a member of AMD's Game Computing Applications Group, where he is the technical lead for the group's demo team. In this role, he focuses on the development of cutting-edge rendering techniques for the latest graphics platforms. Chris has published several articles in the *ShaderX* and *Game Programming Gems* series and has presented his work at graphics and game developer conferences around the world. Many of the projects Chris has worked on may be found at www.chrisoat.com.

Scott Patterson

filter@filtercurve.com

Scott was a contributing author in *Game Programming Gems 2* and *3*, and editor for the audio section of *Game Programming Gems 3*. He started working in the game industry in 1990 for Microprose Software and has also worked for Midway, Naughty Dog, and EA Blackbox. He has worked as a lead programmer on character systems, animation systems, AI systems, user-interface systems, graphics systems, and audio systems. He enjoys creating audio and adding interesting things to the filtercurve.com website.

Nick Porcino

nporcino@ilm.com

Nick Porcino received his bachelor's degree from the University of Victoria, Canada, and has been working in games, computer graphics, artificial intelligence, and robotics since 1981. His adventures have seen him working on autonomous submersibles, robotic toys in Tokyo, and game consoles since the industry's earliest days. He helped create games for Sanctuary Woods, Disney Interactive, and LucasArts. Now he is working at Industrial Light and Magic to bring the worlds of film and game technology together. Nick has had a dozen papers and book chapters published, has taught courses at SIGGRAPH, and is credited on two dozen games and an animated cartoon.

Steve Rabin

steve.rabin@gmail.com

Steve Rabin is a principal software engineer at Nintendo of America, where he researches new techniques for Nintendo's next-generation systems, develops tools, and supports Nintendo developers. Before Nintendo, Steve worked primarily as an AI engineer at several Seattle startups, including Gas Powered Games, WizBang Software Productions, and Surreal Software. He managed and edited the *AI Game Programming Wisdom* series of books, edited the book *Introduction to Game Development,* and has over a dozen articles published in the *Game Programming Gems* series. He has spoken at the Game Developers Conference and moderated the AI roundtables for the last two years. Steve teaches artificial intelligence at both the University of Washington Extension and at the DigiPen Institute of Technology. He earned a bachelor's degree in computer engineering and a master's in computer science, both from the University of Washington.

Aurelio Reis

AurelioReis@gmail.com

For Aurelio Reis, video games have always been a portal for him to visit and enjoy new and exciting worlds. Realizing it as a creative outlet, he decided to pursue it as a career and has since dedicated his life to creating games that evoke awe in their graphical splendor, challenge in their gameplay, and elicit emotions that draw the player into the game. Aurelio is currently a senior programmer at Raven Software, where he specializes in gameplay systems as well as graphics technology. He's currently working on next-generation technologies on multiple platforms for one of Raven's next games. In his (occasional) spare time, he likes to compose music, play sports, and work on graphics demos, as well as design amateur independent games. You can see some of his work at his personal website: www.CodeFortress.com.

Zack Booth Simpson

zack@mine-control.com

Zack Booth Simpson joined Origin/Electronic Arts in 1991 as a programmer on *Ultima*. He left in 1995 as the Director of Technology, and then later returned from 1998 to 1999 as a Research Fellow. In 1995, he co-founded Titanic Entertainment, which created *NetStorm: Islands at War*. In 1997, Zack abandoned the game industry and now creates interactive installation artwork for museums world-wide. He is also a molecular biology research fellow of the Center for Systems and Synthetic Biology at the University of Texas, Austin. His home page is at www.mine-control.com/zack.

Russ Smith

russ@q12.org

Russ Smith is the author of the Open Dynamics Engine, an open-source library for simulating articulated rigid body dynamics. Russ's other simulator work includes the core of MathEngine's game industry products, control research for simulated walking biped robots, and simulation of virtual characters for movie production.

Dr. Finnegan Southey

finnegan@google.com

Finnegan Southey has worked on research in game AI with the University of Alberta GAMES group for over two years as a postdoctoral fellow. His work includes planning, machine learning, opponent modelling, and semi-automated software testing for video games as well as poker. He currently works at Google on user modelling for web search and looks forward to the day when he does not feel compelled to gun down computer-controlled allies in the games he plays.

Marco Spoerl

mspoerl@gmx.de

Marco Spoerl started his professional career in the field of computer graphics as an engine programmer at Codecult Software, working on the Codecreatures Game Development System and Codecreatures Benchmark Pro. After receiving his degree in computer science and a short walk on the wild side as a freelance software developer, he spent a couple of years at Munich-based Krauss-Maffei Wegmann's training and simulation department, developing simulation equipment for tanks, trucks, cars, and trains. Today, he is expanding his horizons engineering custom software.

Bryan Stout

bstout@mindspring.com

Bryan Stout has worked in the fields of artificial intelligence, doing research and applications for the University of Illinois and Martin Marietta, and for computer games, first for MicroProse and then on a freelance basis. Since that time, he has combined both passions as a writer, explaining how AI techniques work and can be applied to games. He has lectured on game AI topics at the GDC, Software Development, and Develop! Conferences, as well as at AAAI symposia and workshops. His articles on game AI have appeared in *Game Developer* magazine and *Game Programming Gems*. His recent activity has been on a book on game AI.

Jan Svarovsky

jan@svarovsky.org

Jan Svarovsky graduated from Cambridge University (England) in 1995, joined Bullfrog, and worked in R&D, writing AI technology, experimental 3D engines, network code, and two of the first-ever 3D-accelerator PC conversions. Since then, he has worked on many games in various genres for several companies, including his own. His homepage can be accessed at www.svarovsky.org/jan.

Andy Thomason

andyt@snsys.com

Andy Thomason has contributed to many game titles since the 1970s. Currently, he is a humble foot soldier at Sony in the U.K., crafting compilers and optimizers for consoles. His goal is to make the gaming experience that much richer every day. Andy has recently been delivering a series of lectures encouraging young people to develop the skills necessary to join the games industry. He has just finished his master's degree in mathematics after five years of brow-furrowing toil, and he enjoys tricky mathematical problems.

William van der Sterren

william.van.der.sterren@cgf-ai.com

William van der Sterren is an AI consultant for games and simulations at CGF-AI. He assisted Guerrilla Games in creating the AI system used in *Killzone* and *Shellshock Nam '67*. William has spoken at the Game Developers Conference and has written about squad AI, AI terrain analysis, and tactical pathfinding for the *Game Programming Gems* and *AI Game Programming Wisdom* book series.

Alex Vlachos

alex@vlachos.com

Alex Vlachos focuses on graphics programming and shader development at Valve. Previously he was Lead Visual Effects Programmer at Naughty Dog, lead programmer on ATI's Demo Team, and was a software developer for the SpaceOrb 360. Alex is a graduate of Boston University. He maintains a website at alex.vlachos.com.

Jon Watte

gpg.bestof@mindcontrol.org

Jon Watte started creating software at 10 years of age and has never stopped. He has delivered several large products, including the CodeWarrior development tools, the BeOS multimedia operating system, and the There virtual world. In addition to contributing to the industry through lectures, articles, and the *Game Programming Gems* series, Jon is a Microsoft DirectX/XNA MVP and moderates the networking and multiplayer forum on www.gamedev.net. Jon currently works as Chief Technical Officer at Forterra Systems, bringing the massively distributed virtual-world platform OLIVE (Online Interactive Virtual Environment) to enterprises all across the real world.

Jason P. Weber

baboon@imonk.com

Jason P. Weber has been working in software for twenty years, starting at the U.S. Army Night Vision Lab. He has done 3D graphics R&D at Intel, game programming for High Moon Studios, and character effects for DreamWorks Animation. His history of projects includes photo-realistic and infrared natural environments, feather systems, fur collision dynamics, garment development, character animation systems, as well as real-time physical simulation of cloth, vegetation, and destructible scaffold structures. Jason has published papers in SIGGRAPH, IEEE CG&A, GDC, and the *Gems* series. His website can be found at www.imonk.com/baboon.

Stephen White

stephenw@suckerpunch.com

Stephen White is a programmer for Sucker Punch and currently working on *Infamous*, an original title for the PS3. Stephen spent the prior 10 years at Naughty Dog, developing the extremely successful *Crash Bandicoot* and *Jak & Daxter* games (over 33 million units sold), filling roles from programmer to programming director to co-president of Naughty Dog. Stephen has worked on a wide variety of platforms over his more than 20 years of professional programming experience in the video game industry. He has developed many critically acclaimed titles, including the multi-award-winning Deluxe Paint ST. In 2002, Stephen was honored with a nomination for Excellence in Programming at the Game Developer Choice Awards for the game *Jak & Daxter*. Stephen has also been a speaker at GDC, as well as other industry events.

Steven Woodcock

ferretman@gameai.com

Steven Woodcock's background in game AI comes from over two decades of ballistic missile defense work building massive real-time war games and simulators. He did a stint in the consumer arena, then returned to the defense world to help develop the AI for the national missile defense system. Steve is dedicated to game AI and is also the author of a number of papers and publications on the subject. He now pursues game AI through a variety of contract work and has had the honor of serving as contributor to and technical editor for several books in the field. Steve lives in gorgeous Colorado

Springs, Colorado, at the foot of Pikes Peak with a crazed pet basenji and an indeterminate number of ferrets. His hobbies include hiking, shooting, writing, and anything related to *Blake's 7* (go figure).

Ryan Woodland

ryanwoodland@att.net

Ryan Woodland is software manager at Zipper Interactive in Redmond, Washington. Previously, he was founder of Cranky Pants Games. He is also a member of the Nintendo Technology Development team at Nintendo of America.

Mark Zarb-Adami

mark@muckyfoot.com

Mark Zarb-Adami has coded games since he was 10 years old, when he got an Atari 800 for Christmas with a BASIC cartridge—but no games. Eight years later, he studied computer science at Cambridge University before working at Bullfrog. He now works at Mucky Foot. Titles he has worked on include *Syndicate Wars* and *Urban Chaos*.

Introduction

In 2000, when the original *Game Programming Gems* was published, there weren't many game development books on the shelf. Game programming was a profession still largely learned by those supremely passionate individuals who stayed up late into the night hacking code, or who gathered in groups with their friends to create demos. The original volume was intended as a book written *by* game developers *for* game developers. The team of 40 programmers who wrote for the first volume did so because of their passion to share what they had learned through many years of trial and error.

Fortunately, the original *Gems* book proved valuable for both professional and aspiring game developers, and eight years later most of the original material is still powerful. There have been nearly 300 contributors to the *Gems* series over the first six volumes—a total of 381 gems! Game programming in the interim has certainly evolved, but the core purpose of the *Game Programming Gems* series has remained the same: to share timeless gems of game programming wisdom with others, to make your life easier, and enable you to tackle bigger challenges by leveraging the algorithms of those who came before you. *Best of Game Programming Gems* contains the articles of the first six volumes of the series that developers have found the most valuable—and the most timeless. On the book's CD-ROM, you'll find sample code to accompany many of the gems, as well as the color plate images referred to in the text.

There are now many places you can find information about game programming: there are all sorts of books, magazines, websites, and conferences. The increasing popularity of game playing has led to the increasing development of games, as well as the rise of game development programs at schools. Even the idea that *everyone* should be able to create games is gaining popularity, with high-profile efforts from the console manufacturers and "Web 2.0" companies to make creating games easier for everyone. It's a great time to learn to make games!

Whether you're new to game programming or a grizzled veteran, you'll find something valuable for you in this book. We all look forward to the day when you're ready to share *your* gems with the world-wide game programming community!

SECTION

1

GENERAL INFORMATION

1.1

The Science of Debugging Games

Steve Rabin, Nintendo of America Inc.

steve.rabin@gmail.com

Debugging a game, or any other piece of software, can be an arduous task. For the most part an experienced programmer can quickly identify and correct even the most difficult bug, but for the novice, it can become a frustrating and insurmountable task. To make matters worse, when you start looking for the source of a bug, you never know how long it will take to find. The trick is not to panic and to instead be disciplined and remain focused on the bug-finding process. Once you are armed with the techniques and knowledge presented in this article, you will be able to beat back even the toughest bugs and regain control of your game.

The difficult chore of debugging can be made simpler by using the *Five-Step Debugging Process* described in this article. The disciplined use of such a process will ensure that you spend a minimal amount of time searching for and identifying each bug. It is also important to have some expert tricks up your sleeve when approaching an especially tough bug, so this article includes some valuable time-tested tips. We will also present a list of tough debugging scenarios explaining what to do when dealing with particular bug patterns. Since good tools are essential to debugging any game, we will discuss specific tools that you can embed within your game to help debug situations that are unique to game programming. Finally, we will review some simple techniques for preventing bugs in the first place.

The Five-Step Debugging Process

Expert programmers have the uncanny ability to quickly and masterfully track down even the toughest bugs. The magical way in which they instinctively know where to find the flaw can be awe-inspiring. While experience plays a significant role in this apparent talent, they have also internalized a disciplined method for investigating and narrowing down possible causes. The following five-step process aims to reproduce that discipline and will help you track down bugs in a methodical and focused manner.

Step 1: Reproduce the Problem Consistently

No matter what the bug, it is important that you know how to reproduce it consistently. Trying to fix a bug that shows up randomly is frustrating and usually a waste of time. The fact is, almost all bugs will consistently occur given the right circumstances, so it is the job of either you or your testing department to discover those circumstances.

Given a fictional game bug, a tester might report, "Sometimes the game crashes when the player kills an enemy." Unfortunately, this type of bug report is too vague, especially since the problem doesn't seem to happen consistently. The player might regularly blast away enemies, so there must be some other correlation to when the game crashes.

For bugs that are nontrivial to reproduce, the ideal situation is to create a set of "repro steps" that show how to reproduce the bug every time. For example, the following steps greatly improve on the previous bug report:

Repro steps:

1. Start a single-player game.
2. Choose Skirmish on map 44.
3. Find the enemy camp.
4. From a distance, use projectile weapons to attack the enemies at the camp.
5. Result: 90 percent of the time the game crashes.

Obviously, repro steps are a great way for a tester to help others reproduce a bug; however, the process of narrowing down the chain of events that lead to a bug is also critical for three other reasons. First, it provides valuable clues as to why the bug is happening in the first place. Second, it provides a systematic way to test that the bug has been fixed. Third, it can be used in regression testing to ensure that the bug doesn't reappear.

While this information doesn't tell us the direct cause of the bug, it does let us reproduce it consistently. Once you are sure of the circumstances that cause the bug to occur, you can comfortably move forward to the next step and begin to gather useful clues.

Step 2: Collect Clues

Now that you can reliably force the bug to occur, the next step is to put on your detective hat and collect clues. Each clue is a chance to rule out a possible cause and narrow the list of suspects. With enough clues, the source of the bug will be obvious, so it's worth the effort to keep track of every clue and understand its implications.

One word of caution—in the back of your mind you should always consider that a gathered clue might be misleading or incorrect. For example, maybe we were told that a particular bug always followed an explosion. While it might be a vital clue, it could be a false lead. Be prepared to discard clues that end up conflicting with other information you gather.

Continuing with the example bug report, we now know that the game crashes during a projectile attack on a particular enemy camp. What is so special about projectiles or fighting from a distance? These are important points to ponder, but don't spend too much time doing so. Get in there and observe exactly how it fails. We need more hard evidence, and mulling over superficial clues is the least efficient way to get it.

In the example, when we get into the game and actually watch the failure, we will notice that the crash occurs in an arrow object when it references a bad pointer. Further inspection shows that the pointer should point to the character that shot the arrow. In this case, the arrow was trying to report back that it hit an enemy and that the shooter should receive experience points for the successful attack. While it might appear that we found the cause, the real underlying cause is still unknown. We must discover what made the pointer bad in the first place.

Step 3: Pinpoint the Error

When you think you have enough clues, it's time to focus your search and pinpoint the error. There are two main ways to do this. The first is to propose a hypothesis for what is causing the bug and try to prove or disprove that hypothesis. The second, more methodical way is to use the divide-and-conquer method.

Method 1: Propose a Hypothesis

With enough clues, you will begin to suspect what is causing the bug. This is your hypothesis. Once it is clearly stated in your mind, you can begin to design tests that will either prove it or disprove it.

In the game example, our detective work has produced the following clues and information about the game design:

- When an arrow is shot, it is given a pointer to the character who shot it.
- When an arrow hits an enemy, it gives credit back to the shooter.
- The crash occurs when an arrow tries to use a bad pointer to give credit back to the shooter.

Our first hypothesis might be that the pointer becomes corrupted sometime during the arrow's flight. Armed with this hypothesis, we now need to design tests and collect data to prove or disprove this cause. One method might involve having every arrow register the shooter's pointer in a backup location. When we catch the crash again, we can check the backup data to see if the pointer is different from when it was originally given to the arrow.

Unfortunately, in this particular game example, this hypothesis turned out not to be correct. The backup pointer was equal to the pointer that caused the game to crash. Thus, we have to make a decision. Do we want to come up with another hypothesis and test it, or revert to looking for more clues? Let's try one more hypothesis.

If the arrow's shooter pointer never became corrupted (our new clue), perhaps the shooter was deleted after the arrow was shot but before the arrow hit an enemy. To check for this, let's record the pointer of every character who dies in the enemy camp. When the crash occurs, we can compare the bad pointer to the list of enemies who died and were deleted from memory. With a little work, it turns out that this was the cause. The shooter died while his arrow was in mid-flight!

Method 2: Divide and Conquer

The two hypotheses that led to finding the bug also demonstrate the concept of divide and conquer. We knew the pointer was bad, but we didn't know if it actually changed values as a result of being corrupted, or if the pointer became invalid at some earlier point. By testing the first hypothesis, we were able to rule out one of the two possibilities. As Sherlock Holmes once said, ". . . when you have eliminated the impossible, whatever remains, however improbable, must be the truth."

Some people might describe the divide-and-conquer method as simply identifying the point of failure and backtracking through the inputs to discover the error. Given a noncrashing bug, there is a certain point at which an initial error cascaded and eventually caused the failure. Identifying the initial error is usually accomplished through setting breakpoints (conditional or not) at all of the input paths until you find the input that breaks the output, thus causing the bug.

When backtracking from the point of failure, you are looking for any anomalies in local variables or in functions higher in the stack. With a crash bug, you should be looking for NULL values or values with extremely high numbers. If it's a bug with floating-point numbers, look for NANs or really large numbers further up on the stack.

Whether you make educated guesses at the problem, test a hypothesis, or hunt down the culprit through a methodical search, eventually you *will* find the problem. Trust yourself and keep your wits about you during this stage. Further sections in this article elaborate on specific techniques that can be used during this step.

Step 4: Repair the Problem

Once the true cause of the bug has been identified, a solution must be proposed and implemented. However, the fix must also be appropriate for the particular stage of the project. For example, in the latter stages of development, it's generally not reasonable to change the underlying data structures or architecture in order to fix a bug. Depending on the stage of development, the lead or system architect should make the decision about what type of fix should be implemented. At critical times, individual engineers (junior or mid-level) often make poor decisions because they aren't looking at the big picture.

Another important issue is that the programmer who wrote the code should ideally fix the bug. When this is not possible, try to discuss the fix with the original author before implementing any remedies. This will give you insight into what might have been done in the past about similar problems and what might break as a result of your proposed solution. It is dangerous to change other people's code without thoroughly understanding the context.

Continuing along in our game example, the source of the crash was a bad pointer to an object that didn't exist anymore. A good solution for this type of game pattern is to use a level of indirection so that this type of crash can't happen. Often, games use handles to objects instead of direct pointers for this very reason. This would be a reasonable fix.

However, if the game must be ready for a milestone or an important demo, you might be tempted to implement a more direct fix for this special situation (like having the shooter invalidate his pointer in the arrow when he is deleted). If this kind of quick hack is made, be sure to make a note of it so that it can be re-evaluated after the deadline. It's a common problem to see quick fixes forgotten, only to cause trouble months later.

While it seems that we've found the bug and identified a fix (using handles instead of pointers), it is crucial to explore other ways that might make the same problem occur. This can take extra time, but it's worth the effort to make sure that the underlying bug was fixed, and not just one particular manifestation. In our game example, it's probably the case that other types of projectiles will also cause the game to crash, but other nonweapons or even character relationships might also be vulnerable to the same design flaw. Find these related cases so that your solution addresses the core problem and not just one symptom.

Step 5: Test the Solution

Once the solution has been implemented, it must be tested to verify that it actually repaired the bug. The first step is to make sure that the original repro steps no longer cause the bug. It is also a good idea to have someone else, like a tester, independently confirm that the bug is fixed.

The second step in fixing the bug is making sure that no other bugs were introduced. You should run the game for a reasonable amount of time and ensure that nothing else was affected by the fix. This is very important since many times a bug fix, especially toward the end of the development cycle, will cause other systems to break. At the very end of a project, you'll also want every bug fix to be reviewed by the lead or another developer as an additional sanity check that it won't adversely affect the build.

Expert Debugging Tips

If you follow the basic debugging steps, you should be able to find and repair most bugs. However, when you attempt to come up with a hypothesis, prove/disprove a cause, or try to find the point of failure, you might want to consider the following tips.

Question Your Assumptions

It is important to keep an open mind when debugging and not make too many assumptions. If you assume that the simple stuff works, you could be prematurely narrowing your search and missing the cause completely. For example, don't always assume that you are running with the most up-to-date software or libraries. It often pays to make sure your assumptions are valid.

Minimize Interactions and Interference

Sometimes, systems interact with each other in ways that complicate debugging. Try to minimize this interaction by disabling subsystems that you believe are not related to the problem (for example, disable the sound system). Sometimes this will help identify the problem since the cause might be in the system that you disable, indicating that you should look there next.

Minimize Randomness

Often, bugs are hard to reproduce because of variability introduced by the frame rate or from actual random numbers. If your game has a variable frame rate, try locking the "time elapsed per frame" to a constant. For random numbers, either disable your random number generator or seed it with a constant so that it always produces the same sequence. Unfortunately, the player introduces a significant source of randomness that you can't control. If player randomness must be controlled, consider recording player input so that it can be fed back into your game in a predictable manner [Dawson01].

Break Complex Calculations into Steps

If a particular line of code combines many calculations, perhaps breaking the line up into multiple steps will help identify the problem. For example, maybe one piece of the calculation is being cast badly, a function doesn't return what you thought it did, or the order of operations is different from what you expected. This also allows you to examine the calculation at each of the intermediate steps.

Check Boundary Conditions

The classic off-by-one problem has bitten all of us at one time or another. Check algorithms for these boundary conditions, especially in loops.

Disrupt Parallel Computations

If you suspect a race condition, serialize the code to check if the bug disappears. In threads, add extra delays to see if the problem shifts. The problem can be narrowed down if you can identify it as a race condition and use experiments to isolate it.

Exploit Tools in the Debugger

Understand and know how to use conditional breakpoints, memory watches, register watches, stack, and assembly/mixed debugging. Tools help you to find clues and the hard evidence that is key to identifying the bug.

Check Code That Has Recently Changed

It's amazing the debugging that can be done with source control. If you know a date when it worked and the date when it stopped working, you can look at which files changed and quickly find the offending code. This will at least narrow your search to particular subsystems or files.

Another way to exploit source control is to create a build of the game before the bug was introduced. This is helpful if you can't eyeball the problem. Running the old and new versions through a debugger and comparing values might be the key to finding the problem.

Explain the Bug to Someone Else

Often, when explaining a bug to someone else, you'll retrace your steps and realize something you missed or forgot to check. Other programmers are also great for suggesting alternate hypotheses that can be explored. Don't underestimate the power of talking to other people, and never be embarrassed to seek advice. The people on your team are your allies and one of your best weapons against truly difficult bugs.

Debug with a Partner

This usually pays off since each person carries different experiences and tactics for dealing with bugs. You'll often learn new techniques and attack the bug from an angle you might not have tried. Having someone looking over your shoulder can be one of the very best ways to track down a bug.

Take a Break from the Problem

Sometimes, you're so close to the problem that you can't look at it clearly any longer. Try removing yourself from the situation and take a stroll outside of your environment. When you relax and come back to the situation, you will have a fresh perspective. Once you've given yourself permission to take a break, sometimes your subconscious mind will work on the problem and the solution will simply dawn on you.

Get Outside Help

There are many great resources for getting assistance. If you are making a game for a console, each console manufacturer has a full team of people ready to assist you when you run into trouble. Know their contact information. The big three console makers all provide telephone support, e-mail support, and newsgroups where developers can help each other.

Tough Debugging Scenarios and Patterns

Bugs often follow patterns in which they give themselves away. In tough debugging scenarios, the patterns are the key. This is where experience pays off. If you've seen the pattern before, you have a good chance of quickly finding the bug. The following scenarios and patterns will give you some guidance.

The Bug Exists in Release But Not Debug

A bug that only exists in a release build usually points toward uninitialized data or a bug in optimized code. Often, debug builds will initialize variables to zero even though you wrote no code to do so. Since this invisible initialization doesn't happen in release builds, the bug shows up.

Another tactic for tracking down the cause is to take your debug build and slowly turn on optimizations one by one. By testing with each optimization, you can sometimes find the culprit. For example, in debug builds, functions are usually not inlined. When they become inlined for optimized builds, sometimes a bug will show up.

It is also important to note that debug symbols can be turned on in release builds. This allows limited (albeit often frustrating) debugging of optimized code and even allows you to keep some debugging systems enabled. For example, you could have your exception handlers perform a full-blown stack trace (which requires symbols) to the crash site. This can be especially helpful when testers must run an optimized version of the game, yet you want to be able to trace crashes.

The Bug Disappears When Changing Something Innocuous

If a bug goes away by changing something completely unrelated, like adding a harmless line of code, then it is likely a timing problem or a memory overwrite problem. Even if it looks like the bug has disappeared, it probably has just moved to a different part of your code. Don't lose this opportunity to find the bug. It's still there and it will most certainly bite you in the future in a subtle or nearly undetectable way.

Truly Intermittent Problems

As mentioned previously, most problems will occur reliably given the correct circumstances. If you truly can't control the circumstances, then you must catch the problem when it rears its ugly head. The key here is to record as much information as you can when you do catch the problem so that you can examine the data later, if needed. You won't get many chances, so make the most of each failure. Another helpful tip is to compare the data collected from the single failure case to data collected from when it worked properly and then identify the differences.

Unexplainable Behavior

There are cases when you will step through code and variables will change without anything touching them. Truly bizarre behavior such as this usually points toward the system or debugger becoming out of sync. The solution is to try to resync the system with "increasing levels of cache flushing."

The following four Rs of cache flushing are courtesy of Scott Bilas:

- **Retry** (flush the current state of the game and run again)
- **Rebuild** (flush the intermediate compiled objects and do a full rebuild)
- **Reboot** (flush the memory of your machine with a hard reset)
- **Reinstall** (flush the files and settings of your tools/OS by reinstalling)

Of these four Rs, the most important is rebuild. Sometimes, compilers don't properly track dependencies and will fail to recompile affected code. The symptoms are usually general weirdness. A complete rebuild often fixes the problem.

When dealing with unexplainable behavior, it is important to second-guess the debugger. Verify the real value of variables with `printfs` since sometimes the debugger becomes confused and won't accurately reflect the true values.

Internal Compiler Errors

Every once in a while you'll run into a situation where the compiler itself has given up on your code and complains of an internal compiler error. These errors could signal a legitimate problem in your code or they could be entirely the fault of the compiler software (for example, if it exceeded its memory limit or can't deal with your fancy templates). When faced with an internal compiler error, here's a good series of first steps to follow:

1. Perform a full rebuild.
2. Reboot your machine, and then perform a full rebuild.
3. Check that you have the latest version of the compiler.
4. Check that you have the latest version of any libraries you're using.
5. See if the same code compiles on other machines.

If these steps don't fix the problem, attempt to identify what piece of code is causing the error. If possible, use the divide-and-conquer technique to pare down the code until the internal compiler error goes away. Once it's identified, examine the code visually and ensure that it looks correct (it might help to have several different people look at it). If the code looks reasonable, the next step is to try rearranging the code to see if you can get a more meaningful error message from the compiler. One last step you might want to try is compiling with older versions of the compiler. It's quite possible that a bug was introduced into the newest compiler version, and an older compiler will compile the code correctly.

If none of these solutions helps, search Web sites for similar problems. If nothing turns up, contact the compiler maker for additional assistance.

When You Suspect It's Not Your Code

Shame on you—you should always suspect your own code! However, if you're convinced that it's not your code, the best course of action is to check Web sites for patches to libraries or compilers that you're using. Study the readme files or search Web sites for known bugs with your libraries or compiler. Often, other people have run into similar problems and workarounds or fixes exist.

However, there is always a remote possibility that your bug is a result of someone else's library or even faulty hardware (and you happen to be the first person to find it). While this is usually not the case, it certainly happens. The fastest way to deal with this is to make a tiny sample program that isolates the problem. You can then e-mail that program to the makers of the libraries or the hardware vendor so that they can investigate the problem further. If it really is someone else's bug, then you can get it fixed the fastest by helping these other people identify and reproduce the problem.

Understanding the Underlying System

To find really tough bugs, you must understand the underlying system. Thoroughly knowing C or C++ simply isn't enough. To be a really good programmer, you must understand how the compiler implements higher-level concepts, you must understand assembly, and you must know the details of your hardware (especially for console development). It's nice to think that high-level languages mask all of these complexities, but the truth is that when something *really* breaks, you'll be clueless unless you understand what lies beneath the abstractions. For more discussion on how high-level abstractions can *leak*, please see "The Law of Leaky Abstractions" [Spolsky02].

So, what underlying details should you know? For games, you should understand the following:

- **Know how a compiler implements code.** Be familiar with how inheritance, virtual function calls, calling conventions, and exceptions are implemented. Know how the compiler allocates memory and deals with alignment.
- **Know the details of your hardware.** For example, understand a particular hardware's caching issues (when memory in the cache might differ from main memory), address alignment constraints, endianness, stack size, and type sizes (such as int, long, and bool).
- **Know how assembly works and be able to read it.** This can help track down problems with optimized builds where the debugger has trouble tracing through the source.

Without a firm grasp of these issues, you will have an Achilles heel when it comes down to fighting the really tough bugs. You must understand the underlying system and know its rules intimately.

Adding Infrastructure to Assist in Debugging

Debugging in a vacuum without the right tools can be very frustrating. The solution is to swing the pendulum in the other direction and build great debugging tools directly into your game. The following tools will help greatly when tracking down bugs.

Alter Game Variables During Gameplay

A valuable tool in debugging and reproducing bugs is the ability to change game variables at runtime. The classic interface for doing this is to use a keyboard to alter variables through a debug command-line interface (CLI) in your game. With the press of a button, debug text is overlaid onto your game screen and a prompt lets you enter input via the keyboard. For example, if you want to change the weather in your game to stormy, you might type "weather stormy" at the prompt. This kind of interface is also great for tuning and checking the value of variables or particular game states.

Visual AI Diagnostics

Good tools are invaluable to debugging and standard debuggers are simply inefficient for diagnosing AI problems. Debuggers give great depth at a moment in time, but they are lousy at showing how an AI system evolves during gameplay. They are also poor at showing spatial relationships in the game world. The solution is to build visualization diagnostics directly into the game that can monitor any given character. By using a combination of text and 3D lines, important AI systems like pathfinding, awareness boundaries, and current targets can be easily tracked and checked for errors [Tozour02], [Laming03].

Logging Capability

Often, in games, we make dozens of characters interact and communicate with each other, resulting in very complex behavior. When these interactions break down and a bug arises, it becomes crucial to be able to log the individual states and events from each character that led to the bug. By creating separate logs for each character, with key events time-stamped, it becomes possible to track down the failure by examining the logs [Rabin00a], [Rabin02].

Recording and Playback Capability

As mentioned before, the key to tracking down bugs is reproducibility. The ultimate in reproducibility would entail recording and playing back player input [Dawson01]. For very rare crashes, this can be a key tool in pinpointing the exact cause. However, to support this capability, you must make your game predictable so that an initial state coupled with player input produces the same result each time. That doesn't mean your game is predictable to players, it just means that you have to carefully deal with random number generation [Lecky-Thompson00], [Freeman-Hargis03], initial state, input, and be able to save the input when a crash happens [Dawson99].

Track Memory Allocation

Create memory allocators that can perform a full stack trace on every allocation. By keeping records of exactly who is requesting memory, you'll never again have to chase down memory leaks.

Print as Much Information as Possible on a Crash

Postmortem debugging is very important. In a crash situation, ideally you'll want to capture the call stack, registers, and any other state information that might be relevant. This information can be printed to the screen, written to a file, or automatically e-mailed to a developer's mailbox. This kind of tool will help you find the source of the crash in a couple of minutes instead of a few hours. This is especially true if the crash happens on an artist or designer's machine and they don't remember how they triggered the crash.

Educate Your Entire Team

While this is not infrastructure that you can program, it's mental infrastructure that must be in place so that your team uses the tools you've created. Train them to not ignore error dialogs, and make sure they know how to gather information so that a found bug is not lost. Spending the time to educate testers, artists, and designers is well worth the investment.

Prevention of Bugs

A discussion of debugging wouldn't be complete without a short guide on how to avoid bugs in the first place. By following these guidelines, you'll either avoid writing some bugs, or stumble upon bugs you didn't know you had. Either way, this will help you eliminate bugs in the long run.

Set your compiler to the highest warning level and enable warnings as errors. Try to fix as many of the warnings as possible, and then `#pragma` the rest away. Sometimes, automatic casts and other warning level issues will cause subtle bugs.

Make your game compile on multiple compilers. If you make sure your game builds with multiple compilers and for multiple platforms, the differences between the warnings and errors of both compilers will usually ensure better code all around. For example, people writing Nintendo GameCube games can also make sure a crippled version runs in Win32. This can also allow you to see if a bug is platform-specific or not.

Write your own memory manager. This is crucial for console games. You must understand what memory you're using and shield against memory overruns. Since memory overruns cause some of the toughest bugs to track down, it is important to make sure they never happen in the first place. Using overrun and underrun guard blocks in debug builds can make bugs show up before they can manifest themselves. For PC developers, writing your own memory manager is not really necessary, since the memory system in VC++ is quite powerful, and good tools like SmartHeap can be exploited to identify errors with memory.

Use asserts to verify your assumptions. Add asserts to the beginning of functions to verify assumptions about arguments (such as non-NULL pointers or ranges). In addition, if the default case of a switch statement should never be reached, add an assertion for that case. Additionally, the standard assert can be expanded to give you much more debugging power [Rabin00b]. For example, it can be extremely helpful if your assertions print out a call stack.

Always initialize variables when they are declared. If you can't assign a variable a meaningful value when it's declared, then assign it something recognizable so that you can spot that it was never properly set. Some ideas for values are `0xDEADBEEF`, `0xCDCDCDCD`, or simply zero.

Always bracket your loops and if statements. This keeps you honest by making you explicitly wrap the intended code, making it more obvious what was intended.

Use variable names that are cognitively different. For example, `m_objectITime` and `m_objectJTime` look almost the same. The typical example of this problem is the use of "`i`" and "`j`" as loop counters. The characters "`i`" and "`j`" are very similar looking and you could easily mistake one for the other. As an alternative, you could use "`i`" and "`k`" or simply use names that are more descriptive. More information on cognitive differences in variable naming can be found in [McConnell93].

Avoid having identical code in multiple places. Having the same code in several different places is a liability. If the code is changed in one place, it is unlikely it will also get changed in the other locations. If it seems necessary to duplicate code, then rethink the core functionality and try to centralize a majority of the code in one place.

Avoid magic (hardcoded) numbers. When a unique number appears in code, its meaning and significance can be completely lost. If there is no comment, then it is unclear why that particular value was chosen and what it represents. If you must use magic numbers, declare them as constants or defines that give a meaningful label to the number.

Verify code coverage when testing. When you write a piece of code, verify that it executes correctly down every branch. If you have never seen it execute a particular branch, there's a good chance it contains a bug. One possible bug that you might catch from this process is discovering that it's impossible to take a particular branch. The sooner this is discovered, the better.

Conclusion

This article has given you the tools you need to effectively debug games. Debugging is sometimes described as an art, but that's only because people get better at it with experience. As you internalize the *Five-Step Debugging Process*, learn to spot bug patterns, integrate your own debugging tools into your game, and build up your repertoire of debugging techniques, you'll quickly become adept at methodically tracking down and squashing tough bugs. With an ounce of prevention, hopefully your game will be smooth sailing and nary a bug will bite you.

Acknowledgments

Thanks go out to Scott Bilas and Jack Matthews for making great suggestions and lending some of their own personal experience and wisdom to this article. There are many different viewpoints with regard to debugging, and their opinions were invaluable in tempering the advice presented.

References

[Dawson99] Dawson, Bruce, "Structured Exception Handling," *Game Developer Magazine* (Jan 1999), pp. 52–54.

[Dawson01] Dawson, Bruce, "Game Input Recording and Playback," *Game Programming Gems 2*, Charles River Media, 2001.

[Freeman-Hargis03] Freeman-Hargis, James, "The Statistics of Random Numbers," *AI Game Programming Wisdom 2*, Charles River Media, 2003.

[Laming03] Laming, Brett, "The Art of Surviving a Simulation Title," *AI Game Programming Wisdom 2*, Charles River Media, 2003.

[Lecky-Thompson00] Lecky-Thompson, Guy, "Predictable Random Numbers," *Game Programming Gems*, Charles River Media, 2000.

[McConnell93] McConnell, Steve, *Code Complete: A Practical Handbook of Software Construction*, Microsoft Press, 1993.

[Rabin00a] Rabin, Steve, "Designing a General Robust AI Engine," *Game Programming Gems*, Charles River Media, 2000.

[Rabin00b] Rabin, Steve, "Squeezing More Out of Assert," *Game Programming Gems*, Charles River Media, 2000.

[Rabin02] Rabin, Steve, "Implementing a State Machine Language," *AI Game Programming Wisdom*, Charles River Media, 2000.

[Spolsky02] Spolsky, Joel, "The Law of Leaky Abstractions," *Joel on Software*, 2002, available online at www.joelonsoftware.com/articles/LeakyAbstractions.html.

[Tozour02] Tozour, Paul, "Building an AI Diagnostic Toolset," *AI Game Programming Wisdom*, Charles River Media, 2002.

1.2

Finding Redeeming Value in C-Style Macros

Steve Rabin, Nintendo of America Inc.

steve.rabin@gmail.com

The lowly C-style macro (`#define`) is a powerful construct that is severely misunderstood. Many people and books characterize it as evil and outdated, replaced by the inline functionality in C++. Unfortunately, that's a simplistic view that doesn't take into account the unique functionality that the macro possesses. Shamefully, many C++ books fail to explain the basic properties of macros or even acknowledge their existence. However, solid explanations can still be found in classic C books such as [Kernighan88].

In a nutshell, the macro is a directive to the compiler's preprocessor to do some creative text replacement. Thus, no type-checking or other safety checks take place, and this is where many programmers get into trouble. As a simple rule, macros shouldn't be used to create function-like behavior or constants. For a discussion of the pitfalls of macros, please refer to [Dalton01], [Hyman99], and [McConnell93].

However, this gem isn't about the problems with macros; it's about proving that macros are useful and desirable in many surprising ways. Macros allow you to perform fancy text replacement before actual compilation, and that's exactly what the following tricks exploit. Note that the source code that appears in each example can also be found on the CD-ROM.

ON THE CD

Disclaimer

With macros, it's easy to be carried away into a world of bad programming practices. However, that's not the intention of this gem. While individuals have their own boundaries as to what is acceptable, it is generally understood that making new *dialects* of C/C++ by using macros is undesirable. Anyone coming onto a project should be able to read your code with a minimal amount of effort. So, as you read these tricks, understand that each one must be carefully weighed for its benefit versus the possibility of obfuscation. Confined use of these examples is probably the most reasonable way to benefit from this gem.

Macro Trick #1: Turning Enums into Strings

There are two special operators that let you do some tricky text manipulation inside of a macro. The first operator is `#`, and it will instruct the macro to put quotes around the argument that follows it. For example:

```
#define CaseEnum(a)   case(a): LogMsgToFile(#a, id, time)

switch( msg_passed_in )
{
    CaseEnum( MSG_YouWereHit );
        ReactToHit();
        break;

    CaseEnum( MSG_GameReset );
        ResetLogic();
        break;
}
```

After the compiler's preprocessing step, the previous code becomes:

```
switch( msg_passed_in )
{
    case( MSG_YouWereHit ):
        LogMsgToFile( "MSG_YouWereHit", id, time );
        ReactToHit();
        break;

    case( MSG_GameReset ):
        LogMsgToFile( "MSG_GameReset", id, time );
        ResetLogic();
        break;
}
```

With this macro scheme, you can easily dump enum names in a reliable and meaningful way, as actual strings, to a log file or the screen. Without this trick, you would need to have a lookup table of all enums-to-strings. Unfortunately, lookup tables are often poorly maintained and, thus, not reliable. The other solution is to use strings in the first place, instead of enums, but it's doubtful you would want to perform routine string compares inside your game. Therefore, the macro trick is a sound solution that is both fast and reliable.

Another variant is to read in the enumeration from a header file and interpret the single list into both an enumeration and an array of string names. The following shows how this can be done:

```
// data.h

DATA(MSG_YouWereHit)
DATA(MSG_GameReset)
DATA(MSG_HealthRestored)
```

```
// data.cpp

#define DATA(x) x,

enum GameMessages
{
    #include "data.h"
};

#undef DATA
#define DATA(x) #x, // make enums into strings

static const char* GameMessageNames[] =
{
    #include "data.h"
};

#undef DATA
```

Macro Trick #2: Compile-Time Constants from Binary Representations

The other special macro operator is ##. This operator lets you paste two arguments together. For example:

```
#define cat(a,b)   a ## b

value = cat( 1, 2 );
```

The preprocessor will turn the previous line into:

```
value = 12;
```

While this simple example is useless (shown just to illustrate the concept), the ## operator can be exploited in very interesting ways. The following trick allows you to create compile-time constants using binary representations. What is especially interesting is that this runs completely in the preprocessor with no runtime code generated. (Special thanks to Jeff Grills who provided this implementation.)

Here's the usage:

```
const int nibble = BINARY1(0101);        // 0x5
const int byte   = BINARY2(1010,0101);   // 0xa5

// 0xa5a5a5a5
const int dword = BINARY8(1010,0101,1010,0101,1010,0101,1010,0101);
```

Macro source:

```
#define HEX_DIGIT_0000 0
#define HEX_DIGIT_0001 1
#define HEX_DIGIT_0010 2
#define HEX_DIGIT_0011 3
#define HEX_DIGIT_0100 4
#define HEX_DIGIT_0101 5
#define HEX_DIGIT_0110 6
#define HEX_DIGIT_0111 7
#define HEX_DIGIT_1000 8
#define HEX_DIGIT_1001 9
#define HEX_DIGIT_1010 a
#define HEX_DIGIT_1011 b
#define HEX_DIGIT_1100 c
#define HEX_DIGIT_1101 d
#define HEX_DIGIT_1110 e
#define HEX_DIGIT_1111 f

#define HEX_DIGIT(a)         HEX_DIGIT_ ## a

#define BINARY1H(a)          (0x ## a)
#define BINARY1I(a)          BINARY1H(a)
#define BINARY1(a)           BINARY1I(HEX_DIGIT(a))

#define BINARY2H(a,b)        (0x ## a ## b)
#define BINARY2I(a,b)        BINARY2H(a,b)
#define BINARY2(a,b)         BINARY2I(HEX_DIGIT(a), HEX_DIGIT(b))

#define BINARY8H(a,b,c,d,e,f,g,h) (0x##a##b##c##d##e##f##g##h)
#define BINARY8I(a,b,c,d,e,f,g,h) BINARY8H(a,b,c,d,e,f,g,h)
#define BINARY8(a,b,c,d,e,f,g,h)  BINARY8I(HEX_DIGIT(a), \
    HEX_DIGIT(b), HEX_DIGIT(c), HEX_DIGIT(d), HEX_DIGIT(e), \
    HEX_DIGIT(f), HEX_DIGIT(g), HEX_DIGIT(h))
```

Macro Trick #3: Adding a Descriptive Comment to Standard Assert

The standard Windows assert (found in assert.h) is already a macro. It's extremely helpful, even indispensable to good software engineering—but it can be improved. The biggest improvement is to add a descriptive string so that a meaningful message is displayed when an assert is triggered.

With the following macro, you can easily expand the standard assert to include a descriptive string:

```
#define assertmsg(a,b) assert( a && b )
```

Example use:

```
assertmsg( time > 0, "Trigger::Set - The arg time must be > 0" );
```

When `time` is less than or equal to zero, the assert will be raised and the embedded message is displayed as part of the failed assertion. You can read more about this trick, as well as other assert tricks, in [Rabin00].

Macro Trick #4: Compile-Time Assert

Occasionally, you'll have a situation where you want a build to immediately fail if a particular condition isn't satisfied at compile time. Depending on the size of your project, this can save a lot of time and trouble. The following macro allows you to verify a statement at compile time, which in effect is a compile-time assert.

```
#define cassert(expn) typedef char __C_ASSERT__[(expn)?1:-1]
```

For example, if you're working on cross-platform code, you might want to check at compile time that enumerations are the same size as an unsigned integer. Given an enumeration such as `MyEnum`, you can check this by writing:

```
cassert( sizeof(MyEnum) == sizeof(unsigned int) );
```

If a false statement is passed into `cassert`, it will fail at compile time because it attempts to define an array with a negative size. Defining a negative-size array is a blatant compile error that will immediately stop the build.

Macro Trick #5: Determining the Number of Elements in an Array

Sometimes it's useful to know the number of elements in an array. However, there is no obvious way to query this, since it is not stored explicitly—only defined at initialization time.

The trick to computing the number of elements in an array is to divide the overall size of an array by the size of a given element. For example, if the total size of an array is 120 bytes and each element takes up 12 bytes, there must be 10 elements in the array. The size of each element, in bytes, is known at compile time, and the following macro neatly returns the number of elements.

```
#define NumElm(array) (sizeof(array) / sizeof((array)[0]))
```

Macro Trick #6: Making `__LINE__` into a String

Several very useful macros exist by default. These include:

```
__LINE__ //an integer of the line number where it appears
__FILE__ //a string containing the file name where it appears
__DATE__ //a string containing the date when it was compiled
__TIME__ //a string containing the time when it was compiled
```

The main use for these macros is to record information that is useful in debugging. For example, when an assert macro is placed in your code, it takes advantage of the `__FILE__` and `__LINE__` macros. Should the assert be triggered, these values are displayed; thus, you know the exact filename and line number where the problem occurred.

Since these values are normally used for printing out debugging information as strings, here are several macros to turn the `__FILE__` string and the `__LINE__` integer into a single string containing both:

```
#define _QUOTE(x) # x
#define QUOTE(x) _QUOTE(x)
#define __FILELINE__ __FILE__ "(" QUOTE(__LINE__) ")"
```

This trick doesn't work with Microsoft Visual C++, since it replaces `__LINE__` *differently than other compilers. Instead of replacing the macro* `__LINE__` *with a simple integer, it is replaced by* `(__LINE__Var+offset)`, *where* `__LINE__Var` *is an internal variable that represents the line number where the function starts, and* `offset` *is an actual integer representing the offset from the start of the function. Therefore, with Microsoft Visual C++, the macro trick might produce a result like:*

```
"C:\project\main.cpp((__LINE__Var+5))"
```

However, this macro trick produces the desired result with both Metrowerks CodeWarrior and SN Systems ProDG (a gcc-based compiler).

Macro Trick #7: Protecting Against Infinite Loops

The possibility of an infinite loop often looms over particular parts of your code, especially parts that depend on outside data or scripts. A practical safeguard is to create a counter that increments every time through the loop and, if it should get too high, asserts. That is exactly what this next trick will do, except that it will be done in a transparent manner that can be optionally compiled out for release builds.

This trick creates a macro called "`while_limit`," which behaves similar to the `while` keyword; however, it takes a second argument that defines the number of iterations at which it will raise an assert. For example, consider the following code:

```
while_limit( node != 0, 1000 ) {
    //some work
    node = node->next;
}
```

The previous example will assert if the loop spins more than 1,000 times. By raising an assert instead of hanging, testers can more easily diagnose bugs. As an added bonus, if the tester chooses to ignore the assert, the `while_limit` will exit the infinite loop and continue normal program execution.

Here's the macro source:

```
static bool while_assert( bool a )
{
    assert( a && "while_limit: exceeded iteration limit" );
    return( a );
}

#define UNIQUE_VAR(x) safety_limit ## x
#define _while_limit(a,b,c) \
    assert(b>0 && "while_limit: limit is zero or negative");\
    int UNIQUE_VAR(c) = b; \
    while(a && while_assert(—UNIQUE_VAR(c)>=0))
#define while_limit(a,b) _while_limit(a,b,__COUNTER__)
```

Note that a new default macro, `__COUNTER__`, is used in the previous code. The macro `__COUNTER__` expands to an integer, starting with zero, and increments by one every time it is used. This allows us to create a unique variable each time we use `while_limit`. This unique variable is used to keep track of loop iterations. The first time a `while_limit` occurs, the variable's name will be `safety_limit0`. (The second time, the variable's name will be `safety_limit1`.) This unique-naming trick is necessary so that multiple `while_limit` macros could be used without their loop-iteration variable names clashing (causing compile errors due to multiple definitions).

The macro `__COUNTER__` is not a standard ANSI C macro and is not implemented in all compilers. However, it is implemented in Microsoft Visual C++ and Metrowerks CodeWarrior. For SN Systems ProDG and other gcc compilers, an alternative trick exists by using the `__LINE__` macro to help create the unique variable name. The following code will work with both SN Systems ProDG and Metrowerks CodeWarrior. (Both variations of `while_limit` work with Metrowerks CodeWarrior.)

This alternate macro source works on both SN Systems ProDG and Metrowerks CodeWarrior:

```
static bool while_assert( bool a )
{
    assert( a && "while_limit: exceeded iteration limit" );
    return( a );
}

#define _UNIQUE_VAR(x) safety_limit ## x
#define UNIQUE_VAR(x) _UNIQUE_VAR(x)
#define while_limit(a,b) \
    assert(b>0 && "while_limit: limit is zero or negative"); \
    int UNIQUE_VAR(__LINE__) = b; \
    while(a && while_assert(—UNIQUE_VAR(__LINE__)>=0))
```

Macro Trick #8: Small, Specialized Languages

Macros can be quite powerful, and this trick probably demonstrates this best. Using the text-replacement property of macros, you can create your own small, specialized language that compiles directly into C/C++. Before you jump to conclusions, remember that we're still striving for readable, maintainable, and debuggable code.

In the article "Implementing a State Machine Language" (*AI Game Programming Wisdom* [Rabin02]), there is an example of a macro language that standardizes the construction of state machines and enforces some good programming practices. Consequently, it makes the state machine easier to build and easier to read. Here is an example of a state machine using the macro language:

```
BeginStateMachine

    State( STATE_Wander )
        OnEnter
            // C++ code for state entry
        OnUpdate
            // C++ code executed every tick
        OnExit
            // C++ code for state clean-up

    State( STATE_Attack )
        OnEnter
            // C++ code for state entry

EndStateMachine
```

While the previous code looks like a completely new scripting language, it compiles into C/C++ only using six macro keywords. The benefit is that native C/C++ code can be freely inserted, and it is trivial to debug, since the full power of the debugger is still available. Once you understand the behavior of the state machine, the macro language actually hides the unnecessary details and lets you code the internals in a simple and natural way.

The six macro keywords are as follows (`OnEvent` is a helper—it's not used directly):

```
#define BeginStateMachine  if(state < 0){if(0){
#define EndStateMachine    return(true);}}else{assert(0); \
                           return(false);}return(false);
#define State(a)           return(true);}} \
                           else if(a == state){if(0){
#define OnEvent(a)         return(true);}else if(a == event){
#define OnEnter            OnEvent(EVENT_Enter)
#define OnUpdate           OnEvent(EVENT_Update)
#define OnExit             OnEvent(EVENT_Exit)
```

If you want to explore this macro-scripting language further, please see [Rabin02] for an in-depth explanation.

Macro Trick #9: Simplifying Class Interfaces

One of the goals of C++ is to separate the declaration of a class from its definition. This is very useful; it allows you to see the interface that a given class exposes—its *declaration*, usually placed in a header file—without having to understand its actual implementation of that functionality (the *class definition*, usually placed in a .CPP file).

Unfortunately, the way C++ implements the separation of class declaration and definition ends up causing a fair amount of extra work. Namely, the signature (function name and parameters) of every non-inline function must be stated twice, once in the class declaration and once in the definition.

```
// class declaration in Elmo.h
class Elmo
{
    void TickleMe(int x, int y = 0);
};

// class definition in Elmo.cpp
void Elmo::TickleMe(int x, int y)
{
    // actual implementation of Elmo::TickleMe() goes here
}
```

Because the signature of `Elmo::TickleMe()` exists in two places, every time we wish to change the parameters of the method—or change the function's name, or change it to be *const*, perhaps—we need to change it in two places.

Usually, this isn't a big deal. In most cases, a method will belong only to one class, and it's not problematic to change it in only two places. However, there are some cases where this aspect of the C++ language can cause you a lot of work. And in some situations it can become very easy to incur subtle bugs when you change a function's signature—bugs that your compiler won't be able to warn you about.

For example, imagine we have a base class named `BaseClass`. There are three classes derived from `BaseClass`—`D1`, `D2`, and `D3`. `BaseClass` declares a virtual function `Foo()`. `BaseClass::Foo()` comes with a default implementation in `BaseClass`; it's not a pure virtual function. Further, let's assume that the derived class `D3` overrides `Foo()`, so that `D3::Foo()` does something different than `BaseClass::Foo()`.

Now, let's say we add a parameter to `BaseClass::Foo()`, and we forget to update `D3::Foo()` at the same time. Sadly, our compiler will now lose the connection between `BaseClass::Foo()` and `D3::Foo()`—it will assume that they are two entirely different functions, and that `D3::Foo()` is an entirely separate function from `BaseClass::Foo()`. When we try to call `Foo()` as a virtual function on objects of class `BaseClass`, `D3::Foo()` will not get called on objects of type `D3`, as we originally intended.

Ideally, we want a method's signature to exist in only one place. It would be nice to be able to declare `BaseClass::Foo()` and provide implementations in both `BaseClass` and `D3` without also having to provide an additional declaration of `D3::Foo()`.

There's also an argument in support of productivity: With inheritance in C++, we often end up making many shallow class hierarchies with a single parent and many children. These generally tend to be much more useful than deep, everything-including-the-kitchen-sink hierarchies, which attempt to artificially conglomerate many unrelated pieces of functionality into a single, massively extended family.

With shallow hierarchies, we begin with a base class that exists primarily to declare an interface—that is, it declares some number of virtual functions, most of which will be pure virtuals. Quite often, we end up with a large number of classes in such a family, with a single base class and perhaps a dozen other classes derived from that base class. The problem is that we need to redeclare all of the methods we want to override in all of the derived classes we implement. If we have a base class with 10 functions, and we derive 10 classes from that base class, that's 100 extra function declarations, all of which essentially exist only to say, "I, too, implement the functionality declared in the base class." All of this extra text can make header files difficult to maintain and hard to read.

Let's imagine we have a class called `Creature`, and we intend to derive various different classes of creatures from this base class. `Creature` defines three pure virtual functions, as shown:

```
class Creature
{
      public:
         virtual std::string GetName() const = 0;
         virtual int GetHitPoints() const = 0;
         virtual float GetMaxVelocity() const = 0;
};
```

Furthermore, assume we derive several different classes of creature (`SnowCrab`, `NordicYeti`, and `SnowshoeBandit`) from this base `Creature` class. Each of our three methods—`GetName()`, `GetHitPoints()`, and `GetMaxVelocity()`—now exists in seven places: once in the declaration of `Creature`, and once each in the declaration and definition of `SnowCrab`, `NordicYeti`, and `SnowshoeBandit`.

So now let's assume we make a minor change and modify `GetHitPoints()` to return a float instead of an int. We now have to go and modify `GetHitPoints()` in *seven different files*—Creature.h, SnowCrab.h, SnowCrab.cpp, NordicYeti.h, NordicYeti.cpp, SnowshoeBandit.h, and SnowshoeBandit.cpp.

One good way to handle this is to wrap the methods into what can be called an *interface macro*. This is a macro that simply declares all of the `Creature` methods, like so:

```
#define INTERFACE_Creature(terminal)                        \
    public:                                                 \
        virtual std::string GetName() const ##terminal \
        virtual int GetHitPoints() const ##terminal     \
        virtual float GetMaxVelocity() const ##terminal
```

```
#define BASE_Creature          INTERFACE_Creature(=0;)
#define DERIVED_Creature       INTERFACE_Creature(;)
```

The beauty of this is that we can now vastly simplify the class declarations of `Creature` and all of the classes derived from it:

```
// Creature.h
class Creature
{
    BASE_Creature;
};

// Skeleton.h
class SnowCrab
    : public Creature
{
    DERIVED_Creature;
};

// NordicYeti.h
class NordicYeti
    : public Creature
{
    DERIVED_Creature;
};

// etc.
```

Now, whenever we want to change one of the methods in `Creature`, we no longer have to touch SnowCrab.h, NordicYeti.h, or SnowshoeBandit.h—all we need to change is the interface macro (`INTERFACE_Creature` in Creature.h). We still need to modify the implementations in the various .cpp files; but given that the function is changing, we'd need to do that anyway.

Furthermore, our class declarations have become much more readable. When we look at the class declaration of `NordicYeti` in NordicYeti.h, we see `DERIVED_Creature` plus some number of other methods specific to a `NordicYeti` and not shared with other creatures. This immediately tells us what functionality belongs specifically to `NordicYeti`, and that if we want to see the declaration of the creature-level functionality, we should look for it in Creature.h, since that's where it properly belongs.

It's important to note that this interface macro is entirely different from the concept of an 'interface' in a language such as Java or C#. In these sorts of languages, you can treat an interface as an object—you can pass it around as a reference and call any of its methods. An interface macro, however, is just a way of encapsulating a set of related function declarations to hide some of the unnecessary duplication that the structure of the C++ language forces you to maintain.

Very special thanks to Paul Tozour for supplying this macro trick.

Conclusion

Hopefully, these examples have given you some renewed hope in macros and have expanded your personal toolbox of solutions. Just remember to carefully weigh the cost versus the benefit; always strive to make your code easier to understand and more robust. Used judiciously, these macros should make your programming tasks just a little easier and the results a little less prone to error.

References

[Dalton01] Dalton, Peter, "Inline Functions Versus Macros," *Game Programming Gems 2,* Charles River Media, Inc., 2001.

[Hyman99] Hyman, Michael, and Phani Vaddadi, *Mike and Phani's Essential C++ Techniques,* APress, 1999.

[Kernighan88] Kernighan, Brian, and Dennis Ritchie, *The C Programming Language,* Prentice Hall, 1988.

[McConnell93] McConnell, Steve, *Code Complete: A Practical Handbook of Software Construction,* Microsoft Press, 1993.

[Rabin00] Rabin, Steve, "Squeezing More Out of Assert," *Game Programming Gems,* Charles River Media, Inc., 2000.

[Rabin02] Rabin, Steve, "Implementing a State Machine Language," *AI Game Programming Wisdom,* Charles River Media, Inc., 2002.

1.3

Inline Functions vs. Macros

Peter Dalton, Smart Bomb Interactive

pdalton@madprog.com

When it comes to game programming, the need for fast efficient functions cannot be overstated, especially functions that are executed multiple times per frame. Many programmers rely heavily upon macros when dealing with common, time-critical routines because they eliminate the calling/returning sequence required by functions that are sensitive to the overhead of function calls. However, using the `#define` directive to implement macros that look like functions is more problematic than it is worth.

Advantages of Inline Functions

Through the use of inline functions, many of the inherent disadvantages of macros can easily be avoided. Take for example the following macro definition:

```
#define max(a,b) ((a) > (b) ? (a) : (b))
```

Let's look at what would happen if we called the macro with the following parameters: `max(++x, y)`. If `x = 5` and `y = 3`, the macro will return a value of `7` rather than the expected value of `6`. This illustrates the most common side effect of macros, the fact that expressions passed as arguments can be evaluated more than once. To avoid this problem we could have used an inline function to accomplish the same goal:

```
inline int max(int a, int b) { return (a > b ? a : b); }
```

By using the inline method, we are guaranteed that all parameters will only be evaluated once because they must, by definition, follow all the protocols and type safety enforced on normal functions.

Another problem that plagues macros, operator precedence, follows from the same problem presented previously, illustrated in the following macro:

```
#define square(x) (x*x)
```

If we were to call this macro with the expression `2+1` it should become obvious that the macro would return a result of `5` instead of the expected `9`. The problem here is that the multiplication operator has a higher precedence than the addition operator. While wrapping all of the expressions within parenthesis would remedy this problem it could have easily been avoided through the use of inline functions.

The other major pitfall surrounding macros has to deal with multiple-statement macros and guaranteeing that all statements within the macro are executed properly. Once again, let's look at a simple macro used to clamp any given number between zero and one.

```
        #define clamp(a)                \
            if (a > 1.0) a = 1.0; \
    if (a < 0.0) a = 0.0;
```

If we were to use the macro within the following loop:

```
        for (int ii = 0; ii < N; ++ii)
            clamp( numbersToBeClamped[ii] );
```

The numbers would not be clamped if they were less than zero. Only upon termination of the `for` loop when `ii == N` would the expression `if (numbersToBeClamped[ii] < 0.0)` be evaluated. This is also very problematic because the index variable *ii* is now out of range and could easily result in a memory bounds violation that could crash the program. While replacing the macro with an inline function to perform the same functionality is not the only solution, it is the cleanest.

Given these inherent disadvantages associated with macros, let's run through the advantages of inline functions.

- Inline functions follow all the protocols of type safety enforced on normal functions. This ensures that unexpected or invalid parameters are not passed as arguments.
- Inline functions are specified using the same syntax as any other function except for the inline keyword in the function declaration.
- Expressions passed as arguments to inline functions are evaluated prior to entering the function body, thus expressions are evaluated only once. As shown previously, expressions passed to macros can be evaluated more than once and may result in unsafe and unexpected side effects.
- It is possible to debug inline functions using debuggers such as Microsoft's Visual C++. This is not possible with macros because the macro is expanded before the parser takes over and the program's symbol tables are created.
- Inline functions arguably increase the procedure's readability and maintainability because they use the same syntax as regular function calls, yet do not modify parameters unexpectedly.

Inline functions also outperform ordinary functions by eliminating the overhead of function calls. This includes tasks such as stack-frame setup, parameter passing, stack-frame restoration and the returning sequence. Besides these key advantages, inline functions also provide the compiler with the ability to perform improved code optimizations. By replacing inline functions with code, the inserted code is subject to additional optimizations that would not otherwise be possible because most compilers do not perform interprocedural optimizations. Allowing the compiler to perform global optimizations such as common subexpression elimination and loop invariant removal can dramatically improve both speed and size.

The only limitation to inline functions that is not present within macros is the restriction on parameter types. Macros allow for any possible type to be passed as a parameter; however, inline functions only allow for the specified parameter type in order to enforce type safety. We can overcome this limitation through the use of inline template functions, which allow us to accept any parameter type and enforce type safety, yet still provide all the benefits associated with inline functions.

When to Use Inline Functions

Why don't we make every function an inline function? Wouldn't this eliminate the function overhead for the entire program, resulting in faster fill rates and response times? Obviously the answer to these questions is no. While code expansion can improve speed by eliminating function overhead and allowing for interprocedural compiler optimizations, this is all done at the expense of code size. When examining the performance of a program, two factors need to be weighed: execution speed and the actual code size. Increasing code size not only takes up more memory, which is a precious commodity, it also bogs down the execution speed. As the memory requirements for a program increase, so does the likelihood of cache misses and page faults. While a cache miss will cause a minor delay, a page fault will always result in a major delay because the virtual memory location is not in physical memory and must be fetched from disk. On a 400-megahertz Pentium II desktop machine, a hard page fault will result in an approximately 10-millisecond penalty, or about 4,000,000 CPU cycles [Heller99].

If inline functions are not always a win, then when exactly should we use them? The answer to this question really depends upon the situation and thus must rely heavily upon the judgment of the programmer. However, here are some guidelines for when inline functions work well:

- Small methods, such as accessors for private data members.
- Functions returning state information about an object.
- Small functions, typically 3 lines or less.
- Small functions that are called repeatedly. For example, within a time-critical rendering loop.

Longer functions that spend proportionately less time in the calling/returning sequence will benefit less from inlining. However, used correctly, inlining can greatly increase procedure performance.

When to Use Macros

Despite the problems associated with macros, there are a few circumstances in which they are invaluable. For example, macros can be use to create small pseudo-languages that can be quite powerful. A set of macros can provide the framework that makes creating state machines a breeze while being very debuggable and bulletproof. For an excellent example of this technique, refer to the "Designing a General Robust AI Engine" article referenced at the end of this gem [Rabin00]. Another example might be printing enumerated types to the screen. For example:

```
    #define CaseEnum(a)    case(a) : PrintEnum( #a )
    switch (msg_passed_in) {
        CaseEnum( MSG_YouWereHit );
            ReactToHit();
            break;
        CaseEnum( MSG_GameReset );
          ResetGameLogic();
          break;
}
```

Here `PrintEnum()` is a macro that prints a string to the screen. The `#` is the stringizing operator that converts macro parameters to string constants [MSDN]. Thus, there is no need to create a look-up table of all enums to strings (which are usually poorly maintained) in order to retrieve invaluable debug information.

The key to avoiding the problems associated with macros is, first, to understand the problems and, second, to know the alternative implementations.

Microsoft Specifics

Besides the standard `inline` keyword, Microsoft's Visual C++ compiler provides support for two additional keywords. The `__inline` keyword instructs the compiler to generate a cost/benefit analysis and to only inline the function if it proves beneficial. The `__forceinline` keyword instructs the compiler to always inline the function. Despite using these keywords, there are certain circumstances in which the compiler cannot comply as noted by Microsoft's documentation [MSDN].

References

[Heller99] Heller, Martin, *Developing Optimized Code with Microsoft Visual C++ 6.0*, Microsoft MSDN Library, January 2000.

[McConnell93] McConnell, Steve, *Code Complete*, Microsoft Press, 1993.

[MSDN] Microsoft Developer Network Library, http://msdn.microsoft.com.

[Myers98] Myers, Scott, *Effective C++*, second edition, Addison-Wesley Longman, Inc., 1998.

[Rabin00] Rabin, Steve, "Designing a General Robust AI Engine," *Game Programming Gems,* Charles River Media, 2000; p 221–236.

1.4

Squeezing More Out of Assert

Steve Rabin, Nintendo of America Inc.

steve.rabin@gmail.com

Almost everybody uses assert, but not everybody is getting the most out of it. This article contains seven cool little tricks that can be used to squeeze more functionality out of assert. If you're already familiar with assert, skip down to "Assert Trick #1." Otherwise, read on. . . .

The Basics of Assert

Every programmer should religiously use the assert macro. The assert macro is a simple, painless way to double-check your assumptions, and it will save you every time. By giving the assert macro a condition to evaluate, you're asserting that this condition should be TRUE. If the condition evaluates to FALSE, assert brings up a dialog box telling you that a problem has occurred. You can then choose to ignore the assert and continue executing your code, abort the program, or break directly into the code where the assert failed.

The assert macro lets you program defensively. If you know a pointer should be NULL, you should assert that it is NULL. By making assert a habit in your code, you'll catch mistakes before they have a chance to bite you.

Vector normalization is an example of an important place to use asserts. In the following function, three assumptions must be met for the code to execute without wreaking havoc. The src and dst vector pointers must both be valid, and the length of the src vector must not be zero.

```
#include <assert.h>
void VectorNormalize( Vec* src, Vec* dst )
{
   float length;

   assert( src != 0 );    // Check that the src vector is not NULL
   assert( dst != 0 );    // Check that the dst vector is not NULL
```

```
    length = sqrt( (src->x*src->x) + (src->y*src->y) + (src->z*src->z) );

    assert( length != 0 );    // Check that the length is not zero
                              // (to avoid dividing by zero)

    dst->x = src->x / length;
    dst->y = src->y / length;
    dst->z = src->z / length;
}
```

Since the `VectorNormalize` function needs to be blazingly fast, we can't afford to waste time checking the assumptions in release builds. However, while the game is in development, we need to be aware of any problems that come up. That's where `assert` makes a lot of sense. The `assert` macro doesn't get compiled in release builds, so assumptions can be tested during development and automatically removed when compiled in release. This allows you to sprinkle `asserts` throughout your code without worrying about removing them before your game ships.

Since the `assert` macro is not compiled under release builds, it's incredibly important that you don't change the state of your program within the `assert`. As a rule, don't call functions or alter any variables inside it. The result would be behavior that differs between your debug and release versions, which could be disastrous.

Why not just put permanent error checking inside the `VectorNormalize` function? This function is so low level that it doesn't have a clue how to remedy any problems. Hopefully (cross your fingers), every piece of code that calls `VectorNormalize` checks for these assumptions because it can directly deal with problems. If a piece of code fails to check those assumptions, the `assert` will be triggered inside `VectorNormalize`, and a programmer can then know to fix the actual code that caused the error.

Assert Trick #1: Embed More Information

One of the drawbacks of the traditional `assert` macro is that it doesn't tell you much information. If `assert(src != 0)` fails, it brings up the string `src != 0` in the `assert` dialog box. Unfortunately, this doesn't give you much to go on. Unless you're running the game from your debugger, it's not very clear what the problem is. One technique is to embed more information inside your condition. Consider the following `VectorNormalize` function:

```
#include <assert.h>
void VectorNormalize( Vec* src, Vec* dst )
{
    float length;

    assert( src != 0 && "VectorNormalize: src vector pointer is NULL" );
    assert( dst != 0 && "VectorNormalize: dst vector pointer is NULL" );

    length = sqrt( (src->x*src->x) + (src->y*src->y) + (src->z*src->z) );
```

```
    assert( length != 0 && "VectorNormalize: src vector is zero length" );

    dst->x = src->x / length;
    dst->y = src->y / length;
    dst->z = src->z / length;
}
```

When the first assert fails in this code, the assert box displays the string `"src != 0 && "VectorNormalize: src vector pointer is NULL""`. Even if your testers are running the game, they can tell you the function name where the assert failed, along with the reason.

Assert Trick #2: Embed Even More Information

Sometimes programmers simply type `assert(0)` if the program execution reaches an ugly spot. You can pull the same trick of inserting a descriptive string simply by negating the string to make it false. For example:

```
assert( !"VectorNormalize: The code should never get here" );
```

This line accomplishes the same thing as `assert(0)` while also giving you some great debugging information.

Assert Trick #3: Make It Less Awkward

The first two tricks can be combined in seconds by writing a simple macro. This macro takes two arguments, the first being the condition to evaluate and the second being the descriptive string. This mimics the first two tricks but makes it easier to type and read:

```
#define Assert(a,b)   assert( a && b )
```

The following two lines use the new macro:

```
assert( src != 0, "VectorNormalize: src vector pointer is NULL" );
assert( 0, "VectorNormalize: The code should never get here" );
```

Assert Trick #4: Write Your Own

Eventually everyone should use an `assert` macro that's been truly customized. The idea is to write your own `assert` dialog box code so that you can have more control over adding features.

A very annoying problem of the standard C `assert` is that it breaks into the debugger in the file assert.c—not the line in your program where the `assert` appears. By writing your own `assert` macro, the debugger breaks directly to the `assert` line that you typed. This avoids the needless step of backtracking up the stack to get to the spot you're actually interested in. The following is an example of a custom `assert` macro:

```
#if defined( _DEBUG )
extern bool CustomAssertFunction( bool, char*, int, char* );

#define Assert( exp, description ) \
   if( CustomAssertFunction( (int)(exp), description, __LINE__,
   __FILE__ ) ) \
   { _asm { int 3 } } //this will cause the debugger to break here on
   PC's

#else
#define Assert( exp, description )
#endif
```

The above macro calls `CustomAssertFunction`, which you have to write yourself. `CustomAssertFunction` should bring up a dialog box stating the `assert` information and allow the user to either continue or break. If the user chooses to break, `CustomAssertFunction` should return TRUE, and the debugger will break on the `Assert` line (that's what the `int 3` instruction does on the PC). Otherwise, the function should return FALSE, and the program will continue executing.

Assert Trick #5: This One Is Priceless

Once you have a custom `assert` macro, you can add an "Ignore Always" option to your `assert` dialog box. This is an amazing feature that lets you ignore an `assert` once and have it remember to never bother you again. It's particularly useful when an `assert` is failing every frame, but you still want to run your game without clicking through a million `asserts`. To implement this feature, each `assert` keeps track of whether it should be ignored and purposely suppresses itself if it should fail in the future.

Practically, the way to implement "Ignore Always" is to place a static Boolean within the `assert` macro. This Boolean then remembers whether the `assert` is to be ignored. Initially, the Boolean is set to FALSE. When the code executes, it checks this Boolean before it even evaluates the `assert` condition. If the Boolean is FALSE, it calls the `CustomAssertFunction` with the pointer to the Boolean as an argument. If the `assert` condition fails and the user selects "Ignore Always" in the `assert` dialog box, it then sets the Boolean to TRUE. The following is the code for the macro:

```
#if defined( _DEBUG )
extern bool CustomAssertFunction( bool, char*, int, char*, bool* );

#define Assert( exp, description ) \
   {  static bool ignoreAlways = false; \
      if( !ignoreAlways ) { \
         if( CustomAssertFunction( (int)(exp), description, \
                                   __LINE__, __FILE__, &ignoreAlways
                                   ) ) ) \
         { _asm { int 3 } } \
      } \
   }
```

```
#else
#define Assert( exp, description )
#endif
```

Assert Trick #6: Only If You're Totally Hard Core

There's a nagging problem with `assert` that shows up clearly in the `VectorNormalize` sample function. The problem is that the source of the error is not inside `VectorNormalize`. The true error is in the function that called `VectorNormalize`, which narrows it down to only several hundred routines! If this type of `assert` fails without the debugger running, the `assert` is virtually useless. Surprisingly, this is a common situation, since testers rarely run games from the debugger.

The simple solution is to provide stack information inside the `assert` dialog box! John Robbins, a writer for *Microsoft Systems Journal*, coined the name *superassert* to describe this implementation.

Assert Trick #7: Make It Easier—Copy and Paste

It's really cool when a simple trick makes work a lot easier. This trick falls into that category. If the `assert` provides tons of great debugging information such as the stack, why not make it really easy for testers to pass it along?

In the Windows environment, you can have a button on the `assert` dialog box that copies the information to the clipboard! With a few simple mouse clicks, anyone can easily copy and paste the `assert` into an e-mail or bug report. This simple, powerful idea will help your testers convey accurate, meaningful information back to programmers.

The following code copies an arbitrary string into the clipboard. You'll want to alter it slightly and put it inside your `CustomAssertFunction`.

```
if( OpenClipboard( NULL ) )
{
   HGLOBAL hMem;
   char szAssert[256];
   char *pMem;

   sprintf( szAssert, "Put assert info here" );
   hMem = GlobalAlloc( GHND|GMEM_DDESHARE, strlen( szAssert )+1 );

   if( hMem ) {
      pMem = (char*)GlobalLock( hMem );
      strcpy( pMem, szAssert );
      GlobalUnlock( hMem );
      EmptyClipboard();
      SetClipboardData( CF_TEXT, hMem );
   }

   CloseClipboard();
}
```

References

[McConnell93] McConnell, Steve, *Code Complete,* Microsoft Press, 1993.

[Robbins00] Robbins, John, *Debugging Applications,* Microsoft Press, 2000.

[Saltzman99] Saltzman, Marc. *Game Design: Secrets of the Sages,* Brady Publishing, 1999.

1.5

Programming with Abstract Interfaces

Noel Llopis, Power of Two Games

llopis@convexhull.com

The concept of abstract interfaces is simple yet powerful. It allows us to completely separate the interface from its implementation. This has some very useful consequences:

- It is easy to switch among different implementations for the code without affecting the rest of the game. This is particularly useful when experimenting with different algorithms, or for changing implementations on different platforms.
- The implementations can be changed at run time. For example, if the graphics renderer is implemented through an abstract interface, it is possible to choose between a software renderer or a hardware-accelerated one while the game is running.
- The implementation details are completely hidden from the user of the interface. This will result in fewer header files included all over the project, faster recompile times, and fewer times when the whole project needs to be completely recompiled.
- New implementations of existing interfaces can be added to the game effortlessly, and potentially even after it has been compiled and released. This makes it possible to easily extend the game by providing updates or user-defined modifications.

Abstract Interfaces

In C++, an abstract interface is nothing more than a base class that has only public pure virtual functions. A pure virtual function is a kind of virtual member function that has no implementation. Any derived class must implement those functions or else the compiler prevents instantiation of that class. Pure virtual functions are indicated by adding `= 0` after their declaration.

This is an example of an abstract interface for a minimal sound system. This interface would be declared in a header file by itself:

```
// In SoundSystem.h

class ISoundSystem {
  public:
    virtual ~ISoundSystem() {};
    virtual bool PlaySound ( handle hSound ) = 0;
    virtual bool StopSound ( handle hSound ) = 0;
};
```

The abstract interface provides no implementation whatsoever. All it does is define the rules by which the rest of the world may use the sound system. As long as the users of the interface know about `ISoundSystem`, they can use any sound system implementation we provide.

The following header file shows an example of an implementation of the previous interface:

```
// In SoundSystemSoftware.h

#include "SoundSystem.h"

class SoundSystemSoftware : public ISoundSystem {
  public:
    virtual ~SoundSystemSoftware();
    virtual bool PlaySound ( handle hSound );
    virtual bool StopSound ( handle hSound );

    // The rest of the functions in the implementation
};
```

We would obviously need to provide the actual implementation for each of those functions in the corresponding .cpp file.

For someone to use this class they would have to do the following:

```
ISoundSystem * pSoundSystem = new SoundSystemSoftware();
// Now we're ready to use it
pSoundSystem->PlaySound ( hSound );
```

So, what have we accomplished by creating our sound system in this roundabout way? Almost everything that we promised at the start:

- It is easy to create another implementation of the sound system (maybe a hardware version). All that is needed is to create a new class that inherits from `ISoundSystem`, instantiate it instead of `SoundSystemSoftware()` and everything else will work the same way without any more changes.
- We can switch between the two classes at run time. As long as `pSoundSystem` points to a valid object, the rest of the program doesn't know which one it is using, so we can change them at will. Obviously, we have to be careful with specific class restrictions. For example, some classes will keep some state information or require initialization before being used for the first time.

- We have hidden all the implementation details from the user. By implementing the interface we are committed to providing the documented behavior no matter what out implementation is. The code is a lot cleaner than the equivalent code full of `if` statements checking for one type of sound system or another. Maintaining the code has also become a lot easier.

Adding a Factory

There is one detail that we haven't covered yet—we haven't completely hidden the specific implementations from the user. After all, the user is still doing a *new* on the class of the specific implementation they want to use. The problem with this is that they need to `#include` the header file with the declaration of the implementation. Unfortunately, the way C++ was designed, when someone `#includes` a header file, they can also get a lot of extra information on the implementation details of that class that they should know nothing about. They will see all the private and protected members, and they might even include extra header files that are only used in the implementation of the class.

To make matters worse, the users of the interface now know exactly what type of class their interface pointer points to, and they could be tempted to cast it to its real type to access some "special features" or rely on some implementation-specific behavior. As soon as this happens we have lost many of the benefits we had gained by structuring our design into abstract interfaces, so this is something that should be avoided as much as possible.

The solution is to use an abstract factory [Gamma95], which is a class whose sole purpose is to instantiate a specific implementation for an interface when asked for it. The following is an example of a basic factory for our sound system:

```
// In SoundSystemFactory.h

class ISoundSystem;

class SoundSystemFactory {
public:
  enum SoundSystemType {
    SOUND_SOFTWARE,
    SOUND_HARDWARE,
    SOUND_SOMETHINGELSE
  };

  static ISoundSystem * CreateSoundSystem(SoundSystemType type);
};


// In SoundSystemFactory.cpp
#include "SoundSystemSoftware.h"
#include "SoundSystemHardware.h"
#include "SoundSYstemSomethingElse.h"
```

```
ISoundSystem * SoundSystemFactory::CreateSoundSystem ( SoundSystemType
                                                        type )
{
  ISoundSystem * pSystem;

  switch ( type ) {
    case SOUND_SOFTWARE:
      pSystem = new SoundSystemSoftware();
      break;
    case SOUND_HARDWARE:
      pSystem = new SoundSystemHardware();
      break;
    case SOUND_SOMETHINGELSE:
      pSystem = new SoundSystemSomethingElse();
      break;
    default:
      pSystem = NULL;
  }

  return pSystem;
}
```

Now we have solved the problem. The user need only include `SoundSystemFactory.h` and `SoundSystem.h`. As a matter of fact, we don't even have to make the rest of the header files available. To use a specific sound system they can now write:

```
ISoundSystem * pSoundSystem;
pSoundSystem = SoundSystemFactory::CreateSoundSystem
               (SoundSystemFactory::SOUND_SOFTWARE);
// Now we're ready to use it
pSoundSystem->PlaySound ( hSound );
```

We need to be careful to always include a virtual destructor in our abstract interfaces. If we don't, C++ will automatically generate a non-virtual destructor, which will cause the real destructor of our specific implementation not to be called (and that is usually a hard bug to track down). Unlike normal member functions, we can't just provide a pure virtual destructor, so we need to create an empty function to keep the compiler happy.

Abstract Interfaces as Traits

A slightly different way to think of abstract interfaces is to consider an interface as a set of behaviors. If a class implements an interface, that class is making a promise that it will behave in certain ways. For example, the following is an interface used by objects that can be rendered to the screen:

```
class IRenderable {
  public:
    virtual ~IRenderable() {};
    virtual bool Render () = 0;
};
```

We can design a class to represent 3D objects that inherits from `IRenderable` and provides its own method to render itself on the screen. Similarly, we could have a terrain class that also inherits from `IRenderable` and provides a completely different rendering method.

```
class Generic3DObject : public IRenderable {
  public:
    virtual ~Generic3DObject();
    virtual bool Render();

    // Rest of the functions here
};
```

The render loop will iterate through all the objects, and if they can be rendered, it calls their `Render()` function. The real power of the interfaces comes again from hiding the real implementation from the interface: Now it is possible to add a completely new type of object, and as long as it presents the `IRenderable` interface, the rendering loop will be able to render it like any other object. Without abstract interfaces, the render loop would have to know about the specific types of object (generic 3D object, terrain, etc.) and decide whether to call their particular render functions. Creating a new type of render-capable object would require changing the render loop along with many other parts of the code.

We can check whether an object inherits from `IRenderable` to know if it can be rendered. Unfortunately, that requires that the compiler's RTTI (Run-Time Type Identification) option be turned on when the code is compiled. There is usually a performance and memory cost to have RTTI enabled, so many games have it turned off in their projects. We could use our own custom RTTI, but instead let's go the way of COM (Microsoft's Component Object Model) and provide a `QueryInterface` function [Rogerson97].

If the object in question implements a particular interface, then `QueryInterface` casts the incoming pointer to the interface and returns *true*. To create our own `QueryInterface` function, we need to have a base class from which all of the related objects that inherit from a set of interfaces derive. We could even make that base class itself an interface like COM's `IUnknown`, but that makes things more complicated.

```
class GameObject {
  public:
    enum GameInterfaceType {
      IRENDERABLE,
      IOTHERINTERFACE
    };
```

```
        virtual bool QueryInterface (const GameInterfaceType type,
                                     void ** pObj );
        // The rest of the GameObject declaration
};
```

The implementation of `QueryInterface` for a plain game object would be trivial. Because it's not implementing any interface, it will always return false.

```
bool GameObject::QueryInterface (const GameInterfaceType type,
                                 void ** pObj ) {
    return false;
}
```

The implementation of a 3D object class is different from that of `GameObject`, because it will implement the `IRenderable` interface.

```
class 3DObject : public GameObject, public IRenderable {
    public:
        virtual ~3DObject();
        virtual bool QueryInterface (const GameInterfaceType type,
                                     void ** pObj );
        virtual bool Render();
        // Some more functions if needed
};

bool 3DObject::QueryInterface (const GameInterfaceType type,
                               void ** pObj ) {
    bool bSuccess = false;
    if ( type == GameObject::IRENDERABLE ) {
        *pObj = static_cast<IRenderable *>(this);
        bSuccess = true;
    }
    return bSuccess;
}
```

It is the responsibility of the `3DObject` class to override `QueryInterface`, check for what interfaces it supports, and do the appropriate casting.

We can finally have a look at the render loop, which is simple and flexible and knows nothing about the type of objects it is rendering:

```
IRenderable * pRenderable;
for ( all the objects we want to render ) {
    if ( pGameObject->QueryInterface (GameObject::IRENDERABLE,
                                      (void**)&pRenderable) ) {
        pRenderable->Render();
    }
}
```

Now we're ready to deliver the last of the promises of abstract interfaces listed at the beginning of this gem: effortlessly adding new implementations. With such a render loop, if we give it new types of objects and some of them implemented the

`IRenderable` interface, everything would work as expected without the need to change the render loop. The easiest way to introduce the new object types would be to simply re-link the project with the updated libraries or code that contains the new classes. Though beyond the scope of this gem, we could add new types of objects at run time through DLLs or an equivalent mechanism available on the target platform. This enhancement would allow us to release new game objects or game updates without the need to patch the executable. Users could also use this method to easily create modifications for our game.

Notice that nothing is stopping us from inheriting from multiple interfaces. All it will mean is that the class that inherits from multiple interfaces is now providing all the services specified by each of the interfaces. For example, we could have an `ICollidable` interface for objects that need to have collision detection done. A 3D object could inherit from both `IRenderable` and `ICollidable`, but a class representing smoke would only inherit from `IRenderable`.

A word of warning however: while using multiple abstract interfaces is a powerful technique, it can also lead to overly complicated designs that don't provide any advantages over designs with single inheritance. Also, multiple inheritance doesn't work well for dynamic characteristics, and should rather be used for permanent characteristics intrinsic to an object.

Even though many people advise staying away from multiple inheritance, this is a case where it is useful and it does not have any major drawbacks. Inheriting from, at most, one real parent class and multiple interface functions should not result in the dreaded diamond-shaped inheritance tree (where the parent of both our parents are the same class) or many of the other usual drawbacks of multiple inheritance.

Everything Has a Cost

So far we have seen that abstract interfaces have many attractive features. But all of these features come at a price. Most of the time, the advantages of using abstract interfaces outweigh any potential problems, but it is important to be aware of the drawbacks and limitations of this technique.

First of all, the design becomes more complex. For someone not used to abstract interfaces, the extra classes and the querying of interfaces could look confusing at first sight. It should only be used where it makes a difference, not indiscriminately all over the game, otherwise it will only obscure the design and get in the way.

With the abstract interfaces we did such a good job hiding all of the private implementations that they actually can become harder to debug. If all we have is a variable of type `IRenderable*`, we won't be able to see the private contents of the real object it points to in the debugger's interactive watch window without a lot of tedious casting. On the other hand, most of the time we shouldn't have to worry about it. Because the implementation is well isolated and tested by itself, all we should care about is using the interface correctly.

Another disadvantage is that it is not possible to extend an existing abstract interface through inheritance. Going back to our first example, maybe we would have liked to extend the `SouncSystemHardware` class to add a few functions specific to the game. Unfortunately, we don't have access to the class implementation any more, and we certainly can't inherit from it and extend it. It is still possible either to modify the existing interface or provide a new interface using a derived class, but it will all have to be done from the implementation side, and not from within the game code.

Finally, notice that every single function in an abstract interface is a virtual function. This means that every time one of these functions is called through the abstract interface, the computer will have to go through one extra level of indirection. With modern computers and game consoles this is typically not a problem as long as we avoid using interfaces for functions that are called from within inner loops. For example, creating an interface with a `DrawPolygon()` or `SetScreenPoint()` function would probably not be a good idea.

Conclusion

Abstract interfaces are a powerful technique that can be put to good use with very little overhead or structural changes. It is important to know how it can be best used and when it is better to do things a different way. Perfect candidates for abstract interfaces are modules that can be replaced (graphics renderers, spatial databases, AI behaviors), or any sort of pluggable or user-extendable modules (tool extensions, game behaviors).

References

[Gamma95] Gamma, Eric et al. *Design Patterns.* Addison-Wesley, 1995.
[Lakos96] Lakos, John. *Large Scale C++ Software Design.* Addison-Wesley, 1996.
[Rogerson97] Rogerson, Dale, *Inside COM.* Microsoft Press, 1997.

1.6

The Beauty of Weak References and Null Objects

Noel Llopis, Power of Two Games

llopis@convexhull.com

Programmers often have a love-hate relationship with pointers. They're small, they're efficient, and they let you manipulate memory in just about any way you can imagine. However, the smallest mistake tends to cause memory leaks, dangling pointers, or, in the worst of cases, program crashes and unhappy users.

This gem looks into the problems caused by moving objects around in memory, something we commonly want to do with game resources. Some of the techniques discussed here also have relevance to the problem of loading and unloading objects in and out of memory. We will look at how weak references are a good alternative to straight C++ pointers. To complement that idea, we will put *null objects* to work, which will allow us to finally stop checking whether a pointer is NULL or not before we use it, as well as having a few other useful side effects.

Using Pointers

Even though they are very convenient, and we have many years of experience using them, pointers are sometimes not the best approach for certain tasks. Let's look specifically at how to deal with dynamic resources in a game. By resources, we mean everything that is loaded from the disk: textures, geometry, sounds, and so forth.

One of the fundamental problems we encounter when dealing with pointers is determining the lifetime of the resource. If you load a large texture, and two models use that same texture, they should both be pointing to the same location in memory. What should we do when one of the models is destroyed? We can't delete the texture because the other model is using it, but how do we know that? Moreover, we can't just leave it in memory, because when we delete both models we'll have a large memory leak.

In situations like these, we're forced to come up with our own solutions. A common approach is to use reference counting. Every time a model gets a pointer to a texture, it increases the reference count of the texture. Whenever the model is deleted, it decreases the texture's reference count. Whenever the reference count reaches zero, the texture is automatically deleted. This sounds great in theory, but it can make for cumbersome code and is frequently the source of programming errors.

Related to that problem is the issue of moving the resource around in memory, or even temporarily swapping it out and loading it later. If that texture is only used in a small section of the world, wouldn't it be great to be able to remove it from memory whenever the player is in a different area, and then load it on the fly as the player approaches that area again? The potential memory savings are substantial, and doing so would allow us to break free of the memory limitations of the machine and the constraints of small levels.

How would we go about swapping out a texture? One way would be to notify the parts of the program that are holding a pointer to the texture so they could invalidate it. Otherwise, if they tried to use the texture, the program would likely crash. Even if the program never had a need to access the texture because it never came into view, by the time we reload the texture, it will probably end up residing in a different memory location. To avoid these problems, we need a way to update the pointer value of all the objects that use it.

If we had a good solution, it would even allow us to load intermediate textures containing just a few mipmaps when the models are far away, and only load the most detailed and memory-intensive versions when the camera is very close to the model.

As is the case with many computer science dilemmas, this problem can be solved by adding a level of indirection. One possible solution is the use of handles. Every resource is identified with a unique ID (probably assigned at load time by the resource management system), which is called a *handle*. The game promises never to keep a pointer to a resource, and keeps the handle instead. Every frame, whenever the game wants to display a model or do any computation that requires accessing the texture, it asks the resource manager to give us the pointer to the texture that corresponds to that handle. We check whether the returned pointer is NULL, and if it isn't, we can proceed as usual.

This gives us the freedom to unload resources or move them around in memory, because the resource manager can keep track of those changes, and the rest of the program always goes through the indirection of the handle before getting a pointer. Unfortunately, this is very cumbersome; having to do the translation between handle and pointer every time, and even having to check whether it's NULL, becomes tedious very quickly. There is also the problem of what happens if we decide to store a pointer "just for a few frames" and then the resource is unloaded out from underneath us.

The rest of this gem presents a solution that provides the feel and convenience of working with straight pointers, but addresses most of the problems discussed here.

Weak References

For the purposes of this gem, a *weak reference* is a reference that has at least one level of indirection between itself and the object it points to. A handle, as discussed earlier, is a good example of a weak reference, since it uses a mapping scheme as a level of indirection. A plain C pointer, however, is a strong reference, because its reference mode is immediate (the pointer contains the actual memory address of the object it is referring to).

Be warned that the term *weak reference* is often used in memory management literature to mean something different. In that context, objects that have no strong references to them are freed by the system, while weak references do not force an object to stay alive.

Our objective is to make a weak reference as convenient to use as a regular pointer. These types of references are usually called *smart pointers*, because they behave like a pointer, but have logic embedded in them that controls the nature of the indirection.

It is possible to build a smart pointer around a handle-based system [Hawkins02], but here we're going to use a slightly different approach. In the interest of simplicity, ease of debugging, and efficiency, we'll use a smart pointer that ultimately wraps a raw C++ pointer, but we'll also enlist the services of some intermediate objects to help us achieve our objective.

Figure 1.6.1 is a UML diagram that shows how the system is going to be organized. Our smart pointer (`ResourcePtr`) is not going to point directly to the resource; instead, it is going to point to an intermediate object (`ResPtrHolder`) that contains a regular pointer to the resource. The resource manager uses a map container to associate resource names with resource pointer holders, so whenever a resource needs to be updated or invalidated, the contents of the holder are changed, and all the smart pointers in the game will automatically use the correct values.

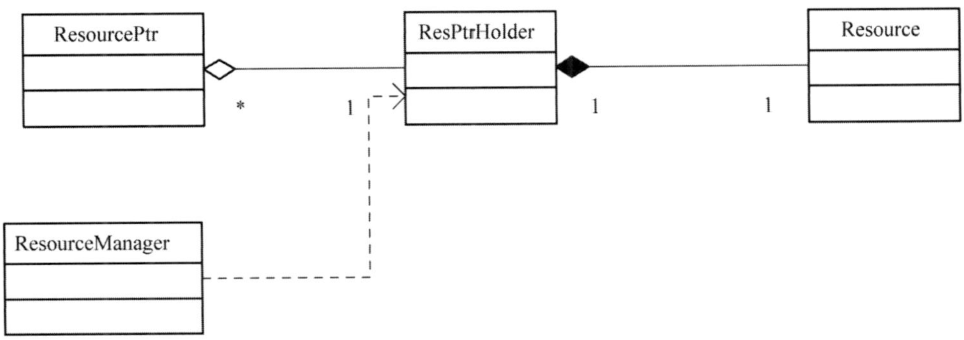

FIGURE 1.6.1 UML diagram.

The Smart Pointer

How can we create this smart pointer that looks like a pointer and behaves like a pointer, but has all this extra logic built in? It's fairly easy, especially if we don't have to deal with some of the headaches introduced by object lifetime determination or copy-on-write semantics. We just need to override certain operators that make it look like a pointer, such as `operator->` and `operator*`. It also makes sense to make it a templated class so it can be type-safe with respect to the type of object it accesses. You can find more information on smart pointers in [Meyers96] and [Alexandrescu01].

ON THE CD

Here are some of the most interesting parts of our smart pointer's interface. The code on the companion CD-ROM includes the full source code along with some unit tests. Notice how the operators to access the data go through the indirection of a pointer holder instead of accessing it directly.

```
template <class ResType>
class ResourcePtr
{
public:
    ResourcePtr(const ResourcePtr<ResType> & ResourcePtr);
    explicit ResourcePtr(ResType * pRes);
    ResourcePtr(ResPtrHolder * pHolder = NULL);
    ~ResourcePtr();

    ResourcePtr<ResType> & operator= (
         const ResourcePtr<ResType> & ResourcePtr);

    ResType * operator->() const
    {
        return static_cast<ResType *>
                        (m_pResHolder->pRes);
    }

    ResType & operator*() const
    {
        return *(static_cast<ResType *>(
                        (m_pResHolder->pRes));
    }

    bool operator==(ResourcePtr<ResType> res) const;
    bool operator!=(ResourcePtr<ResType> res) const;
    bool operator< (ResourcePtr<ResType> res) const;

private:
    ResPtrHolder * m_pResHolder;
};
```

One important aspect of our smart pointer is that it is the same size as a normal pointer (which is currently 32 bits on most platforms). That means that we can efficiently copy it, pass it as a parameter, or do anything with it that we would do with a regular pointer. Moreover, because the smart pointer is pointer-based instead of handle-based, there is very little extra performance overhead. There is no need to perform a handle lookup every time the resource is accessed. Instead, the only cost is an extra pointer dereferencing. It's not free, but it's very cheap, and certainly worth the minor performance cost for what it gets us.

The Resource Pointer Holder

The resource pointer holder class looks very simple. All it needs to do is to hold a pointer to the resource itself. Each holder object will have to be dynamically allocated whenever we need to create one. We can't really put them as part of an array or a vector because we want to be able to create and delete them without ever changing the memory location of other holders, so they have to be dynamically allocated. Doing many small dynamic memory allocations can potentially waste a lot of memory. The best way to deal with that is to override the `new` and `delete` operators for the holder class and make sure they're efficiently allocated out of a memory pool [Llopis03], [Glinker04]. That will result in no memory overhead and very good runtime performance.

It's also worth noting that the `ResPtrHolder` class is not itself a template, even though you might expect it to be. Although it would be nice to make `ResPtrHolder` a template parameterized on `ResType`, and therefore alleviate the need for those ugly static casts in the `ResourcePtr` class, doing so simply moves those same casts into the resource manager class. In fact, pushing these casts into the resource manager class causes a whole series of additional complications, particularly if you want to have a single global resource manager responsible for managing all of your active resources.

Now that we have the extra level of indirection hidden behind the mechanics of a regular pointer, we can solve the resource lifetime problem by adding reference counting to the resource pointer holders. The creation and destruction of smart pointers controls the number of references in a holder, and whenever there are no references left, the holder destroys the resource and then destroys itself (and makes sure to notify the resource manager as well). The companion CD-ROM contains an alternate version of the smart pointer system that uses reference counting in this way.

ON THE CD

The Resource Manager

The resource manager is simply a big map that stores the relation between resource names and the resource pointer holders. It's important that it points to the holders, not the resources themselves; that way, all operations are done on the holder, which prevents us from breaking all the smart pointers in the rest of the game.

Depending on your game's architecture, you could organize a single global resource manager for all the resources in the game, or each type of resource could have a separate manager that keeps track of them. The advantage of the latter approach is that it is easier to implement different algorithms for resource eviction and swapping knowing what type of resource it is and having more information about each.

This map can be implemented in many different ways. A straightforward approach uses a `std::map` of strings and resource pointer holders. On real production code you probably want to make this mapping as efficient as possible, so you would either override the mapping function, or try to use integers as keys. (You can generate these integers at load time from a hash or CRC of the resource's name, or by simply branding your resources with a unique resource ID.) If you're willing to sacrifice a small amount of memory for better performance, you could use a `std::hash_map` and reduce the element access to constant time.

Null Objects

Weak references are great. They allow us to unload resources or move them around in memory with impunity. There is, however, one aspect we haven't addressed: having to check whether our pointers are NULL.

The Concept

We're so used to checking for NULL pointers (either through a conditional or the use of an `assert`) that we might not think much of it. Still, it leads to bloated code, where the intent of the program might be diluted or even overwhelmed by the volume of conditional statements scattered throughout your source files. In addition, while it's an admittedly minor concern, technically you're absorbing a slight performance hit for each of these conditional evaluations.

Wouldn't it be great if we could assume that resource pointers are always valid? The program would never have to check if they are NULL. That might be simple to do if the resources are simply loaded once and then stay permanently in memory, but it becomes harder to do if they are being dynamically loaded.

This is where *null objects* come in. A null object is just a resource, but one that doesn't contain any data, or the minimum amount of data to still function as a correct resource. For example, in the case of texture resources, the null resource could be a small, 4×4 fully transparent texture. This concept can be applied to any type of resource: geometry (a mesh with one vertex), sounds (a short sample with silence), animations (nothing moves), and so forth.

Whenever we decide that we want to evict a resource from memory, we free it, and, instead of setting the pointer inside the resource pointer holder to NULL, we set it to point to the null object for that type of resource. At this point, the program can freely access any resource and never worry about whether it is null. Every resource is guaranteed to be in memory, even if it is a null resource.

The reason to keep null objects as invisible as possible is to avoid artifacts if the program ever tries to display them. For example, if the player rushes into a new area, we might not be done loading the textures for a faraway street sign by the time we display it on the screen. A null object would ensure that the sign is simply transparent until we get a chance to load it, at which point it is likely to pop in. We hope the sign will still be far enough away that the popping won't be too objectionable, but in most cases you also have the option of building out the system so that it can smoothly blend between the depiction of the null object and the loaded resource.

For null objects to work correctly, we need one null resource for every type of resource. That way, the null resource can behave in every way like any other resource of its type. If the program accesses a texture, it will probably try to call texture-specific functions on that resource, which the null texture resource will provide.

Potential Problems

There are just a few issues we need to be aware of when dealing with null objects.

The first is that if the program expects to find some specific data in the resource, the final behavior is unlikely to be correct. For example, if the program tries to access a particular terrain texture that was evicted, it will get the tiny null texture object. However, the program might assume that the texture is 128 × 128, because that's the size of all terrain textures in our game, and try to access a pixel that doesn't exist in the null texture object. Ideally, the program should never try to access a resource that was evicted; doing so probably indicates a bug (more on that later). Even if it does, it is best not to make any assumptions about each resource when working with a system that can freely swap resources around.

The other issue is that of a program that attempts to modify its resources. Fortunately, this is not a very common situation; most resources are treated as read-only because they can be shared. However, this does happen on occasion and we need to be prepared. Perhaps we want to perform some special stamping effect on a texture or modify geometry on the fly. Trying to do that operation on a null resource could have unfortunate consequences, such as causing all of our null transparent textures to become bright red all of a sudden. To avoid this, it would be useful to flag null resources as read-only. Even better, if we want to maintain total transparency, we can allow the program to call functions to modify null resources, but make sure that all those functions have no effect on the resource itself.

Extensions

Now that we have null objects integrated into our resource management system, we can take them one step further and make them even more useful. For example, we can decide that trying to display a null object is something that should never happen, and should be treated as a bug. In that case, we want to make null objects as noticeable as possible. The null texture could become bright pink, the sound an annoying, loud, square wave, and the geometry one big sphere—anything that will catch people's attention right away. Additionally, null objects could even write an entry to the game log indicating which resource the game attempted to display.

In release mode, however, we probably want to revert to the previous behavior and make them as invisible as possible just in case the player ever accesses them in the final shipped game.

Conclusion

This gem presented a flexible alternative to using pointers to keep track of game resources. It allows us to have more control over a resource's lifetime, as well as allowing us to move it around. We can even unload it from memory while the game is running. These new abilities might allow us to have larger game levels or to create a continuous world.

The article also presented the idea of null objects, which are special resources that are put in place of missing resources. These resources behave like any resource of their type, which frees the game code from having to check whether resources are loaded every time one is used. These null resources are often invisible to avoid causing any artifacts if they are displayed, but they can be alternately made very noticeable for debugging purposes.

References

[Alexandrescu01] Alexandrescu, Andrei, *Modern C++ Design*, Addison-Wesley, 2001.

[Glinker04] Glinker, Paul, "Fight Memory Fragmentation with a Templated Freelist," *Game Programming Gems 4*, Charles River Media, 2004.

[Hawkins02] Hawkins, Brian, "Handle-Based Smart Pointers," *Game Programming Gems 3*, Charles River Media, 2002.

[Llopis03] Llopis, Noel, *C++ for Game Programmers*, Charles River Media, 2003.

[Meyers96] Meyers, Scott, *More Effective C++*, Addison-Wesley, 1996.

1.7

Using the STL in Game Programming

James Boer, ArenaNet

james@boarslair.com

In 1997, C++ was officially standardized, ending a nine-year process that not only defined the official language specifications but also gave C++ programmers a massive new set of tools in the form of the standard C++ library. A large portion of this library is the Standard Template Library, or STL. The STL is a collection of container (collections of data) classes, ranging from vectors to balanced binary trees. In addition to the basic containers, the STL provides a massive assortment of algorithms that can operate on those basic containers.

A common concern is whether using STL will slow down your code. The truth of the matter is that the STL was designed with speed as a foremost priority. For instance, vectors do no bounds checking, and iterators are never validated before attempting to access a container. The net result is that, for example, STL vectors can produce code with performance equivalent to that of a simple dynamically allocated array. Other containers fare just as well when put under the performance microscope. The STL was designed for high-efficiency C++ applications. Don't lose sleep about using them extensively in your code.

STL Types and Terminology

The STL is a large and somewhat complex portion of the Standard C++ library. Using the STL effectively requires the understanding of the basic components and how they work together.

Containers

STL containers represent the classic data abstractions and organization schemes such as vectors, lists, queues, and maps. However, we should make a few distinctions between certain types of containers and how they are implemented.

The STL containers vector, list, and deque (pronounced "deck") are implicit data types that both describe an abstract data type and imply a specific method of implementation. A *vector* is, of course, a dynamically resizable array. The *list* is implemented as a double-linked list. A *deque,* or double-ended queue, is implemented in a manner that allows amortized constant time insertion or deletion of elements at either end of a randomly accessible array-type structure. Deques are also known as *sequence containers* because they store ordered sets of data, meaning that the order in which you insert the data affects the order in which they are stored.

Containers such as stack, queue, and `priority_queue` are slightly higher-level abstractions. They describe a container's behavior but allow for different types of underlying implementations. For example, a queue might be implemented using a vector, list, or deque internally. These are known as *container adapters.* Container adapters, because they rely on sequence containers as their underlying data, also fall into that category as well.

Other containers, such as a map, set, multimap, or multiset, are all implemented internally as red-black trees (balanced binary trees) but offer different container behaviors. These are also known as *associative containers* because the data inserted into them is ordered based on a certain sorting criteria.

Iterators

Iterators can be thought of as pointers to elements in the containers, and indeed the STL even uses pointer notation for traversal and access to container data. For instance, the `++` operator moves the iterator to the next element in a container, much the way a pointer to an element in an array can be incremented. In addition, like pointers, the actual data can be accessed by dereferencing the iterator using the `*` operator.

Algorithms

Unlike what you might expect, *algorithms* designed to operate on STL classes do not come in the form of member functions of the container classes. Instead, they exist in the form of stand-alone functions that operate on iterators. Why did the designers of STL choose this seemingly anti-OOP design paradigm?

By separating the data from the algorithms, the designers dramatically reduced the number of combinations of specialized algorithms. Since each container has similar types of iterators, each algorithm had to be written only once instead of once for each container. The downside is that there are sometimes less-than-obvious side effects or suboptimal solutions. In most cases, however, specialized member functions are all you need to perform most basic operations on your containers.

STL Concepts

A few basic concepts are important to working with the STL. First, it is important to understand the methods used to determine ranges when working with a container.

Two methods common to all containers, `begin()` and `end()` return the full range of the container. As you can see in Figure 1.7.1, `begin()` returns the first element in the container, but `end()` returns the position *beyond the last valid element.*

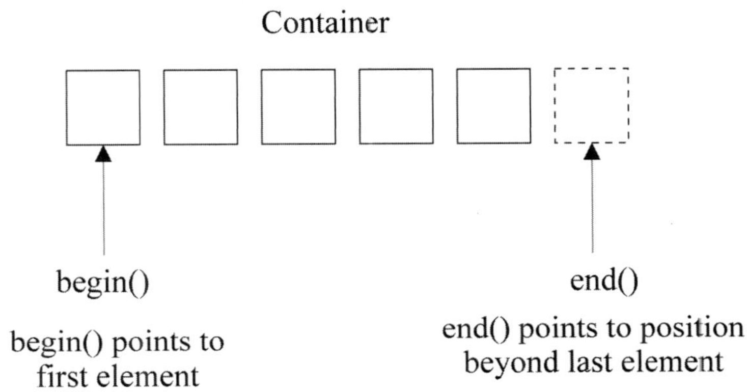

FIGURE 1.7.1 `end()` points after the last valid element.

There are several advantages to organizing the ranges in this manner. First, special-case coding for empty lists is eliminated. Second, iterating through containers has a simple ending criteria: continue as long as `end()` is not reached. The disadvantages of this system are that it is somewhat less intuitive, and reverse iteration requires special members and iterators.

It obviously becomes important to remember not to dereference an iterator that is pointing at `end()`. Such behavior is undefined.

When you use functions specifying a range, functions in STL usually take as parameters two iterators, one specifying the beginning element and one specifying the end element. To pair effectively with `begin()` and `end()`, these functions assume an inclusion of the first element specified and exclusion of the last element specified. Mathematically, the following notation usually designates this sort of range:

```
range [begin...end)
```

There is another aspect of the STL design of which you should be aware. STL containers pass information by value, not by reference. This means that when dealing with small data types, it is acceptable to allow the container to make a copy of the data. With larger data structures or classes, it becomes advantageous to pass in pointers to these objects or structs. Otherwise, every insertion or access results in a copy constructor being called.

Vectors

STL *vectors* are essentially resizable arrays. Note that although the formal C++ standard does not specify what underlying data structures are to be used for containers, the performance and interface requirements leave little ambiguity as to how they will be implemented in practice. Thus, all versions of STL will likely be very similar, with only minor variations in implementation details.

Vectors behave almost identically to standard C arrays, with one major exception: They are dynamically resizable. However, it is important to understand the nature of this resizing.

Vectors are implemented as arrays that periodically need to reallocate memory and transfer data to a new array. This means two things for developers. First, a vector can allocate more memory than it currently needs, due to the requirement that it might be expected to grow at any time. Second, adding an element to the end of a vector is described as *constant time*—it is important to remember that this means *amortized constant time*. In other words, some grow functions can require a substantial amount of resources as they allocate new memory, copy the existing array into this new block, and delete the old memory, but they do not require these extra resources every time. Depending on implementation, a vector can allocate twice its current allocated memory when it runs out of buffer space.

It is also critical that you understand when a vector reallocates memory, since doing so invalidates any iterators currently pointing to elements in the vector. Let's examine the functions to help more precisely manage a vector's internal memory, after viewing the code:

```
#include <vector>
#include <iostream>

using namespace std;

// Typedef the container and iterator names for better
// readability
typedef vector<int> IntVector;
typedef IntVector :iterator IntVectItor;

void main()
{
    // Create a vector object of integers
    IntVector c;
    // Reserve room for 10 integers
    c.reserve(10)

    // Fill the vector with 3 different elements
    c.push_back(3);
    c.push_back(99);
    c.push_back(42);
```

```
        // Now loop and print out all the element values
        for(IntVectItor itor = c.begin(); itor != c.end(); ++itor)
            cout << "element value = " << (*itor) << endl;;



        // Since the elements have been created, we can access or
    // replace them just like a normal array.
            c[0] = 12;
        c[1] = 32;
        c[2] = 999;
        for(int i = 0; i < c.size(); i++)
            cout << "element value = " << c[i] << endl;
    }
```

This example shows most of the basic principles you need to know to start using STL containers. Notice at the top of the listing the inclusion of the appropriate header files for this program. In addition, note the usage of namespace `std`. Like all portions of the C++ library, the STL is part of the `std` namespace and so requires you to declare such in your program.

Next, we see `typedefs` for the type of container and iterator we want to use in the program. This is a very common practice; it not only makes the code easier to read, but it becomes easier to change the underlying data structure, if desired. (We'll see how easy that is next.)

The next section of code creates the vector container object `v` and proceeds to call a vector-only function that reserves 10 integers' worth of memory. The code proceeds to `push_back()` 3 integers onto the back of the vector. Since we have preallocated well over this amount of memory, no additional memory allocation is required.

There are a few routines that you might find helpful when you want to closely monitor and control the allocation of your vector's memory. As shown, you can reserve a buffer in the vector by calling `reserve()` and passing a size parameter. This value can be retrieved by calling `capacity()`. If `capacity()==reserve()` and another element is inserted into the array, a memory allocation will take place and all current iterators will be invalidated. In order to determine the maximum amount of memory that can be allocated for a single vector, use the `max_size()` function.

The `push_front()`, `push_back()`, `pop_front()`, and `pop_back()` functions are common to all basic ordered containers (vector, list, and deque). These functions obviously add and remove elements from the front and back of the container. Due to the implementation of a vector, you want to avoid `push_front()` or `pop_front()` on these types of containers, if possible, due to the `O(n)` performance, but they are available for use if you absolutely need them.

The final portion of sample code demonstrates one of the most commonly used components of STL usage: the iteration loop. We use a `for` loop with an iterator determining the current position. The initial position is set to `begin()`, and the iterator increments with the prefix ++ operator until the iterator equals `end()`, at which point the exit condition of the loop is satisfied. Every container with an accessible iterator can be looped through in this manner.

Since the iterator is the only item keeping track of the current position in the vector, we must use it to extract any information we want. We can see that in keeping with the notion of a pointer, we simply dereference the iterator to access the data.

After the standard iteration loop, we see an example of a vector in use like a typical array. It is important to note that array subscripting cannot be used to insert elements into a list—only to access existing elements.

Lists

The STL *list* is perhaps the most widely used of the basic STL structures. It is implemented as a doubly linked list, so any insertion and deletion of elements is done in true constant time. The tradeoff for this capability is the loss of random access that the vector and deque allow.

One beauty of using STL containers is the consistent naming conventions and methods used throughout the library. Once you learn the basics of manipulating one type of container, you essentially know how to use them all.

Using a list is even simpler than using a vector. The `push_front()` and `push_back()` functions work exactly as you would expect. Iterating through the list also works exactly as we saw in the vector example. In this code, we see many of the same techniques used in the vector class:

```
#include <list>
#include <iostream>

using namespace std;

class Foo
{
public:
    Foo(int i)                  { m_iData = i;    }
    void SetData(int i)          { m_iData = i; }
    int GetData()               { return m_iData; }
private:
    int m_iData;
};

// Typedef the container and iterator names for better
// readability
typedef list<Foo*> FooList;
typedef FooList::iterator FooListItor;

void main()
{
    // Create a list container of integers
    FooList c;
```

```
        // Fill the list with 3 different elements
        c.push_back(new Foo(1));
        c.push_back(new Foo(2));
        c.push_back(new Foo(3));

        // Iterator through the list
        for(FooListItor itor = c.begin(); itor != c.end();)
        {
            if((*itor)->GetData() == 2)
                // demonstrates proper method of removing an
                // element from the middle of the list.
            {
                delete (*itor);
                itor = c.erase(itor);
            }
            else
                ++itor;
        }

        // Make sure to delete all the objects, since the list
        // destructor will not do this automatically for you
        for(FooListItor itor2 = c.begin(); itor2 != c.end();
    ++itor2)
            delete (*itor2);
    }
```

We see in this example the same basic type of container manipulation, but we have added the wrinkle of using user-defined objects instead of built-in data types. This is a much more common usage scenario, so we examine how it differs in practice from inserting data by value.

STL containers do not operate on the data you pass into them. Rather, they make copies of the data they receive and distribute. In order to negate the cost of copying large data structures in memory, you'll want to pass pointers to larger, dynamically allocated objects. Naturally, our objects are ridiculously small for example purposes, but they could conceivably be large enough to seriously affect performance if we copied a large number of them.

There are a few things to remember when working with pointers to dynamically allocated structs or objects. First, and perhaps most obviously, is that you are responsible for freeing any allocated memory when you are finished with the objects. Since the container has no idea what type of data might be used, there is no way for the container to automatically deallocate memory for you.

Second, and perhaps less obvious, is that many operations appear to fail because they are operating directly on the object or struct pointers instead of on the objects or structs themselves. Take the list's `sort()` function, for example. It operates by using the < operator to determine value and sort accordingly. Even if a proper operator is designed for class `Foo`, the list still sorts on the actual value of the pointer, not by the value of the data in the object.

It therefore becomes necessary to design your own compare operator that dereferences the pointers before comparing them. See the sample code in the article "Resource and Memory Management," by James Boer, to see how this comparison can easily be done.

The third "gotcha" is appropriate to all pointer manipulation routines but also bears mentioning in the context of STL. When copying containers, remember that only the pointers are being copied, not the objects. If you create duplicate pointers, it could become extremely difficult to know which objects to delete. There are only two solutions to this problem: Use smart pointers with your objects or avoid STL routines and algorithms that copy elements from container to container.

You should also be wary of removing an element from a list while iterating through the list. Since removing an element to which you are currently pointing invalidates the iterator, you must be sure to make proper use of the `erase()` function's return value, which retrieves the next valid position in the container. By assigning this return value to the old iterator, we essentially skip ahead of the invalidated position. However, this leaves us with another problem. Since we've already incremented the iterator to the next position, we run into trouble when the `for` loop tries to increment it again at the end of the loop. To solve this problem, we remove the increment operator from the body of the `for` loop and place it conditionally inside the loop itself, incrementing only when an element is not erased.

It is often preferable to use algorithms to erase elements from a container instead of iterating through them manually. Algorithms such as `remove_if()` perform the same operation safely and efficiently. Unfortunately, a complete listing and description of the provided algorithms (and how to create your own) could fill up an entire book, so I recommend the resources listed at the end of this article for further study.

Deques

Deques, or double-ended queues, are designed for situations in which inserting and removing elements from either end of the container must be performed, but inserting and removing elements from the middle of the container is not required (or doesn't have to occur often). Like vectors, deques can perform insertions and removals at the front and back of the container in amortized constant time, and inserting or deleting elements from the middle is somewhat slow. Deques also allow random access, but because of the slightly more complex nature of the internal data of a deque, which is arranged in a linked series of memory blocks, random access is not quite as efficient as with vectors. Unlike vectors, though, there is no mechanism in place for determining exactly when additional memory allocations will take place.

```
#include <deque>
#include <iostream>

using namespace std;
```

```
// Typedef the container and iterator names for better
// readability
typedef deque<int> IntDeque;
typedef IntDeque::reverse_iterator IntDequeRItor;

void main()
{
    // Create a deque container of integers
    IntDeque c;

    // Fill the deque with 3 different elements
    c.push_front(3);
    c.push_front(2);
    c.push_front(1);
    c.push_back(3);
    c.push_back(2);
    c.push_back(1);

    // Cycle BACKWARD through the list - special iterators and

    // notation is necessary to do this.
    for(IntDequeRItor ritor = c.rbegin(); ritor != c.rend();
++ritor)
        cout << "Value = " << (*ritor) << endl;

    // remove the first and last elements
    c.pop_front();
    c.pop_back();

    // Accessing elements directly - if needed remember to
    // check to see the deque is not empty. Accessing non-
    // existent elements will lead to undefined behavior;
// probably an access violation
    if(!c.empty())
    {
        cout << "Front = " << c.front() << endl;
        cout << "Back = " << c.back() << endl;
    }
}
```

We see in the preceding listing the familiar code of STL usage, but with a few new twists this time. First, let's introduce the reverse iterator. You might notice that all our iterations up to this point have been in the positive direction. Although bidirectional iterators do exist, it often is much simpler to create a dedicated *reverse iterator* and utilize it as you use the standard iterator.

The reason we need a reverse iterator is that because of the bounding conditions of a container (illustrated in Figure 1.7.1), we can't simply iterate backward and expect to be able to check for the same exit conditions (`itor != begin()`). This would leave the first element in a container out of the iteration loop. Instead, we utilize a reverse iterator combined with the `rbegin()` and `rend()` functions. These functions work exactly like their forward-looking cousins, but `rbegin()` actually accesses the last element, whereas `rend()` points to a position in front of the first valid entry. This exactly mirrors the forward versions of these functions. Because the reverse iterator travels backward when the increment operator is applied, you can use the exact same syntax for looping through all elements in a container.

In this example, we also introduce the opposites of `push_front()` and `push_back()`, `pop_front()` and `pop_back()`. These functions simply remove an element from the front or back of a container, respectively. Note that the value of the element is not returned. You must use two more functions we introduce in this example to access the front or back elements: `front()` and `back()`. These functions return the value of the front or back element in the container. In the example, we check to ensure that the container is not empty using the `empty()` function before trying to access these elements. Accessing elements in an empty list results in "undefined behavior," which you can expect to probably result in some sort of access violation; `pop_front()` and `pop_back()`simply are "no-ops" when performed on an empty container.

Maps

STL *maps* are perhaps the most complex (relatively speaking) of the basic containers to use and perhaps the most versatile. Here we examine maps instead of the other tree-based structures: sets, multisets, and multimaps. Learning the fundamentals of maps allows you to easily use the other container types, so we leave that research up to you.

The map is essentially a value-pairing container. Two arbitrary types of data are paired as a key/value structure and inserted into the container. Looking up the value via the key then can occur in `O(log n)` time. Although not quite as efficient as a hash table, the difference is often negligible and has the advantage of sorting the data during insertion. This process allows iteration of completely sorted data, which is a beneficial consequence of the method of storage (a balanced binary tree, otherwise known as a *red-black tree*).

```
#pragma warning(disable:4786)
#include <map>
#include <iostream>
#include <string>
#include <algorithm>

using namespace std;

// This function object allows us to compare map containers
template <class F, class S>
class value_equals
{
private:
    S second;
public:
    value_equals(const S& s) : second(s)
    {}
```

```
    bool operator() (pair<const F, S> elem)
    { return elem.second == second; }
};


// Typedef the container and iterator names for better
// readability
typedef map<int, string> isMap;
typedef isMap::value_type isValType;
typedef isMap::iterator isMapItor;

void main()
{
    isMap c;

    // Insert key / value pairs
    c.insert(isValType(100, "One Hundred"));
    c.insert(isValType(3, "Three"));
    c.insert(isValType(150, "One Hundred Fifty"));
    c.insert(isValType(99, "Ninety Nine"));

    // display all the keys and values
    for(isMapItor itor = c.begin(); itor != c.end(); ++itor)
        cout << "Key = " << (*itor).first << ", Value = "
 << (*itor).second << endl;

    // You can also access the map like an associative array
    cout << "Key 3 displays value " << c[3].c_str() << endl;

    // Or insert like this as well
    c[123] = "One Hundred Twenty Three";

    // Find and remove a specific element based on the key
    isMapItor pos = c.find(123);
    if(pos != c.end())
        // erasing an element invalidates any iterators
        // pointing to it.  Calling pos++ now would result in
// undefined behavior.
        c.erase(pos);

    // Find and remove an element based on the value
    pos = find_if(c.begin(), c.end(), value_equals
<int, string>("Ninety Nine"));
    if(pos != c.end())
        c.erase(pos);

    // If you must remove elements while iterating through
// the list...
    for(isMapItor itr = c.begin(); itr != c.end(); )
    {
        if(itr->second == "Three")
            c.erase(itr++);
        else
            ++itr;
    }
}
```

We're introduced to a new intermediate data type in this example, the `value_type`, which represents the key/data pair representing every element in the container. For convenience, we've `typedef`'ed this type along with the other usual types.

Inserting combined key/data values uses the `insert()` function like any other container, with the only difference being that you must insert type `map::value_type`. The map sorts every entry as it is inserted, so at any given time the container is always sorted by keys. We can see this as we iterate through the map and display all the keys and their associated values.

Accessing keys and data through iterators means an additional structure to navigate through. Dereferencing the iterator returns the `value_type` structure, which has two data members: first and second. Accessing first gives you the key value; accessing second gives you the data value.

In addition to access through iterators, maps also provide random access via their key values. The map acts like an associative (or sparse) array. Elements can be accessed or inserted using the `index()` operator. Caution must be used when using this operator, however. If you attempt to access an element with an index that does not yet exist, the element is created with a default constructor and is inserted into the map. This might not be the intended behavior and so is something to watch out for.

Moving, on, we see a simple method of finding an element based on the key using the `find()` function. Since the keys are sorted, this function performs in `O(log n)` time.

If we want to find an element based on the value, we must do a bit more work. At best, this work will be performed in linear time, since the data is sorted on the key rather than the value. The solution to this problem gives us our first look at generic STL algorithms. We use the `find_if()` algorithm for this particular problem. The function requires three parameters: an iterator telling where to begin, an iterator telling when to stop, and a function telling when the algorithm should return a true value. The iterators are self-explanatory, but the function object, or *functor*, requires some further elaboration.

In STL, classes with overloaded function operators (did you even know you could do that?) are used in place of functions. This replacement enables both encapsulated and type-safe solutions to generic programming problems. The function object provided in this example simply compares the second value in a value_pair and returns the result. Initializing the object with the result we want to search against provides a clean and completely encapsulated solution. Note that for most solutions, STL provides ready-to-use function objects that you can simply plug into your code. See a comprehensive STL book for a listing of different algorithms and function objects available for use.

The previous paragraph describes the preferred method of searching for values in a container, but if you must iterate through and remove elements manually in a map, we also show you the proper way to do that. Removing elements while iterating through a map poses a special problem because for speed reasons, the designers of

STL neglected to have the erase() function return the value of the next valid position, as other containers do. Unfortunately, because of this failure, we cannot use the simple method of removing elements, as shown in our second code snippet. Instead, we have to resort to a bit of trickery to make sure we don't invalidate our iterator.

In this example, instead of incrementing the iterator inside the for loop, we do it inside the body in a conditional manner. Notice that when an element must be erased, we post-increment the iterator when passing it as the parameter to erase(), but if an element doesn't need to be erased, we perform the standard pre-increment operator instead. Because of the order in which the operations occur, this method allows safe iteration without having to resort to using temporary iterators. Unfortunately, the necessity of this sort of coding creates far more possibility of buggy code than if the designers had just sacrificed a bit of speed in the erase() function. With any luck, the standards committee will consider revising this function in the future to avoid these types of kludgy workarounds.

This might be a good time to answer a question you might want to ask, namely, "Why do you always use the pre-increment operator in your iteration loop?"

The answer is efficiency. The post-increment operator must return a copy of its old value, so it might require the use of a temporary object. The two solutions work the same way, but unless there's a specific reason to use the post-increment (or post-decrement) operator, as in the previous example, you should prefer the pre-increment and pre-decrement operators.

Stacks, Queues, and Priority Queues

We lump together stacks, queues, and priority queues because using them is simple enough that they require little additional explanation. These containers are really examples of *container adapters* because they are implemented as restricted interfaces on top of existing containers.

Stacks

The STL *stack* class provides three primary members—push(), pop(), and top()—for adding and removing elements from the container. These member functions respectively push an element on the stack, pop it off the stack, or retrieve the top element. To check the current state of the stack, size() and empty() are provided.

The stack is implemented as a deque by default, but it allows you to change the implementation in the constructor.

```
// Implements a stack with deque as the underlying
// container type.
stack<int> c;

// Implements a stack with a vector as the underlying
// container type.
stack<int, vector<int> > c;
```

Note that using a vector might not be as poor a choice as it seems, because `push()`, `pop()`, and `top()` actually map to `push_back()`, `pop_back()`, and `back()`. Any container that supports these functions can be used as the underlying implementation for the stack class. Notice that in the second line of code in the preceding example, we make sure to put a space between the two greater-than operators. Otherwise, they would be incorrectly parsed as a single stream operator >>.

It is important to also know that the stack class, like many STL containers, prefers speed to safety. Thus, the class assumes that when you call `pop()` or `top()`, a valid element actually exists. It is therefore important to always remember to use `size()` or `empty()` to verify that a stack is not empty before performing these operations on it. Queues and priority queues work in the same manner, so the same warnings apply to these containers as well.

Queues

The queue class works much like the stack class except that elements are pushed onto the back and popped off the front. The following members are defined for the queue class for element manipulation: `push()`, `pop()`, `front()`, and `back()`. `back()` refers to the location in which elements are inserted, and `front()` refers to the location from which elements are removed.

Like the stack class, the queue also defines `size()` and `empty()` to manage the size. As with the stack class, you can specify a container other than the default deque to be used as the underlying implementation. Unlike stack, a vector used with a deque makes a poor choice due to the bad performance when inserting elements at the front of a vector. However, a list might make sense in some situations.

Priority Queue

The *priority queue* works identically to a queue but differs in one important respect: All inserted elements are immediately sorted in descending order based on a comparison using the < (less than) operator. Because of the sorting functionality, an additional third parameter is offered in the constructor, allowing you to override the default < operator with your own function. This ability could come in especially handy if you are inserting pointers to objects instead of passing in the objects by value. Avoiding sorting the queue based on the value of the pointers requires writing a functor class that calls the < operator after first dereferencing the pointers. There is an example of this functor in the article "Resource and Memory Management," with code sample provided.

Summary

The STL is a powerful new tool available for C++ programmers. By understanding both its strengths and its limitations, you can make the most of the features now available without compromising the speed or integrity of your code.

Entire books have been written explaining how to use the STL. It is therefore obviously impossible to think that this article could do justice to the broad functionality that exists in this library. If you want to fully utilize the power of STL, there is no substitute for a good reference book. Several excellent tutorials and references are listed in the following References section.

References

[Breymann98] Breymann, Ulrich, *Designing Components with the C++ STL,* Addison Wesley Longman, Inc., 1998.

[Nicolai99] Josuttis, Nicolai M., *The C++ Standard Library: A Tutorial and Reference,* Addison Wesley Longman, Inc., 1999.

[Stroustrup97] Stroustrup, Bjarne, *The C++ Programming Language,* third edition, Addison Wesley Longman, Inc., 1997.

1.8

Custom STL Allocators

Pete Isensee, Microsoft Corporation

pkisensee@msn.com

Many games use custom memory allocation strategies, providing their own `malloc` and `free` functions or overriding the globals `new` and `delete`. The C++ STL (Standard Template Library) provides a powerful extension that allows you to use your own allocation and deallocation methods with all standard C++ container objects, including strings. This gem shows how to create custom allocators and integrate them into game code.

An Example

As an example, suppose your game creates a list, manipulates it in some way, then throws the list away—all within a single function:

```
std::list<int> MyList;
for( int i = 0; i < 100; ++i ) // build the list
    MyList.push_back( i );
MyList.reverse(); // manipulate the list
```

If this function is called once per game loop, the penalty you would pay for allocating and freeing list nodes could easily convince you not to use STL lists. Suppose you could customize the list so that all memory allocations came from the *stack* rather than the heap. Deallocations would be free, because stack memory is automatically reclaimed when the stack object goes out of scope. Here's how the stack-based list code might look using a custom allocator:

```
// Create custom allocator object
const size_t nStackSize = 100 * 12;
unsigned char Stack[ nStackSize ];
StackAlloc<int> sa( Stack, nStackSize );

// Tell the list about the custom allocator
std::list<int, StackAlloc<int> > MyList( sa );

// This code is the same
for( int i = 0; i < 100; ++i ) // build the list
    MyList.push_back( i );
MyList.reverse(); // manipulate the list
```

`StackAlloc` is a custom STL allocator. The `StackAlloc` type is specified as a template parameter in the list declaration, and the `StackAlloc` object is passed to the `list` constructor. In this example, the stack is specified as just large enough to allocate 100 nodes. In most STL implementations, a list node consists of the object and two pointers. The full implementation of `StackAlloc` is available on the CD-ROM.

ON THE CD

Performance-wise, this particular optimization produces code that runs *two to three orders of magnitude* faster than the first version, depending on the compiler and platform. Clearly, custom allocators offer huge performance benefits, and the beauty of allocators is that you can write your own implementations that use whatever allocation techniques make sense for your game.

Allocator Basics

STL containers include `vector`, `deque`, `list`, `map`, `set`, `multimap`, and `multiset`. The `basic_string` object also meets the qualifications for a container. All STL containers allocate memory to store objects in the container. These containers allow you to provide custom allocators that define how memory will be managed. For example, `list` is defined as the following:

```
template <typename T, class Allocator = allocator<T> >
class list { ... };
```

The `Allocator` parameter is a default template parameter. In normal usage, it's not specified, and the default allocator, `allocator<T>`, is used. The default allocator will be covered in more detail later.

```
std::list<int> IntList; // uses default allocator<int>
```

Allocator Requirements

Any allocator object must meet the minimum requirements set forth by the C++ standard in Section 20.1.5 of [Cpp98]. These requirements are not difficult to follow and usually involve boilerplate code. However, it's beneficial to understand all portions of the allocator class.

Typedefs

All allocator objects must include the typedef names shown here. These typedefs are almost always defined as listed in this section. However, the C++ standard allows implementations to provide alternative definitions. For instance, the `pointer` typedef might refer to *far* pointers, or some other pointer type particular to the platform. In practice, the freedom to define alternate types is limited, especially since C++ has no way of defining a reference type other than good old `T&`. The moral of the story: Don't alter these typedefs without fully understanding the ramifications.

```
typedef size_t size_type;
typedef ptrdiff_t difference_type;
typedef T*  pointer;
typedef const T* const_pointer;
typedef T&  reference;
typedef const T& const_reference;
typedef T   value_type;
```

Construction and Copying

Allocators are regular C++ objects, so there must be a way to construct them, copy them, and destroy them. Here are the definitions for the constructor and destructor:

```
allocator() throw();
allocator( const allocator& ) throw();
template <typename U>
    allocator( const allocator<U>& ) throw();
~allocator() throw();
```

Notice the unusual template member constructor, which allows an allocator to be constructed given an allocator of another type. Some compilers do not support template members yet, so this constructor may not exist in your implementation. Note also that the C++ standard explicitly requires that neither the constructors nor destructor throw an exception.

Utility Functions

Allocator objects must provide a small set of utility functions. However, the most interesting utility function is `max_size`, which returns the maximum number of objects that could be conceivably allocated via `allocate`.

```
pointer address( reference r ) const
{
    return &r;
}

const_pointer address( const_reference c ) const
{
    return &c;
}

size_type max_size() const
{
    return numeric_limits<size_t>::max() / sizeof(T);
}
```

Allocation

The `allocate` function is one of the two critical functions in the allocator object, and it is the one function that is normally the focus of any custom allocator. The C++ standard says that `allocate` must return a pointer to raw memory of sufficient size to hold n objects of size T, where n is always greater than zero. The function does *not* construct the objects. The second parameter is an allocation *hint*, commonly a pointer to another memory block used to improve locality of reference. The hint parameter is generally not used.

```
pointer allocate( size_type n, const void* pHint );
```

Here's just one example of how this function could be written to conform to the standard:

```
pointer allocate( size_type n, const void* )
{
    assert( n > 0 );
    return pointer( malloc( n * sizeof(T) ) );
}
```

Deallocation

The deallocate function is the second critical function of the allocator object. The C++ standard states that this function must free storage for n objects of size T, where the raw memory of those objects begins at a non-null storage location p. The pointer p must have been previously returned by allocate from an equivalent allocator object, and the function must not throw an exception.

```
void deallocate( pointer p, size_type n );
```

Here's an example of how this function could be written to conform to the standard:

```
void deallocate( pointer p, size_type )
{
    assert( p != NULL );
    free( p );
}
```

In-Place Construction and Destruction

Notice that unlike new and delete, allocate and deallocate don't construct or destroy objects—they only deal with raw memory. For performance reasons, allocators specifically separate out these operations. For instance, vector::reserve() allocates raw memory, but only constructs vector::size() objects. Only if and when vector::resize() is called would uninitialized objects actually be constructed.

The allocator construct function allows existing memory to be used for constructing an object in place. You cannot call a constructor directly in C++, but the *placement new* operator provides the functionality needed. Placement new doesn't actually allocate memory—it calls an object's constructor using existing memory.

```
void construct( pointer p, const_reference c )
{
```

```
        // placement new operator
        new( reinterpret_cast<void*>(p) ) T(c);
    }
```

The `destroy` function allows an object to be explicitly destroyed without releasing the memory. You *can* call a destructor directly in C++, which is exactly what `destroy` does.

```
    void destroy( pointer p )
    {
        // call destructor directly
        (p)->~T();
    }
```

The C++ standard defines these functions very precisely. They must always behave as shown here. The real purpose of these functions is to hide the notational complexity from containers.

Rebind

Suppose you've defined your own allocator object for a list of integers.

```
    list<int, MyAlloc<int> > IntList;
```

You might be inclined to believe that `MyAlloc<int>::allocate` would be called whenever a new item was added to the list. Nevertheless, it is not. Most containers (`vector` being an exception) don't actually allocate the objects they store. They allocate *nodes*. Each node contains an object plus one or more pointers. That means that allocators must have some way of converting from type `T` to type `node`, whatever type `node` may be. The solution is called `rebind`.

```
    template <typename U>
    struct rebind
    {
        typedef allocator<U> other;
    };
```

Rebind simply allows `allocator<T>` to allocate objects of another type, `U`. For example, given allocator `a` of type `T`, you can allocate an object of type `U` with the expression:

```
    T::rebind<U>::other(a).allocate( 1, NULL );
```

Don't worry if you don't understand the gory template details. The important thing to remember is that the allocator you define for a given type has a way to allocate objects of different types (and sizes). The other important thing to know about `rebind` is that it requires a compiler with support for *member templates* in order to work properly. STL implementations that work with nonconforming compilers must provide their own mechanism for allocating nodes. For instance, older versions of the

Dinkumware STL library [Dinkum] provide the function `_Charalloc` to support nonconforming versions of Microsoft Visual C++.

Comparing

The C++ standard says two things about comparing allocators. First, it states that allocators are considered equivalent if, and only if, storage allocated by one can be deallocated via the other. Then, it expresses that STL implementations are *permitted* to assume that allocators "be interchangeable and *always* compare equal to each other." If these statements sound contradictory, that's because they are. What the standard is saying is that allocator comparison is implementation-dependent. Some STL implementations allow allocator comparison. Other implementations always compare allocators as equivalent.

```
template <typename T1, typename T2>
bool operator==( const allocator<T1>&,
    const allocator<T2>& ) throw();

template <typename T1, typename T2>
bool operator!=( const allocator<T1>&,
    const allocator<T2>& ) throw();
```

In many cases, it's perfectly fine to assume that allocators are interchangeable. The classic case is when the allocator has no data members. In other cases, you might really want to compare allocators (for more detail on this issue, see "Allocator State Data" later in this section).

The Default Allocator Object

The C++ standard requires that all STL implementations include a default allocator object called "`allocator<T>`." This is the allocator that's used if a custom allocator is not specified. In other words, this is the allocator that your code is probably using at the moment, so it makes sense to know what it is doing.

The default allocator object is defined in the C++ STL in Section 20.4.1 of [Cpp98]. You can find the default allocator for your version of the STL in the `<memory>` header file (or one of the headers included by `<memory>`).

The standard says the default allocator must call `operator new` to allocate storage. If not enough memory is available, it throws the `bad_alloc` exception. A typical implementation of the default `allocate` function looks like this:

```
pointer allocate( size_type n, const void* )
{
    assert( n > 0 );
    return pointer( operator new( n * sizeof(T) ) );
}
```

The standard says the default `deallocate` function must call `operator delete(p)`. A typical implementation of the default `deallocate` is:

```
void deallocate( pointer p, size_type )
{
    assert( p != NULL );
    operator delete( p );
}
```

As you might expect, the default allocator object simply wraps `new` and `delete`. Implementations are free to provide additional optimizations in the default allocator if needed. You can examine your version of the STL to see how the default allocator is implemented.

Writing Your Own Allocator

As mentioned above, every allocator object must meet the minimum requirements set forth by the C++ standard. To be useful, it also has to function within any compiler-specific limitations. The best way for *you* to meet these requirements (and limitations) is by copying the default allocator from `<memory>` and then customizing the `allocate` and `deallocate` functions, and potentially the constructors, destructors, and comparison operators as well.

ON THE CD

Here's the partial implementation of the `StackAlloc` allocator shown at the introduction of the gem. The full source code is included on the CD-ROM. The `allocate` function simply returns a pointer to the next unused portion of stack memory, then updates the number of bytes that have been allocated. If it runs out of stack space, it throws `bad_alloc()`. The `deallocate` function doesn't need to do anything, because stack space is automatically reclaimed. All of these functions are inlined template functions, so `deallocate` is a no-op in a release build.

```
template <typename T>
class StackAlloc
{
public:

    // boilerplate typedefs here . . .

    // critical ctor
    StackAlloc( unsigned char* pStack,
       size_t nMaxBytes ) throw()
    :
        mpStack( pStack ),
        mBytesAllocated( 0 ),
        mMaxBytes( nMaxBytes )
    {
    }

    // other ctors, dtor . . .

    // utility functions . . .

    // construct, destroy, rebind . . .
```

```
        pointer allocate( size_type n, const void* )
        {
            void* pRaw = mpStack + mBytesAllocated;
            mBytesAllocated += ( n * sizeof(T) );

            if( mBytesAllocated+1 > mMaxBytes )
                throw std::bad_alloc();

            return pointer(pRaw);
        }

        void deallocate( pointer p, size_type )
        {
            assert( p != NULL );
        }

        // member data . . .
    };
```

Potential Uses

When should you write your own allocator? If after profiling your game, you've determined that the default allocator is a bottleneck, consider providing a custom allocator. If your entire game uses a custom solution and you don't want `operator new` being called at all, but you do want to use STL containers, consider writing a custom allocator.

There are far too many allocation strategies to possibly list them all, but Table 1.8.1 lists a selected number of strategies to consider when creating a custom allocator.

TABLE 1.8.1 Allocation Strategies

Tablet Type	Description
`Fixed-Size Pools`	All allocations are the same size; reduces memory overhead per allocation.
`Shared Memory`	Allocations use shared memory. See [Stroustrup97] for an example.
`Multiple Heaps`	Allocations come from different heaps, depending on the allocation size or type.
`Single Threaded`	Allocations and deallocations are not thread-safe; useful within single-threaded code.
`Garbage Collected`	Deallocations don't free memory; garbage collector function is called to free memory.
`Stack Based`	All memory resides on the stack. Useful for containers with short lifetimes.
`Static Memory`	Allocations come from program data space (static memory).
`Never Delete`	Deallocations never free memory; memory is reclaimed when application exits.
`One-Time Delete`	Deallocations never free memory; memory is reclaimed by custom function.
`Aligned`	Memory is aligned to certain requirements, such as SSE instructions that require specific alignment.
`Debugging`	Allocation logging, pinpointing leaks, checking for memory overwrites, peak allocation size, and so forth.

Allocator State Data

As mentioned above, STL implementations might allow any allocator to be equivalent to any other. That implies that unless your particular implementation supports comparable allocators, it's dangerous for allocators to hold per-object data/state of any kind. If you're writing an allocator that must work across multiple implementations, the only safe path is writing allocators with no per-object data. The nice thing about this restriction is that allocators in such implementations generally have no space overhead. The drawback is that it might be more difficult to accomplish your task with a custom allocator.

One of the easiest ways to see if your STL implementation supports allocators with per-object data is to examine the implementation of `list::splice`. In the nominal case, the splice function splices one list to another by shifting pointers, which is very fast. Now, consider the case where the allocators for the lists are truly different—using different heaps, for example. Splice *cannot* simply change pointers, because the resulting list would contain some nodes allocated on one heap and some on another. The resulting list wouldn't "know" how to delete some of its nodes!

In the list `splice` function, if there are two code paths based on the comparison of allocators, it's likely you have an implementation that supports allocators with per-object data. If not, it's likely your implementation assumes that allocators are all equivalent.

Recommendations

Below is a list of recommendations for writing a custom allocator.

Copy the default allocator from `<memory>` and replace `allocate` and `deallocate`. If your allocator has state data, update the constructors and destructor. Don't forget to include the global comparison functions.

Be aware that using `allocator<T>` does not necessarily mean that only blocks of `sizeof(T)` will be allocated. The `rebind` function allows other types—and therefore other sizes—to be allocated.

- Typedefs are your friends, especially when dealing with template code. Use typedefs for allocators and containers that use custom allocators. If you need to make a change, only the typedef will need to be altered.
- Be wary of creating allocators that hold per-object data or that contain "state." Your STL implementation might not support such allocators. Examine the list `splice` function to determine if your implementation supports allocators with per-object data.
- Due to current compiler technology, not all allocator implementations conform to the C++ standard. When in doubt, examine the default allocator in `<memory>` to determine how your implementation works around compiler limitations.
- Don't add custom allocators until you need to. The great thing about the allocator architecture is that allocators can be replaced with very few code changes.

Implementation Details

ON THE CD

The code included on the CD-ROM is designed to work with Microsoft Visual Studio Version 6 and Visual Studio .NET. It was tested with STL implementation Versions 3.08 and 3.10 from Dinkumware. These versions *do* support allocators with per-object data and allow nontrivial comparison functions.

Example allocators are provided for a number of strategies, including multiple heaps, stack-based allocators, and static allocators. There's also an allocator that simply wraps `malloc` and `free`.

Conclusion

Writing a custom allocator is a matter of copying some boilerplate code and customizing a handful of key member functions. Allocators have some curious features, and a working knowledge of these features is critical to understanding how allocators work. It's also important to note that different STL implementations might not support allocators with per-object data and might provide custom member functions to avoid compiler issues. Regardless of the complexities, custom allocators can significantly improve performance and are definitely worth understanding.

References

[Alexandrescu01] Alexandrescu, Andrei, *Modern C++ Design*, Addison Wesley, 2001.

[Austern99] Austern, Matt, *Generic Programming and the STL*, Addison Wesley, 1999.

[Cpp98] ISO/IEC 14882, *ANSI C++ Standard*, August 1998.

[Dinkum] Plauger, P. J., et al., "Dinkumware Standard Template Library," available online at http://www.dinkumware.com.

[Josuttis99] Josuttis, Nicolai, *The C++ Standard Library: A Tutorial and Reference*, Addison Wesley, 1999.

[Meyers01] Meyers, Scott, *Effective STL*, Addison Wesley, 2001.

[Plauger01] Plauger, P. J., et al., *The C++ Standard Template Library*, Prentice Hall, 2001.

[Stroustrup97] Stroustrup, Bjarne, *The C++ Programming Language*, Third Edition, Addison Wesley, 1997.

1.9

Optimization for C++ Games

Andrew Kirmse, Google Inc.

ark@alum.mit.edu

Well-written C++ games are often more maintainable and reusable than their plain C counterparts—but is it worth it? Can complex C++ programs hope to match traditional C programs in speed?

With a good compiler and thorough knowledge of the language, it is indeed possible to create efficient games in C++. This gem describes techniques you can use to speed up games in particular. It assumes that you're already convinced of the benefits of using C++, and that you're familiar with the general principles of optimization (see the references for these).

One general principle that merits repeating is the absolute importance of profiling. In the absence of profiling, programmers tend to make two kinds of mistakes. First, they optimize the wrong code. The great majority of a program is not performance critical, so any time spent speeding it up is wasted. Intuition about which code is performance critical is untrustworthy—only by direct measurement can you be sure. Second, programmers sometimes make "optimizations" that actually slow down the code. This is particularly a problem in C++, where a deceptively simple line can actually generate a significant amount of machine code. Examine your compiler's output, and profile often.

Object Construction and Destruction

The creation and destruction of objects is a central concept in C++, and is the main area where the compiler generates code "behind your back." Poorly designed programs can spend substantial time calling constructors, copying objects, and generating costly temporary objects. Fortunately, common sense and a few simple rules can make object-heavy code run within a hair's breadth of the speed of C.

1. Delay construction of objects until they're needed.

The fastest code is that which never runs; why create an object if you're not going to use it? Thus, in the following code:

```
void Function(int arg)
{
    Object obj;
    if (arg == 0)
        return;
    ...
}
```

Even when `arg` is zero, we pay the cost of calling `Object`'s constructor and destructor. If `arg` is often zero, and especially if `Object` itself allocates memory, this waste can add up in a hurry. The solution, of course, is to move the declaration of `obj` until after the `if` check.

Be careful about declaring non-trivial objects in loops, however. If you delay construction of an object until it's needed in a loop, you'll pay for the construction and destruction of the object on every iteration. It's better to declare the object before the loop and pay these costs only once. If a function is called inside an inner loop, and the function creates an object on the stack, you could instead create the object outside the loop and pass it by reference to the function.

2. Use initializer lists.

Consider the following class:

```
class Vehicle
{
public:
    Vehicle(const std::string &name)  // Don't do this!
    {
        mName = name;
    }
private:
    std::string mName;
};
```

Because member variables are constructed before the body of the constructor is invoked, this code calls the constructor for the string `mName`, then calls the `=` operator to copy in the object's name. What's particularly bad about this example is that the default constructor for `string` may well allocate memory, in fact more memory than may be necessary to hold the actual name assigned to the variable in the constructor for `Vehicle`. Much better is the following code, which avoids the call to `operator=`. Further, given more information (in this case, the actual string to be stored), the non-default `string` constructor can often be more efficient, and the compiler may be able to optimize away the `Vehicle` constructor invocation when the body is empty:

```
class Vehicle
{
public:
    Vehicle(const std::string &name) : mName(name)
    {
    }
```

```
private:
    std::string mName;
};
```

3. Prefer pre-increment to post-increment.
The problem with writing *x* = *y*++ is that the increment function has to make a copy of the original value of *y*, increment *y*, and then return the original value. Thus, post-increment involves the construction of a temporary object, while pre-increment doesn't. For integers, there's no additional overhead, but for user-defined types, this is wasteful. You should use pre-increment whenever you have the option. You almost always have the option in `for` loop iterators.

4. Avoid operators that return by value.
The canonical way to write vector addition in C++ is this:

```
Vector operator+(const Vector &v1, const Vector &v2)
```

This operator must return a new `Vector` object, and furthermore it must return it by value. While this allows useful and readable expressions like $v = v1 + v2$, the cost of a temporary construction and a `Vector` copy is usually too much for something called as often as vector addition. It's sometimes possible to arrange code so that the compiler is able to optimize away the temporary object (this is known as the *return value optimization*), but in general it's better to swallow your pride and write the slightly uglier, but usually faster:

```
void Vector::Add(const Vector &v1, const Vector &v2)
```

Note that `operator+=` doesn't suffer from the same problem, as it modifies its first argument in place, and doesn't need to return a temporary. Thus, you should use operators like += instead of + when possible.

5. Use lightweight constructors.
Should the constructor for the `Vector` class in the previous example initialize its elements to zero? This may come in handy in a few spots in your code, but it forces every caller to pay the price of the initialization, whether they use it or not. In particular, temporary vectors and member variables will implicitly incur the extra cost.

A good compiler may well optimize away some of the extra code, but why take the chance? As a general rule, you want an object's constructor to initialize each of its member variables, because uninitialized data can lead to subtle bugs. However, in small classes that are frequently instantiated, especially as temporaries, you should be prepared to compromise this rule for performance. Prime candidates in many games are the `Vector` and `Matrix` classes. These classes should provide methods (or alternate constructors) to set themselves to zero and the identity respectively, but the default constructor should be empty.

As a corollary to this principle, you should provide additional constructors to classes where this will improve performance. If the `Vehicle` class in example 2 were instead written like this:

```
class Vehicle
{
public:
    Vehicle()
{
}

void SetName(const std::string &name)
{
mName = name;
}

private:
    std::string mName;
};
```

we'd incur the cost of constructing `mName`, and then setting it again later via `SetName()`. Similarly, it's cheaper to use copy constructors than to construct an object and then call `operator=`. Prefer constructing an object `Vehicle v1(v2);` to this `Vehicle v1; v1 = v2;`.

If you want to prevent the compiler from automatically copying an object for you, declare a `private` copy constructor and `operator=` for the object's class, but don't implement either function. Any attempt to copy the object will then result in a compile-time error. Also get into the habit of declaring single-argument constructors as *explicit*, unless you mean to use them as type conversions. This prevents the compiler from generating hidden temporary objects when converting types.

6. Preallocate and cache objects.

A game will typically have a few classes that it allocates and frees frequently, like weapons or particles. In a C game, you'd typically allocate a big array up front and use them as necessary. With a little planning, you can do the same thing in C++. The idea is that instead of continually constructing and destructing objects, you request new ones and return old ones to a cache. The cache can be implemented as a template, so that it works for any class, provided that the class has a default constructor. Code for a sample cache class template is on the accompanying CD-ROM.

ON THE CD

You can either allocate objects to fill the cache as you need them, or preallocate all of the objects up front. If, in addition, you maintain a stack discipline on the objects (meaning that before you delete object `X`, you first delete all objects allocated after `X`), you can allocate the cache in a contiguous block of memory.

Memory Management

C++ applications generally need to be more aware of the details of memory management than C applications. In C, all allocations are explicit though `malloc()` and `free()`, while C++ can implicitly allocate memory while constructing temporary objects and member variables. Most C++ games (like most C games) will require their own memory manager.

Because a C++ game is likely to perform many allocations, it must be especially careful about fragmenting the heap. One option is to take one of the traditional approaches: either don't allocate any memory at all after the game starts up, or maintain a large contiguous block of memory that is periodically freed (between levels, for example). On modern machines, such draconian measures are not necessary, if you're willing to be vigilant about your memory usage.

The first step is to override the global `new` and `delete` operators. Use custom implementations of these operators to redirect the game's most common allocations away from `malloc()` and into pre-allocated blocks of memory. For example, if you find that you have at most 10,000 4-byte allocations outstanding at any one time, you should allocate 40,000 bytes up front and issue blocks out as necessary. To keep track of which blocks are free, maintain a *free list* by pointing each free block to the next free block. On allocation, remove the front block from the list, and on deallocation, add the freed block to the front again. Figure 1.9.1 is an illustration of how the free list of small blocks might wind its way through a contiguous larger block after a sequence of allocations and frees.

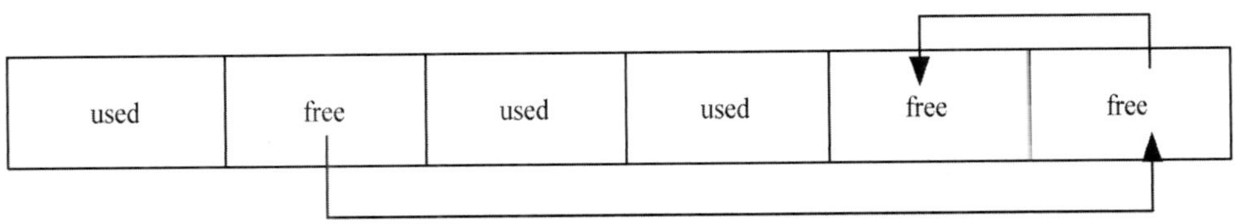

FIGURE 1.9.1 A linked free list.

You'll typically find that a game has many small, short-lived allocations, and thus you'll want to reserve space for many small blocks. Reserving many larger blocks wastes a substantial amount of memory for those blocks that are not currently in use; above a certain size, you'll want to pass allocations off to a separate large block allocator, or just to `malloc()`.

Virtual Functions

Critics of C++ in games often point to virtual functions as a mysterious feature that drains performance. Conceptually, the mechanism is simple. To generate a virtual function call on an object, the compiler accesses the object's virtual function table, retrieves a pointer to the member function, sets up the call, and jumps to the member function's address. This is to be compared with a function call in C, where the compiler sets up the call and jumps to a fixed address. The extra overhead for the virtual function call is the indirection to the virtual function table; because the address of the call isn't known in advance, there can also be a penalty for missing the processor's instruction cache.

Any substantial C++ program will make heavy use of virtual functions, so the idea is to avoid these calls in performance-critical areas. Here is a typical example:

```
class BaseClass
{
public:
    virtual char *GetPointer() = 0;
};

class Class1 : public BaseClass
{
    virtual char *GetPointer();
};

class Class2 : public BaseClass
{
    virtual char *GetPointer();
};

void Function(BaseClass *pObj)
{
char *ptr = pObj->GetPointer();
}
```

If `Function()` is performance-critical, we want to change the call to `GetPointer` from virtual to inline. One way to do this is to add a new protected data member to `BaseClass`, which is returned by an inline version of `GetPointer()`, and set the data member in each class:

```
class BaseClass
{
public:
    inline char *GetPointerFast()
    {
        return mpPointer;
    }

protected:
    inline void SetPointer(char *pData)
    {
        mpData = pData;
}

private:
    char *mpData;
};
```

```
// class1 and class2 call SetPointer as necessary
// in member functions

void Function(BaseClass *pObj)
{
char *ptr = pObj->GetPointerFast();
}
```

A more drastic measure is to rearrange your class hierarchy. If `Class1` and `Class2` have only slight differences, it might be worth combining them into a single class, with a flag indicating whether you want the class to behave like `Class1` or `Class2` at runtime. With this change, (and the removal of the pure virtual `BaseClass`), the `GetPointer` function in the previous example can again be made inline. This transformation is far from elegant, but in inner loops on machines with small caches, you'd be willing to do much worse to get rid of a virtual function call.

Although each new virtual function adds only the size of a pointer to a per-class table (usually a negligible cost), the *first* virtual function in a class requires a pointer to the virtual function table on a per-*object* basis. This means that you don't want to have any virtual functions at all in small, frequently used classes where this extra overhead is unacceptable. Because inheritance generally requires the use of one or more virtual functions (a virtual destructor if nothing else), you don't want any hierarchy for small, heavily used objects.

Code Size

Compilers have a somewhat deserved reputation for generating bloated code for C++. Because memory is limited, and because small is fast, it's important to make your executable as small as possible. The first thing to do is get the compiler on your side. If your compiler stores debugging information in the executable, then disable the generation of debugging information. (Note that Microsoft Visual C++ stores debugging information separate from the executable, so this may not be necessary.) Exception handling generates extra code; get rid of as much exception-generating code as possible. Make sure the linker is configured to strip out unused functions and classes. Enable the compiler's highest level of optimization, and try setting it to optimize for size instead of speed—sometimes this actually produces faster code because of better instruction cache coherency. (Be sure to verify that intrinsic functions are still enabled if you use this setting.) Get rid of all of your space-wasting strings in debugging print statements, and have the compiler combine duplicate constant strings into single instances.

Inlining is often the culprit behind suspiciously large functions. Compilers are free to respect or ignore your `inline` keywords, and they may well inline functions without telling you. This is another reason to keep your constructors lightweight, so that objects on the stack don't wind up generating lots of inline code. Also be careful of overloaded operators; a simple expression like `m1 = m2 * m3` can generate a ton of inline code if `m2` and `m3` are matrices. Get to know your compiler's settings for inlining functions thoroughly.

Enabling runtime type information (RTTI) requires the compiler to generate some static information for (just about) every class in your program. RTTI is typically enabled so that code can call `dynamic_cast` and determine an object's type. Consider avoiding RTTI and `dynamic_cast` entirely in order to save space (in addition, `dynamic_cast` is quite expensive in some implementations). Instead, when you really need to have different behavior based on type, add a virtual function that behaves differently. This is better object-oriented design anyway. (Note that this doesn't apply to `static_cast`, which is just like a C-style cast in performance.)

The Standard Template Library

The Standard Template Library (STL) is a set of templates that implement common data structures and algorithms, such as dynamic arrays (called vectors), sets, and maps. Using the STL can save you a great deal of time that you'd otherwise spend writing and debugging these containers yourself. Once again, though, you need to be aware of the details of your STL implementation if you want maximum efficiency.

In order to allow the maximum range of implementations, the STL standard is silent is in the area of memory allocation. Each operation on an STL container has certain performance guarantees: for example, insertion into a set takes O(log n) time. However, there are no guarantees on a container's memory usage.

Let's go into detail on a very common problem in game development: you want to store a bunch of objects (we'll call it a list of objects, though we won't necessarily store it in an STL list). Usually you want each object to appear in a list only once, so that you don't have to worry about accidentally inserting the object into the collection if it's already there. An STL set ignores duplicates, has O(log n) insertion, deletion, and lookup—the perfect choice, right?

Maybe. While it's true that most operations on a set are O(log n), this notation hides a potentially large constant. Although the collection's memory usage is implementation-dependent, many implementations are based on a red-black tree, where each node of the tree stores an element of the collection. It's common practice to allocate a node of the tree every time an element is inserted, and to free a node every time an element is removed. Depending on how often you insert and remove elements, the time spent in the memory allocator can overshadow any algorithmic savings you gained from using a set.

An alternative solution uses an STL vector to store elements. A vector is guaranteed to have amortized constant-time insertion at the end of the collection. What this means in practice is that a vector typically reallocates memory only on occasion, say, doubling its size whenever it's full. When using a vector to store a list of unique elements, you first check the vector to see if the element is already there, and if it isn't, you add it to the back. Checking the entire vector will take O(n) time, but the constant involved is likely to be small. That's because all of the elements of a vector are typically stored contiguously in memory, so checking the entire vector is a cache-friendly operation. Checking an entire set may well thrash the memory cache, as individual elements of the red-black tree could be scattered all over memory. Also consider that a set must maintain a significant amount of overhead to set up the tree. If all you're storing is object pointers, a set can easily require three to four times the memory of a vector to store the same objects.

Deletion from a set is O(log n), which seems fast until you consider that it probably also involves a call to `free()`. Deletion from a vector is O(n), because everything from the deleted element to the end of the vector must be copied over one position. However, if the elements of the vector are just pointers, the copying can all be done in a single call to `memcpy()`, which is typically very fast. (This is one reason why it's usually preferable to store pointers to objects in STL collections, as opposed to objects themselves. If you store objects directly, many extra constructors get invoked during operations like deletion.)

If you're still not convinced that sets and maps can often be more trouble than they're worth, consider the cost of iterating over a collection, specifically:

```
for (Collection::iterator it = collection.begin(); it !=
collection.end(); ++it)
```

If `Collection` is a vector, then `++it` is a pointer increment—one machine instruction. But when `Collection` is a set or a map, `++it` involves traversing to the next node of a red-black tree, a relatively complicated operation that is also much more likely to cause a cache miss, because tree nodes may be scattered all over memory.

Of course, if you're storing a very large number of items in a collection, and doing lots of membership queries, a set's O(log n) performance could very well be worth the memory cost. Similarly, if you're only using the collection infrequently, the performance difference may be irrelevant. You should do performance measurements to determine what values of n make a set faster. You may be surprised to find that vectors outperform sets for all values that your game will typically use.

That's not quite the last word on STL memory usage, however. It's important to know if a collection actually frees its memory when you call the `clear()` method. If not, memory fragmentation can result. For example, if you start a game with an empty vector, add elements to the vector as the game progresses, and then call `clear()` when the player restarts, the vector may not actually free its memory at all. The empty vector's memory could still be taking up space somewhere in the heap, fragmenting it. There are two ways around this problem, if indeed your implementation works this way. First, you can call `reserve()` when the vector is created, reserving enough space for the maximum number of elements that you'll ever need. If that's impractical, you can explicitly force the vector to free its memory this way:

```
vector<int> v;
// ... elements are inserted into v here
vector<int>().swap(v);  // causes v to free its memory
```

Sets, lists, and maps typically don't have this problem, because they allocate and free each element separately.

Advanced Features

Just because a language has a feature, that doesn't mean you have to use it. Seemingly simple features can have very poor performance, while other seemingly complicated features can in fact perform well. The darkest corners of C++ are highly compiler dependent—make sure you know the costs before using them.

C++ strings are an example of a feature that sounds great on paper, but which should be avoided where performance matters. Consider the following code:

```
void Function(corst std::string &str)
{
}

Function("hello");
```

The call to `Function()` invokes a constructor for a string given a `const char *`. In one commercial implementation, this constructor performs a `malloc()`, a `strlen()`, and a `memcpy()`, and the destructor immediately does some non-trivial work (because this implementation's strings are reference counted) followed by a `free()`. The memory that's allocated is basically a waste, because the string `"hello"` is already in the program's data segment; we've effectively duplicated it in memory. If `Function()` had instead been declared as taking a `const char *`, there would be no overhead to the call. That's a high price to pay for the convenience of manipulating strings.

Templates are an example of the opposite extreme of efficiency. According to the language standard, the compiler generates code for a template when the template is instantiated with a particular type. In theory, it sounds like a single template declaration would lead to massive amounts of nearly identical code. If you have a vector of `Class1` pointers, and a vector of `Class2` pointers, you'll wind up with two copies of `vector` in your executable.

The reality for most compilers is usually better. First, only template member functions that are actually called have any code generated for them. Second, the compiler is allowed to generate only one copy of the code, if correct behavior is preserved. You'll generally find that in the vector example given previously, only a single copy of code (probably for `vector<void *>`) will be generated. Given a good compiler, templates give you all the convenience of generic programming, while maintaining high performance.

Some features of C++, like initializer lists and pre-increment, generally increase performance, while other features, such as overloaded operators and RTTI, look equally innocent but carry serious performance penalties. STL collections illustrate how blindly trusting in a function's documented algorithmic running time can lead you astray. Avoid the potentially slow features of the language and libraries, and spend some time becoming familiar with the options in your profiler and compiler. You'll quickly learn to design for speed and hunt down the performance problems in your game.

Further Investigations

Thanks to Pete Isensee and Christopher Kirmse for reviewing this gem.

Cormen, Thomas, Charles Leiserson and Ronald Rivest. *Introduction to Algorithms.* Cambridge, Massachusetts: MIT Press, 1990.

Isensee, Peter. *C++ Optimization Strategies and Techniques.* http://www.tantalon.com/pete/cppopt/main.htm.

Koenig, Andrew. "Pre- or Postfix Increment." *The C++ Report.* June, 1999.

Meyers, Scott. *Effective C++, Second Edition.* Reading, Massachusetts: Addison-Wesley Publishing Co., 1998.

Sutter, Herb. *Guru of the Week #54: Using Vector and Deque.* http://www.gotw.ca/gotw/054.htm.

1.10

Real-Time Hierarchical Profiling

Greg Hjelstrom, Petroglyph and Byon Garrabrant

greg@hjelstrom.com, byon@byonics.com

When developing most games, a primary goal is to get maximum performance out of your code. Knowing where to spend your optimization effort is key to attaining this goal. We've all heard variations on the old adage: "A program spends 90% of its time in 10% of the code." Profiling is an invaluable tool for finding that 10% of the code that needs to be optimized.

Two types of profiling strategies are often employed—sampling and explicit timing. A sampling profiler works by frequently sampling the position of the instruction pointer while the program runs. This generates a huge amount of raw data that is then processed to generate profiling data. Sampling profilers can often tell you exactly in which line of code most of the time is being spent. Many commercial profilers work this way because modifications to the application code are unnecessary. Unfortunately, it isn't always practical to use sampling in real time, due to the amount of overhead involved in gathering and processing the sampled data.

The other profiling method that is commonly used is to explicitly time blocks of code. These measurements can then be displayed in real time and can aid in finding transient performance problems. This is important because bottlenecks in games are often dependent on many factors. It is useful to see how the profiling data changes as the user plays the game and triggers various events. Also, these profiling samples will typically be logically organized. For example, one might log how much time the code spends processing AI, rendering, and physics. Then, at any point in time, you can see which subsystem in the code is taking the most time. The only drawback to this type of profiling is that it only gives a general idea of where the code-processing time is being spent. For example, once you know the AI is running extremely slow, you typically have to use a sampling profiler or temporarily add more timing measurements to find out why the AI is running slowly.

Ideally, we would like to have the best of both worlds—real-time profiling with as much detail as a sampling profiler. This gem will describe a system that, while not attaining the resolution of a sampling profiler, can efficiently support thousands of profiling samples that are logically and hierarchically organized. A 'profile tree' is constantly updated and can be browsed in real time, and we can find out where the CPU is spending its time.

The Profile Tree

The profile tree is an *N-ary* tree made of profile nodes. An N-ary tree is a tree where each node of the tree can have any number of child nodes. The topology of this tree is determined by the placement of profiling macros in the application's code. Since each node in the tree typically has only a few children, searching and data presentation is efficient.

Each profile node corresponds to a single explicit timing sample of a block of code. Each node tracks the total amount of time spent within that block of code and the total number of times that code has been executed. Samples, which are taken within the scope of another sample, correspond to a child node of that sample. Whenever a new profiling call is made, a new child node is added to or reused in the current node.

For a real-world example, we can examine how this profiling system was used in *Command & Conquer Renegade* (see Figure 1.10.1). *Renegade* had a total of over 1,000 profile nodes. However, the profiler was efficient because there were only an average of 2 children for any given node, and the worst-case node only had 15 children. As we will show later, the cost of this algorithm is proportional to the number of children in a node.

FIGURE 1.10.1 This is a screenshot of the real-time hierarchical profiler running inside of *Command & Conquer Renegade.* Only one node of the tree is shown, but the user can navigate the tree in real time.

Usage

To use this profiling system, `PROFILE` macros must be placed at key points in the code. As will be described later, placing a `PROFILE` macro in the code will cause a profile node to be generated. This node will be responsible for timing the scope of the corresponding code. A good strategy is to place a `PROFILE` macro at the top of each subsystem in the application, and refine it as needed.

It can be helpful to break large routines into several independent profile samples. This is easily accomplished by adding additional scoping brackets to the function, each with their own `PROFILE` macro. Here is an example:

```
void BigFunction(void)
{
    {
        PROFILE("BigFunction Part 1")
        ...
    }
    {
        PROFILE("BigFunction Part 2")
        ...
    }
}
```

It can also be useful to 'flatten' the profile structure of a member function in a class hierarchy. The following example shows how you can combine time spent in a particular layer of an overridden function, even when it is called through many different derived classes. In this example, time spent in `BasePhysics::Timestep()` is not included in `CarPhysics::Timestep()`, and all time spent in `BasePhysics::Timestep()` will be combined into a single profile sample, even when called from other derived classes (assuming they use this profiling strategy).

```
void CarPhysics::Timestep(void)
{
    {
    PROFILE("CarPhysics::Timestep");
    ...
    }
    BasePhyics::Timestep();
}
```

Browsing the Profiling Data

This profiling system generates a lot of data, so the user must have a way to navigate it easily. An iterator is provided that can be used to navigate through the tree and display statistics for the children of the current node. Using this system, a user can chase down a bottleneck in real time by walking up and down the profile tree, and focus on areas of code that are taking a lot of time. For example, a representative profile sample for the main loop of *Renegade* is listed in Table 1.10.1.

TABLE 1.10.1 Profile Data for Main Loop

Name	%Parent	%Total	Ms/Frame	Ms/Call	Calls/Frame
0-Audio	2.01	2.00	0.35	0.35	1
1-Render	51.64	51.40	8.95	8.99	1
2-Network	1.70	1.69	0.30	0.30	1
3-Think	43.19	42.99	7.49	7.49	1
4-Pathfind	0.04	0.04	0.01	0.01	1
Unlogged	1.42	1.42			

In this case, the time is mostly split between Render and Think. Navigating the tree is achieved by assigning a numerical index to each child of the current node. The user is allowed to enter either the parent of the current node or any of its children. Assume the user wanted to investigate the Render child. They would get a new display, as shown in Table 1.10.2.

TABLE 1.10.2 Profile Data for Render

Name	%Parent	%Total	Ms/Frame	Ms/Call	Calls/Frame
0-Switch_Thread	16.39	8.58	1.47	1.47	1
1-Post_Render	0.28	0.14	0.02	0.02	1
2-End_Render	8.04	4.21	0.72	0.72	1
3-DialogMgr	0.09	0.01	0.01	0.01	1
4-Render_Game	49.55	25.95	4.44	4.44	1
5-Begin_Render	1.70	0.89	0.15	0.15	1
6-Shadow_Gen	22.83	11.96	2.05	2.05	1
Unlogged	1.12	0.09			

Since `Render_Game` takes a large portion of this node's time, the user could then descend the tree to get a breakdown of that node. This process can continue as long as there are children of the node you are interested in.

All of the statistics in the profiling system represent running totals and averages. It can be useful to use the reset feature to throw out historical data. For example, when the frame rate drops, we often reset the profiler to get a more accurate measurement of what the code is doing at that time. When the profile system is reset, the tree is not actually destroyed; only the timing data contained in the nodes are zeroed out.

Implementation

The implementation relies on an accurate way to sample time. We used the 64-bit cycle counter feature of Pentium CPUs. This counter is incremented every time the CPU executes an instruction. By saving the state of the counter at the start of a profiling sample and subtracting that value from the state of the counter at the end of a profiling sample, you can very accurately compute the amount of time elapsed. We then divide the number of instructions by the CPU clock speed to determine the amount of time spent. Our profile nodes accumulate the amount of time in a floating-point variable.

CProfileSample

This is a small C++ class whose only task is to call the `Start_Profile()` method of `CProfileManager` in its constructor and the `Stop_Profile()` method in its destructor. This automates the task of starting and stopping a profile sample during the scope of this object. To further simplify the usage, the `PROFILE` macro is used to automatically create a `CProfileSample` object and to easily remove profiling code from release builds.

```
class    CProfileSample {
public:
    CProfileSample(const char * name)
    {
        CProfileManager::Start_Profile(name);
    }
    ~CProfileSample(void)
    {
        CProfileManager::Stop_Profile();
    }
};

#define PROFILE(name) CProfileSample __profile(name)
```

CProfileManager

The profile manager is the external interface to the profiling system. It maintains the `CurrentNode` pointer into the profile tree that corresponds to the scope of the currently executing code. It also contains methods for accessing the profile tree for display purposes.

The `Start_Profile()` method is used to start a profile sample. It detects recursion by comparing the name of the requested profile with the name of the current node. When the subnode that matches the given name is found, it becomes the current node. The overhead incurred in this search will be proportional to the number of immediate children linked to the current node. Typically, this is a small number, rarely as large as 10. In addition, since we use static strings for all of our profile sample names, pointer compares are used rather than slower string compares when looking for a particular profile sample.

In the case that a child with the given name does not exist, a new node will be created and linked to the tree. Note that node creation will only occur on the first pass through a particular code path. In any case, the node's `Call()` method is then called to begin timing.

```
void CProfileManager::Start_Profile(const char * name)
{
    if (name != CurrentNode->Get_Name()) {
        CurrentNode=CurrentNode->Get_Sub_Node(name);
    }
    CurrentNode->Call();
}
```

The `Stop_Profile()` method is used to end a profile sample. The first task is to call the `Return()` method on the current node to complete and record the timing. Since the profile manager has maintained the current node being sampled, no searching overhead is incurred in this operation. Assuming we are not in a recursive function, the parent node becomes the current node.

```
void CProfileManager::Stop_Profile( void )
{
    // go to parent unless recursed
    if (CurrentNode->Return()) {
        CurrentNode = CurrentNode->Get_Parent();
    }
}
```

The remaining methods in the profile manager are either accessors or perform simple administrative functions. For example, the application calls the `Increment_Frame_Counter()` method once per frame in order to support calculation of the number of calls per frame for any profile sample. The `Get_Iterator()` and `Release_Iterator()` methods provide and destroy an iterator that is used to access the profile tree.

CProfileNode

The `CProfileNode` is a C++ class that is private to the profiling system; it stores the total time spent in a block of code and the number of calls of that block of code. When the CPU is in the scope of a node, the node also stores the starting time.

To start a profiling sample, the profile manager calls the `Call()`method on the node. This method simply increments the call counter and, if we are not recursing, records the starting time.

```
void CProfileNode::Call( void )
{
    TotalCalls++;
    if (RecursionCounter++ == 0) {
        Profile_Get_Ticks(&StartTime);
    }
}
```

At the end of a profiling sample, the `Return()` method is called. After checking if we are not recursing, the elapsed time is computed and added to the `TotalTime` variable. This function also returns whether or not the code is recursing, so the profile manager knows if the node is completed, in which case it would return to the parent node.

```
bool CProfileNode::Return( void )
{
    if (–RecursionCounter== 0 && TotalCalls != 0 ) {
        __int64 time;
        Profile_Get_Ticks(&time);
        time-=StartTime;
        TotalTime += (float)time / Tick_Rate();
    }
    return ( RecursionCounter == 0 );
}
```

CProfileIterator

This object provides an easy way to browse the profile tree. It contains methods for navigating the tree and displaying the contents of a particular node. Typically, a node along with its immediate children are displayed to the user. For each child, several statistics are available: total time spent, total number of calls, calls per frame, and time per frame.

Conclusion

With the ability to hierarchically profile code in real time and sample thousands of blocks of code efficiently, we've found this to be a useful tool for code optimization. It is our hope that readers will find this system useful in improving their own code. You will find an implementation of these classes on the CD-ROM.

ON THE CD

References

[GPG00] Rabin, Steve, *Game Programming Gems*, Charles River Media, Inc., 2000.

1.11

A Generic Tree Container in C++

Bill Budge, Sony Computer Entertainment America

billbudge@hotmail.com

After arrays and lists, trees are the most important data structures in game programming. Trees can represent character skeletons, scene graphs, spatial partitions, and hierarchical bounding volumes. In asset processing tools, trees can also be used to represent shaders and parsed script code.

Implementing trees that use memory efficiently and that can be traversed and modified rapidly is not easy. Where performance is critical—for example, in character skeletons and hierarchical collision detection—many games avoid trees altogether, pre-baking them into special arrays. Such representations are fast and efficient but very difficult to modify. That's too bad, because dynamic trees make it easy to add attachments to characters and to update objects during the game. As gamers demand more interactive environments, flexible tree structures will be very desirable.

The only readily available C++ implementations of trees have been too slow or waste too much memory to be suitable for game runtime use [Kovachev02], [Peeters03]. However, it is possible to create a fast and efficient tree library. This article describes the design of such a library.

Reusable Libraries

There are several ways to design a reusable tree container. The simplest is the "C" way—define a tree that can hold void pointers. This is the technique of choice if we are building a C library. It has the obvious problems of type safety, lots of casting, and the overhead of allocating both the tree and its contents as separate objects on the heap.

The "classic" C++ way relies on inheritance—we define a node class and a tree class to contain nodes. The client derives node types from the base node class, which can be added to the tree. Again, we have problems with type safety and the need for a lot of downcasting. Furthermore, clients must define a new node class for each new type of tree.

The "modern" C++ way is to implement containers generically. A template class is created for a tree of objects of type `T`. The C++ Standard Template Library (STL) is the best example of this approach. Generic libraries can be very flexible and efficient. We will follow the example of the STL to create a generic tree library.

A Quick Review of Trees

A tree is a collection of nodes that are linked together in a branching pattern like trees in nature. By convention, trees are drawn upside down (Figure 1.11.1). A tree node contains zero or more child nodes that are themselves trees, so a tree is a recursive structure. A node with children is called an interior or branch node, while a node without children is called a leaf node. The top node of a tree is called the root. For an excellent overview of trees, see *The Art of Computer Programming: Fundamental Algorithms* [Knuth73].

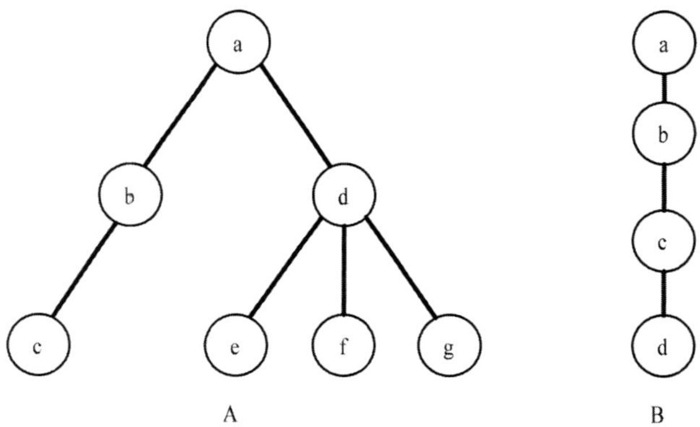

FIGURE 1.11.1 Examples of trees.

There are several different ways in which the contents of a tree can be traversed. A pre-order traversal visits each node first, followed by its children (a-b-c-d-e-f-g in Figure 1.11.1a). A post-order traversal visits the children first, then the node (c-b-e-f-g-d-a). Finally, a level-order traversal visits the root, then its children, then its grandchildren, and so on (a-b-d-c-e-f-g). The most important traversal order in game runtime code is pre-order. This is the natural order for calculating transforms in a skeletal animation system, for culling scene graphs to the view frustum, and for finding intersections of hierarchical bounding volumes. Post-order traversal is useful when interpreting scripts and shaders, where we can't evaluate a parent until all its children are evaluated. Level-order is least useful. One of our design principles is to make pre-order traversal very fast.

In most of our tree applications, the order in which we visit the children is unimportant. Such trees are said to be oriented or unordered, and we can simulate a post-order traversal by performing a pre-order traversal in reverse. If node order is important, the tree is said to be ordered. In that case, we could get the effect of post-order by adding children to the tree in reverse order. In this gem, we will only implement forward and backward pre-order traversal.

Implementing Trees

A very simple way to implement a tree node is to use a list or dynamic vector to hold its child nodes. This makes it easy to perform modifying operations, such as adding or removing nodes. Traversal is also easy. The following code sample shows how we might write the contents of a tree to a stream in pre-order.

```
struct tree
{
    T _value;
    std::vector<tree> _children;
};

void OutputTree(tree& t, Stream& output)
{
    output << t._value;
    int childCount = t._children.size();
    for (int i = 0; i < childCount; i++)
        OutputTree(t._children[i], output);
}
```

A big problem with this approach is that it wastes memory. An efficient dynamic vector implementation will on average waste 25 to 33 percent of the memory it allocates. While it's possible to substitute a linked list for the vector, lists are often implemented with a dummy node. Either way, there is wasted memory at each node in the tree.

Another problem with this design is that we have to write a recursive function to traverse the tree. Recursion is elegant but inefficient. Although we can reduce the function overhead by replacing the recursion with an explicit stack and a loop, it is still costly to traverse the tree. Whatever the traversal method, this code must be duplicated in every additional operation on our tree. This is tedious and a potential maintenance headache. What if we decided to change from using a vector to a list in our implementation? It would be a significant editing chore to change all of the `for` loops in the processing functions. A better design would isolate the traversal logic in the library.

Fortunately, we can make trees more efficient. The following node structure with just two pointers can be used to represent a tree.

```
struct node
{
    T _value;
    node* _first_child;
    node* _next_sibling;
};
```

To visit a node's children, we follow its `_first_child` link, and then the children's `_next_sibling` links, until a `NULL` is encountered. We haven't solved the speed problem, though. We still need a stack to traverse the tree, and there will be serious difficulties implementing tree modification functions. We can fix all of these problems simply by adding more pointers. With just four pointers per node, we get efficient pre-order traversal, and efficient tree modification.

```
struct node
{
    T _value;
    node* _parent;          // NULL for root
    node* _prev_sibling;    // previous sibling
    node* _next;            // next in pre-order
    node* _last_descendant; // leaf points to itself
};
```

The `_next` pointer makes pre-order traversal lightning fast, just a single indirection, but what about in reverse? There is no `_prev` pointer, and in fact, we don't need one. The following node member function will calculate `prev()` in constant time, regardless of tree size.

```
node* prev() const
{
    node* prev = NULL;
    if (_parent)  // root of entire tree has no prev
    {
        if (_parent->_next == this)  // first child?
            prev = _parent;
        else
            prev = _prev_sibling->_last_descendant;
    }
    return prev;
}
```

The following navigation functions can also be performed in constant time.

```
node* first_child() const
{
    node* child = NULL;
    if (_next && (_next->_parent == this))
        child = _next;
    return child;
}

node* last_child() const
{
    node* child = first_child();
    if (child)
        child = child->_prev_sibling;
    return child;
}
```

```
node* next_sibling() const
{
    node* sib = _last_descendant->_next;
    if (sib && (sib->_parent != _parent))
        sib = NULL;
    return sib;
}

node* prev_sibling() const
{
    node* sib = NULL;
    if (_parent && (_parent->_next != this))
        sib = _prev_sibling;
    return sib;
}
```

One wrinkle in this design is that the `_prev_sibling` pointer points to the previous sibling for all child nodes except the first, where it wraps back to the last child to form a circular, singly linked list. This "hack" is necessary in order to get the last child of a node in constant time (see Figure 1.11.2).

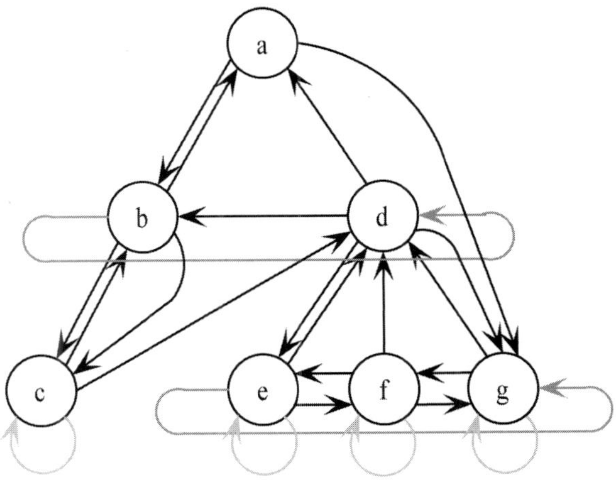

FIGURE 1.11.2 Pointer diagram for tree.

Given these tree navigation functions, it's possible to implement functions to modify the tree. We'll implement all of our tree modifications in terms of the following member functions of our tree.

```
void insert_subtree(TreeT& child, TreeT* next);
void remove_subtree(TreeT& child);
```

An important consequence of having the `_last_descendant` pointer is that adding a node to a tree might require updates all the way back up to the root node. In fact, this is what happens if the tree is built in the usual way by appending new children in pre-order. In the worst case (Figure 1.11.1b), the cost is quadratic in the number of elements in the tree. In practice, this is not a problem, because the worst case is rare and because trees are usually built at initialization time and then modified infrequently. In any case, if it's a problem, the client can insert children in reverse order.

Playing Well with the STL

Now that we know how to implement our tree, it's time to design the interface. We would like to pattern it after the STL for familiarity and to allow us to leverage as much STL code as possible. Can we make a tree look like an STL container?

The STL containers provide iterators to access their contents in sequence without exposing the underlying representation. This concept is what allows the STL to decouple algorithms from containers. An algorithm works for any container that can provide iterators. If we package our tree in the same way, so that our nodes are hidden and our iterators reference the `T` objects, then we can write the following:

```
tree<T> t;
tree<T>::iterator it;
for (it = t.begin(); it != t.end() ++it) {}

// use <algorithm>
void MyTFunction(const T& t);
for_each(t.begin(), t.end(), MyTFunction);
```

Unfortunately, we've also hidden the tree's hierarchical structure, since iterators only expose the `T` objects. That's very inconvenient. When processing a tree, it is often necessary to reference a node's parent or child nodes. In our previous examples, we have no way to access these relatives. Why not add member functions to iterators to get neighboring nodes? That solves the problem in the first example, but not the second. Anyway, it's a bad idea—iterators should look as much like pointers as possible, which means no member functions [Alexandrescu02].

The problem is that the STL container concept is wrong for trees. A tree is not a linear sequence of `T` objects; it's a hierarchical structure that contains `T` objects. We now boldly depart from the STL container concept, and actually emphasize the tree's internal structure. A tree is a linear sequence of trees, and tree iterators expose subtrees.

How do we get to the `T` object? We simply expose it as a public data member of tree named value. It would be silly to encapsulate it, since it belongs to the client. Now we can write code like this:

```
tree<T> t;
for (tree<T>::iterator it=t.begin(); it!=t.end() ++it)
{
    tree<T> subtree& child = *it;
    if (!child.is_root())
        child.value *= child.parent()->value;
}
```

```
void MyTreeFunction(tree<T>& t);
for_each(t.begin(), t.end(), MyTreeFunction);
```

It turns out that it's also useful to be able to iterate over the children of a tree, without descending into the sub-trees. For this purpose, it's easy to provide a `child_iterator`. We can implement it efficiently (constant time increment and decrement) with the `next_sibling()` and `prev_sibling()` functions. Both `iterator` and `child_iterator` are bidirectional, defining increment and decrement operators. Finally, we can leverage some STL machinery to provide reverse iterators and reverse child iterators with just a few lines of boilerplate code.

Given our tree traversal functions, the only difficulty in implementing iterators is handling the end value so that we can iterate backward from it. Dummy nodes that are linked on to the end work well for STL containers like `std::list`, but not for trees. We'd need one per tree node, which is clearly impractical. Instead, our iterators store two pointers, one to the current tree and one to the root tree that produced it. The end position is represented by setting the current pointer to `NULL`. The decrement operator checks for `NULL`, and if so sets current to the last descendant of the root tree. In all other ways, our iterators are similar to `list` iterators, remaining valid until the sub-trees they point to are erased.

Now we know what our tree interface should look like. We define some simple constructors and a destructor. We also define the copy constructor and the assignment operator to give our tree full value semantics. These two functions perform "deep" copies and provide powerful tree-building capabilities.

```
tree();
tree(const T& t);
tree(const TreeT& copy);
~tree();
const tree& operator=(const TreeT& rhs);
```

Because our tree is a linear sequence of trees, it looks and feels a lot like a list. Thus, it's natural to mimic the interface of `std::list`.

```
void push_back(const TreeT& subtree);
void push_front(const TreeT& subtree);
void pop_back();
void pop_front();
iterator insert(iterator it, const TreeT& subtree);
iterator erase(iterator it);
void clear();
iterator splice(iterator it,
    iterator first, iterator last);
iterator splice(iterator it,
    child_iterator first, child_iterator last);
```

The `splice` functions move tree nodes around by manipulating internal pointers. This is much more efficient than copying subtrees and then deleting the originals.

Note that any function that takes a `tree` argument can also take a `T` argument because we defined the constructor `tree(const T& t)` and did not make it explicit. Since there is a natural one-to-one mapping between a `tree<T>` and a `T`, this is one of those rare occasions where allowing the implicit conversion doesn't cause problems.

Finally, we define some tree-specific operations.

```
bool is_root() const;
bool is_leaf() const;
bool is_descendant_of(const TreeT& ancestor);
size_t size() const;   // number of descendants
size_t degree() const; // number of children
size_t level() const;  // depth in tree
```

The STL has a policy of exception safety, which means that containers are guaranteed to remain unchanged when the underlying `T` objects throw certain kinds of exceptions. While most games avoid using exceptions, it doesn't take much work to provide exception safety. This tree container matches the STL guarantees using techniques described in [Sutter00], but throws no exceptions itself.

Memory allocation is always a touchy subject for game programmers. For a library to be suitable for use in game code, it should allow the client to control how memory is allocated. The STL container templates satisfy this requirement. They accept an allocator as an optional argument so that client code can provide custom memory allocation when necessary. We will provide this flexibility as well, although it presents a problem. Our elegant concept of a tree recursively containing trees leaves us no convenient place to store an allocator object. One solution would be to make tree and node separate concepts and store the allocator in the tree. However, the tree would become cumbersome to use, since we couldn't operate on a tree node without the tree object.

If we are less ambitious, we can get most of the benefit of allocators without abandoning our elegant tree concept. We simply make the allocator a static member of our tree class. That limits us to a single allocator per template instantiation of tree, noting that the STL standard makes it hard for implementers to provide much more than this anyway [Plauger01]. Now, with the right custom allocator [Isensee02], `tree` is eminently usable in runtime code.

Conclusion

The tree library we created can generate a tree containing any object type. If we fear template code bloat, we can instantiate just `tree<void*>` and privately derive type-safe tree-of-pointer interfaces from that to get a C-style tree that is type-safe [Meyers98]. Template containers are both powerful and flexible.

The tree library provides powerful facilities for building trees. We can add `T` objects to a tree with a simple interface patterned after `std::list`. Because `tree` has value semantics (a copy constructor and assignment operator), we can copy entire trees in a single assignment. For efficiency, the `splice` functions allow trees to be "glued" together from existing pieces.

Once we've built a tree, we can iterate rapidly in pre-order, forward and backward. We can even perform recursive traversal using child iterators.

```
// preorder traversal, using recursion
void DoSomething(tree<T>& t)
{
    t.value.DoSomething();
    tree<T>::child_iterator it;
    for (it=t.begin_child(); i!=t.end_child() ++i)
        DoSomething(*it);
}

// postorder traversal, using recursion
void DoSomething(tree<T>& t)
{
    tree<T>::reverse_child_iterator it;
    for (it=t.rbegin_child(); i!=t.rend_child() ++i)
        DoSomething(*it);
    t.value.DoSomething();
}
```

ON THE CD

See the source code on the companion CD-ROM for example code that uses `tree<T>`.

References

[Alexandrescu01] Alexandrescu, Andrei, *Modern C++ Design*, Addison-Wesley, 2001.

[Isensee02] Isensee, Pete, "Custom STL Allocators," *Game Programming Gems 3*, Charles River Media, 2002.

[Knuth73] Knuth, Donald, *The Art of Computer Programming: Fundamental Algorithms*, Addison-Wesley, 1973.

[Kovachev02] Kovachev, Alexander, "Tree Data Class for C++," available online at www.codeproject.com/cpp/treedata_class.asp, January 13, 2002.

[Meyers98] Meyers, Scott, *Effective C++*, Addison-Wesley, 1998.

[Peeters03] Peeters, Kasper, "tree.hh: An STL-like C++ Tree Class," available online at www.damtp.cam.ac.uk/user/kp229/tree/, April 17, 2003.

[Plauger01] Plauger, P. J., et al., *The C++ Standard Template Library*, Prentice Hall, 2001.

[Sutter00] Sutter, Herb, *Exceptional C++*, Addison-Wesley, 2000.

1.12

Lock-Free Algorithms

Toby Jones, Microsoft Corporation

thjones@microsoft.com

While game programmers have always driven CPUs to their limits, increasingly they are depending on parallelism to achieve maximum performance. Modern games are expected to take advantage of Symmetric Multiprocessing (SMP) and Chip Multiprocessing (CMP) in PCs and consoles, such as the Xbox 360.

One of the challenges of gaining maximum CPU efficiency is making sure all CPUs are crunching data at all times. One difficulty arises when the CPUs need to share data. While it is best if this is kept to a minimum, at times it can be unavoidable. The traditional techniques involve tools such as mutexes, semaphores, and critical sections to safely serialize access to data and resources.

Mutexes and other lock-based structures are double-edged swords. They allow multiple threads to safely access data, but they are not very scalable. Failing to acquire a lock could cause a thread to spin while waiting for the lock, wasting valuable cycles. In the worst case, they can cause an expensive context switch.

A more modern technique is to use lock-free algorithms. Lock-free algorithms allow access to shared data without needing a lock, but they may restrict what operations are allowed. These algorithms are not wait-free in the sense that all threads will progress immediately, but at least one thread is always able to make progress. Additionally, the algorithms are not necessarily fair; threads are not guaranteed access in order.

One of the primary advantages is that lock-free algorithms can provide a huge boost in speed when used in the right places. They are also invulnerable to deadlock, and terminating a thread in the middle of an operation will not affect the stability of other threads. There are other advantages, but game programmers will generally choose lock-free algorithms due to their speed advantages.

Compare and Swap, and Other Universal Primitives

Implementing a mutex or critical section correctly involves the use of certain atomic primitives, such as a test&set. A thread can repeatedly test&set a memory bit until it succeeds, which would guarantee the thread exclusive access to a resource until the thread clears the bit. However, test&set is not powerful enough for lock-free programming.

Herlihy showed in his seminal paper [Herlihy91] that not all atomic primitives are equal when it comes to choosing primitives for lock-free algorithms. Particularly, test&set, swap, and fetch&add are computationally inadequate. There are primitives that rise to the challenge, which we will call *universal primitives*. These are listed in approximate order of increasing power:

Compare and Swap (CAS): Atomically compares a memory word with a known value, and swaps the memory word with another value if the comparison is equal.

Load Linked/Store Conditional (LL/SC): LL loads a memory word. SC stores a word at the location LL loaded from, provided nothing has written to that location.

Compare and Swap 2 (CAS2): Similar to CAS, CAS2 operates on a contiguous double word.

Double Compare and Swap (DCAS): Similar to CAS2, except the comparison is made on two noncontiguous memory words.

Compare and Swap N (CASN): A generalization of CAS2, which operates on an arbitrary number of contiguous memory words.

Multiword Compare and Swap (MCAS): A final generalization of DCAS, which operates on an arbitrary number of noncontiguous machine words.

CAS can be implemented in pseudo-C code rather easily, as shown in Listing 1.12.1.

LISTING 1.12.1

```
// this function is atomic
bool CAS(uint32_t * ptr, uint32_t oldVal, uint32_t newVal) {
        if(*ptr == oldVal) {
*ptr = newVal;
return true;
        }
        return false;
}
```

Universal Primitives in Practice

It would be wonderful if all universal primitives were available on all hardware. However, most hardware barely supports a subset of these instructions. Generally, one will have either LL/SC or CAS, and perhaps CAS2. This is unfortunate, because many lock-free algorithms require higher-order primitives, such as DCAS.

PowerPC implements two instructions for handling LL/SC. These instructions are Load Word and Reserve Indexed (`lwarx`), and Store Word Conditional Index (`stwcx`). `lwarx` loads a word from memory and stores the address of the word in a hidden register called a reservation. For every memory store, the address is compared against the reservation, and the reservation is cleared if the address matches. `stwcx` attempts to write to the address, but only succeeds if the reservation matches the address. The reservation is then cleared.

x86 supports primitives for CAS and CAS2 through the Compare and Exchange (`cmpxchg`) and Compare and Exchange 8 Bytes (`cmpxchg8b`) instructions. These instructions will compare a memory value against a register (or registers for `cmpxchg8b`), and swap the memory for a second register if the values are equal.

One of the great things about modern C++ compilers is that they often include intrinsics that can be used instead of writing assembly. This can improve portability and still allow the compiler to optimize the code. In Microsoft Visual C++, `_InterlockedCompareExchange()` can be used as a direct replacement for CAS. Other implementations of CAS and CAS2 are available on the CD-ROM.

ON THE CD

Compiler optimizers can cause some problems common to multithreaded code. Lock-free algorithms run in loops, and shared variables may need to be marked with `volatile` in order to be optimized correctly. If available, a better method may be to manually insert read-and-write barriers.

Now that we have some actual universal primitives to work with, we can begin building a lock-free algorithm.

A Lock-Free Parameterized Stack

The stack we will implement will be a general linked-list–based stack. Each node will contain a value and a pointer to the next node as shown in Listing 1.12.2.

LISTING 1.12.2

```
template<typename T> struct node {
        T value;
        node<T> * volatile pNext;

        node() : value(), pNext(NULL) {}
        node(T v) : value(v), pNext(NULL) {}
};
```

We will also define the container itself and a couple of primitive operations, `Push()` and `Pop()`, as shown in Listing 1.12.3.

LISTING 1.12.3

```
template<typename T> class LockFreeStack {
        // NOTE: the order of these members is assumed by CAS2.
        node<T> * volatile _pHead;
        volatile uint32_t _cPops;

public:
        void Push(node<T> * pNode);
        node<T> * Pop();
```

```
        LockFreeStack() : _pHead(NULL), _cPops(0) {}
};
```

When we want to push a new node onto the stack, we need to update the new node to point at the node at the head of the stack. Then, we change pHead to point at the new node. The trick is to do this in a way that maintains the integrity of the stack, even if another thread attempts to push or pop another node (see Listing 1.12.4).

LISTING 1.12.4

```
template<typename T> void LockFreeStack<T>::Push(node<T> * pNode)
{
        while(true)
        {
pNode->pNext = _pHead;
if(CAS(&_pHead, pNode->pNext, pNode))
{
        break;
}
        }
}
```

First, we set the node to point at the head of the stack. Next, we atomically check to see if the head has changed; if not, we point _pHead at our new node. If it has changed, then we start over by grabbing the new head.

Popping an item off the stack is simply the reverse. Get the pointer to the second node from the first node. Then point _pHead at the second node. The first node is now extracted and can be returned. Listing 1.12.5 shows that the implementation is straightforward, but there is a twist:

LISTING 1.12.5

```
template<typename T> node<T> * LockFreeStack<T>::Pop()
{
        while(true)
        {
node<T> * pHead = _pHead;
uint32_t cPops = _cPops;
if(NULL == pHead)
{
        return NULL;
}

node<T> * pNext = pHead->pNext;
if(CAS2(&_pHead, pHead, cPops, pNext, cPops + 1))
{
        return pHead;
}
        }
}
```

Here we see that the implementation is the reverse of the `Push()` method, with the exception of `_cPops`. The reason for this additional check has to do with the ABA problem.

The ABA Problem

A problem that comes up in CAS-based algorithms has to do with aliasing. Consider Figure 1.12.1. Suppose a thread is attempting to pop A. It gets a pointer to B, with the intent of making that the new head. If the thread is preempted at this point, right before the CAS, then the stack becomes unstable. A new thread could pop A and B, and then push A. Now if the original thread attempts its CAS, it will see that the head still points to A, so it will try to make B the new head. The problem is that B is not on the stack!

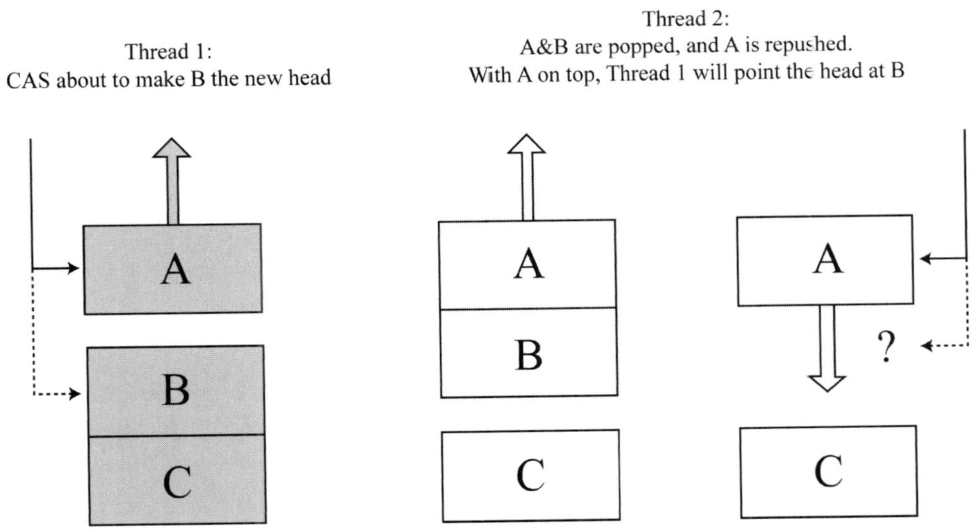

FIGURE 1.12.1 CAS may see that the head is unchanged and consider the stack unchanged. This is the ABA problem.

A solution is to tag the head with a version number. A simple tag counts the number of pops. If the count of pops does not match the expected value, then the head has changed and we must begin anew.

There are other ways to solve the ABA problem. Using LL/SC avoids the ABA problem entirely, as changing the head pointer in a competing thread will invalidate the linked reservation.

Lock-Free Techniques

At this point, the general idea of what is required for a lock-free algorithm may be evident. Work should be done offline in an object outside of the class. When done, CAS the pointer to the shared data. If the CAS fails, start over. The concept, though simple, is complicated in practice.

In the stack example, multiple threads can access the stack, but the content of each node is assumed to be accessed by only a single thread at a time. Allowing concurrent access to the content would require additional lock-free structures for each node, as well as handling the problem of memory management. Reclamation of freed objects is particularly tricky with lock-free structures, but this can be solved by using hazard pointers [Michael04b]. Some of these difficult areas are noted in the code on the CD-ROM.

ON THE CD

Making data access lock-free comes with some restrictions. Not every operation is available as in lock-based algorithms. For example, implementing iteration might be difficult. This would require that each node can be accessed by multiple threads and may require the use of primitives such as DCAS, which are not usually available. As processors begin to include more-powerful universal primitives, additional operations will become available.

What might not be obvious, but should be explained, is that lock-free algorithms cannot be built upon locks. It may be tempting to try, especially when the operations you want are not available.

A Lock-Free Parameterized Queue

A queue is among the most important multithreaded structures and is used in all kinds of situations. We can implement a singly linked lock-free queue with not much more complexity than the previously written stack. Listing 1.12.6 shows the basic container.

LISTING 1.12.6

```
template<typename T> class LockFreeQueue {
        // NOTE: the order of these members is assumed by CAS2.
        node<T> * volatile _pHead;
        volatile uint32_t _cPops;
        node<T> * volatile _pTail;
        volatile uint32_t _cPushes;

public:
        void Add(node<T> * pNode);
        node<T> * Remove();

        LockFreeQueue(node<T> * pDummy) : _cPops(0), _cPushes(0)
        {
_pHead = _pTail = pDummy;
        }
};
```

Here we have a typical definition of a simple queue container. We have pointers to the head and tail; and to avoid the ABA problem, we have version numbers for each end. The significant conceptual change is that we will now add new nodes to the tail of the list instead of the head. We also introduce an initial node into the queue, as suggested in [Michael96].

Adding a node to a queue is more complex than adding a node to a stack. Two operations must be done together. We need to point `pTail` at the new node at the same time that we point the old tail node to the new node. We are now witness to the complexity that comes with lock-free algorithms.

If we had DCAS, the algorithm could follow as in the stack case. Unfortunately, no modern hardware has support for DCAS, so a new method is needed. In this case, we will allow `pTail` to be incorrect, but the threads will cooperate to update `pTail` (in a lock-free way) until it is correct, before we attempt to add the node. This way, we only need to worry about updating the actual tail node atomically (see Listing 1.12.7).

LISTING 1.12.7

```
template<typename T> void LockFreeQueue<T>::Add(node<T> * pNode) {
        pNode->pNext = NULL;

        uint32_t cPushes;
        node<T> * pTail;

        while(true)
        {
cPushes = _cPushes;
pTail = _pTail;

// If the node that the tail points to is the last node
// then update the last node to point at the new node.
if(CAS(&_pTail->pNext, reinterpret_cast<node<T> *>(NULL),
        pNode))
{
        break;
}
else
{
        // Since the tail does not point at the last node,
        // need to keep updating the tail until it does.
        CAS2(&_pTail, pTail, cPushes, _pTail->pNext,
                cPushes + 1);
}
        }

        // If the tail points to what we thought was the last node
        // then update the tail to point to the new node.
        CAS2(&_pTail, pTail, cPushes, pNode, cPushes + 1);
}
```

This approach forces `Remove()` to be aware of the tail pointer in the case that the queue is nearly empty. This is not a problem, as `Remove()` can simply update the tail pointer itself.

In Listing 1.12.8, there are a number of cases to consider. We need to make sure that we atomically retrieve all of the local variables. If the queue appears to be empty, we need to check if `pTail` is simply lagging behind, and retry if so. If the queue is ready to remove a node, it copies the value and attempts to adjust `pHead`.

LISTING 1.12.8

```
template<typename T> node<T> * LockFreeQueue<T>::Remove() {
        T value = T();
        node<T> * pHead;

        while(true)
        {
uint32_t cPops = _cPops;
uint32_t cPushes = _cPushes;
pHead = _pHead;
node<T> * pNext = pHead->pNext;

// Verify that we did not get the pointers in the middle
// of another update.
if(cPops != _cPops)
{
        continue;
}
// Check if the queue is empty.
if(pHead == _pTail)
{
        if(NULL == pNext)
        {
                pHead = NULL; // queue is empty
                break;
        }
        // Special case if the queue has nodes but the tail
        // is just behind. Move the tail off of the head.
        CAS2(&_pTail, pHead, cPushes, pNext, cPushes + 1);
}
else if(NULL != pNext)
{
        value = pNext->value;
        // Move the head pointer, effectively removing the node
        if(CAS2(&_pHead, pHead, cPops, pNext, cPops + 1))
        {
                break;
        }
}

        }
        if(NULL != pHead)
        {
```

```
pHead->value = value;
        }
        return pHead;
}
```

There is an optimization in [Fober05] that removes the need for a node copy at the expense of thread-killing immunity. For game objects that have expensive copy semantics, this may be important.

As you can see, the complexity and availability of certain lock-free algorithms depends greatly on the types of universal primitives that the platform provides.

A Lock-Free Parameterized Freelist

We now have a couple of fundamental algorithms for sharing data. Creating correct lock-free algorithms is very tricky, and often it is more productive to build complex algorithms on top of simple lock-free algorithms.

With these tools, we will build a lock-free freelist. A freelist is used by memory managers to keep track of memory blocks that the game can use. In this context, we will be constructing a fixed-size freelist that has attractive properties such as reduced memory fragmentation [Glinker04].

Our complete implementation in Listing 1.12.9 is a freelist that can create and destroy objects in a lock-free manner. The technique for implementing freelists in a lock-free manner is different from [Glinker04] in that we do not store a list of pointers to the free memory. Instead, we have our lock-free stack manage nodes that include our actual objects. Allocating or deleting objects is as easy as a push and pop!

LISTING 1.12.9

```
template<typename T> class LockFreeFreeList {
        LockFreeStack<T> _Freelist;
        node<T> * _pObjects;
        const uint32_t _cObjects;

public:
        LockFreeFreeList(uint32_t cObjects) : _cObjects(cObjects)
        {
_pObjects = new node<T>[cObjects];
FreeAll();
        }
        ~LockFreeFreeList()
        {
delete[] _pObjects;
        }
        void FreeAll()
        {
for(uint32_t ix = 0; ix < _cObjects; ++ix)
{
        _Freelist.Push(&_pObjects[ix]);
}
```

```
        }
        T * NewInstance()
        {
node<T> * pInstance = _Freelist.Pop();
return new(&pInstance->value) T;
        }
        void FreeInstance(T * pInstance)
        {
pInstance->~T();
_Freelist.Push(reinterpret_cast<node<T> *>(pInstance));
        }
};
```

When a new object is allocated, we pop a node from the stack. Then we use the placement `new()` operator to set up the v-table and call the object constructor. `FreeInstance()` simply calls the destructor and pushes the node back on the stack.

If alignment is a concern, the node pointer could be overlapped on top of the object itself. This should not change the algorithm materially, but you may lose some type-safety.

Other Techniques

Under some circumstances, a lock-free freelist may be useful as an STL allocator. While a thread-safe allocator will not necessarily give you a thread-safe STL container, if the allocator is shared with other game subsystems, there may be some savings.

This freelist is good for allocating fixed-size objects, but there is the question of whether we can do general memory management in a lock-free manner. Object lifetime can be managed with techniques in [Michael04b]. [Michael04a] introduces an incredibly complex but lock-free memory allocator.

Conclusion

The basics of lock-free algorithms are easy to understand but terribly difficult to put into practice. Lock-free algorithms are powerful, but they come at a cost in complexity and restricted operations. Used judiciously, these techniques will allow game creators to squeeze the last bit of performance from their hardware.

When constructing a lock-free algorithm, it might be easiest to build on top of simpler lock-free structures, such as stacks and queues. However, when using low-level lock-free techniques, implement most operations on an outside object and CAS it in. CAS is the foundation of the universal primitives required to build lock-free structures. How these primitives are implemented on different processors may vary.

Lock-free algorithms encompass a new and quickly moving field. Almost monthly, new papers are published that improve techniques and change previous conceptions.

The future is very bright. Investigations are being done to add transactional memory and more powerful universal primitives to processors, which will open the door to more flexible algorithms. The C++ standards committee is also looking at proposals for multithreaded extensions [Alexandrescu04]. Undoubtedly, these proposals will include lock-free semantics.

References

[Alexandrescu04] Alexandrescu, Andrei, Hans Boehm, Kevlin Henney, Doug Lea, and Bill Pugh, "Memory Model for Multithreaded C++." C++ Standard Committee, WG21/N1680=J16/04-0120, September 2004.

[Fober05] Fober, Dominique, Yann Orlarey, and Stéphane Letz, "Optimized Lock-Free FIFO Queue Continued." Laboratoire de Recherche en Informatique Musicale, Technical Report TR-050523, 2005.

[Glinker04] Glinker, Paul, "Fight Memory Fragmentation with Templated Freelists." *Game Programming Gems 4,* Charles River Media, 2004.

[Herlihy91] Herlihy, Maurice, "Wait-Free Synchronization." *ACM Transactions on Programming Languages and Systems,* 13(1): pp. 124–149, January 1991.

[Michael96] Michael, Maged and Michael Scott, "Simple, Fast, and Practical Non-Blocking and Blocking Concurrent Queue Algorithms." 15th ACM Symp. on Principles of Distributed Computing, May 1996.

[Michael04a] Michael, Maged, "Scalable Lock-Free Dynamic Memory Allocation." The 2004 ACM SIGPLAN Conference on Programming Language Design (June 2004): pp. 25–46.

[Michael04b] Michael, Maged, "Hazard Pointers: Safe Memory Reclaimation for Lock-Free Objects." *IEEE Transactions on Parallel and Distributed Systems,* 15(6): pp. 491–504, June 2004.

Resources

[Grove04] Groves, Lindsay, Simon Doherty, Mark Moir, and Victor Luchangco. "A Practical Lock-Free Queue Implementation and its Verification." *FM in NZ,* 2004.

[Pugh90] Pugh, William. "Skip Lists: A Probabilistic Alternative to Balanced Trees." *Communications of the ACM,* 33(6):668–676, June 1990.

[Sutter05] Sutter, Herb. "The Free Lunch Is Over: A Fundamental Turn Toward Concurrency in Software." *Dr. Dobbs Journal.* March 2005.

1.13

Utilizing Multicore Processors with OpenMP

Pete Isensee, Microsoft Corporation

pkisensee@msn.com

CPU clock speeds are not improving at the rates we've become accustomed to over the past decade. The reasons are complex and best left to electrical engineers. The reality is that game players will have machines with multiple processors. Taking advantage of these new architectures requires multithreaded approaches to software development. Game developers now face the complex task of multithreading their game engines.

The high-performance computing industry has been dealing with this problem for some time. This industry often needs to schedule dozens and sometimes hundreds of independent processors that have a shared view of memory. One of their solutions is called OpenMP [OpenMP05]. OpenMP is a portable, industry-standard API and programming protocol for C/C++ that supports parallel programming. Many compilers used by game developers are integrating OpenMP technology. This gem provides a brief overview of OpenMP and examines how games can take advantage of this technology to improve performance.

OpenMP Example: Particle System

Suppose your game has a particle system that recalculates the positions of all particles once per frame:

```
for( int i = 0; i < numParticles; ++i )
    UpdateParticles( particle[i] );
```

On a multiprocessor architecture, it would be nice to split up the loop so that each portion is done on a separate hardware thread. For instance, if there are two threads, you'd like to accomplish something like the following:

```
// run half the loop on thread 0:
for( int i = 0; i < numParticles/2; ++i )
    UpdateParticles( particle[i] );
```

```
// run the other half on thread 1:
for( int i = numParticles/2; i < numParticles; ++i )
    UpdateParticles ( particle[i] );
```

OpenMP allows you to accomplish exactly that, using simple compiler `#pragmas`:

```
#pragma omp parallel for
for( int i = 0; i < numParticles; ++i )
    UpdateParticles ( particle[i] );
```

An OpenMP-enabled compiler generates code that automatically splits this `for` loop into multiple parallel sections, each of which executes independently. The number of parallel sections used depends on the hardware, the OpenMP runtime, and configuration settings that the programmer has established.

Benefits

There are some compelling features to note about this example. First, the technique is totally platform-independent. If the compiler is not OpenMP-enabled, it will ignore the `#pragma`. The code will still compile and work. If the compiler is OpenMP-enabled, the compiler will automatically inject the proper parallelizing constructs for the target architecture. If the target platform doesn't have multiple processors or hardware threads, the overhead of OpenMP likely will be very small.

Second, unlike typical multithreaded code, this code is readable. To the casual observer, it's very clear exactly what this loop is supposed to accomplish. Finally, only a single line of code was required to parallelize this task. Even in the best case with other methods, it would require dozens of lines of platform-specific code to make this loop multithreaded.

Clearly, OpenMP has some big benefits. It can even be used for last-minute optimizations because it's easy to add to existing code.

Performance

What kind of performance can you expect out of OpenMP? The answer depends on the compiler, the platform, and the code being parallelized. However, it's useful to examine a couple of cases to get an idea of potential gains. Consider the previous example. Suppose that `numParticles` is 100,000 and `GetNewParticlePos` takes a small fixed amount of time (see example code on the CD-ROM).

ON THE CD

Table 1.13.1 shows the performance metrics on two different systems using the Visual Studio 2005 compiler. The first system is a desktop PC with dual Xeon processors, each with two hyperthreads. The second system is an Xbox 360, which has three CPUs, each with two hardware threads.

TABLE 1.13.1 Particle System Gain with OpenMP

Hardware	OpenMP Threads	OpenMP Perf Gain	Windows Threads Perf Gain
Dual-core 2.3-GHz Pentium	4	2.9X	2.9X
Triple-core 3.2-GHz Xbox 360	6	4.6X	4.5X

The second column shows the number of hardware threads used by the OpenMP thread team. The third column shows the gain from parallelizing this loop in OpenMP. The gain was very significant: 3X–5X, depending on the target platform. Not bad for a one-line code change! The last column shows the performance when using standard threading techniques. Writing this particular example using Windows thread calls and synchronization primitives required over 60 lines of code (available on the CD-ROM), not to mention considerable debugging and tuning efforts.

ON THE CD

In the end, the performance gain was virtually the same as using OpenMP directly. In fact, on Xbox 360, the overhead of calling Windows synchronization primitives was higher than using OpenMP, because the OpenMP runtime is tuned to call kernel exports directly. What's clear from this simple experiment is that using OpenMP can provide major benefits with a very small investment.

Example: Collision Detection

Here's a more complex example showing how OpenMP could be used in a typical collision-detection loop. Because each iteration through the loop takes a variable amount of time depending on whether the objects actually intersect, dynamic scheduling is used to tell the compiler to schedule the thread team at runtime rather than simply dividing up the iterations evenly between the threads.

```
bool anyCollisions = false;

#pragma omp parallel for schedule( dynamic )
for( int i = 0; i < numObjects; ++i )
{
    for( int j = 0; j < i; ++j )
    {
        if( SpheresIntersect( obj[i], obj[j] ) &&
            ObjectsIntersect( obj[i], obj[j] ) )
        {
            anyCollisions = true;
        }
    }
}
```

It's more difficult to assess the performance of this example, because it depends on so many variables, including the number of objects intersecting and the time to compute each intersection. For the purposes of this example, we assume `numObjects` is 1,000; `SpheresIntersect` takes a small, fixed amount of time; and `ObjectsIntersect` takes 100 times as long as `SpheresIntersect`. We also assume a 10% sphere intersection rate and a 1% object intersection rate. Under these circumstances, Table 1.13.2 shows the resulting performance metrics.

TABLE 1.13.2 Collision Detection Gain with OpenMP

Hardware	OMP Threads	OpenMP Perf Gain
Dual-core 2.3-GHz Pentium	4	3.3X
Triple-core 3.2-GHz Xbox 360	6	5.4X

OpenMP typically adds very little runtime overhead in terms of either size or speed. The Visual Studio OpenMP DLL is only 60K. In this particular example, the performance approached the theoretical maximum. For instance, on Xbox 360, which has six hardware threads, the parallelized version ran 5.4 times faster than the serial version.

Thread Teams

OpenMP is based on a very simple concept: thread teams. Whenever the program enters a parallel section, the thread team goes to work. When the threads have finished their work, the team sits on the bench, waiting for the next parallel section. Because thread creation is somewhat expensive, most OpenMP implementations (including Visual Studio) create the thread team at first usage and then reuse that team throughout the program.

OpenMP allows nested parallel sections. Individual threads can spawn additional thread teams. The number of threads per team is also configurable programmatically. The "OpenMP Threads" heading in the performance tables represents the maximum number of threads in the team on the given platform. This number is programmatically available using the `omp_get_max_threads()` API.

Function Parallelism

Typically, OpenMP is used for data parallelism—that is, parallelizing loops as in the previous example. However, OpenMP can also be used for function-level parallelism. Consider the following implementation of QuickSort:

```
template< typename T >
void qsort( T* arr, int lo, int hi )
{
    if( hi <= lo )
        return;
```

```
        int n = partition( arr, lo, hi );
        qsort( arr, lo, n-1 );
        qsort( arr, n+1, hi );
    }
```

Each of the recursive calls to qsort is completely independent of each other, because they operate on separate sections of the array. It's a perfect opportunity to parallelize those calls. One way is to split the independent recursive calls into their own OpenMP parallel sections:

```
#pragma omp parallel sections
{
    #pragma omp section
    qsort( arr, lo, n-1 );
    #pragma omp section
    qsort( arr, n+1, hi );
}
```

Each recursive call to qsort has been placed in its own OpenMP section. To execute the calls in parallel, they're wrapped in braces so that OpenMP knows what portion to run in parallel. On most platforms, however, the overhead of the recursive parallel sections is likely to outweigh the benefits. A better solution is to calculate a handful of partitions, then do a high-level parallelization on the resulting partitions. Given a decent partition function, each partition will be roughly the same size, and the resulting performance gains can be worth the effort.

```
template< typename T >
void qsortParallel( T* arr, int lo, int hi )
{
    if( hi <= lo )
        return;
    int n = partition( arr, lo, hi ); // 1st-level partition
    int m = partition( arr, lo, n-1 ); // 2nd-level partitions
    int q = partition( arr, n+1, hi );

    #pragma omp parallel sections
    {

        #pragma omp section
        qsort( arr, lo, m-1 ); // serial qsort

        #pragma omp section
        qsort( arr, m+1, n-1 );

        #pragma omp section
        qsort( arr, n+1, q-1 );

        #pragma omp section
        qsort( arr, q+1, hi );
    }
}
```

The performance measurements for this function, given an array of random integers of size 1,000,000, is shown in Table 1.13.3.

TABLE 1.13.3 qsort Gain Using OpenMP

Hardware	OMP Threads	OpenMP Perf Gain
Dual-core 2.3-GHz Pentium	4	1.5X
Triple-core 3.2-GHz Xbox 360	6	1.4X

Gotchas

Like any technology, OpenMP has its flaws. First, OpenMP is not designed to solve all multithreading issues. Complex multithreading scenarios and synchronization are best done using native thread techniques. If you're writing a new engine, using OpenMP is probably not the way to go.

Second, OpenMP-enabled compilers typically don't check to ensure that your code will parallelize correctly. For instance, suppose we naively try to parallelize the partitioning from the `qsort` example:

```
// Evil OpenMP code; don't do this
int n, m, q;

#pragma omp parallel sections
{

    #pragma omp section
    n = partition( arr, lo, hi );

    #pragma omp section
    m = partition( arr, lo, n-1 ); // oh no! n probably undefined

    #pragma omp section
    q = partition( arr, n+1, hi ); // oh no! n probably undefined
}
```

Most compilers will compile this code without errors. The problem is that the second and third sections rely on the top section first completing with a valid value for `n`. OpenMP, however, makes no guarantee about the order in which parallel sections are executed. The results of this snippet are undefined, and it's likely the application will crash. *It's up to the programmer to ensure that OpenMP is only applied to constructs that are not order-dependent.* This applies not only to parallel sections, but also to loops that have order dependencies. Verify that the results given when your code is executed in a parallel environment match the results in a single-threaded environment.

Another gotcha is debugging. When the compiler encounters an OpenMP block, it generates custom code that calls into the OpenMP runtime. Unfortunately, the internals of OpenMP are a black box. This can make debugging devilishly difficult, depending on your compiler and debugger.

Finally, using OpenMP does not guarantee that you will improve performance on multiprocessor systems. Depending on your usage, the runtime overhead of OpenMP can dwarf any benefits. For instance, when `numParticles` in the first example was on the order of 100, performance gains were negligible. As with any optimization technique, profile to verify improvements.

Conclusion

OpenMP is a quick and useful technique for utilizing multicore and hyperthreaded processors. It's easy enough to be used for last-minute optimizations, yet flexible enough to use in cross-platform code. It's not without flaws; but used properly, OpenMP can be an excellent tool in your multithreading arsenal.

Potential applications of OpenMP in games include particle systems, skinning, collision detection, simulations, pathfinding, vertex transforms, signal processing, procedural synthesis, and fractals.

Even though OpenMP has been around for a while, it's a new technology for most game programmers. The best resource is the OpenMP specification, which is available at http://www.openmp.org. The specification is concise and surprisingly readable. The next best resource is typically your compiler documentation.

Reference

[OpenMP05] OpenMP C/C++ specification. Available online at http://www.Openmp.org.

Resources

[Chandra00] Chandra, Rohit, *Parallel Programming in OpenMP,* Morgan Kaufmann, 2000.

[Gaitlin05] Gaitlin, Kang Su and Pete Isensee, "Writing Multithreaded Applications with OpenMP in Visual Studio 2005," *MSDN Magazine* (Oct 2005): pp. 78–91.

[Sutter04] Sutter, Herb, "The Free Lunch Is Over: A Fundamental Turn Toward Concurrency in Software," *Dr. Dobb's Journal,* March 2005: pp. 16–22, available online at http://www.gotw.ca/publications/concurrency-ddj.htm.

SECTION

2

MATH AND PHYSICS

2.1

More Approximations to Trigonometric Functions

Robin Green, Google Inc.

rgreen@google.com

Measuring Error

Before we look at implementing functions, we need a standard set of tools for measuring how good our implementation is. The obvious way to measure error is to subtract our approximation from a high-accuracy version of the same function (usually implemented as a slow and cumbersome, infinite series calculation). This is called the *absolute error* metric:

$$error_{abs} = \left| f_{actual} - f_{approx} \right| \tag{2.1.1}$$

This is a good measure of accuracy, but it tells us nothing about the *importance* of any error. An error of 3 is acceptable if the function should return 38,000. But an error of 3 would be catastrophic if the function should return 0.008. We will also need to graph the *relative error*:

$$error_{rel} = 1 - \frac{f_{approx}}{f_{actual}}, \quad \text{when } f_{actual} \neq 0 \tag{2.1.2}$$

When reading relative error graphs, an error of zero means there is no error; the approximation is exact. With functions like `sin()` and `cos()`, where the range is [–1.0, 1.0], the relative error is not that interesting. But functions like `tan()` have a wider range, and relative error will be an important metric of success.

Sine and Cosine

For most of the examples, implementations of the sine and cosine functions shall be considered, but many of the polynomial techniques, with a little tweaking, are applicable to other functions, such as exponent, logarithm, and arctangent.

Resonant Filter

When someone asks you what is the fastest way to calculate the sine and cosine of an angle, tell them you can do it in two instructions. The method, called a *resonant filter*, relies on having previous results of an angle calculation and assumes that you are taking regular steps through the series (see Figure 2.1.1).

```
int   N = 64;
float PI = 3.14159265;
float a = 2.0f*sin(PI*N);
float c = 1.0f;
float s = 0.0f;

for(i=0; i<N; ++i) {
    output_sine   = s;
    output_cosine = c;
    c = c - s*a;
    s = s + c*a;
    ...
}
```

Note how the value of `c`, used to calculate `s`, is the newly updated version from the previous line. This formula is also readily converted into a fixed-point version, where the multiplication by a can be modeled as a shift (e.g., a multiply by `1/8` converts to a shift right by three places).

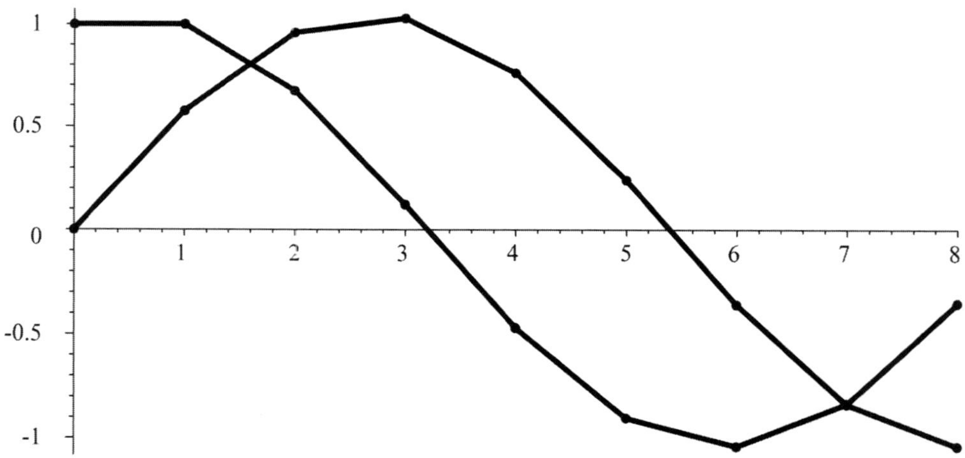

FIGURE 2.1.1 Resonant filter sine and cosine—eight iterations over $3\pi/2$.

If you plan to use this technique to fill look-up tables for later use, you must pay close attention to a (the step size) and to the initial values of `c` and `s`. The technique relies on the previous value feeding back into the system, so the initial values of `s` and `c` affect the final amplitude of the waves (e.g., starting with `s = 0.5` and `c = 0.5` gives a peak value of 0.7). As fast as this technique is for generating sine wave-like signals, you cannot rely on samples at fractions of a cycle returning the accurate values. For example, say we were looking to take seven steps around a quarter of a circle:

```
N = 7;
a = 0.5*sin(PI*N);
...
```

The values for iterations seven and eight (counting from zero) are listed in Table 2.1.1.

TABLE 2.1.1 Testing the Accuracy of the Resonant Filter

Iteration	Sine	Cosine
7	1.004717676	0.158172209
8	0.9917460469	−0.0597931103
...	...	...
27	1.000000000	−0.000000002

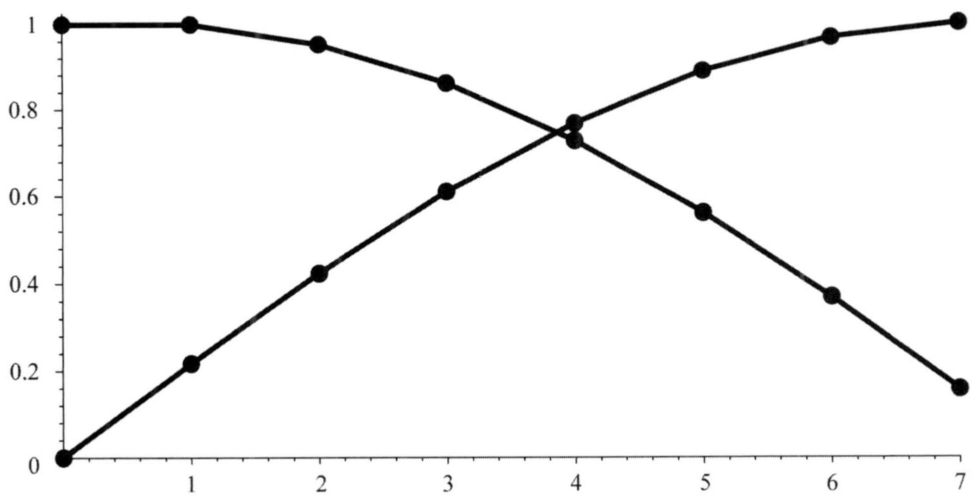

FIGURE 2.1.2 Resonant filter quarter-circle test, seven iterations over $\pi/2$.

The end points of this function miss the correct values of 1.0 and 0.0 by quite large amounts (see Table 2.1.1 and Figure 2.1.2). If, however, we extend the table to generate the whole cycle using 27 samples, we find that the final values for `s` and `c` are correct to nine decimal places. Adding more iterations will reduce this error, but won't make it disappear. Clearly, this approximation is useful for generating long sequences of sine-like waves, especially over entire cycles; but it is not well suited to accurate, small-angle work.

Goertzels Algorithm

A more accurate approach to the same problem is *Goertzels algorithm*, which uses and updates the two previous values (i.e., it's a *second-order* filter). With it, we can calculate a series of sine and cosine values in the series $x_n = \sin(a + n^*b)$ for integer values of n:

```
const float cb = 2 * cos(b);
float s2 = sin(a + b);
float s1 = sin(a + 2*b);
float c2 = cos(a + b);
float c1 = cos(a + 2*b);
float s,c;

for(i=0; i<N; ++i) {
    s = cb * s1 – s2;
    c = cb * c1 – c2;
    s2 = s1;
    c2 = c1;
    s1 = s;
    c1 = c;
    output_sine   = s;
    output_cosine = c;
    ...
}
```

The technique is only slightly more expensive to run than the previous method, but it has greater setup costs. However, if the setup can be done at compile time, the algorithm is still very efficient (see Figure 2.1.3).

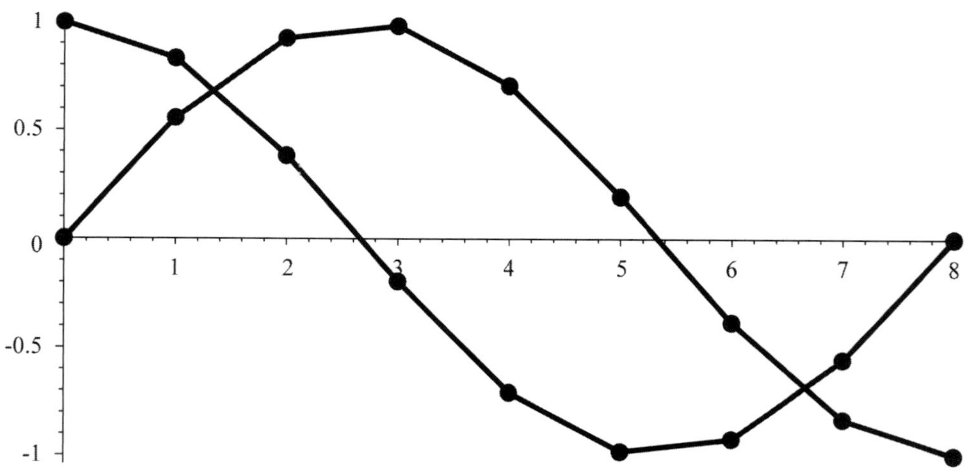

FIGURE 2.1.3 Goertzels algorithm: sine and cosine, eight iterations over $3\pi/2$.

There are some pitfalls associated with this algorithm, as it is a second-order filter. Because the values of s and c are constructed from the two previous samples, the algorithm actually outputs a result three iterations later than you might expect. To compensate for this, we need to initialize the sequence carefully, subtracting three steps from the initial value of a:

```
// step = N steps over 2*PI radians
float b = 2.0f*PI/N;
// minus three steps from origin
float a = 0.0f - 3.0f * b;
...
```

Adding in these alterations and putting Goertzels to the quarter-circle test, we find that it passes the test well, producing more accurate results than the resonant filter for fractions of complete cycles (see Figure 2.1.4).

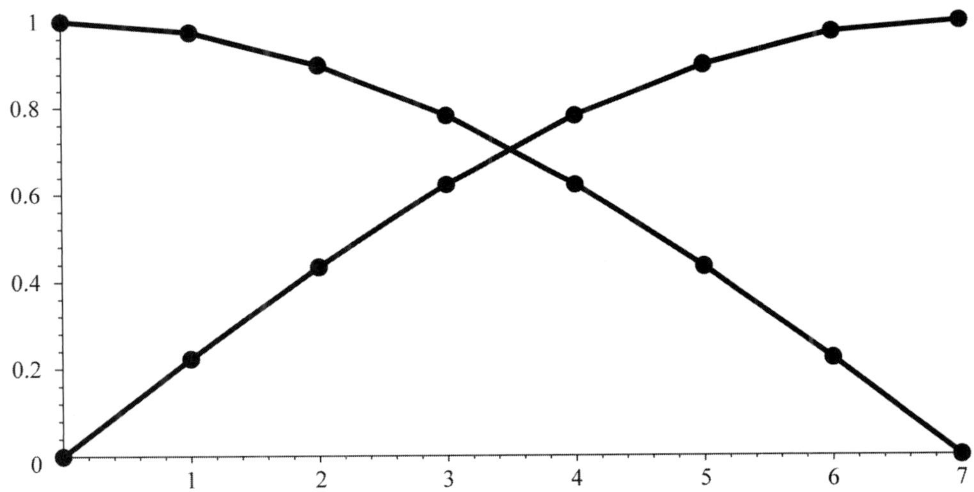

FIGURE 2.1.4 Goertzels quarter-circle test, seven iterations over $\pi/2$.

Table-Based Solutions

As clock speeds rise and memory-access latencies become longer and longer, sine and cosine tables fall out of favor and are no longer the fastest method in all situations. New architectures that provide vector units with closely coupled, fast RAM can still give single-cycle access time for small tables, so the technique must not be discounted and will be with us for some time to come.

The idea is to precalculate a table of samples from a function at regular intervals and use the input value to the function to hash into the table, look up the two closest values, and linearly interpolate between them (see Figure 2.1.5). In effect, we are trading off storage space against speed.

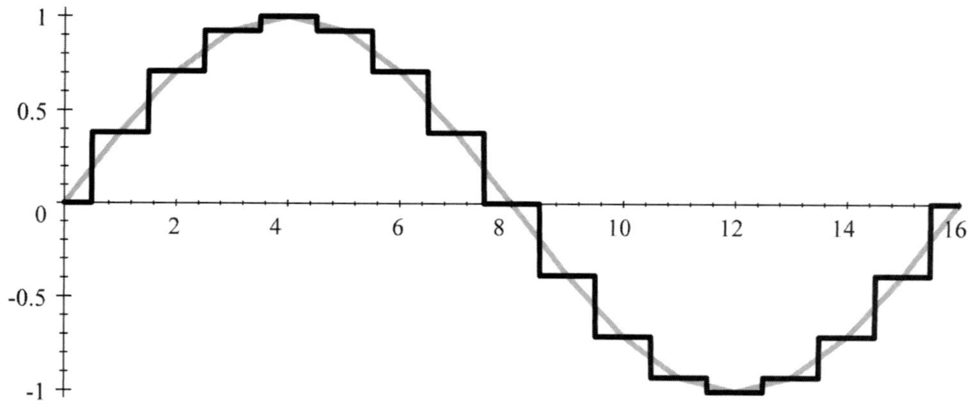

FIGURE 2.1.5 Table-based sine (16 samples) with and without linear interpolation.

In order to speed linear interpolation (*lerp*) between samples, we can precalculate the difference between adjacent samples, saving a subtract per look-up, especially on SIMD machines where a look-up usually loads a four-vector of floats at a time.

$$\begin{aligned}\sin(x) &\approx \text{table}[i] + \Delta * (\text{table}[i+1] - \text{table}[i]) \\ &\approx \text{table}[i] + \Delta * \text{gradient}[i]\end{aligned} \tag{2.1.3}$$

Precalculating these differences turns the lerp operation into a single multiply-add.

Using a table poses the question: How many samples do we need to get N digits of accuracy? The table-based sine with 16 samples is shown in Figure 2.1.5, and the absolute error graph is shown in Figure 2.1.6.

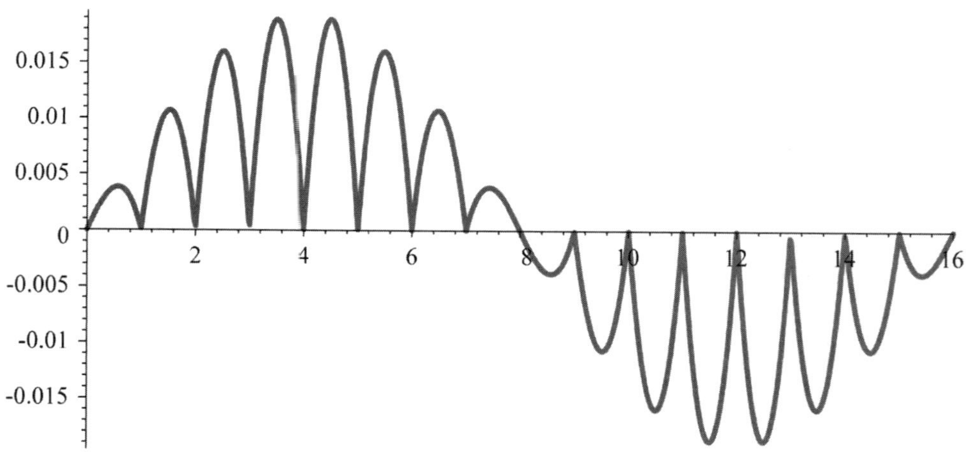

FIGURE 2.1.6 Absolute error of 16 sample, linearly interpolated sine table.

The largest error (or *maximal error*) occurs where the curvature of the function is highest—in fact, when two samples straddle the top of the curve. The size of the maximal error where the step size is $\Delta x = x_{n+1} - x_n$ can be shown to be:

$$E = 1 - \cos\left(\frac{\Delta x}{2}\right) \tag{2.1.4}$$

So, for a table of 16 samples covering one whole cycle, the maximum relative error will be $1 - \cos(\pi/16) = 0.0192147$, giving us just under two decimal places of accuracy in the worst case. Turning the problem around, given a known accuracy, how many entries will we need in the table? We just reverse the inequality. For example, to approximate $\sin(x)$ to 1% error we only need 23 entries:

$$\begin{aligned} E &= 1\% \\ 1 - \cos\left(\frac{\pi}{N}\right) &< 1\% \\ \cos\left(\frac{\pi}{N}\right) &> 0.99 \\ N &> \frac{\pi}{\arccos(0.99)} \\ &\approx 22.19 \end{aligned} \tag{2.1.5}$$

Using a process called *range reduction*, we can reconstruct the whole cycle from just 45° of samples, meaning that we only need a table of 23/8 = 3 entries. Equation 2.1.4 will give you the hard upper bound on the error, an error that almost never occurs. For a slightly looser lower bound, you can use a small-angle approximation to the `arccos()`, as π/N should hopefully be a very small angle, giving you a bound of

$$N = \frac{\pi}{\sqrt{2E}} \tag{2.1.6}$$

Applying Equation 2.1.6 to various error factors gives us a feel for situations where tables would be well used and where more accurate methods must be used. See Table 2.1.2 for some example values.

TABLE 2.1.2 Size of Table Needed to Approximate Sin(X) to a Given Level of Accuracy

	E	360° Range	45° Range
1% accurate	0.01	23	3
0.1% accurate	0.001	71	9
0.01% accurate	0.0001	223	28
1.0°	0.01745	17	3
0.1°	0.001745	54	7
8-bit int.	2^{-7}	26	4
16-bit int.	2^{-15}	403	51
24-bit float	10^{-5}	703	88
32-bit float	10^{-7}	7025	880
64-bit float	10^{-17}	~infinite	8.7e+8

Range Reduction and Reconstruction

The sine and cosine functions have an infinite domain. Every input value has a corresponding output value in the range [0, 1] and the pattern repeats every 2π units. To properly implement the sine function, we need to take any input angle and find out where inside the [0, 2π] range it maps to. This process, for sine and cosine at least, is called *additive range reduction*, and is shown in Figure 2.1.7.

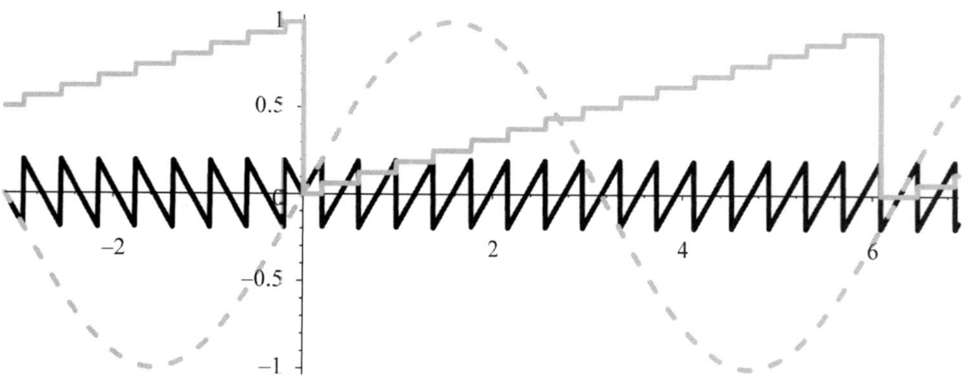

FIGURE 2.1.7 Additive range reduction where $C=2\pi/16$.

To do this, we need to find out how many times we need to subtract 2π from the current value to reduce it to the target range. We divide the input value by 2π, truncate the result toward zero (i.e., convert it to an integer), and subtract that many copies of 2π from it.

```
const float C = 2*PI;
const float invC = 1/C;
```

```
int k = (int)(x*invC);
y = x - (float)k * C;
...
```

In this example, the value of `k` only tells us how many full cycles we need to subtract; but if we were to range-reduce using fractions of a cycle, then the lower digits of `k` would tell us which quadrant the remainder belongs to. Why is this useful? Because of these well-known relationships:

$$\sin(A+B)=\sin(A)\cos(B)+\cos(A)\sin(B)$$
$$\cos(A+B)=\cos(A)\cos(B)+\sin(A)\sin(B) \qquad (2.1.7)$$

If we range-reduce to $y \in [0..\pi/2]$, that means we have four segments to our cycle, and `k mod 4` will tell us which segment to use. If we multiply Equation 2.1.7 through, we find that sin(*B*) and cos(*B*) collapse into the constants zero and one, and we get four special cases:

$$\sin\left(y+0*\frac{\pi}{2}\right)=\sin(y)$$
$$\sin\left(y+1*\frac{\pi}{2}\right)=\cos(y)$$
$$\sin\left(y+2*\frac{\pi}{2}\right)=-\cos(y)$$
$$\sin\left(y+3*\frac{\pi}{2}\right)=-\sin(y) \qquad (2.1.8)$$

These lead to code like the following:

```
float table_sin(float x) {
    const float CONVERT = (2.0f * TABLE_SIZE) / PI;
    const float PI_OVER_TWO = PI/2.0f;
    const float TWO_OVER_PI = 2.0f/PI;

    int k = int(x * TWO_OVER_PI);
    float y = x – float(k)*PI_OVER_TWO;
    float index = y * CONVERT;
    switch(k&3) {
        case 0:  return sin_table(index);
        case 1:  return sin_table(TABLE_SIZE-index);
        case 2:  return -sin_table(TABLE_SIZE-index);
        default: return -sin_table(index);
    }
    return(0);
}
```

Why stop at just four quadrants? To add more quadrants, we need to *reconstruct* the final result by evaluating Equation 2.1.7 more carefully, using either in-lined constants or a table of values:

```
...
s := sin_table(y);
c := cos_table(y);
switch(k&15) {
    case 0:   return s;
    case 1:   return s * 0.923880f + c * 0.382685f;
    case 2:   return s * 0.707105f + c * 0.707105f;
    case 3:   return s * 0.382685f + c * 0.923880f;
    case 4:   return c;
    case 5:   return s * -0.382685f + c * 0.923880f;
    ...
}
```

Note how we have had to approximate both the sine *and* cosine in order to produce just the sine as a result. For very little extra effort, we can easily reconstruct the cosine at the same time, and the function that returns them both for an input angle, traditionally present in FORTRAN mathematical libraries, is usually `sincos()`.

You will find that most libraries use the *range reduction*, *approximation*, and *reconstruction* phases in the design of their mathematical functions, and that this programming pattern turns up over and over again. In the next section, we will generate an optimized polynomial that replaces the table look-up and lerp.

Polynomial Approximations

A person's first introduction to approximating functions usually comes from learning about the *Taylor series* in high school. Using a series of differentials, we can show that the transcendental functions break down into an infinite series of expressions. For example:

$$\sin(x) = x - \frac{x^3}{3!} + \frac{x^5}{5!} - \frac{x^7}{7!} + \frac{x^9}{9!} - \cdots \tag{2.1.9}$$

If we had an infinite amount of time and infinite storage, then this would be the last word on the subject. As we have a very finite amount of time and even less storage, let's start by truncating the series at the ninth power and multiply through to five significant digits:

$$\begin{aligned}\sin(x) &\approx x - \frac{1}{6}x^3 + \frac{1}{120}x^5 - \frac{1}{5040}x^7 + \frac{1}{362880}x^9 \\ &= x - 0.16667x^3 + 0.0083333x^5 - 0.00019841x^7 + 0.0000027557x^9\end{aligned} \tag{2.1.10}$$

This is one of the classic infinite series—it exhibits alternating signs and drastically reducing factors (1/x! plummets toward zero), two signals that this series is going to converge toward the correct value fairly fast. The problems lie in the approximation error. If you graph the absolute error of this function (shown in Figure 2.1.8), you find that it is very accurate for small angles around the origin of the Taylor expansion, but the error increases almost exponentially away from $x = 0$. Truncating the series later will decrease the error; however, it is more costly, opens you up to more danger of numerical error, and each additional term is another load/multiply-accumulate in your program. We need good accuracy across the *whole* range, and we need it using as few terms as possible.

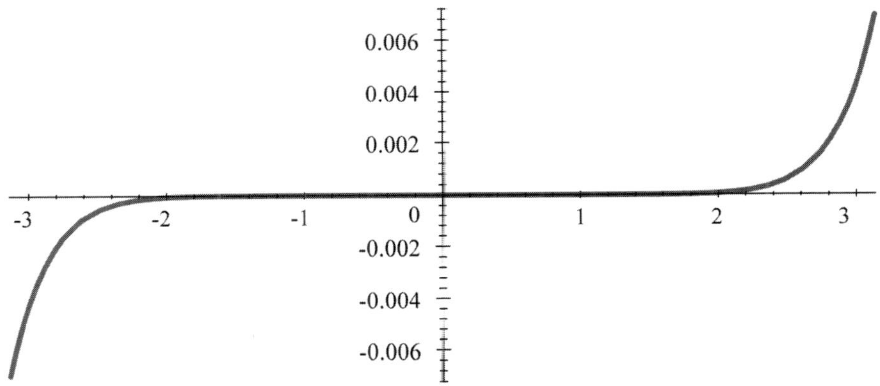

FIGURE 2.1.8 Absolute error of Taylor series over $[-\pi, \pi]$.

How about reducing the input range? If you reduce the range of the sine function that we're trying to approximate, then, yes, we reduce the error because there's less to go wrong! Along with reducing the range, we could also Taylor-expand around the center of the range we want to approximate. This will halve the overall error, but at the cost of doubling the number of constants we need—now we need to calculate every power from zero to nine, not just every second one. We can do better than to use a Taylor series as a technique for generating fast polynomial approximations.

Minimax Polynomials

The Taylor expansion has a poor *maximal error*. If only we could find a way to take some of this error and spread it out across the whole range. In fact, thanks to a theory by Chebychev, it can be shown that every approximation has one special polynomial that has an equal amount of error everywhere, where we have minimized the maximal error, and it's called the *minimax polynomial*. Its characteristics are as follows:

- For a power N approximation, the error curve will change sign $N + 1$ times.
- The error curve will approach the maximal error $N + 2$ times.

The method used to find these polynomial approximations is called the *Remez Exchange Algorithm,* and it works by generating a set of linear equations. For example:

$$\sin(x) - a + bx_n + cx_n^2 = 0, \text{ for a set of values } x_n \in [a..b] \qquad (2.1.11)$$

These are solved to find the required coefficients *a, b,* and *c*; the maximal error is found and fed back into x_n. This highly technical optimization problem is sensitive to floating-point accuracy and is difficult to program, so we call on the professionals to do it for us. Numerical math packages, like Mathematica and Maple, have the necessary environments with the huge number representations and numerical tools needed to give accurate answers.

The arguments needed to calculate a minimax polynomial are as follows:

- The function to be approximated
- The range over which the approximation is to be done
- The required order of our approximation
- A weighting function to bias the approximation into minimizing absolute (weight = 1.0) or the relative error

Let's find a seventh-order polynomial approximation to sin(*x*) over the range [0, π/4], optimized to minimize relative error. We start by looking at the Taylor expansion of sin(*x*), about *x* = 0, just to get a feel for what the polynomial should look like. The result shows us that the series has a leading coefficient of 1.0 and uses only the odd powers:

$$\sin(x) \approx x - 0.166666667x^3 + 0.00833333333x^5 - 0.000198412698x^7 \qquad (2.1.12)$$

A raw call to minimax will, by default, use all coefficients of all available powers to minimize the error, leading to some very small, odd-looking coefficients and many more terms than necessary. We will transform the problem into one of finding the polynomial $P(x) = a + bx + cx^2 + \ldots$ in the expression:

$$\sin(x) \approx x + x^3 P(x^2) \qquad (2.1.13)$$

First, we form the minimax inequality, expressing our desire to minimize the *relative error* of our polynomial *P*:

$$\left| \frac{\sin(x) - x - x^3 P(x^2)}{\sin(x)} \right| \leq error \qquad (2.1.14)$$

Divide through by x^3:

$$\left| \frac{\frac{\sin(x)}{x^3} - \frac{1}{x^2} - P\left(x^2\right)}{\frac{\sin(x)}{x^3}} \right| \le error \qquad (2.1.15)$$

We want the result in terms of every second power, so we substitute $y = x^2$:

$$\left| \frac{\frac{\sin\left(\sqrt{y}\right)}{y^{3/2}} - \frac{1}{y} - P\left(y\right)}{\frac{\sin\left(\sqrt{y}\right)}{y^{3/2}}} \right| \le error \qquad (2.1.16)$$

So, we have reduced our problem to finding a minimax polynomial approximation to

$$P\left(y\right) = \frac{\sin\left(\sqrt{y}\right)}{y^{3/2}} - \frac{1}{y} \qquad (2.1.17)$$

with the weight function

$$W\left(y\right) = \frac{y^{3/2}}{\sin\left(\sqrt{y}\right)} \qquad (2.1.18)$$

In order to evaluate the function correctly in the arbitrary, precision environment of Mathematica or Maple, it is (ironically) necessary to expand the first expression into a Taylor series of sufficient order to exceed our desired accuracy in order to prevent the specially written, arbitrary accuracy sine function from being evaluated:

$$P\left(y\right) = -\frac{1}{6} + \frac{y}{120} - \frac{y^2}{5040} + \frac{y^3}{362880} - \frac{y^4}{39916800} + \frac{y^5}{6227020800} - \cdots \qquad (2.1.19)$$

Our last task is to transform the range we wish to try and approximate. As we have substituted $y = x^2$, so our range $[0, \pi/4]$ is transformed to $[0, \pi^2/16]$. Running these through the minimax function, looking for a second-order result gives us:

$$P\left(y\right) = -0.166666546 + 0.00833216076y - 0.000195152832y^2 \qquad (2.1.20)$$

Resubstituting this result back into Equation 2.1.12 gives us the final result:

$$\sin\left(x\right) \approx x - 0.166666546x^3 + 0.00833216076x^5 - 0.000195152832x^7 \qquad (2.1.21)$$

In order to reconstruct these coefficients as single precision floats, we need only record the first nine significant digits (see proof below), giving us Figure 2.1.9, the absolute and relative error curves over our range with a maximum absolute error of 2.59e-9 at $x = 0.785$.

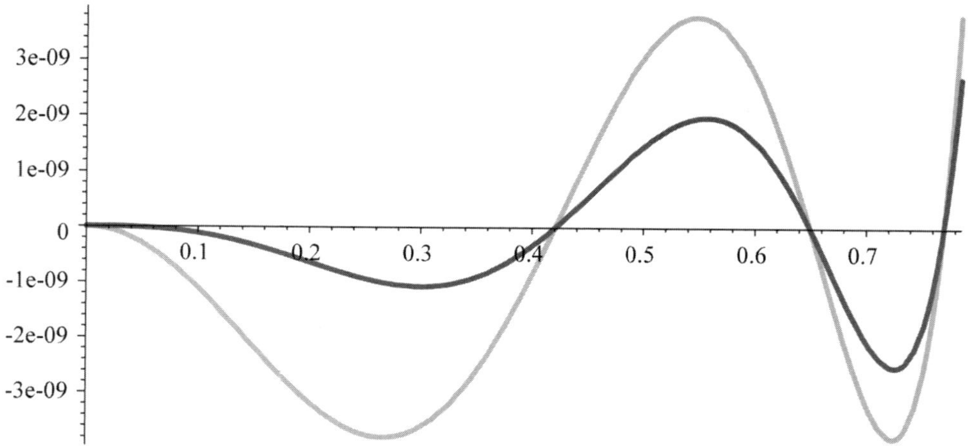

FIGURE 2.1.9 Absolute and relative error of approximation over $[0, \pi/4]$.

Here is a loose proof of this: In single precision, numbers in the range $[10^3, 2^{10}]$ = [1000, 1024] have 10 bits to the right of the decimal and 14 bits to the right. There are therefore $(2^{10} - 10^3)2^{14} = 393{,}216$ representable values. If we use a decimal notation with eight digits, we can represent $(2^{10} - 10^3)10^8 = 240{,}000$ values. We therefore need nine decimal digits to be able to reconstruct the correct binary number. Similar constructions along the number line show a need for between six and nine digits. For more, see [Goldberg91].

Optimizing for Floating-Point

The same technique we used to remove a coefficient can be used to force values to machine-representable values. Remember that values like 1/10 are not precisely representable using a finite number of binary digits. We can adapt the technique above to force coefficients to be our choice of machine-representable floats. Remembering that all floating-point values are rational numbers, we can take the second coefficient and force it to fit in a single precision floating-point number:

$$k = -\frac{2796201}{2^{24}} = -0.16666656732559204101562500000 \qquad (2.1.22)$$

Now that we have our constant value, let's optimize our polynomial to incorporate it. Start by defining the form of polynomial we want to end up with:

$$\sin(x) = x + kx^3 + x^5 P(x^2) \qquad (2.1.23)$$

Now we form the minimax inequality,

$$\left|\frac{\sin(x)-x-kx^3-x^5P(x^2)}{\sin(x)}\right| \le error \tag{2.1.24}$$

which, after dividing by x^5, substituting $y = x^2$, and solving for $P(y)$, shows us that we have to calculate the minimax of

$$P(y)=\frac{\sin(\sqrt{y})}{y^{5/2}}-\frac{1}{y^2}+\frac{k}{y} \tag{2.1.25}$$

with weight function

$$W(y)=\frac{y^{5/2}}{\sin(\sqrt{y})} \tag{2.1.26}$$

Solving this and resubstituting gives us a seventh-degree optimized polynomial over the range [0, π/4] with a maximal error of 3.39e-8 at $x = 0.557$, but with better single precision floating-point accuracy:

$$\sin(x)\approx x-\frac{2796201}{2^{24}}x^3+0.00833220803x^5-0.000195168955x^7 \tag{2.1.27}$$

The absolute and relative error of float-optimized approximation over [0, π/4] are shown in Figure 2.1.10.

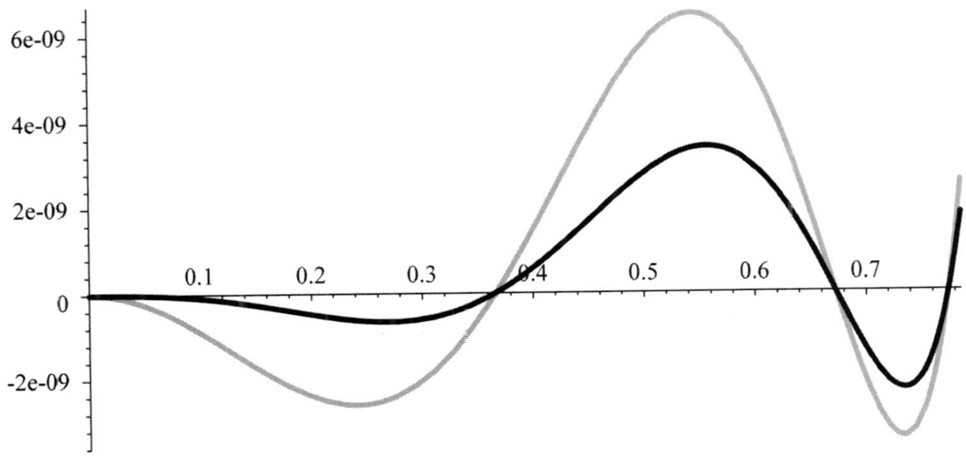

FIGURE 2.1.10 Absolute and relative error of float-optimized approximation over [0, π/4].

A Note on Convergence

How do we choose the degree of polynomial that we need to approximate a function to a given accuracy? We can easily calculate how many bits of accuracy an approximation provides. First, we calculate the maximum error within the range (this will be a small value, typically something like 5e-4) and take the base-2 logarithm of this value using $\ln(error)/\ln(2)$, giving us a negative number that tells us how many bits we will need after the decimal point to be able to represent this value. Generating a table of this value for several important functions shows us some interesting results (see Table 2.1.3).

TABLE 2.1.3 Number of Significant Bits of Accuracy vs. Degree of Minimax Polynomial Approximating the Range [0, 1]

	2	3	4	5	6	7	8
e^x	6.8	10.8	15.1	19.8	24.6	29.6	34.7
sin(*x*)	7.8	12.7	16.1	21.6	25.5	31.3	35.7
ln(1 + *x*)	8.2	11.1	14.0	16.8	19.6	22.3	25.0
arctan(*x*)	8.7	9.8	13.2	15.5	17.2	21.2	22.3
tan(*x*)	4.8	6.9	8.9	10.9	12.9	14.9	16.9
arcsin(*x*)	3.4	4.0	4.4	4.7	4.9	5.1	5.3
$\sqrt{x}$	3.9	4.4	4.8	5.2	5.4	5.6	5.8

Conclusion

The task of writing low-accuracy mathematical functions using high-accuracy techniques has not been covered in any depth in the literature. But with the widespread use of programmable DSPs, vector units, high-speed yet limited hardware, and more esoteric shading models, the need to write your own mathematical functions is increasingly important.

Introductions to polynomial approximation always start by saying how accurate they can be, and this obsession with accuracy continues through to extracting the very last bit of accuracy out of every floating-point number. Why this obsession with accuracy? Because if you can build high-accuracy polynomials with less coefficients, you can also build tiny, low-accuracy approximations using the same techniques. The levels of accuracy you can obtain with just two constants as well as the hugely reduced range can be amazing. Hopefully, this gem has given you the confidence to grab a math package and generate some of your own high-speed functions.

References

[Cody80] Cody & Waite, *Software Manual for the Elementary Functions*, Prentice Hall, 1980.

[Crenshaw00] Crenshaw, Jack W., *Math Toolkit for Real-Time Programming*, CMP Books, 2000.

[DSP] The Music DSP Source Code. Archive available online at http://www.smart-electronix.com.

[Goldberg91] Goldberg, Steve, "What Every Computer Scientist Should Know About Floating Point Arithmetic," *ACM Computing Surveys,* Vol. 23, No. 1, March 1991.

[Hart68] Hart, J. F., *Computer Approximations*, John Wiley & Sons, 1968.

[Moshier89] Moshier, Stephen L., *Methods and Programs for Mathematical Functions*, Prentice Hall, 1989.

[Muller97] Muller, J. M., *Elementary Functions: Algorithms and Implementations*, Birkhaüser, 1997.

[Ng92] Ng, K. C., "Argument Reduction for Huge Arguments: Good to the Last Bit," SunPro Report, July 1992.

[Story00] Story, S. and Tang, P. T. P, "New Algorithms for Improved Transcendental Functions on IA-64," Intel Report, 2000.

[Tang89] Tang, Ping Tak Peter, "Table Driven Implementation of the Exponential Function in IEEE Floating Point Arithmetic," *ACM Transactions on Mathematical Software,* Vol. 15, No. 2, June 1989.

[Tang90] Tang, Ping Tak Peter, "Table Driven Implementation of the Logarithm Function in IEEE Floating Point Arithmetic," *ACM Transactions on Mathematical Software,* Vol. 16, No. 2, December 1990.

[Tang91] Tang, Ping Tak Peter, "Table Lookup Algorithms for Elementary Functions and Their Error Analysis," Proceedings of 10th Symposium on Computer Arithmetic, 1991.

[Upstill90] Upstill, S., *The Renderman Companion*, Addison Wesley, 1990.

2.2

Faster Quaternion Interpolation Using Approximations

Andy Thomason, SN Systems

andyt@snsys.com

Quaternions are used extensively in game development because they provide a simple and effective way to represent a rotation. A quaternion takes up 4/9 of the storage required for a rotation matrix, can smoothly interpolate between rotations, and has many other properties that make it useful for skinned, hierarchical animation. In particular, quaternions are used to represent the joints of characters that can only rotate about a particular point.

As games become more complex, we must move to more advanced methods similar to the linear algebra techniques used by supercomputers. Methods like the Structures Of Arrays (SOA) method can improve computational efficiency by an order of magnitude or more by grouping together similar operations, reducing memory access, and using all available ALUs (Arithmetic and Logic Units) by way of SIMD (Single Instruction, Multiple Data) instructions.

The trouble with using batch linear algebra techniques is that the trigonometric functions normally associated with quaternion interpolation cannot be used. So by using an approximation, not only can we speed up the process by sacrificing some precision, but we can enable the calculations to be done using adds, subtracts, multiplies, divides, and square roots.

In the game *Galleon*, we were able to have dozens of figures fighting hand to hand, each with cloth dynamics, real-time footstep placement, and AI. If we wanted thousands of such figures using the same hardware, the skinning and animation load would dominate, principally because of the cost of quaternion interpolation used for key expansion, animation blending, and collision.

With vertex shaders increasing in complexity, it is now possible to use quaternions for skinning [Hejl04]. We can use approximations to generate batches of quaternions from animation data and quickly feed these results to vertex shaders.

These methods should be suited for use on the specialist vector units that are becoming more common on consoles and computers alike. Examples are provided in C++, but feel free to recode them using native assembly language or intrinsics.

Using Quaternions as Rotations

Recall that a quaternion **q** is a four-component quantity that can be written as follows.

$$\mathbf{q} = \langle w, x, y, z \rangle = w + xi + yj + zk \tag{2.2.1}$$

It consists of one scalar component w and three vector components x, y, and z. Quaternion multiplication is defined using the ordinary distributive law with the following rules for the products of the "imaginary" numbers i, j, and k.

$$\begin{aligned} ij &= -ji = k \\ jk &= -kj = i \end{aligned} \tag{2.2.2}$$

Using these rules, the product of two quaternions **a** and **b** can be expanded to

$$\begin{aligned} \mathbf{ab} = &\left(a_w b_w - a_x b_x - a_y b_y - a_z b_z\right) \\ &+\left(a_w b_x + a_x b_w + a_y b_z - a_z b_y\right)i \\ &+\left(a_w b_y - a_x b_z + a_y b_w + a_z b_x\right)j \\ &+\left(a_w b_z + a_x b_y - a_y b_x + a_z b_w\right)k \end{aligned} \tag{2.2.3}$$

Every nonzero quaternion $\mathbf{q} = w + xi + yj + zk$ has an inverse $\mathbf{q}^{-1}$ given by

$$\mathbf{q}^{-1} = \frac{\overline{\mathbf{q}}}{q^2} \tag{2.2.4}$$

where the quantity $\overline{\mathbf{q}} = w - xi - yj - zk$ is the *conjugate* of **q**. For a unit quaternion, $q^2 = 1$, and the conjugate and inverse are the same quantity.

A quaternion representing a rotation through an angle θ about the unit-length axis $A = (A_x, A_y, A_z)$ is usually written in the following form:

$$\mathbf{q}_{rotation} = \cos\frac{\theta}{2} + \mathbf{A}\sin\frac{\theta}{2} \tag{2.2.5}$$

The way in which a quaternion is used to rotate a vector **v** is to treat the vector as a quaternion with zero scalar component and evaluate the product

$$Rotate(\mathbf{v}, \mathbf{q}) = \mathbf{q}\mathbf{v}\overline{\mathbf{q}} \tag{2.2.6}$$

This leads to the familiar quaternion-to-matrix conversion formula:

$$\mathbf{q}\mathbf{v}\bar{\mathbf{q}} = \begin{bmatrix} 1-2q_y^2-2q_z^2 & 2q_xq_y-2q_wq_z & 2q_xq_z+2q_wq_y \\ 2q_xq_y+2q_wq_z & 1-2q_x^2-2q_z^2 & 2q_yq_z-2q_wq_x \\ 2q_xq_z-2q_wq_y & 2q_yq_z+2q_wq_x & 1-2q_x^2-2q_y^2 \end{bmatrix} \begin{bmatrix} v_x \\ v_y \\ v_z \end{bmatrix} \quad (2.2.7)$$

Note that if we don't make the usual assumption that

$$q_w^2+q_x^2+q_y^2+q_z^2=1 \quad (2.2.8)$$

then we get an alternative formula

$$\mathbf{q}\mathbf{v}\bar{\mathbf{q}} = \begin{bmatrix} q_w^2+q_x^2-q_y^2-q_z^2 & 2q_xq_y-2q_wq_z & 2q_xq_z+2q_wq_y \\ 2q_xq_y+2q_wq_z & q_w^2+q_y^2-q_x^2-q_z^2 & 2q_yq_z-2q_wq_x \\ 2q_xq_z-2q_wq_y & 2q_yq_z+2q_wq_x & q_w^2+q_z^2-q_x^2-q_y^2 \end{bmatrix} \begin{bmatrix} v_x \\ v_y \\ v_z \end{bmatrix} \quad (2.2.9)$$

and we can incorporate a scaling factor s into the quaternions as follows:

$$Rotate(\mathbf{v}, \pm\sqrt{s}\mathbf{q}) = \mathbf{q}\mathbf{v}\bar{\mathbf{q}}s \quad (2.2.10)$$

This only works because we are using the conjugate of the quaternion, not the inverse, for our rotation formula. But clearly, a negative scaling factor cannot be used. Note that negating a quaternion does not affect the rotation that is produced. That is,

$$Rotate(\mathbf{v}, -\mathbf{q}) = Rotate(\mathbf{v}, \mathbf{q}) \quad (2.2.11)$$

For the most part, the techniques described in the following sections assume a unit scaling factor, so be very careful how nonunit quaternions are used. However, the extra scaling factor can be very useful when using quaternions in vertex shaders.

Interpolating Quaternion Rotations

In computer games, animations consist of a series of *keys*, usually rotations representing the angles of joints of a character. To smoothly interpolate between the keys and thus to avoid using precious storage to store a key for each frame, we use a method called *spherical linear interpolation* or *slerp* for short. The goal of the slerp function is to interpolate smoothly between two quaternions **a** and **b**, sweeping a constant angle per unit time and maintaining a constant unit length.

So why can't we just use linear interpolation? The answer is that we need to maintain the unit length of the interpolated quaternion to avoid introducing a scaling factor. Even if we renormalize the result of linear interpolation, the angular velocity of the resulting animation will not be constant, resulting in jerky movement.

An example of a slerp in real life is the great circle taken by a passenger jet over the surface of the Earth. The jet keeps a constant distance from the center of the Earth and moves with a constant speed over the shortest arc. Thus, if we want to fly from Amsterdam to Berlin, we apply the following function:

$$Slerp(Amsterdam, Berlin) \tag{2.2.12}$$

How do we achieve this?

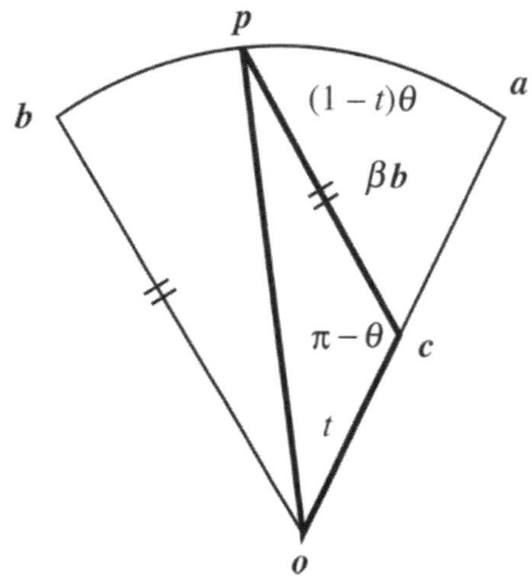

FIGURE 2.2.1 An illustration of the slerp function.

In Figure 2.2.1, Amsterdam is represented by the vector **a** and Berlin by **b**. The position **p** of the jet sweeps out an arc of θ radians during the journey, taking one hour. At time t, we have moved θt radians.

This position can be represented as a linear combination of the vectors **a** and **b**:

$$\mathbf{p}(\theta,t)=\alpha(\theta,t)\mathbf{a}+\beta(\theta,t)\mathbf{b} \tag{2.2.13}$$

We can calculate **a** and **b** by using the triangle drawn on the diagram. Using the sine formula for triangle area in three different ways for the triangle **opc**, with **op** = 1, **oc** = α, **cp** = β,

$$\frac{1}{2}\alpha\beta\sin\theta=\frac{1}{2}\alpha\sin(t\theta)=\frac{1}{2}\beta\sin((1-t)\theta) \tag{2.2.14}$$

These equalities give us α and β leading to the following well-known formula:

$$\mathbf{p}(\theta,t)=Slerp(\mathbf{a},\mathbf{b},t)=\frac{\sin(1-t)\theta}{\sin\theta}\mathbf{a}+\frac{\sin t\theta}{\sin\theta}\mathbf{b},\theta=\arccos(\mathbf{a}\cdot\mathbf{b}) \tag{2.2.15}$$

So if $x = \mathbf{s} \cdot \mathbf{b}$, then

$$\alpha(x,t) = \frac{\sin((1-t)\arccos x)}{\sqrt{1-x^2}}, \beta(x,t) = \frac{\sin(t \arccos x)}{\sqrt{1-x^2}} \tag{2.2.16}$$

because

$$\sin(\arccos x) = \sqrt{1-x^2}. \tag{2.2.17}$$

Figure 2.2.2 shows a plot of $\beta(x,t)$. Notice how the graph is quite flat where $x = 1$ but curves steeply when $x = -1$. This is the source of potential problems with an approximation.

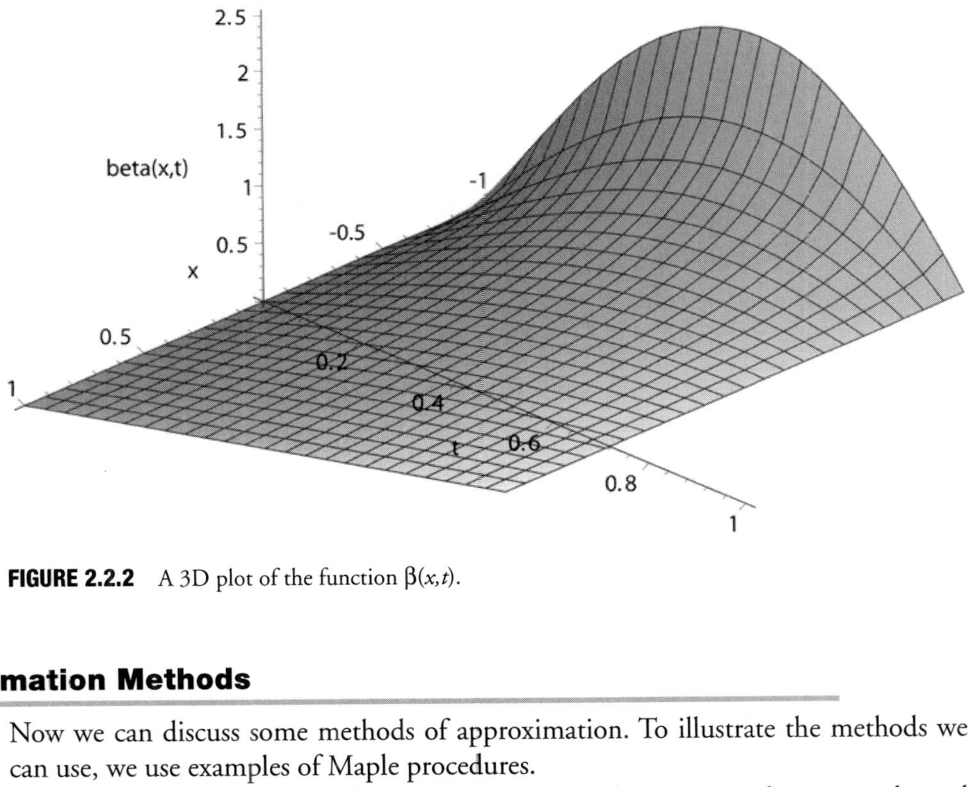

FIGURE 2.2.2 A 3D plot of the function $\beta(x,t)$.

Approximation Methods

Now we can discuss some methods of approximation. To illustrate the methods we can use, we use examples of Maple procedures.

We discuss several methods of approximation and summarize their strengths and weaknesses. One of the golden rules of numerical approximation is that no one method is best. The context in which the approximation is to be used must be considered when determining the specific method.

In computer games, we may have to ask ourselves a number of questions, notably the following:

- How many CPU cycles can we spare?
- How much precision do we need?
- Can we cheaply use functions such as `sqrt(x)` and `exp(x)`?
- Can we use SIMD instructions, like VU macro mode, paired float, SSE, or 3DNow?
- Are we going to be blending more than two quaternions at once?
- What is the maximum angle between our keys?

We present various methods here, but it is up to the reader to decide which is most appropriate for a particular application.

Direct Method

We start with the direct approach. We just examine the beta function formula and approximate the various components. This is actually the best method if very high precision is necessary, but it can be very costly, especially when evaluating large batches of slerps.

Almost every game engine contains something like the code in Listing 2.2.1, and many games spend significant proportions of their time executing it.

LISTING 2.2.1 Reference Slerp Class

```
class SlerpReference
{
public:
SlerpReference( const Quat &a, const Quat &b ) : mA( a ), mB( b )
            {
float adotb = a.X * b.X + a.Y * b.Y + a.Z * b.Z + a.W * b.W;
adotb = Min( adotb, 0.99999f );
mTheta = acosf( adotb );
mRecipSqrt = RecipSqrt( 1 - adotb * adotb );
}

Quat Interpolate( float t ) const
{
float alpha = sinf( ( 1 - t ) * mTheta ) * mRecipSqrt;
float beta = sinf( t * mTheta ) * mRecipSqrt;
return Quat( alpha * mA.X + beta * mB.X, alpha * mA.Y +
beta * mB.Y, alpha * mA.Z + beta * mB.Z, alpha * mA.W +
beta * mB.W );
}
private:
float mTheta;
float mRecipSqrt;
const Quat &mA;
const Quat &mB;
};
```

Here we have used trig functions to create a reference slerp class. The class has a constructor and a method to calculate individual interpolated quaternions. We have taken pains to avoid using branches that will cause lengthy pipeline stalls by using the `Min` function to avoid overflows. Note that although the results near `adotb = 1` will be consistent, if the quaternions point away from each other, the result will be unpredictable.

To turn this into an approximation, we have to approximate `sin(x)` and `arccos(x)`.

The `sin(x)` component is simple, as this responds to traditional polynomial approximation tools. In Maple, there is a package called `numapprox` that contains polynomial approximation tools that can convert an arbitrary function into a polynomial over a certain range of values.

A Taylor series turns a function of x into a polynomial in x that matches the function exactly at one point. Maple has a built-in Taylor series command that gives a result like this:

$$taylorSeries = x - \frac{x^3}{3!} + \frac{x^5}{5!} + O\left(x^7\right). \tag{2.2.18}$$

Unfortunately, Taylor series are not very useful for approximation as they are exact in one place only, but they are simple to calculate and are useful for showing us the general form of a function. A polynomial can be made to be exact in n or more different places, where n is the degree of the polynomial, or highest power term. This can be used to significantly reduce the error.

In the `numapprox` package, Maple has a command called `minimax` that chooses the best places to make a polynomial exact in such a way as the maximum error is minimized, hence the name.

$$\begin{aligned} minimaxSeries &= \text{minimax}\left(\sin\left(x\right), x = -\pi..\pi, 3\right) \\ &= \left(.824535 + \left(-.08692x\right)x\right)x \end{aligned} \tag{2.2.19}$$

Figure 2.2.3 shows a plot of *taylorSeries*, *minimaxSeries*, and `sin(x)`. Here we see that the Taylor series shoots off to infinity when $|x| > 1$. Figure 2.2.4 shows a plot of the error, which shows that the Taylor series is exact only at the origin, whereas the minimax polynomial is exact in five separate places, spreading out the error over the interval.

This is how the built-in functions in C++ are created. The following is an approximation to cos(x) on the interval $x \in \left[\frac{-\pi}{2}, \frac{\pi}{2}\right]$ that we can use to approximate sin(x) on $x \in [0,\pi]$. In this case, cos(x) is an easier function to approximate than sin(x), as it is even and hence uses only terms in x^2.

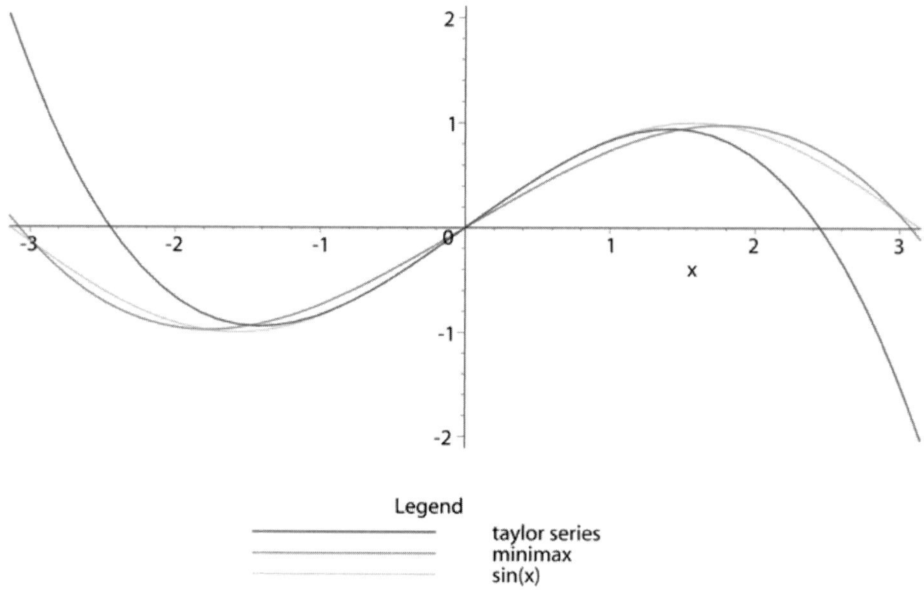

FIGURE 2.2.3 Plot of *taylorSeries*, *minimaxSeries*, and `sin(x)` showing the differences.

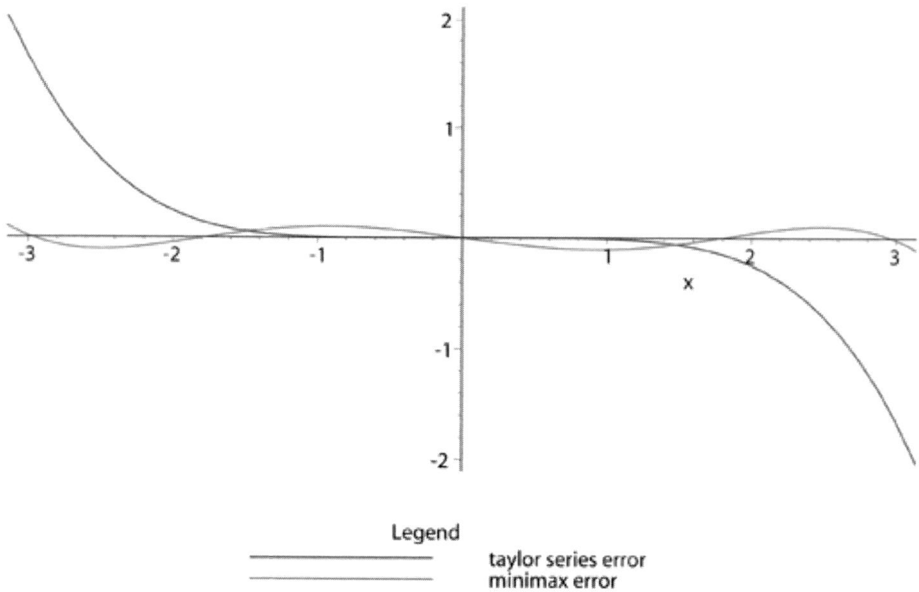

FIGURE 2.2.4 Plot of the error of a Taylor series vs. a minimax series.

$$\cos(x) = \sin\left(x + \frac{\pi}{2}\right)$$
$$\simeq 1 + \left(-.4999991 + \left(.416636 + \left(-.0138537 + .000231540x^2\right)x^2\right)x^2\right)x^2 \quad (2.2.20)$$

Figure 2.2.5 shows a plot of the error for the previous approximation.

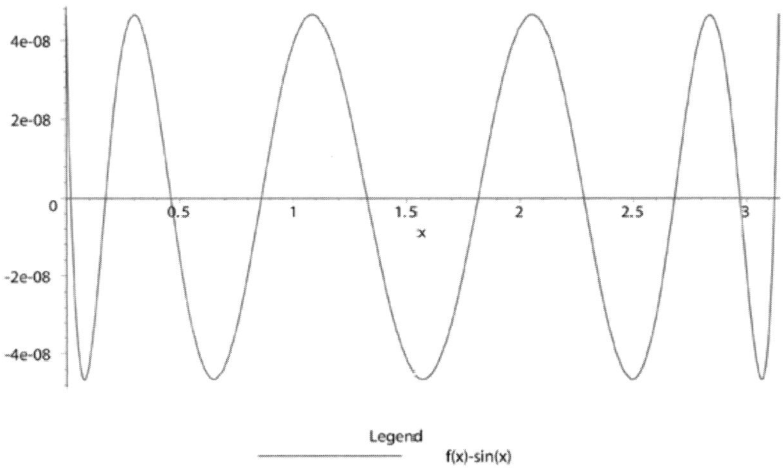

FIGURE 2.2.5 Showing the error in the approximation to cos(x) shifted into the range used by the slerp function.

The `arccos(x)` function does not respond to this kind of treatment. Figure 2.2.6 shows a plot of the error for eight terms, which is shockingly bad.

The reason for this can be seen by looking at the `arccos` function itself, shown in Figure 2.2.7. There are singularities at $x = 1$ and $x = -1$ that behave as $\sqrt{1-x}$ and $\sqrt{1+x}$, respectively. It is very hard for a polynomial to approximate this kind of function. These kinds of behaviors can be discovered using the Maple series command.

Making an approximation in terms of nonlinear terms works much better:

$$\arccos(x) \simeq \sqrt{2.218480716 - 2.441884385x + 0.2234036692x^2} - \sqrt{2.218480716 + 2.441884385x + 0.2234036692x^2} + \frac{\pi}{2} + 0.6391287330x \quad (2.2.21)$$

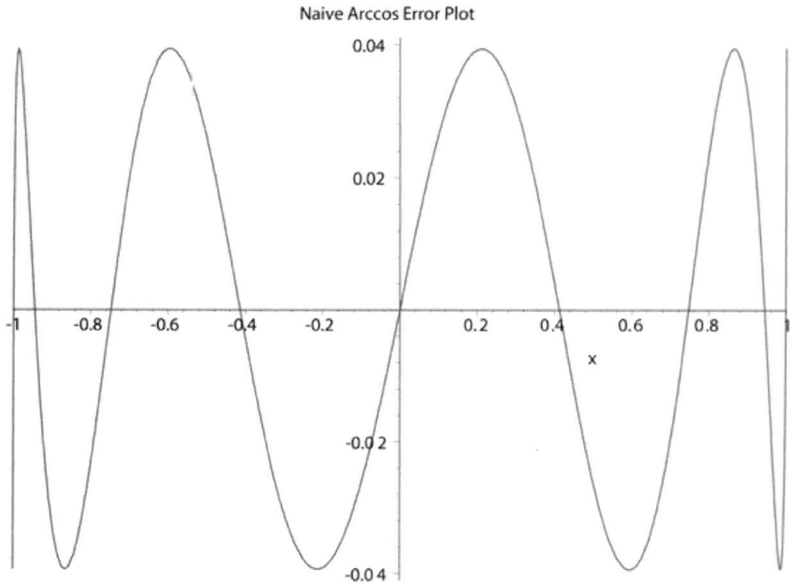

FIGURE 2.2.6 The result of using Maple's *minimax* on the `arccos` function.

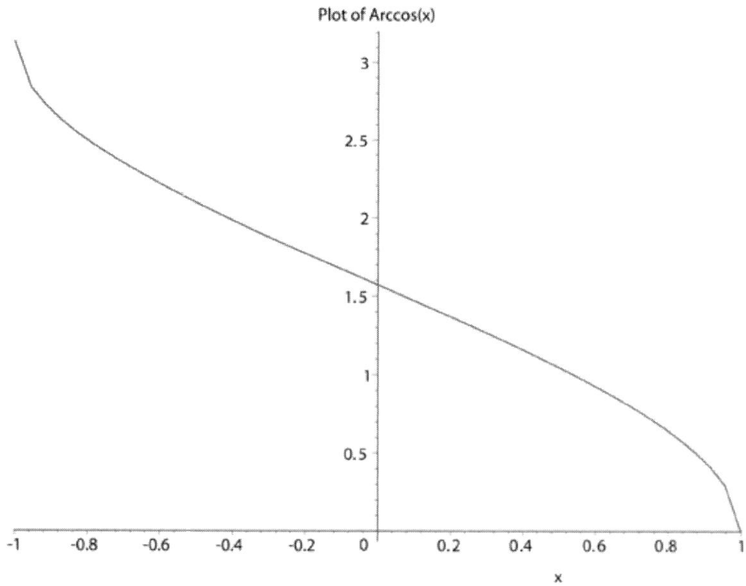

FIGURE 2.2.7 A plot of arccos(x) showing singularities at $x = \pm 1$.

The error for this approximation to arccos(x) is plotted in Figure 2.2.8. Note that these functions only work over our required range. If functions that work over other ranges are needed, they will have to be made separately. The accompanying CD-ROM contains some example Maple worksheets.

ON THE CD

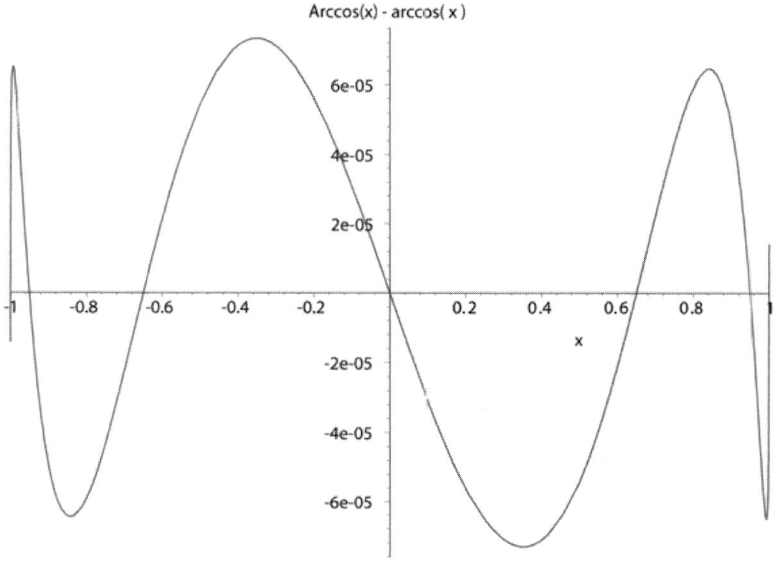

FIGURE 2.2.8 A better approximation to arccos(x).

The reciprocal square root is available on most modern processors using the division unit. One should be careful to allow for latency, however, and calculate this first so that the result is available later. An approximate reciprocal square root is also often available in a single-cycle form to 16 bits with SIMD instructions.

The proportional error in the rotation can be calculated to be of the same order as the error in the alpha and beta functions. To perform this calculation, we may assume an error e in the function and use the Maple "series" command. Decrease the number of series terms until the order $O(e^k)$ is the last remaining term in e.

Figure 2.2.9 shows a series of error plots of beta functions for various angles of separation of the quaternions

$$\frac{\mathrm{Sin}\left(t\,\mathrm{Arccos}\left(x\right)\right)}{\sqrt{1-x^2}} - \frac{\sin\left(t \arccos x\right)}{\sqrt{1-x^2}} \tag{2.2.22}$$

where Sin(x) and Arccos(x) are the approximations.

Use of SIMD architectures enables the calculation of both sine functions together, as shown in Listing 2.2.2.

LISTING 2.2.2 Direct Slerp Method Class

```
class SlerpDirect
{
public:
SlerpDirect( const Quat &a, const Quat &b ) : mA( a ), mB( b )
{
```

```
float adotb = a.X * b.X + a.Y * b.Y + a.Z * b.Z + a.W * b.W;
adotb = Min( adotb, 0.99995f );
float even = 2.218480716f + .2234036692f * adotb * adotb;
float odd = 2.441884385f * adotb;
mTheta = Sqrt( even - odd ) - Sqrt( even + odd ) +
           1.570796327f + .6391287330f * adotb;
mRecipSqrt = RecipSqrt( 1 - adotb * adotb );
}

Quat Interpolate( float t ) const
{
float A = ( 1 - t ) * mTheta - 1.570796327f; A = A * A;
float B = t * mTheta - 1.570796327f; B = B * B;
float sinA = .9999999535f+(-.4999990537f+(.4166358517e-1f
+(-.1385370794e-2f+.2315401401e-4f*A)*A)*A)*A;
float sinB = .9999999535f+(-.4999990537f+(.4166358517e-1f
+(-.1385370794e-2f+.2315401401e-4f*B)*B)*B)*B;
float alpha = sinA * mRecipSqrt;
float beta = sinB * mRecipSqrt;
return Quat( alpha * mA.X + beta * mB.X, alpha * mA.Y +
beta * mB.Y, alpha * mA.Z + beta * mB.Z, alpha * mA.W +
beta * mB.W );
}
private:
float mTheta;
float mRecipSqrt;
const Quat &mA;
const Quat &mB;
};
```

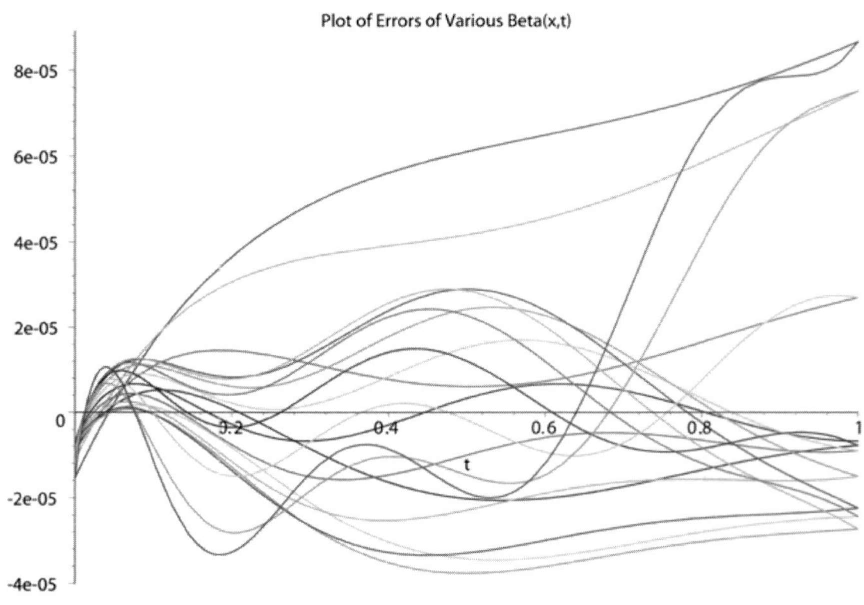

FIGURE 2.2.9 Plots of errors in $\beta(x, t)$ for various x.

This class shows the result we obtain when we simply approximate the component functions of the traditional slerp function.

Matrix Approximation

Because $\beta(x, t)$ is simply a function of two variables, we can, in theory, represent the entire result as a two-dimensional polynomial in x and t. That is,

$$\beta(x,t) = \mathbf{XMT} \tag{2.2.23}$$

where $\mathbf{M}$ is an $N_x \times N_t$ matrix and

$$\mathbf{X} = \begin{pmatrix} 1 & x & \cdots & x^{N_x-1} \end{pmatrix}$$
$$\mathbf{T} = \begin{pmatrix} t & t^3 & \cdots & t^{N_t-1} \end{pmatrix}. \tag{2.2.24}$$

Applying the same process as in the analysis of arccos(x), namely using the Maple series command, we see that we have a problem approximating the whole polynomial because

$$\lim_{x \to -1} \beta(x,t) = \infty \tag{2.2.25}$$

We need to take this singularity out of the function so that we can approximate it with fewer terms. If we instead evaluate

$$g(x,t) = \beta(x,t)(1+x) \tag{2.2.26}$$

then we end up with a much better behaved function over the range $x \in [-1,1]$, as illustrated in Figure 2.2.10. We can then multiply by $1/(1 + x)$ to obtain $\beta(x,t)$.

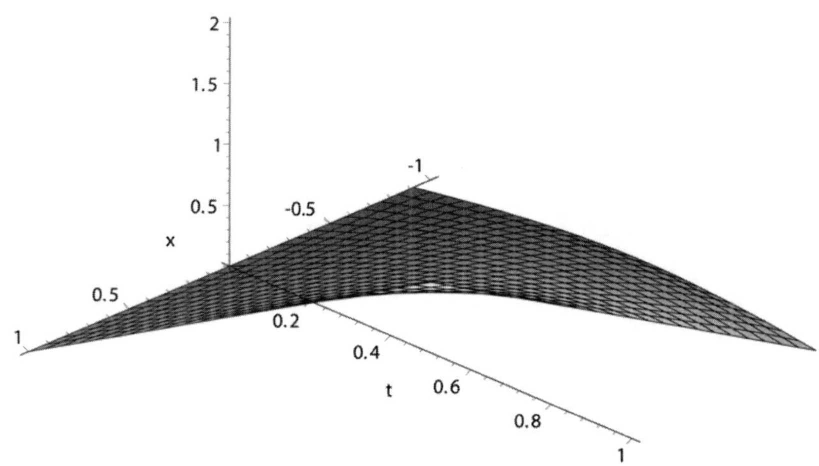

FIGURE 2.2.10 $g(x,t)$, a better alternative to approximating $\beta(x,t)$.

Unfortunately, Maple does not come with a 2D version of the `minimax` command, and besides, uniform error distribution is useful only in certain conditions.

We can make a 2D version of the Chebyshev approximation method, which constructs a function in the form

$$\sum_{j=0}^{N_t} \sum_{i=0}^{N_x} c_{i,j} T(i,x) T(j,t) \tag{2.2.27}$$

where $T(i,x)$ and $T(j,t)$ are Chebyshev polynomials of the first kind, given by

$$\begin{aligned} T(0,x) &= 1 \\ T(1,x) &= x \\ T(2,x) &= 2x^2 - 1 \\ T(3,x) &= 4x^3 - 3x. \end{aligned} \tag{2.2.28}$$

When we have constructed a function of this form, it is easy to convert it to a regular polynomial by multiplying out and collecting terms in x and t. A Maple procedure that does this is included on the book's accompanying CD-ROM.

ON THE CD

Applying this to $g(x,t)$ gives

$$\mathbf{M} = \begin{pmatrix} 1.570994357 & -0.6461396421 & 0.07949824672 & -0.004354110679 \\ 0.5642929825 & 0.5945659091 & -0.1730440015 & 0.01418982936 \\ -0.1783657609 & 0.08610292588 & 0.1079287872 & -0.01567243477 \\ 0.04319948653 & -0.03465102568 & -0.01439451411 & 0.005849053560 \end{pmatrix} \tag{2.2.29}$$

for best accuracy in $0 < \mathbf{a} \cdot \mathbf{b} < 1$. Clearly, more terms can be used, and each row adds two SIMD instructions and more precision to the x expansion.

One of the most useful features of this method is that once the following vector is evaluated

$$\frac{1}{1+x}\mathbf{XM} \tag{2.2.30}$$

multiple $\alpha(t)$ and $\beta(t)$ values can be generated with simple algebra. Listing 2.2.3 shows an implementation.

LISTING 2.2.3 Matrix Slerp Method Class

```
class SlerpMatrix
{
public:
SlerpMatrix( const Quat &a, const Quat &b ) : mA( a ), mB( b )
{
```

```
float adotb = a.X * b.X + a.Y * b.Y + a.Z * b.Z + a.W * b.W;
mRecipOnePlusAdotB = Recip( 1 + adotb );
mC1 = 1.570994357f+(.5642929859f-( -.1783657717f
+.4319949352e-1f*adotb)*adotb)*adotb;
mC3 = -.6461396382f+(.5945657936f+(.8610323953e-1f
-.3465122928e-1f*adotb)*adotb)*adotb;
mC5 = .7949823521e-1f+( -.1730436931f+(.1079279599f
-.1439397801e-1f*adotb)*adotb)*adotb;
mC7 = -.4354102836e-2f+(.1418962736e-1f+( -.1567189691e-1f
+.5848706227e-2f*adotb)*adotb)*adotb;
}

Quat Interpolate( float t ) const
{
float T = 1 - t, t2 = t * t, T2 = T * T;
float alpha = (mC1+(mC3+(mC5+mC7*T2)*T2)*T2)*T *
              mRecipOnePlusAdotB;
float beta = (mC1+(mC3+(mC5+mC7*t2)*t2)*t2)*t *
              mRecipOnePlusAdotB;
return Quat( alpha * mA.X + beta * mB.X, alpha * mA.Y +
beta * mB.Y, alpha * mA.Z + beta * mB.Z, alpha * mA.W +
beta * mB.W );
}
private:
float mRecipOnePlusAdotB;
float mC1, mC3, mC5, mC7;
const Quat &mA;
const Quat &mB;
};
```

Here, we precalculate polynomial coefficients that enable us to simply calculate a series of interpolations. In practice, we would probably recode this using native SIMD instructions.

Renormalization

A quick and dirty approximation, where accuracy is not important, is to simply linear interpolate (lerp) the quaternions and renormalize the result. This produces a result that is good to about four to eight bits in normal use, which is quite often enough. If the angle between the quaternions is very small, the result is quite accurate.

This is the method that has been used in vertex shaders, as it is possible to blend between several quaternions in a way that is superior to conventional matrix blending.

However, except for the setup time, the interpolation is slower than the Matrix slerp method presented earlier and has significantly less precision. Listing 2.2.4 shows an implementation.

LISTING 2.2.4 Simple Lerp and Renormalization

```
class SlerpSimpleRenormal
{
public:
```

```
SlerpSimpleRenormal( const Quat &a, const Quat &b ) :
mA( a ), mB( b )
{
}

Quat Interpolate( float t ) const
{
float alpha = 1 - t;
float beta = t;
Quat result( alpha * mA.X + beta * mB.X, alpha * mA.Y +
beta * mB.Y, alpha * mA.Z + beta * mB.Z,
alpha * mA.W + beta * mB.W );
float recip = RecipSqrt( result.X * result.X +
result.Y * result.Y + result.Z * result.Z +
result.W * result.W );
return Quat( result.X * recip, result.Y * recip,
result.Z * recip, result.W * recip );
}
private:
const Quat &mA;
const Quat &mB;
};
```

The simple lerp can be improved by approximating the following instead

$$\beta(x,t)=\frac{\sin(t\arccos x)}{\sin(t\arccos x)+\sin((1-t)\arccos x)},\alpha(x,t)=1-\beta(x,t), \qquad (2.2.31)$$

and then renormalizing. Alternatively, the angle subdivision methods can be used before the lerp and renormalization operations.

Renormalization can also significantly improve the accuracy of the direct and matrix methods, but at the cost of extra time. Listing 2.2.5 shows an implementation of the improved renormalization method.

LISTING 2.2.5 An Improved (Though Cumbersome) Renormalization Method

```
class SlerpRenormal
{
public:
SlerpRenormal( const Quat &a, const Quat &b ) : mA( a ), mB( b )
{
float adotb = a.X * b.X + a.Y * b.Y + a.Z * b.Z + a.W * b.W;
adotb = Min( adotb, 0.995f );
float even = 2.218480716f + .2234036692f * adotb * adotb;
float odd = 2.441884385f * adotb;
mTheta = Sqrt( even - odd ) - Sqrt( even + odd )
+ 1.570796327f + .6391287330f * adotb;
}
```

```
Quat Interpolate( float t ) const
{
float T = 1 - t, t2 = t * t, T2 = T * T;
float A = ( 1 - t ) * mTheta;
float B = t * mTheta;
float sinA =  -.67044e-5f + ( 1.000271283f + (
-.17990919e-2f + (  -.1621365372f + (
-.556099983e-2f + ( .1198086481e-1f -
.1271209213e-2f * A ) * A ) * A ) * A ) * A ) * A;
float sinB =  -.67044e-5f + ( 1.000271283f + (
-.17990919e-2f + (  -.1621365372f + (
-.556099983e-2f + ( .1198086481e-1f -
.1271209213e-2f * B ) * B ) * B ) * B ) * B ) * B;
float recipAB = Recip( sinA + sinB );
float alpha = sinA * recipAB;
float beta = sinB * recipAB;

// renormalise
Quat result( alpha * mA.X + beta * mB.X, alpha * mA.Y +
beta * mB.Y, alpha * mA.Z + beta * mB.Z,
alpha * mA.W + beta * mB.W );
float recip = RecipSqrt( result.X * result.X +
result.Y * result.Y + result.Z * result.Z +
result.W * result.W );
return Quat( result.X * recip, result.Y * recip,
result.Z * recip, result.W * recip );
}
private:
float mTheta;
const Quat &mA;
const Quat &mB;
};
```

Angle Subdivision Methods

We can bisect the angle between two quaternions by noting the following:

$$\beta\left(x,\tfrac{1}{2}\right)=\alpha\left(x,\tfrac{1}{2}\right)=\frac{\sin\left(\tfrac{1}{2}\arccos x\right)}{\sqrt{1-x^2}}=\frac{1}{\sqrt{2+2x}}. \tag{2.2.32}$$

This is exact for half the angle and can be extended for any value of t that is composed of quarters, eights, sixteenths, and so on. A Maple worksheet is included on the accompanying CD-ROM that calculates the subdivision beta functions in terms of square roots using bisection.

ON THE CD

$$\beta(x,0) = 0,$$
$$\beta\left(x,\tfrac{1}{4}\right) = \frac{1+\sqrt{2+2x}}{\sqrt{2+\sqrt{2+2x}}\sqrt{2+2x}},$$
$$\beta\left(x,\tfrac{1}{2}\right) = \frac{1}{\sqrt{2+2x}},$$
$$\beta\left(x,\tfrac{3}{4}\right) = \frac{1}{\sqrt{2+\sqrt{2+2x}}\sqrt{2+2x}}$$
$$\beta(x,1) = 1. \tag{2.2.33}$$

Comparison of Methods

We compared the classes for accuracy and speed. The test data were three sets of quaternion encodings with large, medium, and tiny rotations.

We expect the small rotations to be more accurate, as the distance between the quaternions is smaller. Large rotations are less common in animation data, but an algorithm must cope with these as well. Table 2.2.1 summarizes the accuracy of the methods for different classes of input data.

TABLE 2.2.1 Approximate Precision in Bits Equivalent

Data Set	Large Angles		Medium Angles		Tiny Angles	
	Worst	Avg	Worst	Avg	Worst	Avg
SlerpDirect	11	13	11	11	11	11
SlerpRenormal	16	18	17	19	19	19
SlerpMatrix	13	16	14	15	15	15
SlerpSimpleRenormal	4	8	11	15	19	19

Table 2.2.2 lists the time taken (in arbitrary units) to slerp 50,000 quaternions. The test consists of one setup and 10 interpolations using a wide range of data.

TABLE 2.2.2 Time Taken (in Arbitrary Units) to Slerp 50,000 Quaternions

SlerpReference	22906
SlerpDirect	13077
SlerpRenormal	24115
SlerpMatrix	7829
SlerpSimpleRenormal	12553

This shows that the approximate functions are quite a bit faster than the reference function, although to get real speed improvement, we would need to code using native instruction sets.

The Matrix method is the clear winner, beating even the simple lerp and renormalization method, probably because of the slow implementation of `sqrt` on the fpu.

This would work especially well on the PS2 VU0 coprocessor, where micro mode could be used to calculate large batches of quaternions for skinning.

Squad Derivative Calculation

We also investigated speeding up the "squad," or spherical quadrangle approximation often mistaken for a Bézier slerp.

Using the approximate arccos and sin functions and a nicely reduced function, we found it was possible to simplify the traditional method that uses log and exponent of quaternions.

Listing 2.2.6 shows a function that contains relatively benign components, easily codeable using SIMD instructions. The approximate functions `ArccosFast` and `SinFast` in Listing 2.2.6 are included on the accompanying CD-ROM.

ON THE CD

LISTING 2.2.6 Elegant Squad Derivative Generator

```
// Squad derivative calculation, optimized by hand
// This is quite fast and gives excellent results (~16 bits)
// try to remove the branches implicit in the ? operators.
Quat DerivativeCompact( const Quat &a, const Quat &b, const Quat &c )
{
Quat bconj = Conj( b );
Quat arel = Mul( a, bconj );
Quat crel = Mul( c, bconj );
float aScale = arel.W > 0.9999f ?
-0.25f : -0.25f*ArccosFast( arel.W ) * RecipSqrt( 1 –
arel.W * arel.W );
float cScale = crel.W > 0.9999f ?
-0.25f : -0.25f*ArccosFast( crel.W ) * RecipSqrt( 1 –
crel.W * crel.W );
float logx = aScale * arel.X + cScale * crel.X;
float logy = aScale * arel.Y + cScale * crel.Y;
float logz = aScale * arel.Z + cScale * crel.Z;
float length = Sqrt ( logx * logx + logy * logy + logz * logz );
float sinLength = SinFast( length );
float cosLength = Sqrt( 1 - sinLength * sinLength );
float xyzScale = length < 1e-5f ? 1 : sinLength / length;
return Mul( b, Quat(
xyzScale * logx, xyzScale * logy, xyzScale * logz,
cosLength) );
}

//    This function can be used like this:
Quat d1 = DerivativeCompact( q0, q1, q2 );
Quat d2 = DerivativeCompact( q3, q2, q1 );
```

```
Quat q12 = SlerpMatrix( q1, q2 ).Interpolate( fract );
Quat d12 = SlerpMatrix( d1, d2 ).Interpolate( fract );
Quat squad = SlerpMatrix( q12, d12 ).Interpolate( 2 * fract *
( 1 - fract ) );

// Where q0,...,q3 are a sequence of keys, fract is the fractional
   time.
```

Further Reading

The reader should read Ken Shoemake's SIGGRAPH paper [Shoe85] for a background to the quaternion slerp process. Not only does this introduce us to the concept, but it is also a very readable introduction to quaternion rotations.

It is worth noting that $\beta(x,t)$ is almost identical to a Chebyshev polynomial of the second kind, unlike the Chebyshev polynomials of the first kind we used for the 2D approximation.

$$\beta(x,t) = U_t(x) \tag{2.2.34}$$

These are solutions of a Sturm-Louiville differential equation:

$$\left(1-x^2\right)\frac{d^2}{dx^2}\beta(x,t) - 3x\frac{d}{dx}\beta(x,t) + \left(t^2-1\right)\beta(x,t) = 0 \tag{2.2.35}$$

Normally for Chebyshev polynomials, the parameter t would be an integer, in which case the function would be a polynomial. However, as our parameter t is a real value, we have a nonpolynomial result.

Read Chapter 11 of [Rich02] for further information. This book contains a good introduction to Maple, power series, and approximate methods.

While doing the research for this gem, we explored using forward differences to solve this equation for $\alpha(t)$ and $\beta(t)$. Although this was not a good method for evaluating the function at a spot value, it would probably be useful for evaluating a series of quaternion interpolations. It is also possible to use multiple-angle formulae to iterate successive slerp results.

Conclusion

We have explored many methods of approximating the quaternion slerp function, which is used extensively in character-based games. We have developed a simple matrix-based method that requires only a few multiplies and adds to produce accurate interpolated rotation quaternions.

Angle subdivision methods using only square roots were also discussed that enable very specific slerp values to be calculated simply.

We have also investigated the squad interpolation function and found a simple function to generate the extra quaternions required for smooth interpolation of a series of keys.

References

[Hejl04] Hejl, Jim, *Game Programming Gems 4*, 5.12. Charles River Media, 2004.

[Rich02] Richards, D, *Advanced Mathematical Methods with Maple*, Cambridge University Press, 2001.

[Shoe85] Shoemake, Ken, ACM SIGGRAPH, 1985.

2.3

Quaternion Compression

Mark Zarb-Adami

Many of today's computer games use large amounts of animation data, and a large portion of the memory used for each animation frame is consumed by the rotation of the bones. Typically, the rotation data is stored as quaternions. In this gem, we propose and compare methods for compressing a four-float quaternion into a 32-bit quantity.

Quaternions

A quaternion $Q(x, y, z, w)$ can be used to represent a rotation matrix. If we consider all rotation matrices to represent a rotation of angle θ about axis $A(X, Y, Z)$, then the quaternion for the rotation would be

$$Q = (sX, sY, sZ, c)$$

where

$$s = \sin(\theta)$$
$$c = \cos(\theta)$$

It is important to note that quaternion $Q(x, y, z, w)$ and quaternion $Q'(-x, -y, -z, -w)$ represent the same rotation. This is because a rotation of θ about axis A is equivalent to a rotation of $-\theta$ about axis $-A$. Also, note that all the quaternions we consider in this gem are normalized. This means that for every quaternion $Q(x, y, z, w)$:

$$x^2 + y^2 + z^2 + w^2 = 1$$

Smallest Three Method

We can compress a quaternion by quantizing each element of the quaternion down to a byte. This is very fast, but it is also inaccurate. Because the quaternion is normalized, we can improve the accuracy of quantization by eliminating one of the elements.

Given three of the elements, we can calculate the fourth one. Now, we have to decide which element to exclude. If we remove the biggest element, we will have smaller numbers to store! In fact, none of the three smallest elements of a quaternion can have an absolute value larger than $1/\sqrt{2}$. To understand why this is the case, consider the following. The *second* largest element of a normalized quaternion will be *largest* when two elements of the quaternion have the same value and the other two are zero, as in $Q(v, v, 0, 0)$. If we normalize this quaternion, then v must equal $1/\sqrt{2}$.

We don't have to store the sign of the largest element, since we can make sure it is always positive. If it isn't positive already, simply negate the quaternion as described previously.

Polar Methods

Since we can store a direction vector (x, y, z) using just two angles, *yaw* and *pitch*, we can also store a quaternion as $(yaw, pitch, w)$. Note that storing (x, y, z) with *yaw* and *pitch* removes information about its length, but we can restore the correct length with w, since the quaternion is normalized. If we ensure that w is always positive, then we don't have to store its sign. Once again, if w is negative, we simply negate the quaternion.

The trouble with storing a direction vector as *yaw* and *pitch* is that the encoded vectors are not evenly dispersed over a sphere. They are instead concentrated at the poles. When the pitch of the vector is $\pi/2$, and the vector points straight up at the pole, we do not want to store a *yaw.* However, when the pitch of the vector is zero and the vector lies along the equator, we want to store many *yaw* values. Say we wanted to use n bits to encode a direction vector. One solution would be to spread 2^n points evenly across the surface of the sphere, store (x, y, z) or $(yaw, pitch)$ for each point in a lookup table, then store an n-bit index into that table. While this is okay for small values of n, the size of the lookup table quickly becomes uncomfortably large!

However, there is an effective method for encoding a direction vector without the use of a lookup table. First of all, we store the signs of x, y, and z separately so that we can assume that x, y, and z are all positive. This reduces the problem to an eighth of the sphere. The next step is to number points inside this eighth of a sphere as in Figure 2.3.1.

Notice that the square numbers appear on the left-hand side of the diagram. This allows us to find the row and column of an encoded number, e, like this:

```
row = floor(sqrt(e));
column = e - row*row;
```

Now, if we let *pitch* be the row of e, and if we let *yaw* be the column of e, we can efficiently store and retrieve these values. Notice how we will not waste any *yaw* values at the pole, and that we have plenty of possible *yaw* values at the equator.

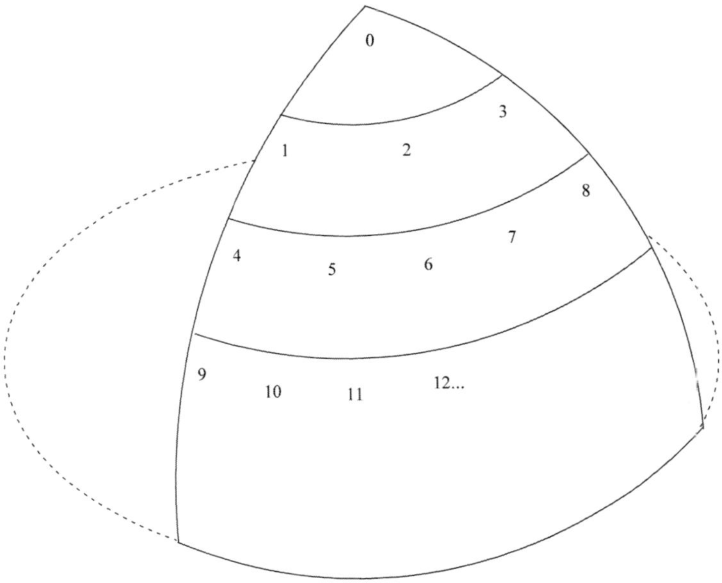

FIGURE 2.3.1 Numbering over an eighth of a sphere.

Implementation

Now, let's discuss the implementation for the methods we have discussed.

Smallest Three

The *smallest three* method neatly stores a quaternion into 32 bits. We need two bits to store the index of the implied (largest) element, leaving 10 bits for each of the three smallest elements. Since we know each of the stored elements lie in the range $\left[-1/\sqrt{2},\ 1/\sqrt{2}\right]$, we can interpolate those values to [0, 1023] so that the values are represented as integers.

Polar

After experimenting with various bit allocations, we found the best compression when we allocated 11 bits to w. We need an additional 3 bits to store the sign of x, y, and z, leaving 18 bits to store *yaw* and *pitch*. If we are encoding *yaw* and *pitch* as a single number, then we can store 512 values. Alternatively, we can allocate 9 bits for *yaw* and 9 bits for *pitch*. We know they are both in the range [0, $\pi/2$], so we interpolate these values to [0, 511] and store them as integers.

Converting from *yaw* and *pitch* to a vector requires sine and cosine calculations for both *yaw* and *pitch*, so we recommend using a fast polynomial approximation [Edwards00] to calculate these values. Moreover, because *yaw* and *pitch* are always within [0, π/2], we can tailor (no pun intended) the approximations to this particular range. We can expand a Taylor series about π/4 (instead of about 0) and use values between [0, π/4] as sample points for a Lagrange series. A Taylor series to order five, or a Lagrange series to order four or five, is sufficient. The order-four Lagrange series is slightly faster, but you lose a bit of accuracy. Also, the order-five Lagrange series gives a more accurate approximation than the order-five Taylor series.

The animation data for our game *Blade II* is stored hierarchically, hence the vast majority of the quaternions have only a small angle of rotation, ι. Since w is $cos(\iota/2)$, w is usually close to 1 for this data. Note that this would be true to a lesser extent even if the quaternions had random angles of rotation, simply because of the nature of the *cosine* function. So, to get more resolution for values near to 1, we store $\sqrt{1-w}$ instead of w and recover w at decompression time.

Performance

To quantify the performance of each compression method, we used the quaternions from our *Blade II* as data. We compressed and decompressed each quaternion Q to get another quaternion, Q'. We converted Q and Q' to matrices, and transformed a set of points with the resulting matrices. Then, for each point, we calculated the distance between the point transformed with Q and the point transformed with Q'. We represent these distances as error for that compression method. We also measured the decompression speed of each method. Figure 2.3.2 shows the relative performance of each compression method on our hierarchical data. The approximation method used for the polar methods was an order-five Lagrange polynomial.

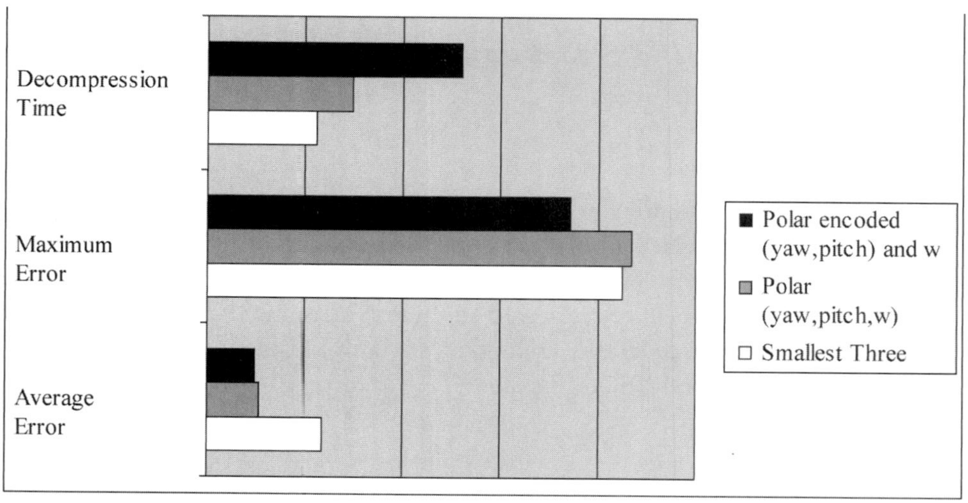

FIGURE 2.3.2 Relative performance of each compression method using *Blade II* quaternion data.

Conclusion

The real test of the compression of each algorithm comes from observing the characters in your game. The worst-case scenario for *Blade II* is when errors accumulate down the skeleton, especially if the character is holding a long lever (like a shotgun) in his hand! There is a visible improvement when using the *polar* methods compared to the *smallest three* method.

Acknowledgements

I want to thank Jan Svarovsky and Mike Diskett for their help in developing the ideas in this gem.

References

[Edwards00] Edwards, Eddie, "Polynomial Approximations to Trigonometric Functions," *Game Programming Gems*, Charles River Media, Inc., 2000.

[Svarovsky00] Svarovsky, Jan, "Quaternions for Game Programming," *Game Programming Gems*, Charles River Media, Inc., 2000.

2.4

Zobrist Hash Using the Mersenne Twister

Toby Jones, Microsoft Corporation

thjones@microsoft.com

In many games, deep and wide searches of game states are used to make decisions. Once a game state is calculated, an evaluation function determines the pros and cons of the state. This has been a popular technique used in games such as chess, go, and reversi, and many of the leading chess games use some variation of it. Strategy games are especially well suited, especially if they are turn-based. High-level character AIs can use these techniques to some degree if their set of discrete states can be bounded.

A good searching technique will generate a large number of game states to be evaluated. Because of the nature of strategy games, game states can repeat, and the same state can result from many different sets of moves. Because running the evaluation function of a game state is often a critical performance factor, we want to minimize the use of this function.

In the case of chess, we can cache the contents of every board state that has previously been evaluated. Before evaluating any new board, the board can be compared against the list of cached boards, and the evaluation can be avoided if the board is already in the list. Searching the list is a linear operation, but the performance can be improved to around constant-time by using a hash.

The Zobrist Hash

The Zobrist hash is a way of rapidly calculating the hash key of a game state from the hash key of a previous game state [Zobrist70]. The Zobrist hash is not a specific type of hash function, but a way to generate keys based on the game state that are incredibly good for hashing. A few of the key points of the Zobrist hash include:

- It is implemented with simple, fast operations.
- Operations can be undone without recalculating the entire hash.
- Collisions are reduced because similar game states result in very different keys.

The exact details of implementing a Zobrist hash tend to vary from application to application, but the concept is the same. Take the game state and combine together random numbers representing parameters of that game state. The combination should be done using a fast math operation. The operation should be associative and commutative, so that operations can be undone in an arbitrary order. Random numbers are used so that similar states will generally have several bits of difference in the hash key.

For example, to generate the Zobrist key for the set of pawns on a chessboard, assign a random number to each square on the chessboard, and then add together the values of all of the positions where pawns sit.

Now consider the act of moving one of those pawns. The beauty of the Zobrist hash is that it allows a new key to be created without much work. Simply subtract the current pawn position value from the current key, and add in the new position's value. Because of the properties of addition, this generates the same key as if the full hash key had been computed. This saves a great deal of time when building search trees.

Implementation of the Zobrist Hash

In chess, a 64-bit key is generally used. Although there are more than 2^{64} valid positions on a chessboard, the number of searchable positions is far smaller, so a 64-bit key gives enough room with which to work.

An n-dimensional *Zobrist table* is constructed and filled with 64-bit random numbers. The number of dimensions depends on the number of game state parameters that are under consideration. The parameters usually considered for chess are piece position, piece type, and piece color. The color to move next could also be a dimension of the table, but since it is a state of the game board, and not a state of each game piece, an added dimension is not warranted. That can be better handled elsewhere.

```
uint64_t m_aZobristTable[BOARD_SIZE]
    [NUM_PIECES]
    [NUM_COLORS];
```

An exclusive-or function is used to combine the piece parameters together. Exclusive-or has the advantage of being reversible using the same inputs. Iterate over all of the pieces on the board, and exclusive-or together values from the Zobrist table using the position, piece type, and color as indices.

```
uZobristKey ^= m_aZobristTable[pos][piece][color];
```

Since the piece values are exclusive-ored together, a fast way to move a game piece is to exclusive-or the value of the old position into the key, and then exclusive-or the value of the new position into the key.

Once the key is created, a 64-bit constant should be exclusive-ored into the key if the current player is black. Alternatively, the constant could always be exclusive-ored in to change the current player. While the side to move could be encoded as a dimension in the Zobrist table, as piece color is, using a constant allows the side to move to be quickly toggled without calculating a complete hash key.

Once the Zobrist key is calculated, the easiest way to use it as a hash key is as an address modulo the size of the hash table. Collisions are rare enough that they are sometimes ignored in practice, which trades off some robustness to gain a speed advantage. In general, when using a Zobrist hash, the primary cause of collisions is that the hash table is too small. The hash table should be as large as physical memory permits without overrunning into virtual memory.

The reason for the minimal number of hash table collisions has to deal with the choice of numbers in the Zobrist table. Because of the use of random numbers, moving a single game piece results in a radically different Zobrist key. These numbers can be carefully chosen, but it is just as valid to use highly random numbers. The C `rand()` function has often been used for generating Zobrist table values. However, the `rand()` function is not actually very random, and it only generates 15-bit numbers. We would prefer a fast, 64-bit, "more random" function.

Mersenne Twister

The Mersenne Twister is a fast pseudorandom number generator that has an extremely long period and high order of equidistribution. While there is no mathematical definition of pseudorandom, the Mersenne Twister does satisfy a number of tests, including the k-distribution test, which is commonly considered a strong pseudorandomness test.

The Mersenne Twister has several nice properties:

- Implementations are easily adapted to generation of 64-bit numbers.
- A 623 dimensional equidistribution property ensures that all bits of a generated number are fairly random.
- It has a huge period of $2^{19937} - 1$, which is the length before repetitions occur.
- It is implemented with simple, fast operations, with consideration to caching, and many implementations are far faster than `rand()`.

These are all great properties for any general-purpose random number generator, but for use with the Zobrist hash, only the first two properties are critical.

Previous generators were flawed in various ways, and the Mersenne Twister was specifically designed to address some of these flaws. It is based on the linear recurrence

$$x_{k+n} = x_{k+m} \oplus \left(x_k^u \middle| x_{k+1}^\lambda \right) A \tag{2.4.1}$$

x is a w-bit word. x_k^u represents the upper w-r bits of x_k, and x_{k+1}^λ represents the lower r bits of x_{k+1}. Exclusive-or and concatenation correspond to $\oplus$ and $|$, respectively. w, r, m, n, and A are all constant parameters.

A is a $w \times w$ matrix of the form

$$\begin{pmatrix} 0 & I_{w-1} \\ a_{w-1} & a \end{pmatrix} \quad (2.4.2)$$

I_{w-1} is an identity matrix, and a is a vector representing $a_{w-2} \ldots a_0$. While all of the Mersenne Twister parameters affect the properties of the generated numbers, this matrix form was chosen because it allows the implementation to be done with fast bit operations.

Each generated word is tempered with transformations to improve the k-distribution:

$$\begin{aligned} y &= x \oplus (x \gg u) \\ y &= y \oplus ((y \ll s) \cap b) \\ y &= y \oplus ((y \ll t) \cap c) \\ y &= y \oplus (y \gg l) \end{aligned} \quad (2.4.3)$$

u, s, t, l, b, and c are all constant parameters of the Mersenne Twister implementation. << and >> are left and right shifts, and $\cap$ is a bitwise AND.

The Mersenne Twister is a parameterized algorithm, and how the parameters are specified will determine the properties of the random numbers. The recommended implementation is MT19937, which defines the parameters as follows:

$$\begin{aligned} &w = 32, n = 624, m = 397, r = 31, \\ &u = 11, s = 7, t = 15, l = 18, \\ &A = \text{0x9908B0DF}, \\ &b = \text{0x9D2C5680}, \\ &c = \text{0xEFC60000} \end{aligned} \quad (2.4.4)$$

Implementation of the Mersenne Twister

To start, a 624-element array, `s_aMT`, is seeded with 32-bit numbers. Any numbers are valid for this array except for all zeros.

Using `m_ix` as an index into `s_aMT`, a 32-bit random number is calculated like this:

```
static const int   MT_W = 32;
static const int      MT_N = 624;
static const int      MT_M = 397;
static const int      MT_R = 31;
```

```
static const uint32_t MT_A = 0x9908b0df;
static const int      MT_U = 11;
static const int      MT_S = 7;
static const uint32_t MT_B = 0x9d2c5680;
static const int      MT_T = 15;
static const uint32_t MT_C = 0xefc60000;
static const int      MT_L = 18;
static const uint32_t MT_LLMASK = 0x7fffffff;
static const uint32_t MT_UMASK = 0x80000000;

uint32_t y;
y = s_aMT[m_ix++];
y ^= y >> MT_U;
y ^= y << MT_S & MT_B;
y ^= y << MT_T & MT_C;
y ^= y >> MT_L;
```

After exhausting all 624 numbers in the array, the array needs to be reloaded. This is perhaps the most complex part of the Mersenne Twister.

```
for(int kk = 0; kk < MT_N; kk++)
{
    uint32_t ui = (s_aMT[kk] & MT_UMASK) |
        (s_aMT[(kk + 1) % MT_N] & MT_LLMASK);
    s_aMT[kk] = s_aMT[(kk + MT_M) % MT_N] ^
        (ui >> 1) ^ ((ui & 0x00000001) ? MT_A : 0);
}
```

In practical implementations, the loop is usually unwound to eliminate the modulus operators.

The Mersenne Twister is not cryptographically strong, although it has a number of good uses, including noise generation or as a fast replacement for `rand()`. Because of its high order of equidistribution, it can be a good choice for populating the Zobrist table, which requires highly random numbers.

Conclusion

The use of a Zobrist hash is a good way to trim the amount of repeated evaluations of a game state. This opens the door to more complex evaluation functions and smarter AI. The Mersenne Twister is a great replacement for `rand()` because it is fast and robust. The algorithm is great when partnered with the Zobrist hash, but it also stands alone for use in other applications.

References

[Zobrist70] Zobrist, A. L., "A New Hashing Method with Application for Game Playing," Technical Report 88, University of Wisconsin, April 1970.

2.5

Solving Accuracy Problems in Large World Coordinates

Peter Freese, Hidden Path Entertainment

peter@hiddenpath.com

Developers creating extremely large continuous worlds will ultimately run into problems due to floating-point accuracy. Nearly every gaming platform uses 32-bit floating-point numbers for coordinates, yet floats cannot represent areas larger than the typical first-person shooter level without significant accuracy errors at larger coordinate values. This article presents a technique for dealing with large coordinates that is fast, efficient, and does not require switching to double precision numbers.

In this technique, world space positions, which normally consist of three floating-point components, are extended to contain an integer *segment*, which allows the *offset*, or traditional position, to be normalized within a desired accuracy range. The names "segment" and "offset" are borrowed from segmented processor address space notation, and many of the concepts, such as renormalization, are similar.

Problem Description

The IEEE 754 standard for binary floating-point arithmetic defines what is commonly referred to as *IEEE floating point* [Goldberg91]. In single-precision 32-bit IEEE format, one bit is designated as the sign bit, the next 8 bits are the exponent field, and the last 23 bits are the fractional parts of the normalized number (see Table 2.5.1).

TABLE 2.5.1 IEEE Floating-Point Bit Layout

Sign	Exponent	Fraction (Mantissa)
S	EEEEEEEE	FFFFFFFFFFFFFFFFFFFFFFF

The accuracy for any given 32-bit floating-point number is equivalent to half the place value, or granularity, of the least significant bit (LSB) of the mantissa for a particular exponent. Since the place value of the leading 1 is 2^E (ignoring the exponent bias) and there are 23 bits of fraction, the place value for the LSB is 2^{E-24}. Very near 1, for example, the granularity is 2^{-24}, or approximately 0.0000001192. At values near 1,000, granularity increases to 0.000061 (2^{-13}), and at values near 100,000, granularity is 0.0078125 (2^{-7}). To put it in practical terms: if units represent meters and our world is 100km square, at the farthest corner of our world, a 32-bit floating point will only allow us to represent space with 7.8mm granularity. The larger the coordinates we need to represent, the less will be our accuracy at its farthest extents. To represent an area the size of the continental United States (approximately 4,500 kilometers east to west), you would be limited to half-meter granularity at the coast farthest from the origin (see Figure 2.5.1).

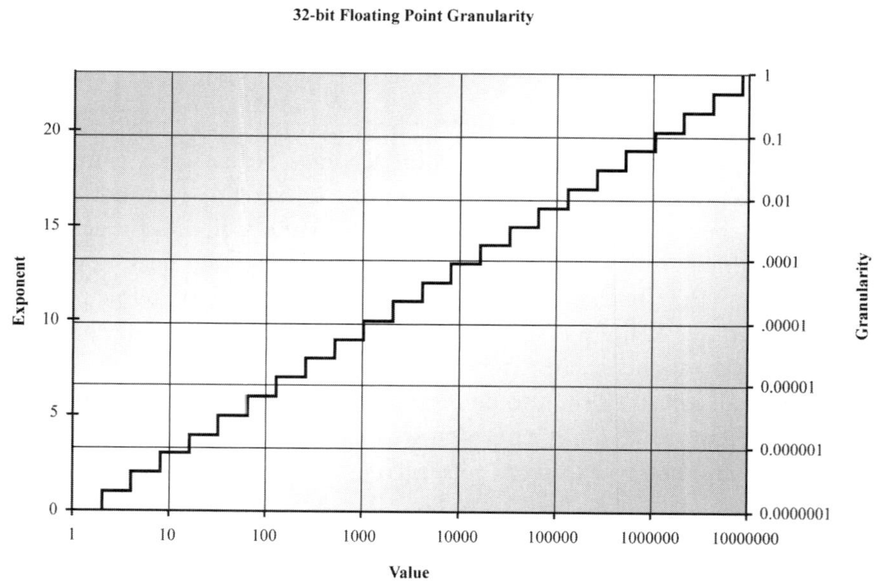

FIGURE 2.5.1 Floating-point granularity.

Symptoms of Accuracy Errors

Does this mean you don't have to worry about accuracy if you're creating an outdoor area only a few kilometers across? Unfortunately, symptoms of accuracy errors can manifest themselves even with numbers that are ostensibly within range to provide more than adequate accuracy. The primary reason for this is that we are most often not simply using numbers to describe positions, but using them in calculations where errors can become amplified. Hierarchical object graphs, such as model skeletons, often rely on a chain of matrix multiplies to determine the position and orientation of a mesh in camera space. After concatenating several matrix multiplies, an accuracy error that would normally be insignificant might have increased to the point at which it introduces visual discontinuities or changes the behavior of a physics simulation.

While it is possible to precisely calculate the amount of error introduced at each step in a set of mathematical operations [Wilkinson94], and thereby determine the maximal error introduced in order to decide whether it is a problem worth solving, it is a rigorous and laborious process. It is far more straightforward to simply deal with the problem of accuracy if and when it becomes apparent. Here are some telltale symptoms of accuracy errors:

- **Inability to align adjacent objects.** This is a symptom of the grossest errors, in that you are actually prevented from setting objects at desired positions or orientations due to numeric granularity. This will be more likely to occur on objects at odd angles.
- **Cracks in mesh seams.** This is a more subtle variation of the first problem, but one in which very slight errors can be visible. Adjacent terrain meshes might exhibit cracks on seams that use coincident geometry, showing sky or fill color through the seams. Character models composed of multiple wearable meshes might fail to completely close, showing ugly gaps.
- **Jittering animations.** Models with skeletal animation might appear to quiver or shake; this will be particularly noticeable when the animations are subtle and don't involve large-scale movement, such as idle animations. The jittering will be more pronounced on bones farther from the skeletal root, such as hands and feet. Foot bones might fail to track properly to ground movement.
- **Collision errors.** All physics systems are subject to numeric instability, but problems can be greatly exaggerated at large coordinates. Similarly, transforms involve matrix inversions, which can cause coordinate accuracy errors to greatly increase in magnitude. Intersection tests can produce large errors that are highly dependent on order of operations. Object A might report that it is penetrating object B, but the reverse test might indicate that B is still some distance from A.

All of these errors can be identified with large numerical values if they are manifest at bigger coordinates, but nonexistent near the world coordinate origin. If you see jittering characters at coordinates (15356, 9436) but animations all look perfect at (0, 0), you can be almost certain your renderer is suffering from floating-point accuracy issues.

Many of the rendering errors described previously can be greatly exaggerated by graphics hardware. To achieve maximum performance, most GPUs perform math in reduced precision modes, such as 24-bit or 16-bit floating-point formats. The s16e7 24-bit format uses a 16-bit mantissa, which is 7 fewer bits than single precision floats. This means that accuracy granularity is 2^7, or 128 times larger. Granularity is yet another 64 times larger for the s10e5 16-bit format.

TABLE 2.5.2 Granularity at Some Common Multiples of Ten

Value	E	23-bit Mantissa	16-bit Mantissa	10-bit Mantissa
1	0	0.00000012	0.00001526	0.00097656
10	3	0.00000095	0.00012207	0.00781250
100	6	0.00000763	0.00097656	0.06250000
1000	9	0.00006104	0.00781250	0.50000000
10000	13	0.00097656	0.12500000	8.00000000
100000	16	0.00781250	1.00000000	64.00000000
1000000	19	0.06250000	8.00000000	512.00000000

It is important to note that the choice of unit has no impact on accuracy errors. In other words, whether you choose a unit measure of one kilometer, one meter, or one millimeter makes no difference as to the scale at which accuracy errors become problematic. As shown in Table 2.5.2, accuracy errors are measured in the same units as the values they are associated with, depending only on the scale of the numbers. If you measure your world in meters, you'll experience the same errors at 10,000 meters as you would at 10 kilometers had you chosen kilometers as your units instead.

Potential Solutions

An ideal solution to floating-point accuracy issues should exhibit the following properties:

- **Improved coordinate precision.** Object placement should not suffer from accuracy granularity dependent on location.
- **Reduction in arithmetic errors.** Numeric manipulation, such as rotational transformation or computation of distance vectors, should not suffer from additional accuracy loss.
- **Minimal performance impact.** Performance overhead should not significantly impact typical operations, such as rendering, collision detection, and picking.
- **Compatibility with graphics pipelines.** We'd like to be able to hand the results of calculations to graphics hardware in a friendly manner, preferably retaining native numerical format.

There are several alternate ways of dealing with accuracy issues that deserve mentioning before we proceed to the solution that is the focus of this article. In some circumstances, they might be appropriate solutions that have minimal code impact.

Larger Float Types

The most tempting solution to accuracy issues is to simply adopt larger float types. IEEE double precision 64-bit floats use a 52-bit mantissa, more than twice the 23 bits of precision in single precision floats. The extra 29 bits increase relative accuracy by a factor of 536,870,912. Whether switching to double precision floats is feasible depends entirely on your platform. Modern consumer CPUs are capable of performing floating-point calculations in single and double precision modes. However, there is a significant performance benefit for calculating in lower precision, which is why most games switch the FPU state to single precision mode and leave it there for the duration of execution. Single precision floats also have half the storage overhead of doubles, which can be significant for highly detailed geometry. Finally, most graphics APIs deal exclusively with single precision floats, and graphics hardware might internally operate at even lower precisions. Even if you could successfully switch your engine to use double precision floats, accuracy issues will still crop up if the graphics hardware does transformations with lower precision.

Eliminating the World Space Transformation

Most graphics pipelines involve a sequential set of transformations applied to vertices similar to the following:

$$M_{world} \rightarrow M_{view} \rightarrow M_{projection}$$

The world transformation (M_{world}) changes coordinates from model space, where vertices are defined relative to a model's local origin, to world space, where vertices are defined relative to an origin common to all the objects in a scene. In essence, the world transformation places a model into the world, hence its name. The view transformation (M_{view}) locates the viewer in world space, transforming vertices into camera space. The view matrix relocates the objects in the world around a camera's position—the origin of camera space—and orientation. At large coordinates, both M_{world} and M_{view} can contain accuracy errors.

Many engines will submit M_{world}, M_{view}, and $M_{projection}$ independently to their rendering pipeline, or M_{world} and a concatenation of $M_{viewprojection}$. By concatenating M_{world} and M_{view} as early as possible, however, and then submitting $M_{worldview}$ and $M_{projection}$, many accuracy issues can be bypassed. This is particularly applicable to solving animation jitter. For example, in a skeletal hierarchy, vertices go through the following transformations:

$$\left[M_{bone} \times M_{parentbone} \times \ldots \times M_{rootbone}\right] \rightarrow M_{view} \rightarrow M_{projection}$$

Normally, all the bone transformations are concatenated left to right, up the hierarchy, resulting in a set of matrices that transform vertices into world space where they can be blended, lit, and so forth. If the root bone matrix $M_{rootbone}$ is combined with the view matrix M_{view} before being concatenated to the child bone transformations, rendering accuracy errors can be isolated to a single operation, combining the root bone and view matrix:

$$\left[M_{bone} \times M_{parentbone} \times \ldots \times \left(M_{rootbone} \times M_{view}\right)\right] \rightarrow M_{projection}$$

For pipelines that require a discrete view matrix to be submitted, the geometry can be submitted with an identity view matrix. All vertex blending, lighting, and primitive calculations are then done in view space, with no additional accuracy errors.

While this can mitigate some of the more conspicuous visual problems in animations, and serves well as an eleventh hour solution for accuracy issues, it fails to solve the basic problem, which is that there simply isn't enough accuracy to represent positions in the world. Furthermore, it introduces an additional CPU level transformation on every mesh whenever the view matrix changes—essentially every time the camera moves.

Far Positions

The solution presented in this article addresses all the requirements outlined previously, and essentially involves a hybrid between fixed-point and floating-point numbers. Position vectors, normally consisting of three floating-point numbers, are extended with an additional integer component representing a floating origin. Because of the way that this data representation resembles the manner in which segmented addresses extended the address space of early 32-bit processors, the components are termed *segment* and *offset*, and the hybrid is called a *far position*. Complete code for the classes and data structures outlined here appears on the companion CD-ROM. For clarity, abbreviated definitions are used here in the text.

ON THE CD

```
class FarPosition
{
private:
    FarSegment m_segment;
    Vector3    m_offset;
    static float      s_segmentSize;
};
```

All positions in space are measured relative to some conceptual fixed point that we call the origin. Because the granularity of floating-point numbers is magnitude dependent, the farther we are from the origin, the greater the granularity. By repositioning the origin so that it is nearer to the position we are measuring, we can reduce the granularity of our measurements. Far positions allow the origin to be repositioned dynamically, maximizing available precision. The segment component of a far position represents an origin in 2D space, which in this case is the XZ plane, assuming a world model in which altitude is represented by the y-axis. The choice was made to limit the segment to the XZ plane because accuracy errors in outdoor rendering environments result from magnitude in horizontal location, not altitude.

Figure 2.5.2 illustrates how a particular segment might exist relative to the world origin. The segment space consists of all points relative to the segment origin. Because we are concerned with making the most use of available precision, we normalize positions so that normalized segment space consists of only those offsets within a segment size of the segment origin (shown in gray).

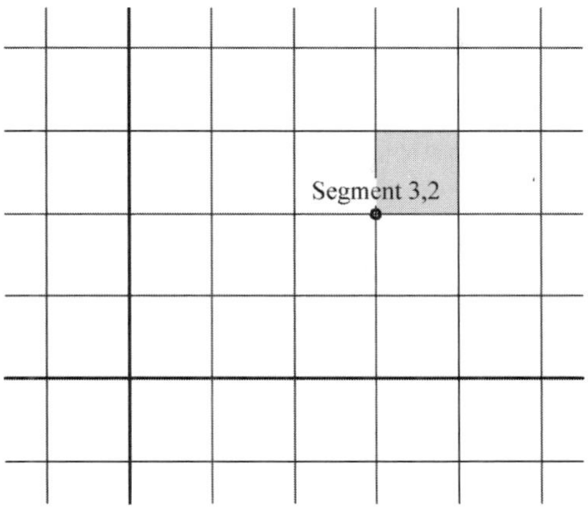

FIGURE 2.5.2 Example segment layout.

Choosing a Segment Size

The choice of units for segment size is somewhat arbitrary. Since this will be encoded in a global constant, it allows us to balance the accuracy we desire with the maximum expressible range and renormalization overhead. When offsets are renormalized, they are limited to a range of up to one segment size; this allows us to put a clamp on the maximum allowable accuracy error. A value of 1024.0f provides a reasonable range for a unit choice of meters for a typical human avatar based outdoor environment. Different choices for units or scale will affect the choice for segment size.

Since the segment value expresses the origin for the offset in integer units, the choice of 1024.0f for segment size gives quite a large working range. We can express the segment with a signed 16-bit value, giving us a maximum expressible segment range of ±33553408.0f (32767 * 1024.0f); this is more than enough to represent a flat projection of the entire earth's surface.

By packing two 16-bit segment coordinates into a 32-bit value, the size of the `FarPosition` structure (which includes three floating-point numbers representing offset) totals 16 bytes, a size friendly to structure alignment and packing. Here is how we define `FarSegments`:

```
union FarSegment
{
      struct
      {
            int16    x, z;
      };

      int32          xz;

      matFarSegment() {};
      matFarSegment( ZeroType ) : xz(0) {};
};
```

The union allows us to treat `FarSegments` as a single 32-bit value, which makes for very simple and fast initializations and comparisons. The `ZeroType` initializer provides a type-based overload for initializing to a known state, which allows us to conveniently provide both an explicit initializing constructor and an empty constructor (useful for storing in standard container classes).

Renormalization Details

The representation of world positions with far positions is straightforward enough, but we need a means of both encoding traditional positions as far positions and converting back. Converting a far position into a traditional vector representation is fairly straightforward; we simply need to add the offset and the segment scaled appropriately by the segment size:

```
Vector3 FarPosition::GetApproximateVector() const
{
    Vector3 v = m_offset;
    v.x += m_segment.x * s_segmentSize;
    v.z += m_segment.z * s_segmentSize;

    return v;
}
```

There is a catch to this simplicity, however. Performing this operation leaves the result in the range of standard floating-point representations, thus in the realm of reduced precision. Conversion operations should be minimized, and only performed when necessary. This is advertised by the name of the member function: `GetApproximateVector()`.

Converting to far positions from traditional representations involves only slightly more work:

```
void SetFromVector( const Vector3& vector )
{
    m_segment.xz = 0;
    m_offset = vector;
    Normalize();
}
```

When we initially store the vector, the far position is in an unnormalized state. The magnitude of the offset is unknown, and could be far larger than what we have determined is an appropriate segment size. Therefore, we invoke a normalization process on the far position:

```
void FarPosition::Normalize()
{
    if ( fabsf(m_offset.x) >= s_segmentSize )
    {
        m_segment.x += FloatToInt(m_offset.x / s_segmentSize);
        m_offset.x = fmodf(m_offset.x, s_segmentSize);
    }
```

```
        if ( fabsf(m_offset.z) >= s_segmentSize )
        {
            m_segment.z += FloatToInt(m_offset.z / s_segmentSize);
            m_offset.z = fmodf(m_offset.z, s_segmentSize);
        }
    }
```

After normalization, the offset *x* and *z* components will be in the range (–`s_segmentSize`, +`s_segmentSize`). Note that the process involves a float-to-integer conversion, so you should use standard optimization tricks for fast conversion.

When converting from Vector3 representations to far positions, the result will only be as accurate as the initial Vector3. To take advantage of the increased accuracy available to us, we need to use far positions for all absolute position representations, not just at render time. This means that object locations should be persisted as far positions, and editors should manipulate objects with far positions. Any time we convert absolute locations to three float vectors, we lose accuracy that cannot be recovered.

Because normalization is based solely on the magnitude of the offset, we can combine it with operations on far positions that might result in unnormalized offsets:

```
void FarPosition::Translate( const Vector3& vector )
{
    m_offset += vector;
    Normalize();
}
```

A key behavior of far positions is the ability to provide their offset relative to a specific segment. This method looks like this:

```
Vector3 FarPosition::GetRelativeVector( const FarSegment& segment )
const
{
    Vector3 r = m_offset;
    r.x += (m_segment.x - segment.x) * s_segmentSize;
    r.z += (m_segment.z - segment.z) * s_segmentSize;
    return r;
}
```

The need for this will become evident when we discuss how far positions fit into the rendering pipeline.

We can measure the distance between two far positions by adding the difference between the offsets and the segments (appropriately scaled):

```
Vector3 operator-( const FarPosition &lhs, const FarPosition &rhs )
{
    matVector3 r = lhs_offset - rhs.m_offset;
    r.x += (lhs.m_segment.x - rhs.m_segment.x) * s_segmentSize;
    r.z += (lhs.m_segment.z - rhs.m_segment.z) * s_segmentSize;
    return r;
}
```

If we want the scalar distance between two far positions, we can simply take the scalar length of the vector returned.

Note that this operation could have been performed by first converting both far positions to world space Vector3 coordinates, and then doing a standard vector subtraction. Doing so, however, could have introduced precision loss, which should be obvious when you consider what happens if the positions are far from the origin.

If the distance between the points is large, a Vector3 might still be incapable of representing the distance vector without accuracy errors. This is probably acceptable, since we are seldom concerned with interactions between objects that are far away from each other. If we need to simply determine the distance between two points, a result with a maximum relative rather than absolute error is usually sufficient.

Render Pipeline Changes

Now that we have a means of representing positions with greatly increased accuracy, how do we make use of it in a rendering pipeline? Rendering engines deal with matrix transformations, not position vectors. How do we create matrices that minimize accuracy errors? The answer turns out to be fairly straightforward: we generate all matrices in the same *segment space*. The devil is in the details, however.

First, let's consider how we represent positions and orientations normally. One natural way of doing this is with a Vector3, representing position, and a quaternion, representing orientation:

```
class Transform
{

private:
     Quaternion        m_quaternion;
     Vector3   m_position;

     mutable Matrix4x4 m_matrix;
};
```

Such a class might also be able to lazily generate a 4×4 matrix on demand, caching the results within the object. We can wrap this class in a new one capable of representing a transform with far positions:

```
class FarTransform
{
public:
    void SetBasisSegment( FarSegment segment );
    const matTransform& GetLocalTransform() const;
    mutable bool      m_bPositionDirty;
    mutable FarSegment m_basisSegment;
};
```

This class combines a local transform with a far position and a *basis segment*. The basis segment is the segment space in which the local transform exists. By generating all rendering transforms, thus all matrices, in the same basis segment or segment space, rendering can proceed as normal. For this to work, all root objects in the scene graph, including the camera, will need to use `FarTransforms`. Nonroot objects, such as individual bone transforms, can continue to use standard transformation representations, since the offsets they contain relative to their parents are usually minimal. This also avoids any additional performance overhead of far positions except where it is necessary.

Lazy Basis Renormalization

What basis segment should we use? The answer depends somewhat on our usage pattern. If we are rendering, choosing a basis segment based on the camera position is the natural choice. If the camera is in motion (which it invariably is), then the segment from the normalized camera position will change only when the camera has moved a distance greater than the segment size. Because we allow the offset to extend both a positive and negative distance from the segment origin, we avoid changing segments unnecessarily when camera motion is in a pathological case, such as tightly orbiting a segment origin.

If we are not concerned with rendering, but instead with interaction among many objects in a region of space (for example, a server dealing with a region in a continuous large world), then choosing a fixed basis segment at the center of the region of interest makes more sense. All objects within the region can be operated on with local transforms, which minimizes accuracy errors.

What happens when the basis segment changes? The first thing to note is that we must make sure that any object we are rendering has a local transform relative to the current basis segment. This can be done by tracking the last basis segment used for the object, as we do for a `FarTransform`. Setting a basis segment that is different from the current one invalidates the local transform:

```
void FarTransform::SetBasisSegment( FarSegment segment )
{
    if ( segment != m_basisSegment )
    {
        m_bPositionDirty = true;
        m_basisSegment = segment;
    }
}
```

When we subsequently request the local transform, the dirty flag is checked, and if set, the local transform is repositioned relative to the new basis segment:

```
const Transform& FarTransform::GetLocalTransform() const
{
    if ( m_bPositionDirty )
    {
        // store position
        m_localTransform.SetPosition(
```

```
            m_position.GetRelativeVector(m_basisSegment));
        m_bPositionDirty = false;
    }
    return m_localTransform;
}
```

World Space vs. Local Space

One of the biggest hurdles in integrating far positions is that we can no longer talk about world space in any meaningful fashion except when dealing specifically with entities incorporating a far position; all other positional representations are relative to the current basis segment. We cannot mix operations on two local transforms unless they are in the same basis segment. If we have a 4×4 matrix or a three-float vector, we know we have a local (basis relative) position or transformation, but we don't know *which* basis it is relative to without inspecting the object that contains it. The notion that everything is relative can cause confusion and is a potential source of bugs.

We also need to distinguish between relative position information and absolute positions when doing calculations. We use far positions to represent absolute positions, and Vector3s to represent relative positions (offsets). This definition puts certain operations off limits to us. For example, we don't have an operator to add two far positions together. Besides the fact that the domain of the result doesn't make sense, providing such an operator puts us at risk of segment overflow. Consider the results, for example, if we elected to independently sum the segment coordinates and offsets for several hundred objects. This might be needed to find the average position of the objects. The segment values could easily overflow the available range. The correct way to handle this problem is to choose a segment in which to sum all of the relative offsets:

```
typedef vector<FarPosition> VFP;
FarPosition FindAveragePosition( const VFP &positions )
{
    if ( positions.empty() )
        return FarPosition(Zero);

    FarSegment segment = positions.front().GetSegment();
    Vector3 offset(Zero);
    for ( VFP::iterator it = positions.begin(); it !=
positions.end(); ++it )
    {
        offset += it->GetRelativeVector(segment);
    }

    FarPosition average;
    average.SetSegment(segment);
    average.SetOffset(offset / positions.size());
    average.Normalize();
    return average;
}
```

This function uses the segment from the first position in the vector as a reference segment. It then sums the relative positions of each of the positions in that segment space. The result should be precise even for thousands of positions, provided they are fairly local. The pathological case of millions of distant objects will work properly without overflow, but will be subject to the same accuracy restrictions of traditional offsets. This is not a significant limitation, as the need for interactions between such remote positions is almost nonexistent.

Translation into Local Space

Often, we will have some construct in absolute world space and we need to translate it into the local space of a nonroot scene graph node. We might need to do this for a collision intersection test or pick ray intersection. In the case of a pick ray, we would start out with a ray origin expressed as a far position, a ray direction that can be expressed as a normal Vector3, and a scalar maximum pick distance. Transforming this into the local object space represented by a `FarTransform` consists of two steps: transforming the ray origin, and transforming the ray direction. Transforming the ray direction is straightforward:

```
// inputs:
// Vector3 vDir = world direction
// FarTransform transform
Transform& localTransform = transform.GetLocalTransform();
Matrix4x4& invMatrix = localTransform.GetInverseMatrix();
Vector3 localDir = invMatrix.TransformVector(vDir);
```

This is identical to the process we would use if we weren't using far positions. Transforming the ray origin involves only a minor change to the normal process:

```
// inputs:
// FarPosition vOrg
Vector3 relOrg = vOrg.GetRelativeVector(transform.GetBasisSegment());
Vector3 localOrg = invMatrix.TransformPoint(relOrg);
```

Before transforming the point by the matrix inverse, we find the position relative to the basis segment of the local transform. It doesn't really matter what this basis segment is; the key thing is that it matches the relative space in which the local transform exists. If we were concerned about maintaining the greatest accuracy in this calculation, we could specifically set the basis segment at the beginning of the operation to the segment from the normalized `FarPosition` in the `FarTransform`. This might be important for systems not involved with rendering that couldn't rely on an appropriate basis segment already being set for the `FarTransform`.

Performance Considerations

There are a few potential pitfalls in implementing far positions. As mentioned previously, maintaining awareness of the relative nature of all transforms is fundamental to avoiding segment-shift bugs. These can be rather insidious, because code that appears to work in simple test cases might fail in the wild when objects, the camera, and the basis segment are all changing.

The performance impact of using far positions is normally quite negligible, for several reasons:

- Normalization tests need only be done on dynamic root node objects, and involve simple floating-point compares.
- For rendering, basis renormalization occurs only when the camera is farther than the segment size along the X- or Z-axis from the origin of the last basis segment used.
- Basis renormalization can be done by simply updating root transform positions. The calculation for this involves just a few integer and floating-point operations.

One potential hitch arises when using multiple cameras to view regions of the world simultaneously. If the cameras are sufficiently remote such that they see completely different sets of objects, the system will work flawlessly. However, if the cameras are near enough to see the same objects, but segments from the camera positions are different, then as each view is rendered, it will update the basis segment in the objects' transforms. The two views will fight over the basis segment to use, and basis renormalization will occur on every render. One case where this might arise is when one camera is used for the user's viewport, and another camera is used to render environment maps for objects within the scene. The solution to this dilemma is to choose a single entity that has control over which basis segment to use for rendering. This could be the primary camera, or it could be based on the position of the player's avatar.

Conclusion

Developers creating large worlds must address problems related to floating-point accuracy. Far positions provide a solution to floating-point accuracy problems that is fast, hardware friendly, and tunable. They don't require higher precision floats or floating-point tricks. They do require a fundamental shift in thinking with regard to what world space means.

References

[Goldberg91] Goldberg, David, "What Every Computer Scientist Should Know About Floating-Point Arithmetic," *ACM Computing Surveys*, March 1991.

[Wilkinson94] Wilkinson, James H., *Rounding Errors in Algebraic Processes*, Dover Publications, 1994.

2.6

Writing a Verlet-Based Physics Engine

Nick Porcino, Industrial Light & Magic

nporcino@ilm.com

Games often sport a physical process that needs to be modeled—weather, crates, vehicles, mechanical systems, characters, and so on. If the process can be modeled with equations, an algorithm can be derived to simulate the process. A class of systems of particular interest for games is rigid body dynamics. Such a simulator models systems of rigid bodies that have physical properties, can contact each other, and collide. Soft bodies such as cloth and hair can co-exist in such a simulation. Forces can be input to the system during a frame, making the simulation particularly interesting.

It can be much easier than you might think to implement a reasonably accurate and sophisticated physics engine. This article describes how it can be done through the description of a simple engine, included on the companion CD-ROM.

ON THE CD

About Physics Engines

There are several kinds of simulation: *offline*, wherein the simulation proceeds slower than the real thing; *online*, which runs as fast as the real thing; *interactive*, which runs fast enough that a person can interact with the simulation from within the loop; and *real-time*, which guarantees that a system will be updated at a certain rate. The physics engine presented here is interactive if there are not too many objects in the simulation.

A game has a number of other components besides a physics engine, including rendering, file systems, AI, and so on. A physics engine provides none of those things, and should have no direct interaction with them. In other words, an AI system or rendering system can query the physics engine to retrieve such things as a body's transformation matrix, but the physics engine does not provide AI facilities or rendering functions.

Most of the literature on physics engines for games focuses either on Verlet integration for nonrigid bodies (such as cloth or rag-dolls) modeled as spring systems [Jakobsen03], or the solution of ordinary differential equations for rigid bodies [Hecker96], [Baraff97]. This article shows that with the incorporation of angular effects, the Verlet integrator can also be applied to rigid body simulations. Furthermore, most presentations of collision within physics engines focus on constraint methods [Smith04] or penalty systems [Jakobsen03]. The engine presented in this article uses the relatively recent technique of impulse-based dynamic simulation and micro-collisions [Mirtich95].

This article does not describe constraint systems, or the simulation of articulated bodies, or the equations of motion. For a grounding in these fundamentals, please refer to Chris Hecker's [Hecker96] or David Baraff's excellent series of articles [Baraff97]. [Smith04] contains a discussion on constraint Jacobians.

Rigid Bodies

A rigid body object is a collection of dynamic and static properties. The dynamic properties of the object are its position and velocity, as well as its orientation, angular velocity, and angular momentum. The static properties of an object are its dimensions, mass, inertia tensor, velocity damping (for friction), and information used for collision calculations. The inertia tensor is a triple integral over the body's volume and mass; it must be recalculated whenever the mass or shape of the body changes. A rigid body object can track other generally useful information such as whether the object can spin, how it participates in collisions, if it is active, and so on.

The dynamic state of the body at the end of the previous time step needs to be tracked while the new dynamic state is built. Forces and torques acting on the body (including friction) are summed into accumulators during a frame for use by the integrator.

The Integrator

There are two major categories of integrators: *implicit* and *explicit*. Implicit integrators must solve a system of equations to determine the present time step, whereas an explicit integrator iterates a system forward using explicit finite differences. The explicit Euler integrator is the simplest of these. The Verlet integrator is a second-order explicit difference based integrator that is created by adding two steps of a Taylor series expansion of the equations of motion, one forward and one backward [Verlet67].

$$x(t+d) = x(t) + v(t)dt + \frac{F(t)dt^2}{2m} + \ldots \tag{2.6.1}$$

$$x(t-d) = x(t) - v(t)dt + \frac{F(t)dt^2}{2m} + \ldots \tag{2.6.2}$$

Adding Equations 2.6.1 and 2.6.2 yields the basic Verlet integrator commonly found in game engines.

$$x(t+dt) = 2x(t) - x(t-dt) + \frac{F(t)dt^2}{m} + O(dt^4) \tag{2.6.3}$$

Equation 2.6.3 requires only object positions; velocities are approximated at each time step. This integrator uses less memory compared to an integrator that explicitly tracks velocities, and has advantages where the velocities cannot be reliably derived. It is particularly suitable for computationally expensive simulations such as cloth and finite element systems. The primary disadvantage of Equation 2.6.3 is that since accelerations due to the application of force are added directly to position and the approximated velocity, the integrator diverges from an accurate solution very quickly.

In many engines, the divergence of the integrator is reduced through heavy damping, but the resulting simulation can suffer noticeably. In particular, energy will rapidly bleed out of the system, making the simulation feel mushy or sloppy. For some applications, such as cloth simulation, the damping of motion is desirable, and the inexpensive computational cost of the basic Verlet integrator is a perfect match. In simulations involving rigid body dynamics, something more robust is in order.

There are two well-known variations of the Verlet integrator: the Leap Frog integrator, and the velocity-based Verlet integrator. The Leap Frog integrator breaks up a single integration step and evaluates the position at the midpoint of the velocity calculation, and the velocity at the midpoint of the position calculation. The Leap Frog integrator offers better numerical precision, but the velocities are still derived instead of explicitly integrated. The velocity-based Verlet integrator explicitly evaluates the position and velocity at each step. It is the most accurate of the Verlet integrators, although it has the added storage cost of the velocities.

The form of the velocity-based Verlet integrator is reminiscent of high school physics.

$$x(t+dt) = x(t) + v(t)dt + \frac{a(t)dt}{2} \tag{2.6.4}$$

In this equation, x is position, t is time, dt is the time step, v is velocity, and a is acceleration. Acceleration is derived from the sum of all the external forces input during the frame, divided by the mass of the object.

$$a = \frac{F}{m} \tag{2.6.5}$$

Forces can come from springs, motors, force fields, gravity, friction, viscosity, and so on.

$$F = F_{external} - \sum_{i=springs} d_i k_i x_i \tag{2.6.6}$$

where the $F_{external}$ term represents externally applied forces except springs, and the rest of the equation describes the springs. The unit length current direction of the spring, *d*, is measured as pointing away from the mass or object connected to the spring, *k* is the spring stiffness coefficient, and *x* is the current length of the spring minus its rest length. If the spring is stretched, it will pull the object in the direction of the spring; if compressed, it will push the object in the opposite direction. A spring damping term, calculated as a per-spring damping constant times the rate at which a spring changed its length during the time step, can be subtracted from Equation 2.6.6.

In reality, the integration step is more complicated than simple high school physics; the velocity update equation includes the calculation of the acceleration at the midpoint, and at the end of the time step.

$$v(t+dt) = v(t) + \frac{\left[a(t) + a(t+dt)\right]dt}{2} \qquad (2.6.7)$$

For soft bodies such as cloth, the integrator's work is done. For rigid bodies, however, there are still the angular effects to integrate. Angular velocity is derived from the angular momentum because the integration of angular momentum is much simpler than the integration of angular velocity [Hecker96]. The angular momentum at the new time step is simply the accumulation of torque times the time step into the angular momentum at the previous time step.

$$L(t+dt) = L(t) + \frac{\left[T(t) + T(t+dt)\right]dt}{2} \qquad (2.6.8)$$

where *L* is the angular momentum, and *T* is the torque. As in the calculation of forces in Equation 2.6.6, springs must be taken into account in the torque term. The attach points of the springs are used to generate the appropriate torques as shown in Figure 2.6.1.

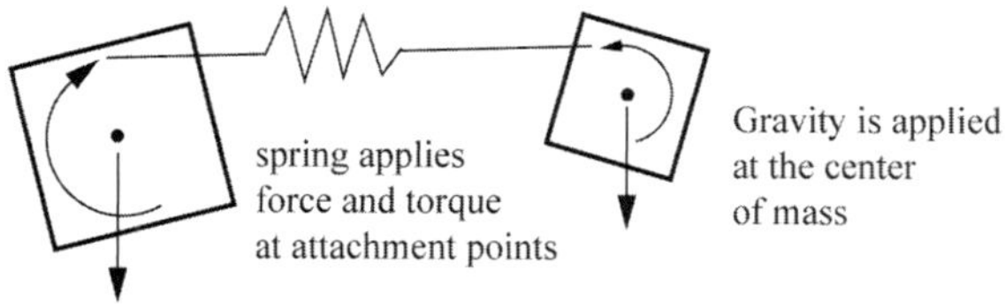

FIGURE 2.6.1 Torques are generated by springs that are not attached at an object's center of mass.

Remember that given a point on a body where a force is applied, the torque is calculated as the cross product of the distance of the point from the center of mass, and the force vector applied at that point. For a rigorous treatment of spring systems in a physics simulator, see [Kaĉić03]. The calculation of angular velocity is as follows:

$$\omega = \frac{\left(RIR^T\right)^{-1} L}{m} \tag{2.6.9}$$

where ω is the angular velocity, *R* is the orientation matrix, *I* is the inertia tensor, *L* is the angular momentum, and *m* is mass. The matrix multiplication in the parentheses moves the inertia tensor from world space to body space. The matrix inversion can be eliminated by pre-inverting the tensor when the rigid body data structure is created. The mass can be divided out at that stage as well. A further optimization is to recognize that dynamically symmetric objects have a tensor with values only on the diagonal, and that spheres have the same value down the diagonal. If those cases are specialized in the integrator, the calculation of angular effects is greatly simplified. The sample code on the companion CD-ROM shows further specialization for quaternions.

ON THE CD

The Physics Engine

The Verlet-based physics engine presented in this article does not support fully general rigid bodies. The following are several simplifications made to improve the system's robustness, minimize the use of system resources, and speed up calculations:

- To simplify the calculation of angular effects, the position of the body corresponds to the center of mass, not the geometric center.
- A full inertia tensor is not maintained; instead, the engine supports only the class of dynamically symmetric bodies (such as boxes, spheres, torii, etc.), for which the inertia tensor is a diagonal matrix. This simplifies the integrator.
- Friction is modeled as a simple opposing force opposite the direction of motion. Surprisingly, Coulomb friction is first-order independent of both speed and area of contact; in Coulomb's model, the force of friction is a function of only the normal force between surfaces.

ON THE CD

Referring to the source code on the companion CD-ROM, the physics engine (PhysicsEngine.h) provides the interface to the rigid bodies, runs the simulation, and resolves collisions. It provides access to the transformation matrix of each of the rigid bodies after the simulation step. Although the position, velocity, and orientation of a rigid body are directly exposed to the user, acceleration, angular velocity, and angular acceleration are not. The reason for this is that the unexposed properties are derived by the engine from initial conditions and force and torque inputs during the frame. These values could be exposed, but in practice, the need doesn't seem to arise often. Figure 2.6.2 illustrates the relationships between the classes used to implement the physics engine.

`PhysicsEngine` is the main interface to the physics engine; `PEAux` is the private implementation. The `RigidBody` has two `DynamicState` objects, and a single `RigidAccumulator`. The static properties of the `RigidBody`, such as mass, are maintained as members of `RigidBody` itself. Note that `PhysicsEngine` does not provide direct access

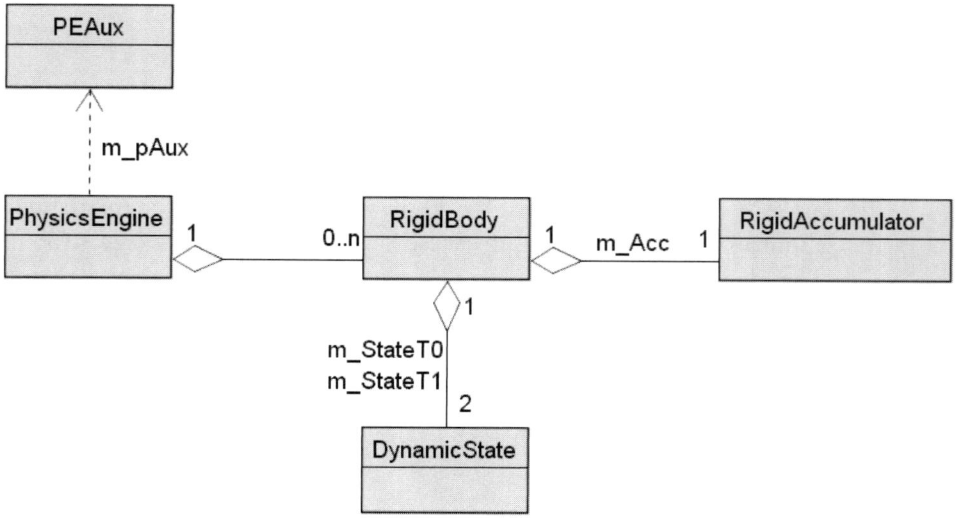

FIGURE 2.6.2 Physics engine classes.

to `RigidBody` object pointers, but instead returns unique identifiers when rigid bodies are created. The game must track all the unique identifiers returned. These identifiers are used to set and get a `RigidBody`'s properties and to retrieve its transformation matrix. This approach is based on the Manager software design pattern.

The Simulation Loop

After adding and initializing all the rigid bodies to the simulation, the application's main loop calls the `PhysicsEngine`'s `Simulate()` method once per frame, supplying the elapsed time since the last invocation. The main loop should clamp the time value at a maximum value, such as 1/20 of a second, so that the simulation remains stable. Similarly, zero should not be passed in as the time step, although very small numbers like 1/120 are fine. A discussion of stability criteria is too lengthy to present here; for more information, see [Kaĉić03].

```
Create rigid bodies and initialize state T1
Simulate
    Copy previous state T1 to state T0
    Velocity += (a * dt) / 2, Equation 2.6.7
    Angular momentum += (T * dt) / 2, Equation 2.6.8
    Calculate position, Equation 2.6.4
    Calculate angular velocity, Equation 2.6.9
    Calculate forces, Equation 2.6.6
    Calculate torques, T, Figure 2.6.1
    Update acceleration, a, Equation 2.6.5
    Velocity += (a * dt) / 2, Equation 2.6.7
    Angular momentum += (T * dt) / 2, Equation 2.6.8
    Collide and Resolve
    Normalize
```

The simulation step is fairly straightforward. First, all internal states are prepared for simulation. Prior to the integration within the `Simulate()` method, a pre-integration step is performed to copy current values to previous, the new values to current, and so on. Then, the equations of motion are integrated. Note that Equations 2.6.7 and 2.6.8 have been broken apart so that forces can be applied, on average, at the midpoint of the integration. If a constraint system is implemented, constraints should also be applied at the midpoint. Collisions (a very specialized form of constraint) are detected and resolved. Internal values are renormalized if necessary to correct for matrices becoming nonorthogonal due to error accumulation and other similar problems.

Collision Detection and Resolution

The `PhysicsEngine` handles collision detection and resolution. For clarity, the version presented here deals with elementary geometry only. In short, all objects are initially not in collision with each other. During the simulation, potential collisions are detected by solving equations describing intersections of swept volumes, and resolved through the application of an instantaneous impulse before movement is applied [Mirtich95]. Since the swept volumes determine the exact point and time of contact, illegal situations are prevented from occurring, and no special resolution heuristics are required (such as stepping backward on the motion path until no collision occurs). The equation governing collision resolution is the impulse calculation derived in part three of [Hecker96],

$$j=\frac{-(1+e)v\cdot n}{n\cdot n\left(M_A^{-1}+M_B^{-1}\right)+\left[\left(I_A^{-1}\left(r_{AP}\times n\right)\right)\times r_{AP}+\left(I_B^{-1}\left(r_{BP}\times n\right)\right)\times r_{BP}\right]\cdot n} \tag{2.6.10}$$

where j is the impulse resulting from the collision, e is the coefficient of restitution, v is the relative velocity between the two bodies, n is the collision normal, M is the mass of bodies A and B, I is the inertia tensor, and r is the vector from the center of mass of bodies A and B to the collision point P.

Since this physics engine relies on impulse-based collision resolution, the engine does not need to switch modes between static and dynamic friction. The engine treats all collisions as dynamic collisions, and deals with sliding contact via micro-collisions [Mirtich95]. This eliminates the calculation of restoring forces. All modes of contact, including continuous contact, are handled by trains of tiny impulses applied to the object, whether they are resting, sliding, or rolling. Under impulse-based simulation, even objects at rest experience tiny rapid collisions with the supporting surface. These collisions are resolved using only information available at the point of contact. When the micro-collision impulses and object's velocity become small enough, the physics engine puts the objects to sleep and doesn't integrate them again until other objects or forces come into play.

In practice, the micro-collision technique converges on the more traditional dynamic/static model [Mirtich95]. It is more numerically stable and robust because there is no discontinuity when switching between different friction modes. All objects go to sleep when they come to rest; in a simulation of a room full of crates it is possible to have hundreds of crates, as they will consume no CPU time until they are moved.

Collision Handling and Game Logic

An application will need to know when two objects have collided with each other. There is a callback interface class provided for that purpose. The callback provides a few interesting values that can be used by the application to determine things like whether a collision was strong enough to break an object. The callback also returns a value to indicate whether the application should respond to the collision. In practice this is very useful, because some collisions might be conditional. For example, alien blood might pass through wood as if it weren't there, but might stop on steel.

The `PhysicsEngine` will report any collisions via the callback object during the simulation step. The application can handle those in any way deemed appropriate, with one exception: the application cannot invoke any `PhysicsEngine` methods, as invalid conditions can result. Finally, after the simulation step, the application can invoke any of the `Get` functions to retrieve the transformation matrices and other useful information associated with each rigid body.

Complex Geometry—A Brief Word

If the `PhysicsEngine` is to be extended with more complex geometry than simple spheres, planes, and boxes, a penalty-based collision resolution method such as that described in [Kaĉić03] is recommended. In such a system, zero-length springs of maximum possible stiffness are introduced at all contact or inter-penetration points, and the system is integrated with small time steps until collisions are resolved to an acceptable degree. These springs are removed when the collision is resolved. The calculation of maximum possible stiffness is related to the stability of the integrator; the reader is referred to [Kaĉić03] for details. Lagrange-multiplier based techniques also work well, as described in [Smith04].

Platform-Specific Considerations

If possible, vector and quaternion objects can be passed by value, not reference. Many Vector3 and quaternion implementations are SIMD: SSE on x86 processors, VU0 on PS2, AltiVec on PPC. Passing by value allows the objects to be passed in a single SIMD register. The example code neglects this optimization and simply uses a Real array. Disassembly reveals that on the current crop of Microsoft and Codewarrior compilers, passing SIMD values by pointer or reference in too many cases invokes unnecessary loads and stores, whereas pass by value is more likely to generate fast code, and is also more likely to optimize operations across function calls. Even so, it is still important to check whether `const` objects passed by value cause the creation of temporaries. Compilers can exhibit better or worse behavior in this regard from version to version.

Extending the Engine

Culling is an important aspect of a physics engine. A typical case that should be dealt with is a portal-based game engine. It doesn't always make sense to iterate physics for an inactive portal region. A unique `PhysicsEngine` could be instantiated for each region; however, a further problem arises. Objects (such as the player character) will sometimes move between regions and thus between `PhysicsEngines`. Removing an object from one engine and putting it in another should be done carefully to avoid discontinuities.

Level of detail could also receive some attention. Many excellent tricks can be implemented here. Gravity can be turned off when an object's upward velocity component is approximately zero (such as a hockey puck momentarily sliding along the ice), eliminating a great deal of collision resolution calculation (the check still needs to be done, but since the object will not have been pushed into the floor by gravity, no resolution is required). Collisions can be reverted to sphere or plane checks to make them less accurate but fast. Collision checks can be turned off entirely. The angular integrator can be switched off. The criteria for putting an object to sleep can be relaxed. Sleeping objects can be left sleeping. In all these cases, objects should be snapped to valid states and positions whenever the LOD changes to a higher level.

A next step in the development of the `PhysicsEngine` would be to incorporate a constraint system. This topic is large enough to warrant its own article. Spring mass systems and articulated figures are nicely described in [Jakobsen03]. Constraint systems are explored in depth by [Smith04].

The collision system could be greatly improved, and generalized, by the incorporation of a sophisticated collision handling system such as OPCODE [Terdiman00]. In this volume, [Moravánszky04] discusses the reduction of contacts for faster processing.

Integration with an animation engine is a fascinating extension, and can be used to achieve rag-doll effects and secondary animation. At some point, the animation engine is turned off, and the physics engine takes over. At that moment, a few quantities need to be derived for use by the physics. Velocities are easy to derive given two previous frames of animation and the time step, but angular momentum is a bigger challenge, and beyond the scope of this article. To get started, model a figure's articulated pieces with primitives the physics engine already knows about such as cylinders and cubes. For more information, see [Baraff97].

Conclusion

This article presented a physics engine incorporating a number of interesting techniques. The velocity-based Verlet integrator for both rigid and soft body dynamics was introduced and streamlined for games applications. Impulse-based dynamic simulation with micro-collisions was described. Most of all, the author hopes to have dispelled some of the mystique surrounding physics engines by showing solutions to many common pitfalls, and by showing how easy it really is to write one from scratch, including such difficult aspects as integration of angular movement.

References

[Baraff97] Baraff, David, "Physically Based Modeling, Principles and Practice, Online SIGGRAPH '97 Course Notes," available online at http://www.cs.cmu.edu/~baraff/sigcourse/index.html, 1997.

[Hecker96] Hecker, Chris, *Game Developer Magazine Physics Series*, available online at www.d6.com/users/checker/dynamics.htm, October 1996–June 1997.

[Jakobsen03] Jakobsen, Thomas, "Advanced Character Physics," available online at www.gamasutra.com/resource_guide/20030121/jacobson_01.shtml, January 21, 2003.

[Kaĉić03] Kaĉić -Alesić, Zoran, Marcus Nordenstam, and David Bullock, "A Practical Dynamics System," *Eurographics/SIGGRAPH Symposium on Computer Animation,* 2003.

[Mirtich95] Mirtich, Brian, and John Canny, "Impulse-based Simulation of Rigid Bodies," in *Proceedings of 1995 Symposium on Interactive 3D Graphics*, April 1995, available online at www.cs.berkeley.edu/~jfc/mirtich/impulse.html.

[Moravánszky04] Moravánszky, Ádám, and Pierre Terdiman, "Fast Contact Reduction for Dynamics Simulations," *Game Programming Gems 4*, 2004.

[Smith04] Smith, Russell, "Constraints in Rigid Body Dynamics," *Game Programming Gems 4*, 2004.

[Terdiman00] Terdiman, Pierre, "OPCODE, Optimized Collision Detection," available online at www.codercorner.com/Opcode.htm, 2000.

[Verlet67] Verlet, L. "Computer experiments on classical fluids. I. Thermodynamical properties of Lennard-Jones molecules," *Phys. Rev.*, 159, 98–103, 1967.

2.7

Constraints in Rigid Body Dynamics

Russ Smith, Google Inc.

russ@q12.org

Modern computer games are immersing the player in increasingly realistic virtual worlds. Part of this added realism comes from sophisticated rendering, part of it comes from AI, and part of it comes from more detailed simulation of game object motion. Cars are expected to skid and tumble as they would in real life, bridges must sway when walked on, brick walls must crumble when struck, and game characters must fall convincingly.

A popular technique for creating these motions is rigid body simulation. Rigid body simulation libraries often come with standard joint types that allow the user to connect bodies together with, for example, hinges and ball-and-socket joints. Some libraries allow users to create their own joint types. When this capability is available, it offers many advantages for simulating novel situations. For example, a new joint type could keep the cart of a roller coaster attached to a track, or it could model a particular kind of suspension that connects the wheel of a car to the chassis.

This article shows how to easily build new joints for the popular Cartesian coordinate/Lagrange multiplier-based rigid body simulators (like [Baraff96]) that use velocity constraints. The description is tailored to the Open Dynamic Engine (ODE), an open-source rigid body simulation library [Smith03]. Other simulation techniques, such as the reduced coordinate method [McMillan94], are not covered. We will see how joints can be created from simple parts, without advanced mathematics. This article assumes that the reader is familiar with the basic concepts of rigid body simulation. If not, there are several good places to start, such as [Witkin97] and [Hecker96].

The Basics

In rigid body simulation, each body starts out with six degrees of freedom (three for position and three for orientation). *Constraints* take degrees of freedom away from the system—they are mathematical restrictions on the ways that bodies can move relative to each other. Constraints are enforced by the simulator, for example by having automatically calculated constraint forces applied to each body. Constraints often take the form of joints that can connect pairs of bodies together. The words *constraint* and *joint* are used interchangeably in this article.

Velocity and Acceleration

We define the linear and angular velocity of a body i to be the vectors $[v_{ix}\ v_{iy}\ v_{iz}]$ and $[\omega_{ix}\ \omega_{iy}\ \omega_{iz}]$, respectively. The linear velocity is measured at the body's point of reference (POR), and the angular velocity is the rotation about this point of reference. A vector $\mathbf{p}_i$ gives the location of the POR. Often, a body's POR is its center of mass. Each body also has linear and angular acceleration vectors, which are the time derivatives of the velocity vectors. For convenience, we group these values together into six-vectors (note that the notation $\dot{x}$ means the time derivative of x).

$$\begin{aligned} \text{velocity}: \mathbf{v}_i &= \begin{bmatrix} \dot{\mathbf{p}}_i & \mathbf{\Omega}_i \end{bmatrix}^T = \begin{bmatrix} v_{ix} & v_{iy} & v_{iz} & \omega_{ix} & \omega_{iy} & \omega_{iz} \end{bmatrix}^T \\ \text{acceleration}: \mathbf{a}_i &= \begin{bmatrix} \ddot{\mathbf{p}}_i & \dot{\mathbf{\Omega}}_i \end{bmatrix}^T = \begin{bmatrix} \dot{v}_{ix} & \dot{v}_{iy} & \dot{v}_{iz} & \dot{\omega}_{ix} & \dot{\omega}_{iy} & \dot{\omega}_{iz} \end{bmatrix}^T \end{aligned} \tag{2.7.1}$$

Equations of Motion

A body i moves under the influence of Newton's law: $\mathbf{f}_i = \mathbf{m}_i\mathbf{a}_i$, where $\mathbf{m}_i$ is the mass matrix and $\mathbf{f}_i$ is the force and torque applied to the body. (From here, the word *force* is used to mean both force and torque.) We normally say that $\mathbf{f}_i = \mathbf{f}_{ir} + \mathbf{f}_{ie} + \mathbf{f}_{ic}$, where $\mathbf{f}_{ir}$ is the rotating torque resulting from nonsymmetric rotational inertia, $\mathbf{f}_{ie}$ is some "externally" applied (or user supplied) force, and $\mathbf{f}_{ic}$ is the constraint force. $\mathbf{f}_{ic}$ is computed by the simulator for each time step so that the rigid body motion will satisfy the constraints.

Velocity Constraints

A velocity constraint on a single body is simply a statement that a body's velocity vector is allowed to have some values but not others. An example of a single body constraint is a hinge that connects the body to a fixed point in space. A single body constraint is expressed with the matrix equation $\mathbf{J}_1\mathbf{v}_1 = \mathbf{c}$. Expanded out, this is

$$\begin{bmatrix} J_{11} & J_{12} & J_{13} & J_{14} & J_{15} & J_{16} \\ \vdots & \vdots & \vdots & \vdots & \vdots & \vdots \\ J_{m1} & J_{m2} & J_{m3} & J_{m4} & J_{m5} & J_{m6} \end{bmatrix} v_1 = \begin{bmatrix} c_1 \\ \vdots \\ c_m \end{bmatrix} \tag{2.7.2}$$

The magic of constraints is that the simulator will compute f_{1c} such that $\mathbf{v}_1$ always satisfies this equation. $\mathbf{J}$, called the *constraint Jacobian*, has m rows, where m is the *order* of the constraint, or the number of degrees of freedom that are removed from the system. The values inside **J** and **c** typically change for each time step, as they often depend on the exact position and orientation of the body. Two body constraints have a similar equation: $\mathbf{J}_1\mathbf{v}_1 + \mathbf{J}_2\mathbf{v}_2 = \mathbf{c}$, where $\mathbf{v}_1$ and $\mathbf{v}_2$ are the velocities of the two joined bodies. Constraints that put three or more bodies in a single equation are possible, but they are rarely useful and ODE does not support them.

Constraint Building Blocks

Constraint code computes **J** and **c** at each time step. **J** and **c** can be designed row by row, where each row acts independently to control the velocity along a particular axis. The following examples start with very simple single body constraints, and then combine them together to make more complex constraints.

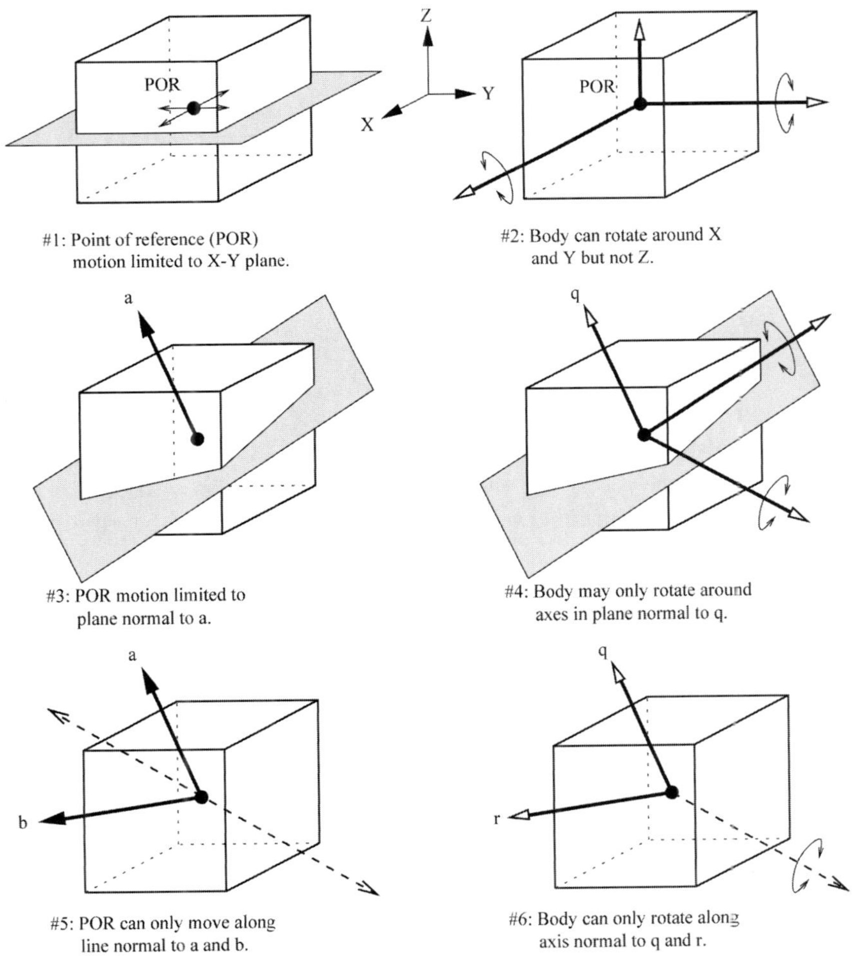

FIGURE 2.7.1 Constraint building blocks.

Constraint #1: No Movement Along Z (POR in X-Y Plane)

Consider the single body constraint (see Figure 2.7.1 #1):

$$\begin{bmatrix} 0 & 0 & 1 & 0 & 0 & 0 \end{bmatrix} \mathbf{v}_1 = 0 \tag{2.7.3}$$

Expanding the multiplication gives v_{1z}, so this constraint sets the body's POR velocity in the Z direction to zero. Another way of saying this is that the body's POR is limited to move in the X-Y plane only. Note that this constraint says nothing about what the Z position actually is, because it is only the velocity that is constrained, not the position.

Constraint #2: No Rotation About Z

Consider the constraint (see Figure 2.7.1 #2):

$$\begin{bmatrix} 0 & 0 & 0 & 0 & 0 & 1 \end{bmatrix} \mathbf{v}_1 = 0 \tag{2.7.4}$$

This says that $_{1z} = 0$. Therefore, this constraint prevents the body from rotating around the Z-axis. It can still rotate around axes that are perpendicular (i.e., normal) to the Z-axis.

Constraint #3: POR in an Arbitrary Plane

This constraint (see Figure 2.7.1 #3)

$$\begin{bmatrix} a_x & a_y & a_z & 0 & 0 & 0 \end{bmatrix} \mathbf{v}_1 = 0 \tag{2.7.5}$$

is similar to constraint #1, except that it zeroes POR velocity along the vector $[a_x \ a_y \ a_z]$. Another way of saying this is that POR motion is restricted to the plane that has $[a_x \ a_y \ a_z]$ as its normal vector. Vector **a** does not have to be a unit vector.

Constraint #4: No Rotation About an Arbitrary Axis

Similar to constraint #3, the following constraint (see Figure 2.7.1 #4) prevents rotation about the axis **q**, allowing rotation around axes in the plane normal to **q**.

$$\begin{bmatrix} 0 & 0 & 0 & q_x & q_y & q_z \end{bmatrix} \mathbf{v}_1 = 0 \tag{2.7.6}$$

Constraint #5: POR Constrained to a Line

To prevent POR motions in two directions simultaneously, we can use two copies of constraint #2, one per row (see Figure 2.7.1 #5).

$$\begin{bmatrix} a_x & a_y & a_z & 0 & 0 & 0 \\ b_x & b_y & b_z & 0 & 0 & 0 \end{bmatrix} \mathbf{v}_1 = \begin{bmatrix} 0 \\ 0 \end{bmatrix} \tag{2.7.7}$$

POR velocity is prevented from having a component in either direction a or b. The result is that the POR is limited to move along the line $\mathbf{a} \times \mathbf{b}$.

Constraint #6: Rotation About a Fixed Axis

Similar to constraint #5, we can prevent rotation about two axes simultaneously, limiting rotation to the single axis $\ddot{\mathbf{o}} = \mathbf{q} \times \mathbf{r}$ (see Figure 2.7.1 #6).

$$\begin{bmatrix} 0 & 0 & 0 & q_x & q_y & q_z \\ 0 & 0 & 0 & r_x & r_y & r_z \end{bmatrix} \mathbf{v}_1 = \begin{bmatrix} 0 \\ 0 \end{bmatrix} \tag{2.7.8}$$

Constraint #7: Fixed POR or Rotation

If we extend constraint #5 to three rows, we can write the following constraint equation,

$$\begin{bmatrix} a_x & a_y & a_z & 0 & 0 & 0 \\ b_x & b_y & b_z & 0 & 0 & 0 \\ c_x & c_y & c_z & 0 & 0 & 0 \end{bmatrix} \mathbf{v}_1 = \begin{bmatrix} 0 \\ 0 \\ 0 \end{bmatrix}, \text{or} \begin{bmatrix} 1 & 0 & 0 & 0 & 0 & 0 \\ 0 & 1 & 0 & 0 & 0 & 0 \\ 0 & 0 & 1 & 0 & 0 & 0 \end{bmatrix} \mathbf{v}_1 = \begin{bmatrix} 0 \\ 0 \\ 0 \end{bmatrix} \tag{2.7.9}$$

which is an explicit statement that $v_{ix} = v_{iy} = v_{iz} = 0$. The result of applying this constraint is that the body's POR stays fixed in space. If the three vectors are not independent (e.g., one vector is a scaled version of another vector), then the simulation might become unstable, as the simulator will be unable to decide how much force to apply along each constraint direction. A similar principle can be applied to limit all rotational motion. Note also that constraints #7 and #6 can be combined to create a simple single-body hinge.

Creating Useful Game Constraints

The previous examples demonstrated the basic constraint principles. Now let's see how we can put these ideas into action and build constraints that might be useful in a game. Along the way, we'll see how to build two-body constraints, how the vector **c** can be put to use, and how force limits can be used to make hard contacts, motors, and brakes.

A Rope-and-Pulley Constraint

Image a game scenario with two platforms connected by a rope and two pulleys (see Figure 2.7.2). The vectors **a** and **b** point in the directions that the platforms can move. If the player steps on to platform A, the platform will fall under the increased weight and platform B will rise. To be realistic, the rate of fall should be proportional to the player weight, and any extra weight piled onto B should slow the fall. These effects can all be created using simple game logic, but unfortunately, each extra piece of physical realism usually requires an extra piece of code to handle it. If rigid body simulation is used, however, all these physical behaviors (and more) come at no extra cost.

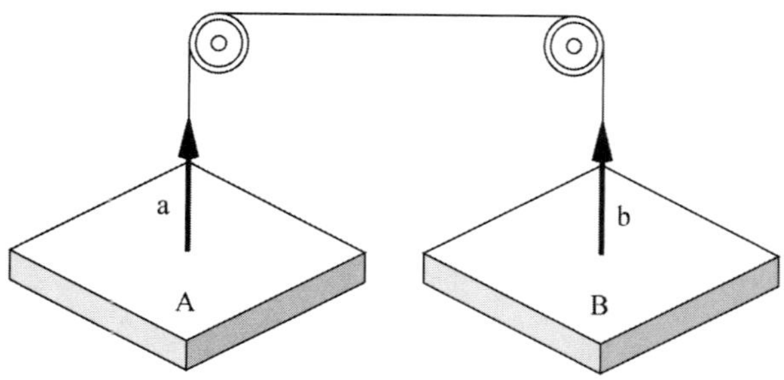

FIGURE 2.7.2 A rope-and-pulley constraint.

How do we create a constraint to model this situation? Recall that two-body constraints have the form $\mathbf{J}_1\mathbf{v}_1 + \mathbf{J}_2\mathbf{v}_2 = \mathbf{c}$. If we set $\mathbf{c} = 0$, we can say that $\mathbf{J}_1\mathbf{v}_1 = -\mathbf{J}_2\mathbf{v}_2$, which illustrates that the velocities of the two bodies along certain directions are traded off against each other. The rope-and-pulley constraint is thus

$$\begin{bmatrix} a_x & a_y & a_z & 0 & 0 & 0 \end{bmatrix}\mathbf{v}_1 + \begin{bmatrix} b_x & b_y & b_z & 0 & 0 & 0 \end{bmatrix}\mathbf{v}_2 = 0$$

This says that the POR velocity of body 1 along direction **a** must match the POR velocity of body 2 along direction –**b** (allowing for the relative lengths of **a** and **b**). Interlocking cogwheels could be simulated using a similar approach, with constraints on the angular rather than linear velocities.

Screw Constraints

A screw constraint forces a body to rotate as it moves in a particular direction, like a nut moving along the thread of a bolt. This effect is achieved by using a constraint row with both linear and angular parts, so that the linear and angular motions are traded off against each other. For example, the constraint

$$\begin{bmatrix} a_x & a_y & a_z & q_x & q_y & q_z \end{bmatrix}\mathbf{v}_1 = \mathbf{a}\cdot\dot{\mathbf{p}}_1 + \mathbf{q}\cdot\blacklozenge_1 = 0 \qquad (2.7.10)$$

is split into linear and angular parts to illustrate that the linear velocity along axis **a** must be some multiple of the angular velocity along axis **q**. In the screw constraint, **a** and **q** point in the same direction.

Ball-and-Socket Joints

Ball-and-socket joints have many uses, like connecting together the links of a chain or the limbs of a rag doll. The joint is shown in Figure 2.7.3, where $\mathbf{g}_1$ and $\mathbf{g}_2$ are vectors from the body 1 and 2 PORs to the ball. Looking along each direction $\mathbf{u}_1$, $\mathbf{u}_2$, $\mathbf{u}_3$ we want the velocity of the ball to be the same when measured from body 1 or body 2, so for each direction vector we have $\mathbf{u}_i\cdot(\dot{\mathbf{p}}_1+\dot{\mathbf{g}}_1)=\mathbf{u}_i\cdot(\dot{\mathbf{p}}_2+\dot{\mathbf{g}}_2)$. This constraint is specified relative to the ball, so we must use the *shifting rule* to make it relative to the body PORs.

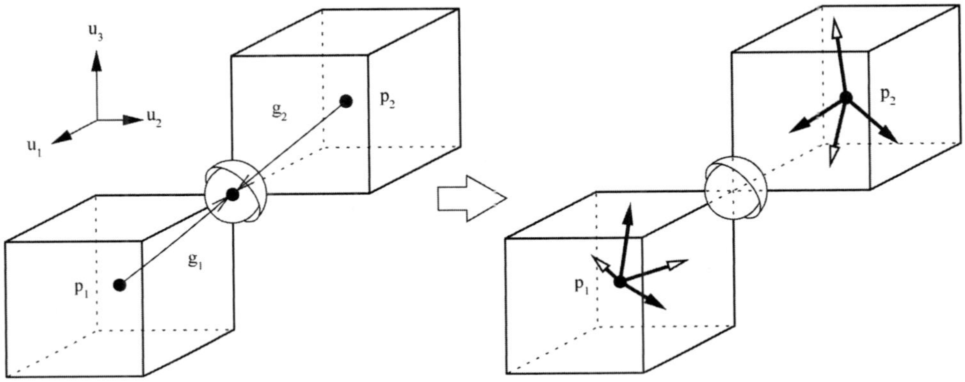

Constraint expressed relative to p+g. Same constraint expressed relative to p.

FIGURE 2.7.3 A ball-and-socket joint created using the shifting rule.

The shifting rule says that if a constraint is specified for points $\mathbf{g}_1$ and $\mathbf{g}_2$ relative to bodies 1 and 2, like this

$$\mathbf{a}_1\cdot(\dot{\mathbf{p}}_1+\dot{\mathbf{g}}_1)+\mathbf{q}_1\cdot\blacklozenge_1+\mathbf{a}_2\cdot(\dot{\mathbf{p}}_2+\dot{\mathbf{g}}_2)+\mathbf{q}_2\cdot\blacklozenge_2=c \qquad (2.7.11)$$

then the equivalent POR-relative constraint is

$$\mathbf{a}_1\cdot\dot{\mathbf{p}}_1+(\mathbf{q}_1+\mathbf{g}_1\times\mathbf{a}_1)\cdot\blacklozenge_1+\mathbf{a}_2\cdot\dot{\mathbf{p}}_2+(\mathbf{q}_2+\mathbf{g}_2\times\mathbf{a}_2)\cdot\blacklozenge_2=c \qquad (2.7.12)$$

This shifting rule correctly trades off linear and angular velocity at the POR. Applying this to the ball-and-socket joint for each $\mathbf{u}_i$ gives

$$\mathbf{u}_i\cdot\dot{\mathbf{p}}_1+(\mathbf{g}_1\times\mathbf{u}_i)\cdot\blacklozenge_1-\mathbf{u}_i\cdot\dot{\mathbf{p}}_2+(\mathbf{g}_2\times\mathbf{u}_i)\cdot\blacklozenge_2=0 \qquad (2.7.13)$$

When we evaluate this for $\mathbf{u}_1$ ... $\mathbf{u}_3$ and write all three constraint rows together, we get the ball-and-socket constraint:

$$\begin{bmatrix} 1 & 0 & 0 & 0 & g_{1z} & -g_{1y} \\ 0 & 1 & 0 & -g_{1z} & 0 & g_{1x} \\ 0 & 0 & 1 & g_{1y} & -g_{1x} & 0 \end{bmatrix}\mathbf{v}_1+\begin{bmatrix} -1 & 0 & 0 & 0 & -g_{2z} & g_{2y} \\ 0 & -1 & 0 & g_{2z} & 0 & -g_{2x} \\ 0 & 0 & -1 & -g_{2y} & g_{2x} & 0 \end{bmatrix}\mathbf{v}_2=\begin{bmatrix} 0 \\ 0 \\ 0 \end{bmatrix}$$

Hinge Joint

A hinge joint is a ball and socket joint with two extra constraint rows that force the bodies to line up along the hinge axis. These extra rows are a generalization of constraint #6 that prevents the bodies from rotating relative to each other along the axes **q** and **r**.

$$\begin{bmatrix} 0 & 0 & 0 & q_x & q_y & q_z \\ 0 & 0 & 0 & r_x & r_y & r_z \end{bmatrix} \mathbf{v}_1 + \begin{bmatrix} 0 & 0 & 0 & -q_x & -q_y & -q_z \\ 0 & 0 & 0 & -r_x & -r_y & -r_z \end{bmatrix} \mathbf{v}_2 = \begin{bmatrix} 0 \\ 0 \end{bmatrix} \quad (2.7.14)$$

Make Stacks of Things with Hard Contacts

Often, a game requires a stack of objects that the player can push over, drive through, or blow up. To stack rigid bodies, we need to model the nonpenetration contact between them. Penalty methods that apply user-calculated restraining forces to each body are difficult to tune and tend to cause instability. What we really want is a hard contact constraint with the following property: when two bodies are pushed together at the contact point, the constraint pushes back with equal force, and when they are pulled apart, the constraint does not resist. This can be achieved with constraint force limits.

First, let's see how force limits work in general. The constraint force vectors $\mathbf{f}_{c1}$ and $\mathbf{f}_{c2}$ that are applied to bodies 1 and 2 are weighted sums of the constraint rows associated with that body. For m rows there are weights $\lambda_1 \dots \lambda_m$ (the Lagrange multiplier values calculated by the simulator) and

$$\begin{aligned} \mathbf{f}_{c1} &= \mathbf{J}_1^T \boldsymbol{\lambda} \\ \mathbf{f}_{c2} &= \mathbf{J}_2^T \boldsymbol{\lambda} \\ \boldsymbol{\lambda} &= \begin{bmatrix} \lambda_1 & \cdots & \lambda_m \end{bmatrix} \end{aligned} \quad (2.7.15)$$

In normal unlimited constraints, the solver will allow $\lambda_1 \dots \lambda_m$ to take any values. In other words, the solver will "do whatever it takes" to make sure that the constraint is satisfied. A force limit restricts the solver so that it only applies constraint forces within a certain range; for example, $\lambda_{iLO} \le \lambda_i \le \lambda_{iHI}$. If larger forces would have been necessary, then λ_i will be clamped to one of the limits and the constraint will not be perfectly satisfied. When limits are present, the simulator must solve a Linear Complementary Problem (LCP) at each time step [Murty88]. Simulators such as ODE allow force limits on any constraint row.

To make a contact constraint we can apply the POR shifting rule to the two-body version of constraint #3, so that the bodies experience a force $\lambda\mathbf{a}$ at the contact point. Let's say that if λ is positive, then $\lambda\mathbf{a}$ pushes the bodies apart. If we set $\lambda_{LO} = 0$, $\lambda_{HI} =$ • and the *required* λ is positive, then the correct reaction force will be applied to keep the two bodies apart. If the required λ is negative, it will be clamped to zero, allowing the two bodies to come apart without resistance. Often, multiple contact points are required to keep two bodies separated; this depends on the geometry of the bodies.

Here's a neat trick to "magnetize" the bodies: set $\lambda_{LO} = -M$, $\lambda_{HI} = \bullet$. This means that some nonzero force M must be exerted to pull the bodies apart.

Making Motors

Making a car go requires some type of motor. The simplest way to model a motor is to apply a torque between a wheel and the chassis. This does work, but there are problems—in particular, it can cause instability when large torques are applied. An alternative model uses a constraint row that sets a constant angular velocity between the wheel and the chassis, using a nonzero value of **c**. In general, when **c** is nonzero it sets the body velocities along the constrained directions (for example, by setting $\mathbf{c} = c_z$ in constraint #3 we are saying that the POR velocity along **a** must be c_z). Let's take the single body hinge obtained by combining constraints #6 and #7, and add the row

$$\begin{bmatrix} 0 & 0 & 0 & s_x & s_y & s_z \end{bmatrix} \mathbf{v}_1 = \begin{bmatrix} c_s \end{bmatrix}$$

where $s = \frac{(q \times r)}{|q \times r|}$ is the unit length axis of hinge rotation. This is a "powered" hinge that has angular velocity c_s around the hinge axis. However, this is a terrible model for a motor because it is infinitely powerful, as it will achieve its target velocity regardless of any restraining torques.

This problem can be corrected by setting lLO = $-f_{max}$, $\lambda_{HI} = f_{max}$ for the motor constraint row. The motor will now not be able to apply more than $\pm f_{max}$ of torque to achieve its target velocity. If the motor is able to bring the body up to speed within a single time step, it will do so; otherwise, it will apply the maximum possible (clamped) torque to bring the body up to speed over several time steps. Any externally applied torque will now be able to compete with the constraint torque, hindering the motor just as it would in real life. Setting f_{max} to zero disables the motor, effectively removing the influence of the motor constraint row. This motor is much more stable than the equivalent direct-torque motor when f_{max} is large. It is also a reasonable model of an engine with an attached gearbox, where internal friction limits the maximum speed (such as the typical drive train of a car).

Brakes and Dry Friction

Cars need brakes as well as motors. As with motors, the simplest braking solution is a torque applied directly to the wheels. As with motors, this can lead to instability. The braking torque at the disc brake of a wheel is caused by dry friction—a constant torque that resists the angular velocity. Dry friction can be modeled well by using a force-limited motor where the target velocity is set to zero. This constraint will apply a torque not exceeding $\pm f_{max}$ to bring the joint velocity to zero. Here, f_{max} is set according to how much the brake pedal is pressed—if no braking is needed, then f_{max}

is zero and the constraint is disabled. If you have a force-limited motor driving the wheel, then you can get braking for free, because the same constraint can be used.

Correcting for Positional Error

If simulators were perfect, we would simply place all the bodies in their starting positions, add some constraints, and the constraints would be enforced perfectly for all time. In practice, simulators are not perfect and numerical errors creep into the body positions and orientations, especially when high rotational speeds are present. A good way to stop this from happening is to allow the constraints themselves to push the bodies back into the correct configuration if they (the bodies) are out of alignment. This is done by using nonzero values in **c**.

A constraint cannot directly affect the position of a body; it can only alter its velocity. However, if the "goal" of a constraint is to maintain a constant position (or to maintain two bodies in a constant position relative to each other), then **c** can be set to force the bodies to move from the incorrect position to the desired one. For example, in constraint #1, if the goal is to keep $p_{1z} = 0$, then we can set $c_z = -kp_{1z}$ so that the correcting velocity is proportional to the positional error. This will exponentially reduce the positional error over time at a rate determined by k. Note that if k is too large, the corrected position will overshoot the mark within one time step, perhaps leading to instability. In general, for each constraint row we set $c = -\text{error}/h$, where the error is measured along the direction vector or axis given in the corresponding row of **J**. For example, in the ball-and-socket joint, the error is measured along directions $\mathbf{u}_1 \ldots \mathbf{u}_3$.

What's on the CD-ROM?

ON THE CD

The companion CD-ROM contains example source code for all the constraints mentioned here, implemented using ODE. It also contains a snapshot of the complete source code, documentation, and example programs for ODE itself. Readers interested in creating their own constraints should refer to the source, as there are several practical details that are not covered in this article.

Conclusion

This article showed how new rigid body velocity constraints can be built from various types of simple constraint rows. You can construct almost any constraint from these building blocks plus the shifting rule, an understanding of the **c** vector, and force limits. Simulation libraries such as ODE that allow user-designed constraints to be used alongside standard ones provide the user with a powerful ability to model new situations.

References

[Baraff96] Baraff, David, "Linear-time Dynamics Using Lagrange Multipliers," *Computer Graphics Proceedings, Annual Conference Series*: pp. 137–146, 1996.

[Hecker96] Hecker, Chris, "Rigid Body Dynamics," available online at www.d6.com/users/checker/dynamics.htm.

[McMillan94] McMillan, Scott, *Computational Dynamics for Robotic Systems on Land and Under Water*, Ph.D. Thesis, The Ohio State University, Columbus, OH, 1994.

[Murty88] Murty, Katta G., "Linear Complementarity, Linear and Nonlinear Programming," available online at http://ioe.engin.umich.edu/people/fac/books/murty/ linear_complementarity_webbook/, 1988.

[Smith03] Smith, Russell, "The Open Dynamics Engine," available online at http://ode.org/.

[Witkin97] Witkin, Andrew, and David Baraff, *Physically Based Modeling: Principles and Practice* (Online SIGGRAPH '97 Course notes), available online at http://www.cs.cmu.edu/~baraff/sigcourse/index.html.

2.8

The Jacobian Transpose Method for Inverse Kinematics

Marco Spoerl

mspoerl@gmx.de

When it comes to goal-oriented movement in games, pre-authored animation data is often inadequate. Haven't we all seen archaeologists, special agents, and other characters trying to grab an object or push a button, only to pick up some imaginary object beyond the real target, or reach into a wall? To fix this, the animation needs to be tweaked at runtime. This is what real-time inverse kinematics is for.

There are plenty of algorithms to solve the inverse kinematics problem. While many of them are good only for offline computations, Chris Welman illustrated two methods suitable for interactive environments in his master's thesis [Welman93]. One of these algorithms, Cyclic Coordinate Descent, or CCD for short, has been explained thoroughly in another article [Weber02]. Our article focuses on the second algorithm from Welman's thesis using the transposed Jacobi matrix. The Jacobian Transpose algorithm usually produces better results than the better-known Cyclic Coordinate Descent, as it always manipulates the complete inverse kinematics chain at once, instead of looking at single succeeding links.

Our Test Bed

For the sake of clarity, we won't bother with a full-blown skeletal animation system to demonstrate the Jacobian Transpose in this article. Instead, we will use a single chain made of articulated joints. Each element in this formation is called a *node*. A node is defined by a pointer to its parent, an array of pointers to its children (if any), and of course its transformation (translation and rotation, but no scale) relative to its parent. We use quaternions to represent rotations in our sample implementation. The first node in the chain is called the *root*, while the last one is called the *effector*. The effector should reach the target with all other nodes down to the root building the inverse kinematics chain, or *manipulator*.

Figure 2.8.1 illustrates the starting configuration of the inverse kinematics chain consisting of five nodes. Note that the effector is only drawn using a simple axis, as it doesn't have a defined length. The axis on the right and the sphere surrounding it denote the target and the threshold allowed to reach its position.

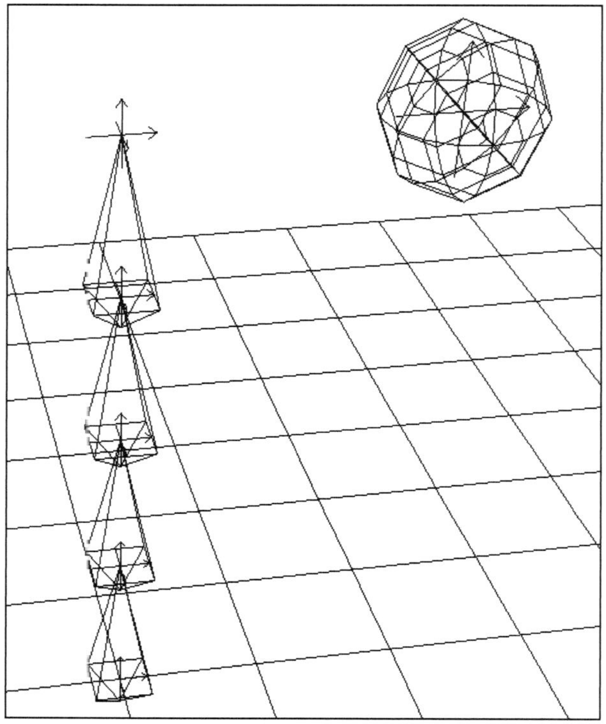

FIGURE 2.8.1 Initial setup of the manipulator.

ON THE CD

The complete source code for the application discussed in this article and our own implementation of the CCD for comparison purposes can be found on the companion CD-ROM.

What Is a Jacobian?

With forward kinematics, the position x of the effector can be computed using

$$x = f(q) \tag{2.8.1}$$

where q denotes a vector of known joint variables (e.g., rotations and translations). In comparison, when using inverse kinematics, the goal is to reach a known position x. Therefore, the inverse of Equation 2.8.1 is needed.

$$q = f^{-1}(x) \tag{2.8.2}$$

The tricky part is that the function f is nonlinear. There's a unique solution from q to x in Equation 2.8.1, but there could be many mappings from a particular x to q in Equation 2.8.2. To solve for this, the problem needs to be linearized. We do so by using the relationship between the joint velocities and the velocity of the effector.

$$\dot{x} = J(q)\dot{q} \tag{2.8.3}$$

The relationship is given by the Jacobi matrix, or Jacobian for short.

$$J = \frac{\partial f}{\partial q} \tag{2.8.4}$$

Simply put, the Jacobian J tells us how the effector changes its position and orientation with changes to the joint variables q. It's an $m \times n$ sized matrix, where n denotes the number of joints in the manipulator and m is the size of the effector vector x. In our case, m is 6 for a general-purpose position and orientation task. That is, column i of the Jacobian describes the incremental change of the effector's position and orientation resulting from changes to joint i. A simple iterative method to solve the inverse kinematic problem can be based on the inverted relationship of Equation 2.8.3.

$$\dot{q} = J^{-1}(q)\dot{x} \tag{2.8.5}$$

In a real-time environment, we want to avoid the expensive inversion required to solve Equation 2.8.5. There is a faster approach using the pseudo-inverse, but that method suffers from problems with singularities when J is not a square matrix. Therefore, our algorithm uses the transposed Jacobian.

The Jacobian Transpose Method in a Nutshell

The goal of an inverse kinematics solver is to reach the specified target. To keep track of its "success," some type of error measurement is necessary. Given the current effector position $x_e(t)$ and target position $x_t(t)$, the error measure or distance vector is

$$e(t) = x_e(t) - x_t(t) \tag{2.8.6}$$

Now consider the error measure e to be a force vector f pulling the effector toward the desired target position. Using that vector f we build a composite force F pulling at our manipulator's tip.

$$F = \left[f_x, f_y, f_z, 0, 0, 0\right]^T \tag{2.8.7}$$

Note that this is different from Welman's version [Welman93].

$$F = \left[f_x, f_y, f_z, m_x, m_y, m_z \right]^T \tag{2.8.8}$$

We ignore the twist m about some axis, as we don't deal with the target's orientation. However, using the principle of virtual work as described in [Paul81], the relationship between the force F and the internal generalized forces τ can be described as

$$\tau = J^T F \tag{2.8.9}$$

So, what does τ represent? Considering an accurate dynamic simulation, τ would be the vector of joint variable accelerations. For our purposes, however, let's think of τ as the vector of joint velocities.

$$\dot{q} = J^T F \tag{2.8.10}$$

Finally, integrating Equation 2.8.10 gives us a new vector q that moves our effector toward the target. In fact, after the integration, q holds rotation angles to be applied to each node. The corresponding axes of rotation are determined while building the Jacobian.

Computing the Jacobi matrix itself is quite simple as well. As we are only using rotational joints (each node's translation is fixed), [Welman93] tells us that the Jacobian column entry for the i'th joint is

$$J_i = \begin{bmatrix} \left[(p - j_i) \times axis_i \right]^T \\ \left[axis_i \right]^T \end{bmatrix} \tag{2.8.11}$$

where p is the world-position of the effector, j_i is the world-position of joint i, and $axis_i$ is the local axis of rotation of joint i.

Recapping, the Jacobian Transpose works like this:

1. Determine the distance vector and magnitude between effector and target.
2. Skip computation loop if distance falls under a certain threshold.
3. Compute the Jacobian and the axes of rotations.
4. Transpose the Jacobian.
5. Determine force f.
6. Compute joint velocities.
7. Integrate joint velocities to obtain joint rotations and apply rotations.
8. Check for criteria to abort.
9. Apply final result to the manipulator.

Implementing the Algorithm

We start solving the inverse kinematics problem with the Jacobian Transpose method by computing the Jacobi matrix itself. In our implementation, getting p and j_i from Equation 2.8.11 is straightforward. However, what about the *axis*? As the nodes don't have a fixed axis of rotation, we'll simply use the vector perpendicular to the two vectors joint → target and joint → effector.

```
for( iColumn = 0, iLinkIndex = 1; iColumn < iLevel;   ++iColumn,
++iLinkIndex )
{

    // Position of current node

    m_arrCurrentTM[ iLinkIndex ].GetTranslation( vecLink );

    // Vector current link -> target

    vecLinkTarget = m_vecTargetPosition - vecLink;

    // Vector current link -> current effector position

    vecLinkEnd = vecEnd - vecLink;

    // Compute axis

    m_arrAxis[ iColumn ] = CVector3::CrossProduct( vecLinkTarget,
       vecLinkEnd );
    m_arrAxis[ iColumn ] .Normalize();

    // Compute upper part of the Jacobian entry

    vecEntry = CVector3::CrossProduct( vecLinkEnd,
    m_arrAxis[ iColumn ] );

    // Set Jacobian entry

    for( iRow = 0; iRow < 3; ++iRow )
    {
      m_arrJacobian[ iRow * iLevel + iColumn ] = vecEntry[ iRow ];
      m_arrJacobian[ ( iRow + 3 ) * iLevel + iColumn ] =
        m_arrAxis[ iColumn ][ iRow ];
    }
}
```

Note that `iLevel` denotes the number of links in the manipulator; that is, the number of entries in the Jacobian. Next, of course, the Jacobian has to be transposed.

```
for( iRow = 0; iRow < 6; ++iRow )
    for( iColumn = 0; iColumn < iLevel; ++iColumn )
      m_arrJacobianTransposed[ iColumn * 6 + iRow ] =
m_arrJacobian[ iRow * iLevel + iColumn ];
```

The force *f* from Equation 2.8.7 is the distance between the effector and the target. Note that this vector has a second purpose as well, as its magnitude is used as a criterion to abort the computation loop.

```
// Determine position of effector

m_arrCurrentTM[0].GetTranslation( vecEnd );

// What do we have to do to reach that?

vecDifference = vecEnd - m_vecTargetPosition;

// How far is that?

fError = vecDifference.GetMagnitude();

// Set force vector

farrForce[0] = vecDifference.GetX();
farrForce[1] = vecDifference.GetY();
farrForce[2] = vecDifference.GetZ();
farrForce[3] = 0.0f;
farrForce[4] = 0.0f;
farrForce[5] = 0.0f;
```

Using Equation 2.8.10, it's easy to get the joint velocities.

```
// Compute q'

for( iRow = 0; iRow < iLevel; ++iRow )
{
    m_arrQDerivate[ iRow ] = 0.0f;

    for( iColumn = 0; iColumn < 6; ++iColumn )
      m_arrQDerivate[ iRow ] += m_arrJacobianTransposed[ iRow * 6 +
iColumn ] * farrForce[ iColumn ];
}
```

Completing the basic computations, we have to integrate the joint velocities and apply the resulting changes.

```
// Integrate and apply changes

for( iIndex = 0, iLinkIndex = 1; iIndex < iLevel; ++iIndex,
++iLinkIndex )
{
    axisAngle.SetAxis( m_arrAxis[iIndex] );
    axisAngle.SetAngle( m_arrQDerivate[iIndex] * 0.01f )
    quatAlign.SetQuaternion( axisAngle );
    quatAlign.Normalize();

    // Store quaternion
```

```
        ...
    }
```

As you can see, we use a simple Euler integration step. While this is not the best way to integrate, it's certainly the fastest. We leave it to the reader to try a more sophisticated scheme like the Runge-Kutta integrator as proposed by [Welman93]. Finally, the resulting value is used as the rotation angle of the specific joint around the axis computed earlier.

As mentioned earlier, we are using quaternions for rotations. In case of the Jacobian Transpose, the consistent use of an axis-angle representation might be better. In that case, the application of the results from the integration would become simpler, and the conversion illustrated earlier would be unnecessary. In our sample implementation, though, the Jacobian Transpose solver shares a common base class with a generic CCD solver that makes heavy use of quaternions.

ON THE CD

The complete Jacobian Transpose implementation can be found on the companion CD-ROM, in the function `CIKSolverJacobianTranspose::Solve()` in the file CIKSolverJacobianTranspose.cpp.

Results and Comparison

As we are using an Euler integration step to solve Equation 2.8.10, careful consideration has to be taken when choosing the step size. A comparison between several different values using our sample implementation is shown in Figure 2.8.2 (the maximum number of iterations is 100).

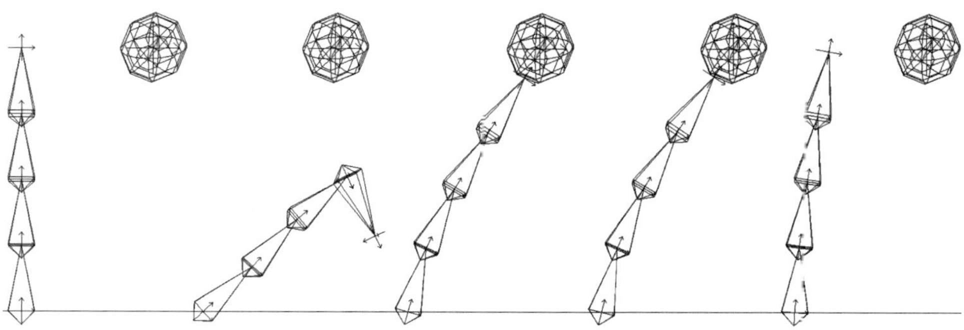

FIGURE 2.8.2 Euler integration step size comparison. From left to right: initial setup, 0.1, 0.01, 0.001, and 0.0001.

With a step size of 0.1, the algorithm doesn't converge at all, regardless of any modification to the iteration limit. When using a step size of 0.0001, the number of iterations has to be increased in order to reach the target. Note that a step size of 0.01 is being used for all of the following tests.

First, let's compare the results generated by the Jacobian Transpose (JT) to that from our generic implementation of the CCD.

In the first case, the target is located just to the right and below the effector. The chain consists of seven nodes with no constraints applied to the rotations. The iteration limit is set to 100. Figure 2.8.3 illustrates the main difference between the two algorithms. While the Jacobian Transpose distributes rotations evenly across the manipulator, the CCD considers each link independently.

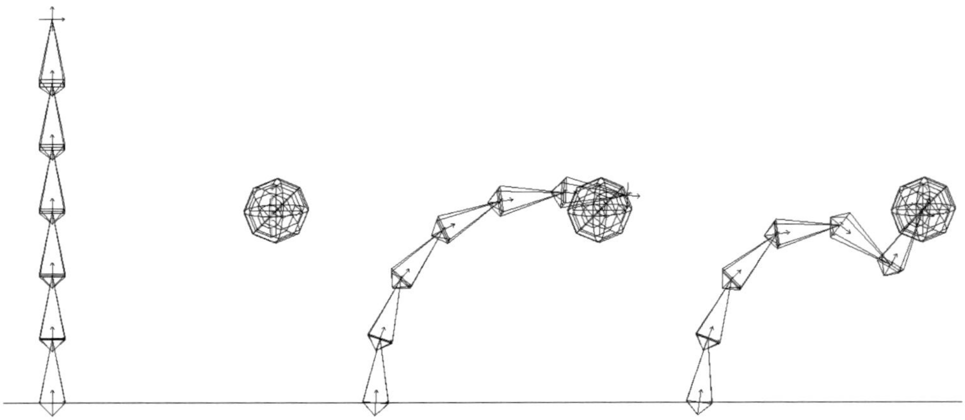

FIGURE 2.8.3 A simple unconstrained setup. From left to right: initial state, JT, and CCD.

The setup from Figure 2.8.4 is almost identical to the previous one, except that in this case, the rotations around the principal axes are limited to ±50 degrees. We see that the CCD result improves, while the JT appears unchanged. Note that in our sample implementation only a simple Euler angle-clamping scheme is used.

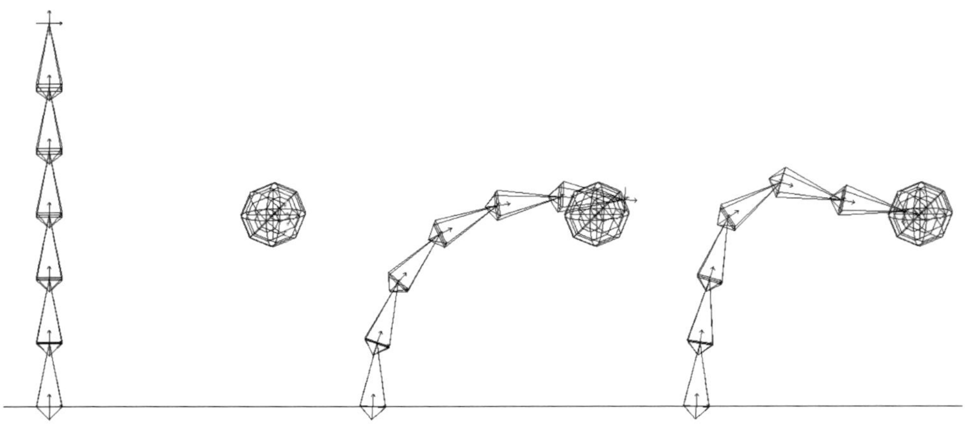

FIGURE 2.8.4 A simple constrained setup. From left to right: initial state, JT, and CCD.

Figure 2.8.5 shows that with tighter limits (±20 degrees), both methods are unable to reach the target and that the CCD's appearance is improved again.

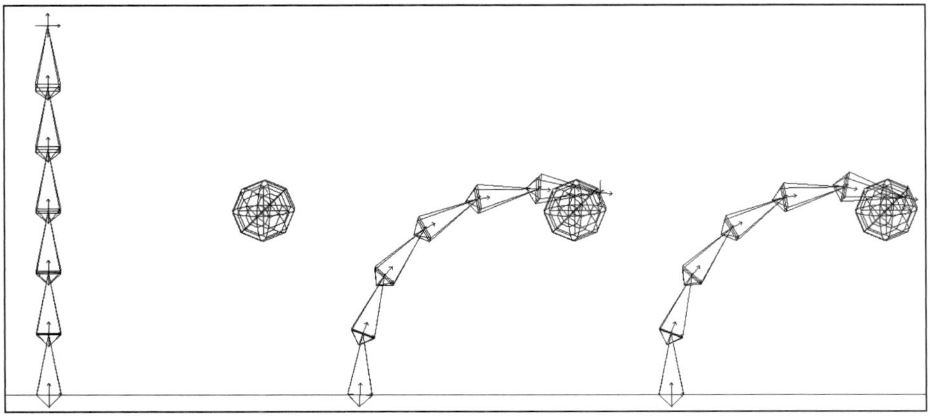

FIGURE 2.8.5 Another constrained setup with tighter limits. From left to right: initial state, JT, and CCD.

Our second test case uses a more sophisticated setup (see Figure 2.8.6). The target is located on the floor away from the effector. The chain consists of nine nodes with no constraints applied to the rotations. Again, the iteration limit is set to 100. While the JT manages to smoothly reach the target, the CCD gives a rather chaotic solution.

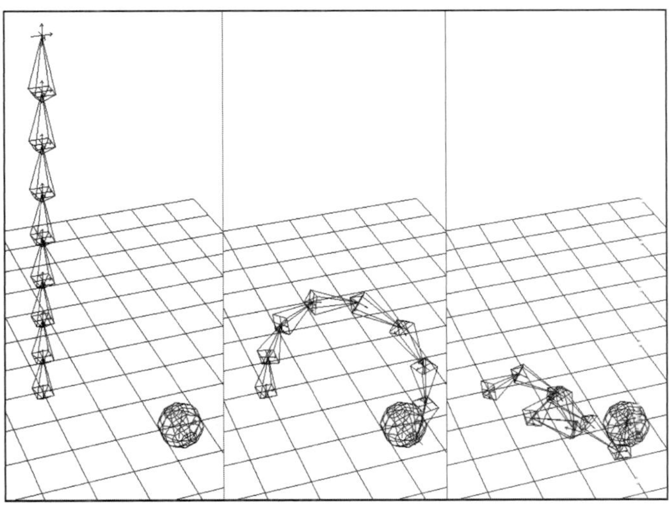

FIGURE 2.8.6 A complex setup without constraints. From left to right: initial state, JT, and CCD.

As in the two-dimensional test, the rotations are clamped to ±50 degrees. Again, Figure 2.8.7 shows that in this case, the JT still manages to appear smooth while the CCD provides a more precise, yet less satisfying solution.

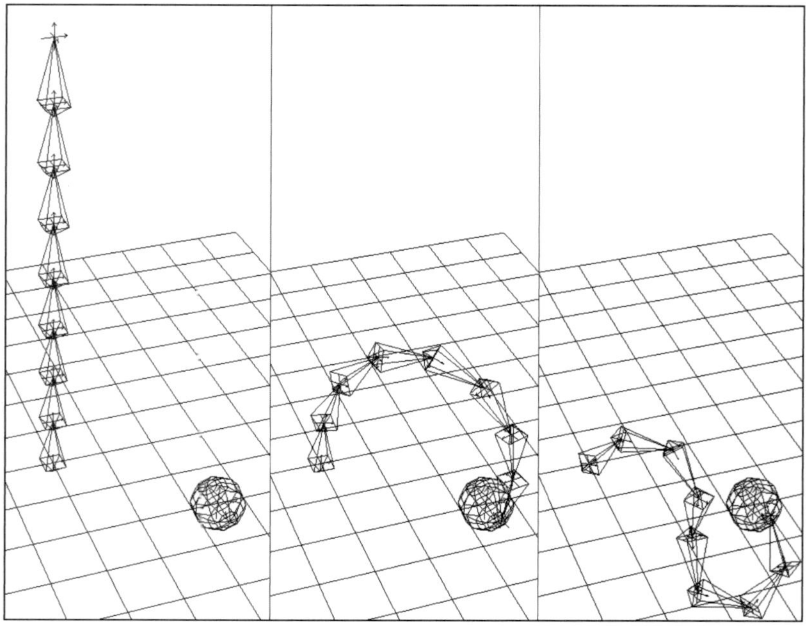

FIGURE 2.8.7 A complex setup with constraints applied. From left to right: initial state, JT, and CCD.

Finally, the last comparison as seen in Figure 2.8.8 proves that the CCD catches up when using tight rotational limits (±20 degrees).

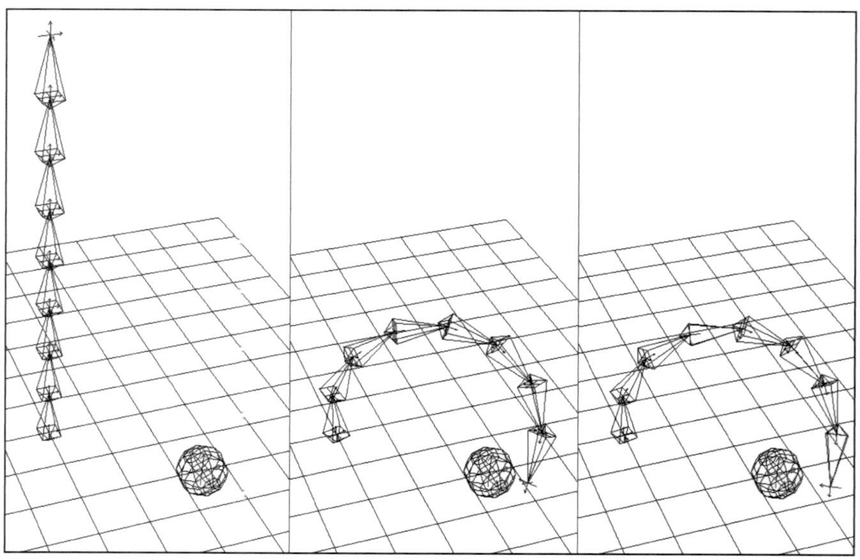

FIGURE 2.8.8 Another complex setup with tighter limits. From left to right: initial state, JT, and CCD.

Conclusion

We presented a powerful alternative to the Cyclic Coordinate Descent (CCD) that dominates in unconstrained environments and when using larger rotational limits. Its evenly distributed node rotations provide superior results.

What we haven't dealt with is the way the degrees of freedom are constrained. In our sample implementation, for the sake of clarity, only the quaternion-to-Euler conversion is used to clamp the rotation (using pitch/yaw/roll limits) before storing the resulting quaternion. Note that this doesn't have any noticeable influence on the convergence criteria, as the Jacobian is recomputed for every step. We strongly encourage the reader to look at texts like [Weber02] or [Blow02] for more advanced methods to clamp rotations. Additionally, [Welman93] contains a chapter on incorporating constraints.

Finally, a last word about matching the target's orientation. As mentioned before, we omit the twisting force from Welman's original Equation 2.8.8 in favor of the simplified Equation 2.8.7. To extend the method presented in this article, one could determine a torque to map the orientation of the effector to that of the target, and put the corresponding axis into the force used to pull at the tip of the manipulator.

References

[Blow02] Blow, Jonathan, "Inverse Kinematics with Joint Limits," *Game Developer* Vol. 9, No. 4 (April 2002): pp. 16–18.

[Paul81] Paul, R.P., *Robot Manipulators: Mathematics, Programming, and Control*, MIT Press, 1981.

[Weber02] Weber, Jason, "Constrained Inverse Kinematics," *Game Programming Gems 3*, Charles River Media, 2002.

[Welman93] Welman, Chris, "Inverse Kinematics and Geometric Constraints for Articulated Figure Manipulation," Master's Thesis, Simon Frasier University, September 1993.

SECTION 3

ARTIFICIAL INTELLIGENCE

3.1

The Basics of A* for Path Planning

Bryan Stout

The Problem

ON THE CD

This article examines the basic solution to the problem of planning a path for an autonomous agent to move from one location in a game world to another, a common situation in computer game AI. On the CD-ROM that accompanies this book is a copy of my PathDemo program, with which you can play to understand how A* (and other path-planning techniques) works.

The most common issue involved in path planning is the avoidance of obstacles, including cul-de-sacs to be ignored (or, sometimes, discovered and explored). The next most common issue is perhaps the awareness of different terrain and seeking out the most efficient path among a variety of choices: exploiting roads or clear terrain, avoiding swamps, and so on.

An Overview of the Solution

The A* (pronounced *A star*) algorithm is an old workhorse in the academic AI community, used since 1968 for solving different kinds of problems, of which the 15-puzzle is the favorite teaching example; fortunately, it is also very useful for the path-planning problem.

A* is an algorithm that searches in a *state space* for the least costly path from a start state to a goal state by examining the *neighboring* or *adjacent states* of particular states. In the 15-puzzle, a state consists of a configuration of the 15 tiles in the 4 × 4 array, and an adjacent state is reached by sliding one tile into the blank area. In the path-planning problem, a state consists of the agent occupying a particular location in the game world, and an adjacent state is reached by moving the agent to an adjacent location.

In essence, the A* algorithm repeatedly examines the most promising unexplored location it has seen. When a location is explored, the algorithm is finished if that location is the goal; otherwise, it makes note of all that location's neighbors for further exploration.

In more detail, A* keeps track of two lists of states, called **Open** and **Closed**, for unexamined and examined states, respectively. At the start, **Closed** is empty, and **Open** has only the starting state (the agent in its current position). In each iteration, the algorithm removes the most promising state from **Open** for examination. If the state is not a goal, the neighboring locations are sorted. If they're new, they're placed in **Open**; if they're already in **Open**, information about those locations is updated, if this is a cheaper path to them; if they're already in **Closed**, they are ignored, since they've already been examined. If the **Open** list becomes empty before the goal is found, it means there is no path to the goal from that start location.

The "most promising" state in **Open** is essentially the location with the lowest estimated path that would go through that location. Each state *X* includes information to determine this: the cost of the cheapest path that has led to this state from the start, which we'll call `CostFromStart(X)`; a heuristic estimate `CostToGoal(X)` of the cost of the remaining distance to the goal; and the total path estimate, defined as `CostFromStart(X) + CostToGoal(X)`. The total path estimate is the lowest `TotalCost(X)` value that it determines is the next state to examine. In addition, each state keeps a pointer to its "parent" state, the state that led to this one and the cheapest path to it; when a goal state is found, these links can be traced back to the start in order to construct the path from start to goal. Please note that in the literature, you'll find `CostFromStart(X)` called **g**(X), `CostToGoal(X)` referred to as **h**(X), and the total path estimate named **f**(X). We'll use our names for greater clarity in this article.

LISTING 3.1.1 The A* Algorithm

In pseudocode form, here is the A* algorithm:

```
Open: priorityqueue of searchnode
Closed: list of searchnode

AStarSearch( location StartLoc, location GoalLoc,
       agenttype Agent ) {
    clear Open and Closed

    // initialize a start node
    StartNode.Loc = StartLoc
    StartNode.CostFromStart = 0
    StartNode.CostToGoal = PathCostEstimate( StartLoc,
GoalLoc, Agent )
    StartNode.Parent = null
    push StartNode on Open

    // process the list until success or failure
    while Open is not empty {
        pop Node from Open    // Node has lowest TotalCost

// if at a goal, we're done
        if (Node is a goal node) {
            construct a path backward from Node to StartLoc
            return success
```

```
        } else {
            for each successor NewNode of Node {
                NewCost = Node.CostFromStart +
                        TraverseCost( Node, NewNode, Agent )
                // ignore this node if exists and no
               //   improvement
                if (NewNode is in Open or Closed) and
                        (NewNode.CostFromStart <= NewCost) {
                    continue
                } else {      // store the new or
                              // improved information
                    NewNode.Parent = Node
                    NewNode.CostFromStart = NewCost
                    NewNode.CostToGoal = PathCostEstimate(
                              NewNode.Loc,
                              GoalLoc, Agent )
                    NewNode.TotalCost =
                              NewNode.CostFromStart +
                              NewNode.CostToGoal
                    if (NewNode is in Closed) {
                        remove NewNode from Closed
                      }
                    if (NewNode is in Open) {
                        adjust NewNode's location in
                                     Open
                    } else {
                        push NewNode onto Open
                    }
                }
            } // now done with Node
        }
push Node onto Closed
        }
        return failure      // if no path found and Open is empty
}
```

Properties of A*

A* has several useful properties. (They are not proved here; readers who are interested in the proofs can look in the References.) First, A* finds a path from the start to the goal, if one exists. Second, it finds an optimal path, as long as the `Cost¯oGoal(X)` estimate is *admissible*, which means `CostToGoal` is always an underestimate—that is, `CostToGoal(X)` is always less than or equal to the actual cheapest path cost from X to the goal. Third, A* makes the most efficient use of the heuristic: No search that uses the same heuristic function `CostToGoal(X)` to find optimal paths examines fewer states than A*, not counting tie breaking among states with equal cost.

Applying A* to Game-Path Planning

Let's now look in detail at how the aspects of A* can be applied to path planning in computer games. Much of this discussion depends on the nature of the game and its internal representation of the world; the following discussion is meant to suggest possibilities.

State

As stated above, the principle component of a *state* in the path search is *location*. However, it need not be the only component. An agent's orientation and/or its velocity can also be important. For example, vehicles can often go only straight ahead or turn slightly, and the amount of turn possible is reduced the faster a vehicle moves. Most vehicles can go backward only after coming to a stop. It is quite possible to plan a route based only on locations, but it could be desirable in some situations to plan based on velocity and orientation as well, to avoid planning a route through terrain or around obstacles that would be difficult to navigate.

Even considering location alone, the issue of which locations to consider is not trivial. In some games, the world is naturally tiled—real-time strategy games often have an underlying square grid, and many war games use a visible hex grid—but many games do not divide the space that way, especially games that use a 3D, first-person, or oblique view of the world. In such cases, it is important to choose a set of locations among which to search. Figure 3.1.1 shows a path-planning situation and several ways of partitioning the space.

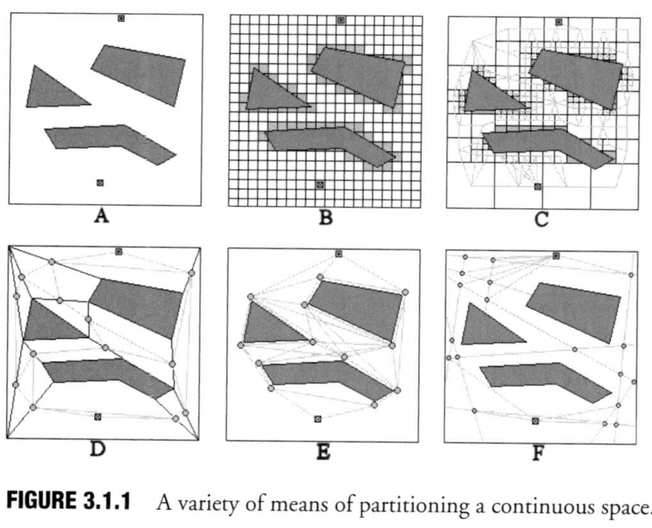

FIGURE 3.1.1 A variety of means of partitioning a continuous space.

The ways of partitioning the space are as follows:

- **Rectangular grid.** The simplest way is to partition into a regular grid of squares, as shown in Figure 3.1.1b. The locations can be either the center points or the corners of the squares; if appropriate for the game, the grid can be considered to consist of the terrain most common to the area it covers.
- **Quadtree.** Another way to partition the space is into squares of differing sizes. The quadtree recursively divides a square into four smaller squares, until each square has uniform (or at least mostly uniform) terrain, as shown in Figure 3.1.1c. Again, the locations for the search can be either the centers or the corners of the squares. This method has a couple of advantages: The larger (and fewer) squares allow for a faster search, and the representation is easy to store.
- **Convex polygons.** A more complex yet possibly more robust scheme is to break up the space into convex polygons made up of uniform terrain. This scheme could already exist in the map's representation, so it can be used directly in the path search. There are several methods that can be used to partition a space into polygons if the existing mesh is useless or inefficient. C-cells are one way to partition the space; each vertex is connected to the nearest visible vertex, and the connecting lines partition the space. Another is maximum-area decomposition, where at each convex vertex the edges connected to the vertex are projected out until they hit an obstacle or wall, and between these lines and the line to the closest other vertex, the shortest is chosen as a boundary. Similar techniques can be used to divide variable-cost terrain into convex polygons of uniform terrain. After the polygons are laid out, search locations can be chosen at their center and/or along various parts of their perimeters.
- **Points of visibility.** Not all techniques divide the space into regions but instead come up with locations directly. Points of visibility are concerned mainly with obstacle avoidance: Place a search location just a little beyond each convex vertex of each obstacle, just far enough away to avoid collision with the obstacles (as in Figure 3.1.1e). The shortest path around obstacles typically passes near these vertices, as though a rubber band connected the start and goal locations. One could possibly extend this method to consider terrain cost by adding these points to those derived from convex uniform polygons.
- **Generalized cylinders.** Another technique concerned mainly with obstacle avoidance is generalized cylinders: The space between neighboring obstacles can be considered a 2D cylinder, the shape of which changes as it goes along. Between each pair of neighboring obstacles (including the walls or boundaries of the map), calculate a central axis (Figure 3.1.1f). The intersections of these lines provide the locations for the search.

For most of these schemes, when a search is done, the start and goal locations are usually not members of the search locations, so they need to be added to them for the duration of that search.

Whichever scheme is used for quantizing a continuous space, it probably must be experimented with and tweaked before it suits the game's demands optimally: There need to be enough locations so that no reasonable route is unconsidered, but not too many, or the search will take too long. Another issue is that most paths found from any quantization scheme seem jagged and a bit artificial, which means the route needs to be smoothed, either before it is assigned to the agent or in the means the agent uses to follow it.

Neighboring States

The neighbors of a state are determined by the map representation and the quantization scheme. Some schemes use only their adjacent locations as their neighbors—a square grid would consider each interior point as having eight neighbors, four if diagonals are excluded—whereas in other schemes, a location's neighbors are all other locations visible to it.

A location's neighbors are also determined by the terrain. Some terrain might be impassable, which means it is not a neighbor to its nearby locations after all. The type of agent could also enter this determination; for example, land vehicles cannot travel on the sea, and infantry can traverse terrain forbidden to some vehicles.

We need an efficient way to compute each location's neighbors, for the sake of search speed. Grids have a natural way of calculating neighbors: The neighbors of (x, y) are $(x+1, y)$, $(x+1, y+1)$, $(x, y+1)$, etc. Most other schemes require that some data structure store the neighbor information for fast lookup, since the neighbor calculations are often expensive.

Cost

The cost function for the path between two locations (`CostFromStart` above) represents whatever it is the path is supposed to minimize—typically, distance traveled, time of traversal, movement points expended, or fuel consumed. However, other factors can be added into this function, such as penalties for passing through undesirable areas, bonuses for passing through desirable areas, and aesthetic considerations (for example, making diagonal moves more costly than orthogonal moves, even if they aren't, to make the resultant path look more direct; see the article on aesthetic optimizations, "A* Aesthetic Optimizations," for more discussion).

Just as with connectivity considered previously, in many games, the cost is not the same for all agents—for example, roads offer a great speedup for wheeled vehicles but little, if any, for infantry. What's more, in some games, travel cost is asymmetric: Going from A to B may be more costly than going from B to A, such as is the case if B is uphill from A. That is why the code in Listing 3.1.1 has the cost functions dependent on the agent traveling as well as the two endpoints of the travel.

Again, these terrain costs need to be quickly looked up during the search and in fact are probably best stored with the connectivity information. In that way, one lookup can determine whether two locations are neighbors, and if so, the cost for the given agent.

Estimate

The estimate of the path cost to the goal is the complement to the known distance from the start. If you want to guarantee that an optimal path is found, this distance should not be overestimated. A common way to do this is to multiply the actual map distance from the given location to the goal times the minimum terrain cost per unit distance. Since the route cannot be shorter than the most direct, "crow's flight" line, this figure will be an underestimate (unless your game has things like instant-transport locations). In many games, this minimum distance is the Euclidean measure between two points in 2D or 3D, but in games with strict square or hexagonal tiles, the shortest tile path is usually a little longer than the Euclidean distance between the tile's center points. Therefore, in a square grid, a tile (3, 5) away has a minimum distance of 2 + 3*sqrt(2), not the Euclidean sqrt(34). This actual shortest distance can then be multiplied by a typical terrain cost. This cost should include all the previously discussed factors concerning the cost between neighboring nodes.

However, guaranteeing an optimum path is not the only consideration; there is also the speed of the search, and the quality of the `CostToGoal` value has a tremendous impact on the search efficiency. Look at Figures 3.1.2 and 3.1.3. In Figure 3.1.2a, the `CostToGoal` has been set to zero, which, after all, *is* an underestimate, and we see that the search spreads in a circle until it hits the goal, because it has no heuristic information to guide it in the correct direction. In Figure 3.1.2b, we see that an accurate heuristic weight of 1 per square sends the search in a straight line to the goal. In Figure 3.1.3, the start and the goal are in costly terrain (8 per square). Since the estimate of 1 per square is a large underestimate, the search frontier is nearly as circular as the uninformed search in Figure 3.1.2a. In Figure 3.1.3b, we see that even an estimate of 5 per square focuses the search considerably. It is therefore important, perhaps crucial, that the estimate be fairly accurate. In fact, in some situations, one might want to *overestimate* the cost to the goal in order to get a fast search, at the risk of getting a suboptimal path (the gem "A* Speed Optimizations" talks about this concept). So rather than using a *minimum* terrain cost per unit, we could use a *typical* cost, which can either be fixed or dynamically determined by sampling the terrain between the stated start and goal.

Goal

The goal is typically a single location, but it does not have to be. For example, if a vehicle low on fuel is trying to plan a route to the closest refueling station, with each new node *N* in the search an estimate is made of the remaining distance to each station, and the minimum of them is used as the `CostToGoal(N)` value. This method

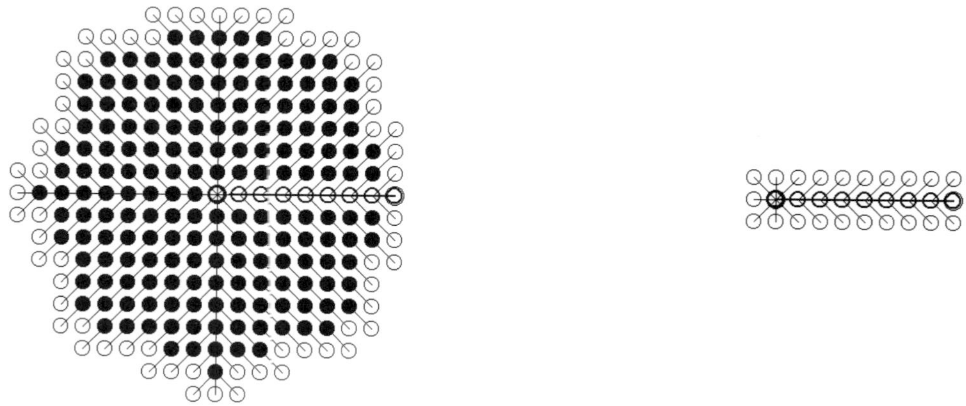

FIGURE 3.1.2 A* search in clear terrain. *a:* With a heuristic weight of 0. *b:* With a heuristic weight of 1.

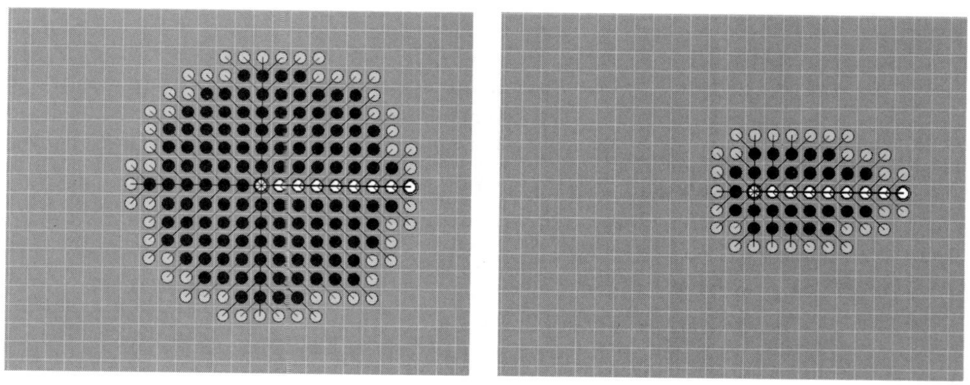

FIGURE 3.1.3 A* search in costly terrain. a: With a heuristic weight of 1. *b:* With a heuristic weight of 5.

guarantees that the search figures out both the closest goal and the best route to it simultaneously.

Weaknesses of A*

Although A* is about as good a search algorithm as you can find, it must be used wisely; otherwise, it can be wasteful of resources. On a large map, hundreds or even thousands of nodes might be in the **Open** and **Closed** lists, which can take up more memory than is available on systems with constrained memory, such as console systems. On any system, A* can take too much CPU time to be affordable.

The case in which A* is most inefficient is in determining that no path is possible between the start and goal locations; in that case, it examines every possible location accessible from the start before determining that the goal is not among them, as shown in Figure 3.1.4. The best way to avoid this problem is to do a pre-analysis of the map, manually or algorithmically, so that the program can look up whether two locations are accessible from each other—say, on the same island. If they are not, the search is not even attempted.

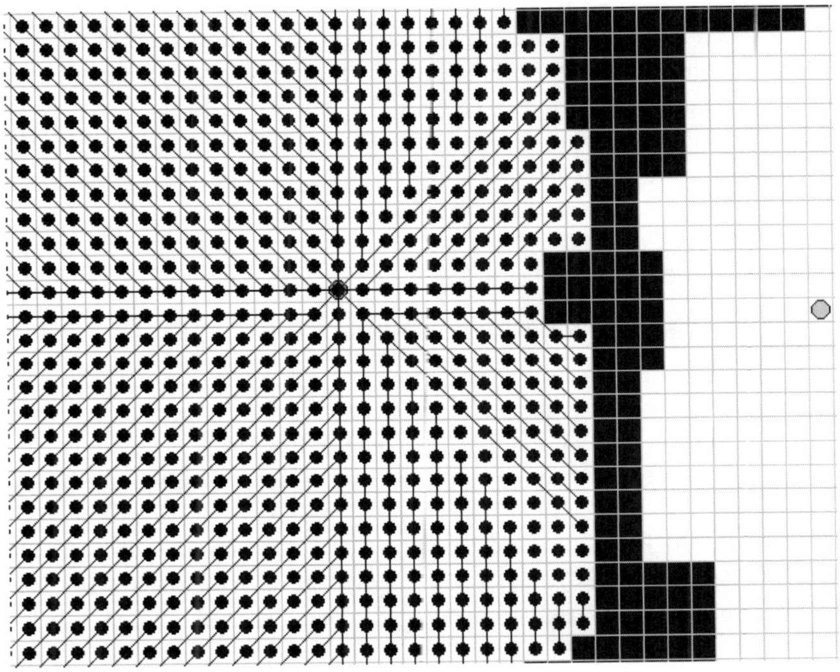

FIGURE 3.1.4 Search in a situation in which there is no path to the goal.

Further Work

There is much more detail that we could cover, because there are many different path-planning and path-following situations. With an understanding of the workings of A*, one can often figure out how to adapt it to their needs. Take a look at the other gems in this volume for further discussion on the ways to partition a floor space for use in A*, as well as efficiency and aesthetic considerations.

References

Websites

[Woodcock] Woodcock, Steven, "The Game AI Page: Building Artificial Intelligence into Games," available online at www.gameai.com. The "Resources and Links" subpage of this site has many links to Web sites that discuss A*, some of which have sample code.

General AI Texts

The following are two very good general AI textbooks, both of which happen to use the agent-centered paradigm for discussing AI:

[Nilsson98] Nilsson, Nils J., *Artificial Intelligence: A New Synthesis*. Morgan Kaufmann, 1998. Since Nilsson was one of the developers of A*, his discussion of it is valuable if one wants to understand the theory behind it. This text presents formal proofs of properties of A*.

[Russell95] Russell, Stuart, and Norvig, Peter, *Artificial Intelligence: A Modern Approach*, Prentice Hall, 1995. Perhaps the best current AI text, it has a couple chapters on search techniques, including A*.

Search Texts

These books discuss the general issues of search, which date back to the early days of AI research:

[Barr81] Barr, Avron, and Feigenbaum, Edward A., eds., *The Handbook of Artificial Intelligence*, volume 1, Addison-Wesley, 1981. A good multivolume survey of major AI issues and important AI programs. This volume includes the discussion of search, including A*.

[Kanal88] Kanal, L., and Kumar, V., eds., *Search in Artificial Intelligence*, Springer-Verlag, 1988. A collection of good articles for those who want to get into the advanced considerations of search, including variations on A* (with imaginative names like B, C, and D!).

[Pearl84] Pearl, J., *Heuristics: Intelligent Search Strategies for Computer Problem Solving*, Addison-Wesley, 1984. This is perhaps the most complete reference on search algorithms and is referenced by practically everyone else.

[Shapiro] Shapiro, Stuart C., and Eckroth, David, eds., *Encyclopedia of Artificial Intelligence*, 2 volumes, John Wiley & Sons, 1987. A truly excellent collection of articles about most aspects of AI research. Good articles pertinent to this article are "Search," "A* Algorithm," and "Path Planning and Obstacle Avoidance."

3.2

A* Aesthetic Optimizations

Steve Rabin, Nintendo of America Inc.

steve.rabin@gmail.com

Computing a path for a character is more than merely an exercise in search algorithms. It also involves creating an aesthetically pleasing path and resulting execution. Computed paths for characters can be improved in three main ways: making the path straighter, making it smoother, and making it more direct. The execution of the path can be improved by simply maximizing responsiveness. All these optimizations result in an experience that is more aesthetically pleasing to the player. Since providing a satisfying experience is the ultimate goal, these things are fairly important and directly impact the code within and surrounding A*.

Straight Paths

Paths calculated by A* often look like they were constructed by someone who was drunk. They weave and bob their way efficiently to the goal, but it sure doesn't look natural. This is a serious problem that undermines the believability of any game's AI. There are two ways to deal with this issue. The first is to promote straight paths within the A* algorithm; the second is to clean up the mess after the path has been calculated.

Promoting straighter paths involves careful cost weighting within the A* algorithm. Consider the two paths computed by A* that are shown in Figures 3.2.1 and 3.2.2.

The amazing observation is that both paths travel the *exact* same distance. Since both paths have identical costs, A* is unable to differentiate between them and simply chooses the first path it stumbles upon. The trick that will make A* choose the straight path is held within the cost function. Simply factor in an extra cost (penalty) if the new step being considered is not straight with the last step. Note that we are not looking at the overall straightness of the path, just penalizing new considerations that are not in line with the last step.

A reasonable penalty is half the normal cost to step in a given direction. The truth is that on a regular grid, any penalty at all (0.0000001) for non-straight choices causes A* to choose the straightest one. However, this is not the case on an arbitrary network.

FIGURE 3.2.1 Typical A* path.

FIGURE 3.2.2 Straightened A* path.

A word of caution: Penalizing non-straight paths results in more work being done by the pathfinder, thus slowing the computation. Obviously, the algorithm has to consider many more permutations in order to find the straightest one. In fact, searches can take significantly more time. However, if hierarchical methods are used, the extra time might not be an issue. Make sure you understand the tradeoffs.

Straight Paths in a Polygonal Search Space

With a polygonal search space, this trick is not very useful. Because triangles aren't uniformly spaced, as a rectangular grid is, similar paths that cost the same are quite rare. Therefore, there is no need to find the straighter path. Instead, there's a different problem: Since triangles can vary greatly in size and proportion, paths are more crooked than ever. The trick is to optimize for straightness after the path has been calculated.

Smooth Paths

Unfortunately, paths computed by A* are usually riddled with sharp turns. Even if you employ a technique to make straighter paths, sharp turns still have the potential to make your characters look like robots. By applying rotational dampening to your turns, you can probably mask them a little, but you'll swing wide on every sharp corner. There's a much better way.

Straight from the field of computer graphics, there's an algorithm that makes your paths (simply a series of points in space) smooth for you. A simple Catmull-Rom spline does the trick because it creates a curve that nails all the control points in the original path (unlike a Bézier curve, which is smoother but doesn't go through the control points). Obviously, it's better to go directly through your points because A* deemed them clear and free of obstacles.

But how do you actually input a list of points and get a smoother list back? The Catmull-Rom formula requires four input points and gives you back a smooth curve between the second and third points. Figure 3.2.3 explains this concept a little better.

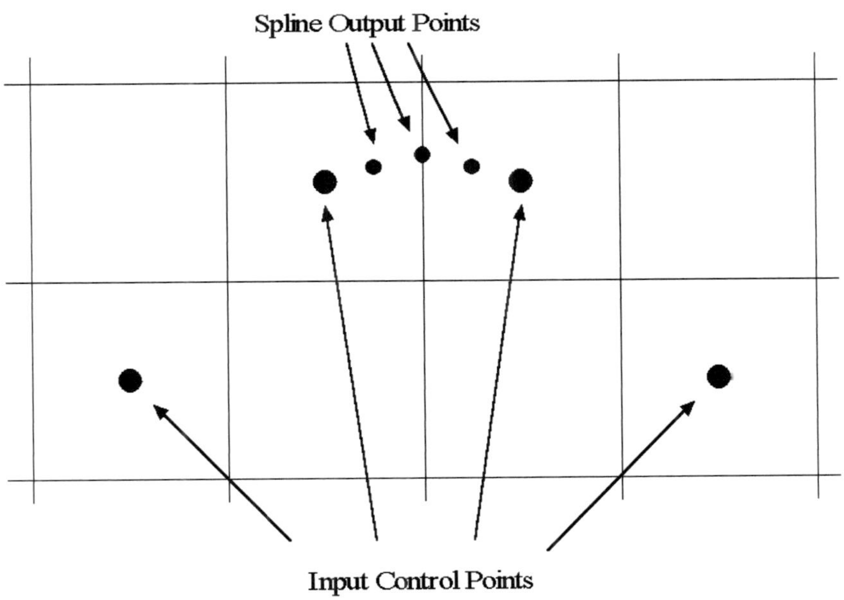

FIGURE 3.2.3 Getting spline points from control points.

To get the points between the first and second input points, you simply give the function the first point twice, then the second and third. To get the points between the third and fourth, give the function the second and third,, and double up on the fourth.

Each time you use the Catmull-Rom formula, it gives you a point roughly **u**% between the second and third inputs, where **u** is a number you pass in. The following is the formula (points can be 2D or 3D):

```
output_point = point_1 * (-0.5f*u*u*u + u*u - 0.5f*u) +
               point_2 * (1.5f*u*u*u + -2.5f*u*u + 1.0f) +
               point_3 * (-1.5f*u*u*u + 2.0f*u*u + 0.5f*u) +

               point_4 * (0.5f*u*u*u - 0.5f*u*u);
```

Note that if **u** is zero, the formula gives you `point_2`. When **u** is 1, it gives you `point_3`. As you can see, the spline really does go directly through the input points.

A Pre-Computed Catmull-Rom Formula

Since speed is an issue, you might want to dictate that you want **u** only at certain intervals, such as 0.0, 0.25, 0.5, and 0.75. By freezing all instances of **u**, you can pre-compute the formula at each **u**. Note that the formulas can take either 2D or 3D points. The following are some formulas at various intervals:

```
// u = 0.0
output_point =    point_2;

// u = 0.25
output_point =    point_1 * -0.0703125f + point_2 * 0.8671875f +
                   point_3 * 0.2265625f + point_4 * -0.0234375f;

// u = 0.5
output_point =    point_1 * -0.0625f + point_2 * 0.5625f +
                   point_3 * 0.5625f + point_4 * -0.0625f;

// u = 0.75
output_point =    point_1 * -0.0234375f + point_2 * 0.226563f +
                   point_3 * 0.8671875f + point_4 * -0.0703125f;

// u = 1.0

output_point =    point_3;
```

Equipped with the Catmull-Rom formula, all you need to do is walk through the path that A* found and create a new path. Remember to double up on the first input point when you start, and double up on the last input point when you get to the end.

If the A* path has only two points to begin with, simply don't apply the spline to the path.

Since you have a new path with four times the number of points, you might want to look into getting rid of redundant points. Running the new path through a function that prunes co-linear points should dramatically reduce your list.

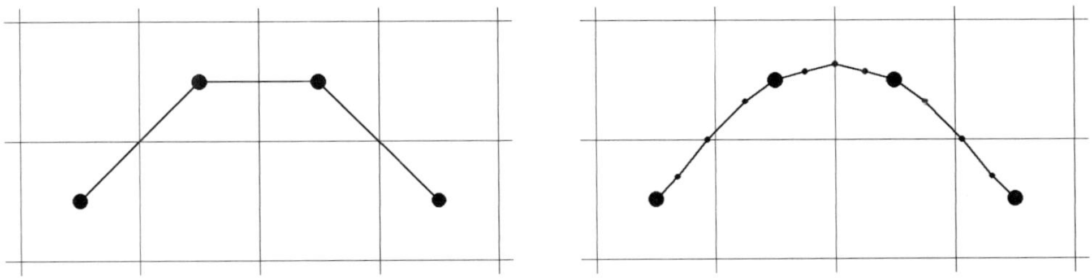

FIGURE 3.2.4 Path points before and after a spline is applied.

Figure 3.2.4 shows a typical path before and after the Catmull-Rom spline has been applied. Notice how it's still just a series of points (piece-wise linear), but the path is now much smoother. In the large scale of things, this path is perfectly smooth.

Improving the Directness of Hierarchical Paths

A very important A* technique is *hierarchical pathing*. However, the problem is that the resulting paths can be less than ideal. In hierarchical pathing, you pathfind in two distinct steps. You first find the large-scale path, and then you pathfind at the local level. For example, a castle might be broken up into rooms. You might want to get from the dungeon to the throne room. The idea is that you first find the large-scale path between the rooms (by running A* on the connectivity graph of the rooms). Once that path is found, you can then pathfind between each connecting room as you encounter it. The result is a huge savings of time. Unfortunately, the overall path can look rather bad because the goal point will always be the door to the next room, thus causing the character to always travel through the center of each door. When doors are arbitrarily large, this can look rather bad. Figure 3.2.5 illustrates the problem.

There is a simple, elegant way to get the ideal path, but it takes roughly twice the computation. The trick is to always path-find to the door beyond the next door. Then, whenever the character crosses through the first doorway, throw away the rest of the path and repeat the process. While the second half of the path is always wasted, it really does create the most direct and aesthetically pleasing route. Figure 3.2.6 shows the final path.

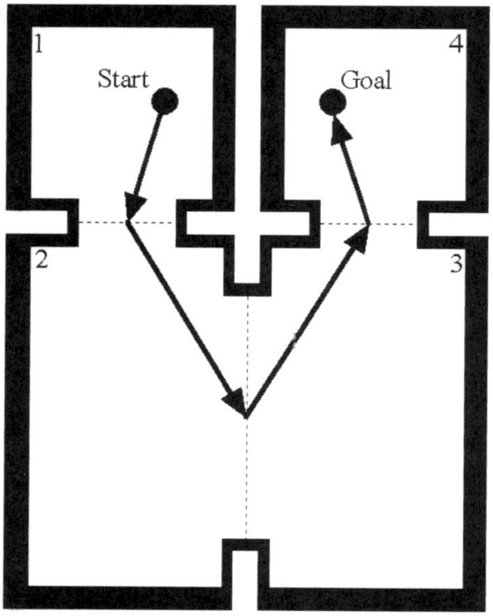

FIGURE 3.2.5 The path through several rooms.

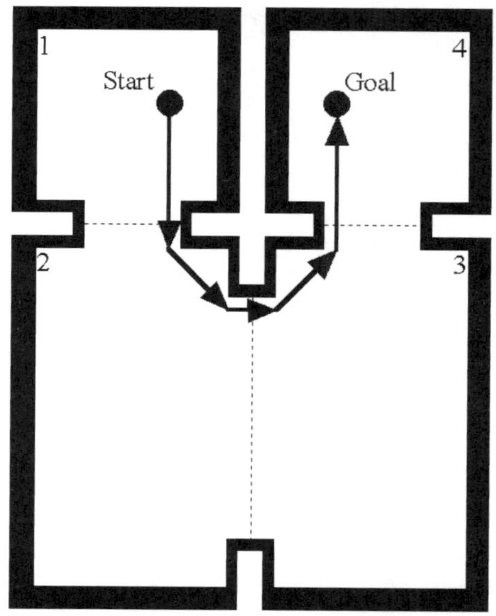

FIGURE 3.2.6 The optimized path through several rooms.

This technique always finds the optimum passage through the doorway because it takes into account the future path. The following is a step-by-step sample path execution guide to show how this method works:

1. Find the best room-to-room path using A* on the connectivity graph of the rooms.
2. The result is to travel the following sequence of rooms: 1, 2, 3, 4.
3. Pathfind from Start to subgoal 1 (Figure 3.2.7a).
4. Let the character walk until he enters Room 2.

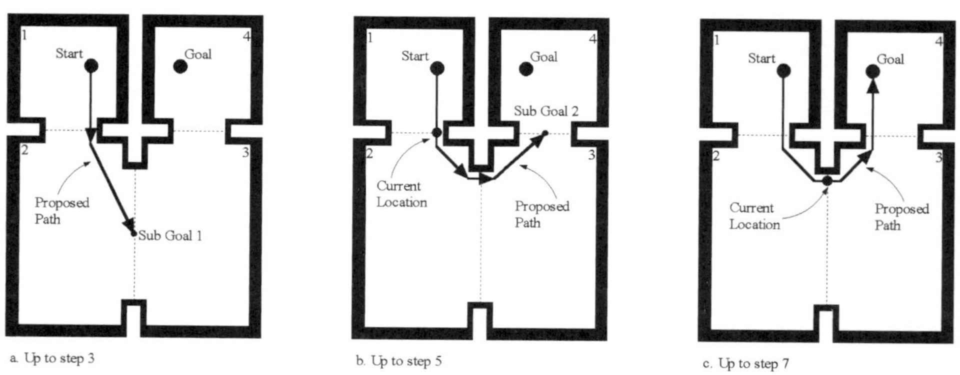

FIGURE 3.2.7 The computed path during various steps.

5. Throw away the remaining path and pathfind to subgoal 2 (Figure 3.2.7b).
6. Let the character walk until he enters Room 3.
7. Throw away the remaining path and pathfind to the final goal (Figure 3.2.7c).
8. Let the character walk to the final goal.

Hierarchical Pathfinding on Open Fields

There is no real difference between a set of connected rooms and a set of connected fields. The same principles apply. The resulting path is not completely straight, but it comes pretty close. You also need to realize that these fields are fairly large relative to the player. Figure 3.2.8 shows the hierarchical steps applied to open fields.

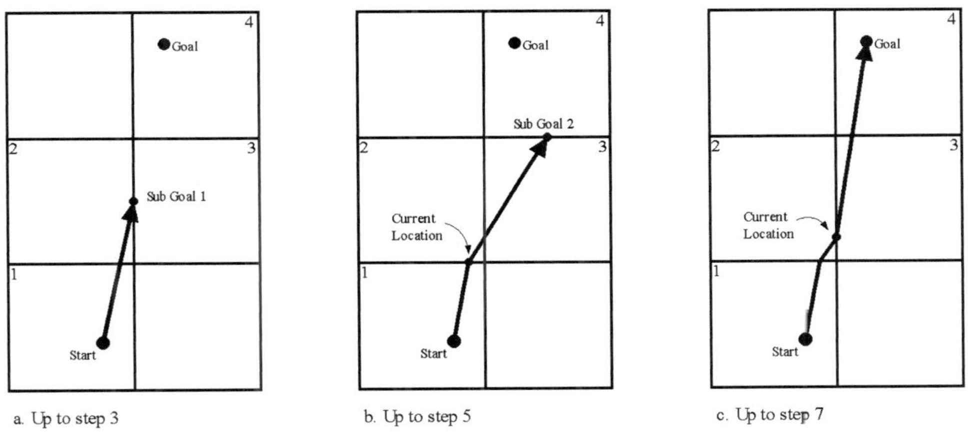

FIGURE 3.2.8 The computed path during various steps.

Eliminating Pauses During Hierarchical Searches

Note that every time the character enters a new room, a new local path must be computed. Since this obviously takes time, the character appears to pause as he enters each doorway. The search itself can't be sped up, but the new path request can be anticipated and computed slightly before it's needed. This simple trick keeps the character motion fluid throughout the path.

Maximizing Responsiveness

Controller responsiveness is critical to game play. When a player issues a move command in an RTS, they expect the unit to respond immediately. However, in the world of pathfinding and search algorithms, sometimes it can take awhile to find that path. That's where we need to pull a few tricks in order to give the feeling of instantaneous response.

The first trick is to stall by playing a sound byte that identifies the unit as having received the command. This trick gives immediate feedback that the unit is aware of the command and will execute it shortly. Meanwhile, the pathfinder is working at full speed trying to find the path.

Another trick is to stall by playing a "get ready to move" animation. The movement of the character signifies that he's going to move—even though he might not actually take any steps. You can even rotate the character to the "best-guess" direction so that he'll be ready to move when the final path is available, thus stalling even longer.

You can take the idea further by moving the character in the "best-guess" direction before the final path is ready. Unfortunately, you could be dead wrong in your guess, and the character will have to backtrack. Unless the pathfinder is extremely slow, it's probably best to avoid using this method.

Moving large groups of people at once can take even longer. If the player grabs 20 units and asks them to move across the map, you could be waiting a long time to get the 20 paths processed. There are two tricks to dealing with this situation. The first is to queue the path requests and let each unit move as its request is serviced. This way, it looks as though there's immediate feedback, because at least some of the units start to move immediately. It looks a bit like popcorn popping as each unit starts to move, but overall, it's fairly satisfying to the player. The second trick is to choose a leader in the group of 20 and find a path for only him. Then tell the other 19 units to follow the leader. However, this method can get complicated because there could be massive bunching, the leader could die halfway through the path, and each unit should eventually stop at a unique destination.

Conclusion

All these techniques are designed to make pathfinding more transparent to the player. The goal has always been to find good, direct paths instantaneously. Since that's a tough problem, hopefully you can apply these gems to your current pathfinder in order to get better-looking paths that ultimately feel better to the player.

References

[Patel99] Patel, Amit J., "Amit's Thoughts on Pathfinding," available online at http://theory.stanford.edu/~amitp/GameProgramming/, November 27, 1999.

[Stout96] Stout, W. Bryan, "Smart Moves: Intelligent Path-Finding," *Game Developer,* October/November 1996, pp. 28–35, also available online at www.gamasutra.com/features/19990212/sm_01.htm.

3.3

A* Speed Optimizations

Steve Rabin, Nintendo of America Inc.

steve.rabin@gmail.com

Traditionally, A* is a slow algorithm that never runs as fast as you'd like. Since there's a long list of optimizations that you could make, it's very important to understand why it's slow so you can wisely use your optimization time.

The first thing to notice about A* is that it is at the mercy of the search space. Usually, the sheer number of connections to search is a good indication of how fast A* works. In a rectangular grid of 1,000 by 1,000 squares, there are 1 million possible squares to search. To find an arbitrary path in that kind of world simply takes a lot of work, no matter how optimized your code. The solution is to optimize the search space.

Once the search space has been optimized, it's time to look deeper into the actual A* implementation. Since A* churns through a lot of memory, it's critical to optimize memory allocation as well as each of the data accesses. A* also demands a lot of sorting, but this can be dealt with quickly and efficiently using some specialized data structures.

Lastly, the best way to speed up A* is by not using it at all for simple cases. Construct some kind of test to determine whether you absolutely need to fire up the pathfinder. Many times, simple routes can be determined without using the full-blown A* implementation. For example, try running a blind straight-line path to the goal, testing to see if it collides with walls or other objects. Undoubtedly, there will be times when this simple solution works amazingly well.

Search Space Optimization

Simplifying the Search Space

The biggest win always comes from searching through less data. If you can represent your world as a simplified connectivity graph, A* will work all the faster. Practically, there are several options to choose from. Since speed isn't the only consideration, some other pros and cons are also discussed here. A simple diagram of each technique is provided in Figure 3.3.1.

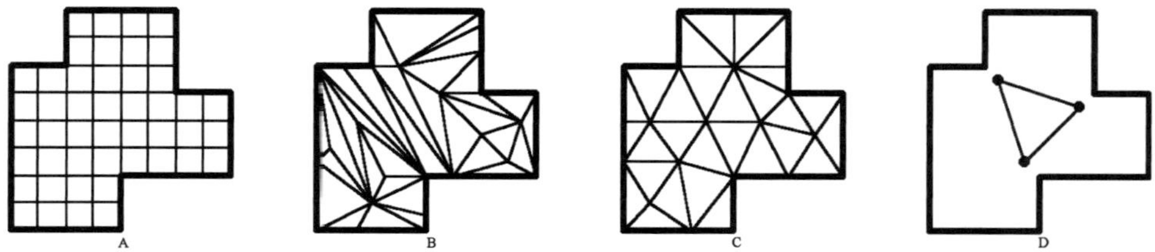

FIGURE 3.3.1 Four options for representing the search space.

Rectangular or Hexagonal Grid

Description

A uniform rectangular or hexagonal grid is overlaid onto the world. The size of each grid space is proportional to the size of the smallest character. Therefore, a character in a grid space blocks that space during the A* search. See Figure 3.3.1a.

Pros

Obstacles and characters can be easily marked in the grid allowing for avoidance. This creates a one-step solution to finding a path through static and dynamic objects.

- Works well for 2D tile-based worlds.

Cons

- Typically results in the largest search space.
- Rectangular grids don't map very well onto 3D worlds.
- Paths tend to look like moves on a chessboard.

Actual Polygonal Floor

Description

In a 3D game world, the floor polygons are specifically marked and used directly as the search space. This polygonal floor is identical to the rendered geometry, thus being arbitrarily simple or complex. See Figure 3.3.1b.

Pros

- Data structure already exists in the 3D world.
- Can be walked through quickly with a BSP tree.

Cons

- Three-dimensional worlds can have arbitrarily high numbers of polygons on the floor.
- Can't represent obstacles such as tables or chairs (because the floor exists beneath these objects).
- Requires algorithmic solution for choosing path points within a polygon.

Polygonal Floor Representation

Description

An artist or level designer creates a polygonal floor representation that is used exclusively for pathfinding. The polygons can be eliminated in places where characters are not allowed to walk, such as under tables or chairs. See Figure 3.3.1c.

Pros

- Small search space representation.
- Can be walked through quickly with a BSP tree.
- Obstacles can be incorporated in the representation.

Cons

- Requires artist or level designer to construct.
- Can't represent characters within the space.
- Requires algorithmic solution for choosing path points within a polygon.

Points of Visibility

Description

Points are placed at convex corners in the world (sticking out a little from each corner). Each point is then connected to all other points that it can "see." This creates a connectivity graph that describes the minimal paths required to get around walls. See Figure 3.3.1d.

Pros

- Creates minimal search space representation.
- Obstacles can be incorporated in the representation.
- Resulting paths are perfectly direct.

Cons

- Requires algorithmic or designer assistance to create the graph.
- Obstacles can't be removed from the graph if they should be destroyed.
- Can't represent characters within the space.
- Doesn't work well with entities that have large widths, such as a wide formation of characters.
- Worlds with curved walls could cause the graph to become unnecessarily complex.

As you can see, there is no obvious choice. Each representation has its trade-offs. If your world is 3D with few dynamic obstacles, then using points of visibility is a reasonable choice. If your world is 2D tile-based or there are hordes of moving characters (as in a large RTS game), a rectangular grid might be the best choice. Just remember that your decision in choosing a search space representation has huge repercussions in terms of speed and flexibility.

Points of Visibility Explained

Since using points of visibility is an extremely viable option, it's worth explaining a little better. The technique requires that you build up a graph that can be used to get around the world. Points are placed at convex corners and connected to all other points they can see. It's as though a freeway system has been constructed for the sole purpose of getting around walls. The problem now is how you get on and off the freeway.

To get on the freeway, you test the visibility between the starting point and every point on the freeway. Since you can potentially compare thousands of points, it's important that you use other space-partitioning techniques (such as hierarchical pathfinding). Once you have a list of potential on-ramp points, you put them on the A* Open list and begin running the algorithm. With each point you explore, you must test its visibility with the goal point. If you find a point that can see the goal point, you have a potential off-ramp. Figure 3.3.2 shows a simple example.

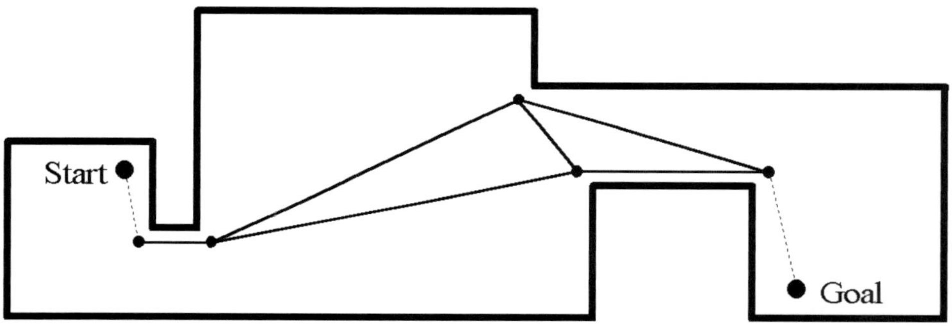

FIGURE 3.3.2 Points of visibility example.

Hierarchical Pathfinding

Hierarchical pathfinding is an extremely powerful technique that speeds up the pathfinding process. Regardless of which search space representation is used, this technique in effect simplifies that space. Therefore, if your world representation is large, there's still hope. The key is to break up the world hierarchically.

Consider a castle. It can be thought of as a single, large building or as a collection of rooms connected by doors (a large-scale connectivity graph). The pathfinder works in two distinct steps. It first finds the room-to-room path, knowing the starting and ending room. Once that room-to-room path is known, the pathfinder then works on the micro problem of getting from the current room to the next room on the list. Thus, the pathfinder doesn't need to compute the entire path before it takes the first step. The micro path is figured out on a need-to-know basis as each new room is entered. This method significantly cuts down on the search space and the resulting time to compute the path.

This technique really shines if your world is already constructed hierarchically. Even a 3D world could be constructed using a simple building-block paradigm. Consider a circular staircase. Normally, a circular staircase causes most pathfinders a lot of grief. The structure is very 3D, mostly circular, and could spiral for a very long distance. A spiral staircase could be built using a quarter-turn piece of the staircase. This piece could then be duplicated indefinitely to create a very tall spiral staircase.

A hierarchical pathfinder could blazingly compute a path up the staircase if it were constructed in this fashion. The pathfinder would first compute the large-scale route through each connecting quarter-turn piece and then would quickly find the local path from the start to the end of each quarter-turn piece. All of a sudden, a complicated path over some rather complicated geometry becomes trivial to compute. Figure 3.3.3 shows an example.

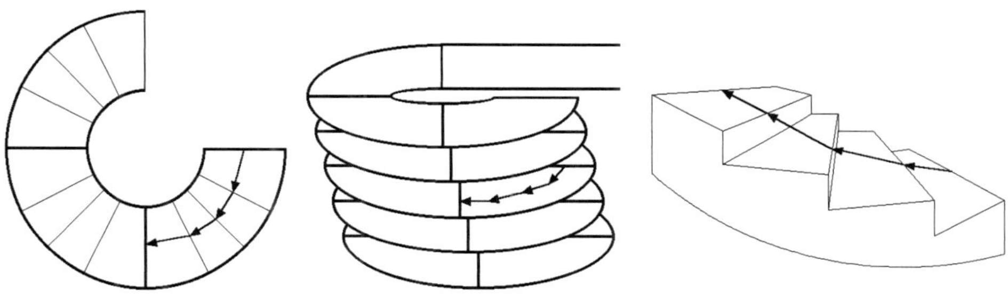

FIGURE 3.3.3 Hierarchical pathfinding on a circular staircase.

Hierarchical pathfinding isn't restricted to rooms with doors. You can easily extrapolate the idea to huge fields of landscape that are stitched together. Although it's true that there isn't one easily identifiable "door" spot anymore, the entire seam from one field to another becomes the door.

Imagine an immense world created with these stitched pieces of land. Now imagine telling a character to walk from one end to the other. No problem! The pathfinder first finds a route through the network of land pieces and then finds the local path from the current land piece to the next. With a little work, you can even imagine planning a route from the throne room of one castle to the ninth-level dungeon below a completely different castle—even though the castles might be 10 miles apart!

Avoiding Pauses While Computing Local Paths

Since a path is computed every time the character enters a new room, it's important that the character not pause at each door while his new path is constructed. In order to avoid a pause, the path request must be anticipated and completed before the character actually needs it. This simple trick keeps the character motion fluid throughout the execution of the path.

Algorithmic Optimization

Playing with the Heuristic Cost

Designing an algorithm for the heuristic cost can at times seem more like voodoo than science. The idea behind the heuristic cost is to estimate the true cost from a particular node to the goal. Here's an interesting fact: If you always knew the true cost to the goal, A* would beeline a path to the goal without wasting any search time going down the wrong path. But if the heuristic estimate happens to overestimate the true cost, the heuristic becomes "inadmissible," and the algorithm might not find the optimal path (and might find a terrible path).

The way to guarantee that the cost is never overestimated is by calculating the geometric distance between the node and the goal. When coding A* for the first time, this is the best thing to do until it's time to optimize. Since the cost will never be more than this distance, the optimal path will always be found.

Overestimating the Heuristic Cost

Interesting fact #2: Using a heuristic that routinely overestimates by a little usually results in faster searches with reasonable paths. However, how much should the cost be overestimated? To answer this question, you need to understand what happens when this remaining path cost is artificially bloated.

If the heuristic part of the total cost (*total cost = cost to node + heuristic cost*) is bigger than it should be, it distorts the reasoning by which nodes on the Open list are picked off. Since A* always picks the node with the least total cost, this distortion promotes nodes closer to the goal to be picked.

When you look at an A* search that's trying to find its way around a wall, you can see a shape that develops from the nodes explored (nodes on the Closed list). This shape is the easiest way to see the effects of playing with the heuristic estimate.

When the heuristic equals zero, the search evolves as a circle around the starting point. When the heuristic uses the Euclidean distance to the goal, the search looks like an oval, with the start and goal points the foci. When the heuristic is overestimated, the shape changes to be more of a diamond or hexagon, with the start and goal points at the extreme corners of the shape. Figures 3.3.4, 3.3.5, and 3.3.6 show the

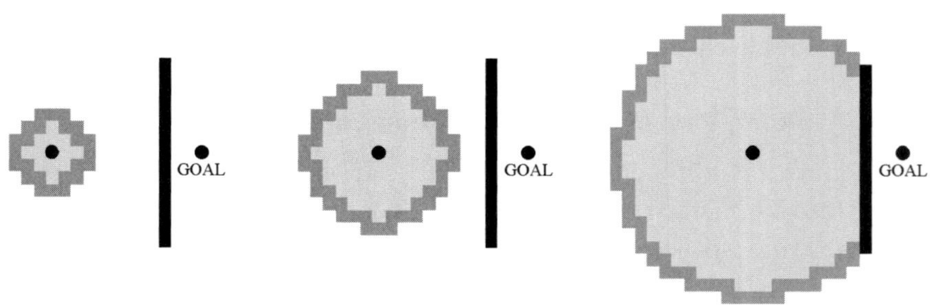

FIGURE 3.3.4 The heuristic cost of zero.

growth of the search using various heuristic costs while trying to overcome a large obstacle.

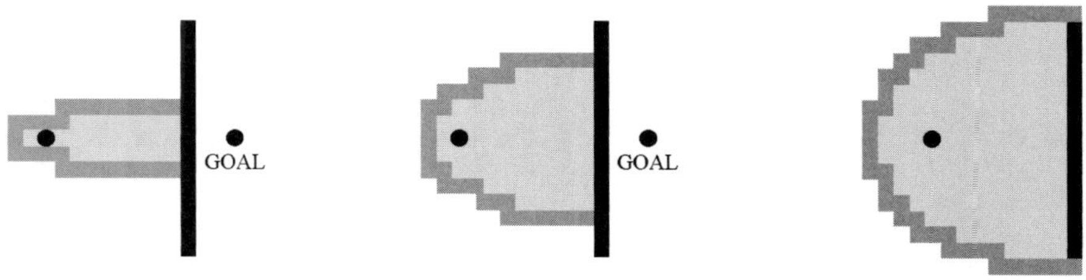

FIGURE 3.3.5 The heuristic cost using Euclidean distance to goal.

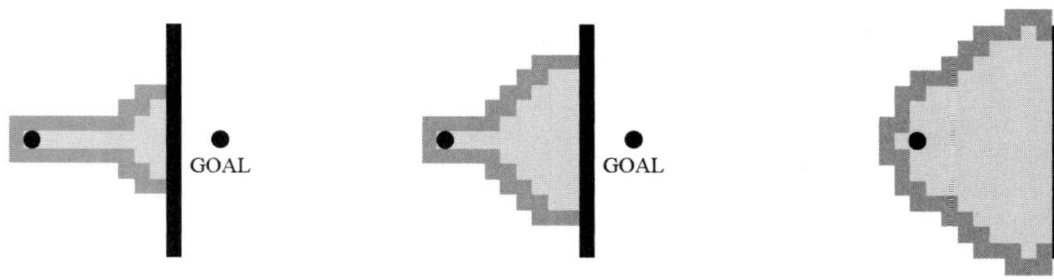

FIGURE 3.3.6 The heuristic cost overestimated.

What does all this mean? It means that by overestimating the heuristic, the search pushes hard on the closest nodes to the goal. This causes pressure for the search to overcome large obstacles that are between the start and goal points of the search. If the actual solution requires backtracking before going to the goal, an overestimating heuristic slows the search. However, if most of the time there's a way to get around large blocking obstacles, the overestimating heuristic is faster. Figure 3.3.7 illustrates this point as the non-overestimating heuristic explores three times more nodes than the overestimating heuristic.

Ultimately, getting the right amount of overestimating requires experimentation. Unfortunately, if the search space is not on a grid, it's probably not possible to accurately observe the shape of the search. Instead, you need to measure indicators such as the size of the Closed list and the maximum size of the Open list.

The final size of the Closed list tells how many nodes were explored; the maximum size of the Open list is a good indicator of how long it takes to explore each node (since Open list operations take a relatively long time as the list grows big). When tuning your heuristic, you can try typical searches and watch the Open and Closed list sizes in order to identify good heuristic values. By testing searches on your actual game, you'll be able to tune the heuristic to something reasonable.

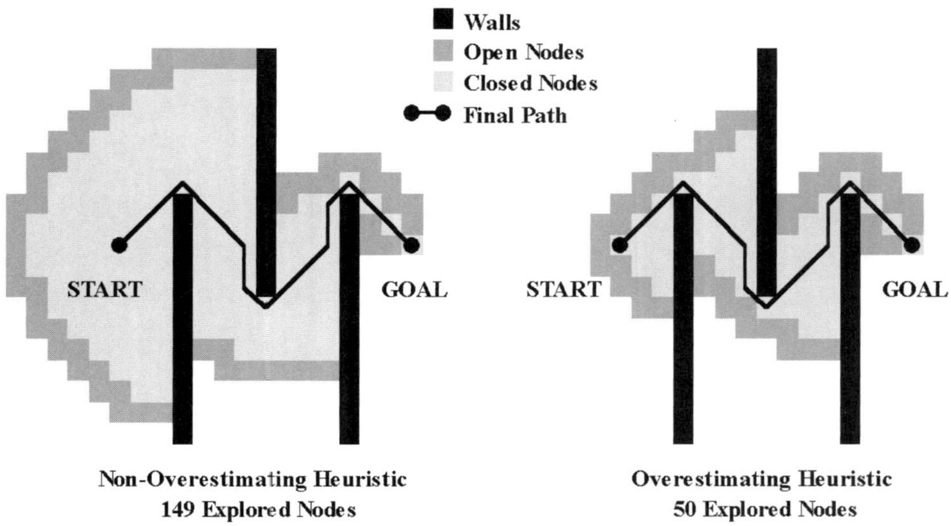

FIGURE 3.3.7 A non-overestimating heuristic vs. an overestimating heuristic.

Decoupling Pathfinding Data from the Search Space

A* requires a large amount of memory in order to store the progress of each search. Traditionally, this memory is held inside each searchable node. If the search space is a rectangular grid, each grid square contains pathfinding node data. If the search space is a polygonal mesh, each triangle contains pathfinding node data. Since an individual search almost never covers every single node in the search space, there is no reason to have this incredible amount of memory dedicated to pathfinding. For example, a 1,000 × 1,000 tiled world has 1 million pathfinding nodes just sitting there unused most of the time.

The solution is to decouple the pathfinding node data from the search space. This solution reduces the huge memory overhead and could also speed up searches. Interestingly, by decoupling the node data from the search space, you allow for simultaneous searches, which can now occur because multiple-node data can point to the same real node in the search space. However, it's generally not a good idea to allow simultaneous searches——still, in certain circumstances, it might be useful.

Pre-allocating a Minimum Amount of Memory

Decoupling the node data from the search space requires that each search use some other chunk of memory. We could simply allocate node data on the fly, but A* can churn through hundreds of nodes each search, so this isn't a reasonable solution. A way around this is to pre-allocate a sufficiently large block of memory that can be recycled for each A* search.

What is A* storing so much of? It's all the data that tracks the progress of the search. For every node explored, the algorithm needs to save the following information:

- A pointer to the parent node
- The cost to get to this node
- The total cost (*cost + heuristic estimate*)
- Whether this node is on the Open list
- Whether this node is on the Closed list

The idea is to pre-allocate a ton of these nodes (call it the *node bank*). The actual number varies depending on the size of your largest search. Now, you don't want to pre-allocate too much memory, so this array should be able to grow if needed—or alternatively, force the search to give up.

When A* explores a new node for the first time, it needs to ask for a free node from the node bank. When it gets a free node back, it needs to fill out the info in order to personalize it for this new node.

Storing Explored Nodes in a Master Node List

Once a node has been personalized from the node bank, it needs to be put somewhere for fast retrieval. The optimal data structure for this activity is a *hash* table. Hash tables allow constant-time storing and looking up of data. Therefore, we store all explored nodes in this *master node list*. This hash table allows us to instantaneously find out if a particular node is on the Closed list or the Open list. Remember, since the node data memory is already allocated, the hash table contains only pointers to these nodes.

At this point you might ask yourself, "Where is the Closed list?" The answer is that it lives inside the master node list. All explored nodes are stored inside the master node list, and the Closed list just happens to be in the same place. This isn't a problem, because each node is clearly marked as whether it's on the Closed or Open list. So where does the Open list live? The Open list is maintained separately, *but* the master node list also contains pointers to all the same nodes that are on the Open list. Why the duplication? Because sometimes it's faster to find the node you want using the master node list, and sometimes it's faster using the Open list. It's all about speed.

When any given node is explored during the A* algorithm, it's possible that the node was already explored during this same search. To make things simple, you'll want a function that gives you back a pointer to that particular node's data, whether its been searched before or not.

This function first checks the master node list to see if the node has been explored before. If it has, the function simply returns a pointer to that existing node. If the node is not in the master node list, a free node is taken from the node bank, it is initialized to represent the desired node, and its pointer is returned. In effect, the function completely hides the details of allocating new nodes from the node bank and getting nodes that already exist.

```
Node* GetNode( MasterNodeList nodelist, NodeLocation node_location )
{
   //GetNodeFromMasterNodeList accesses the hash table of nodes
   Node* node = GetNodeFromMasterNodeList( nodelist, node_location );
   if( node ) {
      return( node );
   }
   else
   {   //Not in the Master Node List – get new one from the Node Bank
      Node* newNode = GetFreeNodeFromNodeBank();
      newNode->location = node_location;
      newNode->onOpen = false;
      newNode->onClosed = false;

      //StoreNodeInMasterNodeList places the node into the hash table
      StoreNodeInMasterNodeList( nodelist, newNode );
      return( newNode );
   }

}
```

Optimizing the Open List

The beauty of A* comes from its ability to direct the search toward the most promising directions. The way it achieves this goal is by putting all nodes it could search next into the Open list. It then orders the list from the most promising to the least promising nodes to search. The problem is that the Open list tends to get big, and each time it goes through the A* loop, the most promising node must be extracted from the list. The node to extract is the one with the lowest total cost (*cost to get to the node + heuristic estimate of the remaining cost to the goal*). As it turns out, the best way to store the Open list is to keep it sorted as a priority queue.

A priority queue can be implemented as a binary heap. A *binary heap* is a sorted tree that has the property that the parent always has a lower value than its children. However, there is no ordering among siblings, so a heap is *not* a completely ordered tree. Because of this interesting property, insertions and extractions (removing the lowest element) take only *O(log n)*. Fortunately, that's pretty much all A* needs to do with the Open list.

Implementing a Priority Queue

It's out of the scope of this gem to implement a priority queue from scratch, but there's an easy way to implement one using STL. Whether you're using STL or not, be sure to check out a great article about priority queues [Nelson96]. It describes priority queues clearly enough that you could probably construct one without the help of STL. Otherwise, consult any standard algorithm and data structure book for more information.

In order to properly use the priority queue, use the following four operations that A* needs to perform on the Open list:

1. Extract the node with the minimum total cost (and resort the list): $O(\log n)$.
2. Insert a new node on the Open list (and resort the list): $O(\log n)$.
3. Update the total cost of a node already on the Open list (and resort the list): $O(n+\log n)$.
4. Determine whether the Open list is empty: $O(1)$.

STL actually implements a priority queue with something called a *container adapter*. However, the operations that can be performed on it are very limiting. In fact, it has no interface to perform operation #3 (updating a node's total cost and resorting the list). Therefore, we can't use the STL implementation of a priority queue. However, we can use the STL heap operations on an STL vector container to make our own priority queue!

Listings 3.3.1, 3.3.2, 3.3.3, and 3.3.4 contain the four Open list operations along with the node object, the heap object, and the STL comparison object—all implemented in C++ using STL. In addition, on the CD-ROM that accompanies this book, you'll find that Greg Snook's pathfinding article, "Simplified 3D Movement and Pathfinding Using Navigation Meshes," contains almost identical code for implementing an STL priority queue.

ON THE CD

A* Using the Optimized Master Node List and Open List

There's nothing too tricky about using the ideas presented, but just in case, the guts of the A* algorithm are implemented in Listing 3.3.5 using the master node list and the Open list. Some other small tricks are also included, such as not searching the node from which the search just came.

Conclusion

Since pathfinding is fundamentally a tough computational problem, the best strategies have always been to simplify the problem. Before any effort is made to optimize the algorithm, ensure that the world is represented in the simplest reasonable way. Once that's decided, it's very important that some kind of hierarchical scheme is also incorporated. Usually this scheme involves some pre-processing that requires level designers and artists to be very involved in the search space representation. Although it adds some overhead to the development of assets, there's no better way to speed up pathfinding.

Once the search space is finalized, it's important to get the pathfinder working correctly in that space before any optimizations are attempted. A* is not a trivial algorithm, and it's extremely difficult to debug if many of the optimizations have been incorporated. When you are ready to optimize, start by decoupling the node memory from the search space. The next step is to implement a priority queue for the Open list and a hash table for the master node/Closed list. Finally, when everything works like a charm and the game is stable, you can play with the heuristic cost. In order to get the best results, you'll want to tune the heuristic several times during development as the game world becomes better defined.

After all these techniques have been implemented, the next step is to cheat. Some techniques for giving the impression of instantaneous pathfinding can be found in the "A* Aesthetic Optimization" gem in this book. The trick involves making the player think that a path has been found when in reality you are just stalling. If the player feels that the game is very responsive, the pathfinder appears to be unobtrusive and transparent, which is the core reason for speeding it up.

LISTING 3.3.1 Node Object

```
class Node
{
public:
   NodeLocation location;    // location of node (some location repre-
sentation)
   Node* parent;             // parent node (zero pointer represents
starting node)
   float cost;               // cost to get to this node
   float total;              // total cost (cost + heuristic estimate)
   bool onOpen;              // on Open list
   bool onClosed;            // on Closed list
};
```

LISTING 3.3.2 Priority Queue Object

```
class PriorityQueue
{
public:
   //Heap implementation using an STL vector
   //Note: the vector is an STL container, but the
   //operations done on the container cause it to
   //be a priority queue organized as a heap
   std::vector<Node*> heap;
};
```

LISTING 3.3.3 STL Comparison Function

```
class NodeTotalGreater
{
public:
   //This is required for STL to sort the priority queue
   //(its entered as an argument in the STL heap functions)
   bool operator()( Node * first, Node * second ) const {
      return( first->total > second->total );
   }
};
```

LISTING 3.3.4 Four Open List Operations

```
Node* PopPriorityQueue( PriorityQueue& pqueue )
{  //Total time = O(log n)

   //Get the node at the front - it has the lowest total cost
   Node * node = pqueue.heap.front();

   //pop_heap will move the node at the front to the position N
   //and then sort the heap to make positions 1 through N-1 correct
   //(STL makes no assumptions about your data and doesn't want
   //to change the size of the container.

   std::pop_heap( pqueue.heap.begin(), pqueue.heap.end(),
      NodeTotalGreater() );

   //pop_back() will actually remove the last element from the heap
   //(now the heap is sorted for positions 1 through N)
   pqueue.heap.pop_back();

   return( node );
}

void PushPriorityQueue( PriorityQueue& pqueue, Node* node )
{  //Total time = O(log n)

   //Pushes the node onto the back of the vector (the heap is
   //now unsorted)
   pqueue.heap.push_back( node );

   //Sorts the new element into the heap
   std::push_heap( pqueue.heap.begin(), pqueue.heap.end(),
      NodeTotalGreater() );
}

void UpdateNodeOnPriorityQueue( PriorityQueue& pqueue, Node* node )
{  //Total time = O(n+log n)

   //Loop through the heap and find the node to be updated
   std::vector<Node*>::iterator i;
   for( i=pqueue.heap.begin(); i!=pqueue.heap.end(); i++ )
   {
      if( (*i)->location == node->location )
      {  //Found node - resort from this position in the heap
         //(since its total value was changed before this function
         //was called)
         std::push_heap( pqueue.heap.begin(), i+1,
            NodeTotalGreater() );
         return;
      }
   }
}
```

```
bool IsPriorityQueueEmpty( PriorityQueue& pqueue )
{
   //empty() is an STL function that determines if
   //the STL vector has no elements
   return( pqueue.heap.empty() );
}
```

LISTING 3.3.5 A* Implemented with a Master Node List and a Priority Queue Open List

```
MasterNodeList g_nodelist;

bool FindPath( GameObject* gameobject, WorldLocation goal )
{
   //Get a path in progress if it exists for this game object with
   //this goal
   //A path may have been started and not finished from last game tick
   //If no path in progress, it returns an empty path structure
   Path* path = GetPathInProgress( gameobject, goal );

   if( !path->initialized )
   {  //The InitializePath function fills out the path structure for
      //this path request
      //It initializes a clean MasterNodeList and a clean Open list
      InitializePath( path, gameobject, goal );

      //Create the very first node and put it on the Open list
      Node* startnode = GetNode( g_nodelist, GetNodeLocation(
         gameobject->pos ) );
      startnode->onOpen = true;      //This node goes on Open list
      startnode->onClosed = false;   //This node not on Closed list
      startnode->parent = 0;         //This node has no parent
      startnode->cost = 0;           //This node has no cost to get to
      startnode->total = GetNodeHeuristic( startnode->location,
         path.goal );
      PushPriorityQueue( path.open, startnode );
   }

   while( !IsPriorityQueueEmpty( path->open ) )
   {
       //Get the best candidate node to search next
       Node* bestnode = PopPriorityQueue( path.open );

       if( AtGoal( bestnode, goal ) )
       {  //Found the goal node – construct a path and exit
          //The complete path will be stored inside the game object
          ConstructPathToGoal( gameobject, path );
          return( true );   //return with success
       }

       while( /*loop through all connecting nodes of bestnode*/ )
       {
          Node newnode;
          newnode.location = /*whatever the new location is*/;
```

```
    //This avoids searching the node we just came from
    if( bestnode->parent == 0 ||
        bestnode->parent->location != newnode.location )
    {
       newnode.parent = bestnode;
       newnode.cost = bestnode->cost + CostFromNodeToNode(
          &newnode, bestnode );
       newnode.total = newnode.cost;

       //Get the preallocated node for this location
       //Both newnode and actualnode represent the same node
       //location, but the search at this point may not want
       //to clobber over the data from a more promising route –
       //thus the duplicate nodes for now

       Node* actualnode = GetNode( g_nodelist,
          newnode.location );

       //Note: the following test takes O(1) time (no searching
       //through lists)
       if( !( actualnode->onOpen && newnode.total >
          actualnode->total ) &&
           !( actualnode->onClosed && newnode.total >
          actualnode->total ) )
       {  //This node is very promising
          //Take it off the Open and Closed lists (in theory)
          //and push on Open
          actualnode->onClosed = false;   //effectively removing
                                            it from
  // Closed
          actualnode->parent = newnode.parent;
          actualnode->cost = newnode.cost;
          actualnode->total = newnode.total;

          if( actualnode->onOpen )
          {  //Since this node is already on the Open list,
             //update it's position
             UpdateNodeOnPriorityQueue( path.open, actualnode
);
          }
          else
          {  //Put the node on the Open list
             PushPriorityQueue( path.open, actualnode );
             actualnode->onOpen = true;
          }
       }
    }
  }

  //Now that we've explored bestnode, put it on the Closed list
  bestnode->onClosed = true;

  //Use some method to determine if we've taken too much time
  //this tick and should abort the search until next tick
  if( ShouldAbortSearch() ) {
```

```
                return( false );
            }
        }

        //If we got here, all nodes have been searched without finding
        //the goal
        return( false );
    }
```

References

A* Algorithm

[Heyes-Jones98] Heyes-Jones, Justin, "A* Algorithm Tutorial," available online at www.gamedev.net/reference/programming/ai/article690.asp, 1998.

[Patel99] Patel, Amit J., "Amit's Thoughts on Pathfinding," available online at http://theory.stanford.edu/~amitp/GameProgramming/, November 27, 1999.

[Stout96] Stout, W. Bryan, "Smart Moves: Intelligent Path-Finding," *Game Developer*, October/November 1996, pp. 28–35, also available online at www.gamasutra.com/features/19990212/sm_01.htm.

Data Structures

[Lewis91] Lewis, Harry R., *Data Structures and Their Algorithms,* HarperCollins Publishers Inc., 1991.

[Nelson96] Nelson, Mark, "Priority Queues and the STL," *Dr. Dobb's Journal,* also available online at www.dogma.net/markn/articles/pq_stl/priority.htm, January 1996.

3.4

Tactical Path-Finding with A*

William van der Sterren, CGF-AI

william.van.der.sterren@cgf-ai.com

If all games were just about getting from point A to point B, AI would solely have to provide the shortest paths. A standard A* algorithm could do the job. However, often when trying to reach point B, the AI also needs to avoid being seen or shot at. This is called *tactical path-finding*, a situation where the AI needs to balance short travel times with avoiding hostile observation and fire (see Figure 3.4.1). Whether handling a tank platoon retreating behind a ridgeline or an XFighter sneaking through a cloud of meteoroids, the AI needs to consider enemy positions and their lines of fire.

Tactical path-finding not only adds a realistic touch to AI movement, but it also presents a more-rewarding and less-predictable opponent for the player. This gem will help you to extend the standard A* algorithm so it generates tactical paths.

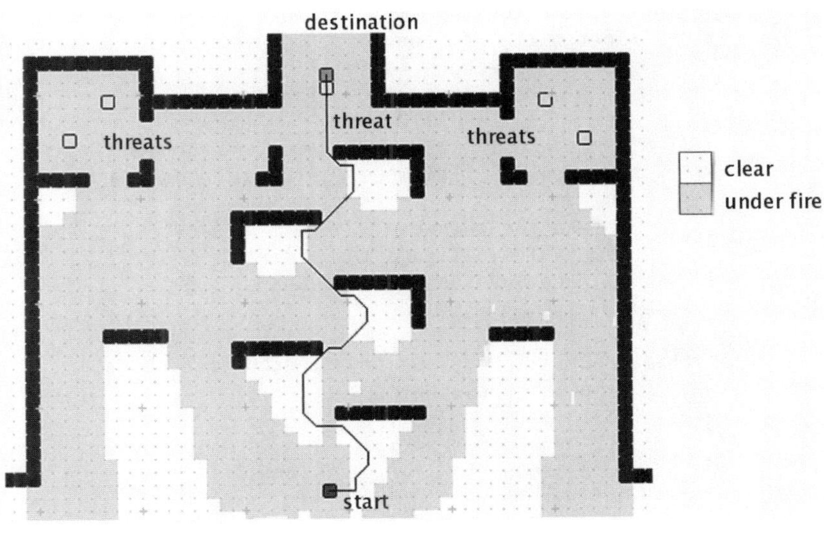

FIGURE 3.4.1 Example of tactical path-finding.

First, we will introduce a small change to the 'shortest-path' A* algorithm by increasing the costs for movement through locations subject to enemy observation or fire. As a result, A* will generate paths that attempt to avoid enemy observation and fire. These attempts, however, often look artificial and are not tactically sound.

We will then look at a few of these 'flawed' tactical paths, figure out why these paths are flawed, and how we can correct this in our A* cost function. We will also compare the computing costs of finding tactical paths with those of finding shortest paths. Obviously, finding tactical paths will be more expensive, but we will look into a few techniques and tricks to limit the overhead of the A* search and the line-of-fire evaluations that need to be done during the tactical path computation.

ON THE CD

On the CD-ROM, you will find an extended version of James Matthews' A* Explorer tool [Matthews01]. With this tool, you can experiment with tactical A* (and follow all the examples included in this gem).

A*, but More Risky

A* is a generic search algorithm. To allow it to find paths for our AI, we equip it with a cost function and a heuristic function [Stout00]. For path-finding, the cost function computes the exact cost of moving from one location to another. These movement costs are computed from the distance traveled and the speed allowed by the terrain.

The heuristic function for path-finding typically provides an estimate of the remaining costs to the destination, such as the vector length divided by the maximum speed. Listing 3.4.1 shows an example of a cost function and a heuristic.

LISTING 3.4.1 Cost Function and Heuristic for Evaluating Shortest Paths

```
float MovementCostNodeToNode(node* aFromNode, node* aToNode) {
    float dist, fromMoveCost, toMoveCost;
    dist = (aFromNode->origin -
        aToNode->origin).Length();

    fromMoveCost  = aFromNode->GetLocalMovementCosts();
    toMoveCost    = aToNode->GetLocalMovementCosts();

    // take the average
    return kTravelTimeFactor * dist *
        (fromMoveCost + toMoveCosts) / 2;
}

float HeuristicNodeToDestination(node* aToNode,
        node* aDestination) {
    float dist;
    dist = (aToNode->origin -
        aDestination->origin).Length();

    return kTravelTimeFactor * dist *
        (minimalMoveCostForAnyLocation);
}
```

Using such a cost function and heuristic A* will find and return a path with the lowest costs to the destination. Typically, the AI is interested in the path that gets it to the destination most quickly, so the costs are expressed as time.

If we now introduce additional costs for visiting locations in the enemy's line of sight and line of fire, the resultant generated paths will also attempt to avoid observation and hostile fire. Our revised A* algorithm will automatically balance short travel time versus visiting risky locations, based on the weights for each type of cost.

You'll find an example of a more-tactical A* cost function in Listing 3.4.2. The additional risk costs depend on the risk sampled at each of the nodes and the travel time needed to move from one node to the other. If the nodes are not too far apart, this approximates the total risk of moving from one node to the other. Otherwise, you might need to sample the risk at additional locations between the nodes.

LISTING 3.4.2 Cost Function for Evaluating Tactical Paths

```
float TacticalCostNodeToNode1(node* aFromNode,
        node* aToNode) {
    float travelTime, riskFrom, riskTo, riskTotal;
    travelTime = MovementCostNodeToNode(aFromNode,
        aToNode);

    // use duration of move, and average risk of
    // both locations
    riskFrom  =
        GetRiskOfEnemyObservationOrFire(aFromNode);
    riskTo    =
        GetRiskOfEnemyObservationOrFire(aToNode);
    riskTotal = (riskFrom + riskTo) / 2 * travelTime;

    // return the weighted combination of travel
    // and risk costs
    return kTravelTimeFactor * travelTime +
        kRiskFactor * riskTotal;
}
```

The `GetRiskOfEnemyObservationOrFire()` function determines the risk of a given node by checking the enemy's ability to observe or fire at that position from all of the known or presumed enemy positions. This typically involves performing a number of ray casts in the game world geometry. Because these ray casts are often expensive, this gem will also discuss how to create small lookup tables of precomputed line-of-fire information.

Listing 3.4.2 explicitly does not provide a tactical version of the heuristic. Because we don't know about the risk in the remaining part of the path, we can only estimate the remaining travel time. The `HeuristicNodeToDestination()` already does this, so we'll just leave it alone.

Have a look at the results in Figure 3.4.2. In Figure 3.4.2a, you see a "traditional" shortest path, happily passing through potential hostile fire (gray areas). In Figure 3.4.2b, you see the result of our `TacticalCostNodeToNode1()` cost function. Just by adding costs for the risk of being under fire, we can obtain paths that show a clever and convincing balance between speed and cover.

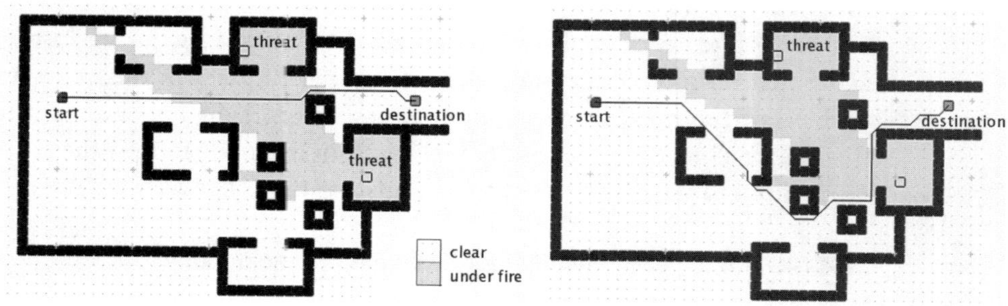

FIGURE 3.4.2 a) Shortest path. (b) Path offering protection and concealment.We are not done yet! In a large number of situations, this simple tactical A* cost function will provide paths that are tactically flawed and break the illusion of intelligence. Another problem is that the 'tactical' nature of path-finding also comes with a (CPU) cost.

In the remainder of this gem, we will first identify and correct a number of tactical flaws in our cost function. Then, we will investigate the additional costs of tactical path-finding and come up with some ways to limit these costs.

Tactical Improvements to Flawed Paths

It only takes one AI flaw to break the illusion of intelligence. When the player has carefully led wingmen, squads, or his tank platoons to an assault position, there is nothing more annoying than seeing them getting killed due to a lack of tactical understanding. Unfortunately, the tactical cost function defined previously lacks this understanding in a couple of places:

- It does not distinguish between long and short exposures to hostile fire, but simply adds up the total exposure;
- It assumes that threats remain static during the path's duration.

We will look into each of these problems and come up with improvements to the tactical-cost function to try to solve them.

Exposure Time and Enemy Modeling

Imagine a helicopter traversing some terrain defended by surface-to-air missile launchers. Imagine that the helicopter can reach its destination via two paths of identical length. One path exposes the helicopter to the missile launcher only once but for

20 continuous seconds. The other path exposes the helicopter for 20 seconds also, but in four stretches of 5 seconds, each exposure separated by at least 5 seconds of concealment. Both paths are equal to our cost function, `TacticalCostNodeToNode1()`, which simply adds up the amount of exposure. So, which one should the helicopter really choose?

To the enemy, the duration of the helicopter's exposure is very important. The single 20-second exposure might just be long enough for a missile launcher to detect *and* lock on to the helicopter so it can launch a smart missile. If the helicopter picks the path with four brief exposures, however, this is less likely to happen. Whether it's missile launchers that need to lock on, snipers requiring time to properly aim, or guards turning around in response to some noise—they all prefer their target to have long exposure times with only brief intervals of cover.

LISTING 3.4.3 A* Node with One Additional Field to Take into Account the Enemy's Aiming Quality

To take into account the enemy's aiming ability, therefore, we need to extend our nodes and cost function:

```
struct node {
    node(): aiming(0) { }; // default ctor: start
                           // with zero aim
    node(float anInitialAim) : aiming(anInitialAim) { };

    float  location[3];
    float  aiming;
};
```

LISTING 3.4.4 Cost Function Tactical Path

In the cost function, we use and update the aiming information detailed in Listing 3.4.3.

```
float TacticalCostNodeToNode2(node* aFromNode,
        node* aToNode) {
    float travelTime, riskFrom, riskTo,
        riskTotal, aiming;

    // compute travelTime and riskTotal
    ...

    // update aiming quality based on risk,
    // and add it to risk
    aiming  = aFromNode->aiming;
    if ( riskTotal > 0 ) { // spotted,
                           // so increase aiming
        aiming = min(kMaxAiming, aiming + travelTime);
    } else { // not spotted, so decrease aiming
        aiming *= power(kAimingDamping, travelTime);
```

```
        }
        riskTotal += kAimingFactor * aiming;

        // store aiming quality at destination
        aToNode->aiming = aiming;

        // return the weighted combination of
        // travel and risk costs
        return kTravelTimeFactor * travelTime +
            kRiskFactor * riskTotal;
    }
```

Figure 3.4.3 shows a simple test case generated against the helicopter path problem, and the graphs below the image show the exposure and aiming quality for each path.

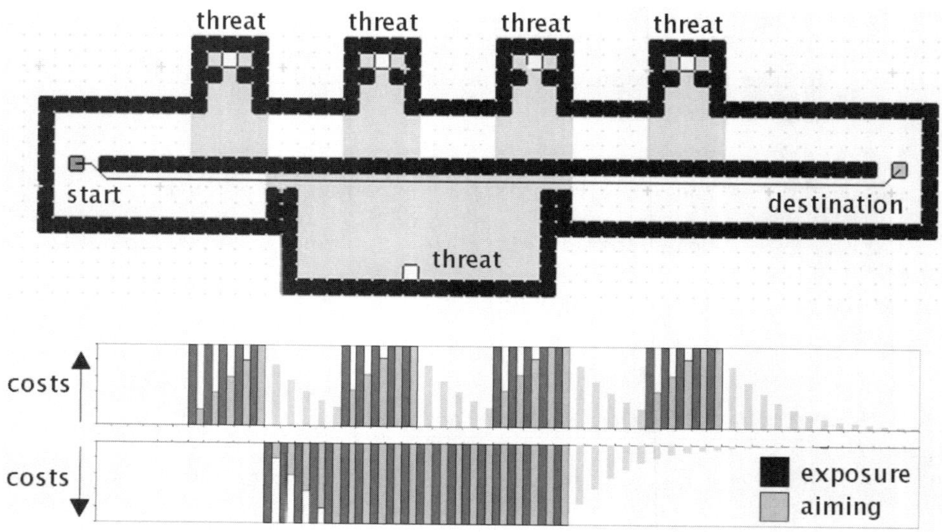

FIGURE 3.4.3 Parts of a simple test case.

Both paths feature the same amount of exposure to hostile fire—20 seconds. In the top path, the exposure (dark bars) consists of four intervals separated by an interval of cover of equal length. In the bottom path, the exposure consists of one interval of 20 seconds. For both paths, aiming by the threat (gray bars) starts as soon as the path is exposed. The aiming quality increases with each exposure until a maximum has been reached. As soon as the path is no longer exposed, the aiming decreases (gray bars). The threat might predict the movement on the covered path for a while, but the aiming decreases with time. For the top path, the total amount of "aiming" when exposed is less (gray bars with borders) than that for the bottom path. The intervals of cover between the exposures decrease the enemy's aiming ability and prevent it from staying at its maximum.

Similarly, when the AI starts a search for a tactical path from a position already exposed to hostile fire, it should start assuming the enemy has a maximum aiming quality. This will result in paths that try to visit nearby cover early on its path.

Thus, by also modeling the enemy's ability to improve its observation and aim in our A* cost function, we get tactically better paths. Our A* now prefers brief exposures separated by long intervals, rather than the alternative of long exposures and short intervals of cover, which definitely looks more intelligent.

Threats Don't Remain Static

Unfortunately, in most games, threats are not static. They patrol an area or move out upon spotting a unit in their path. Our current tactical A* solution, however, will happily plan a movement lasting perhaps 10 seconds, using the exact threat positions at a single moment. By ignoring the threat's movement, much of the "tactical quality" of the path is left to chance, and so is the player's perception of the AI.

To obtain better tactical paths, we must anticipate the enemy's movements. This is less complex than it sounds and can be done without using "chess AI with minmax-trees" to anticipate the most likely enemy movement. Instead, we can just assume that the enemy also occupies each and every position within a few steps of their current position. Have a look at Figure 3.4.4.

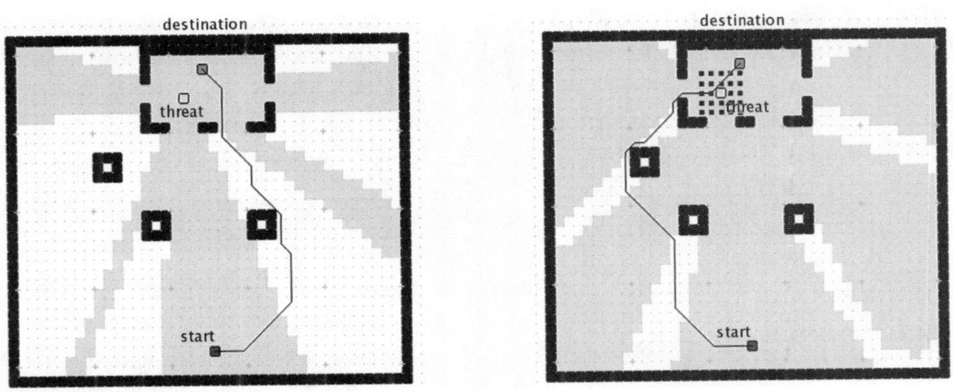

FIGURE 3.4.4 (a) Tactical path assuming threats remain static. (b) A path assuming threats move two steps.

Note how much the path in Figure 3.4.4a depends on the initial position of the threat. The path chosen is not robust against threat movement, and it ignores the larger presence of obstacles and the cover on the left side of the map.

When we assume that threats occupy all positions within two steps of their initial position, we indeed pick a more pessimistic scenario. The result, as shown in Figure 3.4.4b, is more robust against threat movement and also favors the higher availability of obstacles on the left side of the terrain. It's hard to fault the AI for picking this path.

Most game AI implementations provide a fast way to obtain all positions within a few steps of the threat. These usually correspond with the outgoing waypoints or neighboring nodes.

More Tactical Improvements

Going from point A to point B, our AI is now able to use cover and concealment in a plausible and effective way. There's more to tactics than just cover and concealment. Here are some more tactical considerations that can easily be taken into account by our tactical A* cost function.

Not all lines-of-fire are equal. If the AI will face only a few enemies, it is wise to count the number of hostile lines-of-fire to a given path position, rather than just distinguishing "cover" and "risk" positions. The distance to the threat and the threat's weapon might also have a large influence on the risk of being in the line-of-fire.

Games rewarding stealth and/or locations with shade, foliage, or small objects offer important protection from observation. The path-finding algorithm will prefer these locations if the cost function includes a small penalty for all other locations.

Even in the absence of known threats, there can still be tactical path-finding. Rather than avoiding known and suspected hostile lines-of-fire, it is now important to avoid weak combat positions. For example, a tank should not unnecessarily cross ridgelines because its weaker bottom might be exposed, or it might stand out against the skyline. Similarly, a marine should avoid using ladders because his movement on a ladder is very predictable, and he is unable to return fire while climbing it. Visiting the location of a recently shot squad member probably isn't smart either. Many tactical properties of a location can be analyzed and precomputed, as is explained in [Sterren01]. By introducing additional costs for visiting these locations, the paths generated by our tactical A* path-finding will try to avoid them.

Performance

Obviously the added tactical ability of A* described here comes with some additional CPU and memory costs as compared to a standard A*. Our approach compares even less favorably with the fast, yet predictable precomputed path lookup tables used by some games. As a point of reference, finding a tactical path with A* was about 10 times more expensive than finding a shortest path for squad AI in a *Quake*-based game.

On the other hand, most AI movement does not require a tactical path. Often it suffices to replan a squad's tactical path once every three seconds or so. The individual squad members then move in brief, "shortest path" hops along this path, and a few line-of-sight checks are used to find cover.

Let's have a look at the origins of some of these additional costs, what they add, and what we can do to limit them. First, we'll consider the line-of-fire tests, which often add the largest costs. Then, we'll look at A* and its tactical cost function, and the larger search space involved.

Efficient Line-of-Sight/Line-of-Fire Tests

In many games, line-of-sight and line-of-fire (LOF) tests consume considerable CPU time. For tactical path-finding, however, it suffices to use approximations of the actual lines-of-fire (the AI might not have spotted all threats and threats may move or look the other way). Trading CPU time for a lookup table of sampled lines-of-fire might be a good option in this case.

If the terrain is not too large, you might consider using a lookup table with one or more bits per line-of-sight/fire, as described in [Lidén02]. Such a lookup table consumes $O(N^2)$ memory. Alternatively, you can record the incoming lines-of-sight and lines-of-fire per location in terms of sectors, consuming $O(N)$ memory. This approach and the results for our 2D example are illustrated in Figure 3.4.5.

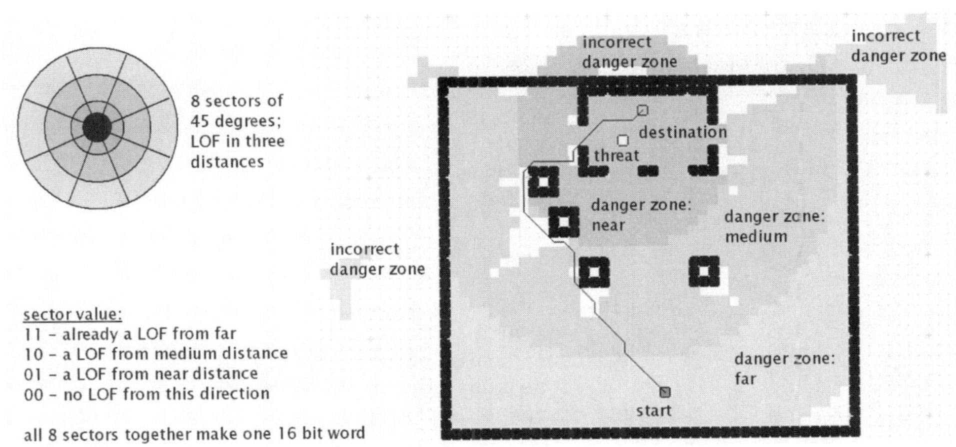

FIGURE 3.4.5 Sector-based LOF lookup and the resulting path.

Using one 16-bit word per location, information is precomputed and stored. For each location, every sector describes the worst-case distance from which a potential enemy in that sector can have a line-of-fire to that location. This worst-case distance is represented using four values, from "no line-of-fire at all in this sector" to a "line-of-fire at the maximum engagement distance." Note that the value stored is a pessimistic one: a single position in the sector that has a line-of-fire is sufficient to mark that sector as having an LOF from locations in that direction.

During an A* search, an approximation of the line-of-fire from a given threat position can be efficiently determined using the sector-based lookup table (see Listing 3.4.5). For the threat and position, the corresponding 45° sector and distance are computed. The lookup table then tells us whether it is possible for the location to be fired at from the threat's sector and for the threat-to-fire into the location's sector. If both lines-of-fire are feasible, the threat likely has a line-of-fire.

Obviously, such a small sector-based lookup table does not represent all lines-of-fire correctly. You can easily verify this by comparing the lines-of-fire in Figure 3.4.4 with the danger zones in Figure 3.4.5. In many cases, the (pessimistic) errors correspond to lines-of-sight easily achieved by the threat if the threat were to move. In other cases, such as the danger zones outside the box, the errors are more serious. With a few more bits and smaller sectors, however, you can easily reduce the number of errors.

For 3D environments and for games offering partial cover (which removes the symmetry in lines-of-fire), you might need to store some more bits. Still, this sector-based lookup approach stores lines-of-sight for some 1,000 locations in a few tens of kilobytes and is generally quite efficient.

LISTING 3.4.5 Computing an Approximate Risk Using Sector-Based, Precomputed LOF Information

```
float GetApproximateRiskFromThreat(node* threat,
       node* location) {
    int   sector = GetSectorForLine(threat, location);
    int   reverse_sector = (sector + 4) % 8;
    float distance =
        GetDistanceForLine(threat, location);

    if (HasLineOfFireFromSector(location->id,
        sector, distance)
            && CanFireIntoSector(threat->id,
                  reverse_sector, distance))
        return distance / kMaxDistance;
    else
        return 0.0;
};

bool HasLineOfFireFromSector(int index, int sector,
        float distance) {
    unsigned int allsectors = sectors[index];
    unsigned int mask  = (0x3 << sector);
    unsigned int value = ((allsectors & mask) >>
        sector);

    return (    (value == 3 && distance < kMaxReach    )
             || (value == 2 && distance < kFarReach    )
             || (value == 1 && distance < kMediumReach));
};
```

```
bool CanFireIntoSector(int index, int sector,
        float distance) {
    // assume firing is symmetric, otherwise
    // an extra table is needed
    return HasLineOfFireFromSector(index,
        sector, distance);
}
```

Extended A* Costs

As mentioned earlier, in its tactical format, A* consumes more CPU and memory, primarily through the tactical cost function and the larger search spaces being explored by A*. One source of additional cost is the floating-point arithmetic in the tactical cost function. You can gain performance by implementing approximate versions of floating-point computations using integer math. You should do this only after having verified and tuned the path-finding with the more "exact" floating-point cost functions to avoid introducing other problems. The space being searched by the tactical A* algorithm is typically much larger than one for a standard A* algorithm, as is shown in Figure 3.4.6.

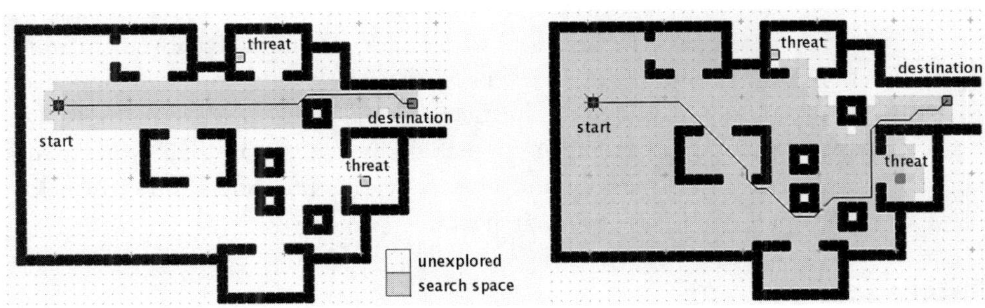

FIGURE 3.4.6 (a) Search space for shortest path. (b) Search space for tactical path.

The larger search space is a result of the added line-of-fire obstacles that typically are placed between the start and destination position of the path. A* will spend a lot of effort exploring locations to the rear and the sides, since those seem safer. It does not help that the heuristic cannot reflect these added line-of-fire obstacles.

One way to reduce the search space is to introduce even more-costly 'virtual' obstacles. If you want your AI to find a tactical path to a forward destination, why not restrict its attempts to evaluate positions deep in the rear or far to the sides by temporarily marking those nodes "off-limits"? Nothing says you can't use the algorithm to ignore these areas.

Another way of reducing the search space is to use hierarchical path-finding, executing the path-finding in "layers." First, generate a shortest path search at a higher level between areas of the map. Then, select the areas used for that shortest path and their neighboring areas, and run the tactical path-finding to the locations within the selected areas. Both Board/Ducker [BoardDucker02] and White [White02] address area navigation in their gems.

The ASE Program

ON THE CD

As an experiment with tactical path-finding, we invite you to play with the A Star Explorer (ASE) application on the CD-ROM. James Matthews [Matthews01] laid the foundation for this A* tool. The tactical enhancements and line-of-fire approximation described in this gem were added. Note that the A* implementation in this ASE is not representative of a high-performance tactical A*. Instead, the algorithm has been designed for hosting alternative cost functions and visualization.

Conclusion

Finding tactical paths with A* is a bit more complex than treating locations under enemy fire as terrain that is expensive to visit. You also should look at the path from an enemy perspective and deal with enemy aiming and movement in the cost function. These features will ensure paths that intelligently use stretches of cover and concealment to limit the risk of hostile fire, even when the enemies move. Using a similar approach, you can extend A* to pick paths that stay in touch with friendly or hostile elements, if that is important. Hopefully, this gem offers sufficient help to add these features to your game with efficiency.

References

[BoardDucker02] Board, Ben and Mike Ducker, "Area Navigation: Expanding the Path-Finding Paradigm," *Game Programming Gems 3,* Charles River Media, Inc., 2002.

[Lidén02], "Strategic and Tactical Reasoning with Waypoints," *AI Programming Wisdom,* Charles River Media, Inc., 2002.

[Matthews01], A* Explorer, available online at http://www.generation5.org, 2001.

[Patel99] Patel, Amit J., "Amit's Thoughts on Pathfinding," available online at http://www-cs-students.stanford.edu/~amitp/gameprog.html, November 18, 2001.

[Rabin00] Rabin, Steve, "A* Speed Optimizations," *Game Programming Gems,* Charles River Media, Inc., 2000.

[Sterren01] van der Sterren, William, "Terrain Analysis for 3D Action Games," Game Developers Conference 2001 Proceedings, paper and presentation available online at www.cgf-ai.com, 2001.

[Stout00] Stout, Bryan, "The Basics of A* for Path Planning," *Game Programming Gems*, Charles River Media, Inc., 2000.

[White02] White, Stephen, "A Fast Approach to Navigation Meshes," *Game Programming Gems 3,* Charles River Media, Inc., 2002.

3.5

A Fast Approach to Navigation Meshes

Stephen White, Sucker Punch Productions; and Christopher Christensen, Naughty Dog

stephenw@suckerpunch.com, christopher_christensen@naughtydog.com

A common problem in video games is how to navigate around objects in a complex environment. In the case of *Jak and Daxter: The Precursor Legacy*, we wanted creatures to be able to maneuver around highly detailed 3D environments, where each level was composed of millions of polygons and filled with many creatures and obstacles. We wanted the creatures to move intelligently and to exhibit several types of movement behaviors. Due to the density of creatures in our world, we needed a system that was faster than the more-common navigation techniques, such as A*; but it still needed to be flexible, accurate, and give the appearance of intelligent movement. To solve this problem, we developed our own navigation mesh technology, which admirably solved our needs, but also had a few interesting limitations.

Static vs. Dynamic Obstacles

The most fundamental problem of navigation is how to get from point A to point B. The shortest distance between these two points is a straight line. However, a straight line isn't appropriate when there is an obstacle blocking a direct movement between the two points. Obstacles can be broken down into two categories: static and dynamic. Static obstacles are obstacles that don't move, ever. These are our favorite type of obstacles since there are many optimizations that can be made to navigate around them. Examples of static obstacles are cliffs, walls, trees, and pillars. Dynamic obstacles are obstacles that can move or be removed, such as other creatures, the player, moving platforms, and crates. Dynamic obstacles are more difficult to deal with since their ability to move makes it difficult to use precomputed solutions. To make things worse, a dynamic obstacle might move in such a way as to invalidate a previously computed path. Since static and dynamic obstacles have so many different advantages and disadvantages, we chose to approach the problems separately.

Nav Meshes

The most common type of static obstacle encountered in *Jak and Daxter* was the terrain. Natural boundaries, such as walls and cliffs, described an area within which a creature could maneuver. Inside that boundary there could be other static obstacles, such as trees, large rocks, pillars, gaps too large to leap across, and other things that the creature should not be allowed to pass through.

To describe where a creature was allowed to maneuver within an area, the artists modeled a *nav mesh*. The mesh was a collection of triangles, and each triangle represented a valid area where the creature could maneuver. The mesh was modeled to the extent of the natural boundaries of the desired area, and holes in the mesh were used to represent areas where the creature could not travel within the natural boundaries. Note that our nav meshes were largely two-dimensional in nature and defined a two-dimensional area where a creature could travel. There was, however, a three-dimensional element to our meshes, which will be explained later.

As an example, suppose there is a clearing that we want a creature to be able to navigate within (see Figure 3.5.1). In this clearing, there is a large rock that the creature should not pass through. The artist would model a nav mesh that would both describe the extent to which the creature can travel as well as a hole cut out around the rock (see Figure 3.5.2). Each triangle in the mesh would describe a valid area where the creature is allowed to travel. By restricting the creature's travel to the two-dimensional space described by the mesh triangles, the creature could neither exit the clearing nor pass through the rock.

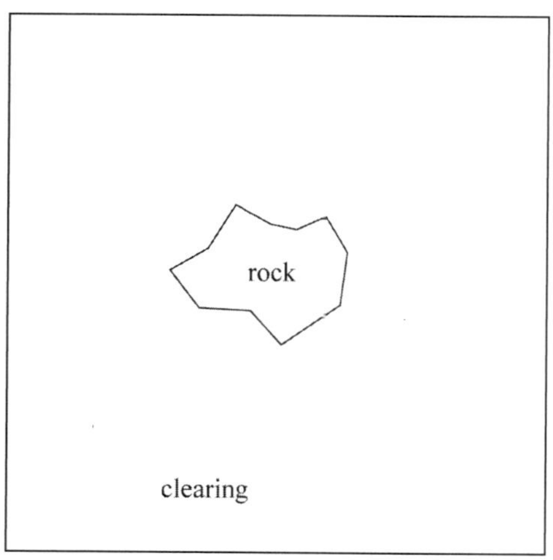

FIGURE 3.5.1 A clearing with a static obstacle.

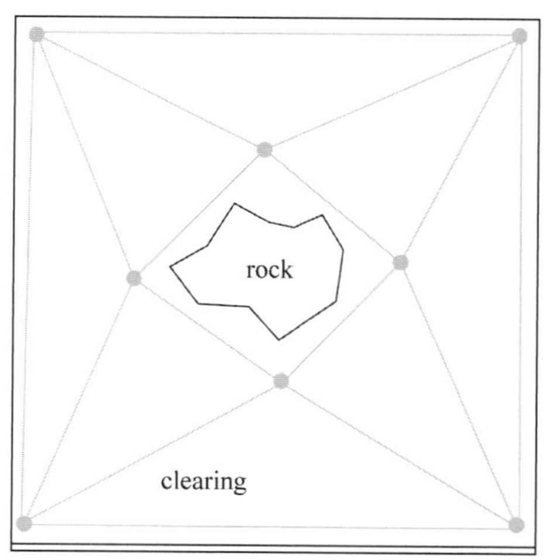

FIGURE 3.5.2 A clearing with a nav mesh added.

The beauty of this system was in its simplicity. Both area-boundary and inner-obstacle problems were solved using the same solution. A fairly simple nav mesh could even represent highly detailed and complicated terrain.

Portals

The triangles of the nav mesh do more than just establish an area where a creature can walk—they also establish what we refer to as "portals." Portals can be thought of as doorways to other triangles. In the case of our nav meshes, the portals were represented by the edges of the triangles. As a simplification, we established that our meshes could not contain any T-junctions, which simply meant that we only allowed an edge to be shared between no more than two triangles. Since a triangle has three edges, this means that a single triangle could be connected to, at most, three other triangles; so a single triangle has at most three portals leading to other connected triangles. This limitation did pose some three-dimensional issues, but it did give us some nice data characteristics. For one thing, we could use two bits to specify a portal of a triangle (first portal, second portal, or third portal) and still have one value left over for other uses.

Suppose our problem is moving from point A to point B. If point A represents the creature, point B represents the desired destination of the creature, and both points are within the same triangle, then we know that the creature can move directly toward point B, since we already know that the creature can move anywhere within the triangle. A problem arises when the destination is not contained within the same triangle as the creature. In this case, the creature might need to choose a direction that will both keep the creature on the nav mesh and intelligently move the creature along a path that will reach the desired destination, even if that path temporarily moves the creature in a direction away from the desired destination.

So, if we're on some triangle and our desired destination is on some other triangle, how do we decide which way to go? The solution that we used was to precompute a two-dimensional array that specified the portal to use to get from any triangle to any other triangle on the mesh. Remember that it only took two bits to specify a portal, so the memory cost of our table was roughly equal to squaring the number of triangles in the mesh and dividing by four. This means that the table for a mesh of 256 triangles (the maximum our implementation allowed) cost only 16 KB of memory. In practice, our nav meshes rarely exceeded more than 64 triangles (one kilobyte of memory) and were often smaller. Also, since multiple creatures typically shared the same nav mesh, there were relatively few nav meshes overall, so the memory cost was not significant. Now, consider the advantages of having this two-dimensional table. Figuring out which portal to use is now extremely fast, since it is a simple table lookup. The entry in the table is found by using the index of the source triangle and the index of the destination triangle. If the table was composed of byte values instead of two-bit values, then the C code might look like the following:

```
portalIndex = portalTable[destTriIndex][srcTriIndex];
```

Of course, using a byte table would quadruple the memory cost for little gain, so our bit-packed table code becomes:

```
bitIndex = 2*(destTriIndex*triCount + srcTriIndex);
byteIndex = bitIndex / 8;
byteShift = bitIndex & 7;
portalIndex = (portalTable[byteIndex] >> byteShift)&3;
```

Once we know the portal to use for a given triangle, we can take the desired direction vector from point A to point B and then solve for the point on the portal that most closely matches our desired direction. The creature then moves in the direction of the point on the portal until it reaches the portal, where it transitions to the triangle on the other side of the portal. If point B is within the creature's new triangle, then the creature can move directly to point B. If point B is still not within the creature's new triangle, then another look-up in the table is done to determine which portal to use next. The logic repeats until the creature eventually reaches the triangle that contains point B.

As an example, refer to Figure 3.5.3. Point A starts the creature out located within triangle 0, and point B (its destination) is located within triangle 3. Since point A is not in the same triangle as point B, a look-up in the table is done to determine which portal to use, and the returned value tells us to use the portal connecting triangle 0 to triangle 1. A point is found on that portal that most closely matches the desired direction of point B, and the creature is moved to that point. The creature is then considered to be within triangle 1. This behavior is repeated until the creature enters triangle 3, which is where point B is located, and the creature can then move directly to point B.

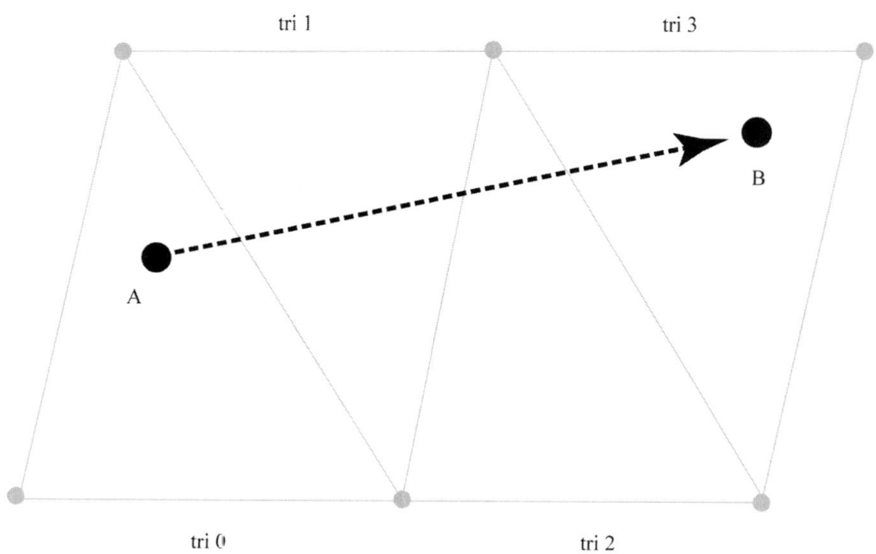

FIGURE 3.5.3 Navigating from A to B on a simple mesh.

Although the above example was fairly simple, the same logic works for far more complicated cases. Consider Figure 3.5.4, which shows the same simple logic applied to navigating a more complicated mesh.

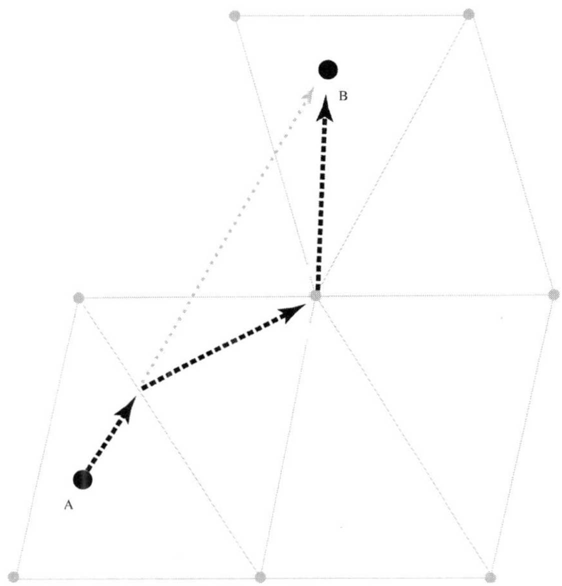

FIGURE 3.5.4 Navigating around a corner.

This logic works for forking and looping paths. When there is more than one portal that can be used to reach a destination, the table entry specifies which portal represents the shortest route to the destination. However, there is actually one complication to consider. A triangle represents an area, and not a single point. This means that the distance between a point on one triangle and a point on another triangle can vary dramatically, depending on where the points are located on their respective triangles. Since the precomputed table tells us how to get from one triangle to another triangle, rather than how to get from an exact position on a triangle to an exact position on another triangle, the precomputed portal might not actually lead to the shortest path to the destination. In practice, however, this was rarely a problem, since if more than one path covered a similar distance, then it really didn't matter that the chosen path wasn't always the shortest.

Building the Table

So, how do you precompute the table? Several methods could be used, but the method that we chose was to compute a point to represent the center of each triangle. Preferably, this was a point that was equidistant to the three corners of the respective triangle. We then used a simple flood-fill algorithm to find the paths connecting the triangles. If more than one path was found between two triangles, then the algorithm would discard the longer path.

An important item to consider when constructing the nav mesh is that it represents a single path to each destination. Each portal should provide a single, clear route between any two areas in order to produce acceptable results. Providing more than one portal to pursue a single path could result in zigzagging movement. Figure 3.5.5 shows a case where it is unclear at precompute time which portal is the best way to get from point A's triangle to point B's triangle. In this example, only one portal is chosen at precompute time, which would be inappropriate at runtime, since it does not intersect a direct path from point A to point B. Figure 3.5.6 shows the proper way to construct this nav mesh, where the direct path is always taken.

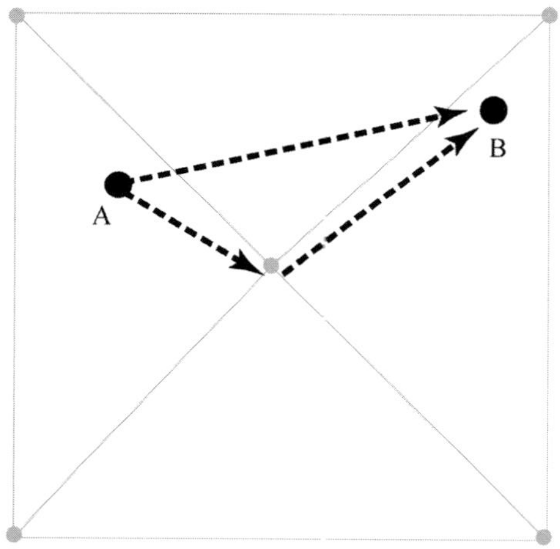

FIGURE 3.5.5 Poor mesh construction.

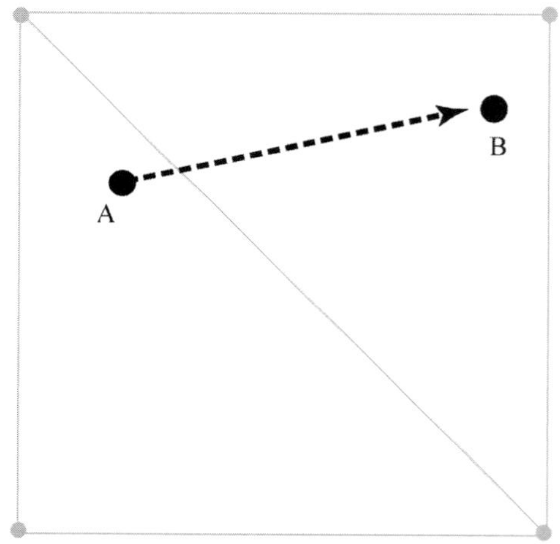

FIGURE 3.5.6 Good mesh construction.

Additional Portal Issues

Although the concept of using portals is quite simple, there are a few complications in their implementation. One such complication is that as point A approaches a portal edge, the test for whether the vector from point A to point B intersects the portal edge might become unreliable. For example, floating-point round-off errors might shift point A outside of the current triangle, causing the test to go awry. Also, when the source-to-destination vector is nearly parallel to the portal edge, the intersection test can give unreliable results. To avoid these problems, we checked to see if the source point was closer than some chosen epsilon distance to the portal edge. When it was, we simply looked ahead to find the next portal on our path that wasn't so close to the source point and used that as our portal.

Another item to consider is choosing alternate directions when the desired direction vector does not intersect the portal. It might not be clear which of the two portal endpoints is the best choice to follow. Choosing an endpoint based on which endpoint most closely matches the desired direction might not be sufficient. For example, if the desired direction vector is perpendicular to the portal and moving away from it, then either of the portal's endpoints is equally desirable. Floating-point precision and other minor variations could cause undesirable oscillations. One method that can resolve this ambiguous situation is to look ahead at successive portals until a portal is found that clearly indicates which endpoint of the current portal is closest to our future path. This "look-ahead" technique also has the added benefit of creating more-direct navigation as the creature travels around winding pathways. Since this technique is rarely needed and usually only requires a few triangles of look-ahead, the extra CPU cost is minimal.

Representing Creatures

Using a nav mesh, we are able to travel intelligently from one point on the mesh to another point on the mesh. Most creatures, however, occupy more space than a single point, and so a question arises about how to account for their thickness. Since efficiency was more important to us than accuracy, we simply used a circle to represent the two-dimensional area of a creature on the nav mesh, where the radius of the circle represented the thickness of the creature. Using circles gave us some problems with creatures that were not very circular in shape. For example, a horse doesn't look very circular when viewed from above. If you made the circle big enough to enclose the entire horse, then other creatures would avoid the sides of the horse, and the horse itself wouldn't be able to squeeze into an area that it visually should fit into. If you made the circle smaller so that creatures could get closer to the horse, then you'd let the ends of the horse poke out of the circle, where they might occasionally overlap something else.

Despite these problems, we felt that the advantages of using circles outweighed the disadvantages. For *Jak and Daxter*, we were always able to find a radius that appeared to be a reasonable compromise between these two adverse effects. Another advantage to using circles was that rotation didn't have to be factored in when checking for collision with the nav mesh or other dynamic obstacles.

Instead of trying to adapt our nice, simple, point-to-point nav mesh logic to a much more computationally expensive circle-to-circle logic, we opted to preshrink our nav meshes to account for the radii of the creatures that may be using it. The concept is simple in that instead of modeling the nav mesh to exactly abut against obstacles, the mesh is modeled to stay at least some radius from all obstacles. Figure 3.5.7 shows how a nav mesh might be modeled for a small creature, and Figure 3.5.8 shows the same scene with a nav mesh modeled for a larger creature. If we guarantee that the distance from the edges of the nav mesh to all static obstacles is greater than or equal to the radius of the creatures that use the nav mesh, then the creature can be represented by a point instead of a circle.

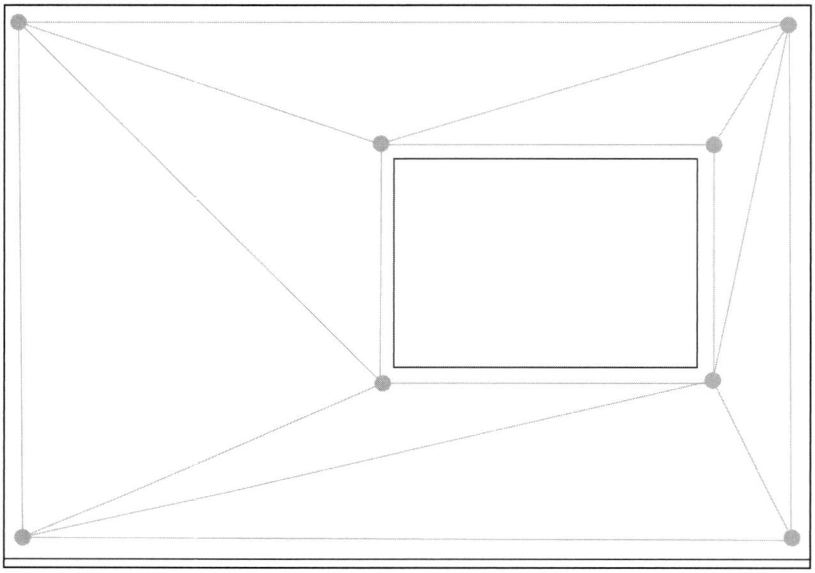

FIGURE 3.5.7 Mesh for small creatures.

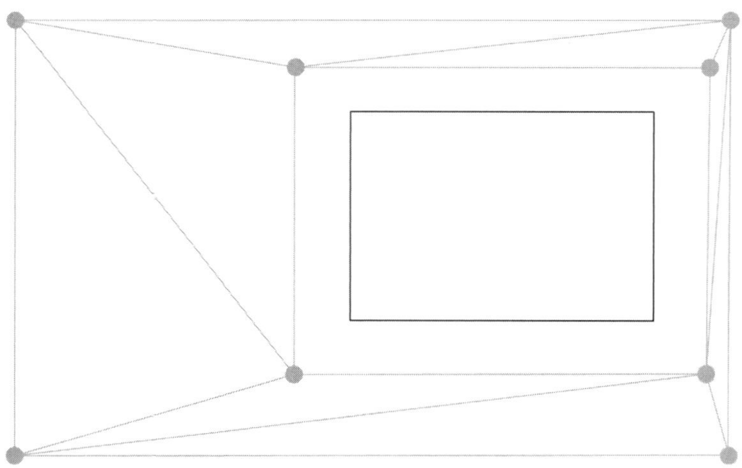

FIGURE 3.5.8 Mesh for large creatures.

This is an enormous optimization, since moving a point around the nav mesh is much simpler than moving a circle around the mesh, though it does come with some problems. The biggest problem is that different types of creatures might want to use the same nav mesh, and some creatures might have significantly larger circles than other creatures. If the nav mesh is modeled to work for the larger creatures, then the smaller creatures might not be able to move very close to the static obstacles. In general, this wasn't a problem for us, but occasionally we had situations where the distance of the nav mesh was far enough from static obstacles that the player could stand next to a wall and a smaller creature couldn't get close enough to the wall to attack the player. To fix this undesirable behavior, we would adjust the distance of the nav mesh to any surrounding static obstacles until we found a compromise in which larger creatures would overlap the static obstacles slightly, but smaller creatures would be able to reach the player.

Our second biggest problem was that it was often difficult to judge what distance to use when modeling a nav mesh. The appropriate distance to use was based on the radii of the circles representing the creatures on the mesh, and the types of creatures and radii of their circles were subject to occasional design and programming changes.

Dynamic Obstacles

Using circles to represent creatures gave us the advantage that we could treat creatures as points when moving them around the nav mesh. This is also true for moving creatures around dynamic obstacles, such as other creatures. Instead of using computationally expensive logic for moving a circle around other circles, we can simply inflate the circles of surrounding obstacles by the radius of the creature currently being moved. For example, Figure 3.5.9 shows a creature of radius r and two dynamic obstacles with different radii, and Figure 3.5.10 shows how we treat the creature as a point by adding its radius to the obstacles. By inflating surrounding circles before moving a creature, we've unified the representation of a creature to being a single point and reduced our navigation issues to the relatively simple problem of moving a point inside the bounds of a mesh while avoiding surrounding circles.

To navigate the point among the circles, we checked to see if the direction that we wanted to travel would cause us to collide with any nearby circles. If not, then we could go ahead and move in the desired direction. If it was determined that a collision would occur, we computed two new vectors that would steer us clear of the collision (see Figure 3.5.11).

These two vectors could be considered as rotations away from the original vector: a rotated vector to steer to the left of the obstacle, and a rotated vector to steer to the right of the obstacle. We would then check these two new vectors to see if either of them would collide with any other obstacles. If so, then we would appropriately rotate the right-most vector to the right or rotate the left-most vector to the left to avoid any additional obstacles. Once all potential obstacles had been accounted for, the two resulting vectors showed two possible ways to move that would avoid the dynamic

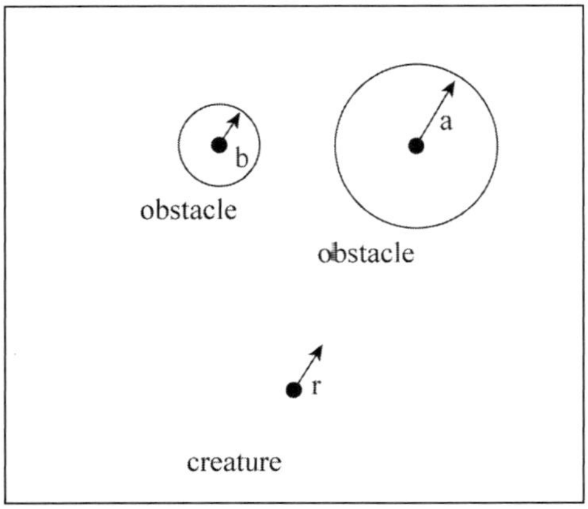

FIGURE 3.5.9 Creature as circle with two circular dynamic obstacles.

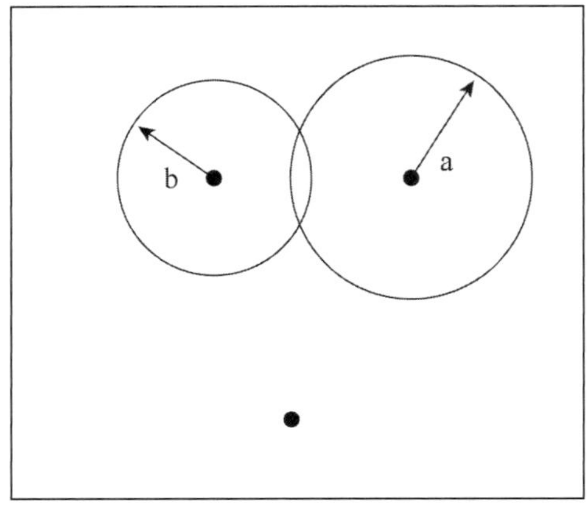

FIGURE 3.5.10 Creature simplified to a point with obstacles enlarged to compensate.

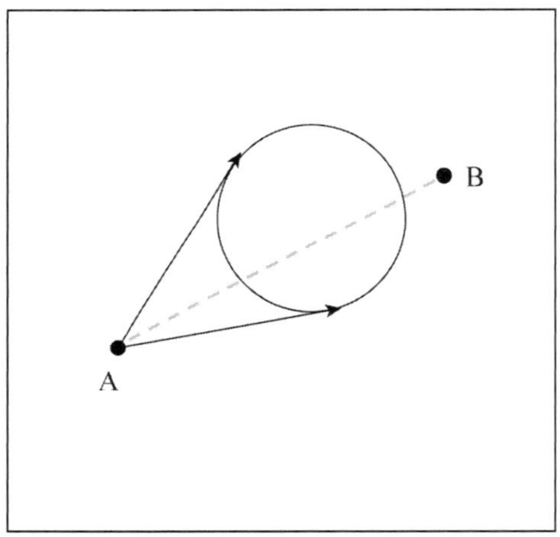

FIGURE 3.5.11 Getting around a dynamic obstacle that intersects our desired path.

obstacles' blocking the originally desired direction of movement. To avoid an undesirable cyclic movement behavior and to keep things simple, we usually chose the vector that more closely matched the creature's last direction.

One problem we had with this approach was that the creature could occasionally become stuck inside of other dynamic obstacles. This was commonly caused by floating-point precision issues, but it could also occur due to various other movement behaviors. Instead of trying to solve the thorny problem of not allowing overlaps to occur under any situation, we opted to have an embedded creature attempt to move away from the obstacles that overlapped it. Basically, we identified which circle the creature overlapped the most, and after computing the directions to avoid the other circles, we blended those results toward the direction away from the overlapping circle, proportionate to the amount of the overlap. This technique caused overlap cases to resolve themselves in a reasonable manner.

Another potential problem was that a creature could become completely surrounded by other dynamic obstacles such that the left and right vectors both faced exactly opposite of the originally desired vector. We chose to ignore handling this case, which meant that a creature could potentially move to a position that would cause them to overlap one of the surrounding dynamic obstacles. In practice, however, this wasn't an issue for us, especially since creatures naturally tended to move away from overlaps.

Navigation of Both Static and Dynamic Obstacles

Our final logic for maneuvering creatures turned out to be quite simple and broke down into the following steps. First, we found the best direction to reach our destination using the nav mesh and its portals. We then checked to see if the resulting direction would hit any dynamic obstacles (circles). If so, we modified the direction to avoid them. Finally, we checked to see if this new direction would lead us off of the nav mesh. If so, we clamped the movement to the nav mesh.

The final step of clamping movement to stay on the nav mesh was done for efficiency and required a little bit of finesse. One problem was that a creature might become blocked and be forced to stop. Another issue was that we sometimes allowed a creature's movement vector to be bent against the edge of the nav mesh instead of being simply clamped. The bent vector allowed the creature to continue moving, but we didn't do an additional check to see if the bent vector would cause the creature to overlap nearby circles; so a creature might subsequently become embedded within another creature. Since our circle avoidance logic made creatures naturally want to move away from overlaps, this usually wasn't an issue between two moving creatures. We did, however, encounter issues when a moving creature overlapped a dynamic obstacle that didn't move, such as a crate. To eliminate this problem, we made sure that nonmoving dynamic obstacles, such as crates, were not placed near the boundaries of a nav mesh.

Additional Nav Mesh Thoughts

Our nav meshes predominantly denoted two-dimensional areas where dynamic obstacles were allowed to move. This sufficed in most cases, since most creature setups can be described using two-dimensional boundaries. However, we occasionally had situations that required three-dimensional information. For example, if we wanted to put a creature on a circular staircase that spiraled upward, it would not be sufficient to use just a two-dimensional nav mesh to describe the staircase. For this type of situation, we had a maximum height that the creature could be from the surface of a nav mesh triangle in order to be considered on that triangle. This gave the ability for a nav mesh to have three-dimensionally crisscrossing triangles, as long as the triangles that occupied the same two-dimensional space were at sufficiently different elevations so that it was clear which triangle a creature was using.

Another enhancement that we made to our nav mesh system was the ability for creatures to jump across certain obstacles to reach the desired final destination. For example, a creature might jump across small chasms in pursuit of the player. Modeling triangles across the chasm and marking those triangles as special "gap triangles" accomplished this ability. When a creature crossed a portal into a gap triangle, a search found the triangle on the far side of the gap, and the creature was sent a message telling it to jump across the gap to that triangle. In order to keep the creature from landing on top of a dynamic obstacle on the other side of the gap, the creature used a temporary circle that reserved a safe landing place.

Conclusion

ON THE CD

Our navigation mesh system admirably fit our needs for the development of *Jak and Daxter* (see Color Plate 1 on the CD-ROM). We were able to create many different types of creatures that exhibited a variety of behaviors while intelligently navigating our complex three-dimensional environments. Although navigational approaches exist that might provide more-robust general solutions to this difficult problem, our system excelled at being both fast and conceptually simple, creating a winning combination for us.

3.6

Flocking: A Simple Technique for Simulating Group Behavior

Steven Woodcock, Raytheon

ferretman@gameai.com

Flocking (sometimes called *swarming* or *herding*) is a technique first put forth by Craig Reynolds in a 1987 paper he did for SIGGRAPH, "Flocks, Herds, and Schools: A Distributed Behavioral Model." In that paper, Reynolds proposed a series of three simple rules, which, when taken together, gave groups of autonomous agents (also called *boids*) a realistic form of group behavior similar to flocks of birds, schools of fish, or swarms of bees. (See Figure 3.6.1 for an example of this behavior in action.) These rules, which Reynolds refers to as *steering behaviors*, are:

- **Separation.** Steer to avoid crowding local flockmates.
- **Alignment.** Steer toward the average heading of local flockmates.
- **Cohesion.** Steer to move toward the average position of local flockmates.

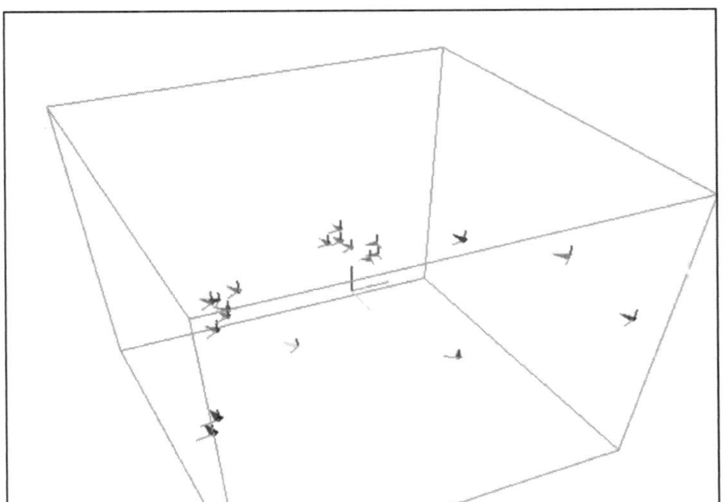

FIGURE 3.6.1 An example image of the flocking demo in action.

Separation gives an agent the ability to try to maintain a certain separation distance from other agents in the immediate vicinity. This helps prevent agents from crowding together while ensuring a "natural-looking" closeness that emulates groups in the real world. The code presented in this gem accomplishes this goal by having each member of a flock test how close it is to its nearby flockmates and then adjust its heading (steering) to obtain a desired distance.

Alignment provides an agent that has the ability to align itself with (i.e., head in the same direction and/or speed as) other agents in its immediate vicinity. As with separation, this gem accounts for alignment through each member of a flock looking at nearby flockmates and then adjusting its heading and speed to match the average heading and speed of its neighbors.

Cohesion gives an agent the ability to "group" with other nearby agents, thus emulating similar behavior seen in nature. Again, this article accomplishes this goal by having each agent examine nearby agents, averaging their positions and then adjust its heading to match.

The Fourth Rule

In later implementations and papers, Reynolds added what has sometimes been referred to as the "fourth rule" of flocking:

- **Avoidance.** Steer to avoid running into local obstacles or enemies.

Avoidance provides an agent with the ability to steer away from obstacles and avoid collisions. This behavior is accomplished by giving each agent the ability to "look forward" some distance and determine whether a collision with some object is likely, then to adjust its heading to prevent it. Similarly, it might be desirable to avoid certain other types of agents (such as rabbits avoiding foxes or doves avoiding hawks), and again this principle would come into play.

No Memory

Note that the steering behaviors say nothing about state information or about a given agent maintaining knowledge of the flock, its environment, where it's headed, or the like. Flocking is a *stateless* algorithm in that no information is maintained from update to update; each boid reevaluates its environment at every update cycle. Not only does this reduce memory requirements that might otherwise be needed to provide a similar behavior using approaches besides flocking, but it also allows the flock to react in real time to changing environmental conditions. As a result, flocks exhibit elements of *emergent behavior*: No one member of the flock knows anything about where the flock is going, but the flock moves as one mass, avoids obstacles and enemies, and keeps pace with one another in a fluid, dynamic fashion.

How Is This Concept Useful for Computer Games?

Flocking provides a powerful tool for unit motion and making more realistic environments the player can explore; it has been used with great success in a variety of commercial titles. For example, both *Unreal* (Epic) and *Half-Life* (Sierra) used flocking algorithms for many of their monsters as well as less life-threatening creatures such as birds and fish. *Enemy Nations* (Windward Studios) used a modified flocking algorithm to control unit formations and movement across a 3D environment. Groups of animals can be made to wander the terrain in real-time strategy games or RPGs more realistically than can be done with simple scripting. Groups of archers or swordsmen can be made to move realistically across bridges or around boulders and other obstacles. Monsters in a first-person shooter can wander the dungeon halls in a more believable fashion, avoiding players where possible but perhaps launching an attack when the flock grows large enough. The possibilities are practically endless.

Implementation

Vectors and Motion

A quick overview of the mechanics of motion for the members of a flock helps in understanding how the code does what it does.

Figure 3.6.2 demonstrates the concept of *local space* (space relative to the boid itself). "Forward" is toward the positive *Z*-axis, "left" is toward the positive *X*-axis, and "up" is vertical toward the top of the boid. Our boid in this article is the classic delta-wing shape often used by Reynolds, but of course it can be any shape desired.

Figure 3.6.3 demonstrates another important principle, *orientation*. Referred to as *roll, pitch,* and *yaw*, orientation is simply an indication of how a given object is oriented in the local space, shown in Figure 3.6.2. Roll is rotation around the local *Z*-axis (the one facing forward and backward). Pitch is rotation around the local *X*-axis (the one running left and right). Yaw is rotation around the *Y*-axis (the one running directly up and down through the boid). Understanding orientation is important because we use it when making decisions about our boid's orientation during movement. The idea presented in this article works by building a *velocity vector* during each update cycle that will adjust the boid's local *X, Y,* and *Z* orientations to match the needs of the four steering behaviors.

Another important aspect of how this idea operates is the manner in which it arbitrates conflicting desires on the part of a boid. Looking at the four steering behaviors for a moment, one can see that there is no guidance on how to prioritize these behaviors—all are considered of equal importance. This loosely matches most normal behavior in the real world: A dove might want to both keep up with its fellows and avoid cutting through a flock of hawks while doing so; however, this concept doesn't take into account life-and-death situations.

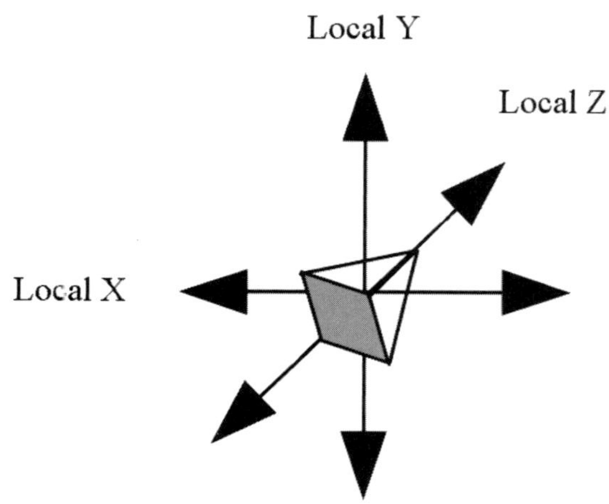

FIGURE 3.6.2 Local space is defined for each boid.

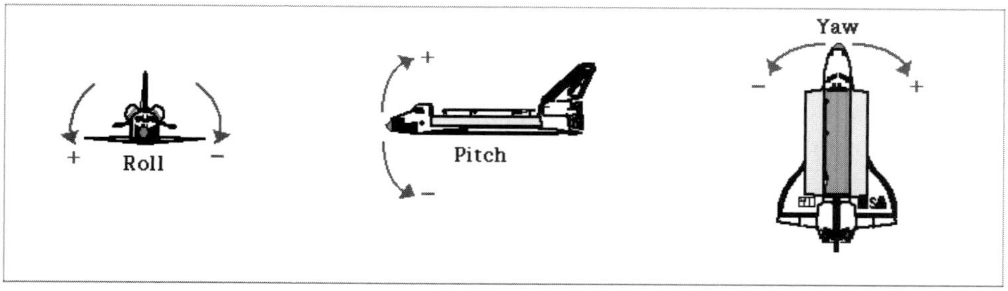

FIGURE 3.6.3 The three axis rotations are defined as roll, pitch, and yaw.

One can solve this problem in several ways—automatically giving higher priority to avoidance, for example—but this article uses a *vector accumulation* approach. The orientation changes that a given boid wants to make to satisfy each of the four steering behaviors are summed in a *change vector* before being applied to the boid's motion. This change vector, by convention, is held to a unit vector so that the accumulated changes are kept in proper proportion. This method allows each steering behavior to have a proportional influence on the boid's final motion changes while enabling the boid to satisfy (at least partially) the needs of two or more conflicting directives. Over time I've found that this approach is generally more satisfactory than others.

Constraints

Several constraints on our boids restrict how they can move and react. Possibly the most influential in this implementation is each boid's *perception range*, which restricts how far a flockmate can "look" around its environment to detect other flockmates, potential obstacles, or enemies. The larger this range, the more organized and coherent the flocks and the better they are at avoiding enemies and obstacles. Making this range smaller results in more erratic flocks, groups of boids splitting off more often when confronted by obstacles or enemies, and so on.

Another constraint on how our agents can move is their *velocity* and *maximum velocity change*. In the real world, animals in flocks are restricted in their ability to keep up with their flockmates by how fast they can move, how fast they can turn, and the like. This article simplifies the problem of motion in a 3D environment somewhat by ignoring acceleration and focusing entirely on velocity; changes to velocity are restricted to some proportion of overall maximum velocity. This helps prevent the agents in our demo from turning on a dime or putting on ridiculous bursts of speed when trying to catch up with their flockmates. It also provides a governing restraint on how quickly they can slow down or alter course to avoid an obstacle. If allowed "infinite response," they might fly directly up to the surface of an obstacle before turning with infinite agility and speed to move around it—not a very realistic behavior.

A final constraint for the purposes of our demo is the world in which our boids flock. For the purposes of this gem, I've arbitrarily created a Box class that defines the world in which our boids can move. Any boid that strays beyond the boundaries of the Box is magically transported to the opposite side, keeping the same motion characteristics it had before. The effect is that flocks that stray too close to the edge of the Box can lose members to the "other side of the world," where they can lose track of the main flock and form a new flock of their own.

Virtually all these parameters are adjustable so that one can see the potential impact of fiddling with them.

The Code

Three classes make up the heart of this gem: `CBox`, `CFlock`, and `CBoid`. Organizationally, these classes can be viewed as described in Figure 3.6.4.

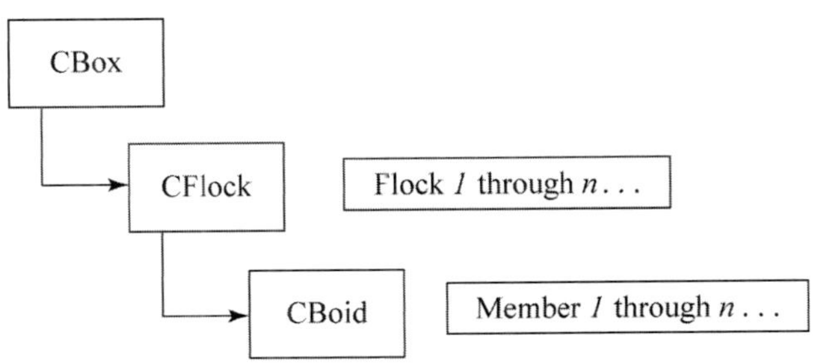

FIGURE 3.6.4 The `CBox` class defines the basic world in which our flocks will fly.

Each flock is represented by an instantiation of a `CFlock` object. There can be multiple `CFlock` objects resident within `CBox`, and they can be created or destroyed at any point (although this gem creates them only at initialization). `CFlock` objects serve to organize and simplify access to the members of the flock.

Similarly, a `CBoid` object represents each member of a flock. There can, of course, be multiple `CBoid` objects associated with each `CFlock` (if there weren't, it would be a pretty small flock), and, like `CFlock` objects, they can be created or destroyed at any point. Although this article creates flock members only at initialization, it wouldn't be hard at all to build in some "lifetimes" for individual members (see the "Limitations and Potential Improvements" section) so that individuals might age and die.

The CBox Class

`CBox` is a rather simple class, as one might expect:

```
class CBox
{

public:

   ////////////////////////////////
   // constructors and destructors
   ////////////////////////////////

   // Constructor #1.
   // Creates a Box with default values of 50 meters
   // on any side not specified.
   CBox (float lv=50.0, float wv=50.0, float hv=50.0);

   // Destructor
   virtual ~CBox();

   //////////////////////////
   // miscellaneous functions
   //////////////////////////

   // GetBoxLength.
   // Returns the length of the Box, in meters.
   float GetBoxLength (void);

   // GetBoxWidth..
   // Returns the width of the Box, in meters.
   float GetBoxWidth (void);

   // GetBoxHeight.
   // Returns the height of the Box, in meters.

   float GetBoxHeight (void);
```

This class provides us with a simple way to parameterize and retrieve the boundaries of our world.

The CFlock Class

The `CFlock` class represents a basic flock of boids and serves mostly as an organizational tool rather than a strict representation of each flock per se. Its various functions are fairly simple and deal primarily with the "bookkeeping" that one might desire when handling flocks. The class definition for `CFlock` can be found in Listing 3.6.1.

Procedurally, flocks are first created and then have one or more boids added to them. The class is built to allow for real-time creation and deletion of flocks, although the demo itself does not do this. A list of all `CFlock` objects is maintained in the simple static array `CFlock::ListOfFlocks[]` (again, simplified for the purposes of this gem). At each update cycle, the flocks' `CFlock::Update()` method is called to update all the members of that flock. New boids can be added at any time using `CFlock::AddTo()`, and members can be removed, if desired, via `CFlock::RemoveFrom()`. `CFlock::GetCount()` and `CFlock::GetFirstMember()` provide methods to obtain specific status information about a given flock, whereas the debugging method `CFlock::PrintData()` provides more exhaustive information.

Flocks can be created at any time, although the demo provided creates them only at initialization. Each flock can have any number of `CBoid` objects as members. Note that members of a flock have no idea what flock they're a member of, but the flock itself *does* know who its members are. For the purposes of this gem, a `CBoid` object remains a member of whatever `CFlock` it is initially assigned to, but it wouldn't be hard at all to add code that would allow boids to change their loyalties if so desired (see the "Limitations and Potential Improvements" section).

The CBoid Class

The `CBoid` class implements the true "meat" of the flocking algorithms and, as such, is fairly beefy. It is contained in Listing 3.6.2. This class handles all aspects of a specific agent's motion and existence: how it moves, how it senses its environment, how it prioritizes its actions.

Each `CBoid` object represents a single individual agent. Much as with `CFlock` objects, `CBoid` objects can be created or deleted at will. Once created, they are indirectly managed through the `CFlock::AddTo()`, `CFlock::RemoveFrom()`, and `CFlock::Update()` methods, as described previously.

Each `CBoid` object is updated via its `CFlock::FlockIt()` method, which begins by building a list of those flockmates that a given boid can see (based on its `perception_-range` value). A list of enemies (members of other flocks) is also built if that option is active.

The method then begins to implement the steering behaviors as described previously, summing an accumulating series of velocity vector changes to accommodate the wishes of the agent. The methods `CBoid::KeepDistance()` (separation behavior), `CBoid::MatchHeading()` (alignment behavior), and `CBoid::SteerToCenter` (cohesion behavior) are called to determine what the boid would like to do. If the option is active, avoidance behavior of members of other flocks is modeled through a call to `CBoid::FleeEnemies()`.

One additional method implemented here is `CBoid::Cruising()`. This method attempts to model a boid's "desired cruising speed," if everything were up to it and it wasn't under any other influences. The primary reason for this method was to give any boids wandering on their own (out of sight of their flockmates) some "purpose" to their motion.

At each stage of the update process, we accumulate all desired velocity vector changes proportionally into an accumulation vector. A check at the end of the `CBoid::Flockit()` method ensures that an individual never exceeds its maximum allowed speed or velocity change.

Two final methods serve as "cleanup" to ensure that everything looks correct. `CBoid::ComputeRPY()` makes calculations necessary to orient our boid properly as a result of its final velocity vector changes. `CBoid::WorldBound()` does some sanity testing to determine whether any agent has strayed outside the bounds of the `CBox` world object in which it resides and, if it has, places it back in its box.

Various private methods handle visibility and linked-list management; there's nothing particularly special about them, nor are they flocking related per se. A debug method, `CBoid::PrintData()`, provides exhaustive information on a given boid on an update-by-update basis.

Limitations and Potential Improvements

Hard reality dictates that any demonstration of flocking behavior has some limitations. This article does not implement obstacle avoidance at all, although it does allow for avoidance in the form of "enemy flocks." Boids remain assigned to the flocks they start with, but one could easily envision code that reassigns a boid dynamically to a new flock should it lose sight of its old one. Similarly, boids in this implementation are blessed with an amazing, 360-degree, full-spherical field of view; there are no restrictions such that they can see only objects or flockmates directly in front of them. A more realistic field of view would probably be desired for any game implementation.

A list of other possible improvements is fairly easy to come up with. Many people who have used flocking behavior and its variations have implemented "life clocks" on individual agents, making boids that die if they stray too far from their mates but that can "breed" new flock members if they remain with their brothers long enough. One could also examine predator and prey behavior, modifying the base code to allow one type of flock to "feed" on another.

Resources and Acknowledgments

It's virtually impossible to study this particular field without quickly discovering that nearly every flocking/swarming/herding application on the Web is somehow related to, derived from, or inspired by some other flocking/swarming/herding application. The implementation described in this gem is no exception. Many thanks to Christopher Kline (Mitre Corporation) for his innovative method for computing roll/pitch/yaw (liberally adapted here), originally published in his *C++ Boids* implementation. Also thanks to Mike Louie (Boeing) for helping with the transformation math (I hate matrices).

There are a number of other excellent references on this subject on the Web and in bookstores. Probably the best single place to start seeking more information is with the "father of flocking" himself, Craig Reynolds. See his article "Flocks, Herds, and Schools: A Distributed Behavioral Model" in *Computer Graphics*, 21(4), SIGGRAPH '87 Conference Proceedings, pages 25–34, 1987.

The *Microsoft DirectX SDK* also comes with two fairly simple-to-follow implementations included on the source CD. On the *DirectX 7a* CD, they are located at *\DXF\samples\multimedia\d3dim\src\boids* and *\DXF\samples\multimedia\dmusic\src\dmboids*. Both versions feature obstacle avoidance using a "force-field" approach that is fairly natural looking.

Finally, an excellent book that addresses the topic of artificial life in general, in addition to discussing both flocking and boids, is Steven Levy's *Artificial Life*, Vintage Books, 1993.

LISTING 3.6.1 The CFlock Class Definition

```
class CFlock
{

   public:

      ////////////////////
      // static variables
      ////////////////////

      // number of flocks
      static int FlockCount;

      // list of flocks
      static CFlock * ListOfFlocks[MAX_FLOCKS];

      ////////////////////////////////
      // constructors and destructors
      ////////////////////////////////

      // Constructor.
      // Creates a new flock.
      CFlock (void);

      // Destructor.
      ~CFlock (void);

      /////////////////////
      // flocking functions
      /////////////////////
```

```
        // Update.
        // Updates all members of a flock.
        void Update (void);

        ///////////////////////////
        // miscellaneous functions
        ///////////////////////////

        // AddTo.
        // Adds the indicated boid to the flock.
        void AddTo (CBoid * boid);

        // GetCount.
        // Returns the # of boids in a given flock.
        int GetCount (void);

        // GetFirstMember.
        // Returns a pointer to the first boid in a
        // given flock (if any).
        CBoid * GetFirstMember (void);

        // PrintData.
        // Dumps all data describing a given flock.
        void PrintData (void);

        // RemoveFrom.
        // Removes the indicated boid from the flock.
        void RemoveFrom (CBoid * boid);

    private:

        int     m_id;               // id of this flock
        int     m_num_members;      // number of boids in this flock
        CBoid   *m_first_member;    // pointer to first member
};
```

LISTING 3.6.2 The CBoid Class Definition

```
class CBoid {

    public:

        ////////////////////
        // static variables
        ////////////////////

        // visible friends list (work space reused by each boid)
        static CBoid * VisibleFriendsList[MAX_FRIENDS_VISIBLE];

        ///////////////////////////////
        // constructors and destructors
        ///////////////////////////////
```

```
// Constructor #1.
// Creates an individual boid with randomized position,
// velocity, and orientation.
CBoid (short id_v);

// Constructor #2.
// Creates an individual boid with specific position,
// velocity, and orientation.
CBoid (short id_v,
       vector * pos_v, vector * vel_v, vector * ang_v);

// Destructor
~CBoid (void);

//////////////////////////
// public flocking methods
//////////////////////////

// FlockIt.
// Used for frame-by-frame updates; no time
// deltas on positions.
void FlockIt (int flock_id, CBoid *first_boid);

//////////////////////////
// miscellaneous functions
//////////////////////////

// AddToVisibleList.
// This visibility list is regenerated for each member each
// update cycle, and acts much like a push-down queue; the
// latest member added to the list becomes the first one
// when the list is sequentially accessed.  Mostly I did
// this for speed reasons, as this allows for fast inserts
// (and we don't delete from this list, we just rebuild it
// each update cycle).
void AddToVisibleList (CBoid *ptr);

// ClearVisibleList.
// Clears the visibility list.
void ClearVisibleList (void);

// GetNext.
// Returns the "next" pointer of the invoking member.
CBoid * GetNext();

// LinkOut.
// Removes a member from a list.
void LinkOut ();

// PrintData.
// Dumps all data describing a given member.
void PrintData (void);
```

```
    // SetNext.
    // Set the "next" pointer of an individual member.
    void SetNext (CBoid *ptr);

    // SetPrev.
    // Set the "prev" pointer of an individual member.
    void SetPrev (CBoid *ptr);

private:

    ///////////////
    // data members
    ///////////////

    // supplied with constructor(s)
    short    m_id;                      // member individual ID
    float    m_perception_range;        // how far member can see
    vector   m_pos;                     // position of member
                                        // (in meters)
    vector   m_vel;                     // velocity of member
                                        // (meters/sec)
    vector   m_ang;                     // orientation of member


    // computed
    float    m_speed;                     // overall speed of member
    u_short  m_num_flockmates_seen;       // # of flockmates this
                                          // member sees
    u_short  m_num_enemies_seen;          // # of enemies this
                                          // member sees
    CBoid    *m_nearest_flockmate;        // pointer to nearest
                                          // flockmate (if any)
    CBoid    *m_nearest_enemy;            // pointer to nearest
                                          // enemy (if any)
    float    m_dist_to_nearest_flockmate; // distance to
                                          // nearest flockmate
                                          // (if any), in
                                          // meters
    float    m_dist_to_nearest_enemy;     // distance to
                                          // nearest enemy
                                          // (if any), in
                                          // meters
    vector   m_oldpos;                    // last position
    vector   m_oldvel;                    // last velocity
    CBoid    *m_next;                     // pointer to next
                                          // flockmate
    CBoid    *m_prev;                     // pointer to
                                          // previous
                                          // flockmate

    ///////////////////
    // flocking methods
    ///////////////////
```

```
// Cruising.
// Generates a vector indicating how a flock boid would
// like to move, if it were all up to him and he was under
// no other influences of any kind.
vector CBoid::Cruising (void);

// FleeEnemies.
// Generates a vector for a flock boid to avoid the
// nearest enemy (boid of a different flock) it sees.
vector CBoid::FleeEnemies (void);

// KeepDistance.
// Generates a vector for a flock boid to maintain his
// desired separation distance from the nearest flockmate
// he sees.
vector CBoid::KeepDistance (void);

// MatchHeading.
// Generates a vector for a flock boid to try
// to match the heading of its nearest flockmate.
vector CBoid::MatchHeading (void);

// SeeEnemies.
// Determines which enemy flock boids a given flock boid
// can see.
int CBoid::SeeEnemies (int flock_id);

// SeeFriends.
// Determines which flockmates a given flock boid can see.
int CBoid::SeeFriends (CBoid *first_boid);

// SteerToCenter.
// Generates a vector to guide a flock boid towards
// the "center of mass" of the flockmates he can see.
vector CBoid::SteerToCenter (void);

// WorldBound.
// Implements a world boundary so that flocks don't fly
// infinitely far away from the camera, instead remaining
// in a nice viewable area.  It does this by wrapping flock
// boids around to the other side of the world, so (for
// example) they move out the right and return on the left.
void CBoid::WorldBound (void);

///////////////////////////
// miscellaneous functions
///////////////////////////

// AccumulateChanges.
// Adds vector values in changes into the accumumlator
// vector. Returns magnitude of accumulator vector after
```

```
        // adding changes.
            float CBoid::AccumulateChanges (vector &accumulator,
          vector changes);

            // CanISee.
            // Determine whether a given invoking boid can see the boid
        // in question. Returns the distance to the boid.
            float CBoid::CanISee (CBoid *ptr);

            // ComputeRPY.
            // Computes the roll/pitch/yaw of the flock boid based on
        // its latest velocity vector changes.  Roll/pitch/yaw are
        // stored in the "ang" data member as follows:
            //   pitch is about the x axis
            //   yaw is about the y axis
            //   roll is about the z axis
            // All calculations assume a right-handed coordinate
        // system:
            //   +x = through the left side of the object
            //   +y = up
            //   +z = through the nose of the model
            void CBoid::ComputeRPY (void);
};
```

3.7

A Finite-State Machine Class

Eric Dybsand

This article defines a generic finite-state machine (FSM) C++ class. *FSMs* are computer science and mathematical abstractions that have been useful for many years in a variety of ways. This article is not a discussion of the theory behind the FSM; instead, it is a simple presentation of a basic building-block tool, the `FSMclass`, which you can use to help develop your own complex artificially intelligent decision-making processes in your computer game.

The first thing you should know about FSMs is that they are simple machines that consist of a finite number of states (obvious, don't you think?). A *state* is really only a condition. For instance, consider a door: its states can be open or closed and locked or unlocked.

The next aspect one should know about FSMs is that there is an input to the FSM, which affects a state transition from one state to another. An FSM can have a simple (or complex) state transition function that determines what state will become the current state.

The new current state is called the output state of the state transition of the FSM, or the state to which the FSM has transitioned based on the input. If this concept is confusing, again think of a door as an example FSM. When the door is in a closed state and a locked state, perhaps the input of use key will cause the door to transition to the unlocked state (the output state of the state transition and the new current state of the door). Then the input of use hand will cause the door to transition to the open state. When the door is in the open state, the input of use hand will transition the door back to the closed state. When the door is in the closed state, the input of use key will transition the door back to the locked state. While the door is in the locked state, the input of use hand would fail to transition the door to the open state, and the door would remain in the locked state. Furthermore, once the door was in the open state, the input of use key would fail to transition the door to the locked state.

So, in summary, an FSM is a machine that has a finite number of states, one of which is a current state. The FSM can accept input that will result in a state transition from the current state to an output state, based on some state transition function, and the output state then becomes the new current state.

Now, how does this concept apply to AI in computer games?

The answer to that question is that the possibilities are really endless! FSMs can form the basis for managing the game world, simulating the emotion of a non-player character (NPC), maintaining the status of the game, parsing input from the human player, or managing the condition of an object.

Consider the attitude of an NPC monster in an adventure game, for example. Let's say that the monster can have the following states: berserk, rage, mad, annoyed, and uncaring. Furthermore, let's say that you have AI game code that does different things based on the state of the monster's attitude. We can use an FSM to manage the monster's attitude and the way it transitions from one state to another based on input from the game itself. Let's further say that inputs are player seen, player attacks, player gone, monster hurt, and monster healed. Then the state diagram shown in Figure 3.7.1 can be drawn.

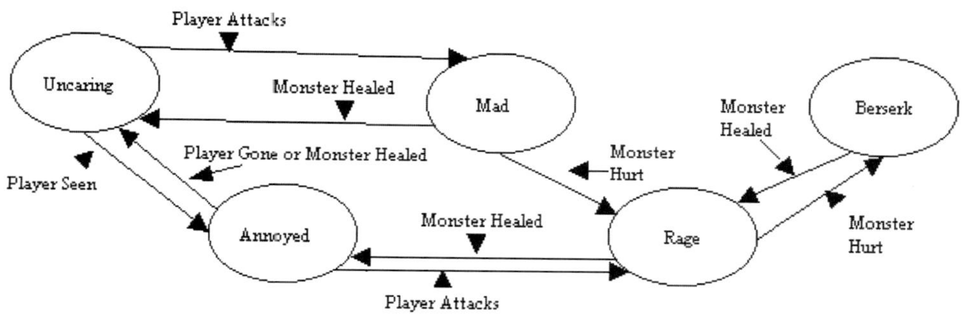

FIGURE 3.7.1 A sample finite-state machine.

Using these inputs and states, we can set up a state transition matrix that looks something like the one shown in Table 3.7.1.

TABLE 3.7.1 A State Transition Matrix for the Monster Game

Current State	Input	Output State
uncaring	player seen	annoyed
uncaring	player attacks	mad
mad	monster hurt	rage
mad	monster healed	uncaring
rage	monster hurt	berserk
rage	monster healed	annoyed
berserk	monster hurt	berserk
berserk	monster healed	rage
annoyed	player gone	uncaring
annoyed	player attacks	rage
annoyed	monster healed	uncaring

So, depending on the current state of the monster's attitude and the input to the FSM, the attitude of the monster will change. Game code that performs behavior based on the attitude of the monster will then cause the monster to act differently.

Obviously, we could add more state transitions, based on more states and inputs. Doing so would affect how our monster's attitude is evaluated and determined, and that is how we create the AI that uses this monster's attitude.

The FSMclass and FSMstate

Now how do we put this idea to work? That is what the `FSMclass` and its subordinate `FSMstate` class will show in the following implementation, as illustrated in Figure 3.7.2.

FIGURE 3.7.2 The `FSMclass` can use any number of `FSMstate` classes.

The `FSMclass` provides structure for any number of states that are provided by the `FSMstate` class. These two classes work with each other to provide the functionality for a *generic* finite-state machine. A generic FSM implies that these objects are generalized, able to support a variety of types of states, a variety of types of state transitions, and any number of state transitions, as well as any number of states within the FSM. With such variety and generalization as a design goal, these classes and their members were selected as you see in the following discussion.

Defining the FSMstate

Here is the class definition we use to represent a state for our FSM:

```
class FSMstate
{
    unsigned m_usNumberOfTransistions;    // maximum number of states
                                             supported
    int *m_piInputs;                    // input array for transitions
    int *m_piOutputState;               // output state array
    int m_iStateID;                     // the unique ID of this state

public:
    // constructor accepts an ID for this state and the number of
    //   transitions to support
    FSMstate( int iStateID, unsigned usTransitions );
    // destructor cleans up allocated arrays
    ~FSMstate();
```

```
        // access the state ID
        int GetID() { return m_iStateID; }
        // add a state transition to the array
        void AddTransition( int iInput, int iOutputID );
        // remove a state transition from the array
        void DeleteTransition( int iOutputID );
        // get the output state and effect a transition
        int GetOutput( int iInput );
};
```

See Listing 3.7.1 for the `FSMstate` class constructor and destructor implementations. The member variables and functions of the `FSMstate` class are as follows:

- The `FSMstate::m_usNumberOfTransistions` controls the number of state transitions that this state is able to support. Setting this value also determines the size of the input and output arrays. Since we are creating a "finite" state machine, this value sets the finite-state transition limit for this state.
- The `FSMstate::m_piInputs` is an array of `m_usNumberOfTransistions` size that contains the input values to be used during state transition. The input array is used by the state transition evaluation function to compare to the input received and determine the corresponding output state.
- The `FSMstate::m_piOutputState` is an array of `m_usNumberOfTransistions` size that contains a corresponding output state identifier that indicates the new transition state during a state transition.
- The `FSMstate::m_iStateID` is a unique identifier used to identify this instance of an `FSMstate` and is the value that would be output by any transition to this state from another state.
- The `FSMstate::GetID()` provides public access to the unique identifier of this instance of the `FSMstate` class. See class declaration for this implementation.
- The `FSMstate::AddTransition()` provides a means to add new input values and output state arrays to this instance of the `FSMstate`. See Listing 3.7.2 for this implementation.
- The `FSMstate::DeleteTransition()` provides a means to delete an existing input and its corresponding output state identifier. See Listing 3.7.3 for this implementation.
- The `FSMstate::GetOutput()` provides the state transition function that uses the input value to determine the transition output state identifier and return it. See Listing 3.7.4 for this implementation.

Defining the FSMclass

Now we need the actual `FSMclass` implementation. The `FSMclass` works by maintaining a collection of `FSMstate` objects.

```
class FSMclass
{
    State_Map m_map;      // map containing all states of this FSM
    int m_iCurrentState;     // the m_iStateID of the current state
```

```
public:
    FSMclass( int iStateID );          // set initial state of the FSM
    ~FSMclass();                       // clean up memory usage

    // return the current state ID
    int GetCurrentState() { return m_iCurrentState; }
    // set current state
    void SetCurrentState( int iStateID ) { m_iCurrentState = iStateID; }

    // return the FSMstate object pointer
    FSMstate *GetState( int iStateID );
    // add a FSMstate object pointer to the map
    void AddState( FSMstate *pState );
    // delete a FSMstate object pointer from the map
    void DeleteState( int iStateID );

    // perform state transition based on input & current state
    int StateTransition( int iInput );
};
```

See Listing 3.7.5 for the `FSMclass` class constructor and destructor implementation. The member variables and functions of the `FSMclass` class are as follows.

The `FSMclass::m_map` is the collection of `FSMstate` objects (pointers to `FSMstate` objects, in this case) and is implemented from an STL <map>:

```
typedef map< int, FSMstate*, less<int> > State_Map;
```

A discussion of the specifics of STL and `<map>` collections in general is beyond the scope of this gem. For information about STL, please see the gem "Using the STL in Game Programming." The preceding function declares `State_Map` to be an STL `<map>` with an `int` for a key; the map contains pointers to `FSMstate` objects, and the comparison function to use during access is the <> operator for `int`.

- The `FSMclass::m_iCurrentState` is the state identifier for the `FSMstate` object that is considered to be the current state of the FSM.
- The `FSMclass::GetCurrentState()` provides public access to the unique identifier of the state of the current `FSMstate` object. See class declaration for this implementation.
- The `FSMclass::SetCurrentState()` provides public access to set the unique identifier of the state of a new current `FSMstate` object for the FSM. See class declaration for this implementation.
- The `FSMclass::GetState()` provides a method to obtain a pointer to any `FSMstate` object contained within the FSM. See Listing 3.7.6 for this implementation.
- The `FSMclass::AddState()` provides a method for adding `FSMobject` pointers to the `<map>` contained within the FSM. This is the method that one uses to record the state relationships within the FSM that are defined by `FSMstate` objects. See Listing 3.7.7 for this implementation.

- The `FSMclass::DeleteState()` provides a method for deleting `FSMobject` pointers from the `<map>` contained within the FSM. This is the method one uses to dynamically remove state relationships from within the FSM. *Note*: When you want to delete the current state from the `<map>`, be sure to set a new current state using `FSMclass::SetCurrentState()` before deleting the old current state. See Listing 3.7.8 for this implementation.
- The `FSMclass::StateTransition()` provides the method for initiating a state transition, using the input value received and returning the output state identifier. See Listing 3.7.9 for this implementation.

Creating States for the FSM

To use our `FSMclass` and `FSMstate` classes in a game, we first build the `FSMstate` objects:

```
FSMstate *pFSMstate = NULL;

// create the STATE_ID_UNCARING
try
{
    // FSMstate( int iStateID, unsigned usTransitions )
    pFSMstate = new FSMstate( STATE_ID_UNCARING, 2 );
}
catch( ... )
{
    throw;
}
// now add state transitions to this state
pFSMstate->AddTransition( INPUT_ID_PLAYER_SEEN, STATE_ID_ANNOYED );
pFSMstate->AddTransition( INPUT_ID_PLAYER_ATTACKS, STATE_ID_MAD );
```

And then create an FSMclass object:

```
// create the FSMclass object
try
{
    // FSMclass( int iStateID )
    m_pFSMclass = new FSMclass(STATE_ID_UNCARING);
}
catch( ... )
{
    throw;
}
```

Now add the `FSMstate` object to the `FSMclass` object:

```
// now add this state to the FSM
m_pFSMclass->AddState( pFSMstate );
```

Repeat the process of creating `FSMstate` objects and adding them to the `FSMclass` object for all the states you want to have in your FSM.

Using the FSM

To use our `FSMclass`, we need only to pass it an input value (which is game dependent) and receive an output state (also game dependent), then act on the output state. So in your game code, you would have something like this:

```
// something happens in the game that causes an input
iInputID = INPUT_ID_PLAYER_ATTACKS;
     .
     .
// have the FSM do the transition to an output state
m_iOutputState = m_pFSMclass->StateTransition(iInputID);
     .
     .
// some game AI code tests for the output state
if( m_iOutputState == STATE_ID_MAD )
{
     // some code for the monster to act mad
}
```

Its usage is that simple!

In conclusion, this `FSMclass` is not an end-all solution to your computer game AI needs. It is a starting point, or a building block, for you to use to create your own FSMs that are specific to your game needs. `FSMclass` objects could even be placed in lists or maps and used to form networks of FSMs that are interrelated.

This `FSMclass` could be expanded to support different input type data or state identification data types. A state or input-specific transition function could be easily added so that, based on the type of input received or the current state, the transition to the output state could be determined uniquely.

Have fun with this concept, and you will gain a powerful tool for making complex computer game AI.

LISTING 3.7.1

```
FSMstate::FSMstate( int iStateID, unsigned usTransitions )
{
     // don't allow 0 transitions
     if( !usTransitions )
     m_usNumberOfTransistions = 1;
     else
     m_usNumberOfTransistions = usTransitions;

     // save off id and number of transitions
     m_iStateID = iStateID;
```

```
        // now allccate each array
        try
        {
            m_piInputs = new int[m_usNumberOfTransistions];
            for( int i=0; i<m_usNumberOfTransistions; ++i )
                m_piInputs[i] = 0;
        }
        catch( ... )
        {
            throw;
        }

        try
        {
            m_piOutputState = new int[m_usNumberOfTransistions];
            for( int i=0; i<m_usNumberOfTransistions; ++i )
            m_piOutputState[i] = 0;
        }
        catch( ... )
        {
            delete [] m_piInputs;
        throw;
        }
}
FSMstate::~FSMstate()
{
    delete [] m_piInputs;
    delete [] m_piOutputState;
}
```

LISTING 3.7.2

```
void FSMstate::AddTransition( int iInput, int iOutputID )
{
    // the m_piInputs[] and m_piOutputState[] are not sorted
    // so find the first non-zero offset in m_piOutputState[]
    // and use that offset to store the input and OutputID
    // within the m_piInputs[] and m_piOutputState[]
    for( int i=0; i<m_usNumberOfTransistions; ++i )
    {
        if( !m_piOutputState[i] )
            break;
    }
    // only a valid offset is used
    if( i < m_usNumberOfTransistions )
    {
        m_piOutputState[i] = iOutputID;
        m_piInputs[i] = iInput;
    }
}
```

LISTING 3.7.3

```
void FSMstate::DeleteTransition( int iOutputID )
{
    // the m_piInputs[] and m_piOutputState[] are not sorted
    // so find the offset of the output state ID to remove
    for( int i=0; i<m_usNumberOfTransistions; ++i )
    {
        if( m_piOutputState[i] == iOutputID )
            break;
    }
    // test to be sure the offset is valid
    if( i >= m_usNumberOfTransistions )
        return;

    // remove this output ID and its input transition value
    m_piInputs[i] = 0;
    m_piOutputState[i] = 0;

    // since the m_piInputs[] and m_piOutputState[] are not
    // sorted, then we need to shift the remaining contents
    for( ; i<(m_usNumberOfTransistions-1); ++i )
    {
        if( !m_piOutputState[i] )
            break;

        m_piInputs[i] = m_piInputs[i+1];
        m_piOutputState[i] = m_piOutputState[i+1];
    }
    // and clear the last offset in both arrays
    m_piInputs[i] = 0;
    m_piOutputState[i] = 0;
}
```

LISTING 3.7.4

```
int FSMstate::GetOutput( int iInput )
{
    int iOutputID = m_iStateID;    // output state to be returned

    // for each possible transition
    for( int i=0; i<m_usNumberOfTransistions; ++i )
    {
        // zeroed output state IDs indicate the end of the array
        if( !m_piOutputState[i] )
            break;
        // state transition function: look for a match with the input
           value
        if( iInput == m_piInputs[i] )
        {
```

```
                iOutputID = m_piOutputState[i];     // output state id
                break;
            }
        }
        // returning either this m_iStateID to indicate no output
        // state was matched by the input (i.e., no state transition
        // can occur) or the transitioned output state ID
        return( iOutputID );
    }
```

LISTING 3.7.5

```
FSMclass::FSMclass( int iStateID )
{
    m_iCurrentState = iStateID;
}

FSMclass::~FSMclass()
{
    FSMstate *pState = NULL;
    State_Map::iterator it;

    // only perform this if there are pointers in the map
    if( !m_map.empty() )
    {
        // first delete any FSMstate objects in the map
        for( it = m_map.begin(); it != m_map.end(); ++it )
        {
            pState = (FSMstate *)((*it).second);
            if( pState != NULL )
                delete pState;
        }
        // let the map dtor() erase the actual pointer out of the map
    }
}
```

LISTING 3.7.6

```
FSMstate *FSMclass::GetState( int iStateID )
{
    FSMstate *pState = NULL;
    State_Map::iterator it;

    // try to find this FSMstate in the map
    if( !m_map.empty() )
    {
        it = m_map.find( iStateID );
        if( it != m_map.end() )
            pState = (FSMstate *)((*it).second);
    }
    return( pState );
}
```

LISTING 3.7.7

```
void FSMclass::AddState( FSMstate *pNewState )
{
    FSMstate *pState = NULL;
    State_Map::iterator it;

    // try to find this FSMstate in the map
    if( !m_map.empty() )
    {
        it = m_map.find( pNewState->GetID() );
        if( it != m_map.end() )
            pState = (FSMstate *)((*it).second);
    }

    // if the FSMstate object pointer is already in the map, return
    if( pState != NULL )
        return;

    // otherwise put the FSMstate object pointer into the map
    m_map.insert( SM_VT(pNewState->GetID(), pNewState) );
}
```

LISTING 3.7.8

```
void FSMclass::DeleteState( int iStateID )
{
    FSMstate *pState = NULL;
    State_Map::iterator it;

    // try to find this FSMstate in the map
    if( !m_map.empty() )
    {
        // get the iterator object of the FSMstate object pointer
        it = m_map.find( iStateID );
        if( it != m_map.end() )
            pState = (FSMstate *)((*it).second);
    }

    // confirm that the FSMstate is in the map
    if( pState != NULL &&
        pState->GetID() == iStateID )
    {
        m_map.erase( it );          // remove it from the map
        delete pState;          // delete the object itself
    }
}
```

LISTING 3.7.9

```
int FSMclass::StateTransition( int iInput )
{
    // the current state of the FSM must be set to have a transition
    if( !m_iCurrentState )
        return m_iCurrentState;

    // get the pointer to the FSMstate object that is the current
       state
    FSMstate *pState = GetState( m_iCurrentState );
    if( pState == NULL )
    {
        // signal that there is a problem
        m_iCurrentState = 0;
        return m_iCurrentState;
    }

    // now pass along the input transition value and let the FSMstate
    // do the really tough job of transitioning for the FSM, and save
    // off the output state returned as the new current state of the
    // FSM and return the output state to the calling process
    m_iCurrentState = pState->GetOutput( iInput );
    return m_iCurrentState;
}
```

3.8

Implementing Practical Planning for Game AI

Jamie Cheng, Klei Entertainment; and Finnegan Southey, Google Inc.

jamie.cheng@kleientertainment.com, finnegan@google.com

The increasing complexity of game worlds and the growing focus on team-based gameplay have pushed the development of game AI beyond the limits of finite state machines (FSMs). FSM approaches are typically brittle with respect to changes in the game design and engine, are hard to debug, and are difficult to extend beyond their originally designed purpose. Designing multiple FSMs to interact intelligently and cooperatively is very tricky, and unforeseen situations during the game can throw the AI into disarray.

Planning addresses these issues by abstracting the reasoning to a new level and expressing them in a concise language that describes the effects of actions in the world. Using planning, most of the reasoning process is handled automatically by the planning engine. Changes to the game design can be quickly reflected in the planning domain, and because the planner reasons explicitly about the goals and subgoals to be obtained, it is able to effectively distribute tasks, allowing cooperative action between multiple agents.

This gem explains our work on the concepts and tools for implementing practical planning, including mixing planning with other types of control (e.g., pathfinding, FSMs, and scripting), communications between the game engine and the planning engine, optimizations, and other important issues.

For the purposes of this introduction, we present a Sims-like game, but one in which the player specifies *goals* for their simulated people instead of specific *actions*. However, the planning approach applies equally well to a wide range of games. We have given substantial thought to its use in RPGs, tactical squad-based FPSs, high-level strategy in RTSs, stealth/espionage games, and we foresee many new types of gameplay both in and out of these genres.

The Planning Framework

Conceptually, a planning framework works with a set of *world states* that contain the essential information about the game world at a given point in time. When we are about to plan, we must provide an *initial state*, describing the world we want to reason about. For example:

- Bob is in the kitchen.
- The cabinet key is in the kitchen.
- The cabinet is in the den.
- The silver plate is in the cabinet.
- The cabinet is locked.

States are transformed into other states via *actions*, so part of our abstract description includes details on how actions alter states. Here, a `move` action would allow Bob to move between the kitchen and the den. Similarly, a `take` action would allow Bob to pick up objects in the same room as himself. If Bob used the `take` action on the key, the new state would be as follows:

- Bob is in the kitchen.
- Bob is carrying the key.
- The cabinet is in the den.
- The silver plate is in the cabinet.
- The cabinet is locked.

Using this model, the designer can specify *goal conditions* such as "Bob is carrying the plate." We are interested in any state where Bob is carrying the plate. We will call these *goal states*. There can be multiple possible goal states, because the only condition we specified is that Bob is carrying the plate. The rest of the world can be in any state.

Planning is a search for a sequence of actions that will transform the initial state into a goal state. During the search, the planner will, explicitly or implicitly, construct many possible world states, heading toward the goal. These states do not map directly to the game engine but are instead based on the initial state fed to the planner. If the planner succeeds, it formulates a *plan*: the set of actions needed to reach the goal state. This is then executed step by step, transforming the actual game world. See Figure 3.8.1.

Planning Domains

We call the abstraction of the game world the *planning domain* for the world. Classical planning views the world as a logical construct where there are certain facts about the world associated with each state. It is common to introduce planning using propositional logic, which simply uses a set of propositions that are either true or false (essentially, a set of Boolean variables). A proposition might consist of a statement like "Bob is carrying the key," and that statement can be either true or false. Think of the

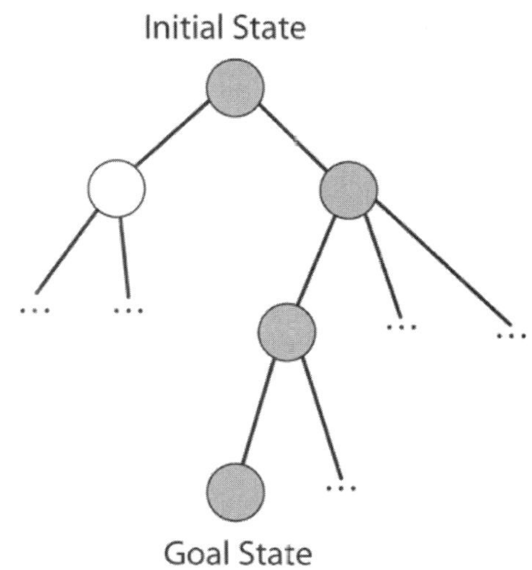

FIGURE 3.8.1 Example of a plan to reach the goal state.

proposition as a Boolean variable named `BOB_CARRIES_KEY`. Propositional logic is the basis for what is probably the best-known planner, STRIPS [Fikes71]. The STRIPS planning language is still used today, along with many variations and extensions.

Predicate logic would instead represent the same statement as a Boolean function that takes objects as arguments. Our example would become something like `carrying( Bob, key )`. This allows for a much more concise planning language and is used in most contemporary planners. The most widely accepted planning language at present is PDDL, used by most contemporary research planners. PPDL uses a LISP-like syntax, which is not widely used in the games industry, so we have developed our own syntax and parser, better suited to the industry at large and more readable by designers who may have only limited programming experience.

Objects

Predicate logic describes truth statements over a set of *objects*. Objects are the entities that make up the world. In our earlier example, objects would include "Bob," "key," "silver plate," "den," "kitchen," etc. These objects are not the same as objects in the object-oriented (OO) sense; they do not have methods or any associated dynamics. However, it is quite natural (and even desirable) to relate planning objects to OO game engine objects in a one-to-one fashion, so that the planner's proposed actions can be translated directly into game object manipulations.

Objects do have *types*, much as in the object-oriented framework. This mechanism affords type checking, so errors can be caught earlier in development. We allow multiple type inheritance, so types form a *lattice*. We identify one special type, "Object," often called the *universal type*, from which all other types inherit. This leads us to the first kind of statement, which declares types to the planner:

```
type Locatable;
type Location;
type Creature isa Locatable;
type Person isa Creature;
type Item isa Locatable;
type Key isa Item;
type ValuablePlate isa Item, Decoration;  // multiple inheritance
```

Once we have declared types, we can declare objects:

```
object alice isa Person;
object bob isa Person;
object cabinetkey isa Key;
object silverplate isa ValuablePlate;
object kitchen isa Location;
object den isa Location
```

Predicates

Predicates help us state facts about the objects in the world. They map tuples of objects to true or false values. For example, we can have a predicate `carrying` that takes two arguments, the first a `Creature` and the second an `Item`. We can now express ideas like the following: `carrying(bob, cabinetkey)` or `carrying(bob, silverplate)`.

Facts expressed as predicates make up the states in our planner. A state is simply a collection of all the facts about the world. In general, we store only the true facts in the world: the predicates that evaluate to true. Every other predicate expression is assumed to be false. This is known as the *closed world assumption*; it is motivated by the expectation that more predicates will be false than true in the world, and so it's more efficient to store the true ones.

There are a few different ways to use predicates. In some cases, we will *assert* predicates, making our expression true in the current state. So we might assert `carrying(bob, cabinetkey)` to add that fact to the state. Alternately, we may use the predicate as a query: "Is Bob carrying the cabinet key?" If that is a fact in the current state, the predicate will return true.

In our planning language, the arguments of predicates have types and predicates must be explicitly declared:

```
predicate carrying(Creature, Item);
predicate inroom(Locatable, Location);
```

Variables

Predicates capture relationships between objects. We can ask whether a relation exists or not, but we can go further and ask for sets of relationships. This is done with variables. For example, if we would like a list of things carried by Bob, we can query `carrying(bob, ?x)`, where `?x` is the notation we use to indicate that `x` is a variable.

It's easiest to think about the process as pattern matching. The query checks all the `carrying` facts in the state, picks only those whose first argument is `Bob`, and sets `x` to each value for the second argument in succession. If the query finds one or more suitable matches, it returns true for each such match and binds the variable(s) accordingly.

Logical Connectors

Using *conjunctions* (logical AND) and *negations* (logical NOT), we can create much more interesting queries. For example, we can check whether Bob and the key are in the same room:

```
inroom(bob, ?x) and inroom(cabinetkey, ?x)
```

Here, the first `inroom()` query finds a match corresponding to `Bob` and binds `?x` to `kitchen`. The second query now becomes `inroom(key1, kitchen)`.

It is also important to allow for a special kind of predicate to represent inequalities, only true if its two arguments are different objects, for example, `?x != ?y`.

Operators

We use operators to transform one state into another. In their simplest form, operators have a *precondition*, a query that must be true before the action can be performed, and *effects*, a set of changes to be made to the world. Both can be stated using simple logic expressions formed from predicates, conjunctions, and negations:

```
operator take(Creature ?c, Item ?i)
    precondition: inroom (?c, ?r) and inroom(?i, ?r)
    effect: not inroom (?i, ?r) and carrying(?c, ?r);
```

This operator takes two arguments (note their types). The preconditions state that the creature must be in the same location as the item. The effect creates a new state, identical to the original state, removing the fact that the item is in the room, and adding the fact that the creature is carrying the item.

Note that the `?r` variable is not one of the arguments of the operator. That's because it isn't really essential to the action, it's just some information we need to know to execute it. Think of it as a local variable for the operator. When the game engine needs to actually execute the action, it only needs to know the creature and the item.

Once we have operators, we can examine a state and automatically determine what actions are possible by testing the precondition for each action. Each match of the preconditions for each operator is a possible action. We now have everything we need to search for a plan except for the actual search algorithm.

A Multi-Agent Planner Example

Putting all this together, we can look at a simple example that clearly shows the power of a planner. In this example, we create a state where there is a trivial solution, and then expand the problem to one that requires two agents working together to solve the problem:

```
type Locatable;
type Location;
type Creature isa Locatable;
type Person isa Creature;
type Dog isa Creature;
type Container isa Locatable;
type Item isa Locatable;
type Key isa Item;
type Plate isa Item;
type ValuablePlate isa Plate, Decoration;        // multiple
                                                    inheritance
type Food isa Item;
```

Once we have declared types, we can declare objects:

```
object alice isa Person;
object bob isa Person;
object cabinetkey isa Key;
object silverplate isa ValuablePlate;
object kitchen isa Location;
object den isa Location;
object cabinet isa Container;
object nelly isa Dog;
object lasagna isa Food;
object fridge isa Container;

predicate inroom(Locatable ?a, Location ?b);     // Object is in
                                                    location
predicate carrying(Creature ?c, Item ?i);        // Creature car-
                                                    ries item
predicate locked(Container ?c);                  // Container is
                                                    locked
predicate unlocks(Key ?k, Container ?c);         // Key unlocks
                                                    container
predicate hungry(Creature ?c);                   // Creature his
                                                    hungry
predicate prepared(Food ?f);                     // Food is pre-
                                                    pared
predicate inside(Item ?i, Container ?c);         // Item is inside
                                                    container

// Pick up something in the room.
operator take(Person ?p, Item ?i)
    precondition: inroom(?p, ?r) and inroom (?i, ?r)
    effect: not inroom (?i, ?r) and carrying(?p, ?r);
```

```
// move to another room
operator goto(Person ?p, Room ?r)
    precondition: inroom(?p, ?o) and ?o != ?r
    effect: inroom (?p, ?r) and not inroom(?p, ?o);

// drop something carried
operator drop(Person ?p, Item ?i)
    precondition: inroom(?p, ?r) and carrying(?p, ?i)
    effect: inroom (?i, ?r) and not carrying(?p, ?i);

// remove something from a container
operator remove(Person ?c, Item ?i)
    precondition: inside(?i, ?v) and inroom(?c, ?r) and
    inroom(?v, ?r) and unlocked(?v)
    effect: carrying(?c, ?i) and not inside(?i, ?v);

// unlock a container with a key
operator unlock(Person ?c, Container ?v)
    precondition: locked(?v) and unlocks(?k, ?v) and carrying(?c,
    ?k)
    effect: not locked(?v);

// prepare some food
operator prepare(Person ?c, Food ?f)
    precondition: carrying(?c, ?f) and not prepared(?f)
    effect: prepared(?f);

// eat some prepared food from a plate
operator eat(Person ?c, Food ?f, Plate ?p)
    precondition: carrying(?c, ?f) and carrying(?c, ?p) and
    hungry(?c) and prepared(?f)
    effect: not hungry(?c) and not carrying(?c, ?f);
```

Now we define our initial state and goal state. The trivial case is that Bob wants the plate and it is in the den while Bob is in the kitchen:

```
//define initial state
inroom(bob, kitchen)
inroom(silverplate, den)


//define goal state
goal carrying(bob, silverplate)
```

Given this, the planner returns the following to us:

```
goto(bob, den)
take(bob, silverplate)
```

Now watch how easily we can expand the problem, defining a new initial state where the plate is locked in the cabinet in the den and Alice carries the key. We will try to achieve the same goal:

```
//define initial state
inroom(alice, den)
inroom(bob, kitchen)
carrying(alice, cabinetkey)
inroom(cabinet, den)
unlocks(cabinetkey, cabinet)
inside(silverplate, cabinet)
locked(cabinet)
```

One possible plan is as follows:

```
unlock(alice, cabinet)
remove(alice, silverplate)
goto(alice, kitchen)
drop(alice, silverplate)
take(bob, silverplate)
```

Now consider a new situation where Alice is hungry and we want her to be fed:

```
//define initial state
inroom(alice, den)
inroom(bob, kitchen)
carrying(alice, cabinetkey)
inroom(cabinet, den)
unlocks(cabinetkey, cabinet)
locked(cabinet)
hungry(alice)
inside(silverplate, cabinet)
inside(lasagna, fridge)


//define goal state
not hungry(alice)
```

A plan to achieve this is the following:

```
unlock(alice, cabinet)
remove(alice, silverplate)
goto(alice, kitchen)
remove(bob, lasagna)
prepare(bob, lasagna)
drop(bob, lasagna)
eat(alice, lasgna, silverplate)
```

These simple examples have immense ramifications. Suddenly, designers can easily create scenarios that may require the AI to cooperate to solve a problem! Even better, as the player changes the world, the AI automatically replans and acts accordingly. Over the course of the game, new predicates can be asserted or operators added that allow creatures to do more things. Other options include designers writing simple scripts that assign goals for the planner to carry out, or players asking a cooperative AI for help. The possibilities are endless.

The best way to see the possibilities is to think about them. Given the earlier domain, spend some time thinking about how you could quickly implement the following:

- Add a way for people to give items directly to each other.
- Describe the layout of the house and add doors.
- Add a thief who only steals valuable stuff and uses unlocked doors.
- Add an operator for the dog to eat food when no people are in the room.
- Make Bob not tall enough to reach the plate in the cabinet, requiring Alice to help.
- Forbid Alice from unlocking the cabinet while Bob is in the room.
- Require two people to move the fridge.
- Require food to be heated before eating.
- Create messes as a result of cooking (e.g., dirty dishes) that require cleaning up.
- Allow only trained people to cook.
- Add driving out to get food to prepare (someone needs a license).
- Require that people like each other or be in the right mood to cooperate.
- Give Alice a sword, Bob some skimpy armor, and the dog three heads to make an RPG.
- Give Alice night vision, Bob a guard's outfit, and the dog a sense of smell to make a stealth game.

Even with automated planning by the agents in our household simulation game, there's plenty of compelling gameplay here: setting a sequence of goals for agents much as actions are set in current games, dropping new objects into the world to help them, adding attributes and training the agents so they can gain new abilities, or directing the actions of one agent with the other working around it.

Planning Search

All these benefits are not without cost. There are overhead costs associated with planning, both in terms of development and machine resources. Developers must specify the planning domain, essentially a secondary description of the game world, and ensure that the actions in the domain do not produce nonsensical states (e.g., the player is in two places at once). Planning domains must be designed and debugged like regular programs. Like a compiler, the planner can only work with what it is given, and if garbage goes in, garbage is all that will come out. However, this development cost is likely to be saved by having simpler low-level mechanisms and, furthermore, we stand to gain more intelligent behavior.

The real expense of planning is search. Depending on the specific methods used, planning search may consume substantial memory. To account for this, planning search can be implemented in different ways.

The first distinction is between forward and backward planning. In *forward* planning, we start from the initial state and consider actions until we discover a goal state. In *backward* planning, we start with the goals and consider those actions that can achieve the goals. The preconditions for those actions now form a new goal, so we continue the search backward. Backward planning has the advantage that it tends to have a smaller branching factor because it never considers actions that do not satisfy some necessary goal, whereas forward planning can conceivably try all possible actions. On the other hand, forward planning is the more natural direction; it only considers states reachable from the initial state, and even an incomplete forward sequence makes sense and can be executed.

The other major difference between search strategies is whether they search in *state space* or in *plan space*. In state space, we explore states, eventually constructing a sequence of states that achieves the goal. We can then extract the plan by listing the actions necessary for each state. In plan space, we consider sets or sequences of actions directly, testing to see whether they achieve the goals, refining and extending the collection of actions as we search.

Most contemporary planners fall into one of three classes: heuristic search planners, planning graph planners, and satisfiability planners. We will briefly describe all three of these but focus on heuristic search planners, which we believe to be the best choice for games for a variety of reasons that will form part of the discussion.

Heuristic Search Planning

Heuristic search planning is a state space planning approach that can run forward or backward. The search is much like pathfinding. Familiar algorithms such as A* can be directly applied, and existing A* code reused. As in pathfinding, it is easy to associate costs with the actions and thus be able to compute "good" plans instead of just feasible plans. It is comparatively easy to encode specific knowledge about the game in the costs and also in the heuristics used by A*.

Another key advantages is that even if forward planning fails to find the goal, either because no sequence exists or because we have limited the running time of the planner, we can always use the best path found so far as a plan so that game characters will at least do something that is likely to reasonable. It is even likely that in subsequent re-planning, these partial actions may have helped to put us in a situation to find a complete plan.

Finally, heuristic search planning offers state-of-the-art performance, especially on nonoptimal planners (optimal planners find plans with minimal plan length or cost, whereas nonoptimal planners search for "good enough" plans; for games, we probably don't need optimal solutions) with planners like FF [Hoffmann01] among recent planning competition winners.

A good introduction to heuristic search planning [Bonet01] is available at www.tecn.upf.es/~hgeffner/index.html.

Graph Planning and Satisfiability Planning

Graph plans are essentially backward planners that work in plan space. From a high-level perspective, they work by constructing a *planning graph*, a data structure that considers the effects of all possible actions starting from the initial state, pretending they never conflict with each other. While constructing the graph, information about mutually exclusive actions is kept, and when the graph is complete, a backward search from the goals takes place to find a set of legal actions within the graph [Weld99].

Graph planning produces partially ordered plans, where the exact ordering of actions is not always specified. Some actions can therefore be performed in any order or, in the case where the actions are performed by multiple agents, at the same time. This is particularly appealing when we wish to control multiple agents. However, the backward planning means that if we run out of time constructing a plan, there is no partial plan to execute. While this approach has potential for games, it not as readily adaptable as heuristic searching. However, it is worth noting that planning graphs are sometimes used to compute heuristics for other kinds of planners (e.g., the FF planner mentioned earlier).

Satisfiability (SAT) planners encode planning problems as SAT problems, which are classic NP-complete problems with lots of high-performance solvers readily available. These planners differ chiefly in how they encode the problem, but once encoded, they can simply call the latest and greatest SAT solver to generate a solution. This means that these planners can be improved from year to year using off-the-shelf components. However, SAT planning is arguably more obscure and less hackable, since the CNF instances are too large to understand and the SAT solver is essentially a black box where it is difficult to encode any extra knowledge you may have about the problem. We will not discuss this approach further here, but it is worth considering because of the rapid advance of SAT solvers.

A good introduction to both graph planning and satisfiability planning [Weld99] is available at www.cs.washington.edu/homes/weld/papers/pi2.pdf.

Practical Issues

The following sections discuss some practical issues.

Limitations

Planning is a powerful tool, one that should be combined with our existing tools to be effective. By using planning, a lot of the complexity being built into FSMs and rules can be better expressed in the planning domain, leaving us with simpler versions of these lower level constructs. However, it also has some limitations:

A symbolic approach like planning is poorly suited to continuous problems (for example, one wouldn't use it to drive a car or aim at targets). Existing mechanisms should be used to handle these tasks, with the planner directing the actions. The planner is best seen as a mechanism to coordinate simple, low-level actions that are implemented in the best way available.

1. In addition to its somewhat limited scope, classical planning makes some strong assumptions. It assumes that a world behaves as described and that actions will succeed. This is clearly not the case because of randomness, because we abstract the gaming world, and above all, because of the human player. This is why we must replan periodically to reflect the changing world and the failure of earlier plans.
2. Classical planning is not adversarial. It does not take into account that someone may be working to thwart it. However, very few game AIs address this problem with more than some basic heuristics and rules. Most of these basic strategies can be reflected as goal selection, with a top-level strategy module picking overall goals that the planner figures out how to accomplish, executing the low-level behavior by instructing FSMs.
3. The symbolic approach is also not good for making value judgements, like the relative strengths of two creatures. Existing heuristic functions should be used in this case and a predicate used in the planner that calls the heuristic and applies a threshold (e.g., a `canKill(Creature, Creature)` predicate might check that one unit's strength is double that of the other unit).

Integration with the Game Engine

In addition to these concerns, it is important to consider how to integrate the planner to the game engine. This depends at least partially on how reusable you want the planning code to be, but we will address a few key points.

We first consider the initial state for planning, which must be obtained by the game engine. Subsequent states generated during planning must be copies of this initial state; we don't want to change variables in the game engine directly while planning. There are a few strategies for getting the facts for the initial state.

In a "pull" strategy, the planner requests information from the game engine to construct states. The planner examines all the predicates when we are about to plan, determines their values from the game engine, and stores them in the initial state. However, the expense of repeated copy operations here is nontrivial, and it is possible that a lot of useless state information will be stored

One solution to this is to use a *read-on-demand* approach. In this case, the value is only read when the predicate is evaluated. Another approach is to use a "push" model, where the game engine sends changes to the planner as they occur. This is a good strategy if planning occurs frequently. With infrequent planning, a lot of update operations will be performed needlessly.

It is also necessary to associate planning objects and actions with the corresponding data structures and functions in the game engine. This mapping is fairly straightforward but should be thought about carefully during design. In addition, different modules should be able to interact with the planner. We built a custom planning language to set up the planning domain (types, objects, predicates, operators) but used Lua, a popular scripting language, to drive the initial state and goals and bind objects and actions to the game engine [Lua]. Our planner can also be controlled directly via C++. Designers can use their favorite scripting language to fine-tune levels and, in the same script, ask agents to solve interesting problems without resorting to loading a separate script with different syntax.

Note that it is possible to skip writing a custom parser entirely and drive the entire planner through Lua scripts (or your favorite scripting language). This gem used a custom parser, because we found it more instructional for the reader and easier to read for development, but it is not essential.

Optimizations

Planning is known to be hard in theory, and it is easy to build hard planning problems. However, games represent an instance where we have a lot of control. In robotics and industry, the world is uncontrolled. In games, the world is perfectly observable and carefully engineered. Games are built to be reliable, and a lot of the qualities QA looks for in a game lead to easy planning domains. Most games are carefully designed so that the player cannot become trapped. Every state of the game should lead to some definite outcome (even if it's just death). This lack of limbo states is good for planning.

Many games also have a lot of *monotonicity* in their actions. This means that once an action is taken, the effect it has on the world is never removed. Examples of this are objects that are never dropped once picked up, doors that can be unlocked but are never locked again, and creatures that do not respawn once killed. Think about the games you have played and you will begin to see a lot of monotonicity. This is because good game design often leads to monotonicity by attempting to keep actions simple. If there is no reason for doors to be relocked or a switch to be flipped twice, making the action monotonic simplifies the controls, the player's options in the game, and debugging/playtesting.

Monotonicity leads to easy planning domains. Moreover, many planning algorithms pretend the domain is monotonic as a heuristic. Such algorithms will be highly effective in largely monotonic game worlds. Nonetheless, nonmonotonicity is going to arise as a natural part of interesting gameplay, and contemporary planning algorithms can still perform well. Exceptionally difficult nonmonotonic subtasks that prove to be a problem can be addressed by a custom solution, a specialized algorithm that solves the hard problem. This can be treated as an action by the planner, effectively removing the hard part of the domain by ensuring that it's done as a single, special action.

For example, an agent might be required to navigate a very complicated maze of doors with switches that must be flipped and reflipped to escape. If the planner is too slow at solving this problem, a specialized algorithm or scripted solution could be associated with a `navigateMaze` action. At the planning level, the action would simply require that the agent be at the start of the maze and the effect would be to put the agent at the end of the maze. Some such problems might be puzzles, which begs the question of whether a game designer should pose puzzles for the game AI to solve. Since the usual point of a puzzle is to challenge humans, it might be better to automatically bypass the puzzle or force the player to solve it.

A lot of other optimizations are possible, such as setting an order in which to explore actions if we have some idea of which might be important. We can automatically reject certain states if they have some undesirable property, thus pruning the search. Finally, there is a large research literature and a range of excellent tutorials that can suggest good optimizations and heuristics.

Conclusion

Planning algorithms can add a new dimension to intelligent behavior in games and reduce the complexity of existing game AI implementations. Planning and games are a great match, and recent A*-based strategies are both familiar to game developers and state of the art in planning research. The time is ripe to adopt planning into games.

For example, Jeff Orkin of Monolith Productions has already incorporated planning into their upcoming FPS game, *F.E.A.R.* It uses a propositional planner, planning for single agents with a small number of facts (around 20), but it provides dynamic, forward-looking AI in the fast-paced, real-time FPS setting [Orkin04]. With more sophisticated heuristics and optimizations, multiple agents and larger scenarios are within reach. Our own planner is more general, and the first iteration took about a month to implement from scratch.

In less immediate games such as RPGs, we believe that much larger environments can be modeled. Tactical and stealth-based games also stand to gain from this technology, addressing the somewhat shortsighted behavior exhibited by their characters. Whether for allies or opponents, a richer and more vivid experience can be offered to the player and a new generation of gameplay opened for designers to play with. We don't just think it's possible, we're sure it's inevitable. A demo is available from www.cs.ualberta.ca/~finnegan/planning4games.

References

[Bonet01] Bonet, Blai and Hector Geffner. "Planning as Heuristic Search." In *Artificial Intelligence—Special Issue on Heuristic Search*, Vol. 129, No. 1–2, 2001. Available online at http://www.tecn.upf.es/~hgeffner/index.html.

[Fikes71] Fikes, R. and N. Nilsson. "STRIPS: A New Approach to the Application of Theorem Proving to Problem Solving." In *Artificial Intelligence*, Vol. 2, No. 3–4, 1971: pp. 189–208.

[Ghallab04] Ghallab, Malik, Dana Nau, and Traverso Paolo. *Automated Planning—Theory and Practice*. Morgan Kaufmann, 2004.

[Hoffmann01] Hoffmann, J. and B. Nebel. "The FF Planning System: Fast Plan Generation Through Heuristic Search." In *Journal of Artificial Intelligence Research*, Vol. 14, 2001: pp. 253–302.

[Lua] "Lua the Programming Language." Available online at http://www.lua.org.

[Orkin04] Orkin, Jeff. "Symbolic Representation of Game World State: Toward Real-Time Planning in Games." In AAAI Workshop Technical Report WS-04-04: *Challenges in Game Artificial Intelligence* (July, 2004): pp. 26–30.

[Weld99] Weld, Daniel S. "Recent Advances in AI Planning." In *AI Magazine* (1999): pp. 93-123. Available online at http://www.cs.washington.edu/homes/weld/papers/pi2.pdf.

SECTION

4

GRAPHICS

4.1

T-Junction Elimination and Retriangulation

Eric Lengyel, Terathon Software

lengyel@terathon.com

Suppose that a scene contains two polygons that share a common edge, as shown in Figure 4.1.1a. When two such polygons belong to the same object, the vertices representing the endpoints of the common edge are usually not duplicated. Instead, both polygons reference the same vertices to save space and bus bandwidth. Graphics hardware is designed so that when adjacent polygons use exactly the same coordinates for the endpoints of shared edges, the rasterizer produces pixels for each polygon that are precise complements of each other. Along the shared edge, there is no overlap between the pixels belonging to one polygon and those belonging to the other; and, more importantly, there are no gaps between the polygons.

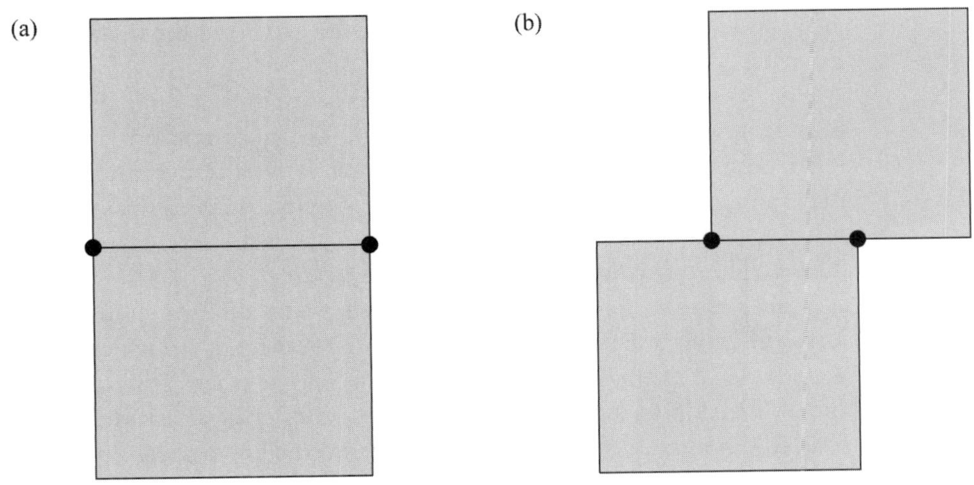

FIGURE 4.1.1 (A) Adjacent polygons sharing a common edge. (B) Adjacent polygons with edges falling within the same line in space, but not sharing the same endpoints.

A problem arises when adjacent polygons belong to different objects that have their own copy of the endpoint vertices for the shared edge. These vertices might greatly differ in each object's local coordinate space. For instance, when the vertices are transformed into world space, floating-point round-off error could produce slightly different vertex positions for each object. Since the vertex coordinates are no longer equal, a seam might appear when the polygons are rasterized.

A greater problem occurs when two polygons have edges that fall within the same line in space, but they do not share the same endpoints, as illustrated in Figure 4.1.1b. In such a situation, a vertex belonging to one polygon lies within the interior of an edge belonging to the other. Due to the shape that the edges form, the location at which this occurs is called a *T-junction*. Because the adjacent edges do not share identical endpoints, T-junctions cause visible seams in any game engine that does not eliminate them.

This gem describes how to detect possible sources of these seams in complex 3D scenes and how to modify static geometry so that visible artifacts are avoided. Since T-junction elimination adds vertices to existing polygons (that are not necessarily convex), we also discuss a method for triangulating arbitrary concave polygons.

T-Junction Elimination

Given an immovable object A in our world, we need to determine whether there exist any other immovable objects possessing a vertex that lies within an edge of object A. We only consider those objects whose bounding volumes intersect the bounding volume of object A. Let object X be an object that lies close enough to object A to possibly have adjacent polygons. We treat both objects as collections of polygons having the greatest possible number of edges. We perform triangulation of these polygons *after* the T-junction elimination process in order to avoid the creation of superfluous triangles.

Before we locate any T-junctions, we first want to find out if any of object A's vertices lie very close to any of object X's vertices. We must transform the vertices belonging to both objects into world space and search for vertices separated by a distance less than some small constant ε. Any vertex $\mathbf{V}_A$ of object A that is this close to a vertex $\mathbf{V}_X$ of object X should be moved so that $\mathbf{V}_A$ and $\mathbf{V}_X$ have the exact same world-space coordinates. This procedure is sometimes called *welding*.

Once existing vertices have been welded, we need to search for vertices of object X that lie within a small distance ε of an edge of object A, but which do not lie within the distance ε of any vertex of object A. This tells us where T-junctions occur. Let $\mathbf{P}_1$ and $\mathbf{P}_2$ be endpoints of an edge of object A, and let $\mathbf{Q}$ be a vertex of object X. The squared distance, d^2, between the point $\mathbf{Q}$ and the line passing through $\mathbf{P}_1$ and $\mathbf{P}_2$ is given by

$$d^2 = (\mathbf{Q} - \mathbf{P}_1)^2 - \frac{\left[(\mathbf{Q} - \mathbf{P}_1)\cdot(\mathbf{P}_2 - \mathbf{P}_1)\right]^2}{(\mathbf{P}_2 - \mathbf{P}_1)^2} \tag{4.1.1}$$

If $d^2 < \varepsilon^2$, then we know that the point **Q** lies close enough to the line containing the edge of object *A*, but we still need to determine whether **Q** actually lies between $\mathbf{P}_1$ and $\mathbf{P}_2$. We can make this determination by measuring the projected length *t* of the line segment connecting $\mathbf{P}_1$ to **Q** onto the edge formed by $\mathbf{P}_1$ and $\mathbf{P}_2$. As shown in Figure 4.1.2, this length is given by

$$t = \left\|\mathbf{Q} - \mathbf{P}_1\right\| \cos\alpha, \qquad (4.1.2)$$

where α is the angle between the line segment and the edge. Using a dot product to compute the cosine, we have

$$t = \frac{\left(\mathbf{Q} - \mathbf{P}_1\right) \cdot \left(\mathbf{P}_2 - \mathbf{P}_1\right)}{\left\|\mathbf{P}_2 - \mathbf{P}_1\right\|} \qquad (4.1.3)$$

If $t < \varepsilon$ or $t > |\,\mathbf{P}_1 - \mathbf{P}_2| - \varepsilon$, then the point **Q** does not lie within the interior of the edge formed by $\mathbf{P}_1$ and $\mathbf{P}_2$. Otherwise, we have found a T-junction, and a new vertex should be added to the polygon of object *A* between $\mathbf{P}_1$ and $\mathbf{P}_2$, precisely at **Q**'s location.

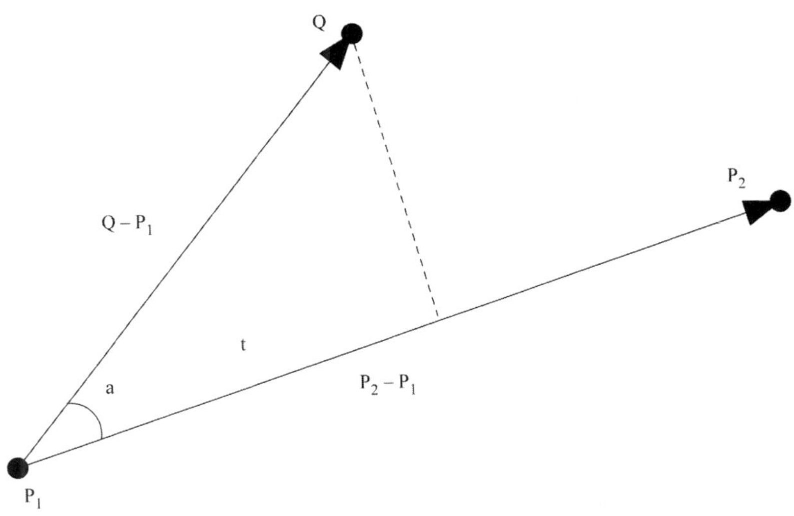

FIGURE 4.1.2 The length *t* is equal to the distance from $\mathbf{P}_1$ to the projection of point Q, onto the edge between $\mathbf{P}_1$ and $\mathbf{P}_2$.

Retriangulation

After all the static world geometry has been processed, we must triangulate the resulting polygons so that they can be passed to the graphics hardware. Any vertex added to a polygon to eliminate a T-junction is collinear (or at least nearly collinear) with the endpoints of the edge for which the T-junction occurs. After all T-junctions have been eliminated for a single polygon, its edges might contain several vertices that fall in a straight line. This prevents us from using a simple fanning approach that might ordinarily be used to triangulate a convex polygon. Instead, we are forced to treat the polygon as concave.

The algorithm that we describe takes a list of n vertices wound in a counterclockwise direction as input and produces a list of $n - 2$ triangles. At each iteration, we search for a set of three consecutive vertices for which the corresponding triangle is not degenerate (not wound in the wrong direction) and does not contain any of the polygon's remaining vertices. Once such a set of three vertices is found, the middle vertex is disqualified from successive iterations, and the algorithm repeats until only three vertices remain.

In order to determine whether a set of three vertices is wound in a counterclockwise direction, we must know beforehand the normal direction $\mathbf{N}_0$ of the plane containing the polygon being triangulated. Let $\mathbf{P}_1$, $\mathbf{P}_2$, and $\mathbf{P}_3$ represent the positions of the three vertices. If the cross-product $(\mathbf{P}_2 - \mathbf{P}_1) \times (\mathbf{P}_3 - \mathbf{P}_1)$ points in the same direction as the normal $\mathbf{N}_0$, then the corresponding triangle is wound counterclockwise. If the cross-product is near zero, then the triangle is degenerate. Thus two of our three requirements for a triangle are satisfied only if

$$\left(\mathbf{P}_2 - \mathbf{P}_1\right) \times \left(\mathbf{P}_3 - \mathbf{P}_1\right) \cdot \mathbf{N}_0 > \varepsilon \tag{4.1.4}$$

for some small value ε (typically, $\varepsilon \approx 0.001$).

Our third requirement is that the triangle contains no other vertices belonging to the polygon. We can construct three inward-facing normals, $\mathbf{N}_1$, $\mathbf{N}_2$, and $\mathbf{N}_3$, corresponding to the three sides of the triangle, as follows:

$$\begin{aligned} \mathbf{N}_1 &= \mathbf{N}_0 \times \left(\mathbf{P}_2 - \mathbf{P}_1\right) \\ \mathbf{N}_2 &= \mathbf{N}_0 \times \left(\mathbf{P}_3 - \mathbf{P}_2\right) \\ \mathbf{N}_3 &= \mathbf{N}_0 \times \left(\mathbf{P}_1 - \mathbf{P}_3\right) \end{aligned} \tag{4.1.5}$$

As shown in Figure 4.1.3, a point $\mathbf{Q}$ lies inside the triangle formed by $\mathbf{P}_1$, $\mathbf{P}_2$, and $\mathbf{P}_3$ if and only if $\mathbf{N}_i \cdot (\mathbf{Q} - \mathbf{P}_i) > -\varepsilon$ for every $i = 1, 2, 3$.

Since we have to calculate the normals given by Equation 4.1.5 for each triangle, we can save a little computation by replacing the condition given by Equation 4.1.4 with the equivalent expression

$$\mathbf{N}_1 \cdot \left(\mathbf{P}_3 - \mathbf{P}_1\right) > \varepsilon \tag{4.1.6}$$

This determines whether the point $\mathbf{P}_3$ lies on the positive side of the edge connecting $\mathbf{P}_1$ and $\mathbf{P}_2$.

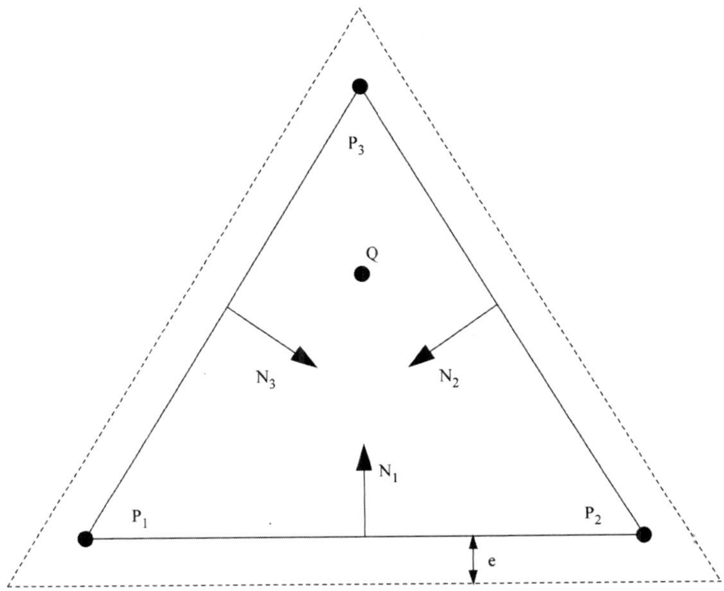

FIGURE 4.1.3 A point Q lies inside a triangle if and only if it lies on the positive side of each of the three edges of the triangle.

Implementation

ON THE CD

The source code provided on the CD-ROM demonstrates an implementation of the retriangulation algorithm. This particular implementation maintains a working set of *four* consecutive vertices and, at each iteration, determines whether valid triangles can be formed using the first three vertices or the last three vertices. If only one of the sets of three vertices forms a valid triangle, then that triangle is omitted, and the algorithm continues to the next iteration. If both sets of three vertices can produce valid triangles, then the code selects the triangle having the larger smallest angle. In the case that neither set of three vertices provides a valid triangle, the working set of four vertices is advanced until a valid triangle can be constructed.

The method presented by the source code was chosen so that the output of the algorithm would consist of a series of triangle strips and triangle fans. Such triangle structures exhibit excellent vertex cache usage on modern graphics processors. The implementation also includes a safety mechanism. If a degenerate, self-intersecting, or otherwise nontriangulatable polygon is passed to it, then the algorithm terminates prematurely to avoid becoming stuck in an infinite loop. This happens when the code cannot locate a set of three consecutive vertices that form a valid triangle.

4.2

Filling the Gaps: Advanced Animation Using Stitching and Skinning

Ryan Woodland, Zipper Interactive

ryanwoodland@att.net

As hardware becomes faster and more feature-laden, game developers are searching for ways to make characters look more compelling. Of the many categories that can be improved, character animation is perhaps one of the most important.

Currently, most 3D games are starting to use some sort of skeletal representation for their characters as their topology for animation. These systems attach geometry to "bones" in a character. The bones are then animated and, consequently, the attached geometry inherits the motion creating adequate animation. Usually, however, the geometry used to represent characters is rigid in nature, which is not the most useful representation for modeling organic creatures that are definitely not rigid in nature.

Because the geometry is completely rigid, any two pieces that are supposed to be connected to each other (an upper arm and a forearm, for example) display blatant discontinuities at the joint at which they are connected. This obviously can become a problem, since the characters we are trying to represent are more often than not made up of a continuous skin that does not show any cracks or separations.

In this article, I will discuss the topics of *stitching* and *skinning* as ways to create more realistic organic animation. Stitching is actually just a less computationally expensive subset of skinning and will therefore be discussed first. Both of these techniques assume one continuous mesh that is attached to a bone structure for a character as opposed to many meshes attached to a single bone in traditional rigid-body animation. This continuous mesh is deformed relative to the character's bone structure, yielding a character that does not create visible (and often very annoying) gaps at joints when animating.

In the following sections, I will be using the example of an arm to demonstrate various features of stitching and skinning. The basic mesh used is picture in Figure 4.2.1.

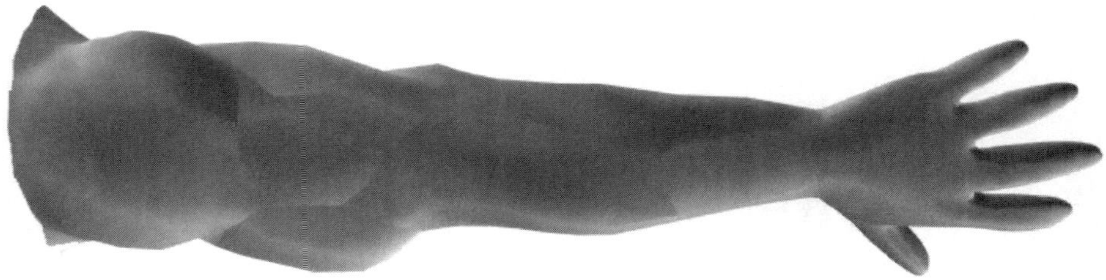

FIGURE 4.2.1 Our basic arm mesh.

Stitching

As mentioned earlier, stitching operates on a continuous mesh attached to a bone structure. In rigid-body animation, a polygon is transformed by one matrix representing the bone to which that polygon is attached. With stitching, each vertex in a polygon can be transformed by a different matrix representing the bone to which the individual vertex is attached. This means that we can create polygons that "stitch" multiple bones together simply by attaching different vertices in the polygon to different bones. When the bones are manipulated, this polygon should fill the gap you would see in rigid-body animation.

One of the major differences between stitching and rigid-body animation is the data topology for representing a character. With rigid-body animation, a bone must simply have a pointer to some geometry it is to animate. The matrix yielded by the corresponding bone then transforms that geometry. For stitching, it is necessary for each *vertex* in the character's skin to keep track of the bone to which it is attached.

```
struct Vertex
{
    float s, t;
    float x, y, z;
    unsigned long color;

    unsigned long boneIndex;
};
```

Before animating a character that has been correctly bound to this data topology, we need to deal with the problem that our vertices are not in the correct space to be properly transformed. The problem is this: a matrix used to transform a bone for animation assumes that the bone starts with its pivot point at the origin of the coordinate space of the character. This makes sense if we consider a hand bone in a normal human. This bone should start with its pivot point at the origin of its coordinate space so that we can easily rotate the bone around that point. The bone is animated (rotated) and then transformed to the end of the forearm bone. This process repeats for the forearm bone—the hand and the forearm are then animated and moved out to the end of the upper arm bone. This continues down through the hierarchy until the entire skeleton has been properly transformed.

Given the spatial relationship between the skin's vertices and the bones of the character, it is necessary to transform the vertices of the skin into the local coordinate space of the bones to which they are attached before transforming them by the bone's animation matrix. To do this, we need to keep a matrix in each bone that tells us how to transform geometry back into the local space of the bone. This matrix should be the inverse of the matrix used to transform the bone from its local space into the character's mesh, given the orientation of the mesh without any animation being applied. See Figure 4.2.2 for a depiction of the local spaces for each bone in our arm mesh.

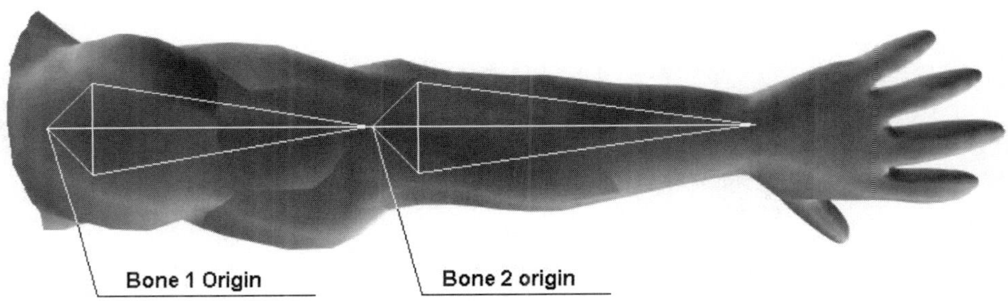

FIGURE 4.2.2 A depiction of the bones in our arm.

Therefore, the data structure of our bones should look like the following:

```
struct Bone
{
    Mtx orientation;
    Mtx animation;
    Mtx inverseOrientation;

    Mtx final;

    Bone *child;
    Bone *sibling;
};
```

Once we have this data, we are ready to animate our character. To do this, we must simply step through the vertex data and transform each vertex by the orientation matrix and then the animation matrix of the corresponding bone.

All of these transformations can be done faster by processing the bone hierarchy and generating a final transformation matrix for each bone concatenating a bone's inverse orientation, concatenated orientation, and concatenated animation matrices together and then transforming geometry by the resulting matrix.

```
void BuildMatrices ( Bone *bone, Mtx forward, Mtx orientation )
{
    Mtx localForward;
    Mtx localOrientation;

    // concatenate the hierarchy's orientation matrices so
        //   that we can generate the inverse
    concatenate(bone->orientation, orientation,
localOrientation);

    // take the inverse of the orientation matrix for this bone
    inverse(localOrientation, bone->inverseOrientation);

    // concatenate this bone's orientation onto the forward
        //   matrix
    concatenate(bone->orientation, forward, localForward);

    // concatenate this bone's animation onto the forward matrix
    concatenate(bone->animation, localForward, localForward);

    // build the bone's final matrix
    concatenate(bone->inverseOrientation, localForward,
bone->final);

    if(bone->child)
        BuildMatrices(bone->child, localForward,
        localOrientation);

    if(bone->sibling)
        BuildMatrices(bone->sibling, forward, orientation);
}
```

Using the preceding technique on the arm mesh, a bend of 45 degrees and 90 degrees to the forearm bone produces the images in Figure 4.2.3.

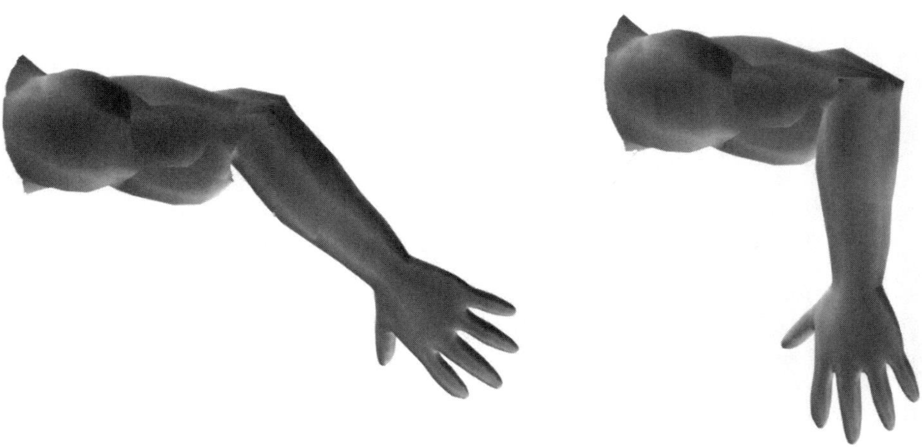

FIGURE 4.2.3 *Left*: Stitched arm mesh bent to 45 degrees. *Right*: Arm bent to 90 degrees.

Stitching is a very valid technique, since it easily takes advantage of any hardware that provides a transform engine. It is necessary to generate the final stitching matrix on the CPU, but the hardware can easily use these matrices to transform any number of vertices we pass it.

As an optimization to this technique, I suggest breaking up the continuous skin so that the vertices exist in the local space of the bone to which they are attached. This prevents us from having to do an extra matrix concatenation per bone per frame of animation.

Skinning

While stitching is a valid technique, it has some problems. In cases of extreme joint rotation, geometry tends to shear massively and appear quite unnatural. Using the techniques discussed earlier, a forearm rotation of 120 degrees displays quite a nasty shear effect at the elbow. This results because we only have one polygon to span the entire gap between the upper arm and the forearm. The larger this gap becomes, the worse the solution looks, as shown in Figure 4.2.4.

FIGURE 4.2.4 Ugly stitched arm mesh bent to 120 degrees.

To prevent this, we can implement a full system of skinning where a vertex is not limited to being affected by a single bone; it can instead be influenced by multiple bones. This makes sense if we look at the behavior of the human body. The skin on a person's elbow is not affected by the orientation of just one bone. The movements of both the upper and lower arm bones affect it. Similarly, skin in the neck and shoulder is affected by the orientations of the arm, neck, and chest.

To enable this, each vertex in a skinned mesh must contain a list of bones that affect it. Each vertex must also carry a weight per bone that tells us how heavily affected the vertex is by the bone. For this example, we will assume linear skinning, which means all of the weights of a vertex must add up to 1.0. Because of this, given n bones by which a vertex is affected, we need to store n-1 weights, since the remaining weight should be 1.0 – ($weight_1 + weight_2 + \ldots + weight_{n-1}$).

```
struct Vertex
{
    float s, t;
    float x, y, z;
    unsigned long color;

    unsigned long boneIndex1;
    unsigned long boneIndex2;

    float weight;
};
```

As mentioned earlier, stitching is a subset of skinning, and therefore suffers from the same local-space transform issues as stitching. Therefore, we should use the same bone representation as shown previously.

In order to do full skinning, we need to transform each bone by each matrix affecting it, then multiply the result by the corresponding weight, and, finally, accumulate the results. The equation for skinning looks like

```
(vertex * matrix0 * weight0) + (vertex * matrix1 * weight1) + ... +
(vertex *
 matrixN * weightN)
```

where the sum of all weights 0..N = 1.0.

What we are effectively doing is a linear interpolation between transformed vertices. Following is the code used to perform this operation on a given mesh.

```
Vector3D TransformVertex ( Vertex *vert, Bone *boneArray )
{
    Vector3D    temp;
    Vector3D    final;

    temp = XFormVec(vert->position,
bone[vert->boneIndex1]->final)
    final.x = temp.x * vert->weight;
    final.y = temp.y * vert->weight;
    final.z = temp.z * vert->weight;

    temp = XFormVec(vert->position,
bone[vert->boneIndex2]->final)
    final.x += temp.x * (1.0F - vert->weight);
    final.y += temp.y * (1.0F - vert->weight);
    final.z += temp.z * (1.0F - vert->weight);
```

```
        return final;
    }
```

Using the technique outlined previously, we were able to generate the following output for forearm rotations of 45 degrees, 90 degrees, and 120 degrees, respectively. Note that even in the extreme 120-degree example (see Figure 4.2.5), the continuity of the elbow geometry is still maintained.

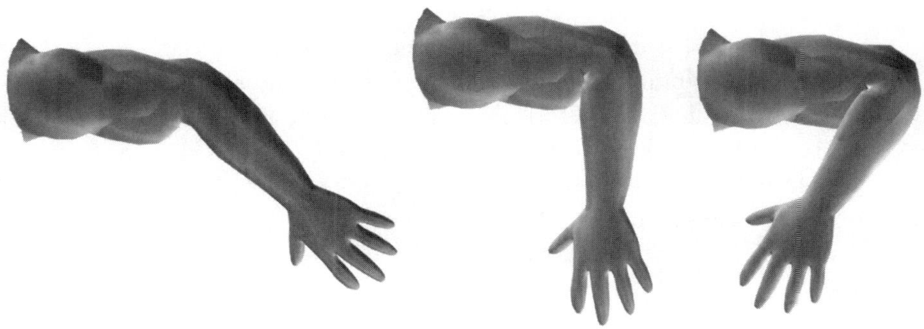

FIGURE 4.2.5 *Left*: Skinned arm mesh bent to 45 degrees. *Center*: Arm bent to 90 degrees. *Right*: Arm bent to 120 degrees.

As you can see, a major problem with skinning is that it is computationally expensive. Unfortunately, these computations are not well supported by today's hardware transform engines. An alternative way of performing the linear interpolation calculations, which potentially takes advantage of some current hardware implementations, is to generate a skinning matrix to be passed to hardware to perform the final transform. To calculate the skinning matrix, simply interpolate the matrices linearly based on the weight

```
(matrix0 * weight0) + (matrix1 * weight1) + ... + ( matrixN * weightN)
```

where the sum of all weights $0..N = 1.0$.

This method is only useful if the same skinning matrix can be used for multiple vertices; in other words, different vertices are weighted identically between the same bones. The less this case is true, the less the gain of this method will be.

It is important to note that the skinning technique outlined previously is not a completely mathematically correct technique. If normals are transformed using this technique, the results are not guaranteed to be normalized. If per-vertex lighting is required for a character using this technique, post-transform normals must be re-normalized before lighting calculations.

Advanced Topics

The skinning example assumes all the weights influencing a vertex must add up to 1.0. It is a possibility, however, to create some compelling special effects with weights that do not sum to 1.0. For instance, it is possible to place an extra bone in an arm that simulates a bicep muscle. All of the vertices in the arm's skin should be weighted normally between the upper arm, lower arm, and shoulder. However, the vertices near the bicep should also be weighted based on their distance from the bicep bone—closer vertices should have higher weight values. When the arm bends, apply a scale to the bicep bone to create the appearance of a muscle flexing.

The skinning technique outlined is not mathematically correct because we are essentially linearly interpolating matrices. Instead of representing bones as matrices, it is possible to represent them as a quaternion. *SLERP* between the quaternions based on the per-vertex weights and then produce a matrix from the result. This should yield a somewhat better-looking skinned mesh.

Sources

[Lander98] Lander, Jeff, "Skin Them Bones: Game Programming for the Web Generation," *Game Developer Magazine*, May 1998: pp. 11–16.

[Terzopoulos87] Terzopoulos, Demetri, et al, "Elastically Deformable Models," *Computer Graphics*, Vol 21, No. 4 (SIGGRAPH 1987): pp. 205–214.

4.3

Improved Skin Deformation Using Kinematic Skeletons

Jason P. Weber, DreamWorks Animation

baboon@imonk.com

Artists can produce beautifully realistic meshes to represent the actors in their games. To bring them to life, these models need to be animated for a wide variety of behaviors. Storing a full set of vertex positions for every frame of animation is not only prohibitively memory-consumptive, it restricts movements to only those actions explicitly created by the artist. So, many applications use a hidden hierarchy of segments that looks and acts very much like a subset of a natural skeleton.

By transforming each vertex of a mesh through multiple matrices instead of just one, and then by doing a carefully weighted average of the results, we are able to deform these meshes to any position and play back the results at any frame rate. This approach permits a significant reduction in the required animation data and allows the skeleton, and thereby the mesh, to be spontaneously adjusted to any pose, perhaps reacting to unpredictable events in its environment.

However, the popular deformation algorithm has some problems when used in its original form. We will demonstrate how large deflection angles cause joints to shrink, potentially even to a point. Fortunately, this can be overcome by adding a small chain of additional bones at troublesome joints, such as the elbows and knees. By carefully reworking the weighting data to account for these "links," we can use the same simple core deformation algorithm and only incur the small additional burden of a few extra bones.

Background

The skeletal structure is a hierarchy of transforms, like a scene graph. At each transform, we define a bone length, which is really a displacement along that transform's local x-axis. By default, the origin of all child bones is positioned at the displaced point on the end of the parent bone. We allow for an arbitrary additional displacement, but in most cases where bones connect end-to-end, it is zero.

A reference pose of the skeleton describes the state of the hierarchy where it aligns with the given undeformed mesh. (Biped, in 3DS Max, calls this the "figure mode.") The motion of the bones away from the reference pose is used to deform the mesh to any arbitrary position. The motion of these bones comes from some driving source, such as motion capture, authored motion, or inverse kinematics [Weber02]. (For a longer description of the background material, refer to the GDC 2000 proceedings [Weber00].)

Simple Methods

The basic skinning algorithm is demonstrated in *Game Programming Gems* by [Woodland00] and is also nicely explained in Jeff Lander's *Game Developer Magazine* article [Lander98]. As an example of this technique, consider vertices on an elbow whose position needs to be affected by the current transform of both the upper and lower arm bones. As we pass each vertex in the elbow through each of the two transforms, we get two different resultant vertices. If we then do a weighted average of these transformed vertices, we get a reasonable "in-between" position. An important guideline here is that these weightings for the vertices should smoothly transition from 100% upper arm to 100% lower arm from the top of the elbow to the bottom. Otherwise, the mesh will stretch abnormally and might appear to tear.

As the deflection angle of the lower arm increases and the difference in the results from each bone increases, serious visual abnormalities could arise. For example, the worst case might be if you twist the child bone 180° about its lengthwise axis. The two transformed resultants are on opposite sides of the elbow, so a 50/50 average is at a point inside the elbow. The overall effect is much like twisting or bending a cardboard paper towel tube. Figures 4.3.1 and 4.3.2 show illustrations of problem cases.

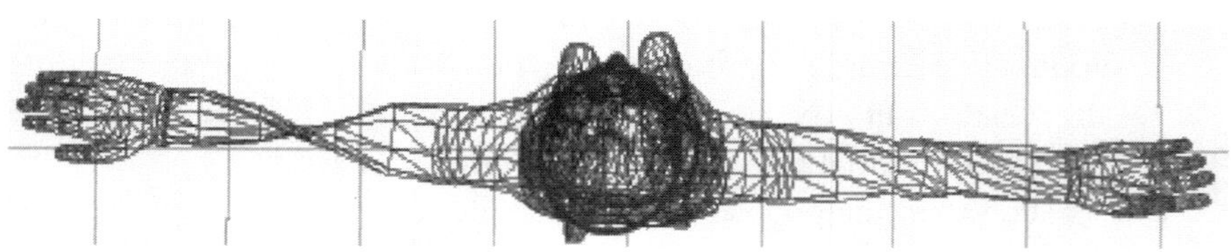

FIGURE 4.3.1 Twisted elbows: a simple skinning method demonstrated on the left arm contrasted with an enhanced technique on the right arm.

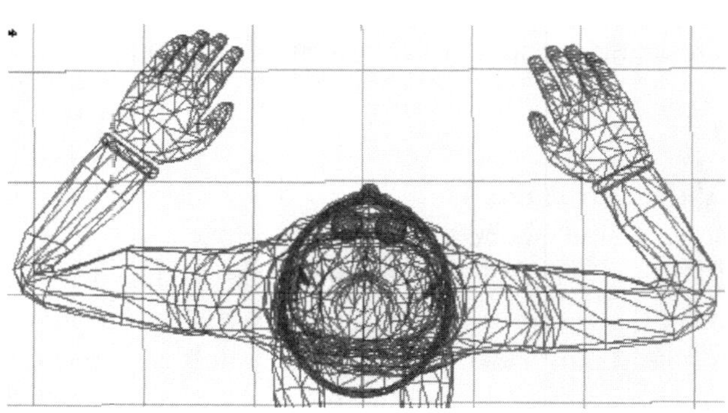

FIGURE 4.3.2 Corresponding effect with elbows bent. The right arm uses the enhanced technique.

Adding the Bones

If large angles cause defects, one solution is to limit all deflections to a small angle. We cannot really restrict the motion of the existing bones, but we can distribute these large angles over several smaller bones conveniently placed at the joints. Since a deflection of 60° seems to be a safe limit, using three or so of these links should usually be sufficient. The length of the links can be left to the author of the model. We are often content with a default value derived from the mesh's cross-sectional radius at the joint and the length of the child bone:

```
total_linklength=0.3*child_length+1.5*joint_radius
```

The placement of the bones should look something like a spline. The bones should stay arranged end-to-end, but they may slide together a little as the joint flexes. We don't have to actually shorten the bones, but the overlap will naturally compress the mesh slightly. Our solution is demonstrated in `GPGBoneNode::CalcBoneLinks()` in GPGBoneNode.cpp on the CD-ROM, and it works as follows.

ON THE CD

To compute the position of the bones, first consider three points, as shown in Figure 4.3.3a—the original joint connection A, the first link center B, and the last link center C. They will form a triangle as the joint flexes. For each link, take two points, one along BC and the other along either BA or AC, depending on whether the link is in the first or second half of the chain. The displacement of these points along these lines is proportional to the ordering of the link along the chain. Once you have these two points, take a weighted average to find the center for the desired link. The weighting goes linearly from 100% of the point on BC at either the first or last link to 50/50 for a link in the exact center. Rotations of the links are computed as the linear interpolation of the overall change in angle so that the total deflection is evenly distributed.

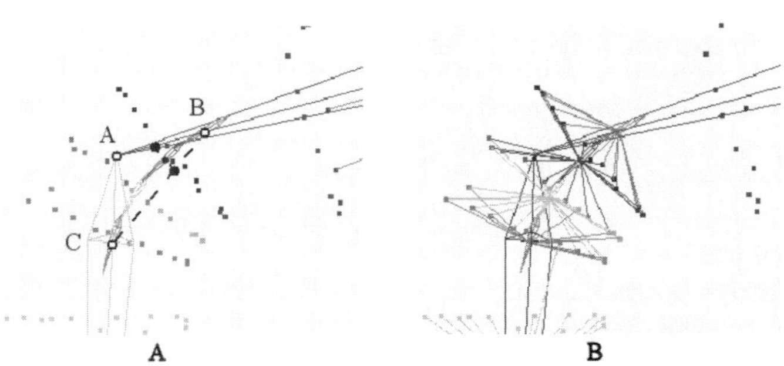

FIGURE 4.3.3 (A) A small chain of bones added to the joint. (B) Example of new weighting relationships.

The instantiation and weighting to the links only need to occur once. The position and rotation of the links need to be recomputed every time the parent or child moves, potentially every frame.

Changing the Weights

Most of the weights around a bone-linked joint will need to be reassigned. The weights should transition smoothly from the original parent to the first link, then along to each element in the chain, and finally to the original child bone. If there is no fork at this joint and all the original influences were assigned only to this parent and child bone, it is sufficient to use the longitudinal (x) position to find which two bones to attach to (including the new link bones). If we look at the links as an integer number line, with the parent bone as zero and the original child as (`number_of_links+2`), then we use the local x position of the vertex along the chain, scaled to the size of the number line. We find the integer numbers above and below where that vertex falls and use the fractional part to determine the weights. For example, if our local x position scales to 2.3 in "bone link space," the new weights will be 70% for the second link bone and 30% for the third link bone.

If there is a fork in the bone hierarchy nearby, more information needs to be considered, even if there is not an explicit sibling to the particular child bone. The hip and shoulder areas are two good examples of this type of situation. The goal for any particular link chain is to only reassign a fair fraction of the parent's influence and leave the remainder of the influence for other bones to consider. For example, a vertex on the chest near the shoulder might be partially influenced by the motion of the upper arm, but it is also well anchored to one or more spinal bones. When adding bones between the clavicle and upper arm, we don't want to reassign the portion that belongs to the spine.

To determine this fair fraction, all the weights are found for the particular vertex that have the same parent as an ancestor to the child in question. These "competitors" reduce how much influence we can reassign for that child. To make sure the effect is not dependent on the order that the weights are processed, only competitor entries that follow the current weight entry on the weight list are considered. Adding up these competitor weights, we determine the fraction as

$$fraction = 1 - competitor \,/\, (competitor + childweight)$$

The weight to be reassigned is then

$$fraction * parentweight + childweight$$

At this point, we continue as in the unforked case. We adjust the existing stored parent weight in place. For our two new weights, we can first overwrite the previous child entry, which has now been entirely reassigned, and then add a new weight entry for the second influence.

Figure 4.3.4a shows a shoulder joint with reassigned weights. This diagram shows which of the given links the vertices are weighted to. It does not show the magnitude of the weights or any weights to other bones, like the spine. A chain of three links connects the clavicle bone to the upper arm. Lines are drawn from each vertex to the center of each bone that the vertex is influenced by. The shade of the line matches the shade of the bone, varied for clarity. Note how the links have influences deep into the chest. These create a gradual stretching of the skin when the arm is moved.

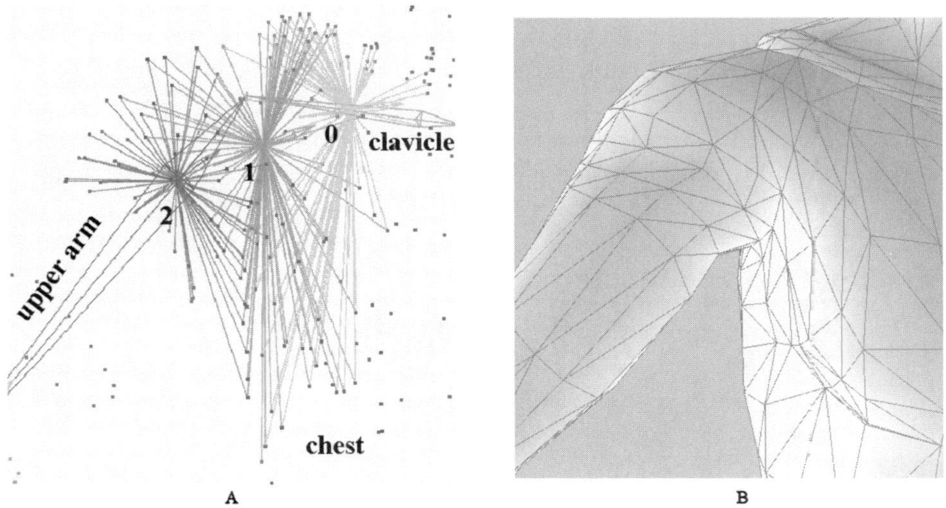

FIGURE 4.3.4 New weighting with three added links (A) for a shoulder mesh (B).

Normal-Derived Influence Fade

There is one side effect we cannot ignore. Since we are reassigning based purely on position, joints with apparent right angles in the mesh can incur excessive bulging. The shoulders tend to display this problem. When the upper arm moves up, the side of the chest will push out sideways, as though it were a very wide region of the arm (see Figure 4.3.5).

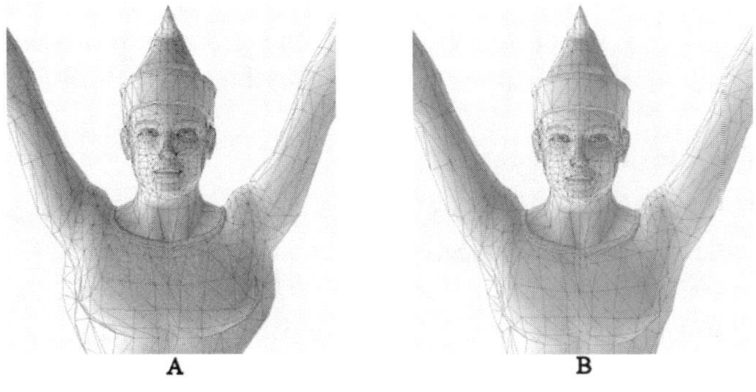

FIGURE 4.3.5 Raised arms (A) without and (B) with normal-derived influence fade.

We can use the inherent difference in the normal direction to correct for this. We take the dot product of a vertex's normal with respect to the longitudinal bone axis. From this result, we subtract the *x* displacement of the vertex along the bone, divided by the approximate radius at the joint (the subtracted value and the result both have a floor of zero). This reduction has the effect of isolating the correction toward the parent side of the joint. The secondary result is a fraction from 0.0 to 1.0, which we square for good measure. This fraction is applied to the weight that was previously destined to reassignment. That portion of the weight is not reassigned, but directly added to the parent's weight. In our example code, see `GPGSkin::RelinkWeights()` in GPGSkin.cpp on the CD-ROM.

ON THE CD

Packing It Up and Making It Fast

In order to process the weights and generate the deformed mesh as quickly as possible, it is critical that we lay out our runtime data in a cache-friendly manner. The biggest decision to make is whether to process the weights in a *bone-major* or *vertex-major* fashion.

For the bone-major method, you have to first clear all the vertex positions and normals in the mesh. Then for each bone, you process all the vertices that the bone influences, accumulating fractional components to their stored positions and normals. While this will probably keep the current matrix in cache, it reads and writes the mesh in a very scattered manner.

In the vertex-major method, we process the vertices in order, pulling in matrices as necessary. While this may incur some scattered access to the matrix array, the advantages are numerous. First of all, there is no clearing stage. We know when the first write to a vertex occurs, so that access can be a pure *set* instead of an *add*. Since the weights for a vertex are clumped together, we can accumulate the results in a local variable and dump them out with one write per vertex, instead of one read and one write per weight per vertex.

We have tried it both ways, and for all our measurements, the vertex-major approach was *at least* twice as fast, and probably much faster, even with all the optimizations we were able to add later on due to the flexibility of the layout.

Transform Matrices

Every bone in the skeleton has a transform, including the added bone links. Until the actual deformation stage, we use quaternions because of their superior interpolative qualities [Bobick98]. However, for raw vertex transforms, using the matrix form is almost four times faster. So, just before the core deformation loop, we fill in a nicely packed array of 3×4 matrices, one for each bone. Each matrix is assigned the inverse of the bone's reference transform, multiplied by the bone's current transform. In this way, we can transform directly from the original, undeformed mesh without having to store vertex offsets relative to each bone.

ON THE CD

The core deformation loop contains only about 50 lines of code. See `GPGSkin::ComputeDeformedVerticesPacked()` in GPGSkin.cc on the CD-ROM.

Packweights

Since the vertex weights will usually be a larger data structure than the matrix array or even the mesh, it is important to keep the weight list small in order to reduce the amount of data we need to process each frame. This not only saves space, but it should really optimize our cache usage. However, we also need to be aware that excessive byte conservation might throw off the word alignment, which would be just as detrimental to the process.

The *packweight* structure is a big byte block with alternating sections of one vertex definition and one or more boneweight influences. The vertex definition contains the vertex index, a copy of the undeformed vertex position and normal, and the number of weights to follow. The boneweight block contains just the bone index into the matrix array and the fractional weight. As we read any block, we can prefetch the next one.

Note that storing the vertex position and normal in the weight list means that we can continuously deform to an output mesh without having to retain an undeformed input mesh. If we wanted to allow outside modifications to the input mesh, such as with a morphing modifier, we would not store that data in the weight list, but we would have to take the penalty of rereading vertices from the input mesh every frame. See the file GPGPackWeights.h on the CD-ROM for our example code.

ON THE CD

Normal Renormalization

We can perform a weighted average of multiple normals just like we do with the positions, but the result will have a reduced magnitude. These differences are easy to fix. Since the reduced normals are known to have a range of magnitude from 0 to 1, you can use a modest table to eliminate the `sqrt()` operation. If you do not renormalize them, they could cause a reduction in lighting intensity. Our observations show very little difference, so you might want to consider leaving them as is or hook the option to a quality toggle.

Conclusion

Bones-based animation can be a key to reducing animation overhead and allowing for spontaneous and unique behaviors. Existing deformation techniques can be made very fast and are easily extended to overcome some inherent limitations.

Additional topics could cover the generation and manipulation of the original vertex weights. Color Plates 2 – 4 on the CD demonstrate improvements achieved by using a completely automated procedure to generate raw weights, remove anomalies, smooth the distribution, and add bone links.

The improvement in the waist is mostly due to the regenerated weights. The upper leg benefits dramatically from using the links to reduce shrinkage. Even the shoulder and knees improve significantly by eliminating excessive stretching. Also, the chest looks more realistic, since using links in the shoulder permits a wider spread of influences over the surrounding mesh.

References

[Bobick98] Bobick, Nick, "Rotating Objects Using Quaternions," *Game Developer Magazine,* February 1998: pp. 34–42. Also available online at http://www.gdmag.com.

[Lander98] Lander, Jeff, "Skin Them Bones: Game Programming for the Web Generation," *Game Developer Magazine,* May 1998: pp. 11–16.

[Weber00] Weber, Jason, "Run-Time Skin Deformation," Game Developers Conference Proceedings (GDC 2000): pp. 703–721.

[Weber02] Weber, Jason, "Constrained Inverse Kinematics," *Game Programming Gems 3*, Charles River Media, Inc., 2002.

[Woodland00] Woodland, Ryan, "Filling the Gaps—Advanced Animation Using Stitching and Skinning," *Game Programming Gems*, Charles River Media, Inc., 2000: pp. 476–483.

The author will make an effort to maintain a long-term archive and link site for some related resources at http://www.imonk.com/baboon/bones.

4.4

Motion Capture Data Compression

Søren Hannibal, Shiny/Collective

sorenhan@yahoo.com

In the video game industry, the stakes increase every year, and budgets can surpass tens of millions of dollars. Often, a large amount is reserved for motion capture sessions, which result in gigabytes of raw key frame data. However, with console memory still one of the scarcest resources in game development, tradeoffs often result in some of the more interesting animations being cut, leaving only the bare minimum.

This article demonstrates a lossy compression system that was developed to improve memory usage for motion capture data. While the system has some features that take advantage of bone hierarchies, a more general solution can be used on any keyframed animation, such as prerecorded camera movements and hand-animated physics objects.

This article focuses on the compression and decompression of animation data, and does not rely on how models are rendered, how animations are blended together, or how curves are interpolated. The techniques presented here can easily be implemented in existing animation systems.

Memory savings depend on how aggressively compression is applied. Animation size can be compressed to below 500 bytes per second for a hierarchical model with 16 bones, compared with over 15,000 bytes per second for uncompressed data. The performance cost for decompression is negligible. Compression is processor-intensive, and requires a small amount of user interaction for optimal results.

Plan of Attack

The compression scheme has a three-step approach:

1. Organize the data so the smallest number of data channels is stored.
2. Reduce the number of keys by removing those that have little or no impact on the animation.
3. Pack the remaining keys by reducing precision.

Each step has several settings available to the animator. With a little experience, the animator will be able to choose settings that will yield good results with minimal tweaking. It is important to keep the number of settings low, so as not to overwhelm the animator.

Organizing the Data Channels

The first step is to figure out which data channels are necessary. For the purposes of this system, a data channel is defined as a series of keys for rotating, moving, or scaling a single bone. For a standard human body, you typically need to store the position of the root and the orientation of every bone. However, when the system has to support facial animation, hand animation, squash-and-stretch animation, or has to render other types of articulated models such as cars or weapons, flexibility in choosing which channels are used becomes more important.

Similarly, if the system has to play multiple animations on a character at the same time, you might not want to calculate all bones for all animations. An example is a character that is running and aiming a weapon at the same time. The character would use a standard running animation for the legs and the torso, and an animation for gripping the weapon for the arms and the shoulders.

Some channels can be further optimized if full freedom of rotation about all three axes is not required. For example, the jawbone, the eyelids, and some finger bones might only rotate around a single axis. You can save a lot of space by storing only a single axis, as you then need only store one-third of the data. Speed is also improved, since creating a local matrix from a single axis is much faster than reconstructing it from three axes or converting it from a quaternion. A single-axis interpolation is also much simpler and faster than a quaternion slerp (spherical linear interpolation) when interpolating between keyframes or blending between animations.

Note that for some animations, some joints might change from single to multi-axis. For example, an animation that shows a character moving her jaw from side to side would not be possible if the jaw were limited to only rotate about a single axis.

Reducing the Number of Stored Keys

Once you have all the data organized, it has to be optimized so keys that have little or no visual impact are removed.

The algorithm itself is simple:

1. Measure the significance of each key.
2. Remove more keys based on some criteria.
3. Remove the least significant key.
4. Recalculate the significance of the two neighbor keys around the removed key.

While the algorithm is simple, it will run very slowly if the data is not organized with the following two questions in mind: which key is the least important, and, for each remaining key, which two keys are its neighbors? This turns out to be easy.

For each channel, an array of keys is stored sorted by frame number. Those keys should also be linked together in a linked list. Whenever a key is removed, it should be taken out of the linked list; thus, knowing which keys are valid and which have been discarded is trivial. You can also quickly find the neighbor keys for each removed key, which is useful when finding the keys that need to be recalculated.

It also helps to have a balanced binary tree sorted by significance of the keys in all channels. This will substantially reduce the amount of time it takes to find the least significant key, and to reposition keys within the binary tree after their significance is recalculated.

Measuring the Significance of Each Key

The one thing that can make or break the compression system is the heuristic for measuring the significance of each key. The heuristic does not matter as much for smaller levels of compression, but becomes increasingly important when higher compression ratios are used. This can mean the difference between a 3D model waving its limbs around unnaturally, and a living, breathing human being.

The animator should be able to tweak the number of keys removed for each animation individually. This can, for example, be input as a target number of keys per second of animation. The optimal amount of compression that can be used varies for each animation, but with a good heuristic, 5 to 10 keys per second can produce natural animations.

The simplest heuristic is simulating the removal of each key from the optimized dataset and comparing the datasets before and after the removal. The simulation is done by decompressing the frames in both datasets and making comparisons between them.

It is not acceptable to find the importance of the key based on the original dataset, because many keys are collinear. The problem collinearity causes is that if any of the collinear keys are removed, the other keys will control the curve through the same path as before. However, if all collinear keys are removed, the curve will change its path.

It is important to use the same interpolation scheme for calculating the significance of the keys and decompressing the frames in the game. Linear interpolation gives the worst results and is not recommended. Animation often looks robotic and unnatural with linear interpolation. Spline interpolation produces much better results by smoothing the animation.

Finding the Right Criteria for Key Removal

Many different removal criteria are possible. The most obvious criterion is to measure how far apart the keys would be in the two datasets. This could be done by using

Pythagoras' method, for example. When using this criterion, all the decompressed frames will closely resemble the frames of the original animation.

However, for the animations to seem realistic, the individual frames do not matter as much as the overall feeling of the final animation. If the heuristic looks only at absolute values, each frame will look correct, but when watched in motion, it might deviate too far from the original animation. Two equally important criteria are speed and acceleration, the first and second derivatives of the curve. For example, a punch animation needs to have the correct acceleration and deceleration to feel fast, yet controlled. Video game players do not know where a punch landed in the original motion capture session, but they do notice if the animation doesn't feel right when they are playing the game.

When dealing with hierarchical animation, the position of each bone matters significantly. Rotational movement affects the extents of an object much more than the center of the object. A one-degree discrepancy in a hand joint would be less noticeable than a one-degree discrepancy on a shoulder joint, because the number of bones between the shoulder and the fingertips is much higher than the number of bones between the hand and the fingertips. This is one area that should not be determined automatically, because in some cases, the animators want the focus to be on certain parts of the body. For example, if there is a close-up of a hand, it is important that all of the bones between the hand bone and the root bone are stored at high quality, but the opposite arm and the legs do not matter as much. Therefore, an easy way to achieve better results is to give the animator control over which groups of the body require more detail.

Finally, if a bone has stored a key on a certain frame, then the child bone and the parent bones should store a key on the same frame. This tends to create a calmer and more precise animation, especially when using linear interpolation.

Recalculating the Importance of the Neighbor Keys

The removal of a key has an impact on its neighbor keys, and they need to have their importance recalculated to eliminate problems with collinearity. If you use spline interpolation, then two remaining neighbor keys on each side of the removed key are affected. With linear interpolation, only one neighbor key on each side is impacted.

If the heuristic takes parent or child bones into consideration, the keys that could be affected for those bones also need to have their importance recalculated.

Packing the Remaining Keys

The hard part is over. Now that you have found which keys you need to store, it's time to think about how to pack the data. Instead of storing everything in 32-bit floating point, significant memory savings can be achieved by storing the final values with less precision.

Quaternions can be packed down to 4 bytes with reasonably good results [Zarb-Adami02]. Similar methods can be developed for positional animation. This type of technique works especially well on fast-moving animations, but on slow animations where the player can pay attention to the details of the character more easily, this can make the animation jittery.

In a hierarchical system, the bones near the root of the character create the majority of the jitter. Therefore, the animations can benefit if you pack the different channels with different levels of precision. Keys for bones near the root should be stored with 8 or 12 bytes of precision, while keys for arms and legs can be stored with only 4 bytes of precision.

Each animation can obviously have a different packing level. If you know that one animation is used in a close-up, or an animation does not look good enough, you can use the highest quality packing. Again, this is something that the animator should be able to control. An easy way to allow the animator to tweak this value is to have a number of predefined settings.

With the key data packed, the only thing left in the compression process is to store the data in a logical format. For each channel, you need to store the remaining keys and their frame numbers. To minimize memory usage, you can store the frame number for each key as an offset from the previous remaining key, in multibyte format. This means that either one or two bytes are used, where the top bit of the first byte will indicate whether a second byte is used. This method works for animations of fewer than 32,768 (2^{15}) frames.

Runtime Decompression

There are two steps required for decompression for each frame rendered:

1. Update the decompression buffers so the keys are in the right frame ranges.
2. Interpolate between the keys in the decompression buffers to get the animation for that frame.

At the start of each animation, the animation player must allocate a decompression buffer for each data channel. The buffers are used to store the unpacked keys that the interpolation routine uses to get the current frame. Each decompression buffer should be large enough for either two or four uncompressed keys per data channel, depending on the type of interpolation that was used during compression. These buffers are kept in memory over the duration of the animation, and each buffer is continuously updated whenever it is not valid for the current animation frame.

The final step is to interpolate between the keys. This is done with the same interpolation routines used during compression. After this step, you are done; you have successfully decompressed a frame of the animation. All that is left is to render the model.

Future Improvements

If you follow the steps in the previous sections, you will have a complete compression system, perfectly capable of delivering good compressed animations. However, as with everything else, there are plenty of ways to improve this system. You can probably come up with some good ideas yourself, but here are a few suggestions and tips:

- **Curve fitting.** After many keys are removed, the curves might no longer be optimal. The curve passes through the values at the frames where a key is stored, but between keys, the curve will be off. By trying to fit the curve to the best result for all keys combined, you will be able to get the overall animation closer to the original, while still keeping the timing unchanged.
- **Storing channels interleaved.** If animation channels are stored interleaved, it might be possible to stream in animations a small piece at a time. This is useful for cut-scenes, as there is no need to have a full animation in memory at once. Regular animations can also benefit, because it will keep random memory access down, as there is only one location in memory that will be read, instead of one location for each channel.
- **Separating key removal from key packing.** Key removal is the slowest part of the system, but it is only one of the parts that animators will need to adjust. By storing an intermediate result between key removal and key packing, animators might be able to tweak the packing parameters and see the result much more quickly than if the system has to recompress the animation from the start.

Conclusion

Every game has memory constraints. Compressing animation data is one path you can take to reclaim some memory. Compression can be a simple process, simply removing keys that are not important for the look and feel of the animation, and packing the remaining keys as much as possible.

The heuristic for measuring a key's significance is the most important, and can be the toughest component to get right. However, even less refined heuristics can result in significant memory savings. Packing the remaining keys is also important, and with high compression levels, the jitter introduced by having packed keys disappears, making the result look better than uncompressed animation with packed keys.

The results vary from animation to animation; there is not one good set of options that can be applied universally. It is therefore important to give animators freedom to tweak compression levels for each animation. However, for the animators to process a large number of animations quickly, it is important to keep the number of options down to a minimum.

While it might seem complicated before you start, making a compression routine is straightforward. Remember that the rules here are not set in stone, but are meant as a guideline—feel free to experiment.

References

[Zarb-Adami02] Zarb-Adami, Mark, "Quaternion Compression," *Game Programming Gems 3*, Charles River Media, 2002.

4.5

Compressed Axis-Aligned Bounding Box Trees

Miguel Gomez

The axis-aligned bounding box (AABB) tree structure has proven to be very useful for accelerating intersection queries on sets of geometry. The data structure is easy to implement, the built structure is numerically well conditioned, and like all binary trees they have *O(log n)* search time [Sedgewick90]. This article explains several techniques that can be used to lower the overall memory footprint of an AABB tree to 11 bytes per triangle.

A Brief Survey of Hierarchical Sorting Methods

This section covers quadtrees, k-d trees, binary space partitioning (BSP) trees, bounding volume trees, and axis-aligned bounding boxes, data structures for sorting three-dimensional sets of triangles.

Quadtrees, k-d Trees, and BSP Trees

Some of the most popular data structures for sorting three-dimensional sets of triangles are the octree, k-d tree and BSP tree. While the octree is probably the simplest to implement, the more sophisticated k-d and BSP trees adapt better to specific sets of geometry. All of these structures use planes to separate space into convex regions, which leads to some serious side effects. First, any triangle that straddles a separating plane must either be split into two pieces, which increases the set of data and can create problematic "slivers," or included in multiple nodes, which removes any upper bound on the size of the node structure. Second, octrees and k-d trees do not separate geometry adaptively, so they may need arbitrary thresholds to terminate a recursive build algorithm. For example, if many triangles share the same vertex, the octree recursion may never achieve one triangle per node and will have to be terminated based on tree depth. This can lead to unnecessarily deep trees. BSP trees that adaptively use the planes of individual triangles for separation do not have this problem, but they still can have problems introduced by splitting.

Bounding Volume Trees

Bounding volume trees approach the problem differently. Instead of dividing space, bounding volume trees recursively divide a set of triangles into two subsets and find a bounding volume that encloses each subset. This approach avoids having to split triangles or include them in multiple nodes, and building a tree simply stops when a subset has only one remaining triangle. For more information on bounding volume trees see [vandenBergen99].

Axis-Aligned Bounding Boxes

An axis-aligned bounding box has a position (its center) and extents. As its name implies, the sides of an AABB are parallel to the *x*-, *y*-, and *z*-axes. Figure 4.5.1 shows how an AABB fits a single triangle.

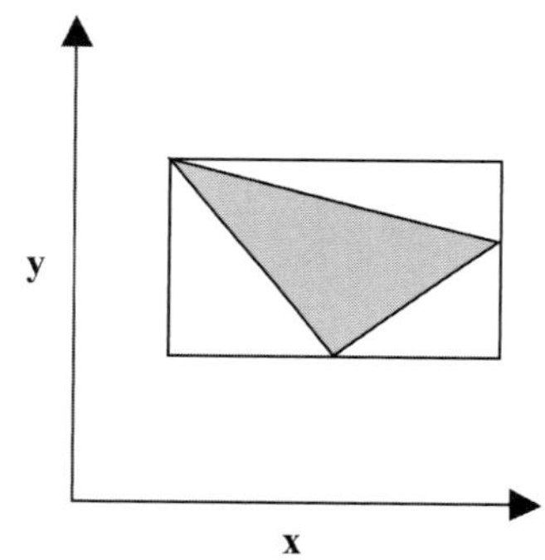

FIGURE 4.5.1 The sides of an AABB are parallel to the coordinate axes.

AABB Trees

The bounding boxes in an AABB can and often do overlap. Figure 4.5.2 shows a shallow tree for a set of two connected triangles, **L** and **R**. Notice that the left and right AABB's overlap one another.

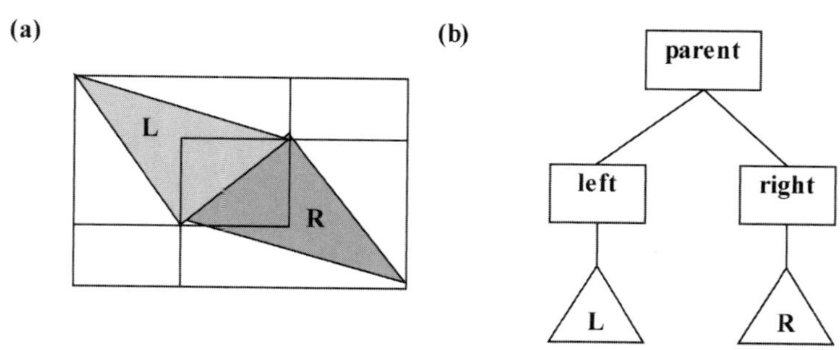

FIGURE 4.5.2 (A) The AABBs for two connected triangles will always intersect. (B) The AABB tree structure for this particular geometry.

Building AABB Trees

An AABB tree is built by successively dividing a set of triangles into two subsets until each subset contains only one triangle. The basic algorithm for building an AABB tree is as follows:

- Find the AABB that encloses the entire set.
- Divide the set into two subsets. This can be done by classifying the centroid of each element along the major (longest) axis of this AABB. If one subset is empty, arbitrarily create two subsets of approximately equal size.
- If a subset contains only one triangle, create a leaf.
- Otherwise, repeat the same process on each subset.

Compressing AABB Trees

In most applications 4-byte floats have sufficient precision (7 digits) for specifying box extents, requiring $6 \times 4 = 24$ bytes at each node. Any binary tree requires exactly $2n$-1 nodes to sort n elements, allowing an array of nodes to be allocated before building the tree. If the data set is large, it might be necessary to specify the indices of the child nodes with 4-byte unsigned integers. To avoid having to store yet another 4-byte integer for a triangle index at each node, we can exploit the fact that the 0th node (the root) is never referenced by another node. Therefore, if one of the child node indices is zero, we can consider the node a leaf and the other integer must index a triangle. This trick gives us a grand total of 32 bytes per node, or about 64 bytes per triangle as n becomes large. If we are willing to limit our triangle count to 2^{15} (giving a node count of $2^{16}-1$), unsigned 2-byte integers can be used for child node indices. This reduces the footprint to 28 bytes per node, or about 56 bytes per triangle. Since most applications can divide triangle sets into chunks of 2^{15}, 56 bytes per triangle will be used as a reference value.

There are two important properties of AABB trees that can be exploited to minimize storage. First, child AABB nodes are fully contained by their parent. This allows us to store child extent values as unsigned 8-bit integer offsets relative to their parent's extents. Second, *at most* six extent values of the child nodes are *not* identical to those of the parent node. This means that we only need to store six values to fully describe the two children.

Approximating Extents

In order to use unsigned bytes as relative extent values for nodes, we must keep track of the floating-point extent values of the parent as the tree is built. By scaling the child extents relative to the parent AABB and then rounding to the nearest integer value, we get a conservative estimate for the child AABB extents (see Figure 4.5.3).

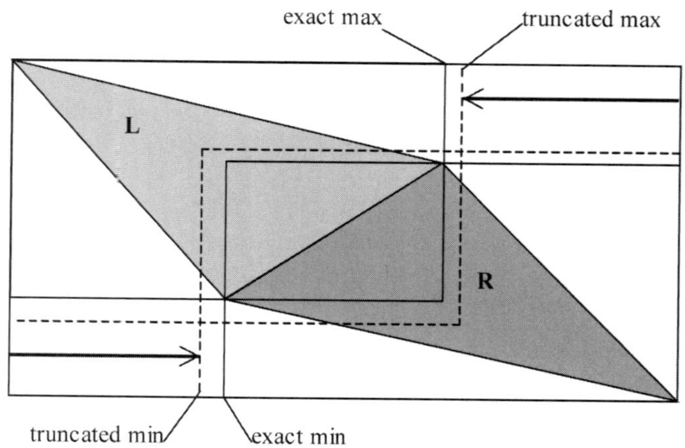

FIGURE 4.5.3 When approximating extents with unsigned 8-bit integers, min values are measured from the left, while max values are measured from the right.

The error of any extent value relative to its parent is never more than $0.5 \times 1/255 \approx 2 \times 10^{-3}$. To put this in perspective, if the extents of the parent node are one meter on each side, we get a resolution of about two millimeters for the child extents. Keep in mind that these numbers scale as the nodes become smaller. The equations for calculating relative offset values are

$$i_{\min} = \operatorname{trunc}\left(255 \frac{\min_{child} - \min_{parent}}{\max_{parent} - \min_{parent}}\right),$$

$$i_{\max} = \operatorname{trunc}\left(255 \frac{\max_{parent} - \max_{child}}{\max_{parent} - \min_{parent}}\right),$$

$$i_{\max}, i_{\min} \in [0, 255].$$

Using one byte instead of four bytes to store an extent value immediately brings the memory consumption down to 10 bytes per node, or 20 bytes per triangle.

Exploiting Redundancy

In order to store only six extent values for both children, we must take a bold step and store both the left and the right child information within one node structure. In this structure, a bit field is used to indicate which extent belongs to which child. A *true* bit means the unique extent value belongs to the *left* child (so the parent's extent value belongs to the right child), and a *false* bit indicates the opposite situation. This requires only six bits, so the other two bits are used to indicate which nodes are leaves.

When information for both children is stored at a single node, the node only consumes 11 bytes (see Figure 4.5.4).

<table>
<tr><td colspan="2">flags (1 byte)</td></tr>
<tr><td colspan="2">extents (6 bytes)</td></tr>
<tr><td>left node/triangle index (2 bytes)</td><td>right node/triangle index (2 bytes)</td></tr>
</table>

FIGURE 4.5.4 The compressed AABB node structure consumes only 11 bytes per node.

In addition, only *n* nodes (including the root) are required to sort *n* triangles, so the tree now needs only 11 bytes of storage per triangle. (Some architectures may require a 12 byte structure for alignment.) This is almost 50% less than if relative values were used alone and about $1/5^{th}$ the storage of our reference value. As an added bonus, we can now keep track of twice as many triangles ($2^{16}-1$ instead of 2^{15}).

In practice, the root node is a separate data type that specifies the floating-point extents of the entire triangle set and is not part of the actual node array, which contains $n-1$ nodes (see Figure 4.5.5).

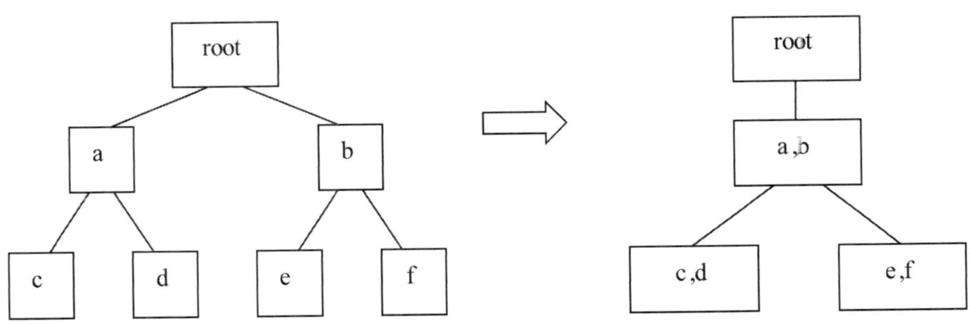

FIGURE 4.5.5 For a set of four triangles, the uncompressed tree requires seven nodes, whereas the tree on the right requires only four.

Runtime Efficiency

The runtime cost of converting the 8-bit values to back to floating-point values is minimal. An experiment in which a line segment was tested for possible intersection with 16K randomly distributed triangles showed that the compressed structure was about 10% slower than the full floating-point representation. It seems that the ability of the significantly smaller data set to fit in the cache nearly compensates for the overhead of converting integers to floating-point values.

Future Work

The compressibility of AABB trees gives them a clear advantage over other structures; however, it may be possible to apply the same techniques to compress other bounding volume tree structures, such as OBB trees. The fact that child AABB nodes are fully contained by their parent volume allows us to easily scale and share extent values. This same property does not hold for OBB trees [Gottschalk96] or even sphere trees. The lack of this property may make it impossible to share redundant extent values; however, it may still be possible to store scaled 8-bit extent values and 8-bit orientation values for OBB trees by propagating the expanded dimensions back up the tree to the root node.

References

[Gottschalk96] Gottschalk, S., Lin, M. C., and Manocha, D., "OBBTree: A Hierarchical Structure for Rapid Interference Detection, *SIGGRAPH Proceedings,* 1996, pp. 171–180.

[Sedgewick90] Sedgewick, Robert, *Algorithms in C*, Addison-Wesley, 1990.

[vandenBergen99] van den Bergen, G., *Collision Detection in Interactive 3D Computer Animation*, Ph.D. Thesis, Eindhoven University of Technology, 1999.

4.6

Textures as Lookup Tables for Per-Pixel Lighting Computations

Alex Vlachos, Valve; John Isidoro, ATI; and Chris Oat, AMD

alex@vlachos.com, jisidoro@csa.bu.edu, chris@chrisoat.com

The latest generation of graphics hardware has brought forth a new level of per-pixel programmability for real-time applications. However, they are limited by both the size and the types of instructions that can be performed. Because of this limitation, programmers need to utilize a new set of tricks to perform more advanced graphics algorithms on a per-pixel basis. In this gem, we show ways to use texture maps as a means to solve functions through a lookup table, focusing on lighting computations. This technique saves precious pixel shader instructions, and in many cases, it is the only way to make certain per-pixel effects possible on the current generation of hardware.

Specular Per-Pixel Lighting Without Using a Cube Map for Normalizing *h* ($n \cdot h/h \cdot h$ Mapping)

A common problem with performing specular lighting calculations in a pixel shader is that the halfway vector, h, can become denormalized when it is linearly interpolated across a polygon. One standard solution is to use a normalization cube map to renormalize the halfway vector. Normalization cube maps have the disadvantages of requiring an additional texture fetch as well as consuming a lot of texture memory. An alternative to using normalization cube maps followed by a 1D specular texture fetch is to use an $n \cdot h/h \cdot h$ map as a lookup table in your shader. This optimization reduces the number of texel fetches required per pixel from two to one. However, the normalization cube map is still used to normalize tangent space light vector, l.

- Fetch n (per-pixel normal) from the normal map (bump map).
- Store the halfway vector (h) as a 3D texture, coordinated and interpolated across the polygon, which will cause it to be denormalized at each pixel.
- Store $n \cdot h$ in the first component of the texture coordinate.
- Store $h \cdot h$ in the second component of the texture coordinate.
- Using this 2D texture coordinate, fetch into the $n \cdot h/h \cdot h$ map. The resulting texel fetched is the specular lighting term raised to some constant power k.

Creating the $n \cdot h/h \cdot h$ map is relatively simple (see Figure 4.6.1). The map is a monochrome image that potentially uses 1/18th of the texture memory required by a normalization cube map (six RGB color faces of a cube). The $n \cdot h/h \cdot h$ map is essentially a lookup table for the following function:

$$f(s,t) = \left(\frac{s \cdot t}{\sqrt{t \cdot t}} \right)^k \tag{4.6.1}$$

which can also be written as

$$\left(\frac{n \cdot h}{\|h\|} \right)^k \tag{4.6.2}$$

FIGURE 4.6.1 $n \cdot h/h \cdot h$ map ($k = 32$). An example of a procedurally created $n \cdot h/h \cdot h$ map that allows for per-pixel specular lighting with a specular exponent of 32.

The following is a DirectX8.1 pixel shader (Version 1.4) that performs the $n \cdot h/h \cdot h$ mapping:

```
;(0.0, 0.5, 1.0, 1.0)
SetPixelShaderConstant 0 psCommonConst
SetPixelShaderConstant 1 ambient
SetPixelShaderConstant 2 diffuse
SetPixelShaderConstant 3 specular
StartPixelShader
    ps.1.4
    texld r0, t0 ;normal map n
    ;tangent space H (not necessarily normalized)
    texcrd r2.rgb, t2
    ;tangent space L (normalizer cube map lookup)
    texld r4, t1
        dp3_sat r4, r0_bx2, r4_bx2 ;(n.l)
        dp3_sat r3.r, r0_bx2, r2 ;(n.h)
        dp3_sat r3.g, r2, r2 ;(h.h)
    phase
    ;Base map
    texld r1, t0
    ;(n.h)/(h.h)^k map lookup
    texld r2, r3
        ;light = n.l * diffuse + ambient
        mad r5.rgb, r4, c2, c1
        ;basemap * light
        mul r5.rgb, r1, r5
        ;(specular * color) + (basemap * light)
        mad_sat r0.rgb, r2, c3, r5
        +mov_sat r0.a, c0.b
EndPixelShader
```

Per-Pixel Specular Exponent Using an $(n \cdot h)^k$ Map

Using a method similar to the one previously described, it is possible to specify a unique specular exponent on a per-pixel basis. This requires some additional math in the pixel shader. A specular exponent (shininess) map, as well as the creation of an $(n \cdot h)^k$ texture, is also required. The grayscale specular exponent map is often stored in the alpha channel of the base texture. This is what an artist paints to define the specular exponent k at each pixel.

- Fetch n (per-pixel normal) from the normal map (bump map).
- Fetch k from the exponent (shininess) map.
- Store the halfway vector (h) as a 3D texture, coordinated and interpolated across the polygon, which will cause it to be denormalized at each pixel.
- Store $(n \cdot h)^2$ in the first component of the texture coordinate.

- Store ($k * h \cdot h$) in the second component of the texture coordinate.
- Store ($h \cdot h$) in the third component of the texture coordinate.
- A projective, dependant texture fetch is required into the $(n \cdot h)^k$ map. The projection causes the first two coordinates to be divided by the third, resulting in $((n \cdot h)^2 / (h \cdot h), k)$. The texel fetched with these coordinates is the specular lighting term raised to the per-pixel power k.

Just like the $n \cdot h/h \cdot h$ map, the $(n \cdot h)^k$ map is used to reduce the amount of math you would otherwise have to do explicitly in the pixel shader (such as normalizing h and raising $n \cdot h$ to a power of k). In this case, $k = [0.0, 1.0]$, where 0.0 corresponds to the minimum k value used during $(n \cdot h)^k$ texture creation, and 1.0 corresponds to the maximum k value in the $(n \cdot h)^k$ texture. When doing the dependent texture fetch, use the projective divide (`_dz` in D3D) to divide the first two coordinates by the third. This projective divide causes the resulting texture lookup coordinates to be

$$s = \frac{(n \cdot h) * (n \cdot h)}{h \cdot h} = \frac{(n \cdot h)^2}{\|h\|^2}$$

$$t = k \tag{4.6.3}$$

For $(n \cdot h)^k$ mapping, the texture lookup table computes the following function:

$$f(s,t) = s^{0.5*t} \tag{4.6.4}$$

By performing the texel fetch from this map, using the preceding coordinates, the equation becomes

$$\left(\frac{n \cdot h}{\|h\|}\right)^k \tag{4.6.5}$$

This results in the standard Phong specular lighting component raised to the exponent k. The beauty of this technique is that the projective texel fetch both normalizes the h vector and performs the exponentiation. The tiled quad at the bottom of Color Plate 5 on the CD was rendered using an $(n \cdot h)^k$ map to achieve varying degrees of specular lighting on a per-pixel basis. The specular exponent varies per-pixel as defined by the exponent map shown in Figure 4.6.4. Figure 4.6.3 is an example of a procedurally generated $(n \cdot h)^k$ map that allows for per-pixel specular lighting with a per-pixel exponential range of [0, 64].

FIGURE 4.6.2 An RGB texture of a tiled surface without any lighting.

FIGURE 4.6.3 A procedurally generated $(n \cdot h)^k$ ($k = [0,64]$) map that allows for per-pixel specular lighting with a unique specular exponent specified at each pixel.

FIGURE 4.6.4 Grayscale specular exponent map that is used in combination with the texture from Figure 4.6.3 to obtain artist-editable per-pixel specular exponents.

```
;(0.0, 0.5, 1.0, 1.0)
SetPixelShaderConstant 0 psCommonConst
SetPixelShaderConstant 1 ambient
SetPixelShaderConstant 2 diffuse
SetPixelShaderConstant 3 specular
StartPixelShader
    ps.1.4
    ;dot 3 map (specular exponent stored in alpha)
```

```
        texld r0, t0
        texcrd r2.rgb, t2 ;tan H
        ;tangent space L (normalizer cube map lookup)
        texld r4, t1
            dp3_sat r4, r0_bx2, r4_bx2 ;(n.l)
            dp3_sat r3.b, r2, r2 ;(h.h)
            dp3_sat r3.r, r0_bx2, r2 ;(n.h)
            mul  r3.g, r3.b, r0.a ;k*((h.h))
            mul  r3.r, r3.r, r3.r ;(n.h)^2
        phase
        ;Base map
        texld r1, t0
        ;Attenuated (n.h)^k map
        texld r2, r3_dz
            ;n.l * diffuse + ambient
            mad r5, r4.r, c2, c1
            ;diffamb = basemap * (n.l * diffuse + ambient)
            mul r5.rgb, r1, r5
            ;diffamb + (specular * specular color)
            mad_sat r0.rgb, r2, c3, r5
            +mov_sat r0.a, c0.b

    EndPixelShader
```

Color-Shift Iridescence

Another rendering effect using texture lookup tables is color-shift iridescence. This type of iridescence can be seen on insects' wings, certain finishes on glasswork, and pearl-like objects. The effect this algorithm simulates is based on the empirical observation that the color at a particular point on an object tends to change in hue depending on the angle between the view vector and the surface normal. This is usually caused by a thin layer of semitransparent film on an object that diffracts different frequencies of incident light in different directions. The base algorithm performs standard Phong lighting and then multiplies the specular highlight color by a texel fetched from a 1D, hue-based gradient texture addressed by $(n \cdot v)$, where n is the per-pixel normal, and v is the tangent space view vector. See Color Plate 6 on the CD for images of hue-based gradient and objects rendered using color-shift iridescence. The following pixel shader performs the color-shift iridescence. Note that this example uses the $(n \cdot h)^k$ technique of the previous subsection.

```
;(0.0, 0.5, 1.0, 1.0)
SetPixelShaderConstant 0 psCommonConst
SetPixelShaderConstant 1 ambient
SetPixelShaderConstant 2 diffuse
SetPixelShaderConstant 3 specular
StartPixelShader
    ps.1.4
    ;dot 3 map (specular exponent stored in alpha)
    texld r0, t0
    ;tan H
```

```
        texcrd r2.rgb, t2
        ;tangent space L (normalizer cube map lookup)
        texld r4, t1
        ;tangent space V (normalizer cube map lookup)
        texld r5, t3
            dp3_sat r4.gb, r0_bx2, r4_bx2 ;(n.l)
            dp3_sat r4.r, r0_bx2, r5_bx2 ;(n.v)
            dp3_sat r3.b, r2, r2 ;(h.h)
            dp3_sat r3.r, r0_bx2, r2 ;(n.h)
            mul  r3.g, r3.b, r0.a ;k*((h.h))
            mul  r3.r, r3.r, r3.r ;(n.h)^2
        phase
        ;Base map
        texld r1, t0
        ;Attenuated (n.h)^k map
        texld r2, r3_dz
        ;Iridescent map 1D tex map lookup
        texld r3, r4
            ;Iridescent * Specular
            mul_sat r0.rgb, r2, r3
            ;n.l * diffuse + ambient
            mad r5, r4.g, c2, c1
            ;diffamb = basemap * (n.l * diffuse + ambient)
            mul r5.rgb, r1, r5
            ;diffamb + specular * specularcolor
            mad_sat r0.rgb, r0, c3, r5
            +mov_sat r0.a, c0.b
    EndPixelShader
```

Per-Pixel Point Lights with Correct Per-Pixel Falloff

Another useful application for texture lookup functions is correct per-pixel light attenuation. Computing distance falloff for point lights is traditionally sampled at the vertices and the distance is then linearly interpolated for per-pixel effects. The problem with this approach occurs when a light is near the surface of a large polygon, and there is no vertex to catch the light near the light source.

The approach for this algorithm is to calculate the distance from each pixel to the light source instead of each vertex. This results in the exact falloff value, based on a given light source, thus avoiding the common problems with the vertex-based approach.

The vertex shader computes the vertex position in *normalized light space* (NLS) instead of directly using the distance from the vertex position. The NLS transform is a translation by (–`lightPos`), then a uniform scaling by (`1/lightFalloff`). This gives us each vertex's position in NLS. The pixel shader then computes the distance squared on a per-pixel basis by simply taking the dot product of this interpolated vertex position with itself. Then, a 1D texture is sampled using the NLS distance squared as the texture coordinate. This allows you to vary the intensity and color of the light using distance in any way possible. The per-pixel nature of the algorithm solves any vertex-sampling issues. Since NLS position is linear by definition, this approach works perfectly without artifacts. This method hides a per-pixel square-root function in a texel fetch (see Figure 4.6.5).

FIGURE 4.6.5 1D point light texture that renders light color and intensity change as a function of distance from the point light source.

Per-Pixel Spotlights and Directional Lights with Correct Per-Pixel Falloff

A natural extension of the per-pixel point light attenuation is to model spotlights and directional lights. This technique is similar to the point light shader above, but it requires slightly different vertex and pixel-shader operations. Instead of creating a 1D texture for the light, a 2D texture is required. The *u* axis of the texture is indexed with distance squared in the same way as a point light. However, the *v* axis of the texture encodes falloff based on the spot angle (the angle between the NLS vertex position vector and the spotlight direction).

To use this 2D texture, we extend the notion of normalized light space to represent a rotation, as well as extending a scale factor and a translation. This rotation matrix is composed of the light's orthonormal basis with the light direction as the *z*-axis.

In the vertex shader, similar to point lights, the vertex position is transformed into normalized light space. In the pixel shader, we can load this new position into a register as a set of texture coordinates and perform a dot product with itself to get the NLS distance squared (exactly like point lights, above). This NLS position is also loaded into a separate register with a projection modifier, causing the first two components to be divided by the first. This will compute the projected position. This projection performs a divide by *z* in NLS, which gives the spotlight its cone-like shape. Then, by doing a dot product with itself, we get a squared, scaled distance from the NLS *z*-axis, which acts like an "angle" in the range 0–1. If the dot product is done without a modifier, this value represents an angle of 0°–90°.

These two dot product values are then used as a lookup into a 2D texture, which is a visually convincing approximation to the usual spotlight distance multiplied by the angle equation, assuming squared values as input.

If we simply do a `dp3` as written below, the 2D texture map represents values within a 0°–90° light frustum. This means that the texture created for the spotlight must encode the full 0°–90° frustum. For lights with larger or smaller cones, texels can be better utilized by selecting an appropriate range. Using scale factor instruction modifiers, the 2D texture can represent other frustum angles. The formula for frustum angle is 2*arctan(1/scale factor). Table 4.6.1 shows the available scale factors and the resulting frustum angle.

TABLE 4.6.1 Available Scale Factors and Resulting Frustum Angles

Scale Factor	_d8	_d4	_d2	None	_x2	_x4	_x8
Frustum Angle (°)	165.7	151.9	126.8	90.0	53.1	28.1	14.3

By using the scale factors for the frustum angle, the *y* resolution of the texture lookup table can be decreased for smaller frustum angles because much less space is being represented. If the desired frustum angle is not listed in the table, just choose the closest table entry that is larger than the frustum to be represented, and make up the difference by scaling down the lookup table in the *y* direction.

```
;(0.0, 0.5, 1.0, 1.0)
SetPixelShaderConstant 0 psCommonConst
StartPixelShader
    ps.1.4
    ;NLS pos
    texcrd r1.xyz, t1.xyz
    ;NLS pos in xy plane scaled by 1/z
    texcrd r2.xy, t1_dz.xyz
        ;distance squared from light
        dp3 r1, r1, r1
        ;Set z = 0
        mov r2.b, c0.r
        ;(dist in xy plane scaled by 1/z)^2
        dp3 r1.g, r2, r2
    phase
    ;Base
    texld r0, t0
    ;Light attenuation
    texld r1, r1
        ;Base*light
        mul r0, r0, r1_x2
        ; " * N.L
        mul r0, r0, v0
EndPixelShader
```

Removing the `_dw` from the second `texcrd` instruction provides a cylindrical directional light frustum. This removes the scaling by $1/z$ of the distance in the *xy*-plane and gives the light's domain a cylindrical shape (see Figure 4.6.6). Note that this light still has a position and a falloff from that position. If positional distance falloff is not desired, just remove the first dot product and use the second dot product to index into a 1D texture.

FIGURE 4.6.6 2D spot/directional light texture that renders how, along one axis, light color and intensity changes as a function of distance from the light source. The other axis renders how the light changes as a function of angle from the light vector. This example assumes a 90° frustum and is a perfect candidate for using the 53.1° frustum to save texture usage.

Conclusion

We have shown a variety of effects using textures as function lookups. Using this idea, many graphics algorithms that have been per-vertex-only techniques can now be performed per-pixel. Of course, these are just a few useful examples of the many effects that can be achieved with this technique.

4.7

Methods for Dynamic, Photorealistic Terrain Lighting

Naty Hoffman, Sony Computer Entertainment America; and Kenny Mitchell, Electronic Arts

gpg@renderwonk.com, kmitchell@ea.com

Current rendering technologies enable us to include expansive and detailed outdoor scenes in our games, using large numbers of triangles. However, an important part of the visual complexity and appeal of an outdoor scene is due to its lighting, not just its geometry. If the lighting is static, it is simple enough to precompute a high-quality lighting solution—but what should we do when the lighting changes dynamically? This gem will present several methods for producing high-quality, physically based lighting solutions for terrain under dynamic lighting conditions.

Background

The first step is to quantify light correctly. Light is electromagnetic radiation in the visible portion of the spectrum (about 400–700 nm). The most common metric for light is *radiance*, or light flux along a ray. To understand how radiance is defined, visualize a small square (area A) centered on the light ray and perpendicular to it (see Figure 4.7.1a).

Light energy continuously passes through this square in all directions and frequencies. In RGB space, this energy (and any quantity derived from it) is specified as three numbers. This can roughly be thought of as dividing it into three "buckets," based on frequency. At a given point in time, we measure the rate of energy over time (light power or *radiant flux* Φ). The amount of flux going through the square depends on the size of the square, and doesn't really indicate the amount of light along the ray. We can measure the flux per area at the intersection point p ($M = d\Phi / dA$, or power

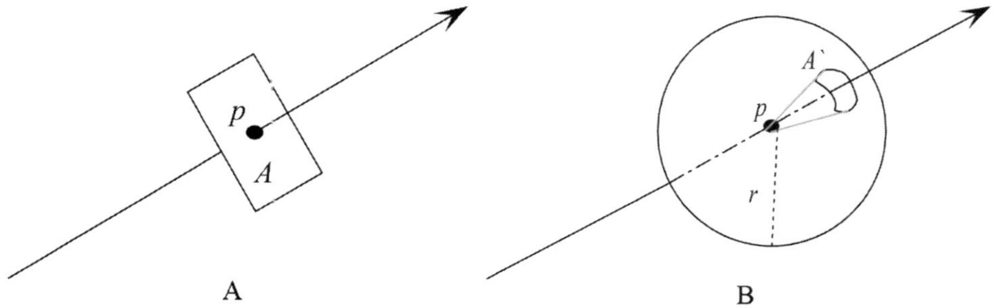

FIGURE 4.7.1 (A-B) Radiance area A along a light ray and patch A' on the radiance sphere.

per area, measured in watts per square meter). However, M includes light going in all directions, not just along the ray. In Figure 4.7.1b, we see a sphere (radius R) centered on p, and a small patch (area A') on this sphere surrounding the ray. A part of M (which we will call M') goes through this patch—M' does not depend on the radius of the sphere, but only on the fraction of the sphere's area covered by the patch. This fraction represents a range of directions and is called a *solid angle* ($\omega = A' / R$, measured in steradians). The quantity of light along the ray is the radiance ($L = dM' / d\omega$, measured in watts per meter squared per steradian). Radiance is power per *projected area* per solid angle—the projected area being measured perpendicularly to the ray. If we use an area that is at an angle to the ray (e.g., when looking at light reflected from a surface), then a correction factor equal to the dot product between the surface normal and the ray is needed.

In outdoor scenes, radiance can vary by six orders of magnitude [Debevec98], but most hardware limits us to a small range of light values. In this gem, we will compress all light values into the [0, 1] range. A related issue is the nonlinear relationship between pixel values and display radiance. The human visual response to light introduces other issues. We have chosen to ignore these problems and deal only with linear radiance values.

Another important quantity used in measuring light is the *irradiance, E*. This is similar to the flux per area, M above (with the same units), except that instead of measuring the total of all the outgoing light at a point, it measures the total incident (incoming) light. Since this is measured at a surface, the incoming radiance at a point p is integrated over a hemisphere $H(p)$ that is centered on the surface normal $\mathbf{N}(p)$:

$$E(p) = \int_{\mathbf{V}\in H(p)} L_i(p, -\mathbf{V})\mathbf{N}(p) \cdot \mathbf{V} d\Omega \tag{4.7.1}$$

Here, $\mathbf{V}$ is an outgoing unit vector in the hemisphere $H(p)$, $L_i(p, -\mathbf{V})$ is the incident radiance at p from $-\mathbf{V}$, and $d\Omega$ is the differential solid angle used for integration. The dot product is the projected area correction factor.

In this gem, we deal only with Lambertian (diffuse) terrain surfaces. For such surfaces, the outgoing radiance L_o is the same in all directions and is equal to the irradiance multiplied by the color *C(p)* divided by π:

$$L_o(p) = \frac{C(p)}{\pi} E(p) \tag{4.7.2}$$

The color is an RGB triple, in which each value is between 0 and 1. A color of 0 reflects none of the incoming energy in the relevant band of frequencies, and 1 reflects all of it.

The problem we are trying to solve here is the calculation of $L_o(p)$ for all the points on a heightfield terrain (at a finite resolution) under changing lighting conditions. Since the terrain is Lambertian, and we assume that *C(p)* is known, this is equivalent to calculating *E(p)*. For this, we need to know the incoming radiances from all directions in *H(p)*. These directions are divided into three groups: those from which the sun is visible, those from which the sky is visible, and those from which other terrain points are visible. We assume that certain data is available at each moment in time: the sun's position, angular size, and radiance. We might also want information about cloud positions, and other data. Note also that the sky's radiance might vary over different parts of the sky.

Now, the directions in which other terrain points are visible pose a difficult problem. In order to know the incoming radiance for these directions, we need to first know the outgoing radiance for other terrain points. If the radiance and positions of the sun and sky were static, we could use an iterative algorithm such as radiosity to precalculate a solution, but this is not practical in the dynamic case.

A Taxonomy of Solutions

We will present a range of techniques to solve the radiance calculations. These techniques will differ in the amount of precalculation and storage needed for the results, their limitations and assumptions, and how well the outcomes approximate the correct results. Most of them require too much precalculation to be usable with deformable terrain (we will note the exceptions). Since there are two sources of light—sun and sky—we can split the problem into a sunlight-only subproblem and a skylight-only subproblem. Most of these techniques solve only one of these subproblems, in which case two techniques must be used and the resulting radiances summed.

Some of these solutions involve calculating light values on the CPU and uploading light maps to the graphics card. In this case, care must be taken so that the CPU and bandwidth consumptions are not too high. Since lighting values usually change slowly, we can amortize the update over multiple frames. We experimented with multithreading for a while; however, we ended up with a single-threaded, double-buffering scheme that calculated and uploaded chunks of an active texture while using the previous texture for rendering. When the active texture was complete, we swapped the active and rendering texture and started again.

Sunlight: Horizon Angles, Shadow Ellipses, and PTMs

The solutions in this section solve the sunlight-only subproblem. Most of the solutions to this subproblem ignore light reflected from other terrain points. Our experience has shown that as long as inter-reflections are taken into account in the skylight subproblem, the results are acceptable. That said, it is preferable to take sunlight inter-reflections into account if possible, and we will show one technique that does so. Without inter-reflections, the sun's contribution to the irradiance at p is

$$E_{sun}(p) = \int_{\mathbf{V} \in S \cap H(p)} L_{sun} \mathbf{N}(p) \cdot \mathbf{V} d\Omega \tag{4.7.3}$$

where S is the set of directions that point at the sun. Since the sun's solid angle, ω_{sun}, is small, then we can assume that the result of the dot product is constant, and we get:

$$E_{sun}(p) = O_{sun}(p)\omega_{sun} L_{sun} N(p) \cdot \mathbf{V}_{sun} \tag{4.7.4}$$

where $\mathbf{V}_{sun}$ is the direction to the sun's center and $O_{sun}(p)$ the percentage of the sun that is outside $H(p)$ or otherwise occluded at p. The two quantities, which vary between terrain points, are the dot product and the occlusion factor. To reduce the cost of calculating the dot product, we quantized the normals of all the terrain points into a 256-entry normal table in a preprocessing stage. Then, for each frame, we calculated the dot product between each entry in the table and the current sun vector. This reduced the dot product calculation for each point to a simple table lookup. Another possibility is to use a normal map and dot3 texture blending in hardware.

There are several methods for calculating the occlusion factor. One of these methods uses *horizon mapping,* which was introduced by Max in [Max88]. This idea is based on storing the angles for each point to the horizon in a given set of directions (see Figure 4.7.2a). If the sun motion is restricted to an arc that passes through the zenith, then two horizon angles suffice. Given this information, determining whether a point is in shadow or not is simply a matter of comparing the angle of the sun to the horizon angle in that direction. If the sun angle θ is below the horizon angle φ, the point is in shadow ($O_{sun}(p) = 0$). Otherwise, it is not ($O_{sun}(p) = 1$). Soft shadows can be supported by tracking two angles for the sun (θ_{top} and θ_{bottom}, the angles to the sun's top and bottom) and comparing both to the horizon angle. If $\varphi \le \theta_{top}$, then $O_{sun}(p) = 0$. If $\varphi \ge \theta_{bottom}$, then $O_{sun}(p) = 1$. If $\theta_{top} > \varphi > \theta_{bottom}$, then $O_{sun}(p) = (\theta_{top} - \varphi) / \alpha$, where α is the angular diameter of the sun. We have had good results with storing the horizon angles as 16-bit fixed-point numbers and doing the calculations on the CPU. You might wish to experiment with 8-bit representations and/or hardware-based implementations. For efficiency, the direction along which the horizon angles are defined should correspond to rows in the heightfield array. This will help when calculating horizon angles. You should scan along the heightfield to a fair distance on each side, since hills can cast quite long shadows when the sun is at oblique angles. Note that horizon angles must always be clamped to *H(p)*, or errors will result (see Figure 4.7.2b).

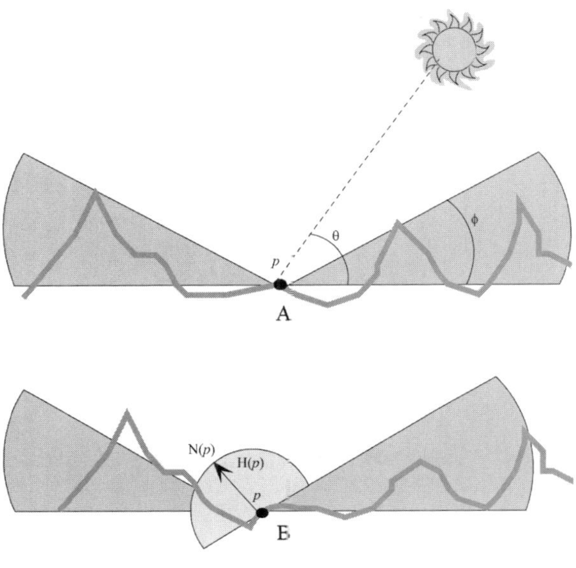

FIGURE 4.7.2 (A) Terrain profile showing sun angle θ and horizon angle φ. (B) Horizon angles must be clamped to $H(p)$.

Of all the sunlight methods, horizon mapping requires the least amount of preprocessing. It would be possible to handle occasional local changes to the heightfield (such as small craters) by recalculating the horizon maps in the affected area and to some distance on both sides.

Occlusion can also be calculated using *shadow ellipses*, introduced in [Heidrich00]. Here an ellipse is fitted to the set of visible angles from each point. This ellipse is parameterized using six numbers, which can be stored in two RGB texture maps. Software, register combiners, or pixel shaders can then be used to evaluate sun occlusion for each point. This method cannot do soft shadows easily. Its main advantage over horizon angles is that it can handle arbitrary sun positions. (See [Heidrich00] for details and [Kautz00] for implementation details using hardware under OpenGL.)

Polynomial texture maps (PTMs), introduced in [Malzbender01], can also be used for evaluating sunlight. This is one of the few techniques that can handle terrain inter-reflections for sunlight. To create a terrain PTM, first render a series of *N* images of the terrain using a radiosity package, with the sun at several different positions. The sun does not need to move in an arc through the zenith as it does in horizon mapping, but it does need to be restricted to a one-dimensional arc. Use a sun color of RGB(1,1,1). Then process the resulting *N* images into a single PTM. The first step is to separate the color and luminance values for each image. Then, fit a quadratic univariate polynomial ($a_0x^2 + a_2x + a_2$) to the N luminance values for each pixel, with the sun's position along its arc as the variable. Finally, generate two RGB textures: One stores one color value per pixel (by averaging across all images), and the other stores the three coefficients of the per-pixel luminance polynomials. At runtime, the polynomials are evaluated with the current sun position, either in software or in a pixel shader. The result is combined with the color value and modulated with the current sun color. (More details on PTMs are in [Malzbender01], and tools for implementing them are available in the download section of the associated Web site. Note that the paper deals mostly with bivariate polynomials requiring six coefficients, which is more complex and expensive than is needed for the purposes of this gem.)

If lighting conditions depend only on a single variable (like the time of day), it is possible to use PTMs to get the full lighting solution. In this case, a separate polynomial will probably need to be stored for each R, G, and B channel to capture the color variations, requiring nine values per pixel instead of six (three and an RGB color).

Skylight: Radiosity Approximations and Patches

The solutions in this section solve the skylight-only subproblem. First, we will handle the case where the entire sky is assumed to have the same radiance. This approximation is not as bad as it would seem. We have used it with good results. In this case, all we need to do is calculate the lighting for our terrain with a sky radiance equal to RGB(1,1,1), and then store the result in a RGB texture. At runtime, we multiply this texture with the current RGB sky radiance to get the desired result. The color in the texture will be relatively subtle, since it will result from inter-reflections with the colored terrain. If space is at a premium, the texture could be converted to 8 bit-per-pixel grayscale with a small loss in quality.

If precalculation time and space are not a problem, then the best way to generate the skylight texture is to use a radiosity package, with the terrain and a hemispherical distributed light source as input. If this is not practical (for time or space reasons, or because the terrain might change), then there is a useful approximation that can generate a very similar result in far less time. Stewart and Langer found in [Stewart97] that in a scene lit by a diffuse hemispherical illuminator, a point p tends to "see" other points in the scene that have a similar radiance value. So, we can assume that for all $\mathbf{V}$ in $H(p)$, where another terrain point is visible, $L_i(p, -\mathbf{V}) = L_o(p)$. Stewart and Langer showed that the error introduced by this approximation is small. The significance of this is that it breaks the interdependence between different terrain points, enabling us to derive a closed-form expression for $E(p)$. Stewart and Langer have derived a closed form using horizon angles to determine which directions are covered by terrain. Their formulation uses any number of horizon angles. We have had good results with eight (which is a convenient number for computation, since it corresponds to the rows, columns, and diagonals of the heightfield array). Assuming there are eight horizon angles (measured from the vertical, and not from the horizontal, as with sunlight) φ_0, φ_1, φ_2, φ_3, φ_4, φ_5, φ_6 and φ_7, the sky's contribution to the irradiance, including interreflections, at p is:

$$E_{sky}(p) = \frac{L_{sky} I(p)}{1 - C(p)\left(1 - \frac{1}{\pi} I(p)\right)} \quad (4.7.5)$$

$$I(p) = \frac{1}{2}\mathbf{N}(p) \cdot \sum_{i=0}^{7}\left(\left(\varphi_i - \frac{\sin 2\varphi_i}{2}\right)\Delta\sin_i \left(\varphi_i - \frac{\sin 2\varphi_i}{2}\right)\Delta\cos_i \frac{\pi}{4}\sin^2\varphi_i\right) \quad (4.7.6)$$

$$\Delta\sin_i = \sin\left(\frac{\pi}{4}(i+1)\right) - \sin\left(\frac{\pi}{4}i\right) \quad (4.7.7)$$

$$\Delta\cos_i = \cos\left(\frac{\pi}{4}i\right) - \cos\left(\frac{\pi}{4}(i+1)\right) \quad (4.7.8)$$

(For details on the derivation of Equations 4.7.5–4.7.8, see either the original paper [Stewart97] or the summary in [Hoffman01].) The horizon angles used here can be scanned to a relatively short distance, unlike those used for sun shadows. Of course, if you are already calculating horizon angles for sunlight shadows, there is no reason not to use those for two out of the eight angles. Since this technique uses relatively little preprocessing, it can also handle occasional minor edits to the heightfield (e.g., small craters) by recalculating the skylight texture in the affected area and a small distance around it.

If assuming a single radiance value for the sky does not produce acceptable results, the sky subproblem can be further broken up into sub-subproblems. For example, the sky could be divided into N patches, and N skylight textures could be calculated, each one based on the terrain being illuminated only by the relevant patch. At runtime, each of the skylight textures is modulated by the radiance of the relevant patch, and the results are summed together. Each of these skylight textures is essentially a basis function for calculating the final skylight solution. These basis functions can be calculated either via radiosity or by Stewart and Langer's method ([Stewart98] derives the necessary math).

Animated Cloud Shadows

Clouds are seldom absent from an outdoor scene, and the shadows cast by clouds are equally important to overall realism. Clouds' shadows are cast onto terrain through the occlusion of light from the sun. With increasing cloud density, sunlight is obscured more, resulting in darker areas on the ground. Therefore, it follows that a simple model of such shadows can be incorporated into a scene by multiplying the inverted cloud density with sunlight and adding the result to the sky's light contribution

$$E(p) = \int_{\mathbf{V} \in H(p)} L_i(p, -\mathbf{V}) \mathbf{N}(p) \cdot \mathbf{V} d\Omega \qquad (4.7.9)$$

where *D(p)* is the cloud density as projected onto the point *p*. Strictly speaking, the mapping of a cloud to its shadow on the ground is a perspective projection from the sun onto the earth's curved terrain at an angle. However, as the sun's distance is very far relative to the area cast in shadow, it is common to assume a planar projection. A less accurate assumption frequently made in the calculation of texture-mapping coordinates for cloud shadows is that the sun is located vertically above the terrain. This assumption permits optimization by directly applying the ground-plane world-space location (G_{pos}) of terrain vertices to texture coordinates using only scale and bias factors:

$$uv = G_{pos} Scale + Offset \qquad (4.7.10)$$

Without this assumption, a more complex texture projection matrix is required, resulting in more cycles per vertex. This per-vertex cost is particularly important with terrain meshes, which involve large numbers of vertices. However, when modeling the change in time of day, the sun's angle should be taken into account in the texture-projection calculation.

With the exception of events like storm clouds and twisters, clouds generally travel in a linear direction. So, animating the movement of clouds is reduced to updating texture offsets in the direction of cloud movement. However, care must be taken in the projection to avoid generating out-of-range texture coordinates.

ON THE CD

On the CD-ROM, a DirectX8 PC cloud-mapping sample demonstrates the use of vertex- and pixel-shading hardware for the method just described. First, the vertex program transforms the world-space vertex position to the screen. Doing this as early as possible is important in order to permit the graphics hardware to determine whether to reject the vertex through clipping.

```
dp4 oPos.x, VPOSITION, c[CV_VIEW_PROJECTION_0]
dp4 oPos.y, VPOSITION, c[CV_VIEW_PROJECTION_1]
dp4 oPos.z, VPOSITION, c[CV_VIEW_PROJECTION_2]
dp4 oPos.w, VPOSITION, c[CV_VIEW_PROJECTION_3]
```

The terrain's color texture is mapped as a planar projection and is performed using the world-space vertex position in the ground plane. This is then scaled and biased using the single multiply add (`mad`) instruction.

```
mad oT0.xy, VPOSITION.xz, [CV_BASE_TEX_PROJ].xy,
  c[CV_BASE_TEX_PROJECTION].zw
```

The sunlight texture is mapped in the same way, but the projection is redone, as it is more efficient to recalculate here than to store the result and copy to the output texture register.

```
mad oT1.xy, VPOSITION.xz, c[CV_BASE_TEX_PROJ].xy,
  c[CV_BASE_TEX_PROJECTION].zw
```

Next, the cloud layer is mapped. Again, this is simply a case of scale and bias operations, with the addition of the animation of the texture offset.

```
mad oT2.xy, VPOSITION.xz, c[CV_CLOUD_TEX_PROJ].xy,
  c[CV_CLOUD_TEX_PROJ].zw
```

The second cloud layer projection is applied to a fourth set of output texture coordinates in the same way, with alternative scale and bias parameters. Note that the only input stream to the vertex program is the world-space location of the vertex. Everything else is generated procedurally from that. This benefits us by reducing the bandwidth to the vertex processor (again this is an important concern with high-density meshes, such as terrains).

In the pixel shader, each texture is combined according to Equation 4.7.9 to yield the final rendered result. After the texture declarations, the average density of the two cloud layers is calculated.

```
add_d2 AVG_CLOUD_DENSITY, TEX_CLOUD_LAYER_0,
    TEX_CLOUD_LAYER_1
```

This is then inverted and multiplied by the contribution from the sunlight texture.

```
mul CLOUD_SHADOW_LUM, TEX_SUNLIGHT,
  1-AVG_CLOUD_DENSITY
```

Next, a constant skylight color factor is multiplied by the terrain texture color.

```
mul SKYLIGHT, TEX_TERRAIN_COLOR, CP_SKYLIGHT
```

Finally, the skylight contribution is added to the shadowed sunlight factor, times the terrain color.

```
mad OUTPUT_REG, CLOUD_SHADOW_LUM, TEX_TERRAIN_COLOR,
  SKYLIGHT
```

For this example, the constant sky radiance factor and sun radiance textures were statically pregenerated using Terragen [Terragen01]. They were extracted from Terragen images using the following methods:

- For the color texture, place the sun vertically above the terrain and disable terrain shadows.
- For the skylight factor, render terrain with a gray surface with sun at an angle, and sample the darkest point in the image.
- For the sunlight texture, subtract the skylight factor from the above image.

The cloud density texture was generated by hand. This texture could also be used to render the clouds themselves.

Video-Based Solution

A brute-force method for generating dynamic terrain lighting is to render canned sequences using an advanced offline rendering tool, then play back the sequence onto a video texture. Any view-independent lighting effects could be represented entirely in the video texture. Certain view-dependent effects, such as fog, might be applied to the video texture with traditional techniques. Furthermore, a novel, detailed bump-map effect can be achieved by applying a lit video texture to the terrain at a smaller scale.

With no time constraints imposed, unlimited complexity could be applied to this solution. However, a serious caveat is the high offline cost of generating video sequences. This time-consuming process must be appropriately budgeted during the developmental process. With that in mind, the remaining challenge of this technique is the efficient playback of video textures in the 3D scene.

PC and console hardware are moving toward accelerated support for video textures in 3D, albeit at a slower pace than vertex and pixel processing. For example, the image-processing unit (IPU) on the PlayStation2 accelerates decompression of mpeg frames. However, the path that video data must take via the IPU before reaching video memory is somewhat convoluted [Hoffman01]. On the PC, such support is presently orthogonal to textured geometry support in 3D, although advanced video-decompression hardware has existed for some time.

An attractive potential hardware solution would be to decompress a video texture format from video memory prior to the pixel shader stage. This would have the benefits of greatly reduced bandwidth and accelerated decompression.

Nonterrain Objects

A large task to consider when rendering outdoor environments with dynamic lighting is the effect of objects, such as buildings and vehicles, on the terrain. Many methods exist for rendering general shadows in real-time [Haines01], which can be applied to terrain shadows in various situations.

In one technique, *decal shadow texture projection*, the texture is pregenerated (or generated by rendering the shadow to a texture surface) and mapped onto the terrain. A slight z-bias is required to avoid z-buffer conflicts when the projected decal mesh does not match the underlying terrain mesh [McNally99]. This method produces detailed soft shadows, can quickly shadow large numbers of static objects (such as trees), and can easily be integrated with a shadow level-of-detail scheme.

For dynamic objects, techniques range from drop shadows to stencil- and shadow-buffer methods. The choice depends on hardware performance and constraints. However, the need for fast projection onto an arbitrary terrain mesh is common among these methods. This can be optimized by assuming an axis-aligned sun position and, in the case of a heightfield, an axis-aligned mesh.

Conclusion

We have presented various methods for achieving photorealistic, quality terrain lighting under changing lighting conditions in real-time. For examples of photorealistic terrain lighting in real-time, see Color Plates 7–10 on the CD. The methods have differing tradeoffs and characteristics in order to fit different types of games, platforms, and development pipelines. If you are developing a game with outdoor environments, we hope at least one of these methods will prove useful.

References

[Debevec98] Debevec, Paul, "Rendering Synthetic Objects into Real Scenes: Bridging Traditional and Image-Based Graphics with Global Illumination and High Dynamic Range Photography," Computer Graphics Proceedings (SIGGRAPH 1998), pp. 189–198.

[Haines01] Haines, Eric, et al., "Real-Time Shadows," GDC 2001 Conference Proceedings.

[Heidrich00] Heidrich, Wolfgang, et al., "Illuminating Micro Geometry Based on Precomputed Visibility," Computer Graphics Proceedings (SIGGRAPH 2000): pp. 455–464. Also available online at http://www.cs.ubc.ca/~heidrich/Papers/.

[Hoffman01] Hoffman, Naty, et al., "Photorealistic Terrain Lighting in Real-Time," *Game Developer Magazine,* July 2001: pp. 32–41.

[Kautz00] Kautz, Jan, et al., "Bump Map Shadows for OpenGL Rendering," available online at http://www.mpi-sb.mpg.de/~jnkautz/projects/shadowbumpmaps/.

[Malzbender01] Malzbender, Tom, et al., "Polynomial Texture Maps," Computer Graphics Proceedings (SIGGRAPH 2001): pp. 519–528. Also available online at http://www.hpl.hp.com/ptm/.

[Max88] Max, Nelson, "Horizon Mapping: Shadows for Bump-Mapped Surfaces," *The Visual Computer,* July 1988: pp. 109–177.

[McNally99] McNally, Seamus, "Treadmarks Engine." Phone conversation available online at http://www.vterrain.org/.

[Stewart97] Stewart, James, et al., "Towards accurate recovery of shape from shading under diffuse lighting," *IEEE Transactions on Pattern Analysis and Machine Intelligence,* September 1997: pp. 1020–1025. Also available online at http://www.cs.queensu.ca/home/jstewart/papers/.

[Stewart98] Stewart, James, "Fast horizon computation at all points of a terrain with visibility and shading applications," *IEEE Transactions on Visualization and Computer Graphics,* March 1998: pp. 82–93. Also available online at http://www.cs.queensu.ca/home/jstewart/papers/.

[Terragen01] Fairclough, Matt, "Terragen." Software available online at http://www.planetside.co.uk/terragen.

4.8

Practical Sky Rendering for Games

Aurelio Reis, Firaxis Games

AurelioReis@gmail.com

As more games shift toward expansive outdoor environments, the sky has become a much more visible part of every scene. When you consider the fact that sky-rendering techniques can be very computationally expensive, you can see the importance of efficient approaches to sky rendering. In this gem, we examine a number of intelligent generic and specific optimizations that can be applied to various sky implementations. These optimizations can be used to ensure that the user has a consistent frame rate, even with the sky in full view at high resolutions.

What We Want vs. What We Get

For a foundation in approaches to dynamic sky rendering, we recommend reading some of the research done by [Nishita00], [Preetham99], or [Jensen01]. Most of the available methods are quite complex, which relates to the fact that they try to emulate real-world physical phenomena. Taking into account a number of atmospheric parameters to simulate the sky is certainly not an easy task, and until just recently has been an approach strictly reserved for offline renderers; but as we continue the move to fully accelerated graphics environments, these techniques have become much more accessible.

Up until a few years ago, sky boxes textured using pre-rendered skies (using an offline renderer like [Terragen]) were the most common way to represent the sky at interactive frame rates. Constrained to advanced flight simulators, dynamic skies were far outside the grasp of most games. However, with the welcome arrival of MMOGs (Massively Multiplayer Online Games) and games like *Grand Theft Auto 3*, which required full day and night cycles, developers delved even further into increasing the realism of the natural environment. Striking a balance between visual quality and performance has been a challenge, and presentation quality has certainly suffered.

There is a stark contrast between what is possible on modern graphics hardware and what should be used in a game. In most demos of sky rendering, you see a very strong presentation highlighting the sky technique itself; but for developers, this isn't as useful a sight as it may seem. The [ATI Atmosphere demo], for instance, while being quite an impressive display of atmospheric scattering, does not present a fully interactive scene, and when coupled with an interactive scene is sure to be restrictively expensive due to the high number of shader instructions used.

The problem is that most demos of these techniques use a sparse world and don't show as detailed a scene as you might find in a real game. This type of scene is an environment populated by other interactive 3D objects that require their own processing power from the CPU or GPU. In a real game, you often have skinned 3D characters, multiple blending operations on the frame buffer, a large triangle count, and heavy per-pixel use.

This gem does not present a new or better sky-modeling technique, but instead describes a number of ways to make the existing techniques work better for you and your game. The main point is to cut through the technical and theoretical specifics, and delve into what bottlenecks are specifically hampering a real-game implementation, and how we can overcome them. The optimizations presented here are completely feasible and easily implemented for use in a real, commercial product. Although this article will delve mostly into the subject of rendering the sky color and clouds efficiently, also it will briefly touch upon such things as efficient lighting techniques for the ever-changing lights emitted by stellar objects. In summary, the end goal is a sky technique that is not only aesthetically pleasing, but which is also efficient to render, leaving enough clock cycles for us to insert a game into our nifty rendering engine.

What's That in the Sky?

Let's first examine the components that make up a dynamic sky, as well as review the terminology we'll be using. First, we have the sky color, which is commonly represented using a sky dome—for us, a hemispherical 3D model. Computations are broken down into discrete points that are performed over the surface of the dome, either per-vertex or per-pixel.

Methods available to determine the sky color at that point can either be a statistical (i.e., using observed and reproduced data) or analytical (i.e., physically based) approach. An analytical model, for instance, might actually calculate the Mie and Rayleigh scattering, as well as ozone and radiant contributions to a particular point. However, it should be noted that most implementations simplify the equations down to the strongest contributing factors, which are usually Mie and Rayleigh scattering. The physics of atmospheric conditions has been well documented, and as mentioned in the previous section, representing it graphically is not a mystery. We will use a few base sources for the sky implementation presented here, which were inspired by other authors.

For the sky color rendering, we will use the optimizations presented by [Spoerl04], which essentially simplified the equations presented by [Nishita00] to only take into account a simplified sky-color algorithm. In this algorithm, only the Rayleigh and Mie scattering terms are calculated (and in a simplified form), and the optical depth is essentially replaced by a scaling factor based on the height of the current sampling point. This is also suggested by [Nielsen03], except that he supplements this approximation with the ability to dynamically change the optical depth to simulate atmospheric darkening for views at varying altitudes. To find the position of the sun in the sky, relative to the observer's position, we'll be using the algorithms outlined by [Jensen01]. To derive an accurate sun color for a specific time of day, the equations outlined by [Preetham99] will be used.

An important aspect of the atmosphere that will not be covered is clouds. A large amount of research has been done on high-quality cloud rendering; however, most of the proposed algorithms just aren't fast enough for real-time use. [Dube05] presented an impressive implementation using what is essentially a ray tracer within a pixel shader to calculate the amount of light absorbed by the clouds at varying depths. The only limitation was that an explicit sunlight direction could not be specified. [Reis05] presented a similar implementation based on the work of [McGuire05], which takes the light direction into account. An efficient solution would be to use the traditional scrolling-sky plane trick, where a texture is mapped to a plane whose texture coordinates are scrolled to simulate movement. This texture could also be projected onto the ground to simulate cloud shadowing.

And last, but just as integral, are the sun and moon. Since we'll only be talking about the sky dome method, the easiest way to get a moving sun and moon is by projecting a sun or moon image onto the geometry using a projective texture matrix. Calculating this matrix takes quite a bit of work, and caching the results for certain times of day could potentially take up quite a bit of memory (depending on the sampling frequency). A possible optimization would be to draw your sun and moon onto a cube map that is then loaded by the game, and rotated based on the current time of day. Rotating a cube map within a shader takes quite a few instructions though, so a cost-effect way of drawing the sun and moon is difficult to find.

The Bottlenecks

When rendering your sky, there are a number of performance-related issues that may arise, depending on the technique you are using. If your approach is done exclusively or even partially on the CPU, you may run into a number of CPU-related bottlenecks that need to be resolved. On the other hand, if you're taking complete advantage of 3D hardware acceleration, you may have an entirely different set of performance bottlenecks.

With the next generation of games making extensive use of pixel shaders, it's quite possible that the majority of them could become pixel-bound. The number of vertices in a scene is variable and based on how the triangles in a scene are constructed (i.e., via triangle lists or strips); and although the number of pixels on the screen is proportional to the screen resolution, the number of times a pixel shader executes for a physical pixel on the screen is also variable because of overdraw. When a mesh is sent to the video card to be drawn, its vertices are projected onto the screen and must be filled. Even though the video card tries to be relatively intelligent about rejecting pixels that aren't visible, the fact that the video card must consider them alone can warrant performance penalty. Although a pixel is not drawn, it can still affect performance; some pixels (due to blending) are always considered, and extreme care must be taken to optimize their shaders. Early depth rejection (through the pre-z pass) and reducing instruction counts through texture lookups (which can be very speedy) are often the way to go to reduce shader expense and complexity.

So let's talk about where a sky implementation may be bound. In the "old" days of sky boxes, one of the biggest concerns was what resolution to use. Pretend we were using a cube map that is 512 × 512 texels in resolution. Depending on the distance to or size of that part of the sky, as well as the texture-filtering method used, you could potentially be drawing either more or less than 512 × 512 pixels. This leads to fill-rate issues, where a large number of texture samples could potentially eat up your performance at high-resolution settings (where there are more pixels to fill in).

Weighing the Benefits of a Vertex- or Pixel-Based Sky

In our situation, where we could be doing quite a number of computations per-pixel, this could really hurt us. The obvious solution would be transfer the possible calculations per-vertex and only take the texture sample hit in the pixel shader. This has its own unique set of issues, however. Assuming we're at least using bilinear filtering, the color values are interpolated across the surface of a triangle between all of its triangles; and although this helps to simulate a smooth range of values, it will also leave you with harsh artifacting due to the low sampling frequency of a low-polygon mesh. This can definitely ruin any chance of nice color gradients across the sky.

So where does this leave us? Well, we could either bite the bullet and eat the potential cost in favor of higher quality, and go with a very low-resolution mesh but do our work per-pixel, or we could use a medium- to high-polygon mesh and do the computations per vertex. The choice is really yours and is based on where your main bottlenecks lie (either vertex or pixel). When talking about the generalized equations, however, we'll assume we're talking about the vertex shader version (for simplicity's sake). In practice, both methods are usable, because they scale effectively for different hardware configurations. Presenting each option individually to the user is way too complex and is certainly not the way to go, so a generic "sky detail" slider as a graphics option could easily toggle between any of the available methods invisibly, with a default value set based on the hardware detected.

Another thing to consider is how you've decided to present precalculated constants and lookup tables for your shaders. In the accompanying demo provided on the

ON THE CD

CD-ROM, we show how to precalculate a pseudo-optical depth needed by the shader to simulate the intense color of the atmosphere near the horizon and the darkening of the sky as the user gains altitude. (The implementation is meant to be very simple, so it forgoes calculating the altitude change to the pseudo-optical depth. [Nielsen03], however, does describe an effective method to simulate this.)

The vertex format for the dome vertex buffer must be prepared to take the optical depth as an additional texture coordinate uniform parameter. Following is the dome vertex declaration:

```
const D3DVERTEXELEMENT9 g_DomeVertexDecl[] =
{
        { 0, 0, D3DDECLTYPE_FLOAT3, D3DDECLMETHOD_DEFAULT,
D3DDECLUSAGE_POSITION, 0 },
        { 0, 12, D3DDECLTYPE_FLOAT3, D3DDECLMETHOD_DEFAULT,
D3DDECLUSAGE_NORMAL, 0 },
        { 0, 24, D3DDECLTYPE_FLOAT3, D3DDECLMETHOD_DEFAULT,
D3DDECLUSAGE_TANGENT, 0 },
        { 0, 36, D3DDECLTYPE_FLOAT3, D3DDECLMETHOD_DEFAULT,
D3DDECLUSAGE_BINORMAL, 0 },
        { 0, 48, D3DDECLTYPE_FLOAT2, D3DDECLMETHOD_DEFAULT,
D3DDECLUSAGE_TEXCOORD, 0 },
        { 0, 56, D3DDECLTYPE_FLOAT1, D3DDECLMETHOD_DEFAULT,
D3DDECLUSAGE_TEXCOORD, 1 },
        D3DDECL_END()
};
```

Specifying additional vertex elements through vertex streams is probably a better way to add the additional elements to the vertex format, but we choose to just use a different usage index. Below you can see how the values are filled in for the model vertex buffers:

```
// Precalculate any constants for the Dome Models.
const float fInv = 1.0f / 5.0f;
for ( int i = 0; i < 3; i++ )
{
        DomeVertex *pVertices;
        g_DomeModels[ i ].LockVertices( (void **) &pVertices );

        int iNumVerts = g_DomeModels[ i ].GetNumVerts();
        for ( int j = 0; j < iNumVerts; j++, ++pVertices )
        {
pVertices->fOpticalDepth
        = 1.7f - powf( fabs( pVertices->vNormal.y ), fInv );
        }

        g_DomeModels[ i ].UnlockVertices();
}
```

In the shader, the vertex input structure has the optical depth as an input parameter:

```
float OpticalDepth : TEXCOORD1;
```

Finally, in the vertex shader, the optical depth is directly read and either used there or sent to the pixel shader as a texture coordinate, where it will be interpolated per pixel. This brings up a good point. Originally this value was calculated as needed in the vertex program, using the vertex position directly. But passing the vertex position to the pixel shader and then calculating this value there often results in much smoother values. The answer as to why should be obvious. Whenever you pass a value from the vertex program to the pixel shader through texture coordinates, that value is interpolated using the graphics hardware. This is why you need to renormalize light or eye vectors when passed there for per-pixel lighting. We need to take this fact into consideration whenever dealing with any data we get on a per-vertex basis. Using this optimization, for instance, leaves us with a low-polygon mesh (100 polygons or less) that will not give us enough range of values to present the sky effectively using the vertex shader technique.

Although we've given quite a few suggestions on ways to increase performance for your sky implementations, as stated previously, the most intensive operations that are being done are those done every frame, either per vertex or per pixel. What we ultimately need to do is find some way of caching a specific state-of-the-sky dome in a way that we can use for at least a few frames. The problem, of course, is that our scene is vibrant and interactive, so the view is changing constantly. The most direct option would be to directly capture the 3D environment to a texture, and project it into the scene in a realistic fashion. How do we do this?

Introducing the Cubic Sky Map

The cubic sky map is essentially a cube map that represents the sky, cached at a specific point in time. By rendering the sky dome onto the six faces of the cube map, we're essentially able to capture its current state and reuse it over a number of frames. Although we still do incur the fill-rate texture sampling cost, this is far better than the cost of all the computations that would have been done each frame either per vertex or per pixel. After the dome has been rendered to the cube map, it is mapped to a very simple box and rendered with the following pass-through vertex shader:

```
VS_OUTPUT_CUBEPASSTHROUGH RenderCubeMapPassthroughVP(VS_INPUT IN)
{
        VS_OUTPUT_CUBEPASSTHROUGH OUT;

        // Transform the position from object space to homogeneous
        // projection space.
        OUT.Position = mul( IN.Position, g_mWorldViewProjection );

        // Pass through the eye vector.
        OUT.TexCoord0 = g_vLocalEyePos - IN.Position;

        return OUT;
}
```

And here is the pixel shader:

```
PS_OUTPUT RenderCubeMapPassthruPS( VS_OUTPUT_CUBEPASSTHROUGH IN )
{
        PS_OUTPUT OUT;

        // Directly sample using the given vector (normalization is
        // implicit through the cube map).
        OUT.Color = texCUBE( CubeMapSampler, IN.TexCoord0 );

        return OUT;
}
```

As you can see, we call this a *pass-through* cube map shader because all it does is calculate the eye vector ray (i.e., the vector from the viewer's eye position to the vertex position) and passes it as an interpolated vector that samples directly into the cube map in that direction. Since the cube map by nature normalizes vectors, you don't even need to renormalize it.

As far as the cube map resolution goes—a high of 512 is imperceptible, while 256 down to 128 are acceptable and certainly worth scaling to, based on the user's hardware specs. At around 64, you start to notice severe banding and artifacts along the sky-color gradients, so quality is severely degraded. This happens most noticeably around the dome borders, but the player should never see them anyway, so it doesn't matter. Anything higher than 512 incurs a pretty hefty cost, so we recommend around 256—and if you've got the horsepower, 512.

Now, although caching the results is a fine optimization, it hardly helps if we need to render to a cube map every frame—the expense, of course, being that we have to render the dome six times for every cube face (five, actually, if you're smart and don't bother with the ground face). So how do we efficiently keep the cube map up to date? We render it sporadically. Depending on what time scale your time-of-day implementation works on (assuming you're using dynamic skies because of its ability for this), you'll want to have an update rate that refreshes the cube map whenever the time changes enough to be perceivable.

Time, on Our Conditions

A reasonable time scale would be about one game minute per one real second—so one game hour every minute, and one game day every 24 real minutes. At this rate, time changes would probably be perceptible around every 30 game minutes or so, possibly even more around dusk or dawn, so let's say every 15 game minutes to be safe. At this rate, you'd need to update your cube map every quarter of a game hour, so about every 15 real-world seconds. Honestly, this is plenty of time to do it, but we're presented with another problem here. Updating six faces of a cube map, never mind the actual scene view itself, can cause quite a chug on your frame rate. What we need to be able to do is spread the cost out. We do this by updating each cube face over a number of frames.

Now, we can either do them successively or sporadically over a fixed amount of time. The former method would involve just rendering each cube view, frame after frame. The latter (and preferred) method would actually calculate the times within the 15-second intervals for us to spread out the computations. Assuming we are only updating five of the faces (as we should be), that gives us a cube face update every three seconds. This definitely spreads out the cost very nicely, but there's still one more issue. Although we're not trying to update the time while rendering out the current time of day, we are rendering a different state for the sky onto separate faces at different times. This can be very obvious, as previously stated, for the times of day when the sky has a lot of perceptible changes. Unfortunately, the only option is to use a swap chain of sorts, where one cube map is being rendered to while the other is being drawn to the sky box, then switching jobs at the next time update. Doing this ensures we won't get any weird color shifting from the updated cube faces.

Dawn of a Demo

The demo and accompanying source code that are included with this gem show off a number of the methods and techniques discussed thus far. The code is highly documented and should be relatively easy to navigate through. Although it's not meant to be a focal point of the demo, a normal mapped terrain is used to make the ground a little more interesting.

The terrain height map was generated by World Machine Basic (www.world-machine.com), the low- and high-polygon meshes and diffuse texture by T2 Terrain Texture Generator (www.toymaker.info/html/texgen.html), and finally the normal map by nVIDIA Melody. (For those unfamiliar with the process of normal mapping, visit the Melody homepage at http://developer.nvidia.com/object/melody_home.html.) We use three sky domes to present the potential aliasing artifacts from using either the per-vertex or per-pixel techniques. In practice, if you've chosen to use a strictly vertex-based implementation, it can help to generate a dome where the number of vertices near the edges is exponentially greater than those at the top of the dome. This can help because although there is not much color variation near the top of the dome, the edges may have very stark color contrasts during dusk and dawn hours, which can be better represented if there are more vertices to simulate these values. This would also help for the pseudo-optical depth described earlier.

ON THE CD

Of particular interest in the code on the CD-ROM: You may want to look at how the `CSceneView` class works, and how the main view is generated and cube map render subview attaches to it. The scene view system basically has one main view and any number of child views that could be attached to it in any order or hierarchy (although a limit is enforced). Each view contains a number of parameters that describe how it will be rendered. Included with values like the view transform and projection matrices is the view target type, which describes where the view will be drawn to. This allows the dependent subviews, or even the main view, to be drawn to any number of textures, which can be used for things like planar water reflections, cube map reflections, (orthographic) GUI views, or even post-process effects over the scene.

As the time of day changes, so does the position and color of our sun or moon. In our scene, we only take into account global illumination from these sky objects. The lighting on the terrain is basic per-pixel phong shading, although a simple ambient term is approximated based on the color of the shadowed pixel. An interesting technique would be to take the cube sky map that we've already generated and use it as a color guide for our ambient. For instance, at dusk when the sky is many different colors, the unlit portion of the terrain might take on some faint color from the sky in its direction, instead of just the globally defined ambient color. We may even want to convolute the cube map to simulate a more proper light diffusion. Doing so, however, can be pretty expensive, as it requires either sampling multiple points and summing their average result at run-time, or downloading and convoluting the cube map on the CPU (which is incredibly expensive).

Sampling the cube map in world space alone is not something you do lightly, and we recommend this merely as an advanced-technique suggestion (i.e., it's probably not practical for games). Using some clever heuristics, it's possible to alter the ambient light values based on the time of day. This could help to "normalize" the lighting contributions over the course of the day so at the sun's highest point, the scene is not too bright, but at night the scene is not too dark. Also, calculating pseudo bump-mapped lighting using some kind of constant light term can help to retain the increased level of detail when using normal mapping with low-polygon models.

For haze/fog, we implemented a simple extinction model that is evaluated for all the objects in the scene. We considered implementing the single scattering model presented by [Sun05] but decided against it, as haze is expensive enough on its own. The haze density value along with a number of other graphics options can be easily toggled from the GUI. We implore the reader, however, to explore any method that may increase the visual realism of aerial perspective, while maintaining reasonable performance.

Down the Horizon

One last thing we'll touch on from the demo is high dynamic range rendering. A real-world scene has an incredible dynamic range—according to [Reinhard02], approximately 10 orders of absolute range and 4 orders of dynamic range from shadows to highlights. Simulating this in an outdoor environment is incredibly important, especially if you want to apply post-processing effects like glare to very bright parts of the scene, like the sun during the day or even the moon at night, when those objects are the brightest parts of the sky. Using tone-mapping with floating-point buffers (and even a floating-point cube map) can be expensive, however, so we urge caution. Using standard glow or intensity-ranged glare (stored in the alpha channel for instance) over a scene can certainly wash out and blur important detail; but at the very least, it can offer better performance in the long run. Also, make sure to choose a standardized range that is able to represent all possible objects in a scene. Although during the day there won't be any objects brighter than the sun, going inside will drastically alter how the values are mapped, so special care must be taken when applying high-intensity lighting values.

Although the demo was made as close to a game environment as possible, there was just no way to present all the elements of a game without actually making one, which is quite an intensive process, as is well known. You can try to be as practical as you like, but in the long run, breathing life into a moving, vibrant environment will definitely require an incredible amount of performance. And as we continue to strive for more-immersive and realistic environments, we must try to balance our graphics pipeline and techniques to take full advantage of the hardware. Although we tried to show how high-level objects might affect performance, there are a multitude of small performance killers left unaddressed. In the long run it pays to be safe, so the special care taken to optimize your sky implementation should definitely take precedence over any additional features that might have been present.

Conclusion

In this gem we went over a number of practical and generic optimizations, and special tricks you may use to increase performance in your sky implementation, and showed them in the sky implementation provided. We also examined some parts of the graphics pipeline and sky rendering techniques to explain why we may be getting unacceptable performance, and how to identify where the bottlenecks may be coming from.

We hope you enjoyed the article and are able to take something from it for your sky implementation. Although we stress performance over visual aesthetics, more-realistic dynamic skies are a noble goal for our games, and we believe they are definitely attainable if modest care is taken to intelligently optimize for best performance on modern systems. Thank you, and best of luck on your sky implementations!

References

[ATI Atmosphere demo] Available online at http://www.ati.com/developer/demos/r8000.html.

[Dube05] Dube, Jean-Francois, "Realistic Cloud Rendering on Modern GPUs." *Game Programming Gems 5*, Kim Pallister, Ed., Charles River Media, 2005.

Intel Vtune. Available online at http://www.intel.com/cd/software/products/asmo-na/eng/vtune/index.htm.

[Jensen01] Jensen, Henrik Wann., et al., "A Physically-Based Nightsky Model." Available online at http://graphics.stanford.edu/~henrik/papers/nightsky/.

[McGuire05] McGuire, Morgan and Max McGuire, "Steep Parallax Mapping." Available online at http://graphics.cs.brown.edu/games/SteepParallax/.

[Nielsen03] Nielsen, Ralf Stokholm, "Real Time Rendering of Atmospheric Scattering Effects for Flight Simulators." Available online at http://www2.imm.dtu.dk/pubdb/views/publication_details.php?id=2554.

[Nishita00] Nishita, Tomoyuki., et al. "Display Method of the Sky Color Taking into Account Multiple Scattering." Available online at http://nis-lab.is.s.u-tokyo.ac.jp/~nis/abs_cgi.html.

[Preetham99] Preetham, A. J., Peter Shirley, and Brian Smits, "Practical Analytic Model for Daylight." Available online at http://www.cs.utah.edu/vissim/papers/sunsky/.

[Reinhard02] Reinhard, Erik., et al., "Photographic Tone Reproduction for Digital Images." Available online at http://www.cs.utah.edu/~reinhard/cdrom/.

[Reis05] Reis, Aurelio, Clouds-rendering demo. Available online at http://www.code-fortress.com.

[Spoerl04] Spoerl, Marco and Kurt Perlzer, "Advanced Sky Dome Rendering." *ShaderX²*, Wolfgang F. Engel, Ed. Wordware Publishing, 2004.

[Sun05] Sun, Bo., et al., "A Practical Analytic Single Scattering Model for Real Time Rendering." Proceedings of SIGGRAPH 2005. Available online at http://www1.cs.columbia.edu/~bosun/sig05.htm.

[Terragen] Terragen, Scenery Generator. Available online at http://www.planetside.co.uk/terragen/.

4.9

Powerful Explosion Effects Using Billboard Particles

Steve Rabin, Nintendo of America Inc.

steve.rabin@gmail.com

Explosion effects are common in games, but often they lack punch or intensity. This article explains how to create an impressive fuel explosion effect out of billboard particles on any 3D hardware platform, including portable devices. Since computers and video game consoles are currently not powerful enough to simulate real explosions or even replay precanned explosion simulations consisting of thousands of particles, game explosions must be caricatures of the real thing. Therefore, the goal is not to directly simulate an explosion, but rather to convey the impression that a powerful explosion has taken place. This requires a careful blend of approximation and caricature. The in-game explosion must attempt to look like a real explosion, but also exaggerate certain aspects to sell the effect.

The explosion effect in this article is a combination of six different particle effects: initial flash, radial flares, white hot inner core, intense fireball, expanding smoke, and debris. The effect is shown in Color Plates 11 and 12, as well as in several videos, on the CD-ROM. While the explosion does not resemble any kind of simulation, research in simulating both explosions and smoke inspired many of the techniques [Fedkiw01, Feldman03, Stam03].

ON THE CD

Initial Flash

When an explosion occurs, there is a moment at the very beginning when the viewer is blinded by light. While this effect is missing from most video game explosions, it is a critical cue that the explosion was both intense and powerful.

One way to simulate the initial flash is to create a single semitransparent particle with a very bright yellow/white glow that falls off completely at the edges. An effective method is to place a Photoshop lens flare in the alpha channel of the texture, as shown in Figure 4.9.1. The color component of the texture should be a solid yellow/white.

At the time of the explosion, the particle should spawn from the center of the explosion and uniformly scale up very quickly, taking up the entire screen. Starting at fully transparent, it should fade up quickly, then after about 0.3 seconds, it should

FIGURE 4.9.1 Alpha channel of a flash texture.

fade down very quickly until it is fully transparent (at which time it can be destroyed). This sequence is shown in the far left column of Color Plate 11 on the CD.

This technique works best for explosions taking place in the sky, since the rapidly expanding flash particles will intersect with the ground, buildings, and other objects, causing the familiar *z*-buffer intersection of the billboard particles with the scene geometry. If this artifact is unacceptable, another option is to create the flash using a post-processing effect on the entire rendered image.

Radial Flares

As you can see in Figure 4.9.1, the initial flash contained some radial flares. However, this technique is so effective that it's worth emphasizing in the explosion. The effect involves creating 10 to 30 pointy flares that are randomly placed around the explosion, as shown in Figure 4.9.2.

These flares won't be scaled but should protrude out enough so that they are seen sticking out of the initial explosion, with each being a random length. Each flare should be started randomly between 0 and 0.2 seconds after the start of the explosion. They should be fully visible on initialization and then start fading out after 0.1 seconds. Note that the explosion will seem cartoonish if the flares are long or if they fade out more slowly than this. If the flares are short and fade out quickly, the effect is almost subliminal yet very effective in conveying the intensity of the explosion. This sequence can be seen in the second column of Color Plate 11 on the CD.

Each radial flare billboard should be a narrow quad that points in the direction of the explosion, as shown in Figure 4.9.3. A solid colored texture with a cloud-like blob in the alpha channel works well for these billboards. A good color scheme is for the flares to be a dusty light gray at the center and then blend to a dirty light yellow at the

FIGURE 4.9.2 Radial flares randomly pointing away from the center of the explosion.

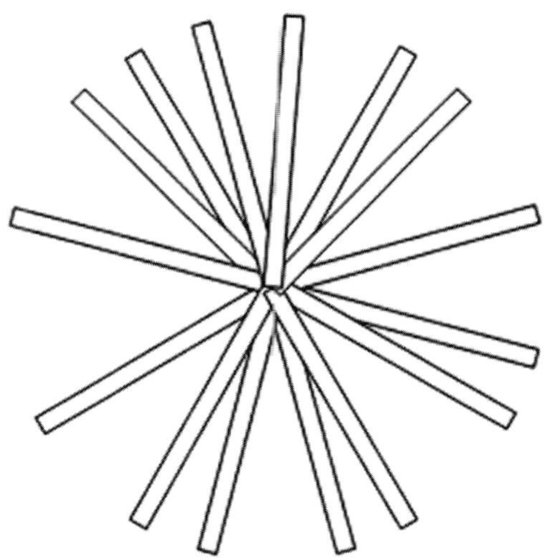

FIGURE 4.9.3 Radial flare billboards made up of quads.

tips. This colorization and gradient can be easily achieved by using a monochrome texture map blended with interpolated vertex colors to provide the yellowish tint.

White Hot Inner Core

The white hot inner core is a key component of the explosion effect. It starts out as a small fully opaque white circle fringed in yellow and orange. It then expands at a very high rate, yet the expansion exponentially decays over time until it ceases to grow. At its largest, the white hot inner core is a cloud-like white, yellow, and orange mass, as shown in the third column of Color Plate 11 on the CD.

From the time of creation, the core should remain at full visibility for about one second and then start fading out very slowly. This effect will act as a backdrop for the fireball and smoke effects, which will be described shortly. As the smoke and fireball expand, this white hot inner core will show through any empty spots and add to the mottled look of the explosion.

There are two ways to render the inner core. The first method is the cheapest, both for the CPU and GPU, and only requires only one particle. The second method is more expensive and requires about 100 particles. As we will see later, games can choose between the cheap and expensive methods in order to scale performance depending on the platform or the complexity of the scene.

The cheap method uses a single texture shaped as an amorphous solid white blob with a very thin fringe of yellow and orange around the edges. The texture should have a sharp but smooth edge in the alpha layer. This single particle will start off rapidly expanding (scaling up), but then slow down exponentially until it stops growing. Then it will fade out slowly after one second.

The expensive method uses about 100 solid white particles, each with a cloud-like blob in the alpha channel. By coloring the vertices of each particle yellow-orange and rendering them using an additive blend, hot white spots will appear on overlapping particles, fading out to yellow-orange at the edges. One effective color scheme is to use bright yellow-orange on the top-right vertex, medium yellow-orange on the bottom-right vertex, medium gray on the top-left vertex, and dark gray on the bottom-left vertex. It also helps to make different octants of the explosion have different intensities of the color scheme so that the core appears less uniform.

With the expensive method, each particle will remain the same size during the entire effect. However, the particles shoot out randomly from the center with a high velocity, exponentially decaying until the particle is motionless. Once all particles have stopped moving, the core will have reached its full size. After about one second, the particles should begin to fade slowly.

In reality, a lingering explosion will rise slowly due to its thermal buoyancy in the air and then drift in a given direction due to the wind. Both of these effects can be simulated by defining a wind force that blows softly in some horizontal direction with a slight vertical component to represent the thermal buoyancy. This wind should be applied to any hot inner core particles. This small touch helps to sell the effect.

Intense Fireball

The fireball is a secondary effect that kicks in after the first three effects. It starts at about 0.1 seconds after the start of the explosion and shoots outward from the center of the explosion. The fireball should start fully opaque and then fade out slowly after 0.3 seconds (as seen in the fourth column of Color Plate 11 on the CD).

As with the hot inner core, there are two ways that you can choose to render the fireball component of this explosion effect. The first method is the cheapest and involves a single particle. The second requires about 50 particles and is more expensive.

The cheap method uses a single texture shaped as an amorphous blob, similar to the cheap hot inner core step. The texture itself should be a mottled red fireball with black cloud-like edges within the texture, while the alpha channel should have a cloud-like density and amorphous shape. This particle will basically crossfade with the white hot inner core, scaling up at a similar rate with the exponential decay. After 0.3 seconds, the particle should slowly fade out.

The expensive method involves spawning roughly 50 particles in the center of the explosion. Each uses a texture similar to the cheap effect and each starts off very small and scales up slowly to a capped size. Each particle shoots from the center at a very high velocity in a random direction. The velocity will then exponentially decay until the particles are still, with only the combined wind and thermal buoyancy causing them to drift. Each particle should then fade out slowly after 0.3 seconds. To make the fireball more mottled, it helps to darken particle vertex colors in particular octants of the explosion.

An important aspect of the expensive method is stretching of the fireball particles in the direction of motion. As each fireball particle moves away from the center, it relaxes into a square shape. This effect is very important in creating the feeling of power bursting from the center. Figure 4.9.4 shows how the billboard quad transforms over the particle's lifetime. Note that the particles become larger and more square as they expand outward and slow down.

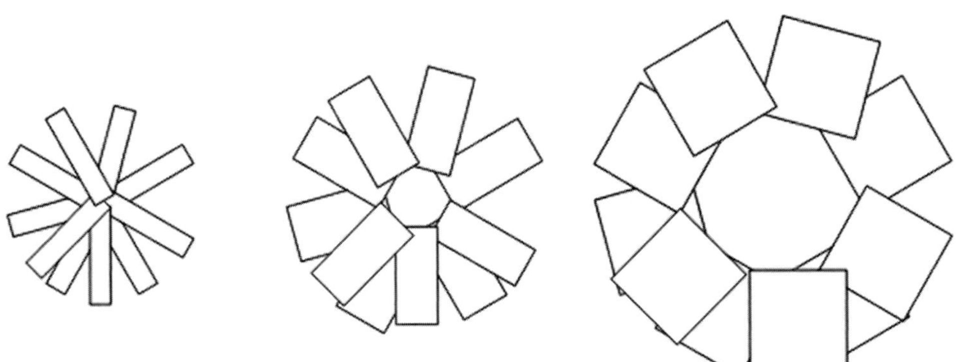

FIGURE 4.9.4 The transformation of the fireball billboard quad over its lifetime. Note how the quad starts out narrow in the direction of the explosion and then relaxes into a square shape.

Expanding Smoke

The expanding smoke is another secondary effect that occurs after the flash, flares, and core. It happens at about the same time as the fireball and generally overlays on top of all the previous effects. Starting at 0.1 seconds, about 30 to 50 smoke particles shoot from the center of the explosion (as seen in the fifth column of Color Plate 11 on the CD). The particle's texture should be a light gray smoke cloud with lots of billowing detail. The alpha channel should have a cloudlike density and amorphous shape.

The smoke effect is fairly important to the explosion since it will expand the farthest and linger the longest. There is no cheap way to create the smoke effect, especially since it provides the cover for the cheap core and fireball effects, masking their simplicity. Even with the expensive core and fireball, the smoke needs to be rather detailed to sell the effect. Many game explosions ignore smoke, but it is a rather convincing detail.

As the smoke shoots out of the center, it will use the same basic technique as the fireball. Each particle will shoot in a random direction with a very high velocity and exponential decay. Each particle should start out stretched in the direction of its velocity and then relax into the shape of a square over time as shown in Figure 4.9.4. After about 0.3 seconds, the smoke should begin to fade out very slowly (slower than the fireball step).

During the course of each smoke particle's lifetime, it should be carried by the wind and thermal buoyancy just like the core and fireball. However, there is one more effect that can add a nice touch. Normally, smoke has lots of billowing and interesting turbulence. This can be caricatured by rotating the smoke particles. The trick is to determine the wind direction as projected to screen space and rotate the particles to simulate subtle vorticity. All smoke particles on the left side of the wind direction should rotate counterclockwise, and all smoke particles on the right side of the wind direction should rotate clockwise, as shown in Figure 4.9.5. The rotations should be very slow, and each particle should have a different randomly determined angular velocity.

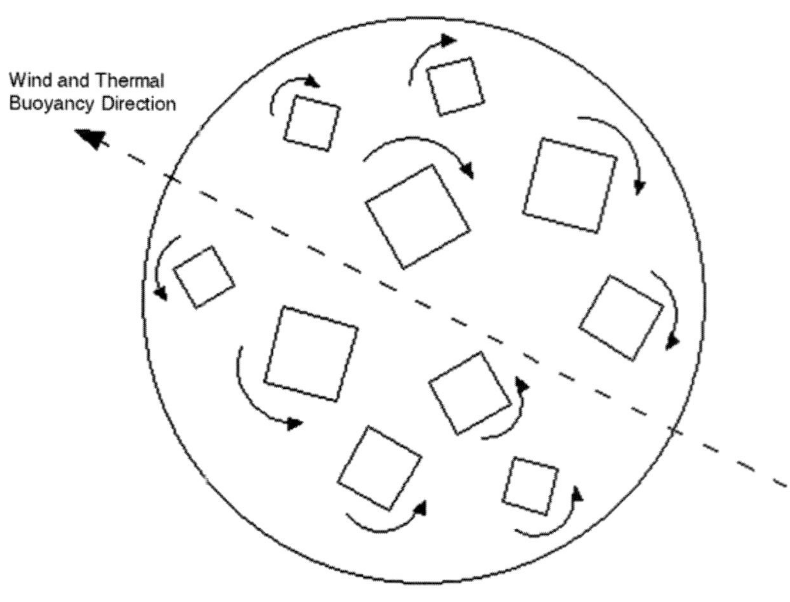

FIGURE 4.9.5 Faked rotational turbulence based on the wind and thermal buoyancy direction.

Debris

No explosion would be complete without debris flying from it. The debris can be embers, small dark chunks of dirt/metal, pieces on fire leaving smoke trails, or whole pieces of whatever just blew up. The debris should be given a high initial velocity and should not decay like the other gaseous effects. Instead, the initial velocity coupled with gravity should drive its motion.

Dark debris is quite effective, since it has a high contrast with the explosion itself. A cartoonish look can be achieved by having chunks of debris give off smoke trails as they sail away from the explosion. Usually these smoke trails give off smoke particles that start off hot white and change over time to yellow, orange, light gray, then finally dark gray. Of course, these smoke trails require rendering of even more particles, so the effect has to be used judiciously to maintain acceptable performance.

Effects Table

The previous effects involved many precise timings, velocities, and forces. Table 4.9.1 lists each effect with all the relevant data so that you can easily compare and recreate the explosion effect. Referring to Color Plate 11 on the CD will also help you understand the precise timing of each effect.

TABLE 4.9.1 Comparison of Effect Timings, Velocities, and Forces

Effect	Particles	Start Time (sec)	Fade Up	Fade Down	Scale Up	Outward Velocity	Other Forces
Initial Flash	1	0.0	Quickly	Very quickly	Very quickly	None	None
Radial Flares	10 to 30	0.0 to 0.2	Instantly	Quickly after 0.1 seconds	None	None	None
White Hot Inner Core (cheap)	1	0.0	Instantly	Very slowly after one second	Quickly with exponential decay	None	Wind and thermal buoyancy
White Hot Inner Core (expensive)	100	0.0	Instantly	Very slowly after one second	None	Very fast with exponential decay	Wind and thermal buoyancy
Intense Fireball (cheap)	1	0.1	Instantly	Slowly after 0.3 seconds	Quickly with exponential decay	None	Wind and thermal buoyancy
Intense Fireball (expensive)	50	0.1	Instantly	Slowly after 0.3 seconds	Slowly until square	Very fast with exponential decay	Wind and thermal buoyancy
Smoke	30 to 50	0.1	Instantly	Very slowly after 0.3 seconds	Slowly until square	Very fast with exponential decay	Wind and thermal buoyancy
Debris	10 to 100	0.0 to 0.2	Instantly	Depends	None	Fast with exponential decay	Gravity

Extra Touches

The billboard effects presented so far will create a nice explosion, but the following extra touches can help make the explosion really come alive.

Randomness

While this article presented a great deal of timing information for start times, fading rates, and velocities, the entire effect is much more effective if each particle is unique and isn't in lockstep with the others. Randomness should be used to tweak all these times, rates, and velocities, but it helps to keep the randomness within narrow ranges. Most of the particles need to behave similarly, so the randomness shouldn't introduce any large variations.

Screen Shake

When a powerful explosion takes place, the perceived intensity can be amplified by briefly shaking the camera up and down (not left and right). Not every explosion might warrant this effect, but close or powerful explosions will certainly be enhanced by the brief shaking.

Efficiency Concerns

There are several efficiency concerns that are raised when many explosion effects occur at the same time. The following explains how to deal with three such concerns.

Controlling the Number of Particles

In a game, it is typically difficult to control how many near-simultaneous explosions occur at a time, due to the unpredictability of the players or AI. Therefore, the cost of each explosion effect should be relatively small since the cumulative cost can skyrocket quickly. Not only must each particle be updated every frame, but all particles from all explosions must be sorted on the CPU in order to blend correctly with the frame buffer. As more particles are drawn, the sorting cost will rise exponentially.

The explosion effect described in this article showed how to make a cheap white hot inner core and a cheap fireball in order to limit the number of particles. The cheaper explosion effect uses about 43 particles (not including optional debris). The more expensive explosion effect uses about 230 particles (not including optional debris) and has considerable overdraw, which can be expensive for the GPU.

Choosing whether to use cheap or expensive explosions is one way to limit particles, but an equally important technique is to put a hard limit on the number of drawn particles and recycle the oldest ones when the limit is about to be hit. For example, a limit of 1,000 particles may be imposed so that the fifth overlapping explosion will start to recycle particles from the first explosion. Since the first explosion is probably far into its lifetime and already fading out, the removal of these older particles is generally not noticeable, especially since new explosions are very distracting to the eye.

Optimizing Billboard Orientation

During gameplay, it might be common to see half a dozen simultaneous explosions represented by thousands of particles. Each particle must recalculate its orientation in order to face the camera each frame. This represents some serious computation, but it isn't necessary or even desirable.

Within a single explosion, if each particle faced the camera based on its center point, the particles would intersect with each other and cause ugly artifacts. Therefore, the particles within an explosion must all be oriented in the same direction. The solution is for each spawned explosion to have a single center point that travels with the explosion during its lifetime (affected by wind and thermal buoyancy). This orientation can be calculated once per frame for each explosion. All particles belonging to a given explosion then use this same orientation, reducing the number of orientation calculations from over a thousand to less than a dozen.

Sorting Particles Within Framerate Constraints

With thousands of potential semitransparent particles, all must be sorted with respect to the camera so that they can be rendered properly. Unfortunately, this task falls on the CPU, so efficiency is a major concern.

It is well known that the quicksort algorithm is ideal for this type of sorting, taking on average $O(n \log n)$. However, the time that quicksort takes can fluctuate wildly each frame, even up to $O(n^2)$ in the worst case. This can be a big problem for games that are trying to maintain a fixed or respectable framerate.

One solution is to use a sorting algorithm that can be stopped after taking a specified amount of time, thus ensuring that it will never take too long. Obviously, this will cause some artifacts, as not all particles are properly sorted on every rendered frame, but this is a concession that may be acceptable in practice. The chosen algorithm must be incremental in that whenever the sorting is interrupted, the list is more sorted than when it started. Since explosions stay confined to small areas and don't move quickly, the sorted list of particles will be relatively unchanged from frame to frame.

One sorting algorithm that can solve the problem is the infamous bubblesort. This very simple sorting algorithm is well known to perform poorly, but it has two nice properties. First, it can steadily sort a list and be interrupted at any time while leaving the list intact and partially sorted. Second, if the list is sorted, it can escape early with as little work as $O(n)$. Therefore, the bubblesort algorithm can be capped, for example, to never take more than 3% of the frame time.

Conclusion

The combined explosion effect presented in this article is a detailed account of one type of explosion, performed completely with billboard particles. Since there are many types of explosions, it will take some careful tuning and creativity to caricature the explosion that you're interested in for your particular game, but hopefully many of the techniques presented in this article can be applied. The key is to study the type of explosion you're trying to recreate. This can be done by looking at reference material from the Internet, movies, and military documentaries.

Many game explosions focus on the white hot core or the fireball but could be enhanced by considering the other effects such as the flash, smoke, and camera shake. One of the key innovations in this article, shown in Figure 4.9.4, was applied to the fireball and smoke. This innovation of making the fire and smoke forcefully explode from the center is very convincing in showing a sense of intensity and power. Without it, the fireball and smoke just seem to be static puffs that quickly move away from the center. This disparity can best be seen in two of the example movies on the CD-ROM. The file explosion1.mpg uses the pointy fireball and smoke technique, while explosion1_alt.mpg does not. The other explosion movies on the CD-ROM are supplied to show different variations.

ON THE CD

Creating good explosions for games is a balancing act of trying to get the best effect within the limits of the hardware. Until we can simulate or replay explosion simulations with tens of thousands of particles per explosion, it will surely take both programming wizardry and artistic creativity to get the most bang for the buck.

References

[Fedkiw01] Fedkiw, R., J. Stam, and H. W. Jensen. "Visual Simulation of Smoke." *The Proceedings of ACM SIGGRAPH*, 2001.

[Feldman03] Feldman, B. E., J. F. O'Brien, and O. Arikan. "Animating Suspended Particle Explosions." *The Proceedings of ACM SIGGRAPH*, 2003.

[Stam03] Stam, Joe. "Real-Time Fluid Dynamics for Games." *Proceedings of the Game Developers Conference*, 2003.

4.10

Rendering with Handcrafted Shading Models

Jan Kautz, University College London

j.kautz@cs.ucl.ac.uk

Quite a few techniques have been proposed on how to implement more complex and more realistic shading models for graphics hardware [Heidrich99, Kautz99], making them useful for games. Still, these techniques are rarely used, probably due to two reasons: complex implementation issues and unintuitive parameters for the shading models used. We propose to use a simple technique called *normal distribution function* (NDF) shading. It allows an artist to handcraft shading models, with the shape and color of highlights simply stored in bitmaps. The technique uses per-pixel shading, and can also be used in conjunction with bump mapping. Anisotropic shading models can also be created.

Shading Models

A shading model determines how much light reflects off a surface, depending on the direction to the light source, l, the direction toward the viewer, v, and the surface normal, n. So far, most interactive rendering systems use the Blinn-Phong [Blinn77] model, due to its simplicity:

$$L_o = k_d\left(n \cdot l\right) + k_s\left(h \cdot n\right)^N \tag{4.10.1}$$

The parameter k_d is the diffuse coefficient, usually stored in a color texture map; k_s is the specular coefficient, often chosen globally, but sometimes stored in a gloss map; and the parameter N is the specular exponent, which changes the shininess of the material. The vector h is the normalized halfway vector between the view and light directions.

As you can see, this model mainly uses simple operations, except for the one exponentiation. On today's graphics hardware it can be implemented with a pixel shader [Mitchell01], since dot products and dependent texture reads are available.

Nonetheless, the lit objects often look like shiny plastic. It is nearly impossible to make a piece of cloth look like cloth. For anisotropic shading, which is used to render materials like brushed aluminum, Blinn-Phong cannot be used at all, since it is only isotropic (i.e., orientation independent).

Previous Methods for Incorporating Better Shading Models

A few methods have been proposed that can incorporate better shading models [Heidrich99, Kautz99], but these usually have limitations, such as unintuitive parameters, or require measured data that is not widely available.

Microfacet-Based Shading Models

Shading models that are based on microfacets (see [Cook81]) assume that the surface consists of tiny specular facets pointing in different directions (see Figure 4.10.1). These microfacets are so small that they cannot be discerned, but the overall distribution of their orientations governs the shape of the specular highlight. Hence, all the microfacet-based shading models use the distribution of the microfacet normals n_m. We denote the NDF with $p(n_m)$. What does this distribution tell us? If we look up a value with $p(h)$, it gives the percentage of the surface's microfacets that face toward direction h.

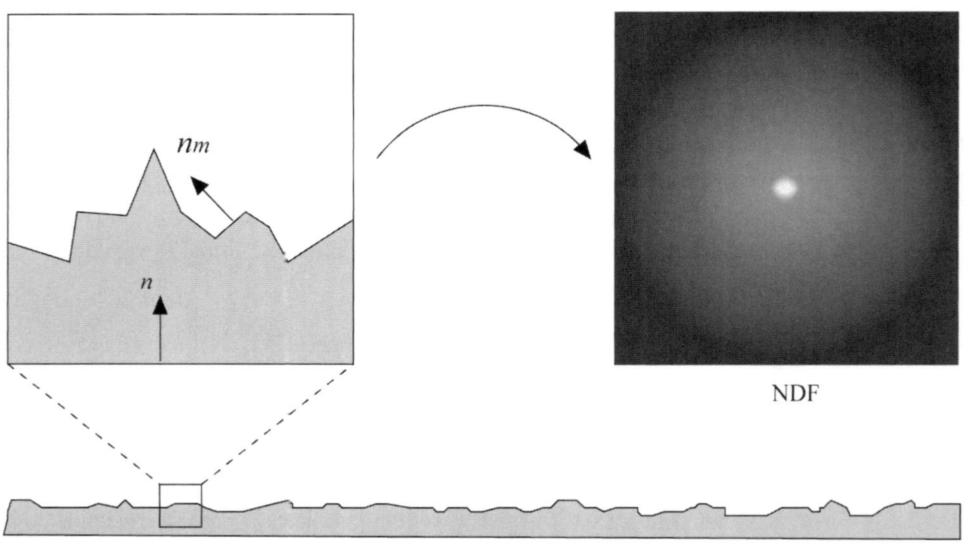

FIGURE 4.10.1 A surface consisting of tiny microfacets and its normal distribution function.

As previously mentioned, microfacet models assume that all the microfacets are small, perfect mirrors. If the halfway vector between the view and light directions is the same as the normal of a perfect mirror, we see the reflection of the light source.

This is almost true for a surface consisting of tiny microfacets. If there are microfacets with a normal n_m that is equal to the halfway vector h between the light and view directions, we see light reflected from the light source, but at the microfacet scale. The distribution function $p(h)$ tells us what percentage of the incoming light is reflected, since not all microfacets are oriented in the same direction.

The specular part of the Blinn-Phong model can be seen as a simple microfacet-based shading model. It assumes that the orientations of the microfacets have a cosine to the power of N distribution.

NDF Shading

The shading model that we want to use is just a slight modification of the original Blinn-Phong model:

$$L_o = k_d\left(n \cdot l\right) + k_s p\left(h_{local}\right), h_{local} = \left(h \cdot t, h \cdot b, h \cdot n\right) \tag{4.10.2}$$

As you can see, the only difference is that instead of the fixed cosine^N distribution, we use an arbitrary normal distribution function. The surface tangent t, binormal b, and the normal n define the local surface coordinate frame, which is also needed for bump mapping. If the normal distribution function happens to be $p(n_m) = (n_{m,z})^N$, we get the original Blinn-Phong model. However, since the normal distribution now depends on the full local halfway vector, instead of only its z coordinate (simply $h \cdot n$), we can also create anisotropic highlights.

How to Store the NDF

How can we store the normal distribution function so that it can be used with graphics hardware? We store it in a 2D texture map. Assuming the microstructure of the surface is a heightfield, the orientations of the microfacets can only vary within the upper hemisphere; in other words, the z coordinates of the microfacets' normals n_m are always positive. Therefore, it is sufficient to use the following two coordinates to index into our 2D $p(n_m)$ texture:

$$u_x = \frac{n_{m,x} + 1}{2}, u_y = \frac{n_{m,y} + 1}{2} \tag{4.10.3}$$

Figure 4.10.1 illustrates an example of a normal distribution function that was stored in such a way. Imagine a hemisphere where all the values of the normal distribution function lie. Now, we project this hemisphere onto a square plane. This is exactly what is shown in Figure 4.10.1 and what the mapping detailed here does.

Rendering Pseudo-Code

So, how do we render an object with this new shading model? Well, it is not much more complicated than the standard Blinn-Phong model. If we have already created a texture by storing a normal distribution function, then we need to do the following to render the specular highlight:

```
Given:
       a light source at position plight
       a viewer at position pviewer
Bind NDF texture
For every vertex vi of a polygon:
       Compute the normalized vector l from vi to plight
       Compute the normalized vector v from vi to pviewer
       Compute the halfway vector h = v+l
       Normalize h
       Retrieve the tangent ti and the binormal bi
       Compute ux = (h*ti+1)/2
       Compute uy = (h*bi+1)/2
       Set texture coordinates (ux, uy)
Render polygon
```

The diffuse term can be added either later or in the same stage if multitexturing is supported. An additional gloss map can also be applied, if desired.

Generating the NDF Texture

So how do we create such an NDF texture? We use a paint program to model our normal distribution, which is equivalent to drawing the highlight itself! Figure 4.10.2 shows a few highlights and how they look on objects.

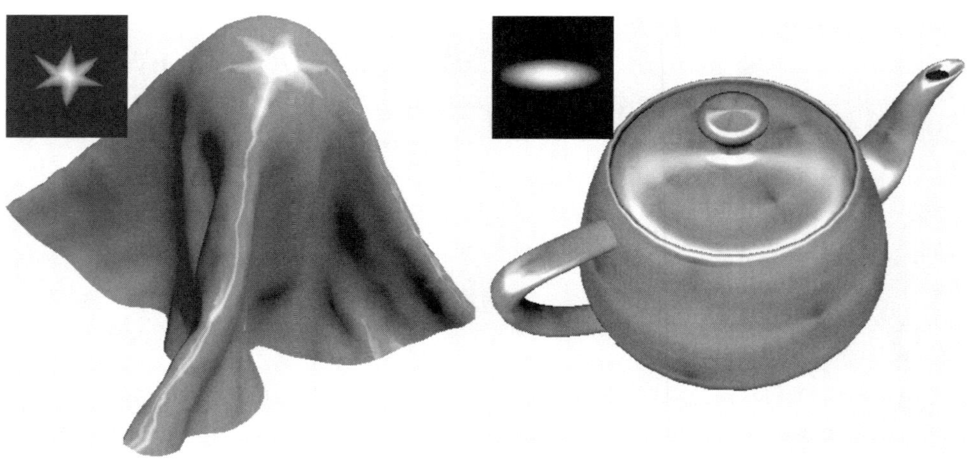

FIGURE 4.10.2 NDFs applied to a piece of cloth and a teapot.

Usage

We now will suggest how to use the diffuse term and the new specular NDF term to generate interesting shading models. If a standard highlight (as in the original Blinn-

Phong model) is desired, then the NDF texture should probably be grayscale, so that you can change its color according to the light source. The texture should not contain a directional diffuse term. In Figure 4.10.2, two different NDFs are applied to some geometry; a standard diffuse term was added as well.

More-interesting shading effects can be achieved by including a (colored) *directional* diffuse term. In contrast to the normal diffuse term, the directional diffuse term depends on $h \cdot n$. Therefore, we can include it in the NDF. This directional diffuse term can, of course, have some color, which makes it possible to achieve interesting effects.

In Color Plate 13 on the CD, on the left, you can see a piece of cloth rendered with a bluish directional diffuse NDF plus a red diffuse term. The cloth looks mostly purple, but at grazing angles, the red diffuse term has more influence than the blue directional term, making the cloth more reddish. In the middle, you can see an NDF that varies from dark red to bright red at grazing angles of the halfway vector, which is the opposite way an NDF usually looks like. Applying this NDF to the piece of cloth gives it a velvet-like look. On the right side, we created an anisotropic NDF, which goes from red to blue. Now the cloth looks like anisotropic satin.

Bump Mapping with NDFs

NDF shading can be easily incorporated with bump mapping, as long as you have dependent texture reads. It is almost equivalent to bump mapping with the Blinn-Phong model, only you have to compute the texture coordinates, u_x and u_y, with the tangent and the binormal for the lookup. This makes it necessary to store them in texture maps as well. Here is a pixel shader (DirectX8.1 notation) that will do this computation:

```
ps.1.4
texld r1, t0  ; Normal (tex1)
texcrd r2.rgb, t1 ; Tangent Space l vector
texcrd r3.rgb, t2 ; Tangent Space Halfangle vector
texld r4, t0  ; Binormal (tex4)
texld r5, t0  ; Tangent (tex5)

dp3_sat r1.xyz, r1_bx2, r2 ; r1 = max(n*l,0)

dp3 r2.x, r4_bx2, r3 ; r2.x = b*h
dp3 r2.y, r5_bx2, r3 ; r2.y = t*h
add_d2 r2.xy, r2, one ; r2 = (r2+1)/2

phase
texld r0, t5   ; tex0.rgb = k_d and tex0.a = k_s
texld r2, r2   ; NDF is in texture unit 2

mul r0.rgb, r0, r1  ; k_d * (Nn*l)
mul r1.rgb, r0.a, r2 ; k_s * NDF()
add r0.rgb, r0, r1  ; k_d * (Nn*lL) + k_s * NDF()
```

Extensions

The shading model could be extended with a Fresnel term and a (so-called) self-shadowing term, which refers to the self-shadowing of microfacets. This is commonly used in more accurate microfacet models [Cook81]. Although these two terms do change the resulting shading, in many cases they do not significantly add to the shading model, especially if point light sources are used for illumination.

One other extension is to include the area foreshorting of incident light for the specular term as well:

$$L_o = k_d(n \cdot l) + k_s p(h_{local})(n \cdot l) \tag{4.10.4}$$

This makes a big difference in the shading, especially if a directional diffuse term is encoded in the NDF texture. In the end, however, the use of this additional term depends on the effect/material you wish to create.

Conclusion

We have presented a shading technique that is easy to implement and easy to use. A wide variety of materials can be simulated. An artist can modify the appearance of an object in an intuitive way by just painting a highlight and/or a directional diffuse term into a texture! Although there is some physical explanation behind this shading technique, it does not accurately model any real world surfaces. Nonetheless, the visual richness that can be achieved with this shading model is fascinating.

References

[Blinn77] Blinn, J., "Models of Light Reflection for Computer Synthesized Pictures," Computer Graphics Proceedings (SIGGRAPH 1977), pp. 192–198.

[Cook81] Cook, R. and K. Torrance, "A Reflectance Model for Computer Graphics," Computer Graphics Proceedings (SIGGRAPH 1981): pp. 307–316.

[Heidrich99] Heidrich, W. and H. P. Seidel, "Realistic, Hardware-Accelerated Shading and Lighting," Computer Graphics Proceedings (SIGGRAPH 1999): pp. 171–178.

[Kautz99] Kautz, J. and M. McCool, "Interactive Rendering with Arbitrary BRDFs Using Separable Approximations," Tenth Eurographics Workshop on Rendering, pp. 281–292, June 1999.

[Kautz01] Kautz, Heidrich W. and H. P. Seidel, "Real-Time Bump Map Synthesis," Eurographics/ SIGGRAPH Workshop on Graphics Hardware, August 2001, pp. 109–114.

[Mitchell01] Mitchell, J., "Advanced Vertex and Pixel Shader Techniques," available online at http://www.ati.com/developer, September 2001.

SECTION

5

NETWORKING

5.1

Overcoming Network Address Translation in Peer-to-Peer Communications

Jon Watte, Forterra Systems

gpg.bestof@mindcontrol.org

Peer-to-peer computing revolutionized the way we compute. From the early research Internet of the late 1970s through the dial-up Internet revolution in the early 1990s to today's bonanza of fat broadband pipes, everyone is using computer networking for fun and for profit. More than 50% of all Internet users will have broadband when this gem is published. Although, with this popularity comes all kinds of problems: self-replicating worms, pings of death, and Windows security problems, coupled with heavy vendor scare tactics, cause most users to set up firewalls to protect their computers. Connection-sharing firewalls are a hot-selling item, as homes with multiple computers find that sharing a single broadband connection is the easiest route; prices having fallen to under $100 for a feature-rich wireless access point with router, switch, and firewall.

Online games are maybe one of the more exciting applications of computer networking technology, where the ability to compete with players from all over the world from the comfort of your own office, living room, or coffee shop has subtly changed how we view the term "buddy" and how we choose to interact online. Companies like Sony Online Entertainment and NCSoft make it their business to run large server clusters where players from all over the world can meet and play together. However, these big server clusters come with big leasing, power, and networking bills, and such services usually come with a monthly price tag for the end user. Thus, another popular form of online gaming is *peer-to-peer gaming*, where one player's computer also serves as the server for the game, and all the other players connect to this player, who is said to be hosting the game.

Unfortunately, some games are not as good at supporting this model of connection as others. Frequently, firewalls and connection sharing software get in the way of hosting games, and sometimes even joining games. While some users may be technical enough to configure a DMZ or port forwarding in their firewalls, many are not.

And even for the technical users, pleading with a Starbucks employee to give you access to their wireless access "hot spot" is unlikely to make that hosted game of *Warcraft III* come any closer. As a developer of a networked game, you would like to do better, and this gem will show you how.

Audience

This chapter is intended for all game programmers who want their game to work as well as possible on the Internet. It is especially important for programmers who want their games to use peer-to-peer, player-hosted servers, and want to extend to as many users as possible without telling users to configure port forwarding, set up a DMZ, or remove their firewall.

We assume that you are familiar with general Berkeley sockets programming (Unix) or Windows WinSock Version 2 (Windows). The technique shown will work equally well under either operating environment. For purposes of this gem, MacOS X (and higher) works a lot like Unix, but the code has not been verified on MacOS X. This chapter uses C++ for its code samples, but the techniques can be expressed in any language capable of using networking at the sockets layer.

IP Addresses

At the core of all networking is the network address. The Internet at large uses an address format called IPv4, which is short for Internet Protocol Version 4. What the first three versions looked like has long since lost its relevance. There is also an up-and-coming version called IPv6 that has so far failed to gain mainstream acceptance. In this article, "IP address" is synonymous with "IPv4 address."

An IP address is simply a series of four bytes. Typically, it will be written out in dotted notation, such as 192.168.1.2. An IP address identifies a specific network card or modem connected to a specific device on the Internet; these individual hardware devices are called *network interfaces*.

Devices connected to the Internet may run multiple services; for example, a Web server will often also run a Secure Shell Daemon (SSHD) that allows administrators to access the command-line interface of the server for monitoring and maintenance. To distinguish network packets destined for the Web server from network packets destined for the SSHD, the two most common Internet protocols add the concept of a port number. Each service uses its own port; for Web servers, the port is 80 unencrypted services and 443 for encrypted services. For the SSHD, the port is 22.

For games, the developer will often choose an arbitrary port within the allowable range. Ports in TCP and UDP addresses are two bytes, and thus the range is between 0 and 65535 inclusive, although tradition dictates that the port number is chosen in the range 1024–49151, inclusive. This tradition likely started with the arbitrary implementation choice on Unix, where ports 1 through 1023 are reserved for the special administrative user "root" on the machine, and only root may open new sockets listening for traffic on these ports. For more information, see [Man3rresvport] and [RFC793].

A UDP or TCP address thus consists of six bytes: four single-byte numbers in the range 0–255, inclusive, called the IP address, and one two-byte number in the range 0–65535, inclusive, called simply the port. The IP protocol suite specifies that all numbers larger than a single byte be sent with the high-order byte first (big-endian), and most sockets implementations supply functions or macros named `htonl()`, `htons()`, `ntohl()`, and `ntohs()` to convert between the local machine representation and the well-defined network representation of numbers.

Sockets Usage

A program running on a machine (we will call these programs "processes" and the machines "nodes" in the rest of this chapter) will typically play one of two roles: server or client. A server process will create a socket using `::socket()` and bind it to a local port and one of many local addresses if the node has multiple network interfaces, using `::bind()`. If the socket is used for TCP connections, the server will then call `::listen()` and enter a loop where it calls `::accept()` to wait for and accept incoming connections from clients. `::accept()` returns a new socket for each new client, and data is exchanged using `::send()` and `::recv()` using this socket. To tell the different connections apart, each TCP connection on the client side automatically allocates a new, unused port for the specific server connection.

If the socket is instead used for UDP connections, the process will enter a loop where it calls `::recvfrom()` on the socket directly after `::bind()`. All incoming traffic from all clients will arrive at the same socket. The network layer has no notion of connectedness, so if multiple, related packets are to be exchanged over UDP, some higher layer software (such as the process itself) has to take care of the coordination thereof. Return traffic for servers using UDP is usually sent using `::sendto()`.

For a client of a TCP service, after calling `::socket()`, the process will call `::connect()` to establish a connection to the intended recipient; once connected, `::send()` and `::recv()` are used for data exchange. The argument to `::connect()` is a TCP address that may have been looked up from a textual name (such as "www.there.com:80"), using name server functions such as `::gethostbyname()`. Meanwhile, clients of UDP just call `::sendto()`, passing in the IP address (again, possibly derived from textual form using the name resolution library), and receive data back using `::recvfrom()`.

In a typical process, many things will be going on at the same time, so thinking of "send" and "receive" as sequential events is usually misleading. Physics simulation, graphics drawing, audio mixing, and disk I/O are examples of other actions often happening at the same time as networking in a typical action-oriented networked computer game. The approach to managing these overlapping tasks is usually either to poll the network using `::select()` to determine what can be productively done, or to spawn multiple threads to deal with operations in different parts of the program. The supporting code for this article uses `::select()`(or on Linux, the `::select()`-like function `::poll()`), because it causes less synchronization overhead and leads to fewer threading bugs; the techniques presented are equally useful in either world view.

A specific process can be a server and a client at the same time. For TCP, this usually means creating at least two sockets; one that is listening and accepting new incoming connections and a separate socket that is connected as a client to some server on the other end. For UDP processes, multiple sockets are not necessary, because it is possible to `::sendto()` and `::recvfrom()` on a socket to and from an arbitrary number of peers. In fact, when using UDP, the concept of "client" and "server" is only visible at the application level, not in the network layers below.

Purists will note that the TCP protocol doesn't specify "clients" and "servers," but in reality, a process that calls `::accept()` is a server, and a process that calls `::connect()` is a client. See [Stevens94] for more details.

Routers, Peers, Protocols

A few more preliminaries are needed to flesh out the background against which to examine peer-to-peer networked gaming.

First, the Internet does not work like a telephone, where a wire is hooked up to the handset on one side and, conceptually, is hooked up through switches to a wire leading to the handset on the other side, forming a closed electrical circuit. Instead, from the point of view of the Internet infrastructure, each IP packet is separate from every other packet. When a process causes a packet to be sent, the local node makes a determination on which interface to send the packet; the packet then makes it through that interface to a router on the other end of that specific connection (the first router along this path is referred to as a gateway for the local node). That router then makes a determination as to where to forward the packet among its possibly many interfaces, passes it along, and so on. The process is repeated until the packet makes it to one of the interfaces on the recipient node and is delivered to the receiving process, or delivery fails. It is important to keep in mind that each router inspects all incoming packets and follows some kind of rule to figure out which interface to forward the packet to, or whether to just ignore the packet (known as "dropping the packet").

Second, because every node participating in the Internet has its own IP address (and, for most services, a socket listening on a specific port), there is no way to inspect just the IP address of a packet and know whether the packet is sent by a client or a server. On the Internet, all nodes are logically equivalent; they are said to be peers of each other. The notion of client and server is something that is constructed by the users of the Internet, typically implemented into the software running the processes on each node.

Third, there are a large number of protocols in use on the Internet. Some of the more common ones include 802.3 (for regular wired Ethernet), IP (packets containing an IP address), UDP (specifying a source and destination port number), and DNS (used for querying name servers to resolve textual node names to IP addresses). A given packet will usually make use of many of these protocols at the same time; a DNS query will be sent on port 53 in a UDP packet to some name server IP address, transmitted over Ethernet through the first jump to the DSL or cable modem. Each protocol is layered on top of the underlying protocols, so UDP is layered on top of IP, and DNS is layered on top of UDP (in this case).

UDP Packet Diagram

An example DNS query packet, as explained earlier, may look like the one in Figure 5.1.1 at the IP layer. Below IP, there will be additional framing, such as Ethernet, ATM, or PPP, which we have excluded for clarity because this gem deals only with phenomena observable at the IP protocol layer and above. We also disregard minutiae like packet fragmentation or van Jacobsen header compression, which do not modify the basic operation of IP networks at the level visible in this gem.

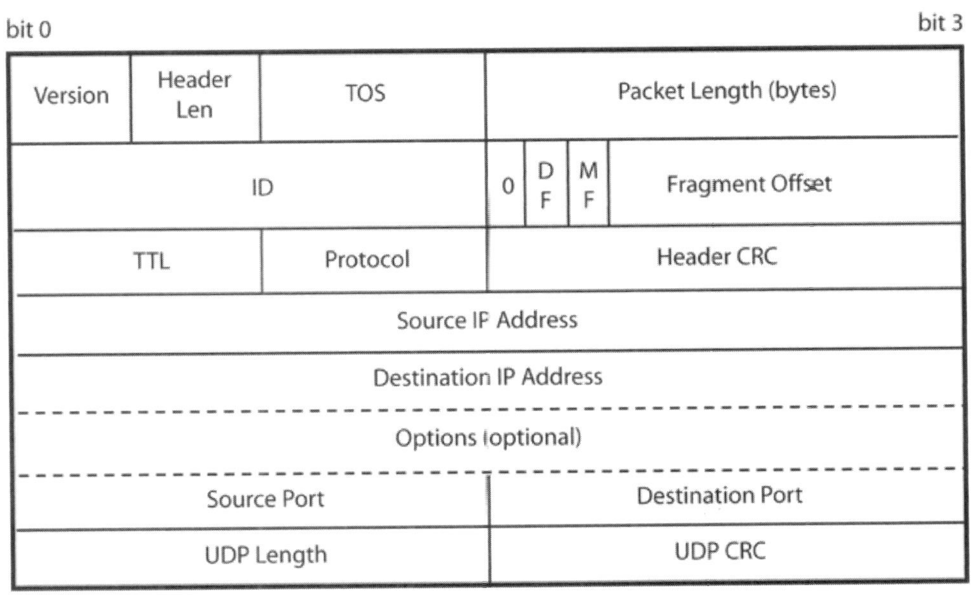

FIGURE 5.1.1 Anatomy of a UDP packet, with IP header, UDP header, and payload data.

Given all this knowledge, you should be able to write a networked game that works over the Internet as it looked in the early 1990s. However, time has moved on, and the introduction of NAT (Network Address Translation) changed all that.

What Is NAT?

The Internet started growing rapidly in 1992 and has kept on growing ever since. Because it is a peer-to-peer network, each node on the Internet needs its own, unique address. These addresses take the form of four bytes, so there is a total of a little over four billion addresses available in the world.

The Problem (IP Address Space)

At some point, we are going to want to add more nodes (or at least interfaces) in the world than supported by four-byte addresses, and even worse, the way that addresses are used at the routing level causes a certain amount of waste. In addition, the allocation between different parts of the world is sometimes grossly skewed; it is said that MIT has more Internet addresses allocated for its internal use than the entire country of China! Whether this is true or not, the Internet has been facing an address crunch, growing faster than the ability to allocate addresses.

Another Problem (Security)

Nodes connected to the Internet are peers to all other nodes. This means that you can type in any URL in a Web browser, and send network traffic to whatever other node that URL resolves to. Unfortunately, it also means that any peer on the Internet can send your node whatever network packet it wishes. Some network services are designed with more careful attention to this fact than others are, and a number of remote exploits (security holes) have been found, using bugs in networked software or even in an OS like Windows itself to take over virtually any node on the Internet, bypassing the need for a password.

Most users will be unable to fix application bugs on their own, and a better way of avoiding security holes through application bugs than just unplugging the machine from the network is necessary.

The Fix

A popular fix to the dual problems of IP address space shortage and keeping unwanted network traffic away has emerged; as previously mentioned, it is known as Network Address Translation, or NAT for short. Most DSL routers, cable modems, and Internet Connection Sharing devices use NAT to work their magic.

The idea is simple: most network protocols use UDP or TCP for their underlying transport. A port number and an IP address identify the endpoints communicating in those protocols. If multiple nodes can share a single IP address but use different port numbers, and the network could somehow distinguish which node to forward a packet to, based on the port in addition to the address, then you would only need a single IP address per household, company, or other subnetwork using less than 65,000 simultaneous connections.

The low-level network protocols like ARP that make the packets flow between nodes do not work well if more than one node share the same IP address, but there's a higher-level entity that fits the bill perfectly to implement this address sharing: the gateway router. If all nodes wishing to share one address (from the point of view of the Internet) sit on one end of the router, and the router is the only visible node to the Internet, then everything will be happy, assuming we can find some addresses for the internal nodes to use when talking to each other and to the router.

Luckily, some address ranges of the IP address space are reserved for experimental or private use. These ranges are `10.x.x.x` (with space for 16 million internal nodes), `172.16+x.y.z` (with space for a million internal nodes), and `192.168.x.y` (with space for about 65,000 internal nodes). These addresses are guaranteed to never be used on the publicly visible Internet, so using those addresses inside a NAT-routed network is guaranteed to not clash with anything outside the NAT. For more information, see [RFC1918].

In our example, the NAT device has address `10.0.0.1` on the inside and address `81.226.155.187` on the outside (with apologies to whoever currently uses that address). The nodes on the inside of the NAT are `10.0.0.2` and `10.0.0.3`, and the sample site we are trying to connect to is `64.125.216.191` (again with suitable apologies to whoever uses that currently). Presumably, the ISP for the user with the NAT box has allocated the `81.x` address, and the `64.x` address has been allocated by the hosting provider for the destination server, and found by the user using DNS.

Putting it all together, when nodes inside the NAT start up, they are assigned addresses out of a private address range, and their gateway is configured to be the NAT router. When they want to communicate with some node on the outside (say, `64.125.216.191:80` for a Web connection), they form their network packets as usual (say, using source address `10.0.0.2:6000`), and forward them to the NAT router. The NAT router then notices that the source address is from within its private network, and substitutes its own, public address as the source address, so for a device on the outside, it looks like the packet comes from the NAT router.

Unfortunately, more than one internal node may use the same port number for the source port. Thus, the NAT router must substitute a new port number for the original port number, in addition to its own IP address for the private source IP address.

Finally, in turn for returning network packets to make their way back to the right node, the NAT router maintains a table of (source IP, source port, substitute IP, substitute port, destination IP, destination port) tuples to be able to rewrite returning packets. In our example, illustrated in Figure 5.1.2, the tuple for a simple Web request is the first line of the table: (`10.0.0.2,6000, 81.226.155.187,11001, 64.125.216.191,80`). Once the port number 11001 has been allocated on the NAT to be used for the node `10.0.0.2` port 6000, this port number should remain allocated for that address/port pair for as long as the connection is open, or a returning packet addressed to `81.226.155.187:11001` will not make it back to the right place.

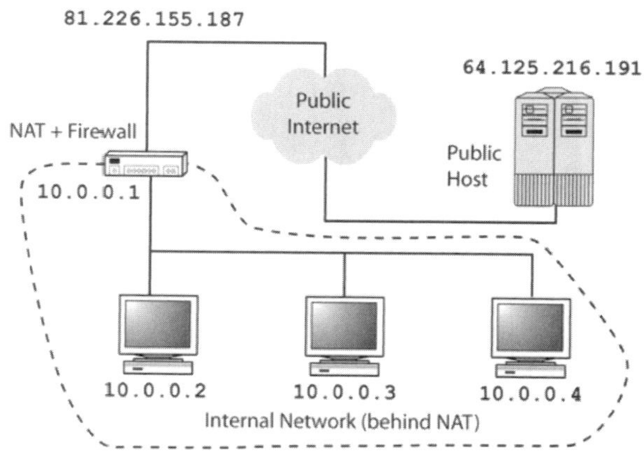

Internal Address	Public Address	Destination
10.0.0.2:6000	81.226.155.187:1101	64.125.216.191:80
10.0.0.2:53	81.226.155.87:53	195.67.199.27:53
10.0.0.2:53	81.226.155.87:53	195.67.199.28:53
10.0.0.4:53	81.226.155.87:11002	195.67.199.27:53

FIGURE 5.1.2 Example NAT-ed Internet connection.

Third parties cannot send traffic to the internal node, because the private address of the internal node makes no sense when interpreted in the open Internet; a packet addressed to `10.0.0.2` from the outside would not even make it to the gateway. Similarly, if a packet arrives at the NAT router with a source address or port that the internal node has not recently sent data to, there will be no tuple recorded in the gateway to translate the destination address to an internal address, and the gateway will simply drop the packet. In this way, a NAT router works a lot like a stateful firewall and often provides all the protection a typical home user needs from remote network attacks. It still cannot protect against attacks that rely on user behavior, such as sending Trojans through e-mail or enticing the user to click on malicious Web links, but it is a good first defense.

How Does NAT Break Client/Server Protocols?

The NAT router substitutes a public source address/port pair for the private address/port pair, remembers the destination address/port, and forwards the packet. For returning packets, it does the reverse translation, and the node on the internal network can communicate flawlessly with the outside world.

Unfortunately, this does not work for all protocols, especially protocols designed before NAT gained widespread acceptance, or without proper understanding of the needs of NAT. One prime example is the File Transfer Protocol (FTP) that is commonly used to download files on the Internet. When FTP was designed, it was designed so that one node could set up a file transfer between two other nodes [RFC959], [RFC1123]. The controlling node C would connect to node A, tell node A to expect a file, node A would start listening on a port, and tell node C what this port is. Node C would then connect node B, and tell node B to connect to node A on that port, sending the file. This also allows the control connection to remain open and issue more commands while data is being transferred on the data connection.

The common case of transferring a file to the controlling node C from the server node B is handled as a special case in the FTP protocol, where the port and address of node C are forwarded to node B, and node B connects back to node C to actually send the data.

The problem is that, because the receiving node listens on a port, rather than actively connecting to the external server, if a NAT router is in the way, the local port and address of node C makes no sense to node B when instructed to connect back. The NAT router translates the source address of the outgoing request to connect back to node C, but it does not have any knowledge of the actual data stream inside the FTP control connection, and thus the internal address and port of the socket waiting for the connection passes through untouched as data on the wire.

An example of how a UDP-based game may make the same mistake as the FTP protocol is found in Listing 5.1.1.

LISTING 5.1.1 Embedded Address Code Sample

```
// An example packet structure for
// connecting to a server.
struct CmdHello {
        char cmd;
        char len;
        unsigned short port;
        unsigned int addr;
};

// Get the local address of a socket; this is not
// something that's generally
// useful on the public internet!
struct sockaddr_in addr;
socklen_t len;
len = sizeof(addr);
::getsockname( sock, (struct sockaddr *)&addr, &len );

// This bad code puts a local address into
// a packet sent to a remote location – do
// NOT do this yourself!
Hello h;
h.cmd = CMD_HELLO;
h.len = sizeof(h);
```

```
h.port = addr.sin_port;   // don't do this!
h.addr = addr.sin_addr;   // don't do this!
::sendto( sock, &h, h.len, 0,
serverAddr, sizeof(*serverAddr) );
```

The Hack

Because FTP is a very common protocol with lots of clients in use, a fix had to be found. Ideally, that fix would not require changing all FTP clients in existence.

The fix that emerged involves adding smarts to the NAT router and having it inspect the data of packets of traffic to certain ports. Most NAT routers today know enough of the FTP control protocol to be able to intercept a control message containing an address and port and rewrite the data of the protocol to contain a public address and port; the router will also add the appropriate tuple in the active NAT session table to allow packets from the serving node to get back in.

While the FTP protocol is so widespread that it enjoys special status in the majority of NAT gateways (but not all), newly designed protocols cannot hope to achieve the same special-case status.

The Fix

The real fix to make a network protocol NAT safe is to structure the protocol so that IP addresses or port numbers do not need to travel within the data stream. The easiest way to make sure that this is sufficient for the protocol's needs is to always create a connection from the client to the server, using UDP or TCP, and always have the server reply back to the client using the address visible on the server when the client connects. No forwarding of connection information should occur over back channels between servers. Correct management of peer addresses is illustrated in Listing 5.1.2.

Some very advanced data center equipment exists that is NAT aware. One kind uses *reverse NAT* to load-balance connections, secure clusters against external attackers, or allow freedom in assignment and management of IP address space. Design of a communication system involving reverse NAT in the face of shared authentication has to be done with utmost care and is beyond the scope of this gem.

LISTING 5.1.2 Correct Address Management

```
// A proposed packet for acknowledging a
// (corrected) CmdHello packet.
struct CmdHelloAck {
        char cmd;
        char len;
};

// The server uses ::recvfrom() to correctly get the
// address of the peer that connects.
struct sockaddr_in addr;
```

```
socklen_t len = sizeof(addr);
union {
        CmdHello hello;
} command;
::recvfrom( sock, &command, sizeof(command), 0,
        (struct sockaddr *)&addr, &len );
// Server registers connected client on a received
// hello packet, and then acknowledges using
// ::sendto() to the received address.
if( command.hello.cmd == CMD_HELLO ) {
        // client_hello() is the function that adds
        // a newly connected client to some internal list
        client_hello( command.hello, addr );
        CmdHelloAck ack;
        ack.cmd = CMD_HELLO_ACK;
        ack.len = sizeof(ack);
        ::sendto( sock, &ack, sizeof(ack), 0,
(struct sockaddr *)addr, sizeof(addr) );
}
```

Other Problems

A variant of this problem is where a game server cluster uses one server for validating logins, and then passes the information about the player to another server, which attempts to return traffic to the client. Even if the public NAT address of the client is used, the NAT router does not expect to see traffic from the new server, so the return traffic is dropped.

Again, the rule to make a protocol fully NAT safe is to always initiate the connection with each individual server from the client, and to never send IP addresses or port numbers as data, but instead relying on `::accept()`, `::getpeername()`, and `::recvfrom()` (but not `::getsockname()`!) to get the address of the node on the other end.

To support the idea of a central login server that validates username and password for a server cluster, you could use a cryptographic cookie. Share a common secret (frequently, a 128-bit strong random number) between the servers. When the player logs in, the login server creates a hash of user ID, login time, and the shared secret, and returns user ID, time, and hash to the client. The client then submits this same information to the other server; that server need only verify that the hash of user ID, time, and secret (not known to the client) matches the hash supplied by the client, to know that the login server properly validated the name/password that goes with the user ID in question, at the time indicated. The strength of this system is mostly dependent on the strength of the shared secret (which should change every so often) and the strength of the hashing algorithm; on Linux, using 16 bytes from /dev/random works well for shared secret, and MD5 is a commonly used strong hashing function.

If you follow this advice, your client/server service will be NAT safe. However, how does this work when using peer-to-peer networking?

How Does NAT Break Peer-to-Peer Protocols?

Setting up and operating large server clusters is expensive. For a smaller game developer, or a game developer who does not want to charge players $14.95 a month for access after the initial purchase, allowing players to host their own game servers is an attractive option. There are security implications in that you can't really trust an arbitrary server hosted in some hacker's bedroom, but the popularity of peer-to-peer networked games all the way from id Software®'s *Doom*™ through Dice's *Battlefield 1942*™ and on validate the peer-to-peer gaming model.

However, the client/server model we have discussed previously only works when the server has a port and address that is publicly visible on the Internet for clients to connect to. Too often, this means that users behind NAT routers cannot host games, only join them, and if the game is not designed to be NAT safe, a user behind NAT cannot even join a game! With the widespread popularity of NAT in modern networks, this is not really a tenable situation. The diagram in Figure 5.1.3 shows a problem where neither node can actually talk to the other (on port 8960, presumably used by some game), because the NAT routers have no appropriate entry for the second node in their respective session state table. Here is where using the technique in this gem will save your game!

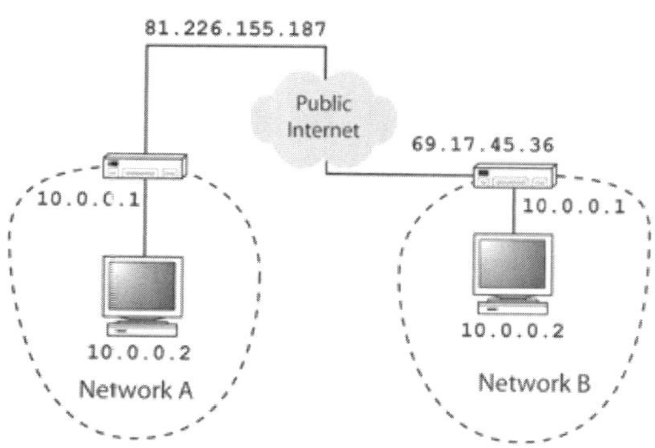

Internal Address	Public Address	Destination
10.0.0.2:8960	81.226.155.187:1101	64.17.45.36:8960

Internal Address	Public Address	Destination
10.0.0.2:8960	69.17.45.36:32768	81.226.155.187:8960

FIGURE 5.1.3 Neither peer can send packets to the other.

The Hack

Read the README.txt of many games today, and you will probably see mention of port forwarding. Port forwarding means going to the NAT router and telling it to make a special case for packets arriving at a specific port. In effect, port forwarding adds a permanent tuple of (internal IP, port, gateway IP, port, any-remote-IP, any-remote-port) to the session state table of the NAT router.

The effect is that any packet arriving at the designated port is only rewritten in the part of the destination IP address and forwarded to the specific machine set up as the port-forwarding target. Games with half a clue will require you to only forward a single port, and may even let you configure which port to use within the game. Games with less flexibility will require a specific port (such that you cannot ever host two games between the same NAT router) or require a whole range of ports to be forwarded. In the latter case, a user may go to the extreme of setting up a De-Militarized Zone (DMZ) host in their NAT router, which negates almost all the security benefits of being behind a NAT gateway, in effect, removing the NAT.

The Fix

Port forwarding is clunky, many consumers have trouble setting it up correctly, and it's often a support hassle for developers and publishers. The core of the problem is that each NAT router is lacking an entry in its session state table for the other peer with whom the internal node wishes to communicate. If we could somehow fool the NAT routers to add such an entry, traffic would flow correctly, and the game could go on!

Remember that when a peer sends a packet out through the NAT router, a tuple is added to the session state table, containing the internal and the external addresses as well as the remote address. As a first approximation, if we assume that a NAT router will preserve the source port of the internal node, assuming that port is not already in use by some other session, we could send packets to the remote node using its public NAT address and the known port. If each node starts sending to the peer in the same way at the same time, and both of them actually get the ports they expect on the NAT router, then the right thing will happen.

The Problem with TCP

This sketch for a solution might work for UDP (assuming we solve the port re-use requirement), but it will not work for TCP. The reason is how TCP connections are allocated: each connection allocates a new port number to uniquely identify the connection. There is no way, in general, to guess which port number will be allocated next, nor how the NAT router will map that port number, so unless you're willing to try 65,536 different port numbers at the same time, you can't really make the three-way handshake work in a NAT for a TCP connection, so we will return to UDP where the prospects for success are very good.

The End-to-End Solution for Games

There are a few too many "ifs" in the previously sketched-out solution. First, how would the peers know to start communicating to each other at the same time? Second, what if the desired port is already in use on the NAT router, and the router chooses to map the internal port to another external port? Maybe the NAT router implementation always remaps the ports, even, for implementation expediency or extra security?

Bonus Problem

Let us start with the first problem: how do the peers know to start sending at the same time? How do the peers even know what the visible (NAT) address of the other peer is? Ideally, the interface we'd like to present to the players is a roster of available, hosted games, where the player can choose to host a new game or join one of the games already being hosted. Good implementations of this game roster system include Blizzard®'s Battle.net® and the Xbox Live™ service by Microsoft®. *Warcraft III®* on Battle.net uses TCP, and peer-to-peer NAT introduction will not work through TCP, because each connection allocates its own local port. Xbox Live uses UDP, however, and experience is that its game hosting will work through most NAT boxes. So how do you find another player to play against?

Matchmaking

Browsing hosted games is not something you can actually do peer-to-peer, unless you do it using broadcast on a local LAN. You'll have to break down and get at least one server onto the public Internet, where games being hosted can register, and players can go to look up hosted games to join. The upside of this approach is that the traffic and performance requirements for this server are very low; a few hundred bytes per game being hosted, and a kilobyte or two per player connecting and getting the list of all games should do it, even for a game with a lot of active players. Ten-thousand players during a single night, consisting of a peak 3-hour period, break down to less than a single player per second; with the suggested bandwidth usage, you could host this on a single dial-up modem! Actually, we would recommend getting into at least a minimal hosting facility, because uptime, availability, and dealing with load spikes is important, and well worth the $100/month or so in hosting fees. As a bonus, you can probably run your corporate Web server on the same machine, given that the load is so low. If your game is wildly successful, scaling this solution up can be an almost trivial operation.

In the code file `sample.cpp`, the available games to join are held in the global set `gHosting` in the introducer server, where they are added in response to a `HOST` protocol command, as shown in Listing 5.1.3, and are returned to presumptive clients in response to the `LIST` protocol command, as shown in Listing 5.1.4 (error checking removed).

LISTING 5.1.3 Adding a Hosted Game

```
enum {
        MAX_NAME_LEN = 32,
};

// For Request::What::HOST
struct HostRequest {
        unsigned char what;
        char name[ MAX_NAME_LEN ];
};

struct Peer {
        std::string name;
        sockaddr_in addr;
        bool operator==( Peer const & o ) const {
return name == o.name;
        }
        bool operator<( Peer const & o ) const {
return name < o.name;
        }
};

std::set< Peer > gHosting;

// When the introducer gets a HOST packet, handle it.
void introducer_host( char * data, int len, sockaddr_in & sin ) {
        // extract the packet and make sure it's terminated
        HostRequest & hr = *(HostRequest *)data;
        hr.name[ MAX_NAME_LEN-1 ] = 0;
        // Record the fact that there's a new guy hosting
        // (in the real world, we'd also add a timeout-at
        // time, and do some login name/password checking).
        Peer p;
        p.name = hr.name;
        p.addr = sin;
        gHosting.insert( p );
}
```

LISTING 5.1.4 Returning Hosted Games

```
struct ListResponse {
        unsigned char what;
        char name[ MAX_NAME_LEN ];
        sockaddr_in addr;
};

// When the introducer gets a LIST packet, handle it.
void introducer_list( char * data, int len, sockaddr_in & sin ) {
        // I just dump all available hosts back – no
        // limiting, no matching, and above all, no re-
        // sending of lost packets.
        ListResponse lr;
        lr.what = Request::LIST_RESPONSE;
        for( std::set< Peer >::iterator ptr =
gHosting.begin();
ptr != gHosting.end(); ++ptr ) {
// Construct a ListResponse packet
strcpy( lr.name, (*ptr).name.c_str() );
// I put an address as data, but that's OK, as the
// address is publicly visible (::recvfrom()).
lr.addr = (*ptr).addr;
// Send the packet, ignoring errors (packet may be
// dropped anywhere, including in the network
// layer – too bad).
::sendto( gSocket, (char const *)&lr, sizeof(lr),
        0, (sockaddr *)&sin, sizeof(sin) );
        }
        // Send a final, empty host name to terminate the
        // list.
        lr.name[0] = 0;
        ::sendto( gSocket, (char const *)&lr, sizeof(lr), 0,
 (sockaddr *)&sin, sizeof(sin) );
}
```

Introduction

Once you have a game browsing server on the public Internet, a client should connect to this server using UDP on a single socket bound to a known port. The publicly visible, NAT-translated address of this socket will be visible to the game browser server when it calls `::recvfrom()` to receive network packets. The browsing server should send this IP address and port to all prospective clients wishing to join the hosted game.

In addition, the browsing server should send the publicly visible IP address and port of clients wishing to join the game to the game host. That way, the game host can attempt to proactively send packets to the joining clients. This will have the effect of adding the appropriate tuple to the session state table in the NAT router to allow the packets being sent from the prospective clients to be allowed through to the hosting server.

A server that acts as a repository of publicly visible IP addresses and ports, and furnishes these to other interested peers for purposes of NAT punch-through, is commonly referred to as an "introducer."

Referring to Figure 5.1.4, the difference from the case where we "correctly guessed" the public port numbers, is that the port used by the NAT router to represent the internal node can be arbitrary, because they are made visible to the other peer using the introducer. The wishful thinking that the port would always be untouched is no longer necessary.

Internal Address	Public Address	Destination
10.0.0.2:8960	81.226.155.187:11002	64.125.216.191:8960

1

Internal Address	Public Address	Destination
10.0.0.2:8960	69.17.45.36:32769	64.125.216.191:8960

Internal Address	Public Address	Destination
10.0.0.2:8960	81.226.155.187:11002	64.125.216.191:8960
10.0.0.2.8960	81.226.155.187:11002	69.17.45.36:32769

2

Internal Address	Public Address	Destination
10.0.0.2:8960	69.17.45.36:32769	64.125.216.191:8960

Internal Address	Public Address	Destination
10.0.0.2:8960	81.226.155.187:11002	64.125.216.191:8960
10.0.0.2.8960	81.226.155.187:11002	69.17.45.36:32769

3

Internal Address	Public Address	Destination
10.0.0.2:8960	69.17.45.36:32769	64.125.216.191:8960
10.0.0.2:2960	69.17.45.36:32769	81.226.155.187:11002

FIGURE 5.1.4 Peer-to-peer communication setup using an introducer.

Implementation Details

There is one fundamental assumption that makes this introducer-based solution work: when a specific (source IP, source port) address is used for source addressing, the NAT router will translate this to a specific (NAT IP, NAT port), no matter what the destination IP and port is. While we still need to send packets both to the introducer, and to the peer we're being introduced to, to create the full session state tuple in the NAT router session state table, if the NAT chose a different port for different destination addresses, even with the same source port and IP, then the return traffic from the remote peer would not arrive at the expected port, and the technique wouldn't work.

Luckily, there are three good reasons for a NAT router to re-use the same NAT port for the same (source IP, source port) pair.

First, on the public Internet, a client process sending a network packet on a socket bound to a specific address and port expects the sender of that packet to remain fixed, no matter what the destination is. After all, the application bound the socket to a specific port and used that same socket to send packets to different remote nodes. Note that this is only possible with UDP, not TCP, which by design allocates new ports on the client side for each connection.

Second, if the NAT router has several nodes on its inner network, it may be called upon to allocate many ports for a lot of simultaneously active sessions. The number of ports available is not unlimited, so the NAT will conserve port space and be able to serve more simultaneous clients if it re-uses the same external port for the same internal address, port values.

Third, NAT introduction is quickly becoming a standard technique. A NAT gateway that does not support this technique will be considered faulty by users, and will have higher return rates and support costs than devices that work properly. This behavior is also actively encouraged for all NAT builders since 2001, through the Internet Society document RFC3022 [RFC3022].

In reality, most gateways work well with this technique, because they do proper port matching. There are reportedly a few that do not; the only one we know of for sure that does not conform to RFC3022 is based on the BSD operating system and not very common in home environments. In 1999, some NAT routers would not deal correctly with a packet being sent from the internal network to an external address that refers to another internal address on the same internal network, as would be the case when two peers behind the same NAT router join through an introducer. This bug has since been worked out of most routers, and most devices on the market today should deal properly with this situation. While there is no workaround for the bug where a NAT gateway does not re-use ports, you can work around a gateway that does not allow internal hosts to communicate through the publicly visible NAT address by initially communicating both using the internal and external address of the peer in question, and respond to the address from which you actually get a reply, and picking the public address if you get a reply from both addresses, as the public address is guaranteed to be unique.

If you find that your client is behind a NAT gateway that is still broken, you can either throw up your hands and tell the user to fix the gateway, or configure port forwarding, or you can decide to eat the bandwidth cost of serving these users (as they are relatively few), and reflect their packets from your well-connected introducer service. Which option you decide on should depend almost entirely on what tradeoff between low support cost and low hosting cost you are willing to make.

Last, there is an implementation flaw in WinSock, the sockets library used on most personal computers connected to the Internet (it is what Microsoft ships with Windows). If you send a UDP datagram to a port that is not listening and receive an ICMP message back saying "port not reachable," WinSock will wedge the socket that sent the initial datagram and return WSAECONNRESET when attempting to use the socket. At this point, you have to close and re-open the socket for it to work again. This is highly inconvenient, because you are very likely to receive at least one port not reachable message when setting up the peer-to-peer NAT punch-through, before both gateways have created the appropriate session state records. Luckily, because UDP is connectionless (as opposed to TCP), the NAT gateway will not know that the socket has been closed and re-opened and bound to the same port on the local machine, and everything will proceed as normal. Typical WinSock code will thus look like Listing 5.1.5 to work around this problem (again, some error checking removed).

LISTING 5.1.5 Working Around WinSock

```
enum {
        GAME_PORT = 8960,
};
#define SOCKET_ERRNO WSAGetLastError()
inline bool SOCKET_WOULDBLOCK_ERROR( int e ) {
        return e == WSAEWOULDBLOCK;
}
inline bool SOCKET_NEED_REOPEN( int e ) {
        return e == WSAECONNRESET;
}
#define INIT_SOCKET_LIBRARY() \
        do { WSADATA wsaData; WSAStartup( \
MAKEWORD(2,2), &wsaData ); } \
        while(0)

SOCKET gSocket;

// Allocate the single, global socket we'll use in all
// roles.
void allocate_socket() {
        if( gSocket != BAD_SOCKET_FD ) {
::closesocket( gSocket );
        }
        else {
INIT_SOCKET_LIBRARY();
        }
        gSocket = ::socket( PF_INET, SOCK_DGRAM,
IPPROTO_UDP );
        // Bind to my port on all local interfaces.
        // Because I want to run multiple instances on the
        // same machine, I try a sequence of ports.
        // Once I've bound to a port, I want to re-use that
        // port if I re-allocate the socket, so remember
        // which port was being used using a static variable
        // (this means I can only open a single socket per
```

```
        // process using this code).
        static int portUsed = 0;
        for( int port = GAME_PORT; port < GAME_PORT+10;
++port ) {
sockaddr_in addr;
memset( &addr, 0, sizeof( addr ) );
addr.sin_family = AF_INET;
if( portUsed ) {
        //  use the old port if set
        port = portUsed;
}
addr.sin_port = htons( port );
// bind the socket to a specific port
int r = ::bind( gSocket, (sockaddr *)&addr,
        sizeof(addr) );
if( r < 0 ) {
        if( portUsed ) {
                //  if I can't re-use the old port, bail out
                break;
        }
}
else {
        portUsed = port;
        break;
}
        }
}

// There's a flaw in WinSock where I'll need to re-
// open the socket if I get CONNRESET on a socket.
// This is because it wedges the socket when it
// receives an ICMP for port-not-reachable, which can
// happen during NAT introduction negotiation.
bool maybe_reallocate_socket( int r ) {
        if( r < 0 ) {
if( SOCKET_NEED_REOPEN( SOCKET_ERRNO ) ) {
        fprintf( stderr,
        "Re-allocating socket because of WinSock.\n" );
        allocate_socket();
}
return true;
        }
        return false;
}

sockaddr_in sin;
socklen_t slen = sizeof( sin );
char data[ 512 ];
//  Wait for an incoming packet
int r = ::recvfrom( gSocket, data, 512, 0,
         (sockaddr *)&sin, &slen );
if( maybe_reallocate_socket( r ) ) {
        continue;
}
```

Conclusion

Using the technique presented here in this gem, your games should be one step closer to offering robust multiplayer gaming that works across a variety of networking configurations. As a result, wizards and warriors should be able to go about the business of saving the world, even from the comfort of their local Starbucks.

Trademark Notes

Starbucks is a registered trademark of Starbucks Corporation.

Warcraft and Blizzard are registered trademarks of Blizzard Entertainment.

Xbox, Xbox Live, Microsoft, and Windows are trademarks or registered trademarks of Microsoft Corporation.

Doom and id Software are trademarks or registered trademarks of id Software.

Battlefield 1942 is a trademark of Digital Illusions CE AB.

BattleZone and Activision are trademarks or registered trademarks of Activision.

References and Further Reading

[Man3rresvport] Unix section 3 manual page for the `rresvport()` library call; found at http://www.gsp.com/cgi-bin/man.cgi?section=3&topic=rresvport.

[Stevens94] Stevens, W. Richard. *TCP Illustrated*. Addison-Wesley Professional, 1994.

[RFC793] USC ISI. Request For Comments document 793. TCP Protocol Specification. Available online at http://www.faqs.org/rfcs/rfc793.html (September 1981).

[RFC959] Postel, J. and J Reynolds. Request For Comments document 959. Available online at http://www.faqs.org/rfcs/rfc959.html (October 1985).

[RFC1123] Braden, R., editor. Internet Engineering Task Force. Request For Comments document 1123. Available online at http://www.faqs.org/rfcs/rfc1123.html (October 1989).

[RFC1918] Rekhter, Y., et al. Request For Comments document 1918. "Address Allocation for Private Internets." Available online at http://www.faqs.org/rfcs/rfc1918.html (February 1996).

[RFC3022] Srisuresh, P. and K. Egevang. Internet Society. Request For Comments document 3022. Available online at http://www.faqs.org/rfcs/rfc3022.html (January 2001).

5.2

Minimizing Latency in Real-Time Strategy Games

Jim Greer, Kongregate and
Zachary Booth Simpson, Mine Control

jim@kongregate.com, zack@mine-control.com

Multiplayer real-time strategy games have different networking requirements than twitchy action games. Rather than transmitting the millisecond-by-millisecond movements of the player, they must manage hundreds of semi-autonomous units. This allows their network protocol to be optimized in ways that action games cannot. In this gem, we will describe *event-locking*, a time-synchronized method well-suited to the coordination of real-time strategy games. The technique could also be applied to simulation games and other non-twitch games.

Frame-Locking Versus Event-Locking

Early networked games, often written for local area network (LAN) play, used a technique called *frame-locking*. Under this method, the clients send out an update every frame; at a minimum, this includes all the user input that occurred during the frame. This update might be sent to all other clients (in a peer-to-peer arrangement) or to a central server that processes it and echoes the results to all clients. In practice, some such frame-locked games render more than one frame before sending an update; but the updates typically happen at some fixed interval. While this method is suitable for LAN play, it does not extend well to Internet play, even under low to moderate latency (150–300 ms).

Consider a network architecture with a central server. As long as all clients are sending in their updates at the same pace, everything is fine. However, if one client's update is not received due to network latency or other reasons, then the server and all other clients must freeze, awaiting the arrival of the update. If they were to proceed without waiting for the delayed client's input, the game would immediately be out of synchronization—the player would see the results of their actions, but no one else would.

Figure 5.2.1 shows an example of this arrangement as an event timeline. For the first update at time 0, Clients A and B send their updates to the server. The server receives both updates at nearly the same instant and sends the results immediately. However, for the second update, Client B's update takes longer in transit due to network latency. The server waits, and so does Client A.

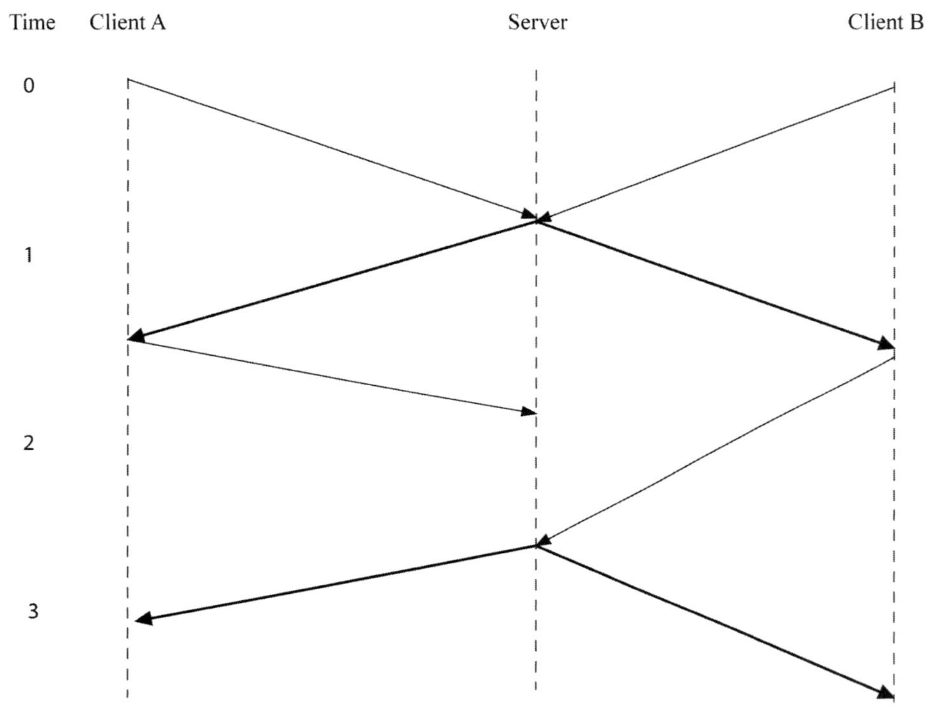

FIGURE 5.2.1 Freezing under frame-locking: Server and Client A are held up by Client B.

This behavior makes pure frame-locking suitable only for LAN games, but with modifications, it can handle longer latencies. For example, *Age of Empires* [Bettner01] used a peer-to-peer architecture with adaptive communication turn lengths. Pauses would occur when communications weren't received from one machine, but then the turn length would be increased to compensate. Instead of more pauses, players would experience slightly diminished responsiveness overall. Unfortunately, the performance of the game was still limited by the slowest network connection among the players.

Event-Locking

What is needed is a method that, in contrast to frame-locking, avoids slowing down all clients to the speed of the slowest one. We propose event-locking as an efficient method. Under this method, each client sends requests for events, which are evaluated by the server and, if approved, broadcast to all clients simultaneously.

For example, imagine a typical real-time strategy game in which one player decides that they want to move a tank. The player issues the movement command on their client, which performs preliminary legality checking. If legal, the client sends a `RequestMoveTank` packet to the server. The server then performs its own authoritative legality check, and upon determining that the movement is legal, sends a `MoveTank` packet to all clients, including the one that originally made the request. (For more discussion about selecting what actions to use as events, see [Dickinson01].)

Note that not all clients will receive the event packets at the same time. Therefore, events must be structured so that clients can begin execution at the appropriate time. For example, a movement event such as the `MoveTank` packet described above might contain a series of waypoints, each encoded with an arrival time. A client that receives the packet later can either warp the tank to the appropriate current position or, if the difference is small, simply animate its movement slightly faster.

It might appear that this arrangement would introduce unacceptable delays for players. If it takes 300 ms or more for their tank to start moving, won't they be frustrated? The answer is to give the player immediate 'request feedback.' In the simplest case, this feedback might be a client-side animation or sound effect. Or, for movement requests, it could be safe to start 'unofficial' movement on the client if server denial is unlikely. For example, in the `MoveTank` example, the tank driver can say "Yes, sir!" and start moving immediately, assuming that the server will confirm the movement the vast majority of the time. Figure 5.2.2 illustrates this example.

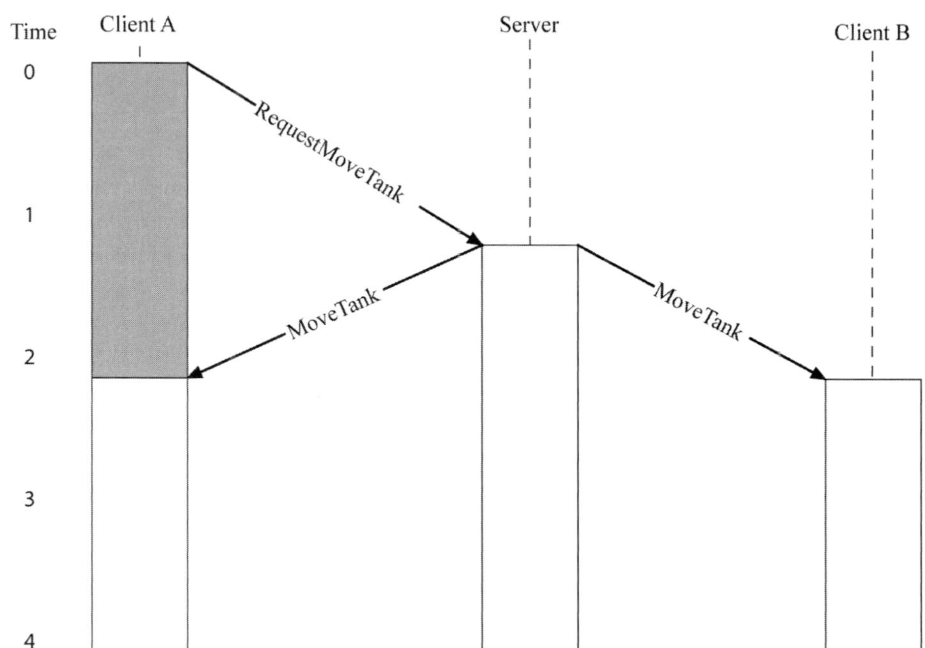

FIGURE 5.2.2 Tank movement example—the tank moves in boxed areas (gray is unofficial movement). All players see the tank arrive at the same time.

There will be cases when the server rejects a client's request or sends a path different than the one the client generated. For example, perhaps just prior to Client A issuing a `RequestMoveTank`, Client B requested the construction of a building near the tank. Client A might create a path that rolls the tank to the north and begins the movement in anticipation of the server's authorization. However, because the server knows that a building now exists in the tank's northerly path, it reroutes it to the west. When Client A receives the correct path, it must warp the tank from the unofficial path to the correct one, and this might be extremely disconcerting to the player. However, unless latency is very high, significant warping will be rare; furthermore, for many games, uncommon but dramatic warping is preferable to the alternative of common, but less-dramatic freezing. Furthermore, the warping will only be experienced by the player with the poorer connection.

The fact that some units might be in unofficial positions on a given client means that all important decisions must be handled by the server. In games that don't have a single final authority, out-of-sync bugs can be a big problem [Bettner01]. In many real-time strategy games, one of the client machines is also the server. Typically, unit creation, destruction, path-finding, and targeting decisions are server-controlled and broadcast. However, movement and attacks are animated independently on each client, generating no network traffic.

The following code illustrates how path-finding packets might be exchanged between the client and server:

```
void MoveableUnit::moveRequest( Coord destination ) {
    // GENERATE a temporary path and
    // begin traversing it. This will
    // probably be the same as the path the
    // server finds but not guaranteed:
    setActivePath(generatePath(destination));

    // SEND a RequestMovement the server,
    // even if this client also happens
    // to be the server:
    sendRequestMovement( destination );
}

void handleRequestMovement(
    MoveableUnit &unit,
    Coordinate destination
) {
    // This is the handler for the destination
    // request packet. Note that all clients send
    // requests, even the client who also happens
    // to be the server

    // This can only run on the client who
    // is also the server
    assert( thisClientIsAlsoTheServer );
```

```
        // ENCODE which unit is to move and compress
        // the path into a compact form:
        Path path = unit.generatePath( destination );
        MovementPacket p = makeMovementPacket(unit, path);

        // SEND the packet to every client
        // including the original sender
        // even if that sender is also the server:
        broadcast( p );
    }

    void handleMovement(MoveableUnit &unit, Path &path) {
        // This function is called in response to
        // a MovementPacket.

        // Note: setting the path may induce warping if the new
        // path is not the same as the temporary path on
        // the requesting client
        unit.setPath( path );
    }
```

Transport Layer for Event-locking—TCP

Assumed in the implementation of event-locking is a reliable delivery protocol, such as TCP [Postel80-2]. In other game protocols—for example, those that might be used in a flight simulator, where units generate traffic as they move—dropped packets are noncatastrophic because newer data will soon arrive to correct the loss. However, in event-locking implementations, the server sends each critical event only once; and therefore, the transport layer must ensure delivery. We have used and were pleased with TCP for this. Some game developers have written their own reliable protocols on top of UDP [Postel80-1], working under the theory that they can reduce latency by 'improving' upon the TCP algorithms. *We strongly advise against this approach.* Not only is the complexity of the task often underestimated, but so also are the ramifications. Smooth operation of the Internet depends upon the well-defined and well-tested flow-control mechanisms of TCP. Attempting to override this flow-control with a custom algorithm can induce catastrophic router feedback and possibly even temporary denial of service. (In the case that the game developer deploys their own centralized servers, this denial-of-service would most likely occur on their own routers.) One final point against UDP is that it is often firewalled on corporate networks because it is more difficult to secure. This implies that game developers will need to consider a TCP connection as a protocol-of-last-resort, even in the case that they implement a custom UDP-based system.

Time Synchronization

Performance of event-locking is significantly improved by time-synchronizing the clients. For example, imagine that when a unit moves, the server broadcasts a message like: "Move unit X such that it will arrive at position P at time T in the future." Without clock synchronization, time T on one client could differ from another client's by as much as the current packet latency (which might be much higher than the average latency). In such a case, a player with lower latency will have an advantage because they will see the world closer to the way the server sees it and are thus less likely to have requests denied.

Existing Clock Synchronization Protocols

Clock synchronization is a topic of major importance, and several well-developed protocols already exist. The simplest technique is incorporated in the Simple Network Time Protocol (SNTP). In this protocol, the client machine to be synchronized sends a datagram (UDP) packet to the server, which then immediately replies to the receiver with the time as it is known to the server. Although simple, the SNTP algorithm is not useful when accuracy is critical and latency is variable, because it does not attempt to measure or compensate for latency.

Unlike SNTP, the Network Time Protocol (NTP) does attempt to compensate for latency by sophisticated statistical methods. Unfortunately, NTP is very complicated and, more importantly, slow to converge on the accurate time delta. This makes NTP less than ideal for network game play where players expect games to start immediately and are unwilling to allow for dedicated synchronization time.

Further complicating matters, NTP and SNTP both use UDP in place of TCP to avoid the anomalous latency measurements induced by hidden retransmits that TCP might generate. As noted above, UDP is often firewalled by many Internet service providers, especially by corporate WANs, and is therefore undesirable.

A Simple Alternative: High Mode Elimination

An alternative to SNTP and NTP is required for games. Ideally, the protocol should be reasonably accurate (150 ms or better), quick to converge, simple to implement, and able to run on stream-based protocols, such as TCP.

We propose the following algorithm, which we call "stream-based time synchronization with elimination of higher order modes":

1. The client stamps the current local time on a "time request" packet and sends it to the server.
2. Upon receipt by the server, the server stamps its time and returns the packet.
3. Upon receipt by the client, a time delta is calculated by *delta* = (*currentTime* – *sentTime*) / 2. (Note that so far this algorithm is very similar to SNTP.)
4. The first received result is immediately used to update the clock, since it will get the local clock at least into the right time zone.
5. The client repeats Steps 1 through 3, five or more times, pausing a few seconds each time. Other traffic might be allowed in the interim, but should be minimized for best results.

6. The time deltas of each packet are accumulated and sorted in lowest-latency to highest-latency order. The median is determined by picking the mid-point sample from this ordered list.
7. All samples above that are approximately 1.5 times the median are discarded, and the remaining samples are averaged using an arithmetic mean.

The only subtlety of this algorithm is the discarding of samples with a time delta more than 1.5 times the median. The purpose of this is to eliminate packets that were retransmitted by TCP. To visualize this, imagine that a sample of 10 packets was sent over TCP, and there happened to be no retransmission. In this case, the latency histogram will have a single mode (cluster) centered on the median latency. Now, imagine that in another trial, a single packet of the 10 is retransmitted. The retransmission will cause this one sample to fall far to the right on the latency histogram, typically more than twice as far away as the median of the primary mode. By simply cutting out all samples that fall far from the median, these stray modes are easily eliminated, assuming that they do not comprise the bulk of the statistics, which is likely that they do not.

One very important consideration in time synchronization is that while the synchronization is running, *time might go backward!* It is extremely critical that any time-dependent checks used during time synchronization (e.g., animations during the startup phase or startup timeouts) do not slave themselves to the clock being synchronized. Failure to heed this warning could result in odd 'lock-up' bugs that will not manifest themselves until play-testing with players who span more than one time zone and are therefore likely to be mysteriously irreproducible within the developer's workplace.

This basic algorithm was tested in *NetStorm: Islands At War*, a real-time, Internet strategy game co-implemented by the authors at Titanic Entertainment (1997). The results were satisfactory and usually resulted in synchronizations of less than 100 ms. Anecdotal evidence in large-scale trials suggested that bad synchronizations due to retransmission were infrequent, and when they did occur, were often symptomatic of an unusually bad Internet connection that would eventually cause more-catastrophic errors (such as dropped connections), rendering the failure due to time-sync moot.

The following code sample demonstrates the statistical technique:

```
// GLOBAL variables holding time samples:
//———————————————————————————
typedef double Time; // or appropriate type for platform
Time timeSamples[MAX_TIME_SAMPLES];
int numTimeSamples;  // Num valid samples in the timeSamples


// CODE that calculate the time correction:
//———————————————————————————
assert( numTimeSamples > 2 );
```

```
// FIND the median:
sort( timeSamples, numTimeSamples );
Time median = timeSamples[ numTimeSamples/2 ];

// FIND mean of samples less than 1.5 times the median:
sum = (Time)0.0;
int count = 0;
for( int i=0; i<numTimeSamples; i++ ) {
    if( timeSamples[i] - median < (Time)1.5 * median ) {
        sum += timeSamples[i];
        count++;
    }
}
```

Conclusion

We had great success using the event-locking method. Our first multiplayer RTS, *NetStorm: Islands at War*, was released by Activision in 1997, and despite having heavy action with hundreds of units animating at once over eight clients, it required only a 9600-baud modem on the server machine and even less on the clients. *Next Generation* magazine described the network play as "smooth as silk" even on terrible connections. We hope you'll have similar results.

References

[Bettner01] Bettner, Paul and Mark Terrano, "GDC 2001: 1500 Archers on a 28.8: Network Programming in Age of Empires and Beyond," Game Developer Conference, 2001, available online at http://www.gamasutra.com/features/20010322/terrano_01.htm.

[Dickinson01] Dickinson, Patrick, "Instant Replay: Building a Game Engine with Reproducible Behavior," Gamasutra.com, July 2001, available online at http://www.gamasutra.com/features/20010713/dickinson_01.htm.

[Postel80-1] Postel, J., "User Datagram Protocol, STD 6," USC/Information Sciences Institute, August 1980, RFC-768.

[Postel80-2] Postel, J., "Transmission Control Protocol, STD 6," USC/Information Sciences Institute, August 1980, RFC-761.

5.3

Real-Time Strategy Network Protocol

Jan Svarovsky, Svarovsky Productions Ltd.

jan@svarovsky.org

This gem aims to explain a simple and practical system for connecting up to 10 computers over the Internet to play dynamic strategy, management, or combat games. *StarTopia* [StarTopia01] is a real-time strategy (RTS) game that supports four-player multiplay over the Internet. Player interaction involves placing and maintaining facilities, interacting with individual characters, and ordering troops around the battlefield. This gem is based on the simple network protocol we used for this game. Although this gem is primarily a description of the general principles, it includes our experiences, both good and bad, in an actual commercial implementation.

First, we will briefly discuss common protocols that we have come across, then cover the basic principles. Following that will be some refinements to the protocol, a description of modules we found useful, and some of the pitfalls we encountered. We will also include a simplified example game. Part of the system found in *StarTopia* is on the CD-ROM.

ON THE CD

Other Protocols

The systems that concern us here are for games involving up to 10 players, rather than those for massively multiplayer online games.

Client/Server: First-Person Shooter

The most common protocol for first-person action games is that each player is sitting in front of a "client" program, which could almost be considered as a dumb terminal. A server runs the game, effectively remote from any client, even if in practice it resides on the same machine as one of the clients. The server tells each client what it can see. Each client tells the server what it wants to happen, based on player controls. There are refinements to smooth out the game, based on the client's prediction of server response.

This protocol benefits from its simplicity and its ability to avoid cheating (since the server can veto some illegal acts). Clients can drop in and out, but the game on the server lives on. However, it does require that the client's visible game state is small enough that it can be repeatedly transmitted. This limitation eliminates this protocol as an option for real-time strategy games where a tremendous amount of game state is involved.

Peer-to-Peer

With the peer-to-peer protocol, no computer in the game is more important than any other. Each computer "owns" a part of the game state and has a final say on what happens to that part (typically, the game-player entity and a few AI agents).

The benefit of this protocol is that the game state owned by the computer is instantly updated. In an ideal world, your computer owns the AI agents that are closest to you, since they are not as important to other players that are farther away. The downside is that any interaction between two characters or objects in the game must have a corresponding network packet so that different computers can establish a consistent outcome. Of course, as the size of the game state increases, the number of packets sent around the network communicating state increases quadratically.

Lockstep

As the name implies, a game using the lockstep protocol runs in lockstep with all computers involved. They start with the same game state, and game time is split into turns. With each turn, each computer models the game world to advance the action by one step. At the end of the turn, each machine tells every other machine what actions the user has performed. Since all of the computers know what all users are doing, they can collectively model the next game turn and stay synchronized.

This is an easy protocol to implement and has a relatively low bandwidth, since user input (which might be idle for many frames) is all that needs to be transmitted. The bandwidth is also unrelated to the size of the game state, which is a big advantage for real-time strategy games.

A problem with this protocol is that the number of game turns per second is limited by the round-trip network delay; at the end of each game turn, the machines must receive at least an acknowledgement from all the other machines before modeling the next turn. Keeping the machines synchronized is also fairly difficult. You have to ensure that no user actions directly affect the game, but rather indirectly affect the game via the network code. This ensures that all machines are acting on the same information, and this discipline must be followed. Similarly, you have to keep their random-number generators synchronized.

In a similar way to the client/server system, some cheats are difficult because any illegal changes enacted on the game state will cause that machine to fall out of sync with the other machines. On the other hand, because the entire game state is available on each machine, other cheats become possible—for example, changing the game to be able to see more of the map than usual.

Our Protocol

We based our protocol on the lockstep system, with several changes to limit its shortcomings. One machine is declared the server in order to keep the network traffic linearly proportional to the number of players. Otherwise, the network traffic is proportional to the square of the number of players. Each client only sends one packet per event (to the server), rather than one to each of the other clients. This method enables the server to be in charge of negotiating the game state when a machine drops its connection.

With lockstep, the clients collect input from the others between each game turn. However, we can remove this round-trip network delay between turns. The server simply broadcasts "advance the turn" packets on a regular basis, and user input from each client is broadcast to all machines upon being received by the server. This means that each user-input event must make the trip to the server and back before it can be processed, but the game turns continue to occur at a steady pace in the meantime (see Figure 5.3.1).

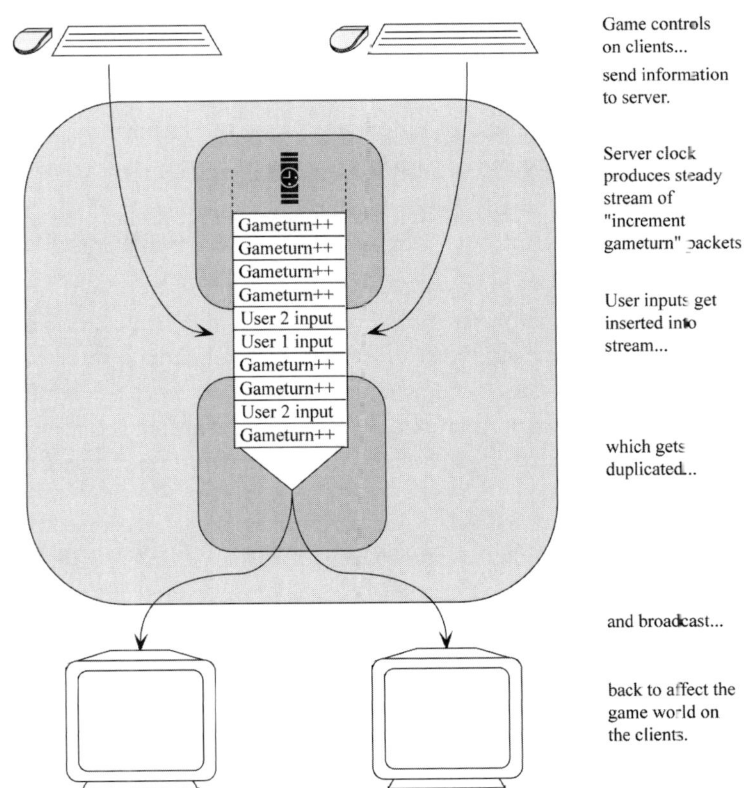

FIGURE 5.3.1 The server/client and game turn/time relations.

The main features of this system are as follows:

- At the start of play, the state of the game on all machines is identical.
- The server then sends an identical stream of packets to the clients. This is a steady stream of "advance the turn" packets, interspersed with user input.
- The game progresses forward based solely on information received from the server, which is identical for all machines. Therefore, the game stays synchronized across the network.
- For this reason, it is vital to decouple local user input from the local game state. User input gets transmitted to the server, which in turn broadcasts them to the other machines so that parallel action can take place.
- Game turns don't necessarily happen absolutely simultaneously on all computers, but game events occur in the same order.
- There is at least one round-trip delay between a user input and its effect on-screen. (This will be discussed in the next section.)
- All network packets must have guaranteed delivery. You want all user actions to get processed, so packets to the server must arrive. In fact, all clients must receive identical event streams, so packets from the server must arrive in order.

Number of Game Turns per Second

Several factors must be considered when deciding how many game turn updates should be issued per second. As will be discussed in the next section, the graphics engine does not draw the game state as it is, but rather as an interpolated version. This means that the number of turns per second is not directly visible to the player, so we must look elsewhere for this design decision.

There is a balance, of course. Lowering the game-turn rate has the following advantages:

- Most of the time, the only network activity that occurs is the server issuing game-turn update packets, so a lower number of turns lowers this expected bandwidth.
- Most game-turn processing is at a constant cost per turn, no matter how many turns per second there are. The simplest example is the movement of objects with a constant velocity. Lowering the game-turn rate reduces the CPU cost of modeling the game.

On the other hand, there are advantages to higher turn rates:

- Some game processing is better performed at a constant cost per second, rather than cost per game turn. For example, if your robots are meant to scan the surrounding area once per second, then halving the number of turns per second will double the amount of scanning that has to be done per turn. In the extreme, the processing of the world will be visible as a pause in the smooth rendering. In *StarTopia*, it was possible to create this effect by running a very low-spec computer with a higher-spec video card and then filling the game area with lots of activity. The frame rate is high, but the computer struggles with processing the game.

- When user input arrives, its effect is only realized in the game the next time it is modeled. This means that, on average, the response time of the game is lagged by half of a game turn. If game turns happen more often, this effect is reduced.

In *StarTopia*, we eventually settled on six turns per second. The *Dungeon Keeper* team [Keeper01] used four turns per second. In both cases, different numbers were experimented with, and in fact varied frequently during game development. A similar number of turns per second should work for most real-time strategy games.

Refinements

Once the basic protocol has been implemented, there are some improvements that will make the whole game much more playable.

Interpolating Between Game Turns

First, the clients anticipate when game turns will arrive from the server and try to interpolate the scene smoothly between turns. In reality, all that is arriving is permission from the server to model the next turn, possibly with some new user input.

Though the world is modeled at a steady number of updates per second, what is shown on-screen can be updated as frequently as each client computer can handle. Players with faster machines get a much smoother view, but the game is the same for all players.

It is impossible to correctly anticipate the precise arrival of the next turn, of course, so any prediction system that comes close is acceptable. We found that basing the prediction on the weighted average of the previous few arrival times was adequate.

This improvement needs no prediction of future game state. You just interpolate between the last two game turns you modeled. This interpolation can be linear for most things, such as object position, even when there are as few as four turns per second. Ideally, the system will correctly anticipate the moment the next game turn occurs, so you can continue with the interpolation. This adds up to one extra game-turn lag, which can be a significant time, but it allows for better gameplay.

Hiding the Lag

The main issue that remains is the very noticeable delay between player actions and their effects on the game world. User input only affects the game after the event has made the trip to the server and back, adding a game-turn delay plus an extra turn for the interpolation.

You can effectively conceal this lag in a management-style game by separating the game into the interface, the network code, and the game state. The game state is the only thing that must stay synchronized. The "interface" is expanded to include as much of the response as possible.

Examples of game state that we (re)classify as interface are as follows:

- In a game where the player creates rooms or buildings, partially designed room layouts are all done locally, and only the final room design is broadcast.
- The AI's response to commands is delayed, but the user interface response to commands, such as flashing circles around targets, gets immediately processed locally. The fact that your tank actually turns to fight its target a quarter of a second later is unnoticeable to the player.
- Camera movement doesn't usually need to be transmitted if where you're looking doesn't affect the game.
- Finishing touches to the GUI should happen only on the local machine. For example, our characters' heads track the mouse pointer around the screen when they are being talked to directly.

It is, in fact, possible to use this protocol in a game that involves more-direct interaction with the world, such as a first-person shooter, but it is awkward. One example is player character movement. The "move left" packet would change to "I want to have moved left on game turn *x*." The image displayed to the local user would update as if the move had been allowed. Every client, on receipt of the event packet from the server, would decide whether or not the move was possible. However, the decisions would be identical on all machines, leaving the local machine with the task of covering up any denied actions.

Host Migration

Since one machine is dedicated as the server, a problem arises when that machine leaves the game. This is quite likely to happen, since players are unlikely to be willing to leave their machines connected for the sake of the others.

To handle this situation, you must first make sure that there is as little state as possible on the server. The system described above is ideal because the server is merely a clock that counts game turns and acts as a short-term holding bay for user input packets.

The remaining clients must decide which machine will host the new server. Different clients might have received different amounts of the event stream from the server. The most up-to-date version must be used because the client that has received the most-recent events will not be able to roll back.

For a more seamless transition, clients should check if they had sent any packets to the server that did not make it into the new broadcast stream. These should then be resent. Storing perhaps five seconds of network packets is not particularly expensive, due to the small nature of the packets.

In *StarTopia*, we supported server dropout to a lesser extent than this. Most games were just one-on-one, so server dropout happened less often than expected. We had a frequent autosave system (every minute or so). If, for some reason, the server left, the remaining machines could just restart from their latest autosave with very little effect on the game.

Handling a Slow Computer

The server will keep generating game turns at a steady rate, which might be too fast for one of the clients, even if only for a short while. If game turn update requests are arriving four times a second, but the client takes half a second to model a game turn, it will never catch up and will freeze, unable to advance the game fast enough.

We simply added an occasional extra packet that clients would send to the server, which would not be rebroadcast. This would tell the server what percentage of CPU time was taken by modeling the game. The server could then slow down gameplay and allow the slower client to catch up by ensuring that the CPU modeling cost had dropped sufficiently for all the clients.

Useful Modules

Next, we will describe four other techniques that we found useful.

Simulating Lag in Single Player

Even in the single-player game, there should be a simulated network lag. This worked wonders for us, because the majority of game development and testing was done in the single-player mode. When we started testing the network game, the testers were very worried about the effect the network lag would have on playability. At this point, we could smugly point out that they'd been playing with lag all along. The game was programmed and tested against network lag by incorporating it from the start.

Pointer-to-Unique-ID

Although the game state might be completely synchronized, pointers won't necessarily be equal across machines, so any object (in C++) that must be referred to by network packets, such as "I'm clicking on this unit" needs a unique ID. This is relatively effortless; simply derive all referenced objects from a base class that contains a unique numerical ID (and a pointer-to-number conversion function), and include a lookup table for number-to-pointer conversion.

There are some subtle pitfalls to watch out for. For instance, when objects are destroyed and new objects are assigned the same number, some network packets might exist that refer to the old object. This is fixed by attaching a small extra number to each ID, which is incremented when the object dies and the ID is used for another object. An alternative is to simply use a much larger number of object IDs and never reuse IDs, or reuse them in least–recently used order. This will increase the size of the lookup table for ID-to-pointer conversion, or it can be turned into a hash table. In *StarTopia,* a surprisingly large number of objects were created and destroyed in a typical session.

Debugging Out-of-Syncs

The major part of network game debugging was tracking down reasons why clients went out of sync with each other. Detecting that the game was out of sync was done by a simple checksum system. The checksum included the number and position of objects, and little else.

Once the game is out of sync, looking at the differences in the game state tells you very little. So, the best strategy is to litter the code with `printfs`, especially around decision points in the code. You then compare the output from the two machines to find where they went out of sync.

Of course, `printfs` are expensive. Hence, since most of what we printed were numbers and constant strings, we kept a large queue of little structures, which could contain either pointers to strings or numbers. The `printf` operation simply wrote onto the end of this queue. The pointers were then dereferenced to produce the "sync dump" only when the game went out of sync. For simplicity, the output was written out to a shared network drive with a machine-specific filename.

Packet Loss

As previously mentioned, all network messages in our system must be guaranteed to arrive in the right order. We found it worthwhile to roll our own guaranteed messaging system, which was effectively a layer under the protocol described here. There is a stream of messages from each client to the server, consisting of user input and some housekeeping packets. There is also one stream from the server to each client, containing game-turn increments and user events. Though each client receives the same information, the streams are handled independently.

Pitfalls in *StarTopia*

We will describe the most common problems we had when implementing this system. Of course, this section is specific to *StarTopia,* but the lessons we learned will hopefully help you with your project.

Out-of-Sync

As mentioned above, this was by far our biggest problem, but it was not insuperable. Although there was a huge amount of detail in the game, we reduced the out-of-syncs to the point that we were unable to find them during testing. At this point, we `#defined` out the "syncdebug" module and put in a message suggesting that people try restarting the game from the latest autosave. This message was never found (unless we cheated to trigger it).

Our main cause of out-of-sync bugs was that, out of necessity, we had written a large portion of the game before the network protocol was incorporated. So, legacy code that was left in by accident would break the rules of the protocol. The most common out-of-sync bugs due to this were [Ireland01]:

- Changing game state directly rather than making the change via a network packet that would be broadcast around to all clients.
- Game code referring to the player that is local to the player's machine.
- Game code referring to the camera.
- Game code referring to the system clock for timing, rather than the game turn.

These problems can be avoided by keeping the interface and game state as far apart as possible. For example, no code that controls game state should know which player is sitting in front of the machine or where the player is looking. Once you have complied with this principle, the remaining common reasons for out-of-sync scenarios are as follows:

- Uninitialized data.
- Different versions of data files. Once the game is shipped, this is less of a problem. But during development, when people can be running many different versions, it is almost worth having a checksum of all data loaded into the game.
- Different executables. Again, the simplest solution is to make the game insist that all players use identical executables, though this can get in the way of some testing.

Event Packets Becoming Irrelevant

The typical instance of this pitfall or bug is that an event packet refers to some object that is destroyed during the time the packet makes the trip to the server and back. Alternatively, a packet describes a change for an object, but the object is no longer in an appropriate state to receive this event. (For a while, we could hire and fire characters in our game, even if they died in the meantime!)

Of course, the tests for this are simple—the unique-ID system described above catches object deaths. In addition, you should always check if your object is in a fit state to respond to an event. What makes this a pitfall is that it happens most often when players are sending many packets or if they are simultaneously referring to the same object. These situations happen more frequently toward the end of game development, when the game is near enough to completion for big showdowns to be played. Hence, these bugs can go unnoticed for an inconveniently long time.

Example Game

ON THE CD

An example game is provided on the CD-ROM. The game is quite primitive in that it only implements the basic protocol. More-complete modules, such as `syncdebug`, have been included, so they are a good basis for a practical implementation. We encourage you to look at the code and comments.

Conclusion

This protocol was easy to implement and worked well for our game. It gave us great freedom to write a game full of many concurrent events, without worrying about their effect on network bandwidth. We hope this gem will help you, should you wish to try our protocol.

I would like to thank the other members of the team who built *StarTopia*, especially Tom Ireland, who gave me helpful comments as I wrote this gem.

References

[Ireland01] Ireland, Tom, list compiled during game development, July 2001.

[Keeper01] Bullfrog, *Dungeon Keeper II*, PC game, information available online at http://www.dungeonkeeper.com, June 1999.

[StarTopia01] Mucky Foot, *StarTopia*, PC game, information available online at http://www.muckyfoot.com, July 2001.

5.4

Secure Sockets

Pete Isensee, Microsoft Corporation

pkisensee@msn.com

Cheating and hacking in multiplayer games is a common problem that can destroy a gaming experience. One way to prevent cheating is by using cryptography, encrypting and authenticating network traffic. This gem explores the Internet Protocol Security (IPSec) standard and shows how games can leverage portions of the standard to protect network packets and prevent spoofing, sniffing, and replay attacks.

IPSec

IPSec is an Internet standard developed by the Internet Engineering Task Force based on academic and government research. It is published in [RFC2401] through [RFC2411], as well as [IPSec2]. IPSec provides services for authentication, integrity, and confidentiality, and is widely used to implement virtual private networks (VPNs). IPSec is designed to be implemented at the network layer (network stack) and is typically hidden from applications. Unfortunately, native IPSec is not a viable option on most gaming platforms. Even when IPSec is available in a given OS (e.g., Windows 2000), it's neither on by default nor required that applications support it. At the time of this writing, the Microsoft Xbox is the only platform that supports IPSec transparently and requires that all games use it exclusively. Nevertheless, game programmers can learn a lot from IPSec, and many of the features of IPSec can be implemented within the context of game network code.

Authentication means verifying who sent a message; integrity means ensuring that a message was not modified. IPSec implements authentication and integrity using keyed cryptographic hashes like MD5 [RFC1321] and SHA-1 [RFC3174]. "Confidentiality" is the term used to describe obscuring data, which implies encryption. IPSec uses symmetric encryption algorithms like DES [RFC2405] and AES. For game traffic, it usually makes sense to choose a high-performance algorithm. Data requiring a higher level of encryption (e.g., player damage packets, tournament scores, etc.) can use stronger, slower algorithms.

Cryptography alone cannot prevent replay attacks. An authentic, encrypted message that is intercepted and resent by an attacker will authenticate and decrypt just fine. Therefore, IPSec also includes a mechanism for preventing replay attacks by using a combination of sequence numbers and a sliding replay window.

Caveats

One of the most critical steps in establishing a secure system is key management. This gem does not cover key-exchange techniques or the proper ways to generate, expire, and update keys. The assumption here is that both ends of a secure connection have the same keys and that the keys were established and exchanged in a secure fashion. Another process essential to secure systems is the proper generation of truly random bits for keys, shared secrets, and initialization vectors [Isensee01]. This gem assumes that keys use cryptographically random values.

The IPSec standard requires the implementer to embed a copy of the IP header into the payload of the packet, which is in turn both encrypted and authenticated. This allows the receiver to verify that the actual IP header wasn't altered. Implementing this level of authentication is both complicated and usually unnecessary, since the authentication of the payload proves that the packet came from someone who knows the proper authentication key. This gem does not cover IP authentication.

IPSec implementations are closely tied to the fragmentation system of the IP protocol. To avoid this issue altogether, this gem assumes that all packets are sent using unfragmented UDP packets and not via TCP, avoiding fragmentation. Most games use UDP packets anyway, so this assumption is not unreasonable. This gem also assumes that all messages are less than the maximum transmission unit (MTU). Applications must implement their own sequence mechanism for messages larger than the MTU.

Security Associations

A security association (SA) is a logical "connection" created for security purposes. The SA defines how traffic is secured from one node to another. An SA includes cipher and authentication keys, modes, algorithms, and other data that define the packet format. The `SecurityAssociation` class included with this gem contains the information shown in Table 5.4.1.

TABLE 5.4.1 Security Association Data

Data	Description
Authentication Algorithm	The cryptographic hashing algorithm used for authentication (e.g., MD5, SHA-1)
Authentication Key	The symmetric key data used for authentication

→

Data	Description
Encryption Algorithm	The symmetric encryption algorithm used when encrypting and decrypting packets (e.g., DES, AES).
Encryption Key	The symmetric key data used by the encryption algorithm.
Sequence Number	The next sequence number to be used by a packet sent on this SA.
Last Sequence Number	The highest sequence number received on this SA.
Replay Window	A bitmask used as the sliding window for rejecting replay attacks.
IV Size	The size of the encryption initialization vector (2–8 bytes).
ICV Size	The size of the integrity check value (8–12 bytes).
Max Padding Blocks	The maximum number of additional random padding blocks (0–4 blocks). The block size is based on the encryption algorithm.

SAs almost always occur in pairs, with an SA on the sender exactly matching an SA on the receiver. In a client-server game, the server might have a list of one SA per client, and each client would have a single SA that matched an SA on the server. In a peer-to-peer game, each peer would have a list of SAs. The list of security associations maintained by a host is called the "security association database" (SAD). For games, this "database" typically resides in the memory of the game or game server.

Prior to sending or receiving secure data, the communicating pair must establish a security association. This gem does not cover the means by which the SA data is exchanged by the sender and receiver. Some of the data, like the algorithms, could be baked into the code. Other data, like the keys, should change on a regular basis for maximum security, and should be exchanged using secure protocols like EKE, Kerberos, or Diffie-Hellman [Schneier96]. Be sure to use different keys for authentication and encryption in order to maximize security.

Packet Format

Implementing secure sockets is a matter of encrypting and stamping a hash on data before sending it, and authenticating and decrypting the data when receiving it. Table 5.4.2 shows the format of a secure packet, detailing which portions of the packet are authenticated and encrypted.

TABLE 5.4.2 Secure Packet Format

Data	Size (bytes)	Default Size (bytes)	Authenticated	Encrypted
Security Parameters Index (SPI)	1–4	2	Yes	No
Sequence Number	4	4	Yes	No
Initialization Vector (IV)	2–8	4	Yes	No
Payload	Variable	Variable	Yes	Yes
Padding	0–255	0–255	Yes	Yes
Pad length	1	1	Yes	Yes
Integrity Check Value (ICV)	8–12	10	No	No

Security Parameters Index

The security parameters index (SPI) is a handle that uniquely identifies a security association in a security association database. An SPI is transmitted in every secure packet so the receiver can select the SA under which the packet will be processed. The size of the SPI is game-specific, and depends on the maximum number of SAs that will be active at any one time. The example implementation included on the CD-ROM generates random, unique two-byte SPIs. The SPI is not, and cannot be encrypted, because it is used to identify the SA that defines the algorithms and keys. If an attacker modifies the SPI, the packet validation will fail, since the SPI is always authenticated.

ON THE CD

Sequence Number

The "sequence number" is a monotonically increasing counter value. The first packet sent using a given security association will have a sequence number of one, the next packet will be number two, and so on. The receiver uses the sequence number to ensure that duplicate packets and "old" packets are ignored. The sender must ensure that if there's a possibility of the sequence number rolling over to zero, the two endpoints of the connection generate a new pair of security associations and expire the old SAs prior to rollover. The sequence number is not encrypted so that replay attacks can be detected without having to decrypt the packet. This can also reduce the effect of a denial-of-service attack. If an attacker modifies the sequence number, the packet validation will fail, since the sequence number is always authenticated.

Initialization Vector

An initialization vector (IV) is a binary blob of random data used to initialize a symmetric encryption algorithm. The IV ensures that even if the same plaintext data is sent multiple times, it will encrypt to different ciphertext. The IV is initialized by the sender with random data and is fed to the encryption algorithm. The receiver initializes its decryption routine using the same IV. Each encryption algorithm defines a standard IV length, with most symmetric algorithms using an IV of eight bytes. To minimize bandwidth at the expense of less security, an implementation can transmit smaller IVs. The example implementation uses four-byte IVs as the default. The remainder of the IV is set to the sequence number when it is used during the encryption or decryption phase.

Payload

Payload refers to the original plaintext data. This data is encrypted in the packet that is sent over the wire.

Padding

Padding is appended to the payload before encryption. Padding is used for two reasons. First, the encryption algorithm might require a certain block size. For instance, many symmetric encryption algorithms use eight-byte blocks. Second, it might be desirable to add a random amount of padding to hide the true size of the payload. Padding bytes are initialized with a series of integer values (starting at one) that can be verified by the receiver, providing an additional level of security.

Pad Length

The pad length is a one-byte field that stores the number of padding bytes in the packet.

Integrity Check Value

The integrity check value (ICV) is a truncated, hash-based message authentication code (HMAC). An HMAC is a keyed hashing algorithm that uses a combination of a standard cryptographic hash algorithm and a secret symmetric key [RFC2104]. Like a thumbprint uniquely identifies a human being, an HMAC uniquely identifies a secure packet. Truncating the HMAC is a well-known security practice. The example implementation on the CD-ROM truncates the hash to eight bytes by default.

ON THE CD

The sender calculates the ICV by hashing the encrypted packet data using the authentication key of the SA. The receiver performs the same calculation and compares the ICV it computed with the ICV that was sent. If they match, the packet is valid—it was sent by someone with a matching SA (authentic) and it was not modified in transit (integrity intact). If not, the packet is bogus and is thrown away.

Sending Data

Sending data is a matter of encrypting the payload and generating a cryptographic hash of the data to be sent. The following sections describe the details used by the example implementation.

Establishing a Security Association

Prior to sending secure data, the sender establishes a security association with the receiver. Once the SAs and SPIs have been set up, each end of the communication link has the data it needs to encrypt, decrypt, and authenticate traffic sent between the two endpoints.

Building the Header

The header includes the SPI, the sequence number, and the encryption IV. The SPI corresponds to the SA used to encode and authenticate the payload. The current sequence number is also found in the SA. Once a sequence number has been used, it is incremented in the SA. The encryption IV is generated randomly. If the SA encryption algorithm requires a larger IV than what is sent in the packet, the remaining bytes are set to the sequence number.

Generating Padding

Padding is generated based on the size of the plaintext payload and the SA encryption algorithm. Additional random padding might be added to hide the true size of the payload. The amount of random padding is configurable. The padding bytes are initialized with a series of integer values, starting at one.

Encrypting the Payload

The encrypted portion of the packet includes the original payload, the padding, and the pad-length byte. The symmetric encryption is initialized with the IV generated above, and the encrypted payload is generated using the SA symmetric encryption key and SA symmetric encryption algorithm. The resulting ciphertext is appended to the header.

Generating the Authentication Code

The last step before sending the data is to generate the ICV. The HMAC algorithm is initialized with the SA cryptographic hash algorithm and authentication key. The hash algorithm is then applied to the packet header and encrypted payload/padding. The resulting hash value is appended to the ciphertext. The hash value is not encrypted.

Sending the Secure Packet

The secure buffer is now ready to be sent using whatever UDP socket mechanism the game uses, typically `send()`.

Receiving Data

On the receiving end, the order of operations is critical for security and performance. The receiver must validate the packet SPI, ICV, and sequence number. The receiver may then decrypt the packet and validate padding. Only after all validation checks are complete can the receiver process the packet payload. If any validation check fails, the packet must be thrown away. If the receiver is a game server, the server might also want to audit the failure event as a way of detecting and tracking cheaters.

Receiving the Secure Packet

The secure packet is received using whatever UDP socket mechanism the game uses, typically `recv()`.

Validating the Packet

The simplest check that can be made on the packet is validating the SPI. If the SPI does not match a security association in the receiver's security association database, the packet is deemed invalid. Assuming an SA match, a quick check is made on the size of the block, based on the minimal amount of data that must be included in the secure packet.

The next step is to validate the packet against the ICV. The HMAC algorithm is initialized with the SA cryptographic hash algorithm and key. The hash algorithm is then applied to the packet header and encrypted payload. The resulting hash value is truncated and compared with the ICV received. If it matches, we have an authentic packet.

The last step prior to decrypting the packet is to check the sequence number. If the packet is a replay or too "old," there's no reason to decrypt it. The example implementation uses a 64-bit sliding window to reject replay attacks and yet still allow out-of-order packets, which can occur with UDP. The "right" edge of the window represents the highest validated sequence number received on the SA. Packets that contain sequence numbers lower than the "left" edge of the window are rejected (they're too old). Packets falling within the window are checked against the list of received packets. If a packet with a matching sequence number is received, it is a replay and is ignored. New packets set the corresponding bit in the window. Packets with a sequence number larger than the right edge cause the window to shift.

Decrypting the Payload

The first step of decryption is to extract the IV. The IV is extended with the sequence number if necessary and then used to initialize the decryption algorithm. The payload and padding bytes are deciphered using the SA symmetric decryption key. The resulting plaintext includes the original payload, padding bytes, and padding size.

Validating Padding

The padding size is validated to ensure that it's reasonable. The padding bytes are then validated to ensure that they contain a series of integer values. Finally, all padding information is stripped from the plaintext, leaving the original payload.

Example Implementation

ON THE CD

The sample code on the CD-ROM, which is included with this gem, includes C++ classes that wrap cryptographic functions, security associations, and secure buffers. Table 5.4.3 shows the list of classes provided.

TABLE 5.4.3 Secure Socket Classes

Class name	Description
`CryptContext`	Win32 CryptoAPI cryptographic service providers
`Key`	Cryptographic keys and algorithms
`Cipher`	Encryption and decryption functions
`Hash`	Hashing algorithms
`Buffer`	`std::string<unsigned char>`
`SecurityAssociation`	Security association data
`SADatabase`	`std::map<SpiType, SecurityAssociation>`
`SecureBuffer`	Functions for encrypting, decrypting, and authenticating payloads

The essential implementation details are contained in `SecurityAssociation` and `SecureBuffer`. The next section shows how the classes are used in a game for sending and receiving secure data.

Creating a Security Association

Create a security association and add it to the security association database (SAD):

```
// One-time association of SAD to SecureBuffers
SADatabase sad;
SecureBuffer::SetSADatabase( &sad );

// Generate random keys. This example uses the
// DES cipher for encryption and MD5 for hashing
Key keyAuth( CALG_DES );
Key keyCrypt( CALG_DES );

// Create a new SA using the specified keys
// and algorithms; other values get defaults
SecurityAssociation sa( keyAuth, keyCrypt, CALG_MD5 );

// Generate a new SPI and add the pair to the db
SpiType nSPI = sad.GenNewSPI();
sad.Insert( nSPI, sa );

// Securely exchange nSPI and keys with other end
// of connection . . .
```

Sending a Secure Packet

Generate and send a secure packet:

```
// Associate SecureBuffer with SA via SPI
SecureBuffer sb( nSPI );
```

```
// Generate the encrypted and authenticated buffer.
// Encryption and hashing happens here.
sb.Create( "payload", 7 );

// Send the secure packet
send( sock, sb.GetDataPtr(), sb.GetSize(), 0 );
```

Receiving a Secure Packet

Receive and process a secure packet:

```
// Receive the secure packet
char pData[ 1024 ];
int n = recv( sock, pData, 1024, 0 );
if( n == 0 || n == SOCKET_ERROR )
   return false;

// Validate the packet
SecureBuffer sb( pData, n );
if( !sb.IsAuthentic() )
   return false;

// Extract the original payload
if( !sb.GetPayload( pData, &n ) )
   return false;

// Adjust the replay window
sb.SetAccepted();
return true;
```

CryptoAPI

The cryptographic algorithms and key management use the Windows CryptoAPI. All of the crypto code is modularized into crypto.cpp so that you can replace the low-level crypto with other implementations. One of the frustrating features of the CryptoAPI is that it doesn't provide direct access to key data. There are no APIs that allow you to directly set or get a key. However, Microsoft KnowledgeBase article Q228786 [KB228786] discusses a method for directly accessing key data, and that method is used by the `Key` class.

Because of the way the CryptoAPI is designed—using cryptographic service providers—not all potential algorithms or key lengths are available on all versions of Windows. Be sure to check the return codes for failure cases.

Performance

There are two major performance issues involved with using secure sockets. The first is additional bandwidth requirements. Using the default settings and an encryption algorithm with eight-byte block requirement (e.g., DES), minimum packet overhead with the sample implementation is as follows:

2 (SPI) + 4 (SeqNum) + 4 (IV) + 0–15 (Padding) + 1 (PadLen) + 10 (ICV) = 21–36 bytes

Those 21–36 bytes are in addition to the standard UDP packet overhead. You can tweak the SA parameters to reduce the overhead, but only at the expense of security. To reduce the effects of the overhead, consider changing from small, frequent payloads to larger payloads sent less frequently. To avoid unnecessary padding, send payloads whose size+1 is evenly divisible by the block size of the SA cipher. (The +1 accounts for the pad length byte.)

The second performance issue is encryption/decryption and authentication. Table 5.4.4 shows the costs of creating, authenticating, and decrypting one kilobyte of payload data, which indicates that performance is not unreasonable. The most important factors at work here are the speed of the algorithms and the size of individual packets. Choose algorithms and key lengths that provide solid security at a reasonable performance cost.

TABLE 5.4.4 Performance

Time to process one kilobyte of payload data

Payload Size (bytes)	Create (ms)	Authenticate (ms)	Decrypt (ms)
64	2.07	0.90	1.07
128	1.06	0.45	0.57
256	0.59	0.24	0.34
512	0.35	0.14	0.23
1024	0.23	0.09	0.16

These values were generated on a Pentium III, 866 MHz, running Windows 2000, and using the default SA settings with DES encryption (64-bit keys) and MD5 hashing. The "Create" column is the time in milliseconds required to repeatedly call `SecureBuffer::Create` on total payload data using the given payload size. The "Authenticate" column shows the time spent in `SecureBuffer::IsAuthentic`, and the "Decrypt" column shows the time in `SecureBuffer::GetPayload`. Performance increases as the payload size increases, since relative packet overhead decreases for larger packets.

Security

The intent of this gem is to present an implementation that strikes a balance between extremely robust security with huge packet overhead and reasonable security with minimal packet overhead. The quality of security provided is primarily dependent on the strength of the algorithms used. Don't use XOR as an encryption or authentication algorithm and expect to have packets that are never cracked. Choose well-known, standard algorithms with solid implementations, like DES, Triple-DES, Blowfish, and AES for encryption, MD5 and SHA-1 for hashing. Understand the security levels and performance trade-offs between the algorithms. Use large keys (128-bits) when they're supported by the algorithm. Change keys regularly. Don't reduce the IV size to less than four bytes or the ICV size to less than eight bytes, or security will be substantially diminished.

Although it's technically possible to turn off encryption and only use authentication, be aware that an authenticated packet without encryption exposes your game to sniffing attacks, which can result in cheating that's just as bad as spoofing attacks (and harder to detect).

Conclusion

As more games support features like tournaments and prize competitions, secure communication not only reduces cheating, but also becomes an essential requirement of the game. The IPSec specification includes security elements that can directly benefit networked games. Although the packet overhead is not insignificant, performance is good, and the benefits of secure traffic are considerable.

References

[Howard02] Howard, Michael and David LeBlanc, *Writing Secure Code*, Microsoft Press, 2002.

[IPSec2] "IP Encapsulating Security Payload (ESP)," updated draft available online at http://www.ietf.org/ID.html, November 2001.

[Isensee01] Isensee, Pete, "Genuine Random Number Generation," *Game Programming Gems 2*, Charles River Media, Inc., 2001.

[KB228786] "How to Export/Import Plain Text Session Key Using CryptoAPI," available online at http://support.microsoft.com/default.aspx?scid=kb;EN-US;q228786, July 2001.

[RFC1321] "The MD5 Message-Digest Algorithm," available online at http://www.ietf.org/rfc/rfc1321.txt, April 1992.

[RFC2104] "HMAC: Keyed-Hashing for Message Authentication," available online at http://www.ietf.org/rfc/rfc2104.txt, February 1997.

[RFC2401] "Security Architecture for the Internet Protocol," available online at http://www.ietf.org/rfc/rfc2401.txt, November 1998.

[RFC2403] "The Use of HMAC-MD5-96 within ESP and AH," available online at http://www.ietf.org/rfc/rfc2403.txt, November 1998.

[RFC2404] "The Use of HMAC-SHA-1-96 within ESP and AH," available online at http://www.ietf.org/rfc/rfc2404.txt, November 1998.

[RFC2405] "The ESP DES-CBC Cipher Algorithm with Explicit IV," available online at http://www.ietf.org/rfc/rfc2405.txt, November 1998.

[RFC2406] "IP Encapsulating Security Payload (ESP)," available online at http://www.ietf.org/rfc/rfc2406.txt, November 1998.

[RFC3174] "US Secure Hash Algorithm (SHA1)," available online at http://www.ietf.org/rfc/rfc3174.txt, September 2001.

[Schneier96] Schneier, Bruce, *Applied Cryptography*, Second Edition, John Wiley & Sons, 1996.

[Schneier99] Ferguson, Neils and Bruce Schneier, "A Cryptographic Evaluation of IPSec," available online at http://www.counterpane.com/ipsec.html, February 1999.

5.5

Bit Packing: A Network Compression Technique

Pete Isensee, Microsoft Corporation

pkisensee@msn.com

Network games often send structures of data containing position, velocity, acceleration, status flags, and other important game state information. Often, many bits of transmitted information do not contain important data. For example, a game might send positions that range from 0 to 100,000 using 32-bit integers. Each position occupies 17 bits, but the remaining 15 bits are wasted. Those unused bits can add up quickly for large data structures.

One of the mantras of the network game developer is to limit the amount of data on the wire. This article shows a bit-packing technique that compresses individual elements of a network data structure into a binary stream where every bit of the stream contains relevant data. This technique can significantly reduce the size of network packets. A secondary advantage of this approach is that elements in the network data structure can be range-checked in debugging versions to verify that they fall within a developer-specified tolerance. Similar packing techniques have been used in existing online games.

An Example

This technique is designed to integrate easily into existing C structs or C++ classes sent on standard sockets. Here's a simplified example of game networking code:

```
struct NetData
{
    unsigned char  MsgType;   // 0 - 28
    unsigned long  Time;              // 0 - 0xFFFFFFFF
    unsigned short Element;   // 148 to 1153
    int            XPosition; // -100,000 to 100,000
    int            Yposition; // -100,000 to 100,000
};

NetData nd;
send( s, (const char*)( &nd ), sizeof(nd), 0 );
```

On a 32-bit platform, the amount of data being sent and received is at least 17 bytes. If the structure is not byte-aligned, the amount of data could be upwards of 20 bytes. If the sender and receiver are on different platforms, there can also be byte ordering issues that require the sender to convert each item to network order before sending and the receiver to convert each item back to host order.

Here's the same structure defined using the bit-packing technique:

```
struct NetData : public BitPackCodec< 5 >
{
    PkUint<unsigned char,5>                 MsgType;
    PkUint<unsigned long>                   Time;
    PkUintRange<unsigned short,148,1153> Element;
    PkInt<int,-100000,100000>               XPos;
    PkInt<int,-100000,100000>               YPos;
};
```

The raw data items are replaced with "packable" data items. Users of these data items can treat them exactly the same as their raw integer counterparts. They can be assigned, read, and written exactly like normal integers. The advantage of a packable item is that it also knows how to pack itself into a bit stream. Moreover, the range of values that an integer can take is now known by the compiler. Because the range consists of template parameters, there's no additional memory overhead, but the compiler can be put to good use doing range checking.

The `NetData` struct derives from a mixin class called `BitPackCodec`, which supports two key functions, `Pack()` and `Unpack()`, along with a registration function that informs the codec which items will be inserted into the stream and in what order they will appear.

Now, rather than sending the raw `NetData` structure, the structure is packed into a bit stream first. The size of the bit stream buffer in this particular example is only 83 bits, versus 136 bits for the original struct, a savings of 40 percent.

```
NetData nd;
int size = nd.GetPackedBytes();
char* pBitStream = new char [ size ];
send( s, nd.Pack( pBitStream ), size, 0 );
```

The target, upon receiving the bit stream, decompresses it back to the original struct format by unpacking it.

```
nd.Unpack( pBitStream );
```

The packing functions automatically handle all the dirty details, including byte swapping. The new `NetData` structure can consist of whatever integer types are most efficient, rather than having to resort to bit fields or other methods of in-memory compression.

Hurdles

There are three tricky issues about this particular technique. The hardest part is the bit packing itself. Although a simple function that packs one bit at a time can be written in a few lines of code, packing bits one by one is inefficient. Writing an algorithm that packs bytes at a time is much more complex. The second difficult part is minimizing the memory footprint of the technique, since it requires a separate buffer for the bit stream, lists to keep track of what to pack, and so forth. The third thorny problem is making the technique flexible enough that it can be easily incorporated into existing game code. The next sections discuss each issue in detail.

Packing the Bits

The algorithm used in this article is based on lining up the source integer and destination bit buffer so that the next available bit in the destination and the first significant bit in the source are aligned. The source bits are copied into the bit buffer one section at a time, where each section is defined by the next nearest byte boundary of either the source or destination. Figure 5.5.1 shows an example. The first available bit in the destination buffer is bit 6. There are 13 bits to copy. Lining up the bits to be copied (the shaded areas), it's clear there will be four copy operations, defined by A, B, C, and D. For example, section B is defined by the first byte boundary at bit 8 in the bit buffer, and the next byte boundary is at bit 8 in the source integer.

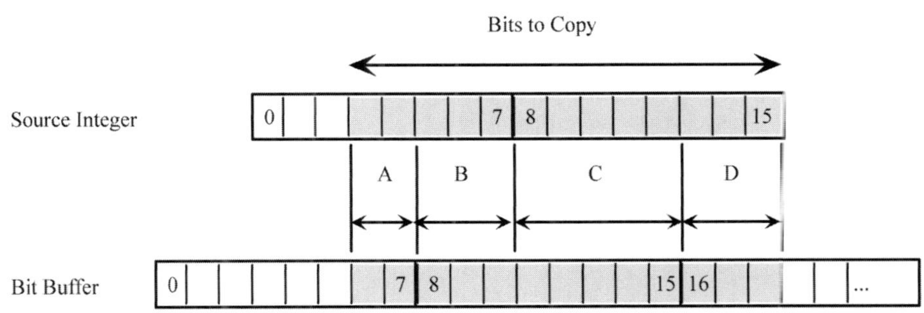

FIGURE 5.5.1 Lining up the source integer and destination bit buffer.

If the byte boundaries of the source integer and the bit buffer happen to be aligned, then up to 8 bits can be copied at a time. If they're not aligned, then each byte is copied in two chunks totaling 8 bits. Unpacking works exactly the same way, but the source and destination are reversed. Prior to copying the bits of an integer to the bit buffer, the integer is converted to network format (big endian). During the unpacking phase, the restored integer is converted back to host format.

The packing algorithm is implemented using a single C++ template function that packs any unsigned integer type from 8-bit to 64-bit integers. The prototype for the function follows. To maintain compatibility with standard socket functions, the bit buffer is a regular char pointer instead of an unsigned char pointer, and the size is an `int` instead of an `unsigned`.

```
template< typename T > // T is any integer type
void Pack( const T& tSrc, int nSrcBits,
           char* pDestBitBuffer, int nDestStartBit );
```

The byte swapping is also implemented using template functions, avoiding unnatural switch statements to determine whether to use `htonl()` or `htons()`. The byte swapping functionality is shown next. It takes advantage of the STL reverse function. An efficient compiler can optimize away the call to `IsPlatformLittleEndian()` and completely inline the reversing algorithm, making these functions highly efficient.

```
inline bool IsPlatformLittleEndian()
{
    const int n = 1;
    return( *((char*)( &n ) ) ? true : false );
}

template< typename T >
T ReverseBytes( T n )
{
    unsigned char* p = (unsigned char*)( &n );
    std::reverse( p, p + sizeof( T ) );
    return n;
}

template< typename T >
T HostToNetworkOrder( T n )
{
    if( IsPlatformLittleEndian() )
        return ReverseBytes( n );
    return n;
};
```

A Generic Interface for a Packable Data Type

Integers are not the only data type that can be efficiently packed. For example, IEEE floating-point values can also be packed by stripping off bits from the mantissa. Strings can be packed using a variety of compression techniques. The approach shown here focuses on integers of various flavors, but is designed to allow the bit packing of any data type. The best way to abstract the notion of packing is via an abstract base class.

```
class Packable
{
public:
    virtual ~Packable() = 0;
    virtual int GetBits() const;
    virtual void Pack( char*, int* StartBit ) const;
    virtual void Unpack( const char*, int* StartBit );
};
```

The `Packable` class includes other helper functions, but the three shown here are the key methods. `GetBits()` returns the number of significant bits in the `Packable` object. These are the bits that will be packed and unpacked by the object. `Pack()` copies `GetBits()` of the `Packable` object into the incoming input buffer starting at the bit specified. It increments the incoming start bit by `GetBits()`. `Unpack()` generates a new `Packable` object from the incoming bit buffer starting at the bit specified. It also increments the incoming start bit by `GetBits()`. The `Packable` interface is designed to be compatible with the socket interface, which uses plain old char pointers.

A Concrete Interface for a Packable Data Type

This article packs integers. Rather than creating a specific class for each integer type (e.g., unsigned char, short, long, etc.), the code is template-based. All integers are supported via one of three different interfaces.

```
template< typename T, int Bits >
class PkUint : public Packable

template< typename T, uint64 Min, uint64 Max >
class PkUintRange : public Packable

template< typename T, int64 Min, int64 Max >
class PkInt : public Packable
```

The `PkUint` class is designed for unsigned integers that hold a specific number of bits. The caller specifies the number of bits as a template parameter. For example, a network message type might be stored using 5 bits (values 0 through 31, or a bitmask with 5 important bits). The `PkUintRange` class is designed for unsigned integers that hold a specific range of values. The range can be zero-based, or it can have a positive minimum value. In either case, the `PkUintRange` class is smart enough to normalize the number before it's packed and denormalize upon unpacking. For example, if the range were 1000–1127, only 7 bits would be used to store the value in the bit buffer. The `PkInt` class is designed for signed integers that hold a specific range of values. This class also normalizes the number and converts the number to an unsigned value before it's packed.

Each of these three concrete classes derives from the `Packable` class and implements the appropriate `Packable` functions. The constructors and conversion operators ensure that users of packable integers can treat them exactly as they would treat normal integers. Because these classes use template parameters, no additional storage is required to hold the bits or range values. The only overhead to these classes is `sizeof(T)` plus the virtual function table pointer required by the `Packable` class.

The Codec

Now all we need is a way to easily pack structs and classes or lists of `Packable` objects. The design goals require that the method be transparent and take as little memory as possible. Enter the `BitPackCodec`. All the `BitPackCodec` needs to know is how many items to pack, the order in which to pack them, and a bit buffer to pack them into. Although the bit buffer could be maintained internally by the class, that would be costly in terms of performance and efficiency. It makes more sense in a game to preallocate a single bit buffer that's large enough to handle the largest network packet and pass that buffer to the codec as needed.

When it comes to maintaining a list of the items to pack, flexible list data types like `std::vector` or `std::list` have memory allocation overhead we'd like to avoid. The solution used in this article is to store the list of `Packable` objects in a C-style array. For maximum flexibility and performance, the array size is a template parameter. The advantages of this solution are that it uses minimal memory, requires no heap allocations, and is very fast. In debug builds, the class can check to ensure that the bounds of the array are not exceeded.

```
template< int N >
class BitPackCodec
{
private:
    Packable* mPackList[ N ];

public:
    void  Register( Packable& );
    char* Pack( char* ) const;
    void  Unpack( const char* ) const;
    int   GetPackedBytes() const;
};
```

`BitPackCodec` is designed as a mixin class. For any struct X containing multiple `Packable` objects, derive X from `BitPackCodec`. `Register()` adds items to the list of packable items. `Register()` is designed to be called by X's constructor. Here's an example using the `NetData` structure:

```
NetData() // NetData ctor
{
    Register( MsgType );
    Register( Time );
```

```
        Register( Element );
        Register( XPos );
        Register( YPos );
    }
```

`Pack()` and `Unpack()` do all the work. They expect an external buffer allocated by the caller that's at least `GetPackedBytes()` in size. Here's the implementation of the `Pack()` function:

```
    char* Pack( char* pPackBuffer )
    {
        memset( pPackBuffer, 0, GetPackedBytes() );
        int nCurrBit = 0;
        for( int i = 0; i < N; ++i )
            mPackList[i]->Pack( pPackBuffer, &nCurrBit );
        return pPackBuffer;
    }
```

`Pack()` clears the bit buffer, and then packs each registered `Packable` item into the bit buffer by calling `Packable::Pack()`. Any object that implements the `Packable` interface can be used by the codec object. This design flexibility allows new data types to become packable as needed.

Evaluating the Tradeoffs

By far the biggest advantage of packing bits is the reduction of network bandwidth. There are a few side benefits, too. Network data structs don't need special alignment, bit fields, or unusually sized data types. There's additional range checking on packed values in debug mode. Finally, packing also helps obfuscate network messages to casual observers.

The cost of packing bits is threefold: readability, performance, and memory. Sending a network struct is simple and easy to understand; packing a struct into a bit stream adds complexity and makes debugging network packets more difficult. In terms of performance, packing and unpacking bits is an $O(N)$ operation, where N is the number of items being packed. In terms of CPU cost, it's quite low considering the relatively small size of network packets sent by most modern games. The classes shown previously have a negligible memory impact. A packable integer is `sizeof(T)` plus a pointer for the `Packable` virtual function pointer table. The codec class introduces an array of size N, and the game must support a bit buffer the size of the largest network packet. All in all, this is not a bad set of tradeoffs for eliminating a significant amount of bandwidth.

Improvements

This article includes code for packing integers from 8- to 64-bit values. The basic technique can be extended to all types of other game data, including floats and strings. Bit packing is a fine lossless compression technique that works well for network data. However, it's not the best you can do. If you're interested in even better methods, check out the arithmetic coders from [Blow03] and [Nelson96] as well as other compression techniques [Bloom].

Conclusion

Bit packing accomplishes the following goals:

- Packs data structures into streams that only contain the "important" bits. All nonessential bits are discarded. The resulting bandwidth savings can be significant.
- Integrates easily into existing code. Existing network data structures can be treated as if they contain the original raw data.
- Allows network data structures to be aligned for speed rather than size.
- Is as transparent as possible.
- Has minimal performance impact.
- Has minimal memory overhead.

References

[Bloom] Bloom, Charles, "Compression Algorithms," available online at www.cbloom.com/algs/index.html.

[Blow02] Blow, Jonathan, "Packing Integers," *Game Developer Magazine* (May 2002): pp. 16–19.

[Blow03] Blow, Jonathan, "Using an Arithmetic Coder: Part 1," *Game Developer Magazine* (August 2003): pp. 14–18.

[Nelson96] Nelson, Mark, and Jean-Loup Gilly, *The Data Compression Book, Second Edition*, M & T Books, 1996.

SECTION

6

AUDIO

6.1

A Basic Music Sequencer for Games

Scott Patterson, Electronic Arts—Blackbox

filter@filtercurve.com

This gem describes how to make a basic music sequencer. First, we will start off with a comparison of music streaming and music sequencing. Then, we will review some important concepts from the MIDI music language, outline a basic computer music language implementation, and then discuss the coding issues that relate to timing and synthesis control.

Streaming vs. Sequencing

Music in games is generally played back in one of two ways: either as a stream of sample data or as a sequence of instructions to an audio synthesis system. It is also possible that music playback may involve a combination of both methods. Individually, the methods have some pros and cons that depend on the hardware systems available. To be combined, synchronization issues must be addressed as well.

Streaming Method Pros

- Audio hardware requirements are minimal.
- Music development and integration with the game is easy.
- Music quality is only limited by the sample rate and number of channels of the stream data.

Streaming Method Cons

- Music data plays the same way each time.
- There can be latency in the start and stop of the stream.
- There may be latency problems when looping a stream or switching streams.
- There may be large memory buffer requirements.
- Certain resources may be tied up during playback such as DMA hardware and storage device hardware.

- If the stream data is not compressed it will take significant storage space.
- If the stream data is compressed it will require hardware or software decompression resources.
- It may not be possible to cross-fade two different streams depending on hardware limitations, so the only choice available may be fading to or from silence.

Sequencing Method Pros

- No latency problems when starting or stopping the music.
- No latency problems when looping or switching music.
- If audio memory is available, sample data memory will not compete with game data memory.
- Resources such as DMA hardware and storage device hardware may not be required for music playback and will be free for the game to use at any time.
- A great deal of music styles and variations can be produced from a relatively small sample data set.
- Music data can by dynamically altered at run-time to create unique game and music interactions.

Sequencing Method Cons

- Voices for music may compete with voices needed for other game audio.
- Music development and integration with the game is more complex.
- Music quality may be limited by synthesis capabilities.
- Music quality may be limited by available sample memory.

Core Computer Music Concepts

Let's now review core computer music concepts, and build our music command language.

Event Blocks

Music can be described as events or commands occurring over time. So we can build our music command language with "event blocks" composed of three elements: time, event type, and event details (see Table 6.1.1). We will store the time relative to previous events and call it a delta-time. The event type will be identified with a number. And the event details will be zero or more parameters that are defined by the event type.

TABLE 6.1.1 Event Block

Delta-Time	Event Type	Event Parameters

By using a sequence of event blocks, we can describe any combination of events and time intervals. So building our computer music language is now a task of choosing how to store the delta-time, choosing the event types to support, and choosing the parameters supplied for each event type.

MIDI (Musical Instrument Digital Interface) Music

The MIDI specification has been around for a long time. Most music composition and sequencing software provides compatibility with MIDI input and output ports for recording and playback. These software products also provide options to save and load MIDI files. Since we are creating our own computer music language, a good place to start will be learning the MIDI specification and its file format. We can then convert MIDI file data to our own custom data.

The word "interface" in MIDI refers to the fact that it is a specification for communication between musical devices. In making a music sequencer for games we aren't as interested in musical device communication as we are interested in music playback on a particular machine. So my introduction to MIDI will include only the parts that relate directly to making our music sequencer for games.

MIDI Event Types

The MIDI specification defines several events called the *channel voice messages* (see Table 6.1.2). MIDI originated as a virtual piano keyboard communication language, so terms such as attack velocity, release velocity, pitch wheel, and key pressure all refer to actions applied to a virtual piano keyboard.

TABLE 6.1.2 MIDI Channel Voice Messages

Event Type	Event Parameters
Note Off	Note Number Release Velocity
Note On	Note Number Attack Velocity
Pitch Wheel	Pitch Bend LSB Pitch Bend MSB
Control Change	Controller ID Controller Value
Program Change	Program Number
Poly Key Pressure	Note Number Pressure Value
Channel Pressure	Pressure Value

The channel voice messages are the core musical control events defined by MIDI. The Program Change event defines what instrument definition to use. The Note On and Note Off events do as they suggest. And the remaining events update various audio playback parameters to new values. Since the Control Change event specifies a Controller ID parameter, it can be used for many different types of audio control. Two of the most commonly used Controller IDs are 7 for Volume and 10 for Pan.

There are also meta-events defined in the MIDI file format 1.0 specification. Table 6.1.3 lists a selection that will be important to us.

TABLE 6.1.3 Selected MIDI Meta-Event Types

Meta-Event Type	Meta-Event Parameters
End of Track	
Set Tempo	Tempo Number
Time Signature	Numerator Denominator MIDI clocks per metronome click 32nd-notes in a MIDI quarter-note
Key Signature	Sharps/Flats Indicator Major or Minor Indicator
Text Event	String Length String Data
Sequence/Track Name	String Length String Data
Instrument Name	String Length String Data
Lyric	String Length String Data
Marker	String Length String Data
Cue Point	String Length String Data

The End of Track meta-event defines the end of a series of event blocks and the Set Tempo meta-event defines how fast to step through the delta-time values of event blocks. The Time Signature and Key Signature meta-events do not change the way that MIDI music plays, but are commonly used for organizing the visual display of music data. We can use these meta-events as special markers for our own organization or synchronization purposes. The remaining meta-events I have listed store string data. We can store custom information in these strings to be used in our conversion from the MIDI format to a custom format.

MIDI Channels and Tracks

The "channel" in MIDI channel voice messages refers to the fact that each MIDI event block also contains a channel number from 1 to 16 (0 to 15). The channel concept makes it possible to send MIDI commands to more than one target over a serial connection. It would also be possible for us to store our music data as a single serial stream and assign channels to each message. An advantage of this method is that processing a single stream of data would work well for CPU caching. A disadvantage of this method is that track data organization would not be flexible and independent.

It so happens that the MIDI file format 1.0 specification defines "format 0" files that have all information combined in one track and "format 1" files that have any number of tracks.

The basic music sequencer that we will present processes any number of tracks independently and does not have a channel concept.

Computer Music Sequencer Implementation

Now we are at the point where we can determine our own custom computer music language. For the purposes of this gem we will choose to implement event types that are very similar to MIDI event types. You can create your own additional event types for your own needs.

Sequences, Tracks, Events, Instruments, and Voices

Let's quickly cover the terminology used in the rest of this paper. A *sequence* is a collection of tracks that run simultaneously. Each *track* is a series of event blocks that we defined earlier. There is always a single current instrument on each track. Every Note On event in a track will start a voice of the current instrument. The corresponding Note Off event will turn this voice off. Many types of events in a track will modify the state of the track's voices.

The sequencer data structures described later show an implementation of these relationships.

Sequencer Event Types

As a first step in creating our basic music sequencer we will come up with a list of event types that we want to support. These are displayed in Table 6.1.4.

TABLE 6.1.4 Event Type Ideas

Event Types	Notes
Note Control	(These work like the traditional MIDI events.)
Note Off	Key Release velocity (optional)
Note On	Key Attack velocity
Immediate Modifications	(These work like the traditional MIDI events.)
SetTrackVolume	Value
SetTrackPitchBend	Value
SetTrackPan	Value
SetTrackEffect	Any effect type Value
SetTrackInstrument	Program change
SetTrackTempo	Value
Target Modifications	(These target an event value rather than setting it.)
SetTarget	Time format and duration to target value Basic modification type and data
Arrangement	
Track End	Ends track playback
Track Marker	Additional entry points, sync points
Jump to Track	Jump to new track data
Gosub to Track	Jump to new track data, returns when done
Callback	
Callback	Calls game code, could change test values

Note Control

It is pretty hard to make music without notes. Following the MIDI tradition we associate a key number and velocity with notes. The MIDI note off message includes a release velocity, but it is our option to include this for our sequencer.

Immediate Modifications

These event types are quite similar to certain MIDI messages. This will make conversion from MIDI files for these events easy. These events also represent immediate updates of synth hardware. Values may be absolute or relative depending on the event type.

Target Modifications

These event types interpolate from current value to destination value over a given time rather than change settings immediately. Target modifications have the advantage of being able to describe a curve of parameter values with a single command rather than the many immediate modification commands needed to achieve the same effect.

Arrangement

These event types switch us to different sections of music data.

Callback

These event types generate callbacks to functions that have been registered with the music sequencer.

Sequencer Data Structures

The abbreviated data structures that we could use for our music sequencer are listed in Listing 6.1.1.

LISTING 6.1.1 Music Sequencer Data Structures

```
typedef list< Sequence_t * > SequencePtrList_t;
typedef list< Track_t * >    TrackPtrList_t;
typedef list< Voice_t * >    VoicePtrList_t;

class MusicSequencer_t {
    MusicSequencerState_t State;
    SequencePtrList_t     ActiveSequencePtrList;
    SequencePtrList_t     FreeSequencePtrList;
    TrackPtrList_t        ActiveTrackPtrList;
    TrackPtrList_t        FreeTrackPtrList;
    VoicePtrList_t        ActiveVoicePtrList;
    VoicePtrList_t        FreeVoicePtrList;
};

class SequenceState_t {
    Tempo_t  Tempo;
    Volume_t Volume;
};

class Sequence_t {
    SequenceState_t State;
    TimeUnit_t      TimeElapsed;
    TimeUnit_t      TimeStep;
    TrackPtrList_t  TrackPtrList;
};

class TrackState_t {
    Volume_t    Volume;
    PitchBend_t PitchBend;
    Pan_t       Pan;
    Effect_t    Effect;
};

class Track_t {
    TrackState_t   State;
    Sequence_t    *pOwner;
    char          *pEvent;
    Instrument_t  *pInstrument;
    VoicePtrList_t VoicePtrList;
};
```

```
class VoiceState_t {
    SynthVolume_t Volume;
    SynthPitch_t  Pitch;
    SynthPan_t    Pan;
    SynthEffect_t Effect;
};

class Voice_t {
    VoiceState_t  State;
    Track_t      *pOwner;
    int           nKey;
};
```

Here we show the `MusicSequencer_t` class that holds the lists of active and free sequences, tracks, and voices. We also see that sequences, tracks, and voices each have a notion of state and some example parameters of those states are shown. A `Sequence_t` has a `TrackPtrList` that holds the tracks owned by the sequence. A `Track_t` has a `VoicePtrList` that holds the voices owned by the track. A `Voice_t` has a `pOwner` that points to the track that owns the voice. A `Track_t` has a `pOwner` that points to the sequence that owns the track. These parent and child data structures help us query and update information up and down our hierarchy whether we are operating on sequences, tracks, or voices.

Event Data Structures

To implement the event type commands we can have the event type command numbers correspond to an array lookup that holds the relevant function pointer and the byte length of the event type and parameters. Listing 6.1.2 shows this code. The function pointers give us a quick way to get to the code associated with each event type. The byte lengths give us a quick way to step to the next event block.

LISTING 6.1.2 Event Type Data Structures

```
// Example Note Off Event Block
typedef struct {
    char nEventType;
    char nKey;
    // no release velocity
}NoteOff_EventBlock_t;

void NoteOff_Function( Track_t *pTrack )
{
    // the pEvent is pointing at our event block
    NoteOff_EventBlock_t *pNoteOffEB =
    (NoteOff_EventBlock_t *)pEvent;

    // walk through this track's voices and turn off
    // any that have pVoice->nKey == pNoteOffEB->nKey
}
```

```
// Example Note On Event Block
typedef struct {
    char nEventType;
    char nKey;
    char nVelocity;
}NoteOn_EventBlock_t;

void NoteOn_Function( Track_t *pTrack )
{
    // the pEvent is pointing at our event block
    NoteOn_EventBlock_t *pNoteOnEB = (NoteOn_EventBlock_t *)pEvent;

    // try to get a voice from the free list or
    // try to get a voice from the active list if possible
    // if we have a voice, turn it on with the pNoteOnEB->nKey
    // and pNoteOnEB->nVelocity and other state information
}

enum enumEventType
{
    EVENT_TYPE_NOTEOFF,
    EVENT_TYPE_NOTEON,
    .
    .
    .
    EVENT_TYPE_COUNT
};

typedef void (*EventFuncPtr_t)(Track_t *);

typedef struct {
    EventFuncPtr_t pFunc;    // pointer to command function
    int            nLength; // byte length of command
}EventTypes_t;

static EventTypes_t aET[EVENT_TYPE_COUNT] = {
    { NoteOff_Function, sizeof(NoteOff_EventBlock_t) },
    { NoteOn_Function, sizeof(NoteOn_EventBlock_t) },
    .
    .
    .
};
```

Here we show that we can give each event type a number that can be used to call up an `EventTypes_t` structure from an array. The `EventTypes_t` structure contains the function pointer to call for the given event type and the length of the command ID and parameters. Being able to define our own command numbers and have them correspond to array entries like this provides an alternative to switch statements.

The Audio Frame and Update Interval

Different computer systems will have different ways of providing timing callbacks or threads that wake up at specific intervals. I will simply assume that we can have a function called at a specific interval referred to as the audio callback. We can think of the time between these callbacks as the audio frame. During each callback we need to update our notion of how much time will pass during the next audio frame and we need to send out all of the commands that are due to occur over this time.

Independent of the audio callback rate we will also have an update interval. The update interval determines the amount of time we will step when sending out low-level commands. So we could have an audio callback that occurs once every second with the update interval at 120 times a second, which would require stepping through 120 time intervals per callback. Another possibility is that we could have an audio callback that occurs 60 times a second with the update interval at 120 times a second, which would require stepping through two time intervals per callback. Listing 6.1.3 is an outline of the audio callback code.

LISTING 6.1.3 The Audio Callback

```
// This function is called by the timer callback
static void OSys_AudioCallback(void)
{
    // protect against callback reentrance

      // determine the number of update intervals required
      // to deliver during this callback

    // begin critical section
    OSys_BeginAudioCriticalSection();

      // for the number of update intervals required on this frame
      // {
    //      iterate over sequences
    //          perform per sequence operations

    //          iterate over tracks
    //              perform per track operations
      //
      //     send low-level commands for this time step
      //     move to next time step
      // }

    // end critical section
    OSys_EndAudioCriticalSection();
}
```

Our callback may happen while other code is executing, which means it might happen when we are changing data structures for the music sequencer. We protect against this by using the critical section method specific to our operating system.

Timing Calculations

In order to play our music data at different rates, we need to work out how to step through our music data based on three parameters: the music tempo, the update interval, and the resolution of our music time format.

- Music tempo is described in beats per minute (BPM).
- The update interval is described in updates per second (UPS).
- Music time resolution is described in parts per quarter note (PPQ).

We are looking for the amount of music time to increment for each audio callback. We can call this parts per update (PPU).

If we consider beats per minute (BPM) to be the same as quarter note per minute (QPM), then the equation is

$$PPU = QPM * PPQ * (1/UPS) * (1Minute/60Seconds)$$

We store this PPU number as a fixed-point number; the final code is shown in Listing 6.1.4.

LISTING 6.1.4 Time Step Calculation

```
unsigned long CalcTimeStep( unsigned short qpm,
                            unsigned short ppq,
                            unsigned short ups)
{
    unsigned long ppu;
    unsigned long temp;
    temp = (unsigned long)qpm * (unsigned long)ppq;
    if( temp < 0x10000 )
    {
        ppu = ((temp * 0x10000) / 60)
              / (unsigned long)ups;
    } else {
        ppu = ((temp / 60) * 0x10000)
              / (unsigned long)ups;
    }
    return(ppu);
}
```

Our calculation here does a little range checking during the calculation to make sure that we obtain as accurate of a 16.16 result as possible given that the input numbers can range in value.

We recalculate the parts per update value any time that a sequence's tempo changes. This parts per update value is placed in our `TimeStep` variable in our sequence structure. Since these time parameters are in the sequence structure, we can only change the tempo for the whole sequence. If we wanted to change tempo for each track individually, we could put these parameters and the tempo setting in the track structure.

Audio Synthesis Control

Connecting Synth to Sequencer

An important issue for our music sequencer implementation is how music event parameters are mapped to audio synthesis parameters. This is where music sequencer code can get very platform specific. In order to keep the code as cross-platform as possible I will call a software synthesizer interface from our sequencer code.

One important part of connecting our audio synthesis to our music sequencer is the `SetInstrument` event type. This command looks up a table of instrument definitions and sets the `pInstrument` field of our track data structure. When a `NoteOn` command occurs, the parameters from the `pInstrument` are transferred to the voice to be started. You can view these details in the accompanying source code.

The capabilities of the audio synthesis system that we are using will determine what kind of control we can have and music will have to be written with these control issues in mind.

The Code

ON THE CD

The example code on the CD-ROM shows how to play music using our custom music sequencer language. This includes how to step through the music data of each track of each sequence and how to code the event types for a particular synth interface.

The example code uses a cross-platform audio engine called CSyn. The CSyn library provided on the CD-ROM is for demonstration purposes only.

Conclusions

We have covered the details of a basic music sequencer. Important MIDI concepts have been presented as well as our custom music language. Implementation details of data structures, event types, and timing have been presented. Finally, the code is there to play with and customize for your own needs. Enjoy!

References

CSyn audio engine can be found online at http://www.softsynth.com/csyn.

6.2

Audio Compression with Ogg Vorbis

Jack Moffitt, Chesspark

jack@chesspark.com

Ever since computers could produce sound, audio has been a part of games in some form or another. Originally, beeps and bloops were all that were possible. MIDI was later used, as it contained a lot of information about the sound in a small amount of space. Then, as sound cards became prevalent, MOD-type files became more popular, offering a combination of sampled sounds with sequencing and limited effects. Once the CD-ROM became the standard media on which games shipped, Redbook audio (normal CD audio) started to become popular, and finally games used high-quality music.

Unfortunately, as the music became better, music files also became larger. While CDs can easily hold an hour's worth of great-quality audio, not much else will share the same disc. ADPCM is one compression standard that has been used in commercial games to try and alleviate the size of music files while retaining the quality, but its size savings are not fantastic. High-quality music is now a must for any game, and since game developers are going to continue to push the envelope with respect to audio and music in games, music files will have to get smaller. Enter psychoacoustic compression.

Psychoacoustic Compression

Psychoacoustic compression works by eliminating all the parts of the sound that the ear can't hear or considers unimportant. Unlike some other forms of compression, psychoacoustic compressors are lossy. The original signal is irreversibly modified, even though to most ears the sound remains the same.

The compression ratios for psychoacoustic compressors are generally between 10:1 and 20:1. This is far better than the ratios offered by the other sound compression alternatives.

How It Works

There are a few basic principles behind psychoacoustics. First, there is the absolute threshold of hearing. This is represented by the graph in Figure 6.2.1.

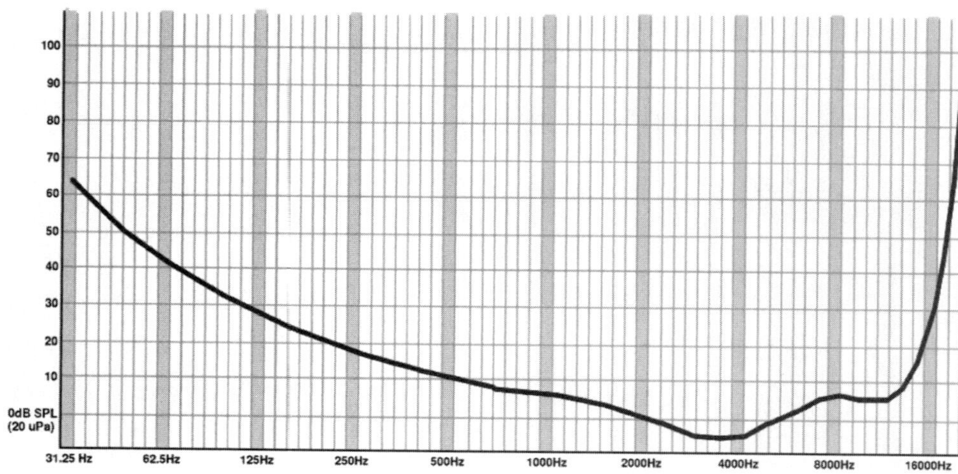

FIGURE 6.2.1 The absolute threshold of hearing. The x-axis represents frequency, the y-axis represents loudness.

The absolute threshold of hearing represents how loud a sound has to be at a certain frequency range in order for the human ear to perceive it. Any sounds that are below the curve can't be heard. If you take away all the sounds that fall under the curve from the original sound, the resulting sound should be perceived identically.

Another basic concept of psychoacoustics is masking. Just as bright background light sources will mask foreground objects, loud sounds will mask quieter ones. A strong tone will mask weaker tones at higher and lower frequencies. Even after a strong tone is gone, it will still mask some sounds, due to temporal masking. Since a fair amount of the sound is masked, psychoacoustic encoders won't include them, and the human ear is none the wiser.

How Do Sound-Compression Techniques Compare?

Now that we have a basic understanding of how psychoacoustic compression works, let's take a look at how it compares to the other forms of audio compression that might be more familiar. Audio is normally transmitted as raw PCM samples. These are uncompressed, so each stereo 16-bit sample takes 4 bytes. For CD-quality audio, there are 44,100 of these every second, or around 10 MB of audio a minute.

Typical ways of reducing the bulk of audio data include downmixing and resampling. Downmixing reduces the stereo channels into one channel, cutting the total size by half. Resampling uses fewer samples per second to represent the sound. Usual resampling rates are 22,050 Hz and 11,025 Hz. Both of these methods result in greatly reduced file sizes, but they come at the cost of quality and the loss of stereo.

ADPCM is a 4:1 compression format that encodes the differences between successive samples. It is sometimes used in games to shrink audio without the unacceptable loss of quality that downmixing or resampling creates. ADPCM is also lossy, though, and does degrade audio quality. It also only compresses audio to one quarter of the size, meaning that an hour's worth of audio can still be almost 200 MB.

There are several lossless methods available as well. While these do not sacrifice any quality, their compression ratios are not very good. Typical lossless compressors get between 1.5:1 and 2:1 in the general case. Many of them can be quite slow, but their compression ratios alone make them unusable for most situations.

Why Ogg Vorbis

Psychoacoustic compression seems to be the clear choice for music compression. High compression ratios and almost no discernable quality loss makes it appealing, but the question still remains—which codec to use of the ones that are widely available?

Ogg Vorbis [OggVorbis02] stands above the rest as the perfect fit for games and other applications. Its royalty-free licensing makes it a much cheaper alternative than the rest of the codecs. Its open-source implementation gives developers the freedom to customize and tweak it if necessary. Also, its broad platform support ensures that the same code will work on Windows, Macintosh (Classic and OS X), Linux, BeOS, and even console platforms.

In addition to these advantages, Ogg also has several unique features that make it specifically appealing to game developers. It supports multiplexing the audio data with other kinds of information. There are already implementations that intertwine MIDI with CD-quality audio for synchronized device control. It also supports multiple channels, meaning that you can encode and play back in surround sound or even something more ambitious.

For example, using Ogg, a game developer could add synchronized mouth movements to compressed vocals, to give a much more-realistic sense of talking or singing. With other formats, this is more difficult and not directly supported.

If game developers want to keep advancing the current state of the art, the audio and sound will not only have to be compact, but also quite flexible. This is where a lot of the other codec options fall short, and this is where Ogg Vorbis shines.

Compression Scenarios

Using Ogg Vorbis as the implementation choice, we can now cover how best to fit compressed music into a game, considering several possibilities about speed requirements and the type of audio being used. Although Ogg Vorbis will be specifically discussed, most of the ideas presented here should work with other codecs.

There are several things to consider when using a codec with a game. Most games have tight speed requirements, so the amount of processor time necessary to decode audio is an important factor. Desktop computers can generally decode psychoacoustically compressed audio in about 2% to 5% of the total processor time on Pentium III-class machines.

Also, the type of sound being decoded is important as well. For instance, background music generally only consists of one stereo track and switches between different tracks. More-complex music might layer tracks together, requiring the decoding of several files at once. Sound effects are generally short sounds and are keyed to events. The latency between the time the event happens and the sound is played is very important. Many sound effects might be playing simultaneously.

With these situations in mind, let's outline some ways that compressed audio can be effectively integrated into games.

Scenario 1: Decoding On the Fly

The most common method of using Ogg in a game would be to decode audio on the fly. This uses a little CPU time, but it allows the files to remain on a mass storage device, such as a hard drive.

In this scenario, an audio stream has been completely encoded in Ogg format and is decoded and played in real time while the game is running. There is no need to make the user wait for entire files to be decompressed before playback, and there's no large, uncompressed audio files sitting around on the player's hard drive. In addition, allowing the player to add his or her own music to a game is simple with this method of integration.

Scenario 2: Decoding to Cache

In some situations, decoding to cache is a better fit. If there are many pieces of audio to be played at once, decoding all of them in real time might not be possible or might use up too much of the processor time. In this case, decoding the files to a cache on level changes or on startup might be the right solution. This allows a game implementation to keep all audio data compressed that is not needed to be immediately available by gameplay.

This is also a nice way to produce sound effects. The game could decode them on-the-fly the first time they were used, and play the already decoded audio on subsequent requests. If latency is a problem with decoding, the sound effects could be decoded on level changes or at startup, as previously described, and then played back with no decoding latency at all.

Scenario 3: Compressed Transport

In cases where none of the previous scenarios make sense, compression can still be used for end-to-end transport. The game distribution CD-ROM and/or downloadable packages can use Ogg to make the download smaller and leave more room for graphics and code. When the game or demo is installed, all of the music can be decompressed to the hard drive. This scenario would also apply well to game patches or additional packages to go along with the game.

Code Examples Using Ogg

A few code examples will illustrate how easy it is to use Ogg Vorbis. To use the vorbisfile library, the code will need to include the following API header

```
#include <vorbis/vorbisfile.h>
```

and link against the vorbisfile, vorbis, and ogg libraries. Under Windows, these can be statically linked or dynamically linked, depending on personal preference (see the SDK files and API reference on the CD-ROM for details).

ON THE CD

Uncompressing Files to Memory

Uncompressing files to memory is easy with the vorbisfile API. First, we declare the `OggVorbis_File` variable:

```
OggVorbis_File vf;
```

Then, we must open the Ogg Vorbis file with an already open `FILE*`. Note that you must open a file in binary mode for vorbisfile. On some platforms, binary files are default for calls like `fopen()`, but on Windows, this is not the case, and you must specify binary mode explicitly.

```
int err;
err = ov_open(fp, &vf, NULL, 0);
```

The `fp` is our `FILE*` to an already open file. The `vf` is the `OggVorbis_File` struct, and the other two parameters are typically set to `NULL` and zero, as in our example. (If you're curious as to what these mean and when you should use them, please consult the API reference.)

The `ov_open` will return zero on success or less than zero on failure. On failure, the return value will map to one of the standard error codes of the API (which you can find explained in the API reference).

Now that the Ogg file has been opened by the vorbisfile library, the library owns the file. It will close the file when it's done, and you should no longer use that file pointer in external file operations. Once the file is opened, the file info must be read:

```
vorbis_info *vi;
vi = ov_info(&vf, -1);
```

The `vorbis_info` struct will contain information about the opened Ogg file, such as its sampling rate, the nominal bit rate, and its number of channels. The second parameter specifies which logical bitstream to return information for (–1 means the current logical bitstream). Optionally, you can read the comments from the file with the `ov_comment()` function.

Before we can decompress the Ogg to memory, we must first allocate some space for it. To find out the total space required, we must call `ov_pcm_total()` to find the total number of PCM samples, and multiply this by the number of channels and the number of bytes per sample (usually 2 bytes for 16-bit audio).

```
int size;
char *buffer;

size = vi->channels * 2 * ov_pcm_total(&vf, -1);
buffer = (char *)malloc(size);
```

Now that we have a buffer allocated for the entire decoded output, `ov_read()` is called in a loop to retrieve PCM samples into the buffer.

```
int eof = 0;
char *buf = buffer;
int current_section;

while (!eof) {
    long ret = ov_read(&vf, buf, 1024, 0, 2, 1,
                  &current_section);

    if (ret == 0) {
        /* 0 return value means end of file */
        eof = 1;
    } else if (ret < 0) {
       /* < 0 return value indicates an error */
    } else {
        /* advance the buffer pointer on success */
        buf += ret;
    }
}
```

The code is fairly simple. It doesn't do any error checking (although when working with Ogg, most errors are normally benign and can be ignored) or overflow checking, but all the hard work is done for you in the vorbisfile library.

Once a file is finished, you must clean up with `ov_clear()`:

```
ov_clear(&vf);
```

Decoding in Real Time

Decoding in real time is very similar to the previous situation of decoding to a memory buffer, except that instead of decoding all at once, real-time decoding takes place a piece at a time. After reading each block from `ov_read()`, the code then sends it to the next stage of the pipeline. In the most common case, this is an audio output device.

For the sake of simplicity, system specifics of audio output won't be covered here. Instead, the code assumes that there is an `audio_output()` function that takes a buffer of samples and a size, and does the right thing.

Using the previous example as a base, the only thing that needs to be modified is the decode loop. At the top of the loop, there is still the call to `ov_read()`:

```
char pcmout[4096];

while (!eof) {
    long ret = ov_read(&vf, pcmout, sizeof(pcmout),
                       0, 2, 1, &current_section);
    /* ... */
}
```

Notice that the buffer is now a fixed size, since the code only processes output in small blocks.

In the `success` clause of the previous example's `if` blocks, we advanced a buffer pointer. Since we only process a block at a time for real-time decode, we just need to send the current block to the `audio_out`:

```
audio_out(pcmout, ret);
```

On `success`, `ret` will be the number of bytes placed into the buffer.

Encoding

The last part to a fairly comprehensive understanding of using psychoacoustic compression in your game is encoding and production. There are several knobs to tweak when making compressed Ogg files, and understanding these will lead to better sounding music and sound effects in your game.

Quality and size are integrally related in Ogg, and both are controlled by a single knob. In most codecs, you adjust the Size knob, which implicitly changes the quality. In Ogg, you adjust the Quality knob, which implicitly changes the size. In general, the bigger you're willing to make the file, the better it will sound; and conversely, the less quality you need, the smaller the file can be. There are some practical limits to this relationship, though.

The size of compressed audio is measured by bit rate: the amount of bits used to store one second of audio. The average gamer is not going to be able to hear subtle quality loss, so pushing the bit rate past a certain point will have diminishing returns. Ogg files should sound quite good at 64 kbps (kilobits per second) and should hardly be discernable from the original, which is around 128 kbps.

Since, with most games, the music is not the primary focus of the gamer's attention, lower-bit-rate Ogg files should be more than enough to give gamers an excellent quality experience.

Two other knobs are the number of channels and the sample rate of the audio. While these affect quality (e.g., mono sound is not as good as stereo), the rate of quality change to size change is not linear. If you halve the size by going from stereo sound to mono sound, the quality is only slightly diminished in most cases. Similarly, if you halve the sample rate, the audio sounds worse, but possibly not much worse. If space is at a premium, you can downmix and resample before compressing with Ogg. This leads to smaller files with an acceptable loss of audio quality.

Conclusion

As game audio grows in importance, it seems obvious that better forms of compression must be utilized to reduce audio's bulk. Since many games are developed on a tight financial budget, an open and royalty-free solution is the natural choice. So, on your next project, consider psychoacoustic compression with Ogg Vorbis.

References

[OggVorbis02] Ogg Vorbis, available online at http://www.vorbis.com, June 2001.

6.3

Using 3D Surfaces as Audio Emitters

Sami Hamlaoui

disk_disaster@hotmail.com

In games today, sound sources are represented by a single point, regardless of the type of sound being represented. Gunshots? Points. Laser beams? Two Points. Rain? Lots of points. Although this has sufficed up until now, the level of detail in games is increasing with each generation of hardware, and while technologies like EAX go some way to improving the realism of game audio, all sound still comes from an infinitely small point in 3D space. We don't want sound that comes from a point anymore—we want sound that comes from an entire surface.

This gem will show you how to create sound that appears to do just that, with almost no extra processing time required and with full hardware acceleration. Intrigued? Then read on.

Method

Instead of using a single point as the location of the sound source, you use a standard geometric primitive such as a line, box, or sphere. Then for each frame, you calculate the closest point to the listener on the primitive and send it to the audio API as the sound's position.

This all seems rather underwhelming until you realize that as the listener moves around these emitters, the sound will travel with him. Move parallel to a line and the sound will move along with you, keeping the same distance until you move past the end of the line, at which point the sound will move behind the listener. As you walk around a sphere, the sound will appear to be a point emitter until you walk inside it and the sound comes from all directions at full volume, as if the sound is really being generated from inside the sphere itself. Use a box to represent rain outside a building, only to walk out into the open and find yourself deafened by the sound of the rain.

The best part of it all is that the sound API and the sound card still think they're working with points, meaning that the audio is accelerated on the hardware. The only thing performed in software is a closest-point algorithm, which is so simple for all the emitters that there won't be any kind of performance hit from using it!

In the following sections, four different emitters are covered: the point, line, sphere, and box. Presented alongside each description is a list of components that make up the emitter (the origin, direction, radius, etc.), the closest-point equation with a line-by-line walkthrough, and a couple of suggestions for what the emitter could be used for in a game.

A Word on Volumes

As mentioned earlier, once the listener is inside a volume emitter (an emitter that has a definable "inside," like a sphere or box as opposed to a line or point), the sound will come from all directions at full volume. This is a deliberate part of the technique and can be used for quite a large number of special effects. They aren't listed here, as they can be found with the appropriate emitter. Suffice to say that the few examples given earlier are only the tip of the iceberg.

A Word on the Math

In the list of components for each emitter will be the mathematical representation of the variable in the closest-point equation. However, there are a few values that will be used in each equation, and it seems daft to include them every time, so they are listed in Table 6.3.1.

TABLE 6.3.1 Standard Variables

Name	Math Notation	Type
Audio Position	**A**	Vector
Listener	**X**	Vector

They are defined as follows:

- **Audio position:** This is the vector that is passed to the audio API. It is calculated by the closest-point algorithm. It is represented by **A** (for audio).
- **Listener:** This is usually the camera's position. It is where the sound is currently being heard from. It is represented by **X** (because **L** is used for the line components).

Two temporary variables are used throughout the equations, too, and they also always have the same meaning. They are listed in Table 6.3.2.

TABLE 6.3.2 Temporary Variables

Name	Math Notation	Type
Direction	**V**	Vector
Distance	d	Scalar

They are defined as follows:

- **Direction:** This is the direction from something to something else. Unless stated, this value is not normalized and therefore contains distance as well as direction information.
- **Distance:** The distance between something and something else. This is a scalar value and is usually used when projecting points towards the listener.

Points

Table 6.3.3 shows the point components.

TABLE 6.3.3 Point Components

Name	Math Notation	Type
Origin	$\mathbf{P}_{\text{origin}}$	Vector

The first type of emitter we are going to cover is the point emitter, because although this gem focuses on alternatives, for the vast majority of the cases you need to play a sound, the point emitter will work fine. It is best if you use the other emitters when it suits the effect being created—and *only* then. Otherwise, stick to the point.

Using a point emitter is exactly like using points for sound sources. Just set the audio position to the value of the point. As points have no properties other than their location, the closest point to the point is itself. For completeness sake, Table 6.3.3 lists components, and Equation 6.3.1 shows the nearest point on the point.

$$\mathbf{A} = \mathbf{P}_{origin} \tag{6.3.1}$$

Set the audio at the same location as the point.

Uses

As mentioned earlier, this is useful for any small sound effect that isn't better suited to the other emitters. So, that'll be the voices, footsteps, gunshots, small explosions, rag dolls hitting things, rocket trails, fire, water dripping, etc.

Lines

Line emitters come in two flavors: infinite lines and line segments. You will probably use the line segments most of the time, but for cases when the line is either very big or infinite, the infinite line emitter will suit you perfectly.

Infinite Lines

Table 6.3.4 shows the infinite line components.

TABLE 6.3.4 Infinite Line Components

Name	Math Notation	Type
Point on Line	$\mathbf{L}_{point}$	Vector
Direction	$\mathbf{L}_{dir}$	Vector

Infinite lines are just that—lines that go on forever. To store them, you only need to keep track of a single point on the line and the direction the line is going in (see Table 6.3.4). To calculate the audio position, you need to orthogonally project the listener's location onto the line. Don't worry if that scares you as it's very simple to do. Just remember that you must use the same point on the line throughout the equation otherwise the audio position will be created in the wrong place!

The closest-point equation for an infinite line is presented in Equation 6.3.2.

$$\begin{aligned} \mathbf{V} &= \mathbf{X} - \mathbf{L}_{point} \\ d &= \mathbf{V} \cdot \mathbf{L}_{dir} \\ \mathbf{A} &= \mathbf{L}_{point} \mathbf{L}_{dir} d \end{aligned} \tag{6.3.2}$$

It is created by the following steps:

1. Create a vector between the listener and any point on the line.
2. Take the dot product between this vector and the direction of the line. This will tell us how far away along the line to create the new point from the test point.
3. Set the new audio location by scaling the direction by the distance and adding it to the point on the line used in step 1.

Line Segments

Table 6.3.5 shows the line segment components.

TABLE 6.3.5 Line Segment Components

Name	Math Notation	Type
Origin	$\mathbf{L}_{\text{origin}}$	Vector
Direction	$\mathbf{L}_{dir}$	Vector
Length	$\mathbf{L}_{length}$	Scalar

Line segments represent a portion of an infinite line. Like the infinite line, they require a point on the line and the direction, but also the length of the segment (see Table 6.3.5). The point on the line should be the start of the line segment, and the length is how far away from this point the line ends.

The audio position is calculated exactly the same as in Equation 6.3.2, except you must clamp the distance between the range of zero and the line's length. If you don't, the result will be exactly the same as the infinite line.

The closest-point equation for a line segment is

$$\mathbf{V} = \mathbf{X} - \mathbf{L}_{origin}$$
$$d = \text{clamp}\left(\mathbf{V} \cdot \mathbf{L}_{dir}, 0, L_{length}\right)$$
$$\mathbf{A} = \mathbf{L}_{origin} + \mathbf{L}_{dir} d \qquad (6.3.3)$$

It is created with the following steps:

1. Create a vector between the listener and the start of the line.
2. Take the dot product between this vector and the direction of the line and clamp it between the range of 0 (zero) and the length of the line. This will tell us the distance to the new point from the line's origin.
3. Set the new audio location by scaling the direction by the distance and adding it to the line's origin.

Uses

Some possible uses include the following:

- **Fluorescent Tubes:** As the tube flickers on and off, you could have a sound effect that plays along with it. Combine it with a dynamic lighting and shadowing system for a very atmospheric set piece.
- **Laser Beams:** Laser beams shot from futuristic rifles are an obvious choice for the line emitter. Instead of the sound being generated at the gun's location and the impact point, the entire beam will hum with energy.

Spheres

Table 6.3.6 shows sphere components.

TABLE 6.3.6 Sphere Components

Name	Math Notation	Type
Origin	S_{origin}	Vector
Radius	S_{radius}	Scalar

The sphere is the first of the volume emitters we will cover. Unlike lines or boxes, there is pretty much only one way to represent a sphere, and that's with an origin and a radius (see Table 6.3.6). As explained in the "Method" section, the volume emitters have a special function that occurs when the listener is inside them—the sound is played at full volume in all directions. There is no special case math required for this, as both the sphere's and the box's closest-point equations take this into account automatically.

Using a sphere for a sound effect like a small explosion will not give you much benefit. In fact, most sphere emitters can be replaced by a point emitter without the player noticing the difference. The spheres become useful only when there is a visual representation of the sound to go with the sphere, and it's one that the player can walk into and out of. Note that the boxes do not suffer from this, as they change the way the sound moves (along a single axis as opposed to spherically, like the points and spheres), and therefore can't be replaced by any other emitter.

The closest-point equation for a sphere is provided in Equation 6.3.4.

$$
\begin{aligned}
\mathbf{V} &= \mathbf{X} - \mathbf{S}_{origin} \\
d &= \min\left(\left|\mathbf{V}\right|, S_{radius}\right) \\
\mathbf{A} &= \mathbf{S}_{origin} + \hat{\mathbf{V}}d
\end{aligned}
\tag{6.3.4}
$$

It is created with the following steps:

1. Create a vector between the listener and the center of the sphere.
2. Take the smallest value between the magnitude of this vector and the radius of the sphere. This will be how far away from the sphere's origin to place the sound source. If the listener is inside the sphere, the magnitude will be the smallest, otherwise, it'll be the radius.
3. Calculate the source position by scaling the normalized vector by the distance and adding it to the sphere's position. This point will be on the surface of the sphere if the listener is outside, otherwise, it will be at the same place as the listener.

Uses

Some possible uses include the following:

- **Explosions:** Although most small explosions are best represented with a point primitive, if the explosion has an expanding radius, the sphere emitter would be the best option. It would be even better if you could tie in the radius of the emitter with the radius of the shockwave on screen.
- **Shields:** When surrounded by a shield, the noise will appear to surround you. To those outside, it will be generated on the surface. The bigger the shield, the more obvious the effect. If the players can walk into and out of the shield, it is another way of letting them know that they're inside it.

Boxes

Table 6.3.7 shows box components.

TABLE 6.3.7 Box Components

Name	Math Notation	Type
Origin	$\mathbf{B}_{origin}$	Vector
Min Bounds	$\mathbf{B}_{min}$	Vector
Max Bounds	$\mathbf{B}_{max}$	Vector

Axis-aligned box emitters are probably the most useful to designers after points. As most game entities already have a bounding box defined, having a sound emit from it doesn't require any extra calculations, other than the closest point! Sound on the box travels on two axes at a time (*xy*, *yz*, and *xz*). This means that as you walk parallel to the box, the sound will always appear to be the same distance away from you until you completely walk past it, at which point it will stick in the corner until you walk down another side. Of course, being a volume, as soon as the listener is inside, sound will come from all directions at full volume, but you should know that by now.

There are two ways of storing bounding boxes: offset and absolute. Offset boxes' bounds are relative to the box's origin, while absolute boxes contain real values in 3D space. Remember that unlike the segmented and infinite lines, both offset and absolute boxes will produce *exactly* the same results—they are just two different ways of storing the same information. Table 6.3.7 provides the list of components for both boxes, although the origin is only used for the offset type.

The two closest-point algorithms for a box are presented in Equations 6.3.5 and 6.3.6.

$$\mathbf{A} = \text{clamp}\left(\mathbf{X}, \mathbf{B}_{min}, \mathbf{B}_{max}\right) \tag{6.3.5}$$

$$\mathbf{A} = \text{clamp}\left(\mathbf{X}, \mathbf{B}_{origin} + \mathbf{B}_{min}, \mathbf{B}_{origin} + \mathbf{B}_{max}\right) \tag{6.3.6}$$

This does the following:

1. Clamp the components of the listener to the minimum and maximum bounds of the box (Equation 6.3.5).
2. If the box's bounds are centered around [0,0,0] instead, you must add the box's origin before the clamp takes place (Equation 6.3.6).

Uses

Some possible uses include the following:

- **Environment effects:** For example, you're standing at the end of a long corridor. At the end is an open door that leads to the outside. You can hear the rain from a distance. As you move closer to the door the rain gets louder and louder until you are outside and the rain is coming from everywhere, deafening you, making you unaware of the masked figure approaching stealthily.
- **The Block Puzzle:** Every time a block is moved into the wrong position, it could flash blue and red and produce a deafening screech at the player.

Summary

This gem has shown you how to create the illusion of sound coming from an entire surface. However, just because only a few different objects are covered doesn't mean that this is all you can use—polygons, planes, cones, and if you really want a challenge, convex hulls for brush-based levels, will all find their place in a game engine. For games using a full physics SDK, you should ideally provide an emitter for every primitive available (and then some).

If you do decide to implement this technique, don't bury the emitters under a mountain of options and menus that the designers will never find, as it defeats the whole purpose of providing them in the first place (unless of course they implement the block puzzle idea mentioned earlier, in which case, bury them as deep as possible!). Make emitter creation and placement as intuitive as possible, and try to provide a way of binding them to the movement of game entities or exposing them to the scripting language so they can be further tweaked and enhanced.

Finally, if you have any comments/questions/praise/flames about this gem, by all means, please e-mail the author.

On the CD-ROM

ON THE CD

In the audio folder on the accompanying CD-ROM, you will find a small demo that shows off the five (the two boxes count as one) emitters covered in this gem. It uses GLUT for the framework and FMOD for the audio processing [FMOD05]. FMOD is one of the easiest to use and fully featured audio APIs out there and is free for non-commercial use. Check out the reference at the end of the gem for more details.

The closest-point algorithms are in Primitives.cpp, and the emitter-management code is in Emitters.cpp. Feel free to play around with the source code and add a few more emitter types to it to test out your ideas. There are absolutely no licenses attached to the source code, so any new code you come up with (and the original code) can be used in a commercial engine without fear of lawsuits, bad press, or hissy-fits.

References

[FMOD05] Firelight Technology. "The FMOD Sound System." Available online at http://www.fmod.org/.

6.4

Introduction to Single-Speaker Speech Recognition

Julien Hamaide, 10Tacle Studios Belgium

julien.hamaide@gmail.com

In the past years, much effort has been made in the fields of 3D and artificial intelligence but not in the area of human-computer interfaces. In a majority of games, our interactions are still limited to traditional peripherals: keyboard, mouse, joystick, or joypad. This gem presents a technique that will introduce a new dimension to these interfaces: the voice. With the recent apparition of recording systems on consoles, this new type of interaction makes sense. Moreover, it can be the basis for a new type of gameplay.

This gem introduces a single-locutor recognition technique based on examples. This technique is easy to implement, does not ask for much processing power, and is easily integrated in existing software. It does not try to understand the meaning of entire sentences, but rather tries to recognize isolated words. Demo software is provided on the CD-ROM so you may evaluate the system.

ON THE CD

Introduction

Speech is a pretty complex signal. Its human origin, made of imprecision, makes it difficult to analyze. In this section, the structure of a speech signal will be briefly introduced. In addition, the acoustic properties that make its recognition more difficult will be pointed out.

Voice is a signal produced by our body and our brain. The latter corrects it and adapts it continuously, thanks to the feedback received trough the ears. The production of voice results from the circulation of the air through the vocal cords of the larynx. As the air passes through the vocal cords, it makes them vibrate, which results in the production of sounds. A speech production model can be seen in Figure 6.4.1.

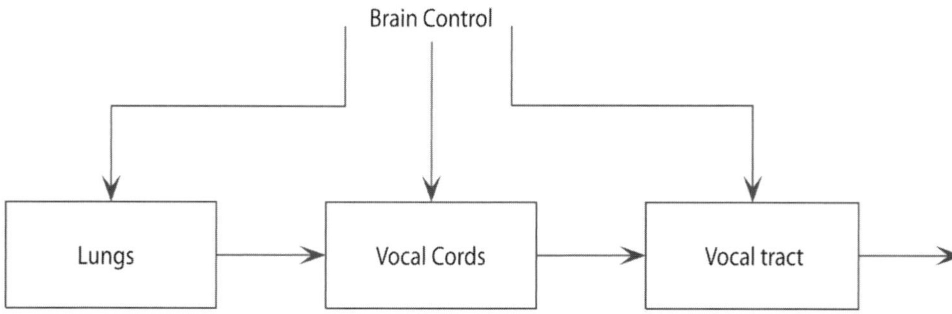

FIGURE 6.4.1 Speech production model.

Our languages use two different types of sound: the voiced sound, produced by the vibration of the vocal cords (for example, vowels); and the unvoiced sound, which does not use the vocal cords (such as consonants *t*, *v*, and *s*). Figure 6.4.2 shows a comparison between voiced and unvoiced sounds. The phoneme *u* is a voiced sound, whereas *t* is an unvoiced sound.

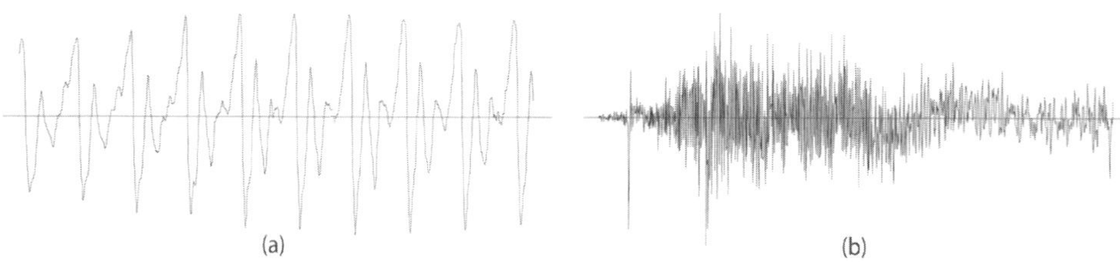

FIGURE 6.4.2 Comparison between (a) voiced sound and (b) unvoiced sound.

The major problem when dealing with speech is the great instability of the produced signal. Actually, the production of speech is dependent on the brain's control of different organs: the lungs, the vocal cords, the tongue, and others. As our ear is insensitive to these weak variations, these are not controlled consciously. For a computer system, it is necessary to extract features as independently as possible from these variations.

An important parameter of a speech signal is its fundamental frequency, also called pitch. The fundamental frequency of a speech signal is the frequency at which the vocal cords vibrate. For a man, it varies from 70 to 250 Hz, while for a woman or a child, it varies from 200 to 600 Hz. Due to the high variability of the pitch, features independent from it need to be extracted.

The other important parameter to take into account is the useful bandwidth. It is common to fix the limit of this bandwidth at 3400 Hz in speech processing. According to Shannon's theorem, the sampling frequency has to be around 8 kHz. Most of the time, we only have access to a 44.1 kHz sampled sound. For speed and simplicity reasons, an 8820 Hz sampling rate is used, that is, 1/5 of initial frequency. The conversion procedure is available on the CD-ROM.

ON THE CD

Recognition System

The recognition chain is composed of two distinct blocks, as shown in Figure 6.4.3. The first one discretizes the whole signal into a discrete set of numeric values. This set is then presented to the input of the second block. A distance measure is performed between the references contained in the database and the signal. The nearest reference is then chosen as the matching one, and its identifier is returned. In the following, the implementation of the system and its limitations will be discussed, and a solution for each limit will be proposed.

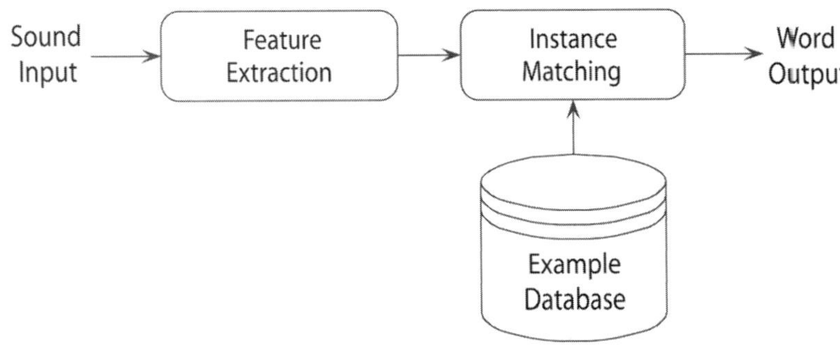

FIGURE 6.4.3 Speech recognition chain.

The technique described here has to be able to detect the presence or absence of a speech signal. In order to not waste computing power, a "push the button when I speak" system can be used. The player pushes the button during the pronunciation of the command. This allows some simplification of the recognition system.

Feature Extraction

Feature extraction is an important step in the speech recognition process. The techniques that give the most accurate results are presented here, but a more general overview can be found in [Schalkwyk]. Actually, feature extraction allows the discretization of a signal slice into a fixed set of numeric values. The length of this slice has to be fixed. The signal within the slice is supposed to be pseudostationary. Experts have decided to take a 20–30 ms slice every 10 ms. A feature vector is produced every 10 ms. The words are then represented as sequences of vectors. Before performing any processing on a slice, a pre-emphasis filter is applied in order to spectrally flatten the signal (Equation 6.4.1). A Hamming's window is then applied to get rid of the border effect.

$$y(n) = x(n) - 0.9 * x(n-1) \tag{6.4.1}$$

Figure 6.4.4 shows the original slice (a), the Hamming's window (b), and the resulting slice. We will now introduce the different feature extractions from this 30 ms of signal.

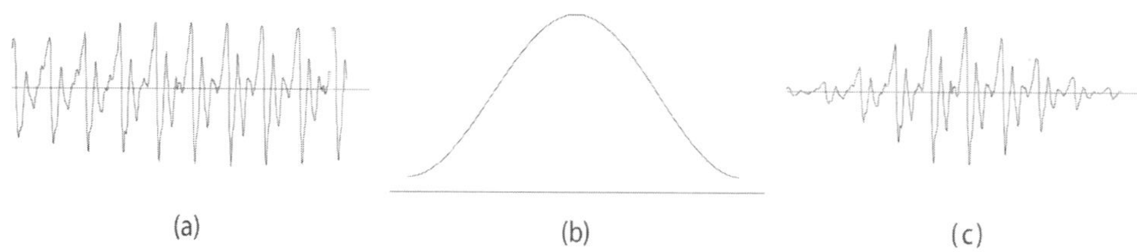

FIGURE 6.4.4 (a) Slice of signal, (b) Hamming's window, (c) result of Hamming's window on the slice.

LPC

The LPC (Linear Prediction Coding) analysis, used in [Edwards02], attempts to model the speech production using a linear system. The method tries to find the linear combination that estimates the best sample $x(n)$ from the t last samples, t being chosen to get the desired precision degree. Equation 6.4.2 shows the estimation function, where $e(n)$ is the residual error. The interesting coefficients are a_i, which represent weights obtained from the linear prediction.

$$x(n) = e(n) + \sum_{i=1}^{t} -a_i x(n-i) \qquad (6.4.2)$$

One can show that the frequency response of the linear filter from Equation 6.4.3 is the envelope of the spectrum of the studied signal.

$$\tilde{x}(n) = \sum_{i=1}^{t} -a_i x(n-i) \qquad (6.4.3)$$

Figure 6.4.5 depicts this phenomenon. This representation has the advantage of being independent from the fundamental frequency of the signal. The order of the method represents the number of samples used for prediction. The number of coefficients a_i is equal to the order of the method. For the recognition process, an analysis with an order equal to the sampling frequency in kHz plus 4 is performed. In this case, an order of 13 will be used. Higher order coefficients are not interesting, because they do not carry enough information.

ON THE CD

The computation details have been treated in [Edwards02], so we will not linger on this problem, as the code is also available on the CD-ROM.

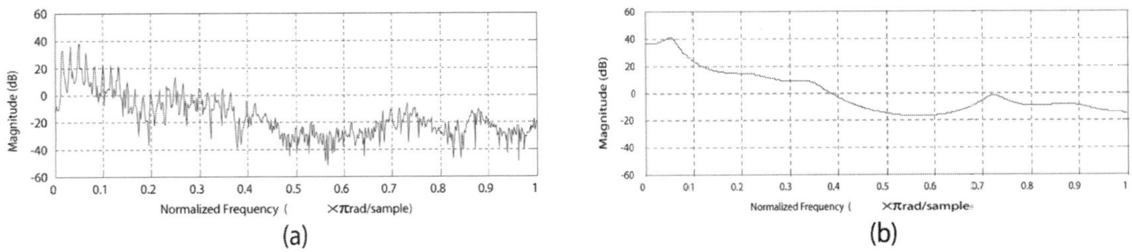

FIGURE 6.4.5 (a) Signal spectrum, (b) frequency response of the LPC filter.

Unfortunately, these coefficients are unstable, and they change significantly for small signal changes. Therefore, they will be transformed into cepstral coefficients *c(i)* with Equation 6.4.4. *p* is the order of the LPC analysis. This recurrence allows us to find more stable coefficients suitable for the recognition process.

$$c(i) = a_i + \sum_{k=1}^{i-1}\left(\left(1-\frac{k}{i}\right) * a_k * c_{i-k}\right);1 < i < p \qquad (6.4.4)$$

These coefficients, although giving good results, do not take into account the nature of human hearing. Another technique, a little more computationally expensive, can be used. This technique is called Perceptual Linear Prediction (PLP).

PLP

This technique is another type of LPC analysis adapted to human hearing. The concept lies on two properties of the human ear:

- The spectral resolution of hearing decreases when the frequency increases.
- The ear is more sensitive to medium frequencies.

This technique will not be explained in detail, given its mathematical complexity. The interested reader can refer to [Boite00] and [Costache02] for more information. The code related to this technique is also available on the CD-ROM.

ON THE CD

Signal Energy

The last introduced parameter is the variance of the signal σ_x^2, an image of the energy of the slice. This parameter allows us to distinguish marked parts of the word (tonic accent, more energetic phonemes, etc.) from others. Equation 6.4.5 shows the evaluation formula for variance.

$$\sigma_x^2 = \frac{1}{N-1}\sum_i^N \left(x(i) - \bar{X}\right)^2$$
$$\bar{X} = \frac{1}{N}\sum_i^N \left(x(i)\right) \tag{6.4.5}$$

Even if the energy is an important parameter, it is not usable in its current form. Actually, if the player speaks louder, the energy increases and moves away from the reference value. Therefore, we will use the relative variation of energy (Equation 6.4.6) instead of its absolute value.

$$\Delta\sigma_x^2(n) = \frac{\sigma_x^2(n) - \sigma_x^2(n-1)}{\sigma_x^2(n)} \tag{6.4.6}$$

Conclusions

To perform speech recognition in video games, two methods can be used: the LPC analysis, which is computationally inexpensive, and the PLP analysis, which demands more processing power but also gives better results. They both produce 13 coefficients. The choice must made considering the available computing power and the desired precision.

Whatever method is chosen, the vector contains 14 coefficients (13 coming from the LPC or the PLP, 1 from the variance) that will compose the identity of the slice. It will be denoted as the acoustic vector in the following sections.

Instance Matching

The set of feature vectors is now available. We will use them to retrieve, among the references, the closest one from the presented word. To measure the distance between two words, called distortion, we have to define a distance between two acoustic vectors. We choose the Euclidian distance (Equation 6.4.7) for simplicity reasons. Other distances, such as city block distance, can be used.

$$d(x,y) = \|x-y\|^2 = \sqrt{\sum_{n=1}^{N}(x_n - y_n)^2} \tag{6.4.7}$$

The first approach is to compare vector to vector for each 10 ms slice and to sum the distances between each vector's couples. Unfortunately, a word is rarely pronounced at exactly the same speed as we expect. The signal is subject to temporal compression and dilatation. Therefore, a technique that automatically adapts the rhythm of the route of the acoustic vector will be used. This technique is called Dynamic Time Warping (DTW).

The goal of DTW is to find the best path in the sequence of acoustic vectors of both words, i.e., the path with the lowest accumulated distance.

The word to recognize will be referenced as X, the words from the database will be referenced as Y_k. Figure 6.4.6 represents the type of awaited path. Each axis represents one of both words to compare. Each point represents a couple of acoustic vectors.

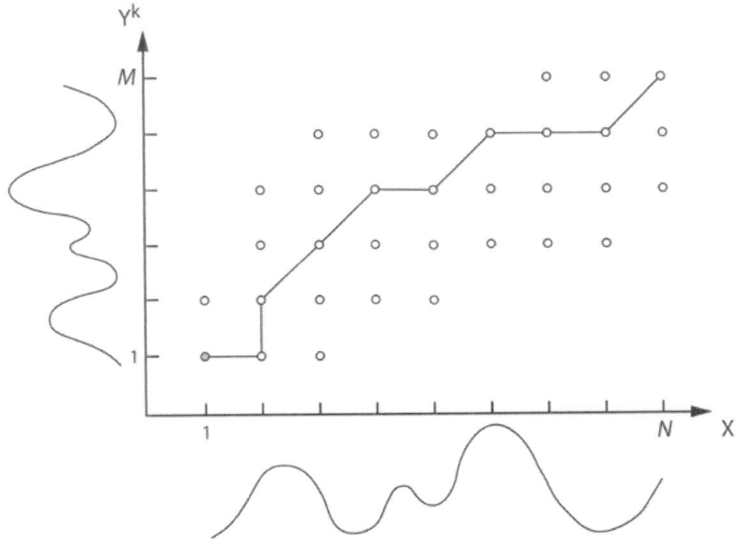

FIGURE 6.4.6 Example of the DTW algorithm path.

To respect the constraints of speech production, the progression of the system has to be limited. Constraints have been chosen to respect the nature of speech. The three main constraints are:

- **The monotonic evolution:** Seen acoustic vectors represent a temporal notion, no return is allowed.
- **The border conditions:** The path begins at (0,0) and finishes at (N,M), N and M are respectively the size of the sequence of the reference and the size of the word to recognize.
- **The progression constraints:** One can find in Figure 6.4.7 some examples of constraints. Only displayed arrows are authorized displacements. The first constraint lets the system be totally free. The second one requires a diagonal progression just before a vertical or a horizontal progression.

Route Algorithm

To compute the minimal distance, we use the property exposed by Equation 6.4.8. The couple (i,j) represents a feature vector couple, i represents the temporal index of

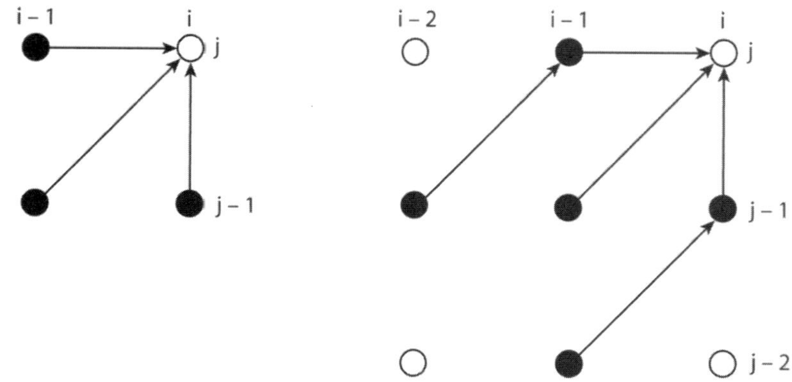

FIGURE 6.4.7 Progression constraints. Black dot = starting point.

the vector to test, and j represents the temporal index of the reference vector, $D(i,j)$ being the minimal distance to access the point (i,j). $p(i,j)$ represents the possible predecessors of (i,j) I (depending on the progression constraints shown in Figure 6.4.7).

$$D(i,j) = d(i,j) + \min_{p(i,j)}\left\{D\left(p(i,j)\right)\right\}$$

$$d(i,j) = \left\|X_i - Y_j^k\right\|^2 \qquad (6.4.8)$$

We have to successively compute the accumulated distance for each (i,j) couple gradually. We do not have to exactly know the traversed path, only the final score is of interest.

Once each reference from the database has been compared to the words to evaluate, the one having the smallest distortion is chosen as the solution. A maximum distortion threshold has to be fixed, to avoid the execution of a command when the user pronounces a word that is not in the reference database.

ON THE CD

More information about the DTW algorithm and implementation can be found in [Keogh03]. The DTW code can also be found on the CD-ROM.

Training

Before being able to recognize words, a database must be constituted. Therefore, the user is asked to pronounce the words to recognize a fixed number of times. The sequences of acoustic vectors are then extracted from the recordings. These vectors will be saved for two reasons. First, we do not have to perform feature extraction again on references, and second, the space needed to save these vectors is smaller than storing samples of the signal. If the recording conditions are good, or if the vocabulary is limited, two or three recordings will be enough. In a noisy environment, or with a bigger dictionary, it could be necessary to record about 10 examples of each word.

Limitations

This very simple system, in adapted conditions of use (using a microphone of sufficient quality, in a quiet environment) gives results near 100%. Unfortunately, it has many limitations.

First, the system is sensitive to environmental noise. Therefore, its use should be limited to a quiet room. Some signal-processing techniques can be applied to remove this environmental noise. If the background noise comes from the game, it is straightforward to subtract it from the signal.

Second, the recognition process is locutor dependent. Other techniques independent from the locutor also exist but need more computation and are greedy for resources.

Third, the complexity of the system depends on the number of words in the database. As the size of the database increases, the number of references the input word will have to be compared to will also increase. The only way to solve this problem is to try to extract phonemes from the signal, rather than comparing the word to examples.

The bigger constraint is the constitution of the example database. The user is asked to record examples of command words. In most cases, three recordings should normally be sufficient.

The solution to the limitations described is the use of more complex systems, based on probabilistic models, neural networks, or Hidden Markov models. These systems are out of the scope of this gem. More information on these systems can be found in [Boite00].

Conclusion

This gem introduces the basics of speech recognition theory and systems. Even if the described system is rudimentary, feature extraction is common to all these systems. The presented technique is simple, quick, and easy to implement. It gives good enough results to be used in video games. In ideal conditions, the method approaches 100% efficiency. The technique has its limitations, but it provides a simple way to introduce speech recognition in an application. For integration in more complex systems, it will surely be necessary to use third-party software, as the problem is far from being trivial. With the apparition of sound-recording systems on most recent consoles, speech recognition might play an important role in the near future.

References

[Boite00] Boite R., H. Bourlard, T. Dutoit, J. Hancq, and H. Leich. "Traitement de la Parole." Presses Polytechniques et Universitaires Romandes, 2000.

[Costache02] Costache, Gavat, Raileanu. "Voice Command System." In *International Workshop Trends and Recent Achievements in Information Technology*. Cluj Napoca, Romania, May 2002.

[Edwards02] Edwards E. "Linear Predictive Coding for Voice Compression and Effects." In *Game Programming Gems 3*, 613–621. Charles River Media, Inc., 2002.

[Keogh03] Keogh, E., and J. Pazzani. "Derivative Dynamic Time Warping." In *Learned Representations in AI*. Division of Computer and Information Sciences, Rutgers University of New Jersey, 2003.

[Schalkwyk] Schalkwyk, J. "Feature Extraction." Available online at http://www.cslu.ogi.edu/toolkit/old/old/version2.0a/documentation/csluc/node5.html. November 27, 1996.

6.5

A Technique to Instantaneously Reuse Voices in a Sample-Based Synthesizer

Thomas Engel, Factor 5 Inc.

thomas.engel@factor5.com

Synthesizers typically offer a limited number of voices that can be active at any given time, so complex allocation schemes are used to make the best use of the voices that are available. Allocating a voice at any given time is easy so long as free voices are available, but this becomes quite tricky when this is not the case, requiring voices to be reused. The difficulty results from the amplitude difference between the current active sample and the next sample to be played, resulting in a sharp pop or click sound (see Figure 6.5.1). This gem presents a technique to accomplish this without any major calculation time or memory overhead.

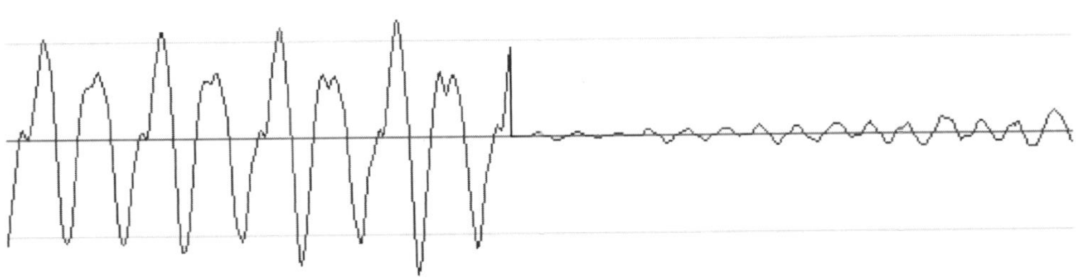

FIGURE 6.5.1 The amplitude difference between samples can create a distracting click.

The Problem

To reuse an active voice for playback of another sample, you might try slowly lowering the volume of the current sample and immediately starting the playback of the new sample. This would nicely avoid any clicks or pops caused by abruptly stopping the old sample and would start the new sample promptly.

This is unfortunately not very practical since two voices are needed to handle this properly—and all this at a time when voices are no longer available. A possible solution to this problem would be to reserve a number of voices for just this case. Unfortunately, this also has major drawbacks. First, hardware resources are lost since you have to guarantee the availability of some extra voices at all times. Also, the number of voices that could be reallocated at once would be limited by the number of extra voices reserved for this purpose, making this a rather impractical solution.

You can remove the need for two voices by serializing the method: first fade out the old sample and then start the new sample on the same voice. This delays the start of the new voice and lowers the volume of the old voice quite a bit earlier than one would like. It also can be very problematic when playing back a musical composition since the delay is very noticeable. The effect of the delay can be minimized by delaying *all* voice starts, no matter if reusing voices or not. This nevertheless introduces an extra global delay to the audio pipeline, and also makes it more difficult to handle the voices due to added complexity.

A more elegant solution is needed.

An Idea for a Solution

The basic idea for the solution is found within a simple question, or rather, the answer to it: What is sound? Answer: Changes in air pressure and, therefore, changes in the amplitude of the output signal. A constant output signal—no matter what the amplitude—will not be audible. The problem with reallocating a voice is this: a sudden, unwanted change in amplitude that generates a sharp pop sound. This sound would also be audible if one were to just switch off the old sample even without starting a second sample.

The idea now is not only to stop any change or oscillation of the old sample, but to keep its last amplitude active in the output sum. A single sample being stopped then would look something like Figure 6.5.2. This output would not generate any click or pop sound since there is no sudden amplitude change.

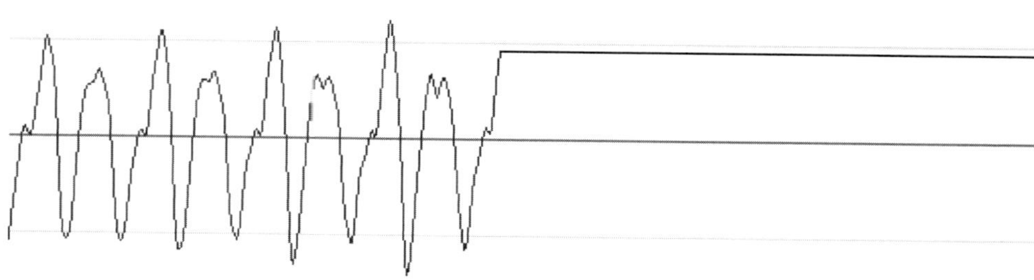

FIGURE 6.5.2 Holding the last amplitude from a sample prevents an undesired pop sound.

The Solution

The effect outlined above can be put to good use to solve our problem. The idea of halting the oscillation of a voice but not dropping its last amplitude simplifies things quite a bit, since all logic concerned with fetching new samples or handling the pitch for the old voice can be dropped as soon as the new sample is started. The output would look something like that shown in Figure 6.5.3.

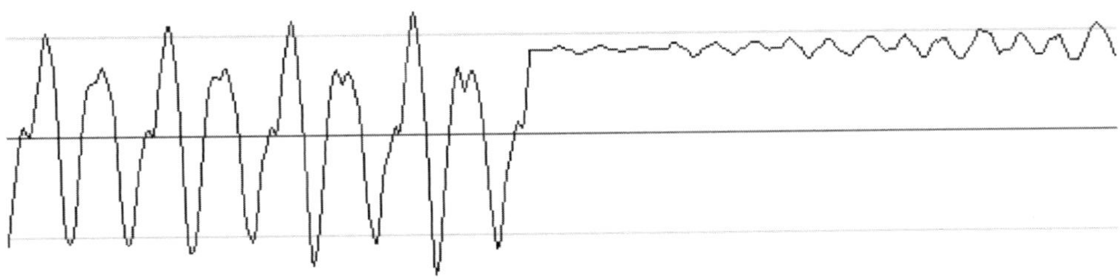

FIGURE 6.5.3 Starting the second sample at the final amplitude of the first.

This has an obvious drawback: by simply halting the old voice we introduce a potentially high DC offset to the output signal, which, due to the limited maximal amplitude of the output sample, may cause the output quality to drop significantly because of clipping artifacts.

There are two simple things that can limit, and, in most cases, completely remove such artifacts. First, one should use a mix buffer of more than 16-bit to generate the final output signal. This extends the maximum amplitude, which can be internally handled. Since the DC offset will be handled together with other voices that again can lower the amplitude, this actually reduces artifacts quite dramatically. The most important step nevertheless is to lower the DC offset quickly to zero. One basically has to fade out the halted old sample, as shown in Figure 6.5.4.

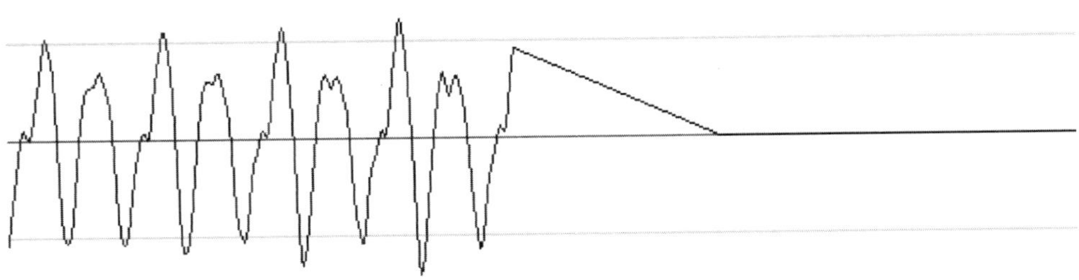

FIGURE 6.5.4 Fading the initial sample to zero.

All this would still require separate logic to handle the halted old sample for each voice to avoid limiting the number of voices that can be reused at once. But is this really true? In fact, one could handle all DC offsets introduced by voices being reused in one very simple handler.

The logic is as follows: Each time a voice is reused the last value mixed into the sum by the old sample on this particular voice will be added onto a global DC offset value. This value in turn will be added to the output signal once all voices are processed.

To get rid of this DC offset, which as outlined above is necessary but unwanted, one lowers the DC offset sum on a per sample basis over a certain time. This can be very efficiently done and does not introduce any further artifacts if not done too quickly. A period of about 5 milliseconds is usually slow enough to lower even a full amplitude DC offset to zero (see Figure 6.5.5).

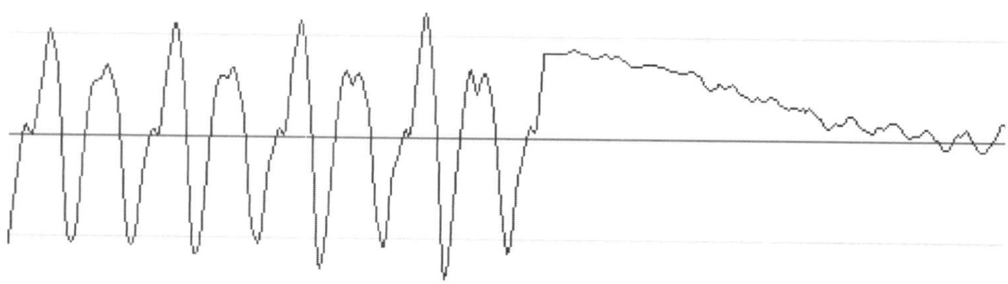

FIGURE 6.5.5 Fading the initial sample to zero while playing the second sample.

Conclusion

In practice, the theoretical negative side effects caused by the DC offset are close to inaudible. One would have to reuse extreme numbers of voices at high amplitudes to actually get some audible effect when using at least a 24-bit mix buffer.

At the same time, the benefits of this method are huge. One can reuse a voice on a moment's notice with no delay and with no audible artifacts in the output signal. The overhead needed to implement this method is minimal. The method can—with some extra work—even be used in systems that feature multi-channel hardware playback of samples. Just one voice has to be set aside to contain the DC offset values to be added in form of a sample data stream generated by the CPU following the algorithm outlined in this gem.

INDEX

License Agreement/Notice of Limited Warranty

By opening the sealed disc container in this book, you agree to the following terms and conditions. If, upon reading the following license agreement and notice of limited warranty, you cannot agree to the terms and conditions set forth, return the unused book with unopened disc to the place where you purchased it for a refund.

License:

The enclosed software is copyrighted by the copyright holder(s) indicated on the software disc. You are licensed to copy the software onto a single computer for use by a single user and to a backup disc. You may not reproduce, make copies, or distribute copies or rent or lease the software in whole or in part, except with written permission of the copyright holder(s). You may transfer the enclosed disc only together with this license, and only if you destroy all other copies of the software and the transferee agrees to the terms of the license. You may not decompile, reverse assemble, or reverse engineer the software.

Notice of Limited Warranty:

The enclosed disc is warranted by Course Technology to be free of physical defects in materials and workmanship for a period of sixty (60) days from end user's purchase of the book/disc combination. During the sixty-day term of the limited warranty, Course Technology will provide a replacement disc upon the return of a defective disc.

Limited Liability:

THE SOLE REMEDY FOR BREACH OF THIS LIMITED WARRANTY SHALL CONSIST ENTIRELY OF REPLACEMENT OF THE DEFECTIVE DISC. IN NO EVENT SHALL COURSE TECHNOLOGY OR THE AUTHOR BE LIABLE FOR ANY OTHER DAMAGES, INCLUDING LOSS OR CORRUPTION OF DATA, CHANGES IN THE FUNCTIONAL CHARACTERISTICS OF THE HARDWARE OR OPERATING SYSTEM, DELETERIOUS INTERACTION WITH OTHER SOFTWARE, OR ANY OTHER SPECIAL, INCIDENTAL, OR CONSEQUENTIAL DAMAGES THAT MAY ARISE, EVEN IF COURSE TECHNOLOGY AND/OR THE AUTHOR HAS PREVIOUSLY BEEN NOTIFIED THAT THE POSSIBILITY OF SUCH DAMAGES EXISTS.

Disclaimer of Warranties:

COURSE TECHNOLOGY AND THE AUTHOR SPECIFICALLY DISCLAIM ANY AND ALL OTHER WARRANTIES, EITHER EXPRESS OR IMPLIED, INCLUDING WARRANTIES OF MERCHANTABILITY, SUITABILITY TO A PARTICULAR TASK OR PURPOSE, OR FREEDOM FROM ERRORS. SOME STATES DO NOT ALLOW FOR EXCLUSION OF IMPLIED WARRANTIES OR LIMITATION OF INCIDENTAL OR CONSEQUENTIAL DAMAGES, SO THESE LIMITATIONS MIGHT NOT APPLY TO YOU.

Other:

This Agreement is governed by the laws of the State of Massachusetts without regard to choice of law principles. The United Convention of Contracts for the International Sale of Goods is specifically disclaimed. This Agreement constitutes the entire agreement between you and Course Technology regarding use of the software.